NATIONS and GOVERNMENTS

SECOND EDITION

NATIONS and GOVERNMENTS

Comparative Politics in Regional Perspective

SECOND EDITION

THOMAS M. MAGSTADT
University of Nebraska at Kearney

ST. MARTIN'S PRESS   New York

EXECUTIVE EDITOR: Don Reisman
DIRECTOR OF DEVELOPMENT: Barbara A. Heinssen
DEVELOPMENT AND PROJECT EDITOR: Douglas Bell
PROJECT SUPERVISOR: Alan Fischer
ART DIRECTOR AND COVER DESIGN: Sheree Goodman
TEXT DESIGN: Gene Crofts
MAP ILLUSTRATIONS: Jeane E. Norton
COMPOSITION AND GRAPHICS: TCSystems, Inc.
COVER ART: Precision Graphics

Library of Congress Catalog Card Number: 92–62748

Manufactured in the United States of America.
8 7 6 5 4
f e d c b

For information, write:
St. Martin's Press, Inc.
175 Fifth Avenue
New York, NY 10010

3 9082 06061316 6

ISBN: 0–312–08644–X

To my beloved sons David and Michael

continents and cultures apart,
in the hope that some day
they will find each other
and inhabit the same world

Preface

The second edition of *Nations and Governments: Comparative Politics in Regional Perspective* follows more closely on the heels of the first than second editions normally do, largely because of the sweeping changes set in motion by the demise of the Soviet Union at the end of 1991. That event not only transformed the Slavic world but also had a profound effect on politics in every other region of the globe.

This new volume thoroughly updates the material in the first edition and goes well beyond it. The basic structure of the book has not been altered, but the content has been revised extensively. Anyone familiar with the first edition will hardly recognize the chapters on Slavic Europe, for example; in regions where changes have been less dramatic, the revisions, not surprisingly, are less sweeping.

Plan of the Book and the Revision   The plan of the book remains essentially unchanged. The world is divided into six regions: Western Europe, Slavic Europe, the Middle East, Asia, sub-Saharan Africa, and Latin America. The importance of historical and contextual differences among regions is reflected in the tripartite structure of this book. Each region is covered in a three-chapter sequence: the first focuses on history, geography, and other factors commonly known as the "political setting"; the second examines contemporary political institutions and processes; and the third looks at the problems and prospects of key nations in each region. To oversimplify slightly, the first chapter looks at the past, the second at the present, and the third at the future. Patterns common to a region as a whole, as well as trends toward greater regionalism, are stressed wherever the facts warrant. In each section, three countries are chosen for special emphasis and are tracked through all three chapters. Other countries are not ignored, of course; they are featured, as appropriate, in the text, in tables, and in sidebars.

The first chapter in *Part I* introduces the study of comparative politics and explores the reasons why comparative inquiry is such a valuable aid to understanding the world around us. *Chapter 2* provides a foundation for the rest of the book by looking closely at various kinds of political systems. *Chapter 3* introduces several theories of economic and political development, with an emphasis on regional patterns and trends. Taken together, these three chapters provide a solid base for the rest of the book.

Part II focuses on Western Europe and the European Community. The results of national elections in 1993 in Great Britain and France and the problems facing a united Germany are among the important new features in this section. The movement toward a unified EC economy also receives due attention.

Part III is a fresh look at the former Soviet bloc, a region that will, for the foreseeable future, continue to experience exhilarating changes and wrenching adjustments. The section is titled "Slavic Europe" in this edition because that term more nearly fits the reality than "Eastern Europe," an epithet too closely associated with the Cold War. Not all the former Soviet bloc nations are inhabited by Slavic-speaking majorities (two obvious exceptions are Hungary and Romania), but the vast majority of people living in this region are Slavic. In contrast to the previous edition, three countries—Russia, the Czech Republic (formerly part of Czechoslovakia), and Yugoslavia (now a rump state encompassing only Serbia and Montenegro)—are used as case studies. The themes in this section include the breakup of several former states (the USSR, Yugoslavia, and Czechoslovakia), the transition from centrally planned to market economies, the attempt to institute liberal democratic governments, and the political instability that has accompanied this remarkable and unprecedented transformation.

The Middle East and North Africa are treated in *Part IV*. The role of nationalism and tradition in Arab politics, the social stability imparted by an ancient and brilliant cultural and religious heritage, the tendency toward political extremism, and the extreme contrasts between fabulously rich Arab states and appallingly poor ones are some of the themes stressed in this section. The countries chosen for special treatment are Israel, Egypt, and Saudi Arabia—a study in sharply contrasting political systems. No consideration of contemporary politics in the Middle East can be complete without a discussion of Lebanon and the Palestinian question—issues so divisive that they impinge on domestic politics, not only in Israel, but also in Egypt, Jordan, Syria, and other Arab countries geographically far removed from the zone of conflict. The ongoing negotiations and yet-to-be-seen results of the 1993 Israeli-PLO peace accord have previously unfathomable implications for the region.

Part V explores politics in Asia, with the spotlight on China, Japan, and India. The challenge of a resurgent China is one of the major new themes in this section. The fact that Japan's sparkling success as a trading nation has not brought commensurate gains in the quality of life for most Japanese is another theme, as is the remarkable staying power of India's embattled democracy.

Part VI examines politics in sub-Saharan Africa. Kenya, Nigeria, and South Africa are given special attention. New pressures for democratic reform throughout the region are illustrated by continuing developments in all three countries. South Africa's abandonment of apartheid and tumultuous transition toward some form of multiracial democracy is one of the themes in this section.

Latin America is the subject of *Part VII*. The process of liberalization that brought popularly elected governments to nearly all the countries of South America in the 1980s has not been reversed, but democracy in many of these societies is under tremendous pressure. The challenges to democratic rule come in many forms: insurgencies, drug-related political violence, corrupt leaders, mushrooming budget deficits, dangerously high inflation and unemployment, and burdensome foreign debts. These problems are examined more closely using Mexico, Brazil, and Argentina as case studies.

The question of whether modern pluralistic societies are governable by democratic (or any other) methods is one of the principal themes of the chapters dealing with Latin America, but it is also relevant to the new democracies in the Slavic world, to incipient democracies in Asia and sub-Saharan Africa, and even to established democracies in Western Europe. Thus, looking at comparative politics from a regional rather than national perspective reveals patterns of interregional as well as international politics. The existence of such patterns is not new; what is new and becoming increasingly important is our growing recognition of them.

One new feature of the second edition is the inclusion of additional maps, tables, and graphs for all regions. These enhancements provide a better regional perspective than the first edition did by painting a statistical and visual picture of each region. They also greatly facilitate cross-regional comparisons.

Acknowledgments   I wish to acknowledge the help of those who assisted in offering helpful suggestions during the revision of *Nations and Governments*: Roger Anderson, Bowling Green State University; Louis Cantori, University of Maryland-Baltimore; Eligah Ben-Zion Kaminsky, Arizona State University; Roger Kangas, University of Mississippi; Charles Miller, Lake Forest College; Phillip Rogers, University of Pittsburgh; James Sundberg, Western Illinois University; and Leonardo Villalon, University of Kansas.

Several individuals deserve special mention for their patience and hard work in carrying this book to a second edition. Only another editor can truly appreciate what painstaking precision this process entails. Doug Bell, who did most of the heavy lifting required to coordinate this project, is at the top of my list: a fine development editor and a world-class diplomat. Doug was ably assisted by Susan Cottenden, Steven Kutz, and Alan Fischer. I also want to thank Bruce Emmer for doing a very thorough job as copy editor: my ego may never recover. Finally, I owe a big debt of gratitude to Stephanie Walker, a former student of mine, who wrote and designed the *Instructor's Manual*.

A project of this magnitude always comes at a high cost to immediate family members. I can only hope that Štěpánka, Michael, David, Amy, Barbara, Casey, and Teddy will never think that my work is more important to me than they are. Nothing could be further from the truth.

THOMAS M. MAGSTADT

Note to Instructors   We would like to note the availability of an *Instructor's Manual* that contains approximately 470 text questions. The manual is available in both print form and in a format for IBM-compatible and Macintosh computers. The software allows randomization of questions and has authoring facilities to permit additions, modifications, and deletions of questions. For more information, please call or write: St. Martin's Press, College Desk, 175 Fifth Avenue, New York, NY, 10010; or call your local St. Martin's sales representative.

Brief Contents

Contents

xviii   Contents

List of Maps

NATIONS and GOVERNMENTS

SECOND EDITION

PART I

Introduction

1

Comparative Politics and the Regional Perspective

"In the development of the city-state Sparta stands apart," according to Raphael Sealey, a distinguished scholar of Greek antiquity.[1] Indeed, Sparta was the great rival of Athens during Greece's Golden Age and led one of the two grand alliances (the other was led by Athens) in the Peloponnesian Wars chronicled by Thucydides.

Lycergus and the Founding of Sparta

Plutarch, in his famous *Lives of the Noble Grecians and Romans,* tells the intriguing story of Lycergus, a heroic figure from Sparta. Lycergus traveled widely, taking note of the features, fine points, and faults of different regimes (this is now known as engaging in "comparative political studies"). On returning to his homeland, he created a new political order, drawing on all that he had learned from his travels. He incorporated the region's particular circumstances (what some modern political scientists would call the "political ecology") in reconstituting the Spartan regime.

Lycergus was especially concerned with security and self-defense. Because in Sparta slaves (*helots*) vastly outnumbered citizens, there was constant fear of a mass insurrection. After the Messenians (enslaved by Sparta in 730 B.C.) revolted, Sparta became an armed camp. It engaged in little commerce with the outside world, stressed patriotism and battlefield valor, glorified physical prowess at the expense of intellectual or artistic pursuits, urged austerity and self-denial, placed the good of the whole above that of the individual, and instituted a kind of crude socialism in which moneymaking (and even money itself) was stigmatized. Obsessed with discipline, physical prowess, and military training, Sparta became the most powerful state in Greece.

Every aspect of life in Sparta—marriage, the birth and education of children, the economy—was geared toward ensuring Sparta's physical security by keeping the citizenry "lean and mean," in a constant state of combat readiness. This siege mentality was a direct response to the numerical superiority of the helots: "The

3

citizens were, in fact, a garrison in their country; and the stability of their political institutions was due to their conscious knowledge that the numbers of that garrison, compared with the numbers of the Helot foe, were perilously small."[2] To this day, the word *Spartan* is synonymous with strict (even severe) discipline, frugal living, and a martial spirit.

Although the Lycergan system was seemingly well adapted to Sparta's unique circumstances, it "illustrates how a rigorous training can turn a people, essentially no braver than the rest of mankind, into an invincible force; it shows, too, how conservatism can stagnate until it becomes a cruel selfishness determined to maintain a system no matter what the cost."[3] Of lasting importance for students of comparative politics is the way in which Lycergus went about founding the new Sparta: thought and analysis—**comparative analysis**—preceded action.

Just as Lycergus is reputed to have built a political order on empirical observation and reason, so two centuries ago the founders of the United States claimed to have constructed a "new science of politics." The theoretical underpinnings of the U.S. Constitution can be found in the *Federalist Papers,* written by Alexander Hamilton, James Madison, and John Jay during the campaign for its ratification.

Before reading on, try this mental exercise: Imagine yourself a Lycergus or a Madison. What sort of a political system would you create? How would you go about it? What purposes would you want it to serve? What dangers would you want it to guard against? Ask yourself these questions as well: Is there one form of government that is best everywhere and always? Or is the best form of government relative to time and place?

Answering these questions should help you develop a sense of what you think good government is all about and how it might best be achieved under different sets of circumstances. Finally, discuss answers with a classmate. The best (and most enjoyable) way to learn is to engage in lively discussions with peers. That's what educated citizens in ancient Greece and colonial America did, with results that left an indelible imprint on world history.

Why Compare?

"Know thyself," admonished the oracle of Apollo at Delphi in the seventh century. These two words, probably the most famous words of wisdom to come out of Greek philosophy, suggest the value of making comparisons. "An age-old idea of philosophers is that knowledge of the self is gained through knowledge of others."[4] What is true of individuals is also true of societies.

Comparison is an excellent antidote to ethnocentrism (a narrow view of the world based on one's own culture, religion, nationality, and so on). Indeed, there is perhaps no better way to gain a perspective on one's own society than to view it from afar, through the eyes of others.

Some of the most penetrating analyses of American political and social institutions have been made by foreigners. Few scholars would dispute that

Democracy in America, an incisive two-volume study written by Alexis de Tocqueville, a Frenchman who visited the United States in the 1830s, retains much of its relevance and validity in the 1990s. Similarly, in the early 1900s an Englishman named James Bryce showed in *The American Commonwealth* how the U.S. system of candidate selection tends to eliminate many of the best-qualified individuals.

By the same token, American observers have made significant contributions to our knowledge of other societies (and their knowledge of themselves). In 1976, Hedrick Smith, Moscow correspondent of the *New York Times,* wrote a best-seller, *The Russians,* on the people, culture, economy, and government of the Soviet Union at the time. I visited the Soviet Union on several occasions in the years immediately following the publication of *The Russians.* Many Soviet citizens inquired eagerly about it. An Intourist guide literally begged for a copy. (Intourist was the official Soviet travel agency for foreign visitors.) A candidate-member of the Soviet Academy of Sciences, who had seen parts of the book, expressed anger and dismay at the hypocrisy of the Party "bosses" and proceeded to relate a personal experience that corroborated Smith's account of a privileged political, managerial, and artistic elite flourishing in the very shadow of the Kremlin. "I have lived here all my life," he said, "and in Smith's book I discovered things about my own country that I did not know."

There are many such examples. French political scientists have long lamented the *incivisme* (lack of civic-mindedness) said to be typical of the French. It took a foreigner, Sidney Tarrow, to observe that the existence of 450,000 municipal councilors in France constituted "an extraordinary phenomenon that demands the revision of certain clichés nourished by many Frenchmen." How accurate is it, Tarrow asked, "to speak of a lack of participation in a country where one out of every sixty citizens is a member of a municipal council?"[5] Why can outsiders so often see things that insiders cannot? Precisely because these things are so obvious. What seems ordinary or natural to native dwellers may in fact be unique.

As human beings, we are often least objective about ourselves. We regularly err in evaluating our own strengths and weaknesses. The same Frenchman who might unfairly decry the civic defects of his compatriots might be just as likely to exaggerate French virtues in other areas. Similarly, Americans are often accused of moral arrogance, of exaggerating our own virtues and treating our own values, beliefs, ideas, and institutions as the embodiment of universal truth. Our belief in the superiority of our institutions coexists paradoxically with widespread cynicism about politics and politicians. In reality, our institutions are not so perfect nor our politicians so imperfect as we commonly suppose.

Almost everyone has a political viewpoint, but few people have the time or inclination to pursue politics intensively. Myths and misconceptions thus abound. The same can of course be said about other fields of knowledge, but there is a crucial difference: *Only in politics does the way we think about the field actually affect the way we conduct our public affairs.*

Unlike the solar system or the life cycle of butterflies, politics is a human system, and government human invention. Faulty understanding in the realm of politics can and frequently does produce faulty policies.

Why do we compare? Let's summarize our answers.

- Comparison is a useful way to evaluate what we see and hear about the world beyond our shores, as well as about our own society.
- What the citizenry believes can have a significant impact on what government does, especially in democratic countries.
- Political myths, to the detriment of the nation (and possibly the world), may be used to prop up policies that have outlived their usefulness.
- An attempt to identify and explain the fundamental patterns of political behavior across different societies and cultures may help us arrive at useful theoretical generalizations.
- Finally, by comparing our own political institutions, processes, ideas, and traditions with those of others, we can learn more about ourselves.

The Logic of Comparative Politics

Comparative politics is as old as political science itself. The Greek philosopher Aristotle (384–322 B.C.), a pioneer in the science of politics, set standards for the discipline that have survived to the present. Aristotle compared existing political systems in order to theorize about the best regime possible. In so doing, he exhibited a mixture of realism (what is) and idealism (what ought to be).

Aristotle appreciated the importance of both theory and method. The term *theory* refers to concepts, ideas, or bodies of thought that purport to explain, predict, or prescribe political systems, patterns, processes, and trends. *Political forms* are sets of institutions or systems that together constitute regimes; political processes include interest articulation and opinion formation, elections, coalition building, and bargaining.

References to methods (or methodology) can be confusing or even intimidating, but they need not be. The so-called scientific method has two aspects—induction and deduction. Regarding the **deductive approach**, John Locke, a seventeenth-century political philosopher, wrote, "Reasoning is nothing but the faculty of deducing unknown truths from principles already known." Deduction involves abstract thought and logical reasoning. For example, that constitutional democracy is the best form of government is a premise that few Americans doubt. Most people would also agree that India is a democracy. Logically, if democracy is good and India is a democracy, then India must have good government.

Although the logic of this proposition is unassailable, its truth is not. Many observers would argue India does *not* have good government. The inference is either that the premise equating democracy with good government is false or that India is not a true democracy.

This example points up the need for an **inductive approach** to analysis. To know whether India does or does not have good government, we must seek empirical (factual) evidence. To do this we can begin with some sort of hypothesis (a proposition to be proved or disproved) and proceed to test it by gathering all relevant data, classifying these data, comparing them with similar data from other countries, and drawing conclusions from concrete facts (rather than abstract reasoning).

Depending on the specific hypothesis being tested, we might subject the data to sophisticated statistical analysis in an effort to discover **correlations** (relationships) among key variables. In the India example, an initial step would be devising a definition of good government that can be operationalized or measured accurately. It would also be important to distinguish between dependent and independent variables. In this example, the form of government might be the **independent variable** and various measures of good government (such as education opportunities, health care, and respect for human rights) might be the **dependent variables**. If we could show that India scores lower on a variety of measures than certain nondemocratic countries, we might conclude either that India is not a true democracy or that the original premise equating democracy and good government is false.

The deductive approach is most often associated with **normative political theory**, whereas the inductive approach is preferred by modern behavioral scientists. Is one approach better or more fruitful than the other? Significantly, Aristotle did not choose between normative and **empirical methods** but instead blended the two, with results that are still studied some 2,300 years later. As a ground-breaking theorist, Aristotle formed hypotheses about political life that he then tested for historical, factual, and logical validity. History provided empirical data for his comparative analyses. A collection of all the constitutions that were available at that time—158—was kept at the Lyceum, where Aristotle taught. In Aristotle's political thought, "The man of science appears again and again behind the student of politics."[6]

Yet Aristotle's ultimate concerns were ethical, or normative. His empirical investigations were driven by such questions as: What is the good life? What form of government is best? What is the relationship between the type of political regime in a given place and the moral character of the people who live under it?

As we embark on this exploration of the contemporary world's major political systems, we should remind ourselves that others, following Aristotle, have been doing the same through the ages. Whether the purpose is to create a new science of politics (like the American founders), to understand what makes a particular form of government tick (as in Tocqueville's *Democracy in America*), or simply to "know the enemy," the comparative study of politics is an essential part of the undergraduate political science curriculum.

A Conceptual Framework: Three Questions

This book adopts a commonsense approach. It combines the ancient Greek penchant for asking fruitful questions with an appreciation of the insights offered by modern-day students of human behavior—in particular, behavior relevant to the problems of governing complex modern societies. Here we ask three questions that together serve as a conceptual framework for this book. The first question deals with political setting, the second with patterns of rule, and the third with problems and prospects. Beginning with Part II, we divide the world into six regions, spreading the discussion of each region over three chapters corresponding to these three questions.

Political Setting

Why does a given form of government prevail in one region and not in another? We will answer this question by asking and exploring a series of related questions (this is known as the **Socratic method**). First, how do environmental factors such as geography, climate, and natural resources affect political values, perceptions, traditions, and institutions in a given region or nation? This avenue of inquiry we will call **political ecology**—the relationship between political institutions and the physical or natural environment to which the societies of a given region have had to adapt.

Second, do religious, ethnic, and linguistic differences complicate the problems of governing? If so, how and to what extent? Do these factors preclude any particular forms of government? Do they necessitate a certain form? The concern here is with the **political culture** and on the process of **political socialization** (the ways in which political culture is transmitted from one generation to the next). Ethnically diverse states are often fragmented into separate communities. In such cases, the larger society tends to lack a unifying political culture. The former Soviet Union and Yugoslavia are two recent examples of multiethnic states that disintegrated due to ethnic conflict and the absence of a common political culture.

Third, are there any particularly traumatic, triumphant, or tragic events in the history of a region or nation that have left an indelible mark on the collective psyche of the people and their leaders? For example, was the region subjected to colonial rule? Was the now-dominant power the victim of foreign invasion, conquest, or subjugation? Did revolution play a role in bringing the present regime into existence? If so, what was the nature of the revolution? Finally, is there danger of war in the region? If so, how long has this danger prevailed? Just as we must know something about a person's history to understand that person's personality, so we must know something of a nation's history to understand its politics.

Two examples of how geography, climate, natural resources, land-population ratios, and of course history influence political institutions help show the importance of these factors. Other examples are found throughout the book (especially in the opening chapter of each part).

In Africa and Asia, resentments against the West occasioned by colonial exploitation have played a major role in shaping attitudes and foreign policies. Colonialism has also impinged on the politics of former colonies. When the European imperialist powers retrenched after World War II, little thought was given to whether the "nation-states" created by the colonizers would be viable. As a consequence, they often were (and continue to be) a congeries of different ethnolinguistic groups, frequently lacking natural resources or arable land and having few or no common folkways, religious traditions, or other shared experiences to hold the people together. Given the poverty and population problems of these nations, it is not surprising that authoritarian regimes have sprung up throughout much of the Third World. These regimes can be seen as a response to pressing needs for internal order, social mobilization, and external security. Moreover, in some cases, the rejection of Western-style parliamentary democracy until very recently may have been a reaction to European imperialism; if we understand the indignity associated with colonial status (and as former colonies we should), we can easily see why many developing nations have not rushed to emulate Western institutions.

In the other example, Russia has been invaded repeatedly throughout its history. The invaders came from two directions: Mongols from the east, French (Napoleon) and Germans (twice in this century) from the west. The empire-building tendencies so evident in Russian history can be explained in part by this vulnerability. Because Russia has no natural barriers to invasion (mountain ranges, oceans, deserts), Russian rulers have sought to insulate the country by grabbing adjacent lands as a buffer zone. The notion that the czars, at least since the time of Peter the Great, sought warm-water ports may also have some validity. The vast wilderness of Siberia, rich in natural resources but inhospitable to human habitation, has no doubt played a role in shaping the Russian psyche and Russian political traditions. Authoritarian patterns of rule probably evolved in response to the exigencies of the harsh climate, the far-flung territory dangerously exposed to attack from without, and the resulting obsession with security. Ironically, despite the heavy-handed authoritarianism that has always been the trademark of Russian rule, a tendency toward rebellion, revolution, and even anarchy surfaces from time to time (most recently in 1991, when a popular revolt against the leaders of an abortive coup led to the collapse of the Soviet empire). The notion that Russians are innately unruly is, in fact, deeply embedded in the political culture. Having internalized the norm of a society that stresses security above all else, Russians not surprisingly tend to equate good government with order and discipline.

Patterns of Rule

How and why do political patterns and trends vary from one region of the world to another?

Surprisingly, by viewing societies and governments in a regional perspective, we can easily observe certain patterns that may be less than obvious if we merely focus on individual countries. For example, most people in the United States know that Great Britain, France, and Germany are democratic republics (governments in which political power is vested in popularly elected representatives). Fewer people know that most Western European countries did not have legislatures elected by universal suffrage (at least male suffrage) until the end of the nineteenth or beginning of the twentieth century or that since the mid-1970s, *all* the nations of Western Europe have been democracies. Fewer still have ever given any thought to the significance of this remarkable fact. Moreover, following the dramatic events of 1989 in Eastern Europe, it may soon be the case that virtually all of Europe will feature pluralistic political systems and market economies.

Of course, not every region displays the uniformity found in Europe; nonetheless, distinct patterns and trends do exist. At the same time, different nations within the same region sometimes display sharply contrasting political traditions and practices. We will note the most significant deviations in each region and attempt to account for them.

Although our main concern is to look at the fundamental forms of government found in a given region, we will not ignore important differences between and among practitioners of a particular form. For example, Great Britain, France, and Germany are all democracies, but they show major differences in the way they conduct elections, organize the government, apportion political power, and choose their chief executives. By contrast, the Middle East displays a wide range of authoritarian forms of government: the theocratic Iranian state, the feudal monarchies of the Arabian peninsula, the modern monarchies of Jordan and Morocco, the personal dictatorships of Syria, Iraq, and Libya, and the mixed regime of Egypt.

In sub-Saharan Africa, too, authoritarianism predominates. In some cases, a military strongman runs the country; in others, civilians rule; and in still others, a civilian or military oligarchy wields power. In a few cases (Botswana, Mauritius, Gambia), parlimentary democracies have been made to work, and there has been movement toward greater pluralism throughout much of sub-Saharan Africa in recent years. Throughout Africa, as in the nearby Middle East during the first two decades after World War II, governments are sometimes brought down by military coups. The political instability implicit in this method of changing rulers has been a persistent problem.

Contemporary Asia displays the greatest variety of regimes in the world—parliamentary democracies (Japan, India, Sri Lanka), Marxist-Leninist regimes (the People's Republic of China, Vietnam, North Korea), authoritarian regimes (Indonesia, Thailand, Burma, Bangladesh), mixed or transitional regimes (South Korea, Taiwan, Singapore, Malaysia), and puppet regimes (Cambodia, Laos). Some of these political systems defy easy classification, and for the region as a whole, it is not possible to discern a definite trend in any particular direction. Yet despite the prevalence of authoritarian, patron-client political traditions throughout the region, Asia is no longer the breeding ground of highly centralized "oriental despotism" that it was once said to be (more on this shortly).

In the 1980s a trend could be discerned in Latin America, particularly in South America. There, one military dictatorship after another gave way to civilian democratic rule. By 1990 almost every country in South America was governed by civilians who had won freely contested elections. In conflict-ridden Central

America, the democratization trend was delayed but gained impetus in the early 1990s. Costa Rica continues to be a model republic, and farther north, Mexico has moved toward a more open, multiparty system.

Describing the patterns and trends of different regions of the globe is relatively simple; explaining them is not. Later chapters will suggest explanations, but clear-cut answers are not always possible in the study of politics.

Problems and Prospects

What are the human consequences of different political traditions, processes, and systems?

Aristotle argued that the proper aim of politics is not simply to sustain life but to seek **the good life.** Philosophers since Aristotle who have contemplated this concept have differed greatly as to its meaning. What exactly is the good life?

For Thomas Hobbes, an English political thinker writing in the seventeenth century, the good life was inconceivable apart from security and order. Anarchy, for Hobbes, was the great enemy of civilization. He watched in horror as the Puritan Revolution, during which Charles I was beheaded, shattered the established order and threatened to sweep away centuries-old customs, values, and institutions. *Leviathan,* his famous treatise on politics published in 1651, remains one of the classic defenses of authoritarian government. In the state of nature, Hobbes wrote, "life would be solitary, poor, nasty, brutish and short." This unruly nature could be kept in check only by an omnipotent state that could "overawe" the great unwashed.[7]

For followers of Jean-Jacques Rousseau, the good life can be equated with the natural life. Rousseau believed that human beings are good at birth and learn, through the socialization process, to be power-hungry and money-grubbing. Hence Rousseau decried the institution of private property and imagined a "state of nature" in which people lived together harmoniously, were not greedy or egocentric, and respected nature rather than exploiting it for personal, short-term gain.[8]

For disciples of Karl Marx, the good life is a function of equality (human misery arises from capitalistic exploitation). Marx agreed with Rousseau about the evils of private property. He went far beyond Rousseau with his theory of "dialectical materialism." According to Marx, slavery gave way to feudalism, which gave way to capitalism. Capitalism, Marx believed, was destined to be replaced by socialism and eventually communism. The engine of change is "class struggle." Thus, in France the middle-class *bourgeoisie,* acting in its own class interest, overthrew the feudal aristocracy in the eighteenth century. Sooner or later, Marx predicted, the exploited working class (or "proletariat") created by the Industrial Revolution would overthrow capitalism and establish an egalitarian—and therefore just—society in which all would enjoy the good life.

For Thomas Jefferson and the other founders of the United States of America, the good life is all about the pursuit of happiness, which, they fervently believed, necessitates liberty. Jefferson was heavily indebted to John Locke, the seventeenth-century English philosopher for whom liberty was the paramount political value. Jeremy Bentham, another English philosopher, believed that happiness—defined as the greatest good for the greatest number—was the true test of a political system. Bentham is the father of utilitarianism, a philosophy that measures the value of things by the pleasure or pain they bring. Bentham was not indifferent to liberty, but he judged all things political against his utilitarian standard. Seen in this light, liberty is instrumental, a means to an end (happiness) rather than an end in itself.

Our study of comparative politics will take account of both the tangible and intangible "goods" implicit in the notion of the good life. Liberty is small consolation for people who are starving or destitute. By the same token, many people who have adequate food and shelter find life empty and monotonous if they lack freedom of speech or freedom of religion.

The difficulty in making comparisons is not one of knowing where people are well off and where they are oppressed or wanting. Rather it is connecting their condition with a particular political order. To what extent is poverty in a given context a function of environment (for example, frequent famines), and to what extent is it a function of politics? Is a trade-off between political freedom and economic well-being a good bargain in some cases (say, where great hardship has historically been the lot of the majority)? Does chronic instability require authoritarian (or repressive) remedies? Where freedoms are denied or curtailed, are popular sacrifices compensated by a steadily increasing standard of living? By greater security? By some other public good? Is social and cultural diversity always compatible with democracy?

These questions defy simple answers. But as Socrates showed long ago, it is worthwhile to grapple with puzzling questions even if clear answers are sometimes beyond our reach.

Politics in Regional Perspective

Domestic political patterns and political development often reflect transnational or regional traits and circumstances. The world can be divided into many relatively small regions or into a few large ones. Regions may be defined by a common cultural core, geographic proximity, economic interdependence, similarity in political traditions, or some combination of these factors. For example, Latin America can either be treated as a single region or as two regions, Central America and South America; South America, in turn, can be divided into three regions—Brazil, the Andean countries (Venezuela, Colombia, Ecuador, Peru, and Bolivia), and the Southern Cone (Chile and Argentina, plus Uruguay and Paraguay). Similarly, Asia can be subdivided into South Asia, Southeast Asia, East Asia, and North or Northeast Asia. Unless a region is defined very broadly (as Asia, Europe, Middle East, Africa, or Latin America), some states will be major players in more than one regional system (China, Japan, and Russia in

Asia, Germany and France in Europe, and Brazil in Latin America are among the most obvious examples).

Nor is there general agreement on how or where to draw the boundary lines for different regions. Should Mexico be included in Central America? Should Japan be included in East Asia or the Western Pacific? Should Turkey be considered part of the Middle East *and* Europe? (Turkey is a member of the North Atlantic Treaty Organization, a European alliance forged by the United States to counter a perceived Soviet threat in 1949.)

Drawing regional boundaries, then, is always difficult and there is no "right" way to do it. This book divides the world into six major regions:

1. Western Europe (Part II)
2. Slavic Europe (Part III)
3. The Middle East (including North Africa and the Persian Gulf) (Part IV)
4. Asia (China, South Asia, Southeast Asia, and Northeast Asia) (Part V)
5. Sub-Saharan Africa (East Africa, West Africa, and Southern Africa) (Part VI)
6. Latin America (Mexico, Central America, and South America—Brazil, the Andean countries, and the Southern Cone (Part VII)

These regions do not correspond precisely to continents, although continental boundaries provide a partial basis for the sixfold division. Geographic location and propinquity are important factors, but so are other commonalities, including history, culture, language, religion, population characteristics, climate, natural resources, economic structure, and quality of life (infant mortality rate, per capita income, life expectancy, and the like).

Regions can also be viewed as subsystems, or subordinate systems, in which regional powers regularly interact with one another. A **subordinate system** consists of "two or more proximate and interacting states that have some common ethnic, linguistic, cultural, social, and historic bonds, and whose sense of identity is sometimes increased by the actions and attitudes of states external to the system."[9] Another characteristic is that regional issues are often at the root of local conflicts (for example, Palestine in the Middle East) and of attempts at collaboration (such as the Common Market in Western Europe).

One scholar has argued that subordinate systems must meet the following conditions:

1. Their scope must be delimited, with a primary stress on a geographic region.
2. There must be at least three actors (or states).
3. Taken together, the members of the subsystem must be objectively recognized as constituting a distinctive community, region, or segments of the global system.
4. The members themselves are conscious of their regional identity.
5. The principal units of power (nation-states) are relatively inferior to the dominant units in the global system.

6. Changes in the global system have greater effect on the subordinate system than vice versa.[10]

This checklist emphasizes the importance of both geography and cultural identity in comparative politics.

In the era of decolonization after World War II, various national governments and international organizations instituted programs of economic and technical assistance to the developing areas in the belief that durable, modern political institutions require economic development and social progress. Often, the hidden agenda was to establish democratic governments that would serve as bulwarks against revolution and would align themselves with the West. The Cold War formed the background for much of the economic and military assistance to the Third World.

Patterns and Trends: A Regional Breakdown

In Western Europe and North America, liberal democracy is solidly established. In the Middle East, authoritarian regimes—mostly monarchies or personal dictatorships—generally prevail. Until recently, military juntas could be found throughout Latin America, and the coup d'état was the normal method of changing the guard. In the 1980s democracy flowered throughout South America—an extraordinary and unprecedented trend for that part of the Western Hemisphere.

In Slavic Europe, a long history of autocratic rule culminated in the highly centralized political structures that remained in place until 1989. In 1929, Stalin launched the first five-year plan and collectivized agriculture. From that time on, Soviet economic policies stressed the primacy of heavy industry, particularly in defense-related areas. After World War II, Stalin imposed this model on the Eastern European "satellite states" (East Germany, Poland, Czechoslovakia, Hungary, Romania, and Bulgaria) as well. In the late 1980s, a trend toward economic liberalization swept the region. Surprisingly, the Soviet Union under Mikhail Gorbachev took the lead (although Hungary had been experimenting cautiously with market-oriented reforms for some years). Soon events outpaced the Kremlin, and in 1989 nearly all the communist regimes of Eastern Europe crumbled. The Soviet Union collapsed in 1991, and Yugoslavia violently split apart in 1991–1992.

Soviet domination of Eastern Europe gave rise to a degree of uniformity unmatched in any other region. Until recently, Czechoslovakia alone in Eastern Europe had experienced democracy. All of the other Slavic nations have a tradition of authoritarian rule.

Trends and patterns are less clear-cut in Asia and Africa. Historically, a brand of extreme authoritarianism known as oriental despotism prevailed. Powerful autocrats (despots) ruled China, India, Cambodia, Vietnam, and Japan. Authoritarian rule and an emphasis on patron-client relations (reciprocal obligations in which individuals of subordinate social status pay deference to a "superior" who assumes some responsibility for their welfare) continue to be common throughout Asia, although there are some notable exceptions. (We discuss these exceptions in Part V.)

Africa is somewhat ambiguous as a regional entity because the continent is split by deserts horizontally into two distinct parts. North Africa is populated largely by Arabs who practice Islam; that is why we include Morocco, Algeria, Tunisia, Libya, the Sudan, and Egypt in the Middle East. The sub-Saharan portion of the African continent—also known as "Black Africa"—has a history of tribalism and ethnic conflict. When the European powers dismantled their colonial empires after World War II, they left behind artificial states that in many cases incorporated ethnic and kinship groups (tribes) that were hostile to one another. Chronic instability has been one legacy, authoritarian rule another. Coups are frequent. Perhaps the most striking pattern has been the predominance of personal rule in one guise or another.[11]

One thing is clear: democracy has fared even worse in Black Africa than in Asia. Indeed, a trivia question that would stump all but experts on African politics is the following: Name one country in sub-Saharan Africa in which a chief executive has handed over the reigns of government to an opposition leader through free elections. (Answer: Zambia.)

Regional Influences on Politics

Many region-linked factors have a bearing on governmental structures and policies. For the sake of brevity we will group these factors first by history and culture and then by resources and demographic characteristics. After that we will consider the effects of the processes of modernization and development.

History and Culture

Professor Jurg Steiner pointed to the importance of region-linked factors when he wrote, "Europe is not only a geographical region, but a cultural concept." European nations, he added, "are bound together by a common culture based on centuries of close interaction."[12] This common culture is rooted in part in a common religious heritage. Before the twentieth century, historians frequently referred to Europe as "Christendom" because Christianity was officially enshrined and popularly embraced as the one true faith throughout the Continent. Indeed, monarchs even ruled by "divine right," meaning that the church was used to legitimize the state.

Language is also an important part of Europe's common cultural heritage. The Romance languages of Western Europe—French, Italian, Spanish, and Portuguese being the major ones—derive their name from their common Latin ("Roman") origins. French emerged as the diplomatic language of Europe: it was spoken at conferences, treaties were written in it, and fluency in it was *de rigueur* for all who aspired to a diplomatic career. Indeed, under Peter the Great,

French became the official language of the Russian royal court! Even today, the ability to speak French is a mark of culture and sophistication throughout Western Europe.

In addition to religion and language, the nations of Western Europe share many common historical experiences. The Renaissance and Reformation, the Enlightenment, and the Industrial Revolution all left a strong cultural imprint on European art, architecture, music, philosophy, and literature. These experiences had a cumulative effect, contributing to the evolution of certain common "European" political values and norms—a kind of moral consensus grounded in humanistic values. One manifestation of this consensus was attempts at conflict management through treaties, the "balance of power" mechanism, and international organizations such as the Concert of Europe and the congress system of the nineteenth century.[13]

What is true of Europe is also true, in varying degrees, of the world's other regions. In the Middle East, for example, Islam and the Arabic language impart a cultural unity that sets the nations of the Arab world apart from other nations. Similarly, in Asia the imprint of Chinese on the languages of Japan, Korea, and Vietnam is unmistakable, and Buddhism and patron-client relations are distinct traditions that have exerted powerful influences on the historical development of most nations of the region. In Latin America, Spanish (except in Brazil, where Portuguese is spoken) and the Roman Catholic religion provide elements of a common "Latin" tradition. The Spanish conquest and, later, the hemispheric dominance of the United States have also aided in the accretion of a common regional political culture.

Finally, even Black Africa, with its rich cultural diversity, exhibits some common historical and sociopolitical patterns. These include animism (a belief in spirits and demons) and tribalism (political and social organization based on ethnic ties or kinship). In addition, the nations of Black Africa—like those of the Middle East and Asia—remained European colonies until well into the twentieth century.

Resources and Demographic Characteristics

Oddly enough, the most obvious explanations of social and political differences are often the least emphasized. Certainly climate distinguishes the nations of the northern latitudes from nations of the southern latitudes in highly significant ways. The French political philosopher Montesquieu, in his famous book, *L'esprit des lois* (*The Spirit of the Laws*), decried "the vices of climate." Climate is detrimental when it causes indolence, as it does (or appears to do) in extremely hot regions. This is particularly true, he believed, in a country like India, where the predominant religion, Hinduism, encourages passivity. Regardless of whether we agree with Montesquieu on this point, it cannot be denied that climatic factors affect food production and that natural events such as droughts and floods can imperil human life.

In Montesquieu's day, agriculture was the economic foundation of society. It is not surprising, then, that he felt that the more the climate induces an individual to shun physical labor, "the more the religion and the laws of the country ought to incite him to it." Thus Montesquieu criticized a law of India because it gave the lands to the princes and destroyed the spirit of property (or free enterprise) among the masses, thereby heightening "the evil effects of the climate, that is, the natural idleness."

Montesquieu went so far as to posit a connection between climate and form of government, arguing that despotism was more natural in hot climates than cold and that liberty was more natural to inhabitants of temperate and cold areas. He pointed out that Asia, with its political tradition of oriental despotism, has no temperate zone, in contrast to Europe (or North America), which has an extensive one.[14]

Differences in the types of crops grown account not only for differences in cultivation patterns, dietary preferences, and nutritional standards but also, in some cases, for differences in the type and level of economic development. Some scholars have even argued that such elemental factors as climate, soil, and water resources may account for contrasting forms of social, economic, and political organization.

In China, for example, where rice has been the staple for centuries, a system of permanent agriculture based on elaborate irrigation networks both necessitated a centralized bureaucracy and reinforced the autocratic tendencies of the imperial court, according to Karl Wittfogel.[15] This "hydraulic" theory of Chinese civilization places the primary emphasis on economic geography: China's autocratic political tradition, Wittfogel argues, grew out of a need to organize and regiment society for the purpose of taming China's great rivers. These rivers, combined with a conducive climate and at least adequate soil, made continuous rice cultivation possible.

Differences in climate and resource availability may also partly account for the dramatic inequalities in wealth from one region to the next. One of the most important natural resources (one we often take for granted) is fertile land. Since the early 1970s, there has been a steady decline in the global land-to-population ratio. According to Lester Brown, founder of the Worldwatch Institute, the period since World War II "breaks into two distinct periods—before and after the 1973 oil price increase." Why 1973? Because that was the year in which the "age of cheap energy" came to an end. Prior to 1973, world food output had been growing at a pace of 3 percent per year, enough to keep food production ahead of population growth. Since 1973, however, the annual growth in food output has dropped below 2 percent, barely matching population increases.[16]

Even so, Brown noted in 1984, the true dimensions of the problem cannot be entirely appreciated without a closer look at the "wide variations in individual geographic regions." Specifically,

> In North America, production has steadily outstripped demand, generating ever-larger surpluses. In the Soviet Union, output has fallen behind demand over the past decade, making the country the largest grain importer in history. And

in Africa, which has a population of 512 million and which has to feed 14 million additional people each year, food production per person has fallen steadily since 1970. Despite a tripling of grain imports since then, hunger has become chronic, an enduring part of the African landscape.[17]

The political and economic implications of this food-population squeeze differ enormously from one region to the next. Africa, Asia, and Latin America are all food-deficit regions with large foreign debts (see Tables 1.1, 1.2, and 1.3). In contrast, North America is the principal food-surplus area and, along with Western Europe and Japan, the major source of foreign aid and investment for the developing nations. As a consequence, low farm prices and a depressed rural economy resulting from overproduction have been major political issues in the United States at the same time that chronic food shortages and periodic famines have plagued Africa and Asia. The same oil crisis that precipitated the worldwide decline in food production also brought an economic windfall to many oil-rich Middle Eastern countries. As we shall see in Part IV, the uses to which this newfound wealth was and was not put have had a profound effect on the region and the world.

Unfortunately, the regions that have the lowest per capita income levels tend to have the highest population growth rates. In most of sub-Saharan Africa,

Table 1.1 Wheat, Rice, and Corn Production in Selected Countries (millions of metric tons)

	Wheat		Rice		Corn	
	1986	1991	1986	1991	1986	1991
World	536	519	470	520	481	478
United States	57	53	6	7	210	189
Argentina	9	9	0.4	0.3	12	8
Brazil	5	3	10	9.5	21	23
China	89	95	177	187	66	93
Egypt	2	4.5	2	3	4	5
France	27	34.5	0.06	0.10	10	13
Great Britain	14	14	—	—	—	—
India	47	54.5	90	111	8	8
Japan	0.9	1.6	15	12	—	1
Mexico	5	4	0.5	0.3	12	13.5
Former USSR	92	80	3	2	13	8.5
*Germany	10	16.5	—	—	1	2

* Figures for 1986 are for the Federal Republic of Germany only. Figures for 1991 include the former German Democratic Republic.

Source: United Nations Food and Agriculture Organization, *1986 FAO Production Yearbook,* vol. 40, and *1991 FAO Production Yearbook,* vol. 45.

Table 1.2 External Debt and Debt Service of Developing Countries (expressed as percent of exports)

	1985	1988	1991
External Debt	150.5	141.9	118.4
(billions of U.S. dollars)	(998.4)	(1,216.4)	(1,313.3)
Africa	188.0	242.5	226.7
Asia	102.9	79.2	64.1
Europe	149.8	146.2	135.0
Latin America	295.6	292.1	250.3
Middle East	89.5	120.8	104.4
Debt Service Payments	20.8	19.0	15.4
(billions of U.S. dollars)	(137.8)	(162.8)	(171.0)
Africa	26.7	25.2	29.0
Asia	14.7	10.7	8.0
Europe	22.3	23.1	17.5
Latin America	41.3	44.9	36.1

Source: International Monetary Fund, *World Economic Outlook* (Washington, D.C.: IMF, 1990), tab. A45.

the average annual population growth rate is more than 3 percent. At that pace, Africa's population will double in just twenty-four years. Kenya currently has the highest fertility rate in the world—eight children per mother and a 4 percent net population increase per year. Nigeria, Tanzania, and Uganda also have potentially disastrous birthrates in excess of 3 percent per year.

These figures suggest that in many African countries, development will have to take a back seat to mere survival—meaning that African governments will find themselves in a defensive rather than an offensive posture in the years to come. In these lands, a vicious cycle is at work, one that is extremely difficult to break. Poverty and malnutrition are pressing problems due to the absence of economic development and little or no new job creation. But the dynamics of rapid population expansion are such that an increasing percentage of society's members are young. Roughly 45 percent of Africa's population is under age 15. In a country with high unemployment, the youth are inevitably the hardest hit. They are also the most rebellious. Lacking opportunities and having no hope for the future, they are like dry kindling waiting to be ignited. The potential for political instability in these circumstances is self-evident.

Latin America faces similar problems. The population of Costa Rica, El Salvador, Guatemala, Honduras, and Nicaragua doubled (to 27 million) in twenty-five years, according to the Latin American Demographic Center (a branch of the United Nations), and is projected to reach 40 million by the turn of the century. In fact, the population growth rate in Central America is one of the highest in the world, according to the executive director of a family planning agency in Guatemala. "Demographic factors," he asserted, "are tremendously

Table 1.3 Population (1991) and Gross National Product (1991) for Selected Countries

	Population (millions)	Gross National Product (billions of U.S. dollars)
Argentina	3	91
Brazil	153	447
China	1,150	424
Egypt	53	33
France	57	1,167
Germany	80	1,516
India	865	284
Japan	124	3,337
Kenya	25	8-9
Mexico	88	252
Nigeria	119	34
Russia	149	479
Saudi Arabia	15-16	34
South Africa	37	105
United Kingdom	57-58	963
United States	252	5,686

Source: World Bank, *The World Bank Atlas* (Washington, D.C.: World International Bank for Reconstruction and Development/The World Bank, 1992). Published by Oxford University Press, Inc., New York.

important, and they will continue to play a major role not only in our social, economic and political situation, but also in the generation of violence."[18] Indeed, it seems likely that the flames of insurgency that engulfed Central America in the 1980s were fanned in part by the poverty and despair that accompanied this rapid population growth.

By contrast, the economic and social problems of Europe and North America are largely unrelated to overpopulation or underdevelopment. On the contrary, they are often part of a "postindustrial" syndrome characterized by a shift from manufacturing to a service-based economy; an emphasis on capital-intensive, high-technology production methods; a tendency toward "stagflation" (economic recession accompanied by inflation); and a growth in trade relations and economic interdependence. Consumerism and commercialism are two other well-known attributes of postindustrialization. In addition, social and environmental problems such as a high crime rate, chronic traffic congestion, air pollution, and a dramatic rise in stress-related health problems generally accompany the urbanization process set in motion by industrialization.

Although concepts like development and modernization are usually associated with the developing nations of Africa, Asia, and Latin America, they have universal validity. Nation-states are the building blocks of the modern international order. Levels of economic and political development vary from one nation or region to the next, but problems such as national integration (or disintegration) are not confined to any one nation or region.

Patterns and Trends

Regional patterns and trends are often multidimensional. Economic patterns quite commonly correlate with population trends and even with environmental changes. The region-by-region sketches that follow illustrate this point.

Western Europe and North America   The wealthiest countries, with per capita GNP averaging roughly $20,000, are nearly all in Western Europe and North America; the most notable exceptions are Japan, South Korea, and Australia. These countries also have the lowest population growth rates, the highest life expectancies, the lowest infant mortality rates, the highest daily calorie supply per capita, the lowest illiteracy rates, and so forth.

Slavic Europe   All the former socialist countries of Slavic Europe have per capita annual incomes under $3,500; most fall between $1,500 and $3,000. (In non-European socialist countries, annual income is below $1,500; in China, Vietnam, Cambodia, and Laos, it is under $500.) Population growth rates are less than 1 percent per year, life expectancy is 70–72, fertility rates are 2.0–2.9, illiteracy rates are less than 5 percent, and the share of agriculture in GDP is at least 10 percent. Perhaps the most striking feature is that per capita GDP in all of the former Soviet bloc states has been shrinking due to the painful adjustments of shifting from centrally planned to market-based economies. The key point here is not that the figures are relatively high or low but that they are relatively uniform throughout the region.

The Arab World   The Arab world (the Middle East and North Africa) is one of two regions in the world (the other being Asia) where the gap between the richest countries and the poorest is a gulf. In 1990, per capita GNP in the United Arab Emirates was just under $20,000; in Egypt, it was $610; in Sudan, $400. This region is the only one in the world that depends so singularly for its wealth on one resource, oil. Because of this lopsided oil dependence, the region as a whole is vulnerable to disruptions in the world market. The oil glut of the early 1980s adversely affected not only the oil-exporting Arab states but also the rest of the world. Countries registering negative per capita growth rates between 1980 and 1991 included Saudi Arabia, Bahrain, Qatar, Syria, Algeria, Iran, Jordan, and Sudan. Only Oman, Egypt, Tunisia, Turkey, and Israel escaped this plight.

A drop in oil prices is only one reason for negative GNP growth rates in the Arab world; the other is high population growth rates that match those of sub-Saharan Africa. The Middle Eastern Arab states grew at a rate of more than 3 percent a year in the 1980s. The North African Arab states grew at rates ranging from 2.2 to 3.0 percent (Libya's rate was 4.1 percent). The average Arab woman, like her African counterpart, bears five or more children. Life expectancy is significantly higher in the Arab world than in sub-Saharan Africa but lower than in Europe, North America, China, Australia, and most of Latin America. The infant mortality rate ranges from 31 to 90—in the same range as Latin America but much higher than in the other regions.

A striking trait common to all Arab countries—one related to Arab culture—is that women constitute less than 25 percent of the labor force (the lowest of any region in the world). The only exceptions in the Middle East or North Africa are two non-Arab countries, Israel and Turkey.

Asia   Asia, like the Arab world, is characterized by glaring disparities between the richest and poorest countries. With a GNP of $3.3 trillion, Japan ranks second in the world as an economic power, trailing only the United States. Its per capita GNP was nearly $27,000 in 1991, also among the highest in the world. By contrast, Bangladesh, with a population nearly the size of Japan's, had a per capita GNP of only $220—one of the smallest in the world. Asia also has the two most populous countries on the planet, China (1.15 billion) and India (865 million), and four other countries—Indonesia (181 million), Japan (123 million), Pakistan (115 million), and Bangladesh (108 million)—that rank in the top ten. These six countries account for over half of the world's current population. But population growth rates have fallen dramatically in Asia—in stark contrast to the continuing high birthrates in the Arab world and sub-Saharan Africa.

Although Asia is still the setting for some of the world's most appalling poverty, it is also the scene of many of the most dynamic economies. In addition to Japan, South Korea, Taiwan, Hong Kong, and Singapore have become "high-tech" trading nations. Communist China had one of the fastest growing economies in the world in the early 1990s, and the economies of Thailand, Malaysia, and Indonesia grew not only in absolute terms but also in per capita terms between 1980 and 1991. Indeed, the phenomenal economic growth in Asia can be viewed as a regional trend. If it continues unabated, it will propel Asia to a dominant position in the world economy within a decade or two.

Sub-Saharan Africa   The countries of sub-Saharan Africa have annual per capita incomes of $500 or less. The share of agriculture in GDP is generally among the highest in the world; the share of investment in GDP is among the lowest. Many countries in sub-Saharan Africa have an average annual population growth rate of more than 3 percent and all are growing by at least 2.2 percent. Life expectancy at birth, with rare exceptions, is less than 55 years (compared to Western Europe and North America, where it is 73 years or more). Also, the fertility rate (the number of children a woman will bear during her lifetime), at 5 or more, is the highest in the world, as is the infant mortality rate (more than 150 per 1,000 children under age 5). The daily calorie supply per capita is the lowest in the world—less than 2,300. (It is highest in the West, where it is 3,300 or more.)

A popular misconception about sub-Saharan Africa is that it is overpopulated. In fact, Africa has the lowest population density of any region in the world. The population problem Africa faces is in the future, due to its dangerously high growth rate. It is also a ratio problem: the ratio of population to resources, jobs, arable land, and so on.

Finally, annual water use per capita is the lowest in the world in sub-Saharan Africa (less than 50 cubic meters per year). Countries with the highest per capita water use (including the United States, Canada, Spain, Portugal, Australia, Argentina, Chile, Egypt, Sudan, Saudi Arabia, Iran, and Pakistan) average more than 1,000 cubic meters per capita.

Latin America   Latin America's richest countries (Mexico, Costa Rica, Panama, Venezuela, Brazil, Argentina, and Chile) have about the same per capita income levels as the most prosperous former socialist countries—around $2,500 a year. On most other social and economic measures, Latin America falls somewhere between North America and Western Europe, on the one hand, and sub-Saharan Africa, on the other.

Any broad overview of regional differences must by definition neglect the many subtle physical and cultural characteristics that distinguish one region from another. Such an overview does, however, illustrate the fact that major geographic, cultural, social, and economic differences do exist and suggests that a regional approach to comparative politics is likely to yield valuable insights into the reasons why nations are not all governed in the same way and why certain patterns of politics are either unique to a particular region or more prevalent in some regions than in others. In other words, a regional approach is an economical one from a pedagogical standpoint: it *summarizes* and allows political *generalizations*. That said, the regional differences painted with broad brush strokes here are examined in greater depth and detail in subsequent chapters.

CONCLUSION

Although the regions of the world are difficult to define precisely, a regional approach to comparative politics has advantages over other approaches. First, it highlights social, cultural, historical, economic, and political features common to all or most of the states within a given geographic area. Second, it provides a basis for comparison not only between and among states but also across regional boundaries. To the extent that generalizations can be made about politics with regions, a regional approach is more efficient than more traditional state-centered approaches. At the same time, choosing key countries as case studies within each major region—Western Europe, Slavic (Eastern) Europe, the Middle East, Asia, sub-Saharan Africa, and Latin America—gives concrete form to abstract generalizations.

KEY TERMS

comparative analysis	empirical methods
comparative politics	Socratic method
deductive approach	political ecology
inductive approach	political culture
correlations	political socialization
independent variable	the good life
dependent variable	subordinate system
normative political theory	

STUDY QUESTIONS

1. What is a region? How important is geography? What other factors are important and why?
2. What are the major regions of the world? Can most "superregions" be divided into subregions? If so, what are some good examples?
3. Is North America a region? If so, what are its boundaries? Are Mexico and Canada natural parts of this region? Why? Is a North American Free Trade Agreement (NAFTA) logical when viewed in a regional perspective?
4. How do history and culture shape political traditions and practices from region to region? Are there any examples of regional patterns that you have read about or perhaps witnessed firsthand? (Suggestion: Ask a foreign student on your campus this question; not only will you learn a lot, but you will probably also make a new friend.)
5. To what degree do variables such as climate, resources, food, and population play a role in shaping political institutions? Do you think that such variables might also influence national character? If so, can you think of any examples?

SUGGESTED READING

Amate, C. O. C. *Inside the OAU: Pan-Africanism in Practice.* New York: St. Martin's Press, 1987.

Ayouty, Yassin, and Zartman, William I. *The OAU after Twenty Years.* New York: Praeger, 1984.

Boyd, Gavin. *Regionalism and Global Security.* Boston: Heath, 1984.

Boyd, Gavin, and Feld, Werner, J., eds. *Comparative Regional Systems.* Elmsford, N.Y.: Pergamon Press, 1980.

Brecher, Michael, "The Subordinate System of South Asia." *Asian Survey,* vol. 15, no. 2 (January 1963).

Burgess, Michael. *Federalism and European Union: Political Ideas, Influences, and Strategies in the European Community, 1972–1987.* London: Routledge, 1989.

Cantori, Louis T., and Spiegel, Stephen L. *The International Politics of Regions: A Comparative Approach.* Englewood Cliffs, N.J.: Prentice Hall, 1970.

Croan, Melvin. "Lands In-between: The Politics of Cultural Identity in Contemporary Eastern Europe." *Eastern European Politics and Societies,* vol. 3, no. 1 (Spring 1989).

Emmerson, Donald. "ASEAN as an International Regime." *Journal of International Affairs,* vol. 41, no. 1 (Summer-Fall 1987).

Haas, Michael. *The Asian Way to Peace: A Story of Regional Cooperation.* New York: Praeger, 1989.

Mazzeo, Domenico, ed. *African Regional Organizations.* Cambridge: Cambridge University Press, 1985.

NOTES

1. Raphael Sealey, *A History of the Greek City-States ca. 700–338 B.C.* (Berkeley: University of California, 1976), p. 68.
2. Cyril E. Robinson, *A History of Greece* (New York: Crowell, 1929), p. 51.
3. Sealey, *Greek City-States,* p. 68.
4. Mattei Dogan and Dominique Pelassy, *How to Compare Nations: Strategies in Comparative Politics* (Chatham, N.J.: Chatham House, 1984), p. 5.
5. Ibid.
6. Aristotle, *Politics,* Ernest Baker, ed. and trans. (New York: Oxford University Press, 1958); see especially the introduction, pp. xxviii–xxix.
7. Thomas Hobbes, *Leviathan* (London: Everyman's, 1965).
8. Jean-Jacques Rousseau, *First and Second Discourses,* Roger and Judith Masters, trans., Roger Masters, ed. (New York: St. Martin's Press, 1964).
9. Louis T. Cantori and Stephen L. Spiegel, *The International Politics of Regions: A Comparative Approach* (Englewood Cliffs, N.J.: Prentice Hall, 1970), p. 6.
10. Michael Brecher, "The Subordinate System of Southern Asia," *Asian Survey,* vol. 15, no. 2 (January 1963), p. 220.
11. See, for example, Robert Jackson and Carl Rosberg, *Personal Rule in Black Africa: Princes, Autocrats, Prophets, Tyrants* (Berkeley: University of California Press, 1982), p. 235.
12. Jurg Steiner, *European Democracies* (White Plains, N.Y.: Longman, 1986), p. 1.
13. See, for example, Hans Morganthau and Ken Thompson, *Politics among Nations: The Struggle for Power and Peace* (New York: Knopf, 1985), pp. 233–240.
14. See, for example, Henry J. Merry, *Montesquieu's System of Natural Government* (West Lafayette, Ind.: Purdue University Press, 1970), especially pp. 51–53.
15. Karl Wittfogel, *Oriental Despotism: A Comparative Study of Total Power* (New Haven, Conn.: Yale University Press, 1957).
16. Lester R. Brown, "Putting Food on the World's Table," in *State of the World, 1984* (New York: Norton, 1984), chap. 10.
17. Ibid.
18. Larry Rohter, "Central American Plight Is People in Abundance," *New York Times,* Sept. 6, 1987, p. 1.

2

Comparing Political Systems

Political systems can be classified in a variety of ways. The most common classifications stress concentration (diffusion) of power or level of economic and political development. Those based on power often make a threefold distinction among democratic, authoritarian, and totalitarian systems. For a long time those based on levels of development featured just two types of nations, developed and developing; more recent studies identify South Korea, Taiwan, Hong Kong, and Singapore as newly industrialized countries (NICs).

A common obstacle to clear thinking in any field of study is the tendency to confuse models of reality with reality itself. This observation is especially pertinent to political science, partly because the stuff of politics is largely intangible. Thus a note of caution is in order at the outset. The political systems (or models) sketched here are *theoretical* constructs—they do not exist in pure form anywhere. Nonetheless, it is useful to discuss different forms of government in the abstract before moving on to describe and analyze concrete forms. Hence this chapter will rely more heavily on deductive reasoning than subsequent chapters (which will be heavily inductive).

Two modern forms of government, constitutional democracy and totalitarian dictatorship, have left an indelible mark on world politics in the past half century. What are the historic forerunners of these two models? Is traditional authoritarian rule likely to supplant Stalinism in the former Soviet Union and Eastern Europe in the long run, or will the forces of liberalism that so dramatically burst forth there in 1989 transform these societies into authentically pluralistic systems? Is democracy really on the advance worldwide? Can totalitarianism now be relegated to the dustbin of history? Is military rule or some other form of authoritarian dictatorship inevitable in developing nations that have never experienced democracy? Are conditions in different regions of the world naturally conducive to different types of regimes?

We take a closer look at these questions—and others that they raise—in the pages that follow.

Political Models: Yesterday and Today

For thousands of years, political thinkers have tried to design the perfect government—or to dissect the imperfect ones—by conceptualizing the relationships between rulers and ruled. Aristotle was perhaps the most gifted model builder of all time. His classic work, *Politics,* was the first comparative study of political systems. Aristotle identified six possible forms of rule based on a threefold distinction: rule by one, rule by the few, and rule by the many. Each of these alternatives, in turn, can occur in two opposite forms, depending on the moral character of the ruler or rulers. Corrupt rulers, Aristotle taught, use power to further selfish interests or "special interests"; worthy rulers, on the contrary, place the good of all above the good of a privileged few or of narrow self-interest. Thus rule by one in his or her own interests is **tyranny**—Aristotle's worst form. **Monarchy** (or rule by a benevolent dictator) is the opposite of tyranny. Aristotle considered monarchy the best form in an ideal world, although he recognized that it was rare in the real world. He called self-interested rule by the few **oligarchy** and contrasted this form with **aristocracy**—rule by the few in the interests of all. Finally, Aristotle warned against the tyranny of the majority (selfish rule by the many), which he disdainfully called **democracy**. The opposite of democracy in Aristotle's typology was a **polity**—rule by the many in the interests of all. Although polity was the least efficient form of good government, according to Aristotle, it was the best form possible in many (if not most) societies.

Although he abhorred tyranny, Aristotle was no great enthusiast of democracy because he feared that it would degenerate into **mob rule**—rule by the masses in their own narrow self-interest. Such rule, Aristotle reasoned, would celebrate mediocrity and scorn excellence. **Justice**—a political condition in which society's members are rewarded in proportion to their individual merit—was regarded as incompatible with popular rule.

To his great credit, Aristotle did not get hung up on his own models. He recognized that reality is usually much more complex and varied than any theoretical construct, that the range of possibilities is broader than simplistic typology, and that if avoiding the worst regimes is difficult, creating the best is impossible.

Aristotle argued that a constitutional system combining elements of monarchy, oligarchy, and democracy is the best form of government possible under most circumstances. Such a **mixed regime**, he believed, would give the middle class a key role in government—that of mediating between the rich (whom they admire without resenting) and the poor (whom they pity without either fearing or embracing). This type of regime would offer the best means of achieving equilibrium between the class interests of the two extremes, especially where the middle class was large. The middle class, he reasoned, was not so affluent as to lack all sympathy for the poor nor so destitute as to revolt or seek to dispossess the rich—moderate wealth would produce moderate political opinions. (By the same token, extreme poverty would produce political extremism.) In this manner, Aristotle made a logical connection between social class structure and political stability.

Aristotle's model of a mixed regime resembles many contemporary governments—often called **democratic republics**—in which power and wealth are widely distributed (and, in the modern welfare state, redistributed). A strong executive similar to a monarch is often present in even the most democratic of these regimes. The strong presidencies built into the American and French constitutional systems are two cases in point.

The secret of success of a mixed form of government lies in its realism. What Aristotle sketched was a kind of internal balance of power among competing interests. Although he did not elaborate a Madisonian theory of checks and balances like that found in the *Federalist Papers,* he provided the conceptual underpinnings for such a theory. Indeed, Aristotle drew up the blueprints for constitutional democracy as it is widely practiced today—a form of government in which power and wealth are broadly (albeit unequally) dispersed and the right to rule derives from set procedures, including, above all, periodic popular elections.

Regimes characterized by a concentration of power and wealth, whether run by a single despotic ruler or a ruling clique, are normally described as authoritarian. They may be headed by a military or civilian strongman, a military junta, or a party-based directorate (for example, the *politburo* in the former Soviet Union).

Aristotle's models are germane to the modern world in large part thanks to their elasticity. They can be stretched into an almost infinite variety of specific forms. In fact, until the twentieth century, there was no political system that did not fit into one model or another. The rise of Soviet Russia and Nazi Germany, however, forced political thinkers to reevaluate the adequacy of the authoritarian model. Today, totalitarianism has receded and authoritarian rule is again the major alternative to democracy. At the same time, democracy has sprouted in many countries and in several regions where it has not flourished in the past.

Constitutional Democracy

A look at broad historical trends over the past hundred years leads to a striking conclusion: the fading of monarchy has been accompanied by the coming of age of democracy. Whereas there were many monarchs and few republics in the nineteenth century, today the situation is reversed. Democracies now flourish throughout Western Europe and have recently flowered in Latin America as well.

In the contemporary world, there are two basic forms of democracy: presidential and parliamentary. The United States exemplifies the former, Great Britain the latter.

Presidential Democracy

In a **presidential democracy**, the chief executive is popularly elected by the nation as a whole. The executive, legislative, and judicial branches are distinct structures with special constitutional functions, and a system of checks and balances is built in. No member of the government can serve in more than one branch at any given time.

In this system, the president is both head of state and head of government. The president leads the nation at home and abroad but must sell favored policies and programs to the legislature, which has the power of the purse (final taxing and spending authority). In the United States, at least, constitutional questions, including those involving disputes between the executive and legislative branches, are decided by the Supreme Court exercising its power of judicial review.

Parliamentary Democracy

In a **parliamentary democracy**, the chief executive is usually a prime minister rather than a president. The British Westminster model provides a convenient starting point for any discussion of parliamentary government. The British prime minister is chosen by the majority party in the legislature (or parliament). To become prime minister, one must first win a seat in the parliament by standing for election in a local constituency and must then be chosen by one's peers in the legislature. Note that there is no separation of powers in this type of democracy; rather there is a fusion of powers. The prime minister and cabinet are chosen from the leadership of the majority party or coalition in the legislature. They retain their legislative seats while they simultaneously serve in executive posts in the government.

A British-style parliamentary system has several distinct advantages. First, the government rarely has great difficulty getting its budget approved by the legislature because it almost always has a legislative majority (otherwise it would not have become the government in the first place). Second, if the government falters for whatever reason, it can be forced out at any time by a "no confidence" vote in the parliament (although this device has not been used in Britain in recent decades). Third, the government can dissolve the parliament at any time and call for new elections. The power to terminate a parliament is important for two arguable reasons: it may help keep party discipline in hand (although scholars disagree on this), and it sometimes gives the party in power the opportunity to choose an auspicious time for new elections. (In the British system, a government must call new elections at least once every five years.)

Contrary to a widely held notion, the British parliamentary system is *not* closely copied by many other countries. In fact, Canada, Australia, and New Zealand are among the few that have emulated the United Kingdom in any considerable detail. Most countries do not require that cabinet ministers be members of parliament; the Netherlands actually forbids them to be. Nor are the cabinet members necessarily top party leaders. Most parliaments serve for fixed terms, and some cannot be prematurely dissolved. Usually parliamentary governments are underpinned by majority parties or coalitions, but in some cases (for example, in the Scandinavian countries), minority governments are frequent.

Many variations of both the U.S. and the British models exist. Some countries combine features of both systems. The most notable example of this approach is France, which has both a popularly elected president and a prime minister chosen by the majority party in parliament. Whether nations choose one model or the other (or some combination of the two), the goal is always essentially the same: limited government—a government of laws, not of men. A sharper contrast with personal dictatorships and authoritarian regimes of all kinds is difficult to conceive.

Today constitutional democracies can be found in every part of the globe including regions such as Slavic Europe and Latin America where pluralism made few inroads until recently. Two of the oldest and largest democracies coexist harmoniously in North America; in fact, the United States and Canada share the longest unguarded border in the world. Western Europe is democratically ruled without exception. The most populous democracy, India, is located in Asia. Western-style government has not flourished in the rest of Asia, although Japan has successfully adapted the parliamentary system—virtually imposed by the United States after World War II—into a unique form of **patron-client democracy**. Sri Lanka (formerly Ceylon), an island neighbor of India, is the other notable exception. Australia and New Zealand have long been solidly democratic nations; recently, the Philippines also lurched toward democracy following the overthrow of the nation's corrupt president, Ferdinand Marcos, in early 1986. Marcos's successor, Corazon Aquino, vowed to preserve democracy despite continuing guerrilla warfare against the government by communist insurgents.

Democracy has had the least success in Africa and the Middle East. Popularly elected civilian government has not taken firm root in any Arab state with the possible exception of Lebanon prior to the civil war of the mid-1970s. In Africa there are only two established democracies, Gambia and Botswana, but several other African nations, including Zambia, have moved toward multiparty constitutional rule.

Modern Mixed Regimes

Aristotle favored the mixed regime, with elements of both democracy and oligarchy. In fact, what we normally sanctify as democracy is not pure and unadulterated democracy at all but a watered-down version (known as a republic) in which elected representatives of the people, not the people themselves, actually make laws and decide policy. These elected officials form a kind of political class—a legislative oligarchy, if you will. Presidents and prime ministers typically possess some of the same powers as tyrants; in times of crisis, they often become virtual dictators. A case in point was Indira Gandhi, who as prime minister of India declared a national state of emergency in 1975 and exercised dictatorial powers for nineteen months. France under General Charles de Gaulle during the formative years of the Fifth Republic—a period that coincided with Algeria's war of independence against France—also illustrates this point. The trouble in Algeria brought about a domestic political and constitutional crisis in France in 1958; de Gaulle stepped in (at the invitation of key politicians) and guided the nation through this difficult time. He ruled with a firm hand, but his methods were no more autocratic than those of, say, Abraham Lincoln in the Civil War or Presidents Woodrow Wilson and Franklin Roosevelt in World Wars I and II, respectively.

If democracies have elements of oligarchy and even tyranny, dictatorships may have elements of democracy. Elections are held, though they may be rigged. Sometimes they are little more than plebiscites designed to demonstrate how much the masses adore the dictator. In many dictatorships, at least limited civil liberties exist. There may even be token political opposition—perhaps a small maverick party in a rubber-stamp legislature or a relatively independent newspaper that dares to criticize the government. For example, the government of Egypt is more authoritarian than democratic, but many of the trappings of democracy are undeniably present.

This mingling of different forms of government is even more evident when we look at different types of the same form. Categorization can be difficult, particularly in the case of authoritarian regimes. For example, in South Korea, elections are held, some civil liberties are permitted, and people move about freely. But until 1987, South Korea was in reality part military junta and part personal dictatorship. Following a coup in 1961, General Park Chung Hee ran the country as a military strongman (although he was "elected" president in 1962). In 1972 a referendum allowed him to be elected to an unlimited number of six-year terms. He was assassinated by one of his own lieutenants in 1979 and was succeeded by another military strongman, General Chun Doo Hwan. In 1987, student-led popular demonstrations against the government, backed by pressure from the U.S. Reagan administration to democratize, compelled Chun Doo Hwan to allow popular presidential elections. These recent developments are dramatic and unprecedented in Northeast Asia; however, the tender shoots of democracy in South Korea will remain fragile for many years to come.

Market and Mixed Economies

Both democratic and authoritarian forms of government are typically associated with **market**, or **mixed**, **economies**. Market economies regard **free enterprise** as the key to self-sustaining growth and general prosperity. They feature a minimum of state interference in commerce, finance, industry, and agriculture, a policy known as *laissez faire*. The forces of supply and demand are allowed to operate without extensive state regulation or subsidization. The profit motive provides the incentive for individuals to work hard, compete vigorously, improve the quality of the services or products they deliver, and strive for excellence. In theory, coercion and exhortation are unnecessary because everyone in a free-enterprise system is *self-motivated*.

The whole concept of *laissez faire* as originally expounded by the Scottish economist Adam Smith in the late eighteenth century posited a natural harmony of interests in society. Individuals behaving rationally (trying to get rich) in a free-enterprise system would unwittingly serve the needs of society as a whole. By working hard, earning as much money as possible, spending some and saving the rest, investing soundly, and playing by the rules so as not to jeopardize the legal order on which contractual obligations ultimately depend, individuals would create a synergy that could be expected to maximize creativity, ingenuity, and productivity. It would do so, in part, by rewarding innovation and invention.

In reality, no pure market economies exist. All market economies are mixed free-enterprise systems, meaning that the operation of market forces is regulated in varying degrees by government. For example, the money supply is generally controlled by a central bank (in the United States, the Federal Reserve Board performs this function). Governments use fiscal as well as monetary policy to regulate the economy. They raise taxes and cut spending to cool down an "overheated" economy or lower taxes and increase spending to resuscitate a slumping economy. They also typically give extensive subsidies to agriculture and tax breaks to business and industry. In many developing countries, the government heavily subsidizes the general populace by providing food, fuel, and other necessities at prices well below actual cost. Subsidies are a major source of government indebtedness in Africa, Asia, and Latin America, but ruling elites in these regions are reluctant to discontinue them because of the hardships that would result and the danger of provoking riots and regime-threatening unrest.

Authoritarian Regimes

Authoritarianism has been around as long as government itself. It is indigenous to every region of the world. It remains the most prevalent form of government in Africa, the Middle East, and Asia. Until the 1980s, it was also the norm in Latin America. Even in Western Europe it was present on the Iberian peninsula (Spain and Portugal) until the mid-1970s.

There are many forms of authoritarian government, but most share certain characteristics. First, there is usually a wealthy, elite class closely linked to the ruler or rulers. No radical transformation, restructuring, or penetration of society is attempted, and the regime is often quite content to let the free market operate unmolested (it may even be closely allied with domestic business and banking interests). The ruling elite aims, above all, to maintain the status quo. In doing so, it assumes a defensive posture: tolerate no challenges from opposition parties or autonomous interest groups, but otherwise let sleeping dogs lie. To this end, popular participation is often deliberately kept to a minimum (in contrast to Marxist-Leninist regimes, which mobilize or manipulate the masses for particular economic and political ends). For this reason, too, political and sometimes civil liberties are curbed or denied. Finally, the military often has a key governing role, even where it does not rule directly.

Authoritarian systems can be classified in various ways, none of which can accommodate all relevant cases with equal precision. But generally, contemporary authoritarian regimes take the following forms:

1. Personal dictatorships (tyrannies)
2. Military oligarchies (juntas)
3. Dynastic regimes (monarchies)

Personal Dictatorships

Personal dictatorships have long dominated the pages of history. Indeed, they were prevalent in Aristotle's day (he called them *tyrannies,* rule by a tyrant), and the twentieth century has had its share. Totalitarian tyrants like Hitler and Stalin appear to have read and digested at least one passage from Aristotle. In his *Politics,* Aristotle noted that tyrants were famous (or infamous) for "the 'lopping off' of outstanding men, and men of spirit."[1] Some other methods of personal rule, according to Aristotle, included the following:

> the forbidding of common meals, clubs, and anything of a like character—or, in other words, a defensive attitude against everything likely to produce the two qualities of mutual confidence and a high spirit . . . the adoption of every means for making every subject as much of a stranger as is possible to every other . . . [requiring] every resident to be constantly appearing in public . . . endeavouring to get information about every man's sayings and doings. This entails a secret police. . . . (Men are not so likely to speak their minds if they go in fear of a secret police; and if they do speak out, they are less likely to go undetected.)[2]

In summary, Aristotle believed that tyrants have three basic aims:

1. To break the spirit of their subjects
2. To breed mutual mistrust ("Tyranny is never overthrown until men can begin to trust one another.")
3. To make their subjects incapable of action ("Nobody attempts the impossible.")

Not all personal dictators are equally tyrannical. Fortunately, few modern tyrants can hold a candle to Hitler or Stalin when it comes to brutality and an insatiable appetite for power.[3] Nonetheless, personal dictatorships are often associated with extreme political repression and arbitrary rule.

Personal dictators come in many guises. They usually gain power through force or fraud, often by means of a coup d'état or a rigged election. They may start out as military officers, charismatic politicians, or even religious gurus.

One of the first military officers to seize power and then establish a highly personalistic dictatorship was Egypt's Gamal Abdel Nasser. Military officers who have become personal dictators include Saddam Hussein (Iraq), Muammar al-Qaddafi (Libya), Mengistu Haile Miriam (Ethiopia), Samuel Doe (Liberia), Jerry Rawlings (Ghana), Hafez al-Assad (Syria), Muhammad Zia ul-Haq (Pakistan), Muhammad Ershad (Bangladesh), Manuel Noriega (Panama), and Alfredo Stroessner (Paraguay). Uganda under Idi Amin and the Central African Republic under Jean-Bedel Bokassa were two fairly recent instances of cruel and arbitrary tyranny at the hands of personal dictators who began as military officers. (Both were ousted in 1979.) General Rafael Trujillo of the Dominican Republic ruled as a brutal tyrant for thirty years until his assassination in 1961. General Anastazio Somoza of Nicaragua, overthrown by the Sandinistas in 1979, is yet another example of a modern-day tyrant.

In recent times there have also been some notorious civilian tyrants. They are often demagogues or visionaries with a gift of eloquence and a lust for power. Several of the charismatic Third World figures who led their nations to independence three or four decades ago were able to translate their popularity into a formula for personal rule. Most are now gone. Several of the most notable were Sukarno in Indonesia (1945–1966), Kwame Nkrumah in Ghana (1957–1966), and Ahmed Sékou Touré in Guinea (1958–1984). Sukarno and Nkrumah were ousted by military coups. Several civilian dictators have fallen more recently. The Shah of Iran was ousted in 1979; seven years later, Ferdinand Marcos in the Philippines and the notorious Jean-Claude ("Baby Doc") Duvalier in Haiti met a similar fate. Habib Bourguiba became Tunisia's president for life following independence in 1956 and remained in power for more than three decades until he was ousted in a bloodless coup in 1987. At the time, only Jordan's King Hussein had ruled longer.

Regardless of background, tyrants must rely on a military ("praetorian") guard to keep them in power. As two observers of this phenomenon in Africa have noted, "The key to tyranny is the relations between the tyrant and his mercenaries, without whom tyranny is impossible."[4] Personal dictatorships in which the military plays a key role, however, should not be confused with military rule, which is a separate type of authoritarian system.

Military Juntas

Only where military rule has been institutionalized can a military regime be said to exist. In this type of authoritarian government, there is almost always a figure who is "first among equals" because someone must perform the ceremonial and symbolic functions of a chief executive. But one way in which a typical military regime differs from a tyranny, even one dominated by a military strongman, is that rule is collegial rather than personal.

Personalistic rule cannot be institutionalized. The reason is simple: a ruler who has risen to power by his own wiles cannot succeed himself—even the most absolute dictator is mortal. But choosing an **heir apparent** is risky because the anointed one may become an impatient rival. Thus a system dominated by a military strongman would fit the description of a tyranny better than that of a military regime.

Where the military rules as an institution, there is seldom a charismatic or popular leader. The powers of the chief executive are shared by several high-ranking military officers who form a **junta**, or ruling oligarchy. Military juntas have a long history, particularly in Latin America, where military intervention in domestic politics is a widespread tradition.

Nations with governments in which the army frequently intervenes and has the potential to dominate are often called **praetorian states**.[5] Military regimes typically come to power in a **coup d'état** (power seizure), often bloodless. In some parts of the world, coups occur with astonishing frequency. One scholar counted eighty-eight military coups in fifty-two countries between 1958 and 1969.[6] According to Eric Nordlinger, since the 1920s, the military has intervened in every Latin American country except Mexico and Costa Rica.[7] Nordlinger further notes:

> Between 1945 and 1976, soldiers carried out successful coups in half of the eighteen Asian states. By 1976 the soldiers had made at least one successful or unsuccessful attempt to seize power in two-thirds of the Middle Eastern and North African states. They established military regimes in Egypt, Syria, Iraq, the Sudan, Libya, and Algeria. . . . By 1976 coups had occurred in more than half of the African countries, and in that year the military occupied the seat of government in half of them.[8]

The study of military regimes, Nordlinger concludes, "is the study of one of the most common, and thus characteristic, aspects of non-Western politics."

In Latin America (and to a much lesser extent, in Africa), the picture has changed in recent years. Until the 1980s, Latin America was the most coup-prone region in the world. Military juntas were the rule, representative democracies the exception. Only in Mexico, Costa Rica, Venezuela, and Colombia were democratic institutions well entrenched. One by one South America's military rulers relinquished power to popularly elected civilian governments, beginning with Ecuador in 1979, followed by Peru (1980), Bolivia (1982), Argentina (1983), Uruguay (1985), and Brazil (1985). Despite regional tensions arising from civil wars in El Salvador and Nicaragua, several Central American states that were previously under military sway have also moved toward civilian government in the 1990s.

As a form of authoritarian rule, juntas appear to be on the decline. The same cannot be said of dynastic regimes, which continue to demonstrate surprising resilience in one region (the Middle East) despite their increasingly anachronistic character.

Dynastic Regimes

Dynastic rule, or monarchy, was the most common form of authoritarianism (which, as noted, has always been the most common form of government) nearly everywhere in the world until the twentieth century. Monarchs have gone by different names in different places—king, emperor, caliph, sultan, emir, mogul, and czar, to name but a few. Whatever their title, monarchs rule as a birthright—they inherit absolute power. In Europe and elsewhere, kings and emperors often reinforced this dynastic claim by asserting a God-ordained **divine right** to rule. Only in parts of the Middle East has this form of authoritarianism continued to thrive. (The remaining monarchs in Europe reign but do not rule.)

Monarchs continue to rule as well as reign in Jordan (King Hussein), Saudi Arabia (King Fahd), and Morocco (King Hassan II). The oil-rich "ministates" of Kuwait, Bahrain, Oman, Qatar, and the United Arab Emirates are also governed by autocratic rulers, called sultans or emirs. Beyond the Middle East, monarchies are few and far between. Only in such obscure places as Swaziland, Nepal, Brunei, Bhutan, and Tonga can they still be found.

Is monarchy a vanishing species of authoritarianism? This particular type of dynastic rule has undergone a precipitous decline since the nineteenth century, one that accelerated after World War II. Countries in which monarchies have fallen or been displaced in recent decades include Afghanistan (1973), Burundi (1966), Cambodia (1955), Egypt (1952), Ethiopia (1974), Iran (1979), Iraq (1958), Libya (1969), and Tunisia (1957). And unlike military regimes, which come and go, monarchs, once deposed, are seldom, if ever, restored to power.

Totalitarianism

Totalitarianism is a concept of relatively recent vintage. It was first applied to the system established in the Soviet Union during the long and bloody reign of Joseph Stalin and to the Nazi regime in Germany under Adolf Hitler in which millions of European Jews and other people were put to death in extermination camps. The term is appropriate because the political systems set up by Stalin and Hitler were characterized by a *total* concentration of power at the center (in Stalin's case, in the hands of a single individual).

A pivotal feature of the totalitarian model is the presence of an all-encompassing and monolithic party organization that functions like a state within a state. This party is controlled by an omnipotent dictator with the help of a handpicked oligarchic elite. Members of the elite make decisions in secret and rely heavily on secret police to intimidate and mobilize the society. In the Stalinist variant, the party apparatus and the state bureaucracy are inextricably intertwined; the bureaucracy implements policies while the party acts as the dictator's whip hand and watchdog.

Carl Friedrich and Zbigniew Brzezinski list the following six characteristics of all totalitarian regimes:

1. An official ideology covering all aspects of human existence to which every member of the society must adhere, not only by outer forms but also by inner convictions.

2. A single mass party led by one person and consisting of relatively small proportions of the total population, which acts as the official ideology's priesthood.
3. A system of terroristic police controls making full use of modern technology for spying and surveillance.
4. Centralized state control of the mass media.
5. Confiscation of all arms and explosives previously in private hands.
6. Centralized state control of the economy through bureaucratic coordination of all productive enterprises.[9]

In the full-blown totalitarian state, political liberties and other human rights are nonexistent. Dissidence and nonconformity are not tolerated; citizens who do not submit often vanish in the night, dispatched to labor camps or the firing squad. The press is state-controlled, and the performing arts are tightly regulated. Newspapers, books, movies, and radio and television programming are censored. No independent group or association of any kind is permitted. The educational system is geared to the regime's political objectives, and the curriculum is infused with ideological content.[10]

Totalitarian rulers, by definition, aim at a radical restructuring of society. To achieve such ambitious goals as rapid industrialization, social transformation, and territorial expansion, they must resort to mass mobilization. As a consequence, passive obedience on the part of the masses is not enough; active participation is required. Ardor is an order. Sloth is treason. In true Orwellian fashion, society must be infiltrated and controlled so that no one can hide anything from the state, including subversive thoughts or feelings. Today air transportation systems, mass communications systems, computerized information management systems, electronic surveillance systems, and increasingly sophisticated internal security systems place formidable new means and methods of control at the disposal of the modern state.

The *potential* for totalitarian rule would appear to be inherent in the processes of economic and political development. Has any tendency toward totalitarian rule been apparent in the developing countries in recent decades? Are industrially developed and technologically advanced societies more susceptible to totalitarian blandishments under some circumstances than more traditional societies? The answers to questions such as these can be found only through comparative political analysis. For now it will suffice to note that the Stalinist example demonstrates the danger of totalitarianism in a largely agrarian, traditional setting, and the Nazi example shows clearly that advanced industrial societies are not immune to this contagion. At present, few totalitarian regimes remain, but there is no guarantee that totalitarianism will not rear its ugly head again.

Marxist-Leninist Regimes

Prior to its collapse in 1989–1991, the Soviet Union was the prototype for the **Marxist-Leninist** form of government. Lenin readily acknowledged his intellectual debt to Karl Marx, but he took Marxism and recast it into an ideology suitable for use as a kind of state religion. Ever since the triumph of Lenin's *Bolsheviki* (as the original Russian Communists were known) in the October Revolution of 1917, the propagation of a state-sponsored ideology, Marxism-Leninism, imposed on society by means of intimidation and censorship has been a trademark of Marxist-Leninist regimes.

During the heyday of Stalinist rule, such regimes were strictly totalitarian. In the 1980s, under the influence of Mikhail Gorbachev's *perestroika* (restructuring) campaign in the Soviet Union, several Communist states implemented market-oriented economic reforms and relaxed internal police-state controls (press censorship, foreign travel restrictions). In 1991, tumultuous events in the Soviet Union brought the edifice of Communist one-party rule there crashing down. Two years earlier, popular uprisings had culminated in the downfall of Communist governments in Eastern Europe and the dissolution of the Warsaw Treaty Organization (Warsaw Pact). What follows is a sketch of the Marxist-Leninist system as it existed in Europe and still operates in modified form in several Asian countries and in Cuba.

Power is concentrated in a single, all-encompassing party organization that rules through a subservient state bureaucracy. Elections are held regularly, but in the absence of a competitive party system, they are little more than window dressing. Civil liberties (free speech, freedom of the press, freedom of association and assembly, freedom of movement, and so on) may not be entirely repressed but are severely restricted. Periods of relative leniency toward dissenters alternate with crackdowns on dissent.

Before World War II, the Soviet Union was the only Communist regime in existence. At the end of that war in 1945, with the Red Army in control of Eastern Europe, Stalin installed Soviet-type puppet governments in Poland, East Germany, Czechoslovakia, Hungary, Romania, and Bulgaria. These countries had been ravaged, overrun, and occupied during the war, first by Nazi Germany and then, under the guise of "liberation," by Soviet forces. Only in Yugoslavia, which had liberated itself from Hitler's armies, was an independent—albeit Marxist—state established.

Communist dictatorships also sprouted in Asia, sub-Saharan Africa, the Middle East, and Latin America in the decades after War II. By the early 1990s, only a few of these regimes were still in power.

Command Economies

In a **command economy**, public goods (and state interests) take priority over private interests, industry and commerce are owned and operated by the state, and central planning, rather than the marketplace, regulates the flow of goods and services. The state heavily subsidizes consumption: people live in subsidized public housing, depend on subsidized public transportation, and receive free education, medical care, and many other social services. Nearly everyone works in the public sector (for state-run enterprises). The same government that provides the subsidies pays low salaries that make the subsidies necessary.

Command economies are so named because businesses respond to instructions from above rather than consumer preferences (demand) from below. An overall plan is developed each year, setting production targets for every sector of the economy that are broken down into monthly quotas. Every factory, farm, and enterprise is expected to fulfill its monthly quota. Rewards, in the form of bonuses, are given for overfulfillment; underfulfillment can derail the career of the plant manager, who is ultimately held responsible.

This system maximizes state (or party) control, which is the chief reason why Stalin created it. It enables the ruler to shape the economy, extract and allocate resources (including land, labor, and investment capital), and concentrate on a particular objective, such as military-industrial development. Stalinist political economy stressed the primacy of heavy industry, which meant everything from coal and steel production to hydroelectric power and machine tools for heavy construction and infrastructure (roads, bridges, dams, and the like). "Heavy industry" was also a euphemism for a major Soviet arms buildup, the genesis of a permanent wartime economy that eventually created a superpower arsenal rivaled only by that of the United States.

The command economy is particularly well suited to rapid industrialization based on forced labor—the model of economic development Stalin patented. The system has major liabilities, however. For example, it becomes increasingly cumbersome to administer as the economy modernizes and diversifies. Although Stalin proved that the initial stages of industrialization can be forced by *quantitative* inputs—massive amounts of conscript labor, capital squeezed from agriculture, and the export (for hard currency) of raw materials extracted without regard to human costs or future needs—it is now glaringly apparent that sustained economic growth in an age of rapidly advancing technology requires *qualitative* inputs (applied research, managerial skills, innovative ideas and attitudes, entrepreneurship, vision, investment strategies, risk taking). In the 1970s and 1980s, command economies fell farther and farther behind the most dynamic market economies. This economic decline was the major reason Mikhail Gorbachev launched the Soviet reform movement in the mid-1980s; it is also the reason for the collapse of communism in Europe a few years later.

CONCLUSION

Aristotle's ancient classification scheme accommodates nearly all forms of modern government. It works for a full range of political systems from highly pluralistic democracies to highly autocratic dictatorships. Totalitarian regimes represent the one notable exception. In the next chapter we turn our attention to the problems of political development: how do societies create the political cultures and the political structures without which a modern nation-state cannot exist?

KEY TERMS

tyranny	mixed economy
monarchy	free enterprise
oligarchy	*laissez faire*
aristocracy	authoritarianism
democracy	personal dictatorship
polity	heir apparent
mob rule	junta
justice	praetorian states
mixed regime	coup d'état
democratic republic	dynastic rule
presidential democracy	divine right
parliamentary democracy	totalitarianism
patron-client democracy	Marxist-Leninist
market economy	command economy

STUDY QUESTIONS

1. What are some major differences between presidential and parliamentary democracies? What are the advantages and disadvantages of each? In your opinion, which system is better?
2. What is authoritarianism? What modern forms has it assumed? Where is it most prevalent, and why?
3. How does totalitarianism differ from authoritarianism? What principal forms has totalitarianism assumed, and where has it prevailed? In your opinion, is totalitarianism a thing of the past? Why or why not?

SUGGESTED READING

Arendt, Hannah. *Totalitarianism*. Orlando, Fla.: Harcourt Brace, 1968.

Aristotle. *Politics*. Ernest Barker, ed. and trans. New York: Oxford University Press, 1962.

Bailey, Sydney. *British Parliamentary Democracy,* 3rd ed. Westport, Conn.: Greenwood Press, 1978.

Conquest, Robert. *The Harvest of Sorrow: Soviet Collectivization and the Terror-Famine*. New York: Oxford University Press, 1986.

Crick, Bernard. *Basic Forms of Government: A Sketch and a Model*. London: Macmillan, 1980.

Diamond, Martin. *The Founding of the Democratic Republic*. Itasca, Ill.: Peacock, 1981.

Dicey, A. V. *Introduction to the Study of the Law of the Constitution*. New York: St. Martin's Press, 1982.

Friedrich, Carl. *Limited Government: A Comparison*. Englewood Cliffs, N.J.: Prentice Hall, 1974.

Friedrich, Carl, and Brzezinski, Zbigniew. *Totalitarian Dictatorship and Autocracy.* New York: Praeger, 1965.

Hamilton, Alexander, Jay, John, and Madison, James. *The Federalist.* New York: McGraw-Hill, 1964.

Latey, Maurice. *Patterns of Tyranny.* New York: Atheneum, 1969.

Machiavelli, Niccolo. "The Prince." In *The Prince and Other Discourses.* New York: McGraw-Hill, 1950.

Macridis, Roy C. *Modern Political Systems: Europe.* 7th ed. Englewood Cliffs, N.J.: Prentice Hall, 1990.

Menze, Ernest, ed. *Totalitarianism Reconsidered.* Port Washington, N.Y.: Kennikat, 1981.

Moore, Barrington. *Social Origins of Dictatorship and Democracy.* Boston: Beacon Press, 1966.

Orwell, George. *Nineteen Eighty-four.* New York: New American Library, 1983.

Ponchaud, François. *Cambodia: Year Zero.* New York: Holt, 1978.

Rubin, Barry. *Modern Dictators.* New York: New American Library, 1988.

NOTES

1. Aristotle, *Politics.* Ernest Barker, ed. and trans. (New York: Oxford University Press, 1958), p. 244.
2. Ibid., pp. 244–245.
3. For a discussion of the magnitude of the suffering and deaths caused by totalitarian dictators (Hitler, Stalin, Mao Zedong in China, and Pol Pot in Cambodia), see Thomas Magstadt and Peter Schotten, *Understanding Politics: Ideas, Interests, and Issues,* 3rd ed. (New York: St. Martin's Press, 1993). For a more detailed discussion see C. W. Cassinelli, *Total Revolution* (Santa Barbara, Calif.: ABC-Clio, 1976).
4. Robert Jackson and Carl Rosberg, *Personal Rule in Black Africa: Princes, Autocrats, Prophets, Tyrants* (Berkeley: University of California Press, 1982), p. 235.
5. Amos Perlmutter, ed., *The Military and Politics in Modern Times* (New Haven, Conn.: Yale University Press, 1977), p. 4.
6. Samuel H. Finer, *Comparative Politics* (London: Penguin, 1970).
7. Eric Nordlinger, *Soldiers and Politics: Military Coups and Governments* (Englewood Cliffs, N.J.: Prentice Hall, 1977), p. 6.
8. Ibid.
9. Carl J. Friedrich and Zbigniew Brzezinski, *Totalitarian Dictatorship and Autocracy* (Cambridge, Mass.: Harvard University Press, 1956), p. 9.
10. Any systematic set of political beliefs can be called an ideology; in the totalitarian state there is an elaborate *official* ideology that is force-fed through propaganda and education.

3

Politics and Development: Nationalism or Regionalism?

No treatment of theories, patterns, and approaches in the study of comparative politics is complete without a discussion of **development**. The Western concept of development is sometimes used as a synonym for **modernization**. Used in this way, development theory can be seen as an intellectual outgrowth of the idea of progress. Anyone who believes in progress must also believe that human beings are capable of building a better world. This belief is often associated with optimism, idealism, rationalism, faith in the future, or some combination of these.

Optimistic development theorists have usually assumed that sovereign states are here to stay. Not surprisingly, therefore, the modern state provides the framework for most models of development. But progress is no longer automatically set in the context of the modern state, both because of the decay of several societies in recent times and because of the economic success of the European Community; as we shall see, progress is also coming to be associated with regional structures in other parts of the world.

The Idea of Progress

Neither ancient peoples nor medieval Europeans believed in progress. The Judeo-Christian tradition emphasized the fall of man and his eventual redemption through a messiah rather than through reason or science. The Greeks were still more pessimistic: the predominant Greek view was that human societies are organisms that go through cycles, returning time and again to their original starting point. Indeed, one school of thought holds that it was to break this vicious cycle that Plato wrote his *Republic;* in this view, Plato was trying to save what he considered a good society from otherwise inevitable decay.

It follows that development was anathema to Plato, whose purpose in writing *The Republic* was to freeze society and prevent all change. Plato wanted the state to restrict the emergence of specialized occupations and professions. According to modern development theory, one of the keys to development is the increasing differentiation and specificity of roles. Plato understood that, and to prevent development, he prescribed that this differentiation and specificity should be artifically restricted, even prohibited.

Thus Plato was an early pioneer of development theory, but in a negative sense: his purpose was to prevent rather than promote development. The idea that human beings are capable of infinite progress is a product of the modern era—specifically, the Enlightenment.

What Is Development?

Development can be defined as "the increasing capacity to make rational use of natural and human resources for social ends."[1] It is a key concept in all the natural and social sciences.

Anthropologists and sociologists stress sociocultural aspects of development such as values, beliefs, taboos, attitudes, and orientations. They also focus on interpersonal and group relations (families, clans, and tribes or ethnic, religious, and other distinct groups in society). Economists stress changes in patterns of production and distribution, consumption, and investment. Political scientists focus mainly on changes in patterns of power and authority. As societies develop, how do power relationships change? What new institutions emerge? What old ones disappear? What is gained and what is lost? How is political stability affected? What is the relationship between political development and economic development? Are certain kinds of government more suitable for developing societies than others? Is there a close correlation between regime type and economic development? Finally, political economists combine the disciplines and analytical tools of economics and political science. The study of political economy is logical because global and national markets are never free of state intervention and regulation.

Development and World Politics

World War II was a watershed. First, it ushered in a bipolar, global balance-of-power system that replaced the previous regional (European) system. Although Europe continued to be the focus of international tensions for a time, the once dominant powers of the Continent were now militarily, economically, and psychologically dependent on the United States. One reason was the menacing presence of the Soviet Union—half European and half Asian—in the East. Post–World War II East-West rivalry became known as the **Cold War**.

A second (and closely related) change after World War II was the breakup of the European colonial empires. Indeed, the dissolution of these empires was one sign that the former great powers of Europe were in an era of decline. Internationally, this new state of affairs meant that Europe no longer controlled, and could no longer easily exploit, Asia, Africa, and the Middle East.

Third, the United States and the Soviet Union, which confronted each other across an ideological chasm symbolized by Winston Churchill's famous "iron curtain" metaphor, looked to other regions of the world for allies, trading partners, military bases, strategic minerals, and investment opportunities. The Third World became a new battleground in the East-West conflict. Each superpower urged developing nations to imitate its institutions; each offered a variety of inducements, including economic and military aid; and each pressured aid recipients to choose sides. The developing nations often resisted these pressures, preferring to play one side off against the other and insisting that the economic divide between North and South was more important than any ideological rivalry between East and West.

How Many Worlds?

Never have regions played a more prominent role in international affairs than after World War II. Europe and North America became known as the First World; the Soviet Union and its allies, especially the satellite states of Eastern Europe, constituted the Second World; and the former colonial areas (located mainly in the Southern Hemisphere) formed the **Third World**. These three "worlds" corresponded to regions to some extent, but this way of dividing the globe was always artificial and somewhat arbitrary. Since the fading of the Cold War, an approach that takes account of politically significant patterns in various geographic regions makes more sense.

In the 1950s, similarities among the former colonies, irrespective of their regional location, were more apparent than differences:

> As the newly emergent states of Asia, Africa, and Latin America took their place in the international community, it rapidly became apparent that they were not states in the Western sense of the word. They were desperately poor. Their economies were based upon subsistence agriculture and the export of raw materials to the industrial powers of the West. Their political systems were fragile and subject to frequent coups d'état. More often than not, they were ruled by narrow elites whose strength came from tribal support or large landholdings. Socially, they were fragmented into a multitude of poorly integrated ethnic and religious factions. Culturally, their populations, largely illiterate, clung to the ways of the past.[2]

Although this description is oversimplified (witness the success of South Korea, Taiwan, Hong Kong, and Singapore in Asia), a great economic gulf remained between the North (primarily the West) and the South. The seven most prosperous industrial democracies (the United States, Great Britain, Germany, France, Italy, and Japan) contain only about one-seventh of the world's population but use about two-fifths of its energy, garner half of all export earnings, and consume over half of the world's production of goods and services every year. Poverty plagues much of the rest of the globe:

> Three hundred million 6–11-year-olds in developing countries do not go to school. Fifty percent of all children who actually enter elementary school will not stay to the end of the second year. Only 25 percent will finish elementary school. Only 10 percent . . . are immunized against the six basic childhood diseases.[3]

From the perspective of impoverished nations in regions formerly under European colonial rule, the blame for their dire straits rests squarely on the shoulders of the West (and particularly the United States as the leading Western power).

This common perspective should not obscure the fact that there is enormous diversity *within* these nations and regions. The growing economic differentiation is relatively new; the geographic, historical, cultural, racial, ethnic, social, religious, and linguistic differences are obviously very old.

The substance of these differences will be elucidated in following chapters. Here our aim is to set the stage for that in-depth discussion. Accordingly, we now consider some competing theories and approaches in the study of political development.

The Study of Development

Various disciplines, ranging from the oldest, philosophy, to the comparatively new behavioral sciences, have shed light on the phenomenon of political development. We turn first to philosophy.

Development and Political Philosophy

As we have seen, Plato believed that a state constructed along the lines he proposed in *The Republic* would be perfect, and therefore any change or "political development" would be change for the worse—regressive rather than progressive. But some of Plato's ideas have nonetheless been useful to founders and builders of new states. For example, Plato's ideal society was predicated on a myth (which Plato preferred to call a "noble lie"):

> I shall try to convince, first the Rulers and the soldiers, and then the whole community, that all that nurture and education we gave them was only something they seemed to experience as if it were in a dream. In reality they were the whole time down inside the earth, being molded and fostered while their arms and all their equipment were being fashioned also; and at last, when they were complete, the earth sent them up from her womb into the light of day. So now they must think of the land they dwell in as a mother and a nurse, whom they must . . . defend against any attack, and of their fellow citizens as brothers born of the same soil. . . . It is true, we shall tell our people in this fable, that all of you in this land are brothers; but the god who fashioned you mixed gold in the composition of those among you who are fit to rule, so that they are the most precious quality; and he put silver in the auxiliaries, and iron

and brass in the farmers and craftsmen. . . . They will appeal to a prophecy that ruin will come upon the state when it passes into the keeping of a man of iron or brass.[4]

Plato understood that without such a myth, it would not be possible to preserve and perpetuate his ideal society. But just as Plato comtemplated the use of a noble lie to prevent development, the leaders of developing countries often use an emotionally appealing oversimplification (anticolonialism, Marxism, nationalism, pan-Arabism) to *promote* development.

Plato's idea of rule by the wise and gifted has a present-day echo in the theory of Steven Chilton.[5] Chilton posits the evolution of a universal moral philosophy. As people mature, their capacity to engage in abstract moral reasoning increases (the research of development psychologists supports this part of Chilton's argument). Some individuals, however, have a greater innate ability to engage in such reasoning than others do. Political systems that manage to put these gifted individuals into leadership and policymaking positions are most likely to develop in accordance with universal moral values.

Karl Marx provided the basis for another theory of political development. His concept of the "withering away of the state" holds that as societies evolve, government will eventually become superfluous. The need for coercive political institutions to control society will disappear. Under socialism (and then communism), society's members will internalize collective values rather than the individualistic values associated with capitalism. What we know as government will be replaced by the "administration of things." A contemporary version of this idea has been espoused by sociologist James Davies. In his view, the best developed societies are those whose members most universally and thoroughly internalize rules associated with sharing and fair play. Davies argues that governments arose to combat anarchy and will be replaced by mere administration as societies evolve to a level where everyone internalizes the rules.[6]

Other political philosophers have embraced ideas, especially about human nature, that have far-reaching implications for theories of political development. Thomas Hobbes believed that life in the state of nature would be "solitary, poor, nasty, brutish and short." An imposing state was thus necessary to "overawe" the masses and maintain order and stability. Societies that lacked such a strong state were, by definition, politically underdeveloped.

Rousseau took quite the opposite view: that the modern state represented political degeneracy, not progress. "Man is born free," he declared, "and everywhere he is in chains." Rousseau believed that human beings are also born innocent but are soon corrupted by society. He decried the institution of private property and viewed political systems as elaborate devices for perpetuating inequality based on property ownership. Remove the political and social props that both support the existing system and create a culture of greed and self-aggrandizement, and the natural goodness of human beings would blossom.

Rousseau was no admirer of the modern nation-state, but other philosophers have taken the opposite view. In the nineteenth century, for example, Friedrich

Hegel argued that the nation-state (in particular, Prussia) represented the highest stage of development in world history. Hegel's famous dictum that "what is real is rational and only the rational is real" has a special relevance here. Hegel thought that the nation-state most closely approached true reality (the Absolute Idea) because it was the most rational worldly organization. Because of this exaltation of the state, Hegel has sometimes been blamed for the rise of twentieth-century totalitarian ideologies.

More recently, John Herz propounded the theory that political units expand in response to the changing security needs of society.[7] When these needs could be satisfied by the family, clan, or tribe, there was no need for the modern state. But when traditional forms of sociopolitical organization were no longer adequate for protection, they were replaced by the modern nation-state. Herz argues that the nation-state is now inadequate due to new threats such as nuclear war and ecological disaster. Only world government can deal effectively with these new challenges, in this view; hence the next major stage of political development must go beyond the nation-state to establish a new global order.

Although the argument that whatever is necessary is possible in human affairs has some appeal, one can question whether world government is in fact necessary. Evidence is mounting that nation-states are becoming increasingly interdependent. Evidence also suggests that the most plausible alternative to the nation-state at this historical juncture may be regional rather than global government. The most obvious case in point is the European Community (EC), but others are the Association of Southeast Asian Nations (ASEAN), the North American Free Trade Agreement (NAFTA), and the Southern Common Market (MERCOSUR) linking Brazil, Argentina, Uruguay, and Paraguay.

For many countries, regionalism is sometimes the only good alternative to the nation-state (which may no longer be viable) or world government (which is unattainable). The success of the EC, the largest trading bloc in the world, can be expected to spur intensified efforts at regional integration elsewhere. In later chapters, we will see that this "demonstration effect" is already at work, especially in North and South America. The trend toward geographically de-limited free-trade zones makes a regional approach to the study of comparative politics especially appropriate at this time.

Empirical Theories of Development

More than two centuries ago, the French philosopher Montesquieu (1689–1755) argued that complete understanding of a political system would require a careful examination of the environmental and cultural context of politics.[8] Such an approach would look at geography, population, climate, resource endowments, the economy, and cultural characteristics.

Incorporating all of these variables into one theory is, of course, easier said than done. Nonetheless, Montesquieu's argument still serves as a foundation for traditional approaches to development. These approaches vary greatly, but they all view development as an *evolutionary process,* one that occurs in increments over an extended period of time. Various conceptual schemes placed countries on a developmental continuum, classifying them according to level of economic development or prevailing mode of production (agriculture, industry, services). Different studies share the assumption that economic development leads to physical wellbeing derived from the increasingly efficient organization and mechanization of production. This process is usually viewed as inseparable from social and political modernization.[9]

Development theorists often attempt to evaluate and compare the performance of different political systems by looking at goal attainment capabilities and success in extracting and distributing resources or regulating social, economic, and political activity. Societies are then proclaimed to be developed and "modern" to the degree that they are able to perform such functions. Not surprisingly, political instability and economic stagnation are often cited as evidence that Third World nations are underdeveloped, that is, incapable of managing society so as to extract and distribute resources efficiently.[10]

The Perspectives of Sociology and Psychology

Some theorists stress that economic development reflects a state of mind more than anything else, that it is essentially psychological and cultural. Explanations of this kind are found in the works of sociologists Talcott Parsons, Daniel Lerner, and Amitai Etzioni; psychologist David McClelland; anthropologist Clifford Geertz; and political scientist Edward Banfield.[11] In different ways, these authors have suggested that personality structures conditioned by social and cultural norms must change from within for development to be possible.

Daniel Lerner observed the traditions of Middle Eastern society and concluded that lack of empathy (inability to put oneself in another's place) is the key factor inhibiting economic development in Arab societies. Lerner's thesis is that this lack stifles individual and group motivation.[12]

McClelland studied individuals in Western societies, using a psychological measure of the need to achieve. McClelland discovered that individuals with low scores had a low ambition for acquiring wealth or other attributes of success and concluded that for this reason, societies vary in achievement levels, the principal expression of this variation being economic development or underdevelopment. He observed, "In a century dominated by economic determinism in both communist and Western thought, it is startling to find concrete evidence for psychological determinism, for psychological developments as preceding and presumably causing economic changes."[13]

From the study of a traditional village in southern Italy, Edward Banfield attempted to explain backwardness in terms of specific behavior patterns of individuals and families. Banfield attributed backwardness to the villagers' orientation toward life and society. He described them as now-oriented and self-centered people who feared death, lacked interest in outside affairs, and embraced a world view bounded by self or family. Banfield attributed their underdevelopment to these causes.[14]

The Perspective of Political Science

In political science, development theory often stresses the political prerequisites for economic development—political order and stability—which are in turn a function of viable institutions and enforceable rules. Development thus entails an increase in the capability of the political system to expand the range of individual freedoms, opportunities, and choices.[15]

According to **input-output theory**, the political system receives inputs in the form of public demands and supports, as well as pressure from its various environments, and converts them into outputs expressed as policies, programs, and priorities. This view holds that institutionalization of the functions of the political system (in the form of universal rules and regular and reliable operations) will create a climate conducive to domestic peace and prosperity.

For proponents of **evolutionary theory**, a solution to the problem of underdevelopment lies in changing the psychology and culture of the society, as well as its political rules. To induce such changes, these theorists often call for stepped-up foreign aid, trade and investment, and the introduction of modern technology. A country that absorbs Western products and capital, the theory goes, will modernize not only its means of production but also its consumption patterns and lifestyle. Greater popular participation is likely to follow. This, in turn, will both galvanize the society and spur the government to higher standards of performance.

Normative versus Scientific Approaches

Political development means different things to different people. One reason is that concepts of development often conceal **normative** assumptions and assertions. If, for example, order is given the highest priority, states capable of suppressing dissent or socializing citizens into cooperative rather than competitive behaviors could be considered the most developed. If liberty is prized most highly, states that encourage individuality, private enterprise, and self-expression might be deemed the most mature.

Approaches of this kind tend to be not only normative but also prescriptive. Normative theorists make moral choices—freedom over order, equality over liberty, and so on. On the basis of these choices, they prescribe developmental models and policies designed to produce the type of society they prefer. Political systems that manifest the traits they value most highly are labeled progressive or developed; regimes that display the opposite traits may be labeled traditional, primitive, regressive, despotic, bourgeois, or reactionary.

An alternative approach to economic and political development, dominant until 1970, uses the **scientific method**. It spurns moral or ethical judgments in favor of careful observation and analysis. Often espoused by behavioralists, this approach sticks to the facts, stresses scientific objectivity, conscientiously seeks to verify its findings, and avoids sweeping generalizations.

A third approach is **deterministic**. Marx argued that one historical stage would follow another inexorably. Free choice plays little or no role here. But

Marxists are not the only ones who tend to be deterministic. Many developmental theorists stress forces and factors beyond human control. Most, however, fall somewhere between the extremes of free will and determinism.

The approach used in this book combines normative and prescriptive elements with description and analysis. It acknowledges the claims of determinism but recognizes that determinism can too easily become an excuse for defeatism and self-fulfilling prophecies. The persistent appeal of determinism serves to remind us that powerful impersonal forces are at work in the world and that there are limits to politics.

Political Economy and Development

Comparative politics on a global scale has benefited from the contribution of scholars who look at the world through the prism of political economy—politics and economics as two sides of the same coin. From this perspective, economic inequality among nations and regions is a stark fact of international political life. Three patterns are particularly noteworthy.

First, the world's material wealth is grossly maldistributed between the North and South, especially between the nations of North America, Western Europe, and much of the Pacific Rim on the one hand and the nations of South and Southeast Asia, sub-Saharan Africa, and much of Latin America and the Middle East, on the other.

Second, economic growth rates have declined in many regions of the world over the past three decades, but this decline has hit the Third World the hardest. The full impact of declining growth rates on developing countries can be gauged by comparing them with population growth rates, which yields the average annual per capita GNP growth rate. By this measure, many low-income countries in Asia, Africa, and Latin America experienced negative growth rates in the 1980s.

Third, the distribution of wealth is more unequal within developing nations and regions than within the developed nations and regions. For example, the top 10 percent of the population owns 50 percent of the wealth in Brazil and 40 percent of the wealth in countries such as Kenya, Zambia, Peru, and Mexico. In the United States and Japan, by contrast, the top 10 percent owns considerably less than 25 percent of the wealth. The economic problems endemic throughout Africa, Latin America, and much of Asia are exacerbated by—and reflected in—the world debt crisis. This phenomenon, which grew to ominous proportions in the 1980s, accentuated the inequalities between North and South. In the late 1980s, the debt burden on the developing nations and regions reached $1.3 trillion! The biggest debtor nations, Mexico and Brazil, owed over $100 billion each; Argentina (over $50 billion), Indonesia ($40–$45 billion), and Venezuela ($30–$35 billion) were also major debtors. Other countries as far-flung as Poland, Nigeria, and the Philippines shouldered debt burdens that far exceeded their capacity to repay. The threat of a debt-induced global financial crisis receded somewhat in the early 1990s due to large-scale debt rescheduling, tough austerity measures taken by many debtor nations, and a drop in world interest rates.

The causes of the debt crisis of the 1980s were of two types: proximate and systemic. The proximate (immediate) causes were skyrocketing oil prices in the 1970s (rising from $2.50 per barrel to $34.00 per barrel), the availability of foreign loans (due in large part to huge OPEC oil profits), and, at the beginning of the 1980s, a sharp rise in interest rates (reaching a high of 21 percent) in the United States associated with oil-fueled inflation.

The systemic causes are more difficult to identify and more controversial. The International Monetary Fund (backed by the U.S. government) pointed to structural problems within many of the debtor nations' economies—hyperinflation and chronic budget deficits due to state subsidies, high arms spending, capital flight, and a porous tax collection system. It offered hard-currency loans to financially stricken governments willing to implement spending cuts, restrict the money supply, offer new incentives for domestic and foreign investment, and adopt free-market reforms. Many debtor countries put IMF-approved policies into practice in the early 1990s. These policies were invariably unpopular. As a consequence, the external debt crisis eased, but internal tensions mounted.

The traditional Third World perspective stands in sharp contrast to that of the IMF. It is a mixture of ideas drawn from the writings of Marx and Lenin and more recent works by scholars who subscribe to a school of thought known as **dependency theory**.

Dependency Theory: A Regional Perspective

Dependency theory starts with the proposition that the world has finite resources. The rest of the argument flows from certain assumptions and observations about the nature of the global political economy.

Dependency theorists have adapted Marxist class analysis. The world, they contend, is divided into three basic classes: the *industrial core* (the United States, Western Europe, and Japan), the *semiperiphery* (or so-called newly industrialized countries such as South Korea, Taiwan, Singapore, and Brazil), and the *periphery* (the vast majority of countries in the former colonial areas of Asia, Africa, and Latin America). The states of both the periphery and the semiperiphery are dependent on the industrial core for markets, capital, and technology. The industrial nations have a vested interest in perpetuating this state of dependency.

The dependency system has several salient features. First, the core states produce expensive manufactured goods, and the peripheral states supply cheap raw materials (foodstuffs and minerals). The price structure is manipulated by the dominant economic powers. The **terms of trade** thus heavily favor the core states.

Closely related is the fact that commodity prices fluctuate widely from one year to the next, and many developing countries are dependent on the export of one or two commodities (such as sugar, coffee, bananas, or jute). Thus export revenues are extremely sensitive to price fluctuations beyond the control of the export countries. But the developing countries must continue to import and must pay for imports with hard currency (foreign reserves). Often they must borrow, with no option but to pay whatever interest rates international financiers in the core states choose to charge. Further, if they seek foreign aid, they are forced to accept all the strings attached. Finally, in a crisis, they are left with little choice but to accept the conditions imposed by the IMF for short-term loans. Called **conditionality**, this practice of imposing austerity measures has been a major bone of contention in the North-South conflict.

An especially insidious aspect of this whole system, according to dependency theorists, is the collusion between capitalists in the core states and a small economic elite in the peripheral states. This elite typically profits enormously from the arrangement, but it is mutually beneficial: the core states back "anticommunist" regimes, which maintain order and stability and ensure access to domestic markets. Grants of military and economic aid, seen in this light, are payoffs and props that reap larger dividends for the donor nations than for the recipients in part because corrupt rulers often siphon off most of the funds.

Not all political economists embrace dependency theory. Particularly in the West, development scholars tend to blame the developing nations themselves for most of their problems and argue that these nations must find their own solutions. Typically, they stress that many developing nations have been plagued by weak institutions, corrupt or incompetent leaders, and chronic sociopolitical instability. Hence the path to economic development is essentially political.

Politics and Economic Development

Political instability is the bane of economic health and social progress. Instability takes a variety of forms, including military coups, riots, and insurgencies; it is especially prevalent in Africa, Asia, and Latin America. Its economic consequences are myriad, including disruption of communications and transport, diversion of scarce resources to internal security needs, and large-scale capital flight. Instability is anathema to investors. In the mid-1980s, *Business Week* estimated that without capital flight, Argentina's foreign debt would have been $1 billion rather than $50 billion, Mexico's would have been $12 billion rather than $100 billion, and Venezuela's would have been nonexistent.[16] Political failure leads to economic failure, but the reverse is also true. Poverty begets instability by undermining economic development.

Political factors that impinge on the pace and direction of economic development include (1) the quality of leadership, (2) the capabilities of existing political structures, (3) the availability of necessary resources, (4) the quality of the citizenry, and (5) the threats and opportunities presented by a changing regional and international environment.

Leadership quality is reflected in the attitudes and attributes of political elites. Are they progressive or tradition-bound? Do they want economic development even if it is accompanied by other changes that might be destabilizing? Are they more concerned about income distribution or economic growth? Do they value social justice, or are they interested only in feathering their own nests? In short, as Aristotle might ask, do the leaders rule in their own interest or in the interest of all?

Beyond moral character, of key importance are the skills and abilities of political elites—those who implement policy as well as those who formulate it. Do these elites understand basic principles of economics? Are they familiar with appropriate technologies in agriculture, industry, and the service sector? Do they have administrative experience and skills? The answers to these questions are crucial to the economic prospects of developing nations and regions.

The concept of institutional capacity is particularly important in the comparative study of politics. Are viable institutions already in place, or do they have to be built from scratch? Can these institutions perform essential functions? For example, can they facilitate the processes of controlling, extracting, and mobilizing human and material resources? Institutionalization of the various functions all governments must perform is one measure of political development.

The availability of resources may appear at first blush to be unrelated to political leaders and institutions. But such is not the case. Here one must distinguish between potential and actual resources. Some political systems are more effective than others at extracting and developing resources. A nation with oil reserves will not benefit from this resource until the oil has been discovered and the financial and technological wherewithal to develop it have been obtained. In addition, the infrastructure—canals, harbors, bridges, railroads, storage facilities, pipelines, and communications systems—must be built. Clearly, such an effort requires a great deal of planning, coordination, and expertise.

Equally important, human resources must be developed. Education and training are essential; so is the fulfillment of basic human needs such as food, shelter, and medical care. Otherwise, human resources will be wasted, and population growth will become a liability.

The quality of citizens is reflected in their values, attitudes, and behaviors, which can help or hinder economic growth, social harmony, and political stability. One crucial variable is the presence or absence of the **work ethic**. Are people highly motivated or nonchalant on the job? Do people feel a sense of responsibility to the state and society, or are they sullen and cynical? The quality of citizens is no less vital to the future of nations and regions than the quality of leaders.

Finally, the regional and international environment gives rise to certian political possibilities and constraints. The ability to coordinate foreign policies regionally so as to present a united front to the rest of the world can be critical. The success of the Organization of Petroleum Exporting Countries (OPEC) in the 1970s is one example. The desultory efforts of debtor nations in Latin America to devise a common strategy show the costs of failing at policy coordination. Constraints arise in various forms, but nationalism is the most prevalent and persistent. Citizens and leaders continue to identify primarily with national symbols, interests, and causes, even though awareness is growing that regional and global action is needed to solve or alleviate many common problems.

The Strains of Economic Development

Economic development alleviates some causes of instability, but it also creates new stresses and strains. The dislocations (urbanization, anomie, unemployment, and so on) that accompany economic development typically give rise to social conflict as well as feelings of personal alienation. Governments must be able to mediate between and among new social groups (students, workers, professionals), accommodate competing demands, and manage conflict.

Examples of countries that have not been able to deal with the forces unleashed by modernization are legion. A classic case is Iran both before and after the fall of the Shah, an ardent modernizer, in 1979. Another involves a regime that had for decades appeared to be immune to outbreaks of political instability. In 1989, Communist China was rocked by a massive student-led rebellion. Over a million protesters gathered in Tiananmen Square in Beijing, demanding an end to press censorship and official corruption. They also wanted new leadership and broad democratic reforms. After days of tense confrontation, the government ordered a bloody crackdown. In the end, the regime again proved its ability to manage internal conflict—a capacity greatly exceeding that of most developing nations.

In sum, the capacity to mobilize resources and manage social conflict are necessary (but probably not sufficient) conditions of economic development. The revolt in China demonstrates that no developing nation is immune to political instability but that some governments are more capable of coping with conflict than others. Industrial democracies also experience occasional unrest, but in contrast to Second and Third World nations, domestic tensions in the First World rarely even strain the capacity of political institutions to accommodate conflict.

The State and the Economy

Market economies predominate in the most affluent regions of the world, including North America, Western Europe, and the western Pacific (Japan, South Korea, Taiwan, and Hong Kong). During the Cold War era, centrally planned economies operated in the Soviet Union and Eastern Europe. These countries are now going through a painful transition, but command economies still operate in the People's Republic of China, Vietnam, and Cuba. The majority of developing nations combine some free enterprise with varying degrees and kinds of state intervention.

The free-enterprise model places primary emphasis on private incentives and private investment. The engine of economic growth is the profit motive. The marketplace determines prices and allocates profits—competition is the key. The most efficient producers prosper by being able to offer a quality product at a relatively low price. The private sector predominates.

In developing nations, national pride and political goals have often taken precedence over economic rationality. Building a large steel mill or a sports stadium, starting a national airline, or acquiring sophisticated jet fighters can have more to do with politics than economics or defense. Above all, most developing nations want to escape the external dependency they associate with colonialism. In practical terms, this desire translates into policies aimed at economic self-reliance.

State intervention in the developing regions and nations has taken three principal forms: **etatism** (state socialism), **export promotion**, and **import substitution**. Etatism involves a conscious effort by the state to form a partnership with private capital with the aim of spurring and guiding economic development. Turkey in the interwar years and Mexico more recently are two prime examples of this strategy. Export-led growth is a strategy most often associated with Japan's "economic miracle." It has also been adopted and adapted by South Korea, Taiwan, Hong Kong, Singapore, and many other nations in the developing areas. Import substitution is especially attractive in the early stages of industrialization. The United States followed this strategy in the early nineteenth century when it protected its infant industries. Ultimately, import substitution must be accompanied by export promotion because most countries do not have adequate internal markets to support sustained economic growth.

Development and Regime Type

Are some types of regimes more adept than others at implementing policies aimed at rapid economic development? Common sense and experience both suggest that regimes in which power and authority are centralized or concentrated are more effective at mobilizing society and dealing with conflict (most often by crushing opposition). Such regimes are sometimes called **mobilization systems**. They may be authoritarian or totalitarian in form. If the leadership fastens on to economic development as its supreme goal, a mobilization regime, by definition, is well equipped to do the job. By the same token, if the leaders set some other goal, such as military conquest or international prestige, they can also divert resources and postpone purely economic priorities indefinitely (as Germany and Japan did in the interwar period).

Democratic governments place social harmony and personal liberty above rapid economic development. They typically try to accommodate competing interest groups. Public policy is the result of compromises cobbled together on an ad hoc basis rather than of rational plans predicated on clearly articulated goals. The pace and direction of economic growth depends heavily on consumer choice. Regimes of this type are sometimes called **reconciliation systems**.

In the early stages of economic development, mobilization regimes can accomplish rapid growth. But beyond a certain point, reconciliation regimes now appear to be the more successful and sustainable of the two.

The Time Crunch

Whatever the type of regime in power, its leadership will face a dilemma. What is needed to ensure stability in the long run is a prosperous society in which the benefits of economic growth are widely enjoyed. The austerity policies often urged on developing nations by the IMF are aimed at achieving this result. These policies, however, are often at odds with the leaders' short-run objectives of staying in power and avoiding destabilizing and disruptive social conflict. Cutting subsidies for food and other necessities is one way for the government to divert scarce resources from unproductive social programs to growth-sustaining development projects. In some countries where the government has taken such steps (including Egypt, Sudan, Tunisia, Morocco, and Zaire), massive food riots have erupted, and austerity measures have had to be softened or rescinded to quell the unrest.

Latin American governments have faced a similar dilemma. For example, in 1985, Peru's newly elected president, Alan Garcia, blamed the country's economic and political problems (hyperinflation, widespread poverty, and a ferocious insurgency movement) on the IMF and the United States. And when Venezuela, one of South America's most stable democracies, became the scene of major riots in early 1989, the new president, Carlos Andres Perez, attributed the violent outburst to the country's heavy foreign-debt burden and to IMF-prescribed economic policies.

Hence time is not always on the side of economic development. In poverty-stricken developing countries, immediate needs (food, shelter, medicine, and other basics) are likely to take precedence over longer-range goals and objectives. If the government decides to cut short-term consumption when many citizens live on the edge of starvation, the moral and political consequences are dire. But if the government takes care of basic needs, there may be little or nothing left over for long-term investment. And even in affluent countries, high-consumption policies are always more popular than high-investment policies. More than a century and a half ago, this tendency toward immediate gratification was noticed by Alexis de Tocqueville, who considered it a defect peculiar to democratic governments. In truth, it may be a trait inherent in the very nature of the development process.

The Causes of "Underdevelopment"

Developing nations and regions are often assumed to have certain characteristics in common. According to the stereotype, they have little investment capital and small domestic markets, depend on one or two cash crops (produced for export rather than local consumption), and lack infrastructure (schools, hospitals, roads, communications networks, and the like). They are tied to tradition, village, and family; resistant to change; and mired in myth and superstition. They do not understand the idea of private property, and the profit motive is alien to them. This is the meaning of the term **underdevelopment**.

In contrast to the Madisonian model of constitutional democracy, developing countries are plagued by divisiveness. As James Mittelman has noted, "In most parts of the Third World, the receding colonial power sought to graft Western parliamentary and party institutions on to indigenous cultures, which are based on other historical realities." This "often aggravated existing class and ethnic rivalries." Issues of religion, language, and culture tore at the social fabric. In most cases, "the replicas of Western polities could not withstand the swirl of these centrifugal forces." Not surprisingly, spasmodic repression, accompanied by burgeoning bureaucracies in which loyalists are rewarded with government jobs, has been the response. The riots, insurgency, secessionist movements, and civil wars seemingly endemic to the Third World are symptomatic of the popular discontent bred by these conditions.[17]

Despite persistent stereotypes, developing nations are not all alike, nor have their leaders all pursued the same ends, used the same means, or embraced the same strategies. Three patterns can be discerned. Some developing nations, including the People's Republic of China, North Korea, Cuba, and Vietnam, have pursued egalitarian policies (equitable income distribution) more avidly than economic growth. Others, such as Brazil, Mexico, and Argentina, have pursued high-growth policies with scant regard for equality or living standards. And a few developing countries have been able to achieve both high growth and a high general standard of living. The shining example is Taiwan, but South Korea, Hong Kong, and Singapore also fall into this charmed category.

These patterns will be discussed in greater depth in Parts IV through VII. For now, it is enough to note that the Third World encompasses scores of nations in four distinct regions and that these nations are at different stages of economic and political development.

Nations and Regions: The Challenge of Integration

In this chapter we have discussed the regional context of politics and the problems of nation-building, which cut across regional boundaries, particularly in the Third World. Despite similarities, we have noted that patterns vary from nation to nation and from region to region. Hence the nation-building tasks and problems confronting most of sub-Saharan Africa are not identical to those facing most Slavic European countries, and the development issues that are most pressing in Latin America are very different from those facing Western Europe.

The very idea of economic and political development may seem irrelevant to the technologically advanced nations of the West. But development is an ongoing, never-ending process, and the challenges of postindustrial development are widely recognized in countries like Great Britain, France, and the United States, whose economic achievements were once the envy of the world. Some scholars assert that there are limits to growth that the advanced industrial nations are approaching. The failure to recognize these limits, they warn, will lead to overdevelopment (air pollution, urban congestion, and high crime rates are among the symptoms) and ultimately to social, economic, and political decline. The merits of this argument will not be explored here, but its proponents do raise important questions for students of comparative politics: What is the future of the industrial democracies? Have they exhausted their potential? Do affluent, mass-consumption societies face inevitable decline?

These questions are explored in Part II. For now let us note that Western Europe has moved rapidly toward economic unification. In the 1960s and 1970s, the nations of Central and South America, Southeast Asia, and other regions took cautious first steps in this direction as well. Many of these efforts have gained new momentum in the early 1990s. In 1992, Mexico joined the United States and Canada in a plan to establish a common market in North America. Finally, there has been talk of a western Pacific free-trade area involving Japan and the "four little dragons" (South Korea, Taiwan, Hong Kong, and Singapore).

These and other developments around the globe hint at the possibility that the twenty-first century will be the age of regionalism much as the nineteenth and twentieth centuries have been the age of nationalism. Regionalism will not replace ethnic particularism or nationalism any time soon, but the success of the European Community and the prospect of an even larger North American common market are likely to stimulate similar efforts in other regions of the globe. In politics, as in fashion, trends are often set by the rich and powerful, and imitation is the sincerest form of flattery.

CONCLUSION

Postindustrial societies in Europe, North America, Asia, and elsewhere are the products of a long process of political development. In Europe and North America, this process was largely driven by internal forces. Societies in the former colonial areas (the so-called Third World) have been undergoing rapid political and economic development in the second half of the twentieth century. The pace of change has been much faster than it was in Europe and North America, and the forces of change were (initially, at least) largely external rather than internal. Similarly, the models urged on Third World states by First and Second World powers were alien models that often did not fit easily into indigenous Third World cultures. These developmental differences are among the factors that have led to the emergence of regional institutions and a growing emphasis on regional economic trade, aid, and development. The success of the European Community is another factor. If this trend continues, it will profoundly affect political life as we know it on both the national and international levels.

KEY TERMS

development	terms of trade
modernization	conditionality
Cold War	work ethic
Third World	etatism
input-output theory	export promotion
evolutionary theory	import substitution
normative theory	mobilization systems
scientific method	reconciliation systems
determinism	underdevelopment
dependency theory	

STUDY QUESTIONS

1. Define development as it relates to states and societies.
2. How do different disciplines view development?
3. What are the various theories and approaches to development? Which, if any, are especially illuminating?
4. From a developmental perspective, what is the relationship between politics and economics? Politics and culture? Politics and society?
5. What is the nature of the debate over the proper role of the state in economic development?
6. What are the causes of "underdevelopment"? What are some of the symptoms? Are the major causes internal or external? (Does it really matter? If so, why?) Who or what is to blame for the maldistribution of wealth that results from differences in levels and kinds of development?

SUGGESTED READING

Almond, Gabriel, and Coleman, James, eds. *The Politics of the Developing Areas.* Books on Demand.

Apter, David. *The Politics of Modernization.* Books on Demand.

Banfield, Edward, and Banfield, L. F. *The Moral Basis of Backward Society.* New York: Free Press, 1967.

Caporaso, J. S. "Dependence, Dependency, and Power in the Global System: A Structural and Behavioral Analysis." *International Organizations,* vol. 32, no. 1 (Winter 1978).

Chilcote, Ronald. *Theories of Development and Underdevelopment.* Boulder, Colo.: Westview Press, 1984.

Chilton, Stephen. *Grounding Political Development.* Boulder, Colo.: Reiner, 1991.

Easton, David. *The Political System.* New York: Knopf, 1977.

Enloe, Cynthia H. *Ethnic Conflict and Political Development*. Lanham, Md.: University Press of America, 1986.

Fanon, Frantz. *Wretched of the Earth*. New York: Grove Press, 1988.

Gamer, Robert E. *The Developing Nations: A Comparative Perspective*. 2nd ed. Madison, Wis.: Benchmark & Madison, 1982.

Huntington, Samuel. *Political Order in Changing Societies*. New Haven, Conn.: Yale University Press, 1969.

Jaguiribe, Helio. *Political Development: A General Theory and a Latin American Case Study*. New York: Harper, 1973.

Lerner, Daniel. *The Passing of Traditional Society: Modernizing the Middle East*. New York: Free Press, 1958.

McClelland, David. *The Achieving Society*. New York: Halstead Press, 1976.

Mittelman, James H. *Out from Underdevelopment: Prospects for the Third World*. New York: St. Martin's Press, 1988.

Myrdal, Gunnar. *Asian Drama*. New York: Twentieth Century Fund, 1968.

Palmer, Monte. *Dilemmas of Political Development*. 4th ed. Itasca, Ill.: Peacock, 1989.

Pye, Lucian. *Aspects of Political Development*. Boston: Little, Brown, 1966.

Rostow, W. W. *The Process of Economic Growth*. 2nd ed. New York: Norton, 1962.

Ward, Barbara. *The Home of Man*. New York: Norton, 1976.

NOTES

1. James H. Mittleman, *Out from Underdevelopment: Prospects for the Third World* (New York: St. Martin's Press, 1988), p. 22.
2. Monte Palmer, *Dilemmas of Political Development,* 4th ed. (Itasca, Ill.: Peacock, 1989), p. 2.
3. *World Development Forum 2,* Nov. 15, 1984.
4. Plato, *The Republic of Plato,* Francis MacDonald Cornford, trans. (London: Oxford, 1945), pp. 106–107.
5. Stephen Chilton, *Grounding Poliltical Development* (Boulder, Colo.: Reiner, 1988).
6. Palmer, *Dilemmas,* p. 10.
7. John H. Herz, *International Politics in the Atomic Age* (New York: Columbia University Press, 1959).
8. Melvin Richter, *The Political Theory of Montesquieu* (Cambridge: Cambridge University Press, 1977), pp. 98–100.
9. See, for example, W. W. Rostow, *The Stages of Economic Growth: A Non-Communist Manifesto,* 2nd ed. (Cambridge: Cambridge University Press, 1966). Rostow delineates five stages of growth: (1) traditional, (2) precondition for take-off, (3) take-off, (4) drive for maturity, and (5) high mass consumption. See also A. F. K. Organski, *The Stages of Political Development* (New York: Knopf, 1967).
10. Robert A. Nisbet, *Social Change and History: Aspects of the Western Theory of Development* (New York: Oxford University Press, 1969).
11. Talcott Parsons, *The Social System* (New York: Free Press, 1964), especially pattern variables, pp. 46–51 and 58–67; see also Daniel Lerner, *The Passing of Traditional Society: Modernizing the Middle East* (New York: Free Press, 1958), pp. 47–52; Amitai Etzioni, *The Active Society* (New York: Free Press, 1968); David C. McClelland, *The Achieving Society* (New York: Halstead Press, 1976); Clifford Geertz, *Islam Observed*

(New Haven, Conn.: Yale University Press, 1968), p. 107; and Edward Banfield and L. F. Banfield, *The Moral Basis of Backward Society* (New York: Free Press, 1967).

12. Lerner, *Passing of Traditional Society,* pp. 47–52.
13. McClelland, *Achieving Society,* pp. 103–105.
14. Banfield and Banfield, *Moral Basis,* pp. 10–11, 83–101, 139, 155–158.
15. Among the most highly respected developmental theorists in political science are David Easton, *The Political System* (New York: Knopf, 1977), and "An Approach to the Analysis of a Political System," *World Politics,* April 1957; Gabriel Almond and James Coleman, *The Politics of the Developing Areas* (Princeton, N.J.: Princeton University Press, 1960); Gabriel Almond and G. Bingham Powell, *Comparative Politics: A Developmental Approach* (Boston: Little, Brown, 1966); Samuel Huntington, *Political Order in Changing Societies* (New Haven, Conn.: Yale University Press, 1969); and Lucian Pye, *Aspects of Political Development* (Boston: Little, Brown, 1966).
16. *Business Week,* Apr. 21, 1986.
17. Mittleman, *Out from Underdevelopment,* p. 16.

PART II

Western Europe

4

N. Ireland

Ireland

Great Britain

Netherlands

Belgium

Luxembourg

Germany

France

Switzerland

Austria

Italy

Portugal

Spain

GREAT BRITAIN

Area: 94,399 square miles
Population: 57.5 million
Density per square mile: 609
Languages: English, Welsh, Gaelic
Literacy rate: 99%
Religions: Protestantism, Roman Catholicism
Monetary unit: pound sterling
GNP: (1991) $963 billion; $16,750 per capita

FRANCE

Area: 210,038 square miles
Population: 57 million
Density per square mile: 271
Languages: French
Literacy rate: 99%
Religions: Roman Catholicism (76%)
Monetary unit: franc
GNP: (1991) $1.2 trillion; $20,600 per capita

GERMANY

Area: 137,753 square miles
Population: 80 million
Density per square mile: 580
Languages: German
Literacy rate: 99%
Religions: Protestantism, Roman Catholicism
Monetary unit: Deutsche mark
GNP: (1991) $1.5 trillion; $23,650 per capita

4

The Western Political Heritage

During the heyday of the Cold War, it was common to divide Europe into two parts: Western Europe, rooted in classical Greek and Roman civilizations, and Slavic (or Eastern) Europe, a commingling of Slavic, Scandinavian, Mongolian, and Byzantine cultures. The division resulted from a specific set of historical circumstances, above all the ideological rivalry between the capitalist United States and the communist Soviet Union.

For more than forty years, East-West tensions ran high; suddenly, after 1989, a year of momentous events in Europe, they evaporated. Several milestones marked this sudden end of the Cold War, including the overthrow of communist regimes throughout Eastern Europe, the demolition of the Berlin Wall, the reunification of Germany, Soviet troop withdrawals from the territory of former Warsaw Pact allies, and major conventional force reductions on the Continent. At the same time, however, the north-south split within the European Community (EC), the reemergence of the Balkan states as independent actors, and the presence of historic, geographic, and economic antecedents for a distinct Mediterranean subregion all point to the conclusion that Europe in the next century may be more appropriately viewed as a single region with several subregions and that new obstacles to the creation of a unified Europe are likely to appear in the post–Cold War era.

Regional Overview

Although every society has its unique features, there are many similarities among contemporary Western European states, similarities so striking that they can only be attributed to a certain cross-fertilization and overlapping of linguistic, cultural, religious, literary, and intellectual experiences. Democratic government is one striking feature common to all—this cannot be said of any other region

65

of the world, with the exception of North America (which, of course, is closely tied to Western Europe, historically and culturally). By the same token, all of the Western European countries embrace market-oriented capitalism, as opposed to the state-centered economic planning long associated with Soviet-style command economies. Moreover, all of these societies boast a large, well-educated, relatively affluent urban middle class employed increasingly in the service sector (law, medicine, education, banking, insurance, and the like), rather than agriculture or manufacturing. The south, however, can be said to lag behind the north; Spain, Portugal, Greece, and the southern regions of France and Italy have been the least prosperous parts of Western Europe in modern times.

Urbanization and economic diversification throughout Western Europe have been accompanied by the growth of materialism and secularism. Religion is still important to many individuals and families, but it is no longer the chief determinant of public or private morality. At the same time, ever greater faith has been placed in the power of science and technology to solve human problems. This reliance on reason and science as opposed to divine providence is, as we shall see, a salient feature of Western civilization, one that lends coherence and continuity to the history of social, economic, and political development in Latin-influenced Europe at least since the Renaissance (beginning in the late fifteenth century).

Western Europe also has a distinctive intellectual tradition. The effects of the Renaissance, the Reformation, and the Enlightenment were confined almost exclusively to the West. Profoundly influential in modern European history, these formative cultural and spiritual movements merely rippled the surface of Russian society, culture, and politics. The overthrow of czarist rule in 1917 brought to power a band of revolutionaries who espoused a Western ideology (Marxism), but the institutions that replaced czarism had little in common with the ideals of humanism and liberalism inspired by the Enlightenment.

The broad patterns just noted are familiar to anyone who has grown up in a Western country. What is not familiar is how these patterns evolved and why they are unique to the West. In Part II we will trace the outlines of this evolution. By the end of the book, we will have done so for every region of the world and every cluster of historical and cultural experiences in the interest of gaining a clearer understanding of the context of politics in each.

Environmental Influences

The great peninsula of Western Europe is not separated from the continental interior by any obvious natural barrier; the topographic grain of the region runs east-west rather than north-south. A crescent of low mountains, the Carpathians, however, "present their convex front to the Russian plain in the form of steep slopes," and north of the Carpathians a vast plain extends to the Baltic Sea. "In this belt lies a huge morass, the Pripet Marsh, a barrier equal to or surpassing the mountains." Nonetheless, "wide-open gateways" of firm ground flank it.[1]

The significance of this geography for European history is something of a paradox. On the one hand, there have been intermittent communication and contact between the two parts of Europe—peninsular and interior—for many centuries; on the other hand, the parts developed along largely separate lines. There is no solid line that divides Europe, but rather

> several kinds of transitions: the break between Roman-German culture and Greek-Slavic culture; the broad span where hill-bordered lowland on or near salt water gives way to featureless inland plains; the coarse versus fine mesh of transport routes; the dominance of continental over marine climate; the political boundary of Russia.[2]

The European Nursery

For most of the modern era, Western Europe has been the seedbed of innovative ideas in science, technology, and politics. Not surprisingly, no part of the globe was left untouched by the power of these ideas and the institutions they spawned:

> Beginning with very small areas, uniform in climate and resources and isolated from neighbors, the Western tradition has moved into larger spaces, adapted itself to varied climates and landforms, and learned to use a multiplicity of resources. In the process, isolation has given way to a worldwide net of communication. Possessing a unique combination of favorable natural conditions, Europeans maintained political dominance and economic leadership in the successive worlds of which they have been a part.[3]

Although the metaphor of Europe as a nursery may overstate European influence and understate indigenous developments in many other regions of the world, the concept holds more than a grain of truth. From the beginning of the great European explorations during the fifteenth-century Renaissance to the Age of Imperialism and the Industrial Revolution four hundred years later, Europe made a deep imprint on every region of the world. Indeed, as Table 4.1 shows, Europe accounted for over three-fifths of the world's total manufacturing output by 1900; what is more, this dramatic shift had resulted in the economic eclipse of the Third World, including China and India.[4] Why did Western Europe display such enormous vigor during this protracted period? Could physical, geographic, or climatic factors have contributed to this burst of creative energy?

Nature's Benevolence

Western Europe does enjoy certain natural advantages over most other regions of the world. Its climate displays a wide variety without extremes. "No area of equal size on earth is so favored in climate—both in its variety and in its suitability for human life."[5] Its soils and climates are generally conducive to agriculture, yet minerals are also abundant:

> Two of the three most critical soil fertilizers are present in large quantities, and the third can be manufactured from local resources. Rich coal fields occur from Scotland to Poland, and ample iron ores for steelmaking lie not far from coal. The Western economic order since the Industrial Revolution has been based on these two minerals.[6]

Table 4.1   Relative Shares of World Manufacturing Output, 1750–1900 (percent)

	1750	1800	1830	1860	1880	1900
Europe	23.2	28.1	34.2	53.2	61.3	62.0
United Kingdom	1.9	4.3	9.5	19.9	22.9	18.5
Hapsburg Empire	2.9	3.2	3.2	4.2	4.4	4.7
France	4.0	4.2	5.2	7.9	7.8	6.8
German States/Germany	2.9	3.5	3.5	4.9	8.5	13.2
Italian States/Italy	2.4	2.5	2.3	2.5	2.5	2.5
Russia	5.0	5.6	5.6	7.0	7.6	8.8
United States	0.1	0.8	2.4	7.2	14.7	23.6
Japan	3.8	3.5	2.8	2.6	2.4	2.4
Third World	73.0	67.7	60.5	36.6	20.9	11.0
China	32.8	33.3	29.8	19.7	12.5	6.2
India/Pakistan	24.5	19.7	17.6	8.6	2.8	1.7

Source: Paul Kennedy, *The Rise and Fall of the Great Powers* (New York: Random House, 1987), p. 149.

Northwestern Europe thus became the center of the Industrial Revolution. Coal deposits and rivers were crucial. According to a scholar of the 1920s:

> Modern industry is based upon the use of coal and to a [lesser] degree on "white coal," or waterpower. Coal is necessary in the making of iron and steel and for the operation of the machines in factories. Since coal is bulky and expensive to transport, it is usually easier to bring raw materials that are to be converted into manufactured articles to the vicinity of the mines than vice versa. As a consequence, many of the great manufacturing centers, particularly those of Germany, England, and Belgium, cluster near the coal fields. . . .
>
> It is a very important fact that there is almost no coal at all in the Alpine-Mediterranean Region. This circumstance, perhaps no less than the reorientation of the world's trade routes to the Atlantic which followed the discovery of America and the sea route to the Indies, helps explain why the Mediterranean countries have not experienced the tremendous industrial development and the growth of huge cities so characteristic of Northwestern Europe.[7]

It was no accident, for example, that in the 1920s, twenty-seven of Great Britain's forty largest cities were situated near coal deposits and that eleven of Germany's forty-seven cities of 100,000 people or more were on coal beds.[8] Rivers were important as a source of hydroelectric power and, like the sea, as a means of commerce, communication, and transport. The main waterway of modern Europe has run along the Atlantic Coast of the Continent rather than the Mediterranean. With only a few exceptions, the principal seaports are located on or near the mouths of rivers.

The accessibility which many districts of Northwestern Europe have acquired through their nearness to river and sea routes was a powerful stimulus to commerce, to movements of people, to the spread of institutions, and to the exchange of ideas for centuries before the Industrial Revolution.[9]

Historical and Cultural Factors

Why did Western Europe develop differently from other regions? One reason often given is that Europe was able to develop at its own pace. This "modernization from within" contrasts sharply with the externally induced social change that occurred in the Middle East, Africa, Asia, and Latin America. Europe in the Middle Ages was very much like today's developing countries were a century ago. But unlike the Third World, Europe was not conquered and colonized by more technologically advanced invaders. It is true that the Chinese and Ottoman empires were both ahead of medieval Europe in state organization and technology. Indeed, the Ottoman Empire pressed the periphery of Western Europe, reaching the outskirts of Vienna in the sixteenth century. But by this time the Ottoman state was overextended and past its zenith.

Thus Western Europe could evolve slowly, with less urgency and along lines that were natural to its indigenous peoples and cultures. It is noteworthy that the European countries most immune to outside incursion (Britain and Scandinavia) evolved quite differently from Germany and Italy, which in turn have followed paths different from Eastern Europe and the Balkans.

The fact that Western Europe has a feudal Christian background and the United States does not also deserves brief mention here. Because the castelike relationships of **feudalism** never existed in the New World, Americans often fail to understand the political implications of class structure. The feudal heritage and the pervasiveness of Roman Catholicism led eventually to struggles over class and religion in Europe and the rise of church-based political parties. By contrast, there is no feudal or aristocratic tradition in the United States, and the constitutional separation of church and state has limited the role of organized religion in American politics.

Also striking is the absence in the United States of the labor-based, left-wing parties so commonplace in Western Europe. The lack of such parties in the United States is due in part to the early establishment of universal white male suffrage. In Europe, with the major exception of France, the working class had to fight for the franchise, and to this end it supported political movements that persisted for decades afterward.

Religion, Reformation, and Renaissance

From the standpoint of religion, all of Western Europe has been part of Christendom since the early days of the Holy Roman Empire (800–1806). Until the Reformation in the sixteenth century, Roman Catholicism was the universal religion. The **Reformation** was a revolt against Rome, not against Christianity. Quite the opposite: it was a revitalizing of Christianity as the one true faith. Martin Luther, John Calvin, Huldrych Zwingli, and other great church reformers were determined to rescue the church from a corrupt papacy. The Reformation, then, was a time of spiritual and temporal tumult and change, but it reaffirmed the dominance of Christianity in the moral and spiritual life of the West.

It would be a mistake to regard the Reformation as a cause of secularization. We must instead examine its antecedents. Certainly, the Renaissance and the ensuing age of exploration paved the way for the spirit of adventure, inquiry, iconoclasm, and intellectual ferment that lay at the core of the Reformation.

The **Renaissance**, originating in Italy, was revolutionary in its notion of human beings as the center of all things. Whereas Christianity stressed that divine providence sets the shape and course of history, the giants of the Renaissance (exemplified by Leonardo da Vinci in art, science, and technology; Michelangelo in art and architecture; and Machiavelli in political philosophy) believed in the surpassing powers of the human will and intellect.

The Renaissance and the Reformation together fed into powerful new intellectual, economic, and political undercurrents that emerged in the form of mercantilism, the Scientific Revolution, the Age of Enlightenment, the Industrial Revolution, and the Age of Imperialism.

Mercantilism

Mercantilism refers to the means devised by England and France to deal with the economic challenge posed by Holland in the seventeenth century. As formulated in France under Jean-Baptiste Colbert, Louis XIV's famous minister, mercantilism was a policy aimed at impeding or preventing the importation of Dutch products by imposing high tariffs, banning the use of third-country ships in foreign trade and commerce, and subsidizing domestic shippers and manufacturers. Mercantilism equated wealth with money and judged nations by the size of their balance-of-trade surplus or deficit.[10] Mercantilism also reflected the desire to promote national producers and manufacturers (an early version of the "infant industries" development strategy).

In Holland, England, and France, mercantilism provided the impetus for the acquisition of colonial empires. The instruments of this early empire-building rivalry were the great merchant companies, notably the Dutch East India Company and the English East India Company. (A French Company of the Indies was also established later.)

> It was the company, not its members, which conducted the business, sent out its ships—the great *East Indiamen*, bought and sold beyond the seas, and exercised rights of sovereignty in its colonial possessions by delegation from its own government.[11]

The key role of economic factors in the rise and fall of the great powers in Europe during this period has been well documented by historians.[12]

The Scientific Revolution

The urge to conquer new worlds in the sixteenth and seventeenth centuries was no less evident in domestic than in international affairs. The **Scientific Revolution**, as this period has come to be known, was a time of tremendous intellectual vitality. Leonardo da Vinci, Copernicus, Galileo, Johannes Kepler, René Descartes, Francis Bacon, Robert Boyle, and Sir Isaac Newton gave new meaning to the humanistic impulses associated with the Renaissance. In little more than a century and a half, they revolutionized our understanding of the physical world and laid the foundations of the natural sciences, including physics, chemistry, biology, and astronomy. In so doing, they also laid the foundations of modernity, with all its implications for good or evil. They gave future generations the tools to conquer nature and paved the way for the **secular humanism** of today, a philosophy that stresses the potential of humankind, using scientific as well as political means, to solve social and economic problems.

The Enlightenment

The **Enlightenment** of the eighteenth century followed naturally on the heels of the Scientific Revolution. And the Industrial Revolution developed side by side with the Enlightenment in a kind of symbiotic relationship.

As an intellectual movement, the Enlightenment was a significantly new way of looking at humanity and the world, emphasizing human reason over blind faith. (Indeed, this period is also known as the Age of Reason.) The morality linked to Enlightenment ideas and ideals was readily identifiable in the Judeo-Christian tradition and the ethical systems of Greek and Roman antiquity: the Golden Rule of the New Testament, the Golden Mean of the Greek philosophers, the emphasis on honesty and other conventional virtues. Two elements of Roman Catholic dogma, however, were rejected. One was the key role of the holy sacraments (such as the ritual breaking of bread and drinking of wine known as Holy Communion, and the giving of last rites at the time of death) as the path to salvation; the other was the central importance of asceticism, self-deprivation, and resistance to temptation (broadly defined as worldly pleasures).

In place of the notion that one must endure suffering and self-sacrifice to get to heaven, Enlightenment thinkers (principally the French *philosophes*) developed the doctrine of **ethical hedonism**, which held that ordinary human desires were natural and good, not things to be denied or ashamed of. The orthodox Christian teaching on the inherent evil in human beings (the doctrine of original sin) was replaced by a belief in innate goodness.

The ultimate dream of the Enlightenment thinkers, although they disagreed on many points and seldom set forth their aspirations for the future in a fully explicit picture, focused on a world without conflict, without harshness, with men of intelligence and goodwill working independently, each for his own welfare, yet all together for common interests as well.[13]

The French *philosophes*—most notably Montesquieu, Voltaire, Diderot, and Rousseau—set about to do for the social sciences what the giants of the Scientific Revolution did for the natural sciences. They emphasized the empirical world (fact and experience) and sought the truth about human nature and society through introspection. By this method the *philosophes* developed trenchant critiques of established social values and political institutions. Their overriding aim, however, was not to disparage existing customs and beliefs but, in Jeremy Bentham's felicitous phrase, to seek "the greatest good for the greatest number."

Politically, the *philosophes* seem surprisingly moderate (and modern) by today's standards. In general, they did not advocate anything so radical as the dismantling of the nation-state system or even the overthrow of Europe's absolute monarchs. Instead they envisioned a new social order in which the rule of law bound rulers and ruled alike and all citizens were guaranteed equal rights. They did not seek economic equality or common ownership of property—indeed, they seldom called for the abolition of noble titles and ranks—but they did favor eliminating aristocratic powers and privileges.

The transformation that the rational thinkers of the eighteenth century sought, though temperate in its ends and means, was achieved only after a protracted period of civil strife. The first upheaval occurred in France.

The French Revolution

The **French Revolution** of 1789 was not the inevitable result of the intellectual dissent associated with the Enlightenment but rather the product of complex social, economic, and political difficulties. It began as a rebellion of the nobility against what this class regarded as unfair and onerous taxation imposed by King Louis XVI. The execution of this monarch in 1793 was a turning point in French (and European) history. The revolution progressed through several stages. First, a limited constitutional monarchy was created by charter; then the monarchy was abolished altogether. Next, radical **Jacobins**, led by Maximilian Robespierre, set about creating a "republic of virtue"—a thinly veiled tyranny run by ideological zealots with a vision of a utopian society.

The "fever" stage of the French Revolution did not last long: it soon gave way to the so-called Thermidorean reaction. The Thermidoreans rejected both popular government, which they saw as synonymous with mob rule, and absolute monarchy rooted in heredity and privilege. Under the guise of republicanism, they set up an oligarchic mechanism known as the Directory. This regime lasted about five years before giving way to the dictatorship of Napoleon Bonaparte.

The French Revolution makes for a fascinating study. For our purposes, the essential point is that this revolution, despite its failure in France, was a presentiment of the far-reaching demands for political liberalization that would accompany the social and economic changes wrought in eighteenth- and nineteenth-century Europe by a revolution of a different sort.

The Industrial Revolution and Its Consequences

The rise of liberalism in nineteenth-century Europe was facilitated by the application of science to production. The new economic frontiers opening up made constitutional democrary attractive to the rising commercial middle class, which would now have the political means to protect and expand its economic interests. At the same time, the new technologies, and the factory system they spawned, had enormous socioeconomic implications. The emergence of an urban, industrial class of wage laborers transformed the structure of previously rural, agriculturally based, aristocratic societies, with consequences that could hardly have been imagined at the time.

The use of mechanical energy to increase labor productivity was a key feature of the **Industrial Revolution**. Textile manufacturing and mining were the first industrial sectors to be mechanized; virtually all others followed. One of the early social consequences was the exploitation of the labor of adults and children for profit; another, as Karl Marx noted, was the concentration of labor, which in time gave rise to new social forces that changed Western European politics forever.

The widespread industrial application of mechanical energy provided the impetus for the construction or refurbishing of roads and canals. It revolutionized the modes of transportation and communication and paradoxically made farming far more efficient and productive yet far less labor intensive. Industrialization led to the rise of the modern urban centers—a process that occurred in a relatively short time span in Europe (see Table 4.2, page 74).

Today we can see the results of the Industrial Revolution all around us, especially urbanization and its accompanying ills. Big cities, elaborate highway systems, mammoth shopping malls, a depopulated countryside, chronic agricultural surpluses, air and water pollution, urban sprawl, traffic congestion, and high crime rates—these are just a few of the economic and social consequences of the Industrial Revolution.

Liberalism

Along with socioeconomic changes came changes in political thinking—in particular, the rise of **liberalism**. This philosophy represented a middle way between the extreme egalitarianism of the Jacobins and the inherited wealth, power, and privilege of the old aristocratic order. It was ideally suited for the emerging middle class, for whom liberty ranked above equality in the hierarchy of political values. Politically, liberalism decried arbitrary and repressive rule, press censorship, laws conferring special privilege on hereditary aristocracies, and discrimina-

Table 4.2 Urban Population of the Powers (in millions) and as a Percentage of Total Population, 1890–1938

	1890	1900	1910	1913	1920	1928	1938
1. Britain	11.2	13.5	15.3	15.8	16.6	17.5	18.7
(1)	(29.9%)	(32.8%)	(34.9%)	(34.6%)	(37.3%)	(38.2%)	(39.2%)
2. United States	9.6	14.2	20.3	22.5	27.4	34.3	45.1
(2)	(15.3%)	(18.7%)	(22.0%)	(23.1%)	(25.9%)	(28.7%)	(32.8%)
3. Germany	5.6	8.7	12.9	14.1	15.3	19.1	20.7
(4)	(11.3%)	(15.5%)	(20.0%)	(21.0%)	(35.7%)	(34.4%)	(30.2%)
4. France	4.5	5.2	5.7	5.9	5.9	6.3	6.3
(3)	(11.7%)	(13.3%)	(14.4%)	(14.8%)	(15.1%)	(15.3%)	(15.0%)
5. Russia	4.3	6.6	10.2	12.3	4.0	10.7	36.5
(8)	(3.6%)	(4.8%)	(6.4%)	(7.0%)	(3.1%)	(7.1%)	(20.2%)
6. Italy	2.7	3.1	3.8	4.1	5.0	6.5	8.0
(5)	(9.0%)	(9.6%)	(11.0%)	(11.6%)	(13.2%)	(16.1%)	(18.2%)
7. Japan	2.5	3.8	5.8	6.6	6.4	9.7	20.7
(6)	(6.3%)	(8.6%)	(10.3%)	(12.8%)	(11.6%)	(15.6%)	(28.6%)
8. Austria-Hungary	2.4	3.1	4.2	4.6	—	—	—
(7)	(5.6%)	(6.6%)	(8.2%)	(8.8%)			

Source: Paul Kennedy, *The Rise and Fall of the Great Powers* (New York: Random House, 1987), p. 200.

tion against individuals on the basis of race or religion. Economically, it stressed property rights and other middle-class interests.

Following the teachings of Adam Smith, Thomas Malthus, and David Ricardo, nineteenth-century liberals embraced the view that free competition among nations and individuals, unrestrained by tariffs and monopolies, would inevitably produce the greatest prosperity for the largest number; that unemployment, hunger, and deprivation were nature's way of regulating population growth; and that wages are determined not by capitalists seeking to maximize profits and minimize costs but by the "iron law" of supply and demand.

Because liberalism represented rather narrow economic interests (by contemporary standards, nineteenth-century liberalism was stiffly conservative), advocates of democracy and republicanism stepped forward—in England they were called radicals. And as the Industrial Revolution came of age, the working class also came of age. For the champions of this underclass, "bourgeois" democracy was too cautious and too compatible with capitalism. Charles Fourier, Louis Blanc, Robert Owen, and, of course, Karl Marx considered socialism the answer.

Socialism

Socialism is an ideology that views private ownership of the means of production as the root of all evil in society. It disdains the profit motive and advocates extreme equality in the distribution of material goods. It takes an optimistic view of human nature and blames greed, envy, corruption, and crime on injustices built into the nature of capitalistic society. Remove the social causes of antisocial behavior, and domestic tranquillity will surely follow.

Conservatism

While liberalism, republicanism, and socialism were vying for the allegiance of newly emerging social forces in Great Britain and on the Continent, the advocates of **conservativism** were trying to preserve traditional values and protect the old order. The most important (and prescient) of the conservative thinkers was Edmund Burke (1729–1797). In his book *Reflections on the French Revolution,* written in 1790, Burke warned that nations that discard customs, beliefs, and institutions rooted in the past in their endeavor to build a perfect society risk chaos and political catastrophe. No doubt the victims of the Jacobin terror would have agreed.

Against the background of the advancing Industrial Revolution, these cross-currents—liberalism, socialism, and conservatism—competed for primacy in Western Europe during the nineteenth century and most of the twentieth.

Social Class and Politics

As the foregoing discussion suggests, the political spectrum in Europe is much broader and more diversified than in the United States. The conventional American understanding of "class" can be misleading when applied in the European setting. There social class has played a major role in defining ideological positions and creating political parties. To a much greater extent than in the United States, class consciousness is a motive force in European politics, and ideological divisions are just as important in election campaigns and outcomes as policy differences.

Historically, political parties in Europe have reflected the evolving class structure of European society. Center-right parties—the Christian Democrats in Germany, the Gaullists and neo-Gaullists in France, the Conservatives (Tories) in Great Britain—have historically represented conservative farming and business interests—the middle class. Center-left parties (Social Democrats and Socialists) have sought to appeal to the commercial and professional classes. And the far-left Communist party has represented the working class and intellectuals. Center-right parties often support "welfare state" policies of the kind most conservative Republicans in the United States consider anathema. Parties of the far right were very popular in Europe during the tumultuous period between World War I and World War II. As we will see in Chapters 5 and 6, far-right parties were discredited and even outlawed after World War II, but in recent years, have made a comeback—especially among youths and blue-collar workers. Center-left parties are ideologically similar to the most liberal elements of the U.S. Democratic party. Far-left parties have never had much appeal in North America.

Why would some Europeans identify with the Communist party? First, throughout Europe, the Communists have historically fought for the rights of workers, as have the Socialists and the Social Democrats. Second, in World War II, the Communists generally put up the strongest resistance to the Nazis and Fascists, and many voters in France and Italy showed their appreciation by voting for Communist party candidates in the elections held after the war. Third, the Communist parties of Europe are not subversive or revolutionary organizations. In most cases, they disavow violence and participate in elections like any responsible political party. In the 1970s, Western European Communist parties made a major effort to distance themselves from the Soviet Union, Stalinism, and revolution; this movement became known as **Eurocommunism**.

Nonetheless, Communist parties have fallen on hard times in Europe, both East and West. In the West, the reasons are not difficult to discern: the industrial work force—the Communists' main constituency—has dwindled in proportion to service-sector jobholders in recent decades; measures protecting workers from exploitation or abuse at the hands of profit-minded capitalists are in force; and the Communist parties have failed to broaden their base or build lasting coalitions with other parties. But the severest blow to Eurocommunism was the toppling of Communist governments in Eastern Europe and the disintegration of the Soviet Union in the span of only three years (1989–1991).

Some examples will clarify the class character of European political parties. In Great Britain, the Labour party emerged as the champion of the working class around a century ago. The party has always been closely linked to the British trade union movement. The absence of a significant Marxist party in Great Britain is due partly to the rise of the Labour party and partly to the fact that British ruling elite pursued relatively progressive policies, making economic and political concessions to the workers. On the Continent, Socialist and Communist parties competed with each other and with Social Democratic parties for the allegiance of the workers.

The Christian Democratic party in Germany exemplifies another ideological strand in European politics. Throughout Europe, religion has long been a politically potent force. In Germany, both Roman Catholics and Protestants have viewed Marxism with alarm, in part because of its atheistic bent. Christian Democrats are strong advocates of democracy and free enterprise. Hence they represented a coalition of middle-class elements (farming, business, banking, the professions) and working-class people for whom religion was as important as bread-and-butter issues. Today, with the fading of the "Communist threat," the religious dimension of politics in Germany is no longer of great significance. Instead, both the Christian Democrats and the Social Democrats are essentially centrist parties, the former stressing free enterprise and the latter advocating state intervention to share the nation's considerable wealth more equitably. But it is important to recognize that many "conservative" parties in Western Europe, including the Christian Democrats, strongly support welfare-state policies, in sharp contrast to the right in the United States.

New problems and changing conditions have produced new parties, one example being the Greens. Green parties sprang up throughout Western Europe in the 1960s and 1970s in response to growing fear of a nuclear catastrophe. In the 1970s and 1980s, the Greens became increasingly concerned with other environmental concerns. In the Federal Republic of Germany, where they had some electoral success, they continued to oppose nuclear weapons and nuclear power plants but began to focus more and more on air and water pollution. Their support is drawn largely from the universities—both professors and students—and white-collar workers. Their main opponents are farmers (who use large quantities of pesticides and chemical fertilizers), industrialists, and developers (who tend to place economic growth ahead of environmental protection).

Imperialism and the European System

The second half of the nineteenth century is often called the **Age of Imperialism**, for at this time began a new wave of European colonial expansion. Earlier in the same century, people had become disillusioned with empires and colonies, due in part to successful revolutions in the Americas against England, Spain, and Portugal. Industrialization diverted attention from external expansion to internal development, and the new emphasis on free trade removed much of the rationale for global empire-building. British Prime Minister Benjamin Disraeli expressed the tenor of the times in 1852. "These wretched colonies," he said, "will all be independent too in a few years and are a millstone around our necks."

Theories of Colonial Rule

As industry grew, Europe's economic and political leaders began to seek new sources of raw materials and new markets for their products. After 1870, free trade gave way to protectionist policies, and soon a race for new colonies began. A plethora of theories defending colonial expansion were expounded. Alfred T. Mahan's geopolitical concepts were used to "prove" that great powers could not survive without overseas possessions. Charles Darwin's concept of the survival of the fittest was used to "prove" that colonialism was in accordance with the inexorable laws of nature. Rudyard Kipling wrote about the "white man's burden" (to spread civilization to a benighted world). Even U.S. President McKinley claimed that God had spoken to him on the eve of the Spanish-American War (1898), commissioning the United States to take the Philippines and Christianize "our brown brothers."

By the end of the nineteenth century, all of Asia and Africa had been colonized. Even China had lost its sovereign status: it was subjugated through a series of treaties that gave various European powers special rights and prerogatives. Africa in 1914 was under the colonial sway of no fewer than seven European nations—Belgium, France, Germany, Great Britain, Italy, Portugal, and Spain. In fact, only two independent nations remained—Ethiopia and Liberia.

The Classical Balance of Power

Paradoxically, as Eurpoe approached the zenith of its power, it was also reaching the end of its preeminence in world affairs. For centuries the international system had been synonymous with the European system. Since the Treaty of Westphalia (1648), the rulers and statesmen of Europe had recognized the existence of a **balance of power**, a system that preserved order and prevented the hegemony of any one state over the others.

This uniquely European system grew out of shared values forged over the centuries. In 1871, Edward Gibbon, author of *The Decline and Fall of the Roman Empire,* proposed

> to consider Europe as one great republic, whose various inhabitants have attained almost the same level of politeness and cultivation. The balance of power will then continue to fluctuate, and the prosperity of our own or the neighboring kingdoms may be alternately exalted or depressed; but these events cannot essentially injure our general state of happiness, the system of arts, and law, and the manners which so advantageously distinguish, above the rest of mankind, the Europeans and their colonies.

During the heyday of the European balance-of-power era, many of the great thinkers made implicit reference to the intellectual and moral foundations that undergirded a de facto political unity. For example, Fenelon noted, "Christendom forms a kind of general republic which has its common interests, fears, and precautions"; Rousseau asserted, "The nations of Europe form among themselves an invisible nation"; and Vattel, the great Enlightenment philosopher of international law, wrote that "Europe forms a political system, a body where the whole is connected by the relations and different interests of nations inhabiting this part of the world."[14] In sum, the fuel that kept "the motor of the balance of power moving," according to this thesis, "is the intellectual and moral foundation of Western civilization, the intellectual and moral climate within which the protagonists of eighteenth-century society moved and which permeated all their thought and action."[15]

Beyond a common world view, the main features of the European balance-of-power model can be summarized as follows:

1. Numerous sovereign powers—five to ten significant state actors are present at any given time.
2. Flexible alliances—state actors are pragmatic and unencumbered by ideological baggage.
3. Limited objectives—state actors do not pursue goals that threaten the existence of other states.
4. Limited means—strategies, tactics, and armaments employed in pursuit of national interests are circumscribed by both the state of technology and moral constraints.
5. A keeper of the balance—as an island power aloof from the affairs of the Continent, Great Britain was ideally situated to play this role.

The Demise of the Eurocentric System

Ironically, the globalization brought about by imperialism hastened the demise of this Eurocentric international system. In the years leading up to World War I, the European system showed signs of decrepitude: alliances turned rigid, an unrestrained arms race occurred, ideological divisions sharpened, and nationalism spread.[16]

U.S. President Woodrow Wilson conceived of the League of Nations as an alternative to nationalism and the European balance-of-power system. Although it never worked, it prefigured the emergence of a new global system with the United States and Japan (later the United States and the Soviet Union) as the major non-European powers.

The Totalitarian Interlude

A dark shadow fell across the political landscape of Europe after World War I. An extreme left-wing ideology, the Marxist-Leninist form of **communism**, triumphed in Russia in 1917, and an extreme right-wing ideology, **Fascism**, gained ascendancy in Italy a few years later. But it was in Germany between the two world wars that the battle lines between extremist ideologies of the left and right were drawn most sharply and fatefully.

The German defeat in World War I was humiliating, and harsh peace terms were imposed. Following an unconditional surrender, Germany was forced by the Treaty of Versailles to accept a "war guilt" clause, in effect an admission of responsibility and liability for the death and destruction caused by the war. The treaty imposed a parliamentary democracy on Germany (the ill-fated Weimar Republic), assessed heavy reparations and indemnities against Germany, and called for permanent unilateral German disarmament.

Understandably, this treaty was never popular in Germany. Nor was the Weimar Republic, which carried the stigma of Versailles. But it was the draconian economic burdens imposed by the treaty that proved to be the undoing of the Weimar government and the making of Adolf Hitler's Nazi party.

In the early 1920s, hyperinflation left the German middle class impoverished. The worldwide stock market collapse of 1929 delivered the coup de grace. Foreign banks called in their loans to Germany, and a wave of protectionism brought international trade to a near standstill. Depression spread across the industrialized world, and unemployment grew to epidemic proportions. In the chaos and despair that ensued, extremism found fertile soil. Germany became a hothouse for radical ideologies, especially National Socialism.

National Socialism (Nazism) had much in common with other extreme right-wing (fascist) ideologies. It was ultranationalistic, glorifying the German *Volk* as a chosen people and enshrining a mythical *Volksgeist* (popular spirit) as the force that defined, united, and guided the German nation. Among its highest values were loyalty to the leader, obedience to authority, and courage in the face of danger. The Nazis glorified power; for true believers, violence was a virtue, and war would bring triumph rather than tragedy.

Hitler came to power legally; indeed, his Nazi party had a larger following in the early 1930s than any of its competitors. The Nazi leader was popular in part because he told the German people what they wanted to hear. For example, he attributed Germany's defeat in World War I not to German failings but to a stab in the back by Communists and Jews (he tended to equate the two). He also pandered to German prejudices, particularly anti-Semitism. Jews became a convenient scapegoat for nearly everything that was wrong with German society. In sum, National Socialism was a doctrine of hatred, prejudice, violence, and revenge.

Such dark sentiments were not confined to Germany. The roots of European fascism were in Italy, and the branches reached far and wide. Fascism triumphed in a relatively mild form in Spain in the 1930s. It also took hold in Eastern Europe; fascist regimes in Hungary, Romania, and Bulgaria collaborated with Hitler in the early stages of World War II. Moreover, even where fascism failed to gain the upper hand, its sympathizers occasionally made their presence felt. In southern France, for instance, the upstart Vichy regime, headed by Marshal Philippe Pétain, collaborated with Hitler during the war. On the other side of the globe, a militaristic, expansionist, and fanatically nationalistic regime closely resembling the fascist model came to power in Japan in the 1930s.

War and Revolution: An Ambiguous Legacy

Critics of the European balance-of-power system call it the "war system." If its purpose was to prevent war and bloodshed, they argue, it failed miserably. Wars have been a recurring phenomenon in Europe since the nation-state system emerged from the morass of the Middle Ages.

Defenders of the European system argue that in the absence of a balancing mechanism, war would likely have been more frequent and less restrained. They point out that prior to the twentieth century, when the classical balance-of-power system broke down, wars were generally limited in scope, if not in duration. By contrast, several all-out wars have been fought since, suggesting that once the old European order collapsed, there was nothing equally efficacious to take its place.

One thing is certain: war has played a major role in shaping the modern history of Western Europe. As we have seen, revolution—the domestic equivalent of war—has also been an integral part of European history during the past two centuries. (More recently, terrorism has intruded on the political scene as well.) The unmistakable conclusion is that collective violence is a political tradition in Europe, its rich aesthetic, religious, and intellectual legacy notwithstanding.

The implications of this dark side of Europe's heritage are far from obvious. We might assume that a violent history predisposes individuals or societies to violence. But this is not necessarily the case. Indeed, the cataclysmic events that

⦿ European Economic Community Member Nations (*Western Europe*):

Belgium	Ireland
Denmark	Italy
France	Luxembourg
Germany	Netherlands
Great Britain	Portugal
Greece	Spain

◎ Nations Applying for EEC Membership:

Austria
Cyprus*
Finland
Malta
Sweden
Switzerland
Turkey

☐ European Free Trade Association Members:

Austria
Finland
Iceland*
Norway
Sweden
Switzerland

▲ Nations with Nuclear Weaponry: France, Great Britain

*not shown

have torn Europe asunder in the twentieth century could just as well have the opposite effect: to make succeeding generations determined not to repeat the mistakes of their elders.

Similarly, the nations of Western Europe have firsthand experience with the burdens of imperialism and the pitfalls of unrestrained nationalism. It may be that these lessons will be forgotten or that they were never properly learned. From the vantage point of the 1990s, however, it appears as though Western Europeans, chastened by the sanguinary episodes of their recent past, are determined to find a different pathway to the future. (It is a different story in the Balkans, as the bitter wars between the peoples who once comprised Yugoslavia have recently demonstrated.)

World War II sealed the fate of the European system and, for a time at least, relegated the former great powers (and colonial overlords) of Europe to second-rate status. As a result of two devastating wars on the Continent, France, Germany, and Great Britain—the core countries of Western Europe—were forced to turn to the United States for succor and security. The Marshall Plan and the North Atlantic Treaty Organization, two American postwar initiatives, symbolized the decline and fall of Western Europe.

As we will see in the following chapters, obituaries for Western Europe were premature. The recovery of the Continent, highlighted by economic miracles in Germany and Italy, the resurgence of democratic rule, and the integration of national economies into a single trading bloc called the **European Community** (popularly known as the **Common Market**), has brought into being a new economic superpower.

Case Studies: The United Kingdom, France, and Germany

In the early 1990s, the United Kingdom, France, and Germany had a combined population of roughly 190 million and a combined GDP second only to that of the United States. They form the inner core of the European Community, the world's largest trading bloc. Along with Russia, they are the major European military powers—France and Great Britain boast their own nuclear weapons, and Germany has the economic and technological capability to field Europe's most formidable conventional forces.

The United Kingdom

Roughly the size of Oregon, the United Kingdom is a relatively small island nation that has played a disproportionately large role in modern European history. The distance from the northern tip of Scotland to the southern coast of England is slightly less than six hundred miles. Because it is long and narrow, the ocean is never very far away—even in the so-called Midlands, the coast is less than a two-hour drive away.

The United Kingdom is comprised of four distinct regions, the ancestral homelands of the country's four major ethnic groups: England in the south,

Scotland in the north, Wales in the west, and Northern Ireland, a few miles west of Scotland across the North Channel of the Irish Sea. The island on which England, Scotland, and Wales are located is known as Great Britain. By far the majority of the population lives in England (about 47 million, or 84%). The U.K. is one of the most densely populated countries in the world; its population density is greater than India's and ten times that of the United States. In England, there are more than nine hundred people per square mile, more than in Japan. Overcrowding is now a fact of life that has serious implications for politics and public policy.

The political, financial, and cultural center of the nation is London: in this respect, few nations are more highly centralized. With a population in excess of 7 million, London is one of the largest cities in the world. Not only is London the capital, but most of the major banks, corporations, newspapers, and television networks are located there. So, too, are the British equivalents of Wall Street, Broadway, and Hollywood. Finally, many of Britain's most famous historical and cultural landmarks and tourist attractions—Buckingham Palace, the Tower of London, Westminster Abbey, Big Ben, the British Parliament, St. Paul's Cathedral—are in London.

England First   The historical domination of Great Britain by England and England by London would presumably have created strong pressures toward homogenization and can easily give rise to the impression that the British people are, in fact, all alike; that there is an extremely high degree of social harmony; and that whatever political problems the nation might have, disunity is not one of them. All of these are false. As noted earlier, the U.K. has four distinct nationality groups: the English, the Scots, the Welsh, and the Irish. Although English is spoken throughout the country and the political system is a unitary one, each region has its own separate identity, including language, history, customs, and folkways. There is no large nonwhite minority in Great Britain, but the influx of immigrants from former British colonies has led to racial tensions and tighter restrictions on immigration in recent times.

Island of Stability   Of great importance, historically, is that England became a unified kingdom under a strong centralized government much earlier than most of the continental states. England was already a single kingdom before the Norman Conquest in 1066; William the Conqueror then consolidated the monarchy in such a way that feudalism could not interfere with royal policies. One effect of this early unification has been to give the English a more secure sense of nationality (expressed in a less militant form of nationalism) than either the French or the Germans. Another effect is that British statesmen in modern times have been able to concentrate on taming the power of the central government rather than trying to build a state. By contrast, France was not consolidated as a firm kingdom until the fifteenth century, and then only after great and prolonged struggles. Until recently, the French had to work on creating a state that could overcome the great nobles, assimilate the various subcultures in the provinces, and eventually impose republicanism on conservative sections of the country that preferred the church and the king to bourgeois politicians. Germany was unified for the first time only in 1870, and then, of course, reunified only in 1991. The Russian Empire, as we can now see clearly, was never truly unified. Countries that have to concentrate on unification almost inevitably have to stress power at the center, regardless of its potential for repression.

Great Britain's political stability derives in part from its geography. Separated from the Continent by the English Channel, its internal boundaries have changed very little over the centuries. Wales has belonged to England since the thirteenth century and was formally united with England in 1535, but has its own capital, Cardiff, and its own distinct national language, Welsh, still spoken by perhaps one-fourth of the population. Scotland was joined to England in 1707 but has its own legal, educational, and local government systems. Ireland accepted union with England in 1800, but religious differences (Ireland is Roman Catholic; England, Anglican) and economic disparities made the marriage unworkable. In 1922, following years of bloody civil war, Ireland became independent, but the six northeastern counties of Ulster (Northern Ireland) remained in the United Kingdom and were granted home rule.

Historically speaking, the lack of boundary disputes and incursions by external enemies has meant that Britain has avoided the destabilizing effects of having to digest new chunks of territory, assimilate new populations, or adjust to foreign rule. Problems arising from the presence of disaffected or displaced minorities have likewise been relatively few. These circumstances created an environment conducive to the comparatively peaceful evolution of the British political system from a monarchy to a parliamentary democracy.

England's Channel   Externally, the English Channel, a mere twenty miles wide at its narrowest point, has played a major role in shaping British political history. For centuries it was a geographic barrier to invasion (the last successful invasion was the Norman Conquest). It also enabled England to remain aloof from many of the conflicts on the Continent. England's advantageous geopolitical position meant that the British crown could act as the keeper of the balance, choosing when and when not to get involved in the game of power politics on the Continent.

Because the threat of invasion was minimal, the British never had to maintain a large standing army, and the military was never a serious threat to civilian rule. Instead, the nation concentrated on building a powerful naval force that enabled it to dominate the seaways in the eighteenth and nineteenth centuries. One consequence of the small-army, large-navy system was that the absolute power of the monarchy was never so absolute in England as on the Continent. Unlike armies, navies are useful only against *external* challenges; at home, the British monarch had to negotiate power.

A Maritime Tradition   Great Britain's geography goes far toward explaining its historic rise to economic prowess. A strong maritime tradition and an auspicious location at Europe's gateway to the North Atlantic placed the British in an ideal position to establish a foothold in the New World. The opening of new Atlantic trade routes made Britain a major international financial and commercial center. The need to protect these routes in both war and peace in turn provided the incentive to build a strong navy. Sea power made possible the growth of a colonial empire, which counteracted any temptation to lapse into the isolationism of an island fortress.

Even so, the United Kingdom did not seek to become an integral part of Europe until recently. Instead, the British have traditionally been self-reliant and independent in both domestic and foreign affairs, setting their own agenda and viewing entanglements on the Continent with a mixture of disinterest and disdain. This tradition of aloofness helps explain why the U.K. did not join the Common Market until 1973, fifteen years after it was formed.[17] It also explains why many British subjects continue to be wary of the European Community and question whether the benefits of membership outweigh the burdens. Although Prime Minister John Major is more pro-EC than his predecessor, Margaret Thatcher, it seems likely that this issue will stir controversy in British politics for years to come.

Another legacy of Britain's strong maritime tradition is an attachment to the doctrine of free trade. Tariffs were steadily reduced, and by the middle of the nineteenth century, British agriculture was largely unprotected. The existence of overseas colonies, British naval supremacy, and the cost-effectiveness of oceanic transport encouraged the importation of food, and this in turn freed up domestic resources for industrialization. Today the United Kingdom is highly dependent on agricultural imports.

Not surprisingly, the British have long paid close attention to their **balance of payments**. Food imports must be balanced by the export of manufactured goods; fluctuations in exchange rates, domestic inflation, foreign competition, and changes in consumer habits at home and abroad can all have serious political and economic ramifications in a country so deeply enmeshed in the international economy. If British industrial goods lose their competitive edge, the impact on the economy (and on the consumer) would be profound. Similarly, if the price of food imports increases, the impact would be direct and immediate. Thus, regardless of the party in power, governmental intervention in the economy—through price and wage regulation, budget measures, taxation, currency controls—is likely to be needed, if for no other reason than to manage external trade and maintain adequate foreign reserves.

The Origins of Parliament   British history has clearly been influenced by geography, but geography also exerts a force of its own on contemporary British politics and government. The British are not descendents of the island's original inhabitants. Their ancestors were Angles, Saxons, and Jutes from Germany who invaded the island after the Romans withdrew and seized it from the Celtic Britons (ancestors of the Welsh, Scots, and Irish).

Until the eleventh century, Britain was invaded repeatedly. The Danes ruled the country from 1016 to 1042. In 1066, William the Conqueror invaded from Normandy (in what is known as the Norman Conquest), established a monarchy, and introduced the **feudal system**. Under this system, a hereditary nobility was granted certain rights and privileges (land entitlements, access to the royal court, and others) in exchange for loyalty to the king and the acceptance of various duties and obligations (paying taxes, defending the realm, keeping the peace). Disputes over these rights and duties were settled in a council of lords convened by the king. From these humble origins evolved the concepts of constitutionalism and parliamentary government.

The years 1100 to 1135 saw a great expansion of royal administrative power during the reign of Henry I. In 1215 the Magna Carta was signed at Runnymede. Contrary to a popular notion, this document had nothing to do with government by the people. Rather, it was the instrument by which the barons enforced their rights under feudal contract (*magna carta*) with King John. From this point forward, the lower nobility had the right to be represented in decisions (especially tax levies) directly affecting them. As early as 1265 (in "De Montfort's Parliament"), townspeople were also given the right to representation in the great council (which was known as **Parliament** by this time).

But the right to be represented is not the same as the right of consent. The king was not obligated to heed the wishes of any of his subjects, including the nobility, and he did not even have to convene the Parliament at regular intervals. Nor were the representative bodies truly representative—the idea of popular elections was still centuries away. Representatives of commoners were not allowed to meet with the king or nobles or to take any direct part in decision making. By the fifteenth century (the reign of Henry V), commoners were able to elect a "speaker" and to put their views in the form of a petition to the monarch (an early version of a legislative bill).

Hence in the beginning Parliament was a kind of royal sounding board and advisory council. It was never intended to be a check on the monarch's power and authority. In time the right of barons to approve taxes became the right of the Parliament to originate all revenue and spending bills. Along the way there were occasional battles between the Parliament and the king—none more fateful than the one begun in 1629 when Charles I dissolved the Parliament and proceeded to rule as a tyrant. In 1650, Oliver Cromwell led a revolution that overthrew the monarchy (Charles I was beheaded) and established a short-lived republic.

The Puritan Revolution   The issue of religion was also a factor in the revolution. As a result of a doctrinal dispute with the pope, the Anglican church had replaced the Roman Catholic Church as the established religion in England more than a century earlier, but controversy over the break with Rome still raged. When James II, a Roman Catholic, tried to reopen the religious question, forcing a showdown between the Parliament and the monarchy, he was deposed in a bloodless coup. Rather than abolish the monarchy, Parliament invited the king's Protestant daughter, Mary, and her husband, William, to share the crown. By accepting, they implicitly recognized the supremacy of Parliament. Since 1689, no British monarch has challenged this constitutional principle.

In the nineteenth century, the franchise was gradually extended. Whigs (liberals) and Tories (conservatives) evolved from factions in the seventeenth century into full-fledged political parties. Finally, the idea of **cabinet** rule, in which the leaders of the majority party in Parliament form a kind of board of directors (called the "government") to set policy and manage the bureaucracy, emerged as an integral part of the British constitutional system.

France

About the size of Texas, France is located in a pivotal position on the Continent. Although it shares a border with six other countries (Spain, Italy, Switzerland, Germany, Luxembourg, and Belgium), France is demarcated by natural boundaries (except, as we shall see, in one border zone). To the north is the English Channel; to the west, the Bay of Biscay; to the southwest, the Pyrenees Mountains; to the south, the Mediterranean Sea; and to the southeast, the Alps.

In the northeast, however, France and Germany have historically engaged in confrontation and conflict over disputed territories along the southern Rhine River (particularly in a resource-rich region known as the Saar) and in Alsace-Lorraine. There are no insurmountable barriers to invasion in this region: even Belgium, which poses no direct military threat, was a geostrategic liability for France prior to World War II because it could (and did) serve as a springboard for German armed aggression.

Internally, France has no formidable geographic barriers to communication or transportation. A well-developed network of navigable rivers, canals, and railways, combined with a compact geography and natural land and sea boundaries, has contributed to a strong sense of national identity and a high degree of political and economic integration. French is the native language and Roman Catholicism the religion of the overwhelming majority of the population.

Even so, the French people are far from homogenous; indeed, customs, attitudes, and opinions vary significantly from region to region. Historically, the south of France was heavily influenced by Roman civilization; the north, by Germanic culture. Economically, too, there is an important division: the south and west are rural, conservative, and relatively poor, whereas the north and east are industrially developed, growth-oriented, and relatively prosperous.

France has remained a nation of shopkeepers, artisans, and small farmers longer than most other Western industrial democracies. Although the actual numbers of self-employed producers and proprietors in traditional sectors of the economy have declined sharply since the 1950s, the vaunted individualism of the French citizenry lingers on.

Paris versus the Provinces   Paris is to France as London is to Great Britain. Nearly one-fifth of France's total population, some ten million people, live in Paris or its suburbs, and the city dominates the political, economic, cultural, and intellectual life of the country. It is the banking center and industrial hub. More than one-third of all commercial and financial profits are earned in Paris, which also accounts for over half of France's domestic wholesale and retail trade. Paris is also one of Europe's most popular tourist attractions, with its rich historical heritage, magnificent architecture, world-famous art museums, beautiful parks, and fine restaurants. The Louvre, the Cathedral of Nôtre-Dame, the Eiffel Tower, Montmartre, and the Champs-Élysées are only a few of the landmarks that give Paris its distinctive character.

The division between Paris and the provinces is etched deeply into French culture, society, and politics. The contrast between the high culture and hustle-bustle of Paris and the rustic and relatively relaxed pace of life in the provinces is made all the more significant because France remains less urban than other industrialized countries. France has only six cities with populations over 500,000, in which only about one-third of the French people live (by comparison, fully one-half of the British population lives in big cities).

Economic Development   Despite a diversified manufacturing industry and state-initiated efforts at technological modernization, French farmers—numbering 2.5 million, or about 8 percent of the labor force—remain a powerful force in domestic politics. France has an abundance of arable land and a variety of climates conducive to farming. As a consequence, France is not only agriculturally self-sufficient but also a major food exporter, accounting for a quarter of the European Community's total agricultural output. As we shall see, France's desire to protect its farm producers and buttress its position as the Continent's paramount food exporter has long been a source of tension within the Common Market.

Although France kept pace with industrialization elsewhere on the Continent during the nineteenth century, the French economy (and society) stagnated in the first half of the twentieth century. One reason is that, unlike Great Britain, which stressed free trade and welcomed competition, France instituted protectionist policies to *prevent* competition, both foreign and domestic. Tariffs, quotas, cartels, and subsidies were the chosen instruments of France's autarkic development strategy. Prior to the Fifth Republic in 1958, roughly one-third of the French national budget was allocated to direct or indirect subsidies.

French business practices also impeded growth and change. The family firm (along with the family farm) was the foundation of the French economy. Turning a bigger profit, capturing a larger market share, opening up new product lines, modifying consumer habits, expanding, diversifying, modernizing—these were not primary considerations. In fact, competition was regarded as unethical. A business was viewed as a family tradition, a way of life. Many businesses were owned and operated by the same family for generations, even centuries.

Unfortunately, respect for tradition is often accompanied by resistance to change; until the 1960s, French business practices reflected this truth. Profits were seldom reinvested; quality was stressed over quantity, which meant limited production and high unit costs; and the concentrations of capital necessary for research and development, aggressive marketing, and technological retooling were hard to come by. The resulting stagnation was not easily overcome.

Indicative Planning after World War II   After World War II, the French government took the lead in directing the reconstruction effort and revitalizing the economy. Through so-called indicative planning and modernization commissions, the state set targets for growth in specific industries. Both consultation and incentive methods were used to persuade the private sector to comply.

The results were spectacular! A French economic miracle occurred. Industrial production doubled between 1952 and 1963, then grew by another 70 percent in the next decade. By the early 1980s, the French economy had surpassed Great Britain's and was gaining on that of West Germany. France's GNP per capita was higher than Japan's, and it was increasing faster than that of any other major Western democracy. A relatively high rate of inflation was a chronic problem (running at 8.4 to 13.4 percent per year between 1975 and 1984), but that has since been brought under control (averaging 3.1 percent per year between 1985 and 1990).

Population Blues   France experienced zero population growth long before it was fashionable. Between 1860 and 1940, France's population held steady while that of surrounding countries, especially Germany, was taking off. For France this situation was particularly alarming because both its population and its per capita income had fallen far below that of Great Britain and France on the eve of World War I (see Table 4.3). France was the only Roman Catholic nation in the world in which population was not increasing. Between the wars, it actually started shrinking (in part reflecting the loss of 1.5 million Frenchmen in World War I).

After 1945 the population began to rebound; nevertheless, the fertility rate in France remains low, possibly below replacement level. Paradoxically, nearly one-third of France's population is under 20, which means considerable pressure on educational facilities and the prospect of serious problems of unemployment or underemployment in the future. Women make up about 40 percent of the

Table 4.3 France and the Other Great Powers in 1914: A Three-dimensional Comparison

	National Income (billions of U.S. dollars)	Population (millions)	Per Capita Income (U.S. dollars)
United States	37	90	377
Britain	11	45	244
Germany	12	65	184
France	6	39	153
Italy	4	37	108
Japan	2	55	36

Source: Paul Kennedy, *The Rise and Fall of the Great Powers* (New York: Random House, 1987), p. 243.

labor force, largely in low-prestige (and low-paying) occupations in the clerical, sales, and service sectors.

To the extent that France's population has grown in the past decade, it is largely the result of immigration from former French colonies in North Africa. Some 5 million immigrants had sought refuge in France by 1990, at a time when unemployment in the nation was nearing 10 percent. The destabilizing effects of this influx of foreigners into a previously homogeneous society will be discussed in subsequent chapters.

Religion and Society   That France is today a predominantly Roman Catholic society speaks volumes about French history but says little about the role of religion in France. Religion has long been at or near the center of civil strife. In the sixteenth century, French Protestants (called Huguenots), who wanted to bring the Reformation to France, fought church loyalists, who wanted to preserve Catholicism as the one true faith. The Edict of Nantes (1598) brought religious toleration and peace, but the struggle resumed in the next century, culminating in the decree of King Louis XIV that all of France would be Roman Catholic. Religion was a factor in the French Revolution (1789), but this time it was Catholics against anticlericals (denouncers of the church) rather than Catholics against Protestants. Historically, the church has been a conservative force in French society, opposed to republicanism and allied with the monarch, its protector. Religious controversy in general and anticlericalism in particular thus have deep roots in French political history. This fact helps explain why both Communist and Socialist parties have, at different times, enjoyed a large popular following in postwar France, despite the incompatibility of Marxist and Christian doctrines.

Hence the appearance of religious unity in present-day France is deceptive. The great majority of the French people are Roman Catholic (over 70 percent are baptized in the church), but most are nonpracticing.

Even so, the church plays a significant role in French society through its extensive primary and secondary private school system. Since the early 1950s, church and state have cooperated closely in the area of education, with the state providing considerable financial support for parochial schools and the church accepting state-defined regulations and curricular standards. But in the 1980s, when the ruling Socialist party proposed further steps to integrate (and possibly absorb) the Catholic schools into the public school system, a mass protest in Paris persuaded the government to drop the idea.

France's Turbulent History   As the discussion so far suggests, to understand French politics, it is necessary to know a little about French history. France was ruled by a monarch for some eight hundred years, until the French Revolution. This long stretch of royal absolutism, which reached its zenith during the reign of Louis XIV (1643–1715), is one reason why France, early on, developed a strong sense of national identity.

But the political system degenerated under the despotic Louis XVI, and French society became increasingly polarized. A kind of representative assembly, the Estates General, had been in existence since the fourteenth century, and judicial bodies called *parlements* occasionally served—at the pleasure of the monarch, of course—as sounding boards or advisory councils. Thus the mechanisms for political accommodation were available but were little used; unlike their British counterparts, French monarchs were loath to compromise with the aristocracy or the rising middle class.

One event that precipitated the French Revolution was Louis XVI's decision to suspend the *parlements*. The privileged classes sided with the *parlements*, never dreaming that the so-called Third Estate, which represented middle-class commoners and peasants, would eventually seize the initiative. This is not the place to recount the story of the French Revolution. We will simply note that it was a watershed in European history; its impact went far beyond France and outlasted the tyranny of Robespierre and the Jacobins. The revolution was the prelude to a century of turmoil and started a tradition of division and disunity.

The First Republic gave way to the First Empire under Napoleon Bonaparte. Napoleon continued to pay lip service to the republican ideal and held occasional plebiscites to underscore his popular mandate, but in reality he established a personal dictatorship not much different from an absolute monarchy.

After Napoleon's defeat in 1815, the House of Bourbon was restored to the throne. The Bourbons were said to have learned nothing and forgotten nothing. In 1848 a revolt again toppled the monarchy and led to the short-lived Second Republic. Louis Napoleon, the nephew of Napoleon Bonaparte, emerged as the new popular leader; following in his uncle's footsteps, he crowned himself emperor in 1852.

The Second Empire lasted until 1870, when France was defeated by Germany in the Franco-Prussian War. This defeat and the election of a large number of reactionary monarchists to the National Assembly alarmed progressive elements of all persuasions. Radicals violently opposed to the monarchy and the church, perhaps influenced by Marxism, set up a rival government in the capital, the so-called Paris Commune. A bloody civil war ensued in which 20,000 people died during the last week of fighting alone.

The Third Republic came into being in 1876 and lasted until World War II—the longest-surviving political structure in France since the French Revolution. But the Third Republic was always troubled, plagued by divisive party politics and a weak executive. In the early years it survived a major challenge in the form of General Georges Boulanger, a dashing figure who preached revenge against Germany and railed about the need for political reform. Boulanger might have become France's third Bonapartist dictator in a century; facing charges of treason, however, he was forced to flee the country in 1889 and subsequently committed suicide.

A Contradictory Legacy   World War I caused great damage in France, but the Third Republic somehow survived. World War II, however, sounded its death knell. We will look at France's two post–World War II republics in Chapter 5. Here we simply note that France has tried a dozen different political systems since 1789, including five republics. The contradictory politics of modern French history can be said to have had the following characteristics:

1. A belief in republicanism combined with a mistrust of government expressed in the insistence on a weak executive under the Third and Fourth republics
2. A susceptibility to Bonapartism expressed in the occasional emergence of a "white knight on horseback" (Napoleon Bonaparte, Louis Napoleon, Georges Boulanger) and the use of periodic plebiscites to renew the leader's popular mandate
3. A tendency toward polarization expressed in the historic dichotomies of reactionary versus revolutionary, royalist versus socialist versus communist, the church versus the anticlericalists, and republican versus *dirigiste* (an advocate of strong central government and broad executive powers)
4. A durable, efficient, and centrally run system of law courts and public administration combined with a tendency toward governmental paralysis and drift
5. A high level of patriotism and national pride combined with a marked tendency toward popular revolt against the symbols and substance of national authority

Compared with Great Britain, France has been less stable or socially cohesive and has lacked the continuity that is the hallmark of British parliamentary rule. France's economic policies have until recently been autarkic and protectionist, in contrast to the British stress on free trade and competition.

Germany

A century ago, Germany was the preeminent military power on the Continent. For forty-five years following World War II, it was divided into two distinct parts—the Federal Republic of Germany (West Germany) and the German Democratic Republic (East Germany). After a popular uprising against Communist rule in East Germany and the subsequent opening of the intra-German border in 1989, the movement toward German unification proceeded rapidly and was completed in October 1990.

Germany's Precarious Geography   Germany's geographic position on the Continent places it at the crossroads of Europe. Unlike Great Britain or France, Germany does not have natural boundaries, and this fact shaped the nation's fate in several ways. For centuries, whenever wars were fought in Europe, German territory was apt to be a battleground. There are at least three reasons for this: Germany is centrally located; until late in the nineteenth century it was divided into many principalities, most of them small; and the absence of geographic barriers made German lands accessible to the armies of neighboring states.

Having no natural boundaries, however, also meant that industrious Germans (many of whom were successful entrepreneurs) could spread out and settle in adjacent territories without being cut off from their homeland. As a result, German culture became disseminated well beyond Germany proper. When Hitler seized the Sudetenland from Czechoslovakia, he did so on the grounds that most of the people there were Germans. He justified Nazi aggression in general on Germany's ostensible need for *Lebensraum* (living space). This argument was specious, but it made sense to a nation long accustomed to migrating into neighboring areas.

Germany's geographic vulnerability influenced its history in other ways as well. If, as is often said, the best defense is a good offense, then one logical response to the danger of invasion is to go on the offensive. For hundreds of years, the fragmented Germany was unable to follow such a strategy. In the eighteenth century, however, the German state of Prussia emerged as a major power under Frederick the Great, who ruled from 1740 to 1786. Frederick enlarged Prussia considerably (he took Silesia from Austria and acquired another large chunk of territory from Poland). From this time forward, the ideal of the military state was a prominent part of the German *Weltanschauung* (world view).

The Concept of Germany   Due largely to the struggle against the empire-hungry Napoleon, the concept of a German nation began to emerge. The German Confederation created at the Congress of Vienna in 1815 was a modest precursor of the modern German state, but rivalry between Austria and Prussia, distaste for reform, and the claims of German princes combined to block an early move toward German unification. The loose confederation, which awarded Vienna the permanent presidency, encompassed 39 sovereign entities running the gamut from the formidable Austrian Empire and Prussia to four free cities. For example, the diet that was supposed to meet at Frankfurt was more a council of ambassadors than an elective assembly, and a unanimous vote was required on important matters. Also, the confederation's legislative powers were severely restricted. In practice the league was important in German politics only on the rare occasions when Prince Metternich, the great Austrian statesman, found it convenient.

Metternich used the confederation, for example, to suppress student protests inspired by pan-German nationalism and liberalism, both anathema to the ruling elites. After the assassination of a reactionary writer, the confederation was used as the vehicle to launch the Carlsbad Decrees of 1819; these measures intensified censorship, banned radical professors and students (including Karl Marx), and outlawed political clubs. They also required each member state to appoint commissioners to monitor and certify the universities for ideological reliability. Although there was considerable ferment in intellectual circles, German society as a whole—still largely rural but with a growing urban-industrial labor force—remained rather more tranquil than elsewhere in Europe.

Prussia and German Economic Development   In Prussia, the landowning Junkers were allied with the crown. The noble Junker class supplied most of the officers for the royal army and for the top posts in the state administration:

> Sons of burghers filled state posts in the lower echelons and shared in decision making on municipal affairs. The skillful and efficient bureaucracy of Prussia set standards that other German states sought to imitate. The peasant masses in overwhelmingly rural "Germany" seemed content to allow public business to be conducted by their social betters.[18]

Prussia was an efficient monarchy. Under the enlightened rule of Frederick William III, the state continued to support education and promote economic growth. A common tariff, established in 1818 in all its territories, lowered duties (discouraging smugglers as well as opening up the economy to competition) and allowed free entry of raw materials (a spur to industrial development). These progressive measures worked remarkably well—so well that nearly all the German states except Austria soon joined Prussia's customs union, the *Zollverein.* "By 1834 over twenty-three million Germans, living in an area larger than New York, Pennsylvania, and New England combined, were exchanging goods freely."[19] Revenues were collected by Prussian inspectors, shared by all *Zollverein* members, and used primarily to build roads (creating essential infrastructure for a future German state). In retrospect, the Prussian experiment in economic integration can be seen as an early forerunner of the European Community.

The *Zollverein* was a tonic to commerce, and by midcentury, manufacturing and trade were also stimulated by an intricate railroad network built and subsidized mainly by Prussia. Economic integration facilitated political unification; that is, new economic relationships preceded political change. (Is it not possible that the new Europe of the 1990s, under the impetus of the European Community, which began as a customs union too, will repeat that same pattern? At the very least, there may be a parallel between the role Prussia played in the formation of the modern German state and the key role Germany is now playing in Europe.)

Economic development brought social dislocations as modern factories, both foreign and domestic, displaced the old trades. Signs of popular discontent and political disturbances began to appear, rooted in a newly emerging commercial-industrial class structure as dissidents and agitators demanded what were then radical reforms, including a graduated income tax and guarantees of the right to work.

Limited concessions to liberalism, mainly in the guise of constitutional reform, were made in some parts of the confederation. In Prussia, Frederick William IV, the most liberal of the Prussian monarchs, convened a united *Landtag* (a representative assembly) in 1847 but soon had second thoughts. The revolutionary turmoil that erupted throughout Europe in 1848 brought class conflict to the surface in German society. Landed gentry were pitted against the middle class (factory owners, bankers, lawyers, professors), the middle class against the workers, and peasants against liberals of all stripes. The revolts in the German states (and Austria) failed to depose the rulers, who were supported by loyal armies.

The clamor for constitutional change in Prussia and elsewhere mingled with nationalistic fervor. Talk of German unification in time became commonplace to the point where even the Prussian Hohenzollern and Austrian Hapsburg rulers paid it lip service. Ironically, dreams of a united German state—a "superpower"—continued to be associated with a desire for liberal democratic government.

From Bismarck to Hitler   Otto von Bismarck unified Germany in 1871, having gained wide popular support at home following impressive military victories over Austria (in 1866) and France (in 1870). The German Empire (called the Second Reich, the Holy Roman Empire having been the First) was the product of triumph and the prelude to tragedy for the German people. Germany under Bismarck became the most powerful state in Europe. In 1878, Bismarck masterminded the Three Emperors' Alliance (Germany, Austria-Hungary, and Russia) at the Congress of Berlin as a bulwark against liberal reform. Over the next seventy-five years, Germany would fight and lose two world wars, undergo a tumultuous revolution, and embrace the totalitarian designs of a raving tyrant, Adolph Hitler.

Whether or not German aggression was the real cause of World War I, the allied powers placed this stigma on Germany when they insisted on a "war guilt" clause as a pivotal feature of the Versailles Treaty ending that war. U.S. President Woodrow Wilson spoke for many of his contemporaries when he blamed the war on two prominent features of prewar German politics: nationalism and autocracy. He believed that one way to prevent future wars in Europe was to remake Germany (and other autocratic regimes) in the image of a parliamentary democracy. Where there are popular controls on government, Wilson theorized, war is likely to be a last resort because if people are given a choice, they will choose not to fight and die except in self-defense.

The Weimar Republic, Germany's first constitutional system, was born in these inauspicious circumstances. The new German government had several marks against it from the start. First, it was a symbol of Germany's humiliating defeat in World War I. Second, it was imposed by the victorious powers—the German people were never consulted. Third, it was un-German: Germany had no prior experience with republican government, and there was little in German history or culture to underpin any kind of democracy. Fourth, it was associated with a draconian peace that extracted onerous and punitive war reparations and indemnities from Germany. Fifth, it was powerless to protect legitimate German interests against continuing foreign encroachments (for example, Germany was required to finance an allied army of occupation in the Rhineland for fifteen years). Not surprisingly, when the economy went into a tailspin (as it did at least twice in the 1920s), popular disenchantment with the form of government opened the door to demagoguery and dictatorship.

Hitler's Third Reich was an aberration made possible by the impact of a worldwide depression on an already beleaguered German economy and society. Although Hitler came to power legally, he had no respect for laws and constitutions. As chancellor, he quickly obtained an enabling act from the German *Reichstag* (parliament). Thus armed with the power to rule by decree, Hitler instituted one of the most repressive and brutal tyrannies in history.

At a conference in Munich in September 1938, Hitler demanded that the Sudetenland be ceded to Germany. The following year Hitler and Stalin made an infamous deal, known as the Molotov-Ribbentrop Pact. Ostensibly a nonaggression pact, it was the device by which the two dictators divided up Poland and Hitler "conceded" the Baltic states and Bessarabia (now called Moldavia, at the time part of Romania) to the Soviet Union. The Holocaust—the genocidal murder of nearly six million Jews and a like number of others (including Poles, Gypsies, and Magyars—stands as the most heinous symbol of Nazi totalitarian rule.

A lively academic debate about Germany's role in the outbreak of World War I continues, but there is little question that Germany was the aggressor in World War II. Nonetheless, the Allies (except for the Soviet Union) did not seek a punitive peace after Germany's defeat in 1945; in fact, the United States and Great Britain, viewing a viable Germany as a valuable future ally against Soviet military expansion, actually shielded West Germany from Soviet and French demands for huge reparations payments.

CONCLUSION

Europe is a mix of many cultures and nations with distinct languages, cultures, histories, and political traditions. Nonetheless, Western Europe has a common core of values and beliefs due to the pervasive and enduring influence of Christianity, the Renaissance and Reformation, the Scientific Revolution, the Enlightenment, the Industrial Revolution, and the Age of Imperialism. The salubrious climate and compact geography of the Continent and the accessibility of maritime highways to the world outside have also contributed to the development of a distinctly Western outlook among the peoples of this region. In Chapter 5 we explore contemporary patterns of politics and government, which are the fruits of this heritage.

KEY TERMS

feudalism
Reformation
Renaissance
mercantilism
Scientific Revolution
secular humanism
Enlightenment

philosophes
ethical hedonism
French Revolution
Jacobins
Industrial Revolution
liberalism
socialism

conservatism
Eurocommunism
Age of Imperialism
balance of power
communism
Fascism
National Socialism (Nazism)

European Community (Common Market)
balance of payments
feudal system
Parliament
cabinet

STUDY QUESTIONS

1. What are the seminal features of European civilization relative to the shaping of the political cultures of the Continent?
2. In what sense has totalitarianism shaped both the history and the political landscape of Europe in the twentieth century?
3. Why was Europe so prone to war in the first half of the twentieth century? Why has it been immune from war during most of the second half?

SUGGESTED READING

Carr, Edward Hallett. *The Twenty Years' Crisis, 1919–1939: An Introduction to the Study of International Relations.* New York: Harper, 1964. (Originally published in 1939.)
Cipolla, Carlo M. *Before the Industrial Revolution: European Economy and Society, 1000–1700.* New York: Norton, 1980.
Dehio, Ludwig. *Germany and World Politics in the Twentieth Century.* New York: Norton, 1959.
Dehio, Ludwig. *The Precarious Balance: Four Centuries of the European Power Struggle.* New York: Vintage Books, 1962.
Kenndey, Paul. *The Rise and Fall of the Great Powers: Economic Change and Military Conflict from 1500 to 2000.* New York: Random House, 1987.
Kissinger, Henry. *A World Restored: The Politics of Conservatism in a Revolutionary Age.* New York: Grosset & Dunlap, 1964.
Plumb, J. H. *The Italian Renaissance.* New York: Harper, 1961.
Slavin, Arthur J. *The Way of the West: The Era of World Dominion, 1760–Present.* Lexington, Mass.: Xerox Corp., 1974.

NOTES

1. Derwent Whittlesey, *Environmental Foundations of European History* (Norwalk, Conn.: Appleton & Lang, 1949), p. 140.
2. Ibid., p. 141.
3. Ibid., p. 132.
4. See Paul Kennedy, *The Rise and Fall of the Great Powers: Economic Change and Military Conflict from 1500 to 2000* (New York: Random House, 1987), pp. 148–150.
5. Whittlesey, *Environmental Foundations*, p. 138.
6. Ibid.

7. John Kirtland Wright, *The Geographical Basis of European History* (New York: Holt, 1928), pp. 78–79.

8. Ibid.

9. Ibid.

10. Bryce Lyon, Herbert H. Rowen, and Theodore S. Hamerow, *A History of the Western World* (Skokie, Ill.: Rand McNally, 1969), p. 443.

11. Ibid., p. 444.

12. See Kennedy, *Rise and Fall of the Great Powers*.

13. Lyon et al., *History of the Western World,* p. 509.

14. Hans Morganthau and Kenneth Thompson, *Politics among Nations: The Struggle for Power and Peace,* 6th ed. (New York: Knopf, 1985), p. 235.

15. Ibid., p. 238.

16. See Ludwig Dehio, *The Precarious Balance: Four Centuries of the European Power Struggle* (New York: Vintage Books, 1962).

17. The British rejected membership in the Common Market in 1958; several years later they tried to join but were thwarted by President de Gaulle of France. Only after de Gaulle's departure from government (and subsequent death) was the United Kingdom admitted to the European Community.

18. Arthur J. May, *The Age of Metternich* (New York: Holt, 1963), p. 40.

19. Ibid., p. 44.

5

The Triumph of
Parliaments and Pluralism

The political systems of Western Europe are not identical, but the similarities far outweigh the differences. Since the mid-1970s, when dictatorships in Spain and Portugal and military rule in Greece ended, every country in Western Europe has been governed by civilian rulers who came to power through free elections. Hence the governments of the region display a remarkably consistent pattern too uniform to be mere coincidence.

Prior to the 1980s, when many Latin American nations converted from military to civilian rule, fully half of the world's constitutional democracies could be found in Western Europe: Great Britain, France, Germany, Italy, Belgium, the Netherlands, Luxembourg, Denmark, Norway, Sweden, Finland, Austria, Switzerland, Spain, Portugal, and Greece. As noted, the governments of these countries are not identical, but they have several salient features in common. They are based on clearly defined principles and ruled by representatives elected by universal suffrage; in other words, they are all democratic republics grounded in constitutional law. With the exception of Great Britain, all the states of Western Europe have written constitutions. Many also continue to have monarchs who now serve as figureheads, having long ago lost political power. For this reason, some of these governments are described as **constitutional monarchies**. Spain, Belgium, Luxembourg, the Netherlands, Denmark, Norway, Sweden, and Great Britain are in this category. In these countries, the monarch *reigns* but does not *rule*—the king or queen is the ceremonial head of state, but an elected parliament makes the laws and chooses the government, consisting of the prime minister and the cabinet, who make policy and oversee the day-to-day operations of

99

the bureaucracy. A constitutional monarch could theoretically intercede in the political process, but to do so might place the institution of the monarchy at risk.

Great Britain, a **parliamentary democracy** that is also a constitutional monarchy, has never bothered to adopt a written constitution. Yet it has a "constitution" that is more deeply entrenched than most written ones.

Great Britain: Mother of Parliaments

In contrast to the United States, whose founders developed elaborate theoretical underpinnings for the political system, in Great Britain the political tradition is an outgrowth of centuries of history, experiment, and legal precedent. A theory of British constitutionalism can be found in the writings and speeches of Edmund Burke, who in the late eighteenth century celebrated the role of continuity and stability in the development of Britain's evolving political system. Burke stressed the importance of Great Britain's long, unbroken chain of political development, during which economic equality and political liberty evolved side by side.

The Unwritten Constitution

Great Britain's constitution is not recorded as a single document. Rather it is the product of four elements: statutory law, common law, custom and convention, and works of authority. Today the normal method of amending and augmenting the British constitution is **statutory law**, which originates from acts of Parliament. The Parliament Act of 1911, which reduced the legislative role of the House of Lords, is an example of a statutory law that amended the constitution. Other examples include the Bill of Rights of 1689 and the European Communities Act of 1972. Statutory law is made by elected **members of Parliament (MPs)** in the **House of Commons** (lower house). The role of the House of Lords (upper house) in the legislative process will be discussed shortly.

Common law is judge-made law. It is based on legal rulings and decisions passed down through generations that are generally upheld in the courts. At one time common law played a crucial role in the evolution of the British system. For example, it is the basis of the principle of parliamentary sovereignty. A. V. Dicey, a great nineteenth-century British political thinker, considered this principle one of the two main pillars of the British constitution (the other being the rule of law). Common law now plays a secondary role.

Custom and **convention** are long-standing practices not based on statutory or common law. They are rooted in nothing but the perceived logic of the system itself: they must be observed in order for the government to run smoothly and efficiently, the British believe. For example, it is important for symbolic reasons that the British crown give its royal assent to acts of Parliament. A law that did not have the royal stamp of approval would seem somehow not legitimate. The last time a British monarch refused to give assent to an act of Parliament was in the 1700s. Another custom is the monarch's dissolving Parliament and calling for new elections, at the prime minister's request, if the government receives a vote of no confidence.

A final source of constitutional law is **works of authority**, tracts esteemed for the quality of reasoning they exhibit and the reputation of the scholars who produced them. In addition to Dicey, prominent British constitutional authorities include John Austin, Walter Bagehot, Sir Ivor Jennings, Sir Kenneth Wheare, O. Hood Phillips, and E. C. S. Wade.

There is no power of judicial review in Great Britain. Government ministers, judges, and administrative officials can interpret the constitution in specific instances, but in general, acts of Parliament are supreme. And there are no extraordinary procedures for amending the British constitution; statutes and common law are changed by ordinary legislation (that is, they require a simple majority in the House of Commons).

Two seminal ideas undergird British politics: parliamentary sovereignty and the rule of law. Dicey defined **parliamentary sovereignty** as "the right to make or unmake any law whatever; and, further, that no person or body is recognized by the law of England as having a right to override or set aside the legislation of Parliament." The **rule of law**, according to Dicey, means two things. First, "no man is punishable . . . except for a distinct breach of law established . . . before ordinary courts of the land." Second, "no man is above the law . . . whatever his rank." Dicey also observed that "the constitution is pervaded by the rule of law" in the sense that the general principles of the constitution are themselves "the result of judicial decision determining the rights of private persons in particular cases brought before the courts."[1]

The British parliamentary system has four salient characteristics. First, the British system is a centralized or **unitary system**, in contrast to the federal system found in the United States or Germany. The central government possesses all the powers of government and delegates to local governments only as much authority as it deems necessary and proper. Consequently, London has complete power over the local authorities; the concept of reserved powers has no relevance whatever in the British system.

Second, a **fusion of powers** obtains at the national level rather than the separation of powers found in the United States. The U.S. presidential system bars members of Congress from concurrently holding a cabinet office. In contrast, the British cabinet consists of the leaders of the majority party in the House of Commons. Thus under normal circumstances, election to Parliament is a prerequisite to becoming a cabinet member. After an election, the head of the victorious party in Parliament (the prime minister) names the other members (ministers) of the new cabinet; following a pro forma vote of approval by the party's majority in the House of Commons, a government is formed. (In a multiparty system, the government will often be formed by a coalition of two or more parties.) The cabinet, headed by the prime minister, is responsible for formulating and initiating legislation. Although all members of Parliament, including the opposition, are free to question and criticize the government, the majority party is virtually assured that its legislative proposals will pass.

A third key feature is **collective ministerial responsibility**. The prime minister and cabinet (the government) are members of Parliament and exercise executive power only so long as they are supported by a parliamentary majority. The government must be prepared to answer the questions about its policies before both houses of Parliament. The collective aspect of ministerial responsibility relates to the fact that cabinet members are expected to support all policies, actions, and decisions of the government in public; they may dissent only in private. You might say that governing is a team sport in Great Britain. The prime minister is the coach, team captain, and head of the cheering section. Grandstand plays by individual cabinet members are frowned on, and prime ministers do not like being circumvented or upstaged by their players. Prime ministers handpick their cabinets and can make cabinet changes whenever they wish.

Fourth, the system is a **two-party system**. This does not mean that there are only two political parties in existence but rather that two major parties tend to alternate in power. (In contrast to the situation elsewhere in Europe, the victorious party in British elections never finds it necessary to enter into coalitions with smaller parties.) Furthermore, British political parties present relatively clear policy alternatives to the electorate, to a far greater extent than the two major parties in the United States. British political parties also display considerably more party discipline in Parliament than their U.S. counterparts (the reasons for this are discussed later in this chapter). Consequently, when a party wins an election and forms a government, it can put its program into effect expeditiously.

Westminster: The British Parliament

In Parliament the British have fused the political symbols, ceremonies, and conventions of the past with the changing realities of the present. They have retained an element of aristocracy in the House of Lords but since 1911 have lodged primary legislative power in the House of Commons. Westminster, where Parliament sits, is virtually synonymous with the British government.

The **House of Lords** consists of approximately eleven hundred members, of whom about four-fifths are hereditary peers. The remaining members include the bishops of the Church of England, Lords of Appeal in Ordinary (equivalent to the Supreme Court in the United States), and other life peers (distinguished British subjects appointed by the monarch). Typically, only about two hundred to three hundred members of the Lords attend sessions regularly. The upper chamber has been precluded from vetoing money bills since 1911 and was restricted to a suspensive veto of one year on all other bills in 1949. (In other words, the Lords can delay bills for one year but cannot block legislation if the government is determined to have it passed.) Nonetheless, the precarious position of the Lords is suggested by the fact that it rarely tries to obstruct the House of Commons. As a result, it has been overruled only four times in more than eighty years, most recently in 1991 over a controversial measure (called the War Crimes Bill) that cleared the way for prosecution of several alleged Nazi mass murderers living in Great Britain. That was the first time the Parliament Act of 1911 had been invoked in four decades. The Lords fear that if they ever try to exert much influence by obstructing or delaying legislation, the upper house will be abolished.

In the early 1990s, the House of Commons consisted of 650 members elected by plurality vote in single-member districts for five-year terms, subject to dissolution of Parliament. The seats are apportioned according to population, so England's share is slightly more than 80 percent of the total. The House of Commons approves or rejects legislation and provides an "oratorical battle-ground" where the opposition can and often does go on the offensive, forcing the prime minister and cabinet to defend the government's actions and policies.

Parliament is the sole source of legislative power in the British system. It alone can make new laws and repeal or revise old ones. This power gives the majority party enormous leverage; theoretically, it could reshape the entire political system by one simple parliamentary act. But the political obstacles to drastic structural change are formidable. The existing system has broad national support. Any attempt to reorder the system would risk a tumultuous outpouring of public indignation. In Great Britain, when the government loses public support, it is expected to resign.

Moreover, the opposition party would join the public in protesting any fundamental change in the system. The role of the opposition is, quite simply, to oppose—if it does not do so, it is acting irresponsibly. Thus the majority party and the opposition both have a vital role to play. No major party is ever irrelevant, win or lose. This point is underscored by the traditional name given to the party out of power: Her Majesty's Loyal Opposition.

The government controls the legislative process. After a bill is formally introduced in the House of Commons, the government decides when it will be debated. Except for the nineteen "opposition days" during each session of Parliament, the government has control of the legislative agenda. Bills go through three readings—one when they are introduced, another when they are debated, and a third when they are voted on. Floor debate occurs after the second reading. This is a crucial point in the process: bills approved at this stage usually have clear sailing the rest of the way. Following debate, bills go into standing committees.

In contrast to the committee system in the U.S. Congress, British committees are often very large (up to fifty members) and are not specialized. (However, because the personnel of a committee changes with each bill and members can volunteer for each bill, members with expertise or special concerns do get to consider bills of particular interest to them. In this way the party leaders are able to satisfy membership demands for participation without actually conceding any power of great importance.) Committees' powers are narrowly circumscribed: they refine the language of legislation, but they may not redefine the legislation itself. They rarely pass amendments unless they are proposed by the minister of the department concerned. The majority party always controls the committees by the same margin that it enjoys in the full House of Commons.

Next comes the report stage, during which amendments can be approved or rejected. The government's amendments are almost always passed; any private member's amendment at this stage is generally rejected unless it has the blessing of the government. Bills dealing with constitutional issues are handled differently:

they go to a "committee of the whole"—the entire House of Commons is the committee. If a bill of this nature is passed without amendments, it does not have to go through the report stage.

The third reading in the House of Commons occurs when a bill is voted on in final form. If it passes, it goes to the House of Lords, which can amend it, but only if the House of Commons approves. The final step is the granting of royal assent by the crown—a mere formality but one that preserves the symbolism so important to the legitimization of government in Great Britain.

It may sound as though the legislative process is cut and dried, with the government holding all the trump cards. In point of fact, the opposition has ample opportunity to criticize, embarrass, and call the government to account. The most important opposition device is question time. Every day, Monday through Thursday, government ministers must answer questions on the floor of the House of Commons; twice a week, the prime minister must answer questions as well. Question time makes politics something of a spectacle in Great Britain. It puts a premium on debate skills and forces policymakers to justify their actions and decisions continually—not only to Parliament but to the British people as well.

If the government loses its popular support, it may either resign or risk a vote of no confidence in Parliament. If Parliament passes such a motion or defeats a government bill with a vote of confidence attached, the government must, by convention, resign and either permit another party leader to form a government or ask the monarch to dissolve Parliament and call new elections. This procedure was last invoked in 1979, when the Labour party lost on a vote of confidence, resigned, and opened the door to the Conservative party, which subsequently won the elections and has held power ever since.

Under normal circumstances, the government need not worry about losing important votes in Parliament. The majority party members are led by the government's chief whip, who holds a salaried position. The chief whip helps the government set the schedule in Parliament and keeps the cabinet briefed on developments there. Above all, the chief whip is responsible for party discipline, which in the British context means ensuring that majority-party MPs support government policy and vote to pass government bills. (The opposition and minor parties also have whips who perform the same disciplinary functions.)

The House of Lords passes on legislation and can offer amendments, but its lawmaking powers are quite limited. It can delay money bills for no more than one month and all other legislation for no more than one year. Generally, the Lords confine themselves to scrutinizing legislation, refining the language, and occasionally offering an amendment to reinforce rather than weaken the bill's original intent.

As noted earlier, the British system features a fusion of powers. This fusion is particularly evident in the judicial functions of the House of Lords, which serves as the highest court of appeals in Great Britain. In that it is similar to the U.S. Supreme Court, except that the House of Lords does not have the power to declare legislative acts unconstitutional.

Some critics argue that the House of Lords is an anachronism and should either be abolished altogether or replaced by a democratically elected upper house. One proposal would reconstitute Parliament so that representation would be based on geographic areas or regions in one house and on population in the other, something like the federal-style bicameral legislatures found in the United States and Germany. The opposition Labour and Liberal Democratic parties issued new calls for electoral reform in 1991 and 1992, advocating proportional representation. But the British remain steeped in tradition, and there is little popular support for far-reaching political reform.

The British Cabinet System

The British system has sometimes been called "cabinet government." The prime minister holds the most powerful position, acting simultaneously as chief executive, majority party leader, and principal adviser to the crown. The prime minister appoints and dismisses cabinet members, sets the legislative agenda, decides major policy issues, directs the bureaucracy, and manages the nation's diplomatic affairs. Being both head of government and leader of the parliamentary majority, the prime minister has enormous authority. Some critics have asserted that the British prime minister is a virtual dictator, but this charge is greatly exaggerated. Besides the ever-present possibility of a no-confidence vote, there are systemic liabilities that tend to offset a prime minister's powers. For instance, a prime minister cannot blame Parliament for failed government policies the way U.S. presidents can blame Congress. As British prime ministers have discovered, the more power a chief executive wields, the more responsibility he or she must bear for the outcome.

British voters do not vote for the prime minister in national elections the way American voters vote for the president; rather, the majority party in Parliament chooses a prime minister. The choice is always a foregone conclusion, however, because each party selects a leader at its convention before a general election. This part of the process is similar to the nominating conventions in the United States, except that future prime ministers do not have to face grueling primaries.

The formation and functioning of the cabinet illustrate the fusion of legislative and executive powers in the British system. The prime minister chooses leading MPs to serve in the cabinet. There is no limit on the size of the cabinet; each prime minister decides which departments will have cabinet representation, although certain ministers, among them Chancellor of the Exchequer (treasury), Foreign Secretary, and Home Secretary, are always included. The cabinet's functions were defined in 1918 by the Haldane Committee on the Machinery of Government as follows: final determination of the policy to be submitted to Parliament, supreme control of the national executive, and continuous coordination of the administrative departments.

As noted, the cabinet operates under the principle of collective responsibility. Publicly, all cabinet members must support the government's policies without reservation, even if they disagree among themselves in private. A cabinet member who cannot support a decision is expected to resign.

The cabinet generally convenes once a week in the Cabinet Room at the prime minister's residence, 10 Downing Street. The chief whip normally attends cabinet meetings, which are chaired by the prime minister. Votes are rarely taken, the prime minister preferring instead to seek consensus or to listen to the discussion and then declare a decision. The precise nature of cabinet meetings is shrouded in mystery: tradition, self-restraint, and the Official Secrets Act keep leaks to a minimum.

There are two schools of thought regarding the extent of the prime minister's powers. One school views the prime minister as omnipotent, having the final authority to decide all matters and appoint or dismiss cabinet members at will. The other school stresses that any politician who gets a cabinet post is powerful in his or her own right. Creating a cabinet is a political act: the prime minister must placate the party's power brokers in Parliament while preserving party unity.

Coordination and communication between the cabinet and the subordinate levels of the government are done through cabinet committees and the Cabinet Office. Originally, the committees were created to deal with particular issues; today there are about twenty-five permanent cabinet committees responsible for interdepartmental coordination and oversight in various issue areas. There are also over one hundred ad hoc committees set up to handle specific issues and facilitate two-way communication between the cabinet and the appropriate government departments.

The Cabinet Office also houses a secretariat that handles the cabinet's administrative affairs. It assists in coordinating the operations of government, keeps noncabinet ministers informed of cabinet decisions, prepares and circulates the agenda for cabinet meetings (and cabinet committee meetings), and the like. With the growth of the powers, functions, and responsibilities of the executive, the secretariat has become an indispensable part of the government's administrative apparatus.

Whitehall: The Administrative Departments

The cabinet is the keystone in the arch of the central government, but the departments are the building blocks. Headquartered in Whitehall, the departments run the day-to-day business of the government. They are supervised by a minister or by a secretary of state. (Recall that not all departments enjoy cabinet status.) Each departmental minister is assisted by at least one junior minister called a parliamentary secretary. The largest departments may also have parliamentary undersecretaries. All of these officials are members of the majority party, and all are appointed by the prime minister (about a hundred, plus the cabinet posts).

Department ministers are in charge of main administrative units of the government and must perform a variety of managerial functions, including motivating and monitoring the large number of civil servants who staff the department. The minister's chief aide is the permanent secretary, a senior civil servant who has the broad administrative experience and substantive expertise that a politically appointed minister may lack. Nevertheless, ultimate responsibility for departmental performance rests squarely on the minister's shoulders.

At times a minister's most important and difficult task is to persuade, bully, cajole, and otherwise induce the civil servants at the working levels of government to implement policy according to the government's wishes, but British civil servants, unlike top bureaucrats in the United States, have but one master, the government. Hence a determined minister can prevail unless held back by colleagues, and the government as a whole can completely dominate policy if it knows what it wants to do. By contrast, even the most determined U.S. president and cabinet officers may be utterly frustrated by federal bureaucrats backed by powerful members of Congress, especially key committee members, who are in turn often buttressed by powerful special interests. British ministers simply have to deal with the inevitable complications of any large, complex organization. The American president has to deal with bureaucrats who are in some instances powers unto themselves. There are no British bureaucrats with the kind of clout exercised by, say, the director of the Federal Bureau of Investigation. Also, in the United States, both independent commissions and the judiciary are given wide-ranging policy powers, to the point that, for example, federal judges have more to say about regulating telecommunications than either the president or Congress; there are no parallels in Great Britain. In general, the fragmentation of power in the American federal government gives bureaucrats much more discretion than the centralization of power in the British cabinet gives to British civil servants.

Parties and Elections

Traditionally, Great Britain has had a two-party system, but throughout most of the twentieth century there have been three major national political parties: the Conservative (Tory) party, the Labour party, and the Liberal (now Liberal Democratic) party. A Social Democratic party was launched recently, but it has had very limited electoral success. Since the early 1900s, control of the government has alternated between the Conservatives and Labour.

The Conservatives dominated British politics during the 1980s. In 1987, Margaret Thatcher became the first British prime minister in the twentieth century to lead a party to three consecutive election victories. Facing criticism from the public over a highly unpopular poll tax and opposition from within the Tory party over her lack of enthusiasm for broader British participation in the European Community, Thatcher stepped down in November 1990. John Major was then chosen to lead the party. In the spring of 1992, the Conservatives held on to power, winning a narrow majority in Parliament.

In terms of doctrine, the British Conservative party can be loosely compared to the Republican Party in the United States. Margaret Thatcher and Ronald Reagan shared a common belief in the benefits of the free-enterprise system. Both advocated a strong national defense and tended to embrace containment as the best way to deal with Soviet Communism. Prime Minister Thatcher was also instrumental in winning NATO support for the Intermediate Nuclear Force (INF) treaty negotiated by the two superpowers in 1987. Thatcher and Reagan were highly compatible in matters of both principle and policy.

As prime minister, Thatcher sought to reduce the size of government, curb spending, denationalize (or reprivatize) industry, cut taxes, maintain a strong independent nuclear strike force, and remain in the European Community (EC). She also encouraged private home ownership and self-reliance, advocated partial privatization of the National Health System (NHS), and opposed modernizing Britain's railway system. In addition, she tried to break the grip of the trade unions on the nation's domestic economic policy. In pushing this ambitious program of governmental retrenchment and economic revitalization, Thatcherites were helped by the fact that the Conservative party is relatively cohesive, without deep ideological divisions or warring factions. Rather there are certain divergent "tendencies" over policy; hence Thatcher's successor has shown somewhat greater flexibility in both domestic and foreign policy, dropping Thatcher's poll tax, promising not to privatize health care, and adopting a more benign attitude toward the EC.

The Labour party is a coalition of disparate interests. Originally an outgrowth of the British trade union movement, it was founded as the party of the working class. It became the main opposition party in the 1920s. From the outset, it distanced itself from the once-powerful Liberal party by embracing a moderate form of socialism.

Today Labour is no longer simply a working-class party. It is an umbrella organization appealing not only to workers but also to middle-class civil servants, teachers, housewives, peace activists, welfare recipients, students, pensioners, the jobless, the homeless, and the otherwise poor and downtrodden. Because the Labour party's constituency is so diverse and unity is lacking, its programs are difficult to summarize. Policies advocated in recent years have included renationalization of industry, unilateral nuclear disarmament, withdrawal from the EC, closing of U.S. military bases, expansion of the social welfare system, higher taxes for the wealthy, and concessions to organized labor. But after its third electoral loss in a row in 1987, under the leadership of Neil Kinnock, the party shifted toward the center in an effort to get back into the political mainstream.

The Labour party last controlled the government in 1979. After its electoral defeat that year, a struggle between the left-wing and moderate factions ensued. The moderates opposed both the party's stance favoring British withdrawal from the EC and a change in the party's method of selecting its leader. The new Social Democratic party, founded by disaffected Labourites, was the bitter fruit of this struggle. The defection weakened the Labour party but did not give rise to a viable alternative.

Just how badly the Labour party was weakened by its lurch to the left and fractured leadership became newly apparent in April 1992 when it again lost parliamentary elections, capturing only 35 percent of the popular vote to the Conservatives' 43 percent. This defeat came at a time of prolonged economic recession and high unemployment and despite the lackluster performance of

Tory Prime Minister John Major. It occasioned yet another round of soul search-ing and, following Kinnock's resignation as party leader, an ideological power struggle between two factions. Trade union leaders and others who favor tradi-tional Labour policies (high taxes on the middle class as well as the rich, state ownership of strategic industries, cradle-to-grave social welfare programs) pushed the candidacy of John Smith, while those who wanted to move away from Labour's "core collectivist philosophy" leaned toward Brian Gould.[2] Some critics also argued that Labourites were doing Conservatives a favor by refusing to form an alliance with the Liberal Democrats—together the parties had gained an absolute majority (52 percent) of the popular vote in the 1992 elections.

But British political parties have not shown much enthusiasm for fundamen-tal realignments or even temporary coalitions. In the 1983 elections, for example, the Social Democrats and the Liberals formed such a coalition, which they called the Alliance. The two parties kept their campaign finances separate but issued a joint manifesto urging government action to relieve unemployment, cuts in military spending, redoubled arms control efforts, expanded welfare programs, continued membership in the EC, and incentives for private enterprise. The Alliance was designed to offer the British voters a middle-of-the-road alternative to the right-leaning Conservatives and left-leaning Labourites. It met with little success at the polls. The possibility that a new political party will come along to challenge the old established ones still remains, but it is still premature to write the obituary for Great Britain's celebrated two-party system.

The minor parties in Great Britain—the Greens, the Scottish Nationalist party, the Unionist party, the Nationalist Front party, and the Communist party—are all marginalized by such factors as extremism, a narrow popular base, a lack of resources, poor leadership, or internal bickering.

In addition, minor parties face two systemic obstacles—tradition and the "first past the post" electoral system, in which candidates run in single-member districts and whoever gets the most votes wins. On tradition, Sydney Bailey's observation is apposite:

> There is nothing sacred in the number two, but the fact is that for by far the greater part of the three centuries during which parties in the modern sense have existed in Britain there have been two major parties, a Government party and an Opposition party.[3]

On the electoral system, some elaboration is necessary. Parliamentary elec-tions must be held at least every five years, but the prime minister has the prerogative of calling elections sooner if so desired. Negative circumstances, such as a vote of no confidence or a scandal, can force early elections. More often, the prime minister will try to capitalize on a momentary surge in public approval to win another five-year term. For example, in 1983, when the British defeated Argentina in a war over the Falkland Islands, Prime Minister Thatcher called early elections to take advantage of the resulting surge in her personal popularity. By contrast, John Major did not call early elections in 1991 because public displeasure with the Tory government at that time was high (as evidenced by the loss of some 890 town hall seats in local elections held in England and

Wales in May 1991). By waiting to hold parliamentary elections until the spring of 1992, Major was able to ride out the storm, and the Conservatives won a fourth consecutive term in office—the first British party to do so in 150 years.

Elections in Great Britain are short and simple compared to those in the United States. In the United States, president, senators, and representatives are elected to terms of different lengths, and national elections are staggered, taking place every two years. As a result, campaigns are frequent, and it seems like one election barely ends before the next begins. In Great Britain there is normally one national election every four or five years.

Elections are held when the prime minister formally asks the monarch to dissolve Parliament, a procedure that usually takes about ten days. Next a royal proclamation summons a new Parliament. The election must be held within three weeks of the proclamation. As a rule, the prime minister dissolves Parliament before the five-year term is up. Because the government can decide precisely when the next election is to be held, however, the party in power has an advantage over the opposition. Elections are often held in May or October, but no law requires this.

All British subjects 18 years of age or older are eligible to vote, provided that they have registered. Because voting registers are produced only once a year now, it can take up to sixteen months for a voter to qualify. However, in Great Britain, local officials have an obligation to get everybody registered, which is not the case in the United States. The result is that virtually every adult is registered in the United Kingdom, in sharp contrast to the United States, where only half of the eligible voters may be registered at any given time. There are currently 651 seats in Parliament, each representing a local constituency. Every fifteen years the Boundary Commission redraws the boundaries of the constituencies to reflect population changes.

The electoral system is based on the "**first past the post**" **principle**, meaning that each party in a district fields a single candidate, and whoever gets a plurality of the votes wins. If there were ten candidates, for example, one might win with only a small fraction of the popular vote.

This system has been widely criticized on the grounds that it distorts the actual voting results. To cite one example, in 1979 the Conservative party won 339 seats in Parliament, a clear majority; if the seats had been distributed in proportion to the votes, however, the Conservatives would have won only 279, well short of a majority. In fact, only in 1900, 1906, 1931, and 1935 would the government have won a working majority in Parliament if the seats were distributed in direct proportion to the votes.[4]

There has been considerable debate in Great Britain over changing the way MPs are elected. The advocates of change want a proportional representation system of one kind or another. Tradition is a formidable obstacle to such a change. Another is the logic of the British two-party system, which ensures that one party or the other will have a working majority in Parliament. The electoral system sometimes magnifies the winning party's parliamentary majority by a large margin. Hence in 1983 the Conservatives won an overwhelming 144-seat majority with well under half the popular votes. In the 1987 elections they captured only about 43 percent of the popular vote but still ended up with a 101-seat majority in Parliament. In the 1992 elections, by contrast, the Conservatives won roughly the same percentage of the popular vote but gained only a 22-seat majority—a much smaller magnifier effect but enough to give the Tories more than half the seats.

Changing the system would reduce the odds that any single party would win a working majority. For a new government to be formed, parties would be forced to enter into coalitions. This outcome is greatly desired by smaller parties like the Liberal Democrats. Others, however, fear that it would undermine the stability and capacity to act that have been the hallmarks of the British system.

Thus British elections are like those in the United States in regard to the method of election (plurality vote in single-member districts). But that is where the similarity ends. British elections are much shorter and much less expensive. And national elections in Great Britain are more party-oriented than in the United States, where the personality, reputation, and charisma of the individual candidate are often paramount. Because the government can put its programs into effect in the British system, the party in power is held strictly accountable for the condition of the country. That is why in 1979, when the British economy was in the doldrums, the voters ousted the Labour party and put the Conservatives in power.

Public Opinion and Pressure Groups

We have already alluded to the role of public opinion in the British system. Prime ministers often decide when to call new elections on the basis of opinion polls. Conversely, when a government's popular approval rating falls, it may be forced to resign. Thus public opinion is likely to have a more direct impact on government in Great Britain, where the prime minister and cabinet have an indefinite term of office, than in the United States, where the president and administration have a fixed term.

Public opinion polling can be critical in any democratic society, but it is especially important in the British system, where success or failure in elections is often a question of timing. It is also important because a steady or sudden drop in the government's popularity can induce it to resign or prompt a confidence vote in Parliament. Consequently, the accuracy of polls is more than a matter of theoretical interest. The 1992 elections demonstrated that polls and pollsters are no more infallible in Great Britain than elsewhere. All the polls on the eve of the elections predicted that the outcome would be very close and that Labour would have the edge. They also predicted that the outcome might be a "hung Parliament," with neither major party attaining a clear majority in the House of Commons. That made the vote for the Liberal Democratic party, the potential holder of the balance, critical. Even if Labour beat the Tories, the pollsters pointed out, Labour leader Kinnock might have to cut a deal with the Liberal Democrats in order to form a government.[5] These predictions all turned out to be wrong.

Pressure groups began gaining influence in Great Britain after World

War II. In fact, prior to the Tories' victory in 1979, the trade unions, in particular the Trades Union Congress (TUC), and the business interests, especially the Confederation of British Industry (CBI), had become so powerful that some experts began to describe the system as "corporatist." The heralds of corporatism argued that Parliament was losing its relevance as the new "triple alliance" of big government, big business, and organized labor was shaping policy and dominating the political system.

The **corporatist model** as it applies to postwar British politics has some merit, but there is little reason to believe that the parliamentary system itself is in jeopardy. Indeed, Prime Minister Thatcher greatly reduced organized labor's clout in economic policy formulation, and union membership declined by more than 20 percent between 1979 and 1986 in Great Britain.[6]

British pressure groups find that they are most effective when they can establish lines of communication with the civil service. In contrast to the United States, where lobbying Congress is as important as establishing contacts within the bureaucracy, in Great Britain, where policy emanates almost exclusively from the executive branch (the cabinet and the various ministries and departments), pressure groups generally bypass Parliament altogether.

France's Fifth Republic

That France has been governed by five different republics in two centuries (during which time the United States has had but one) is indicative of the political turmoil that has characterized so much of modern French history. France has had no fewer than *fifteen* constitutions since the French Revolution in 1789. The latest one has lasted more than three decades—a noteworthy achievement, considering that its predecessor, adopted in the wake of World War II, endured only twelve years. During that time, French governments lasted an average of only six months! Small wonder that political instability was both the cause of the Fourth Republic's early demise and the principal malady the Fifth Republic's Constitution was designed to cure.

A Hybrid System

The Constitution of the **Fifth Republic** is a composite of France's earlier constitutions. It incorporates presidential, plebiscitarian, parliamentary, and republican features, along with certain innovations insisted on by the Fifth Republic's founder and first president, General Charles de Gaulle.

The hallmark of the current Constitution is the majestic presidency, which contrasts sharply with its predecessors. Under the Third and Fourth Republics, the president was little more than a figurehead who rubber-stamped measures passed by French parliament. The president was chosen by the legislature acting as an electoral college and tended to be a captive of that body. French parliaments

Italy: Success without Stability

The core of the ancient Roman Empire, Italy emerged as a modern nation-state only in the 1860s. After World War I, Benito Mussolini, head of the ultranationalist Fascist movement, gained control of the government and created a police state. In 1935, Italy invaded Ethiopia, while the world looked on. The League of Nations failed to take collective military action or even to make economic sanctions stick. Italy joined the Berlin-Tokyo Axis and fought on the side of Germany and Japan at the start of World War II. After Fascism was overthrown in 1943, Italy declared war on Germany and Japan and contributed to the Allied victory.

After World War II, Italy's economy was in shambles. Aided by the American Marshall Plan, Italy was able to accomplish the tasks of postwar reconstruction in record time—the German "economic miracle" was matched by an Italian miracle no less impressive.

In 1991, Italy had a trillion-dollar economy that was comparable in size to that of France and bigger than that of the United Kingdom (which had dwarfed Italy economically a century earlier). Italy's average per capita GNP was over $18,500—larger than Great Britain's but lower than France's or Germany's. In the 1980s, Italy's economy actually grew at a slightly faster rate than that of France or Germany.

Italy's economic success, however, did not bring political or governmental stability. A freewheeling parliamentary democracy, Italy has been a cauldron of fractious parties, left-wing political violence, and scandal-ridden governments. In the late 1970s, a wave of terrorist attacks, including kidnappings and assassinations, threatened to destabilize Italy. In 1978, former Italian Prime Minister Aldo Moro was brutally murdered by members of the terrorist Red Brigade. Although terrorism continued into the 1980s, the government responded with an effective antiterrorism program.

In the early 1990s, Italian politics was marred by scandals involving alleged collusion between the Sicilian Mafia and some of Italy's most prominent political figures, including two former prime ministers, Giulio Andreotti and Bettino Craxi. Andreotti had served as prime minister seven times, and had become an emblem of the Italian state.

Italy's Referendums, April 1993

Referendum	Percentage of Votes Cast	
	Yes	No
Electoral reform	82.7	17.3
Abolish subsidies to political parties	90.3	9.7
Drug reform	55.3	44.7
Abolish local environmental competence	82.5	17.5
Abolish Ministry of State Industry	90.1	9.9
Abolish Ministry of Agriculture	70.1	29.9
Abolish Ministry of Tourism	82.2	17.8
Abolish political controls over savings banks	89.8	10.2

Source: Economist, Apr. 24, 1993, p. 53.

Italian voters were disgusted enough to demand fundamental political reform. In Italy, this meant, above all, changing the method of electing members of the legislature from strict proportional-representation to the first-past-the-post system used in Great Britain and the United States. The proportional-representation electoral system turned the Italian parliament into a political circus and helped make Italy's government the most unstable in Western Europe: by the spring of 1993, Italy had no fewer than fifty-one postwar governments and a variety of political parties.

In April 1993, a referendum on a proposal to change the electoral system for the Senate (upper house) was overwhelmingly approved (82.7 percent of the people voted yes; see table). The vote also showed clearly that the electorate wanted a similar change in the method of electing the Chamber of Deputies (lower house). Though this change is probably a good idea, it is unlikely that electoral reform will be the magic bullet that cures all of Italy's political ills.

were notoriously fragmented and ineffectual, which meant that the French government was often adrift. Presidents had the power to appoint prime ministers (with legislative approval) and to dissolve parliament, but that power was negative; positive power, to the extent that it existed at all, was lodged in the prime minister and cabinet, who were often paralyzed by a perpetually divided parliament.

General de Gaulle stressed the need for a strong and dignified president who would be aloof from fractious party politics and could guide the nation, mediate among the parties, and discipline (or circumvent) the parliament in the interests of unity, stability, and efficiency. As a champion of French nationalism who despised the narrow particularism of petty politicians, de Gaulle was both admired for his leadership abilities and reviled for his allegedly Bonapartist tendencies. Recent scholarship casts doubt on the view that de Gaulle was dictatorial in his exercise of power.

The plebiscitarian aspect of the present Constitution has its historical roots in the populist nature of Napoleon Bonaparte's rule and, more specifically, in the French Constitution of 1852. A **plebiscite** is a direct vote of the people on some issue of political importance to the nation. The idea of taking issues directly to the people sounds democratic, but in the hands of a charismatic leader, it can be an instrument of dictatorship. Hence a popular president can use plebiscites to get around parliament, in effect establishing a personalistic (and deliberately antirepublican) form of rule.

An example of how President de Gaulle used this power was the 1962 referendum on the direct election of the president. De Gaulle decided somewhat belatedly that it would strengthen the hand of the French president (namely, himself) to be directly elected to a seven-year term of office. (Originally in the Fifth Republic, the French president was indirectly elected to a shorter term by an electoral college.) The referendum was popular, and to nobody's surprise, it passed—President de Gaulle had somewhat highhandedly announced that he would resign if it failed. Whether this amendment was constitutional is debatable but now moot.

The republican facet of the French system is evident in the **National Assembly**, whose members are directly elected by secret ballot on the basis of universal suffrage. Under the Fifth Republic's Constitution, however, the legislative branch can be circumvented by a popular and willful president.

Finally, the quasi-parliamentary nature of the system can be seen in the presence of a cabinet-style executive in which the leader of the majority party in parliament (or of a coalition) chooses a cabinet and forms a government (as in Great Britain). The Consitution divides executive powers between the prime minister and the president. This **dual executive** arrangement can give rise to a constitutional crisis if the two executives are not on parallel tracks.

The present Constitution was approved by 70 percent of the French voters and has now weathered decades of storm and stress. It has thus gained legitimacy by virtue of its longevity. The mix of authoritarian, populist, republican, and parliamentary characteristics mirrors both the complexities of France's political history and the ideological diversity of the French electorate.

Who Rules? President and Prime Minister

France has a unique dual executive: a president with ample constitutional prerogatives to act and a prime minister who is the head of the government. This arrangement may seem impracticable, but it has worked reasonably well in the French context.

Almost all West European governments are of the parliamentary variety in which the executive is chosen by the parliament and cabinet members are also party leaders in the legislature. Parliamentary rule can lead to governmental instability, especially where a multiparty system and an ideologically fragmented or polarized electorate prevent any single party from gaining a clear majority. Coalition governments are often vulnerable to votes of no confidence on controversial issues. Under some conditions, they can even produce the expectation of instability, which may in time become a self-fulfilling prophecy.

In a presidential system, the chief executive is chosen by the people for a fixed term. Except in extraordinary circumstances using cumbersome procedures, the legislative branch does not have the power to oust the president. Thus in one sense the presidential system has greater stability than the parliamentary system. By contrast, presidential government lacks the flexibility of the parliamentary system. In the former, if a scandal occurs or public support wanes, the government cannot simply resign and call for new elections; it can do so in the latter.

The French system tries for the best of both worlds, combining a strong president with a parliamentary form of government. Both fusion and separation of powers are present: the prime minister and cabinet are linked by party ties and constitutional logic to the National Assembly, but the president is elected separately and is not directly affected by the vicissitudes of parliamentary politics. The government can be censured and forced to resign; the president can dissolve parliament as often as once every twelve months. (This power has been used very sparingly.)

In general, the Constitution positions the president as an arbitrator charged with settling differences among conflicting interests. Elected for a seven-year term and eligible for reelection, a popular president may dominate the political system for many years without facing the rigors of frequent campaigning or the vagaries of party politics. To win, a presidential candidate must gain an absolute majority of the votes cast; if no candidate wins such a majority, a runoff election is held. This **two-ballot system** ensures that whoever is elected will be the first or second choice of the majority of voters and thus that the president will have a national mandate. Having a president endorsed by only a minority of the electorate would not be an auspicious start for a new government, especially in a country like France with a tradition of divisive politics.

Today, thanks to de Gaulle, the French president possesses in practice all the powers that the British monarch has in theory. These include the power to appoint the prime minister (although the president must carefully weigh the balance of power among the parties in parliament before making this choice). The president has the power to dissolve the National Assembly and can even exercise dictatorial powers simply by declaring a state of emergency (after consultation with the Constitutional Council). The power to call a national referendum in certain key areas also places the president in a strategic position to manage political conflict and manipulate the system to produce the desired outcome.

In dealing with the National Assembly, the executive branch (president and prime minister) has several constitutional weapons at its disposal. For example, the prime minister (most likely in close consultation with the president) can ask for broad "decree" powers and combine such a request with a vote of confidence: in other words, the National Assembly must either grant the request, which means that the government can make laws by fiat (without parliamentary approval), or face dissolution. The government can put a controversial bill into a bundle with other legislation expected to win easy approval and demand a **package vote**. This tactic forces the National Assembly either to approve a single measure that many members may oppose or to vote down legislation that the majority favors.

During most of the Fifth Republic, prime ministers have played a subordinate role. Even so, their current powers are far greater than their predecessors held under the Third and Fourth Republics. President and prime minister can cooperate to push legislation through the National Assembly or block measures they oppose.

Although prime ministers are overshadowed by presidents, they do have important political and administrative functions. The prime minister typically takes the lead in policy areas of little interest to the president, supervises and coordinates the work of the cabinet ministers, acts as the principal liaison between the executive and legislative branches, and, in the absence of a parliamentary majority, mediates among the parties in the governing coalition. This was one of the main responsibilities of Michel Rocard, who became prime minister in 1988 after the Socialists gained sixty-one new seats in parliamentary elections but failed to win a majority. Another normal function of the prime minister is to direct and lead the election campaign in the National Assembly; it is considered undignified for the president to participate excessively in legislative elections.

Unlike presidents, prime ministers have no job security. Rocard's term in office was plagued by economic problems; he resigned in May 1991 and was replaced by Édith Cresson, France's first female prime minister. Cresson was controversial from the start; having failed to halt a downslide in Socialist popularity, Cresson resigned ten months later, after the Socialist party made its worst showing since World War II in local and regional elections.

The power of the French cabinet, along with that of the prime minister, was reduced by the de Gaulle Constitution. As a rule, cabinet members owe their positions and the scope of their power to the president. The number of cabinet members has ranged from twenty-four under President de Gaulle (1958–1969) to forty-three under Prime Minister Chirac (1986–1988). Cabinet members are drawn from diverse walks of life; many come from the civil service. Unlike their British counterparts, members of the National Assembly must formally resign from the legislature to take a cabinet position. In practice, however, cabinet ministers only temporarily relinquish their parliamentary seats to a surrogate; as soon as they leave the government, they typically go back to the National Assembly. Another French wrinkle is that ministers are often simultaneously mayors of major cities as well. When Jacques Chaban-Delmas was prime minister (1969–1972), he continued as mayor of Bordeaux, and when Jacques Chirac became prime minister for the second time (1986–1988), he stayed on as mayor of Paris.

Ministers act under the direction of the president and prime minister. Their primary duty is to oversee the implementation of policy by the part of the bureaucracy for which they are responsible. The French government has traditionally been highly centralized, although the main thrust of President Mitterrand's administrative reforms has been to decentralize the system.

French Technocracy: The Civil Service

The basic components of the French civil service are the so-called *grands corps,* which include the Council of State, the Court of Accounts, the Finance Inspectorate, two corps of engineers, and the diplomatic service. The civil servants in these organizations are graduates of prestigious public-policy and engineering schools known as *les grandes écoles,* of which the most famous is the *École Nationale d'Administration* (ENA). They dominate virtually all segments of the French administration. In many cases, top officials in the government (and chief executive officers of major French corporations as well) are recruited from *les grands corps* (about one-third of France's ambassadors are graduates of ENA, for example). Famous French ENA alumni include former President Valéry Giscard d'Estaing and Prime Minister Laurent Fabius.

Until recently, France's highly centralized unitary system precluded any large role for local government. In the classical French system, most decisions were made in Paris, and **prefects** (officials appointed by Paris) supervised the mayors of municipalities in the various *départements* (intermediate administrative districts). In this traditional **tutelage system**, prefects were powerful go-betweens, but their position has been undermined by decentralization, with more power given both to the cities and to regional governments. Today the big-city mayors are important figures in French government—so much so that some politicians are giving up national political office in order to devote full time to local politics.

The Taming of Parliament

The French parliament wielded most of the power under the Third (1871–1940) and Fourth (1946–1958) Republics. The instability and paralysis of parliamentary government during that often turbulent era led directly to the curbing of the powers of parliament by the present Constitution. The fulcrum of French government moved to the presidency under the Fifth Republic.

The legislature comprises an upper and a lower house—the National Assembly and the Senate, respectively. In 1986 the former had 577 deputies elected from multimember districts on the basis of a complex system of proportional representation. The new electoral system was introduced by the Socialists after Mitterrand won the presidency in 1981; after the 1986 elections, it was changed back to the earlier two-ballot system. Deputies are once again elected in single-member districts; the two highest voter-getters on the first ballot then compete in a runoff election to determine the winner in each district. This system has an interesting twist: parties can form alliances for the second vote, in effect dividing up voting districts according to which party's candidate has the best chance of winning in each.

With two exceptions, the National Assembly and Senate share power equally. The former has the right to examine the budget first, and the cabinet is responsible to the National Assembly rather than to the Senate. Almost all legislation originates in the executive branch; private members may not even introduce budget measures.

In a sense, the French parliament is more interesting for the powers it does *not* have than for the powers it has. First, it cannot meet for more than six months each year. Second, it has no power to introduce financial bills—if it fails to approve the government's budget by a certain deadline, the budget can be enacted by executive decree. (It is normal in parliamentary countries for members to be forbidden to propose spending money or reducing taxes.) Moreover, as noted earlier, it can be compelled by the executive to cast a package vote on several pieces of legislation at once. Also, the government can make any particular vote a vote of confidence. In a confidence vote, a measure is considered approved unless the National Assembly passes a censure resolution by an absolute majority of the members. This means that only the votes in favor of censure are counted; abstentions have the effect of opposing censure. So the deck is stacked, so to speak, in favor of the government.

President de Gaulle creatively combined provisions of the Constitution to maximize presidential leverage over the parties in parliament. Thus, for example, he was not above calling for a package vote on some part of his overall program and then making the vote itself a matter of confidence!

The committee system in the Fifth Republic is a cross between the U.S. Congress and the British House of Commons. As in the British system, there are only six standing committees; but as in the United States, they are specialized. Most committees have more than one hundred members. Membership on committees is apportioned according to party strength in the parliament. Unlike their American counterparts, committees in the French parliament cannot change the substance of government bills. There are other differences as well. Investigative committees can be created to probe government actions, but they have limited powers. The length of time they may investigate is set, they cannot investigate matters that are being handled by the judiciary, their findings must be reported to a standing committee for approval or rejection, and, to minimize leaks, they may meet only in closed sessions. Committee assignments are used as a means to distribute power among the parties and to give the opposition a formal role in the political process.

The **Senate** is indirectly elected by an electoral college consisting of members of the National Assembly and representatives of local governments. Its members, numbering around three hundred, serve nine-year terms; Senate elections are staggered at three-year intervals. The Senate is autonomous and cannot be dissolved by the president.

The French Senate gives disproportionate representation to rural areas and thus acts as a counterweight to the urban-oriented National Assembly. Although it is weaker than the Assembly, the Senate may reject government bills. (The Assembly can override a Senate veto, however.) The Senate's chief role is to keep the government honest by using question time to challenge policymakers and decision makers.

A Multiparty System

France continues to have a panoply of political parties ranging across the spectrum from extreme right to extreme left. Traditionally, the Socialists and Communists have been the two main parties on the left. From the end of World War II until the late 1970s, the Communist party generally received at least 20 percent of the popular vote. The 1980s saw a steady erosion of Communist party strength.

The Socialist party was the major beneficiary of this moderating trend within the French left. In 1981 it not only won the presidency but also gained a clear majority in the National Assembly. Although support for the Socialist party dropped in the 1986 elections, France's Socialist president, François Mitterrand, easily won reelection to a second term in 1988. (Mitterrand won 54 percent of the popular vote on the second ballot, to Jacques Chirac's 46 percent.) In the June elections to the Assembly, the Socialists fell short of the legislative majority that pollsters were predicting; they nonetheless won 276 seats, giving them the largest block of votes (only 13 short of the 289 needed for an absolute majority in 1988). Moderate Socialist leader Michel Rocard formed a minority government with the support of an autonomous group of fifty centrist and independent deputies known as the Center for Social Democrats (CDS).

The Socialists have adopted policies favoring expanded social welfare programs, concessions to free-market forces (especially business and banking interests), and strong support for the Western alliance system and the European Community. After the 1988 elections, President Mitterrand outlined a series of goals for the new government: working toward a united Europe, supporting further superpower nuclear arms reductions, investing more in research and education, accelerating modernization of French industry, and protecting France's elaborate social security system. There appeared to be a national consensus behind this mix of liberal and conservative measures, but by 1990 rising unemployment (10 percent) and budgetary constraints that hit traditionally left-leaning lower-income groups hardest sent the Socialists' popularity into a nosedive.

On the political right, Gaullist parties under various names predominated for several decades. De Gaulle himself never founded a party; indeed, he was contemptuous of political parties in general. Nonetheless, his followers kept the Gaullist legacy alive for a time under the banner of the Gaullist Union of

Democrats for the Republic (UDR) and later under a neo-Gaullist party, the Rally for the Republic (RPR), headed by former (and future) prime minister Jacques Chirac.

In 1978, then President Valéry Giscard d'Estaing created a new political formation, the Union for French Democracy (UDF), a coalition of several center-right parties and some smaller groups. An RPR-UDF alliance produced a center-right victory in the 1978 national elections, despite a determined effort by the Socialists and Communists to close ranks and enforce "republican discipline" in the second round of balloting. The RPR and UDF shared many elements of a common political philosophy, both favoring strong presidential government, a centralized administrative system, and free-market economic policies, but personal ambitions and myopic leadership prevented them from cooperating fully and helped the Socialists gain power in the 1980s.

In addition, splinter parties on both the left and right have arisen from time to time. One such party, the National Front, has become firmly rooted in a disenchanted segment of the French electorate. Several other new parties, including the Greens and the *Génération Écologiste,* appear to be gaining an equally solid foothold to the left of center. In regional and local elections held in March 1992, the traditional parties were challenged by these upstart parties to a degree never before witnessed under the Fifth Republic.

Perhaps the most ominous threat comes from the National Front, whose leader, Jean-Marie Le Pen, did surprisingly well in his presidential bid in 1988. In the subsequent legislative elections, his party—which espouses nationalistic, racist, anti-immigrationist policies—made a very poor showing, but in the 1992 balloting Le Pen's party polled nearly 14 percent, only about 4 percentage points behind the governing Socialist party. At the same time, the two environmental parties together garnered about 15 percent of the popular vote, prompting some commentators to conclude that France's party system was being transformed in the early 1990s.[7]

Mitterrand's France: Testing the System

In 1964, Prime Minister Georges Pompidou described the delicate institutional balance of the Fifth Republic:

> France has now chosen a system midway between the American presidential regime and the British parliamentary regime, where the chief of state, who formulates general policy, has the basis of authority in universal suffrage but can only exercise his function with a government that he may have chosen and named, but which in order to survive, must maintain the confidence of the Assembly.[8]

The Fifth Republic has provided France with unprecedented political stability. The personality of de Gaulle was certainly a factor in the early years. De Gaulle's influence extended well beyond his presidency. His opposition to domestic communism, his emphasis on France's sovereign independence (symbolized by the French nuclear strike force), his concern with enhancing French prestige in Europe and beyond, and his desire for economic growth without extensive nationalization of industry were all continued by his two presidential successors, Georges Pompidou (1969–1974) and Valéry Giscard d'Estaing (1974–1981). The National Assembly and the French voters have also broadly supported these policies.

But in 1981 this national consensus was challenged. For the first time, the Socialist party won a clear majority in the Assembly, and a Socialist, François Mitterrand, was elected president. The Socialist victories portended a turn to the left in the form of expanded welfare programs, deficit spending on a grand scale, greater nationalization of French industry, worker participation in management (*autogestion*), administrative decentralization, and abolition of capital punishment. The realization of this agenda, however, was hampered by deepening domestic difficulties—in particular, high unemployment and economic stagnation—which adversely affected the Socialists' popularity.

While France was experiencing these political changes, the system itself came under fire. The president was criticized for being too aloof from political pressures and public opinion, the system for being overly politicized. Because the president was elected every seven years and the National Assembly was chosen at least every five years, elections—and preparations for them—came to dominate French politics. Legislative or presidential elections were held twelve times between 1962 and 1988. One authority asserted that "long-range programs gave place to expediency, and party alignments obeyed the logic of electoral tactics rather than policy making."[9]

A severe test of the system came in 1986, when the center-right parties won a narrow majority in the legislative elections. France's Socialist President Mitterrand was compelled to choose a conservative prime minister. He asked the leader of a neo-Gaullist party, Jacques Chirac, to form a new government. The Fifth Republic had been created with a built-in time bomb that seemed about to detonate: a **divided executive** was in power. The president and the prime minister belonged to different parties, had different agendas, and looked to different constituencies.

This predicament produced *cohabitation,* the coexistence of a divided executive without bringing the system down. There were tensions at times, and the machinery of government did not run as smoothly as it might have, but Mitterrand and Chirac both displayed enough flexibility and mutual tolerance to avert a major constitutional crisis for two years. In 1993 history repeated itself when the center-right again won a majority (roughly 80 percent) of the seats in parliamentary elections and Mitterrand was again forced to name a leader of the archrival neo-Gaullist RPR, Édouard Balladur, to head a new government. The fact that the system faced this challenge once before and survived suggests something of historic importance to the French nation: both major political configurations, left and right, have a commitment to the Constitution that transcends ideologies. The system itself has perhaps acquired a legitimacy the likes of which no other French republic has ever known. This newfound institutional stability could be of critical importance in the 1990s as France undergoes major social and political changes.

Germany's Unified Federal Democracy

On October 3, 1990, West Germany and East Germany were united as one country, after more than four decades as separate entities. The East German Communist regime was swept away, and the West German system of government was extended throughout the new nation. Thus despite a tradition of autocratic rule, Germany is today a thriving democracy. Before unification, the Federal Republic of Germany (West Germany) comprised ten states, or *Länder* (singular, *Land*), plus West Berlin.[10] It encompassed an area about the size of Oregon. The new unified Germany encompasses 16 *Länder* and a land area of 137,838 square miles, slightly larger than Montana. Its population has gone from just under 62 million to just over 79 million (see Table 5.1). The capital has been officially moved from Bonn back to Berlin, historically the center of Germany's political life, although the process of physically moving the machinery of government will take several years.

The *Länder* are the building blocks in a system designed to ensure a high degree of political decentralization. *Land* governments have the primary responsibility to enact legislation in specific areas such as education and cultural affairs. They alone have the means to implement laws enacted by the federal government, to command most of the administrative personnel to accomplish this task, to exercise police power (taking care of the health, welfare, and moral well-being of the people), to direct the educational system, and to ensure that the press does not violate constitutional rules.

Table 5.1   The New German Federation

Land	Capital	Area (square miles)	Population
Baden-Württemberg	Stuttgart	13,803	9,432,709
Bavaria	Munich	27,283	11,049,263
*Berlin	Berlin	341	3,379,000
*Brandenburg	Potsdam	15,044	3,441,000
Bremen	Bremen	156	661,992
Hamburg	Hamburg	291	1,603,070
Hesse	Wiesbaden	8,151	5,568,892
Lower Saxony	Hannover	18,311	7,184,943
*Mecklenburg–West Pomerania	Schwerin	6,080	1,509,000
North Rhine–Westphalia	Düsseldorf	13,149	16,874,059
Rhineland-Palatinate	Mainz	7,658	3,653,155
Saarland	Saarbrücken	992	1,054,142
*Saxony	Dresden	6,839	4,989,000
*Saxony-Anhalt	Halle	7,837	3,027,000
Schleswig-Holstein	Kiel	6,053	2,564,565
*Thuringia	Erfurt	5,872	1,980,000

* Formerly part of East Germany: estimated populations.

Though the *Länder* have considerable clout, the federal government is the main repository of political authority in the constitutional system. The central government has the exclusive right to legislate in foreign affairs, citizenship matters, currency and coinage, railways, postal service and telecommunications, and copyrights. In other areas, notably civil and criminal law and laws relating to the regulation of the economy, the central government and the *Länder* share power.

Germany is more "federal" than the United States; the *Länder* run more of their own affairs and receive a larger proportion of taxes than American states do. For example, individual and corporate income taxes are split between Berlin and the *Länder* in equal 40 percent shares; the cities get 20 percent. The *Länder* also receive one-third of the value-added tax, the large but hidden sales tax used throughout Europe. As a result, although some additional funds are transferred from Berlin to the *Länder* and cities, the local governments are not reduced to begging the national government for money, as their counterparts in the United States so often are. The most imposing institutional expression of German federalism is the **Bundesrat**, the upper house of the national legislature.

The Basic Law

Germany's charter is called the **Basic Law** rather than the Constitution because it was designed as a temporary document to be supplanted by a true constitution upon reunification of the two Germanys. Its last article states, "This Basic Law loses its validity on the day on which a Constitution that has been freely decided on by the German people comes into effect."

The drafting of the Basic Law was extraordinary in part because it was done under the watchful eyes of the powers occupying Germany after World War II. The United States, Great Britain, and France served as models from which the West Germans borrowed freely. From the United States they took the principles of federalism and bicameralism. From Great Britain they adapted the parliamentary system. They imitated the French electoral system, using proportional representation to fill some of the seats in the **Bundestag** (lower house). The preamble to the Basic Law proclaims West Germany's right of self-determination, and there is no mention of the Occupation. Remarkably, a few short years after World War II, a sovereign, independent, and democratic government became fully operational in West Germany.

The Basic Law and Individual Rights   Significantly, the first nineteen articles of the Basic Law deal with the inalienable rights of every West German. As one student of German politics has observed, "The relevant historical experience was that of the Third Reich with its oppressive flouting of all human liberties."[11] The Weimar Constitution made it possible for the government to suspend constitutional rights during times of emergency. Abuse of these emergency powers by the Nazi regime eventually led to the revocation of the Constitution itself. Accordingly, Article 19 of the Basic Law proclaims, "In no case may the essential content of a basic right be encroached upon." The guarantees contained in the first nineteen articles are entrenched: no act of the executive, legislative, or judicial branch of government can revoke or abridge them. If a question arises as to whether or not a statutory law conflicts with the Basic Law, the issue is resolved by the Federal Constitutional Court.

The rights guaranteed under the Basic Law include equality before the law; freedom of speech, religion, assembly, and the press; academic freedom; freedom of association; freedom from unlawful searches; private property rights; the right of asylum; freedom from discrimination based on race, sex, or political convictions; and the right to refuse military service as a matter of conscience. Article 18 attaches a caveat to these rights, stipulating that they cannot be used "to attack the democratic order." This proviso was clearly aimed at the two extremes of left and right, Communism and Nazism, which have so afflicted German life in the twentieth century. Doubtless it reflected most of all the postwar preoccupation with Soviet Communism that prevailed throughout the Atlantic Community and was particularly pervasive in West Germany. However, fear of the reawakening of neo-Nazi ultranationalism has never been far beneath the surface in the Federal Republic, as evidenced by the fact that neo-Nazi activity has generally been interpreted as constituting an attack on the democratic order.

The Amendment Process   Amending the Basic Law requires a two-thirds majority vote in both houses of parliament, but the fundamental principles and guarantees cannot be revoked or amended. In addition to the civil liberties enumerated in the first nineteen articles, the federal, republican, democratic, and welfare-state features of the political system are deliberately set in stone to prevent a recurrence of the Nazi nightmare.

Article 23   From its inception, the Basic Law of the Federal Republic looked ahead to a time when Germany would be united. Under Article 23, East Germany (the German Democratic Republic, or GDR) could be merged with West Germany at any time, the only proviso being that the GDR accept the Basic Law. Prior to 1989, this part of the Basic Law seemed irrelevant in the context of the Cold War. But with the overthrow of Communist rule in East Germany at the end of 1989, Article 23 became the vehicle by which the two states were united.

The Chancellor

Germany has a parliamentary form of government with a dual executive. The president is a figurehead, indirectly elected and endowed with ceremonial powers. The true chief executive is the **chancellor**, who obtains the position in the same way as the British prime minister—by being leader of the majority party in the lower house (the Bundestag). If no one party enjoys an absolute majority, as has often been the case in Germany, the leader of the major party in the ruling coalition becomes the chancellor.

The chancellor, with parliamentary approval, appoints and dismisses cabinet members. Together with the cabinet, the chancellor sets policy guidelines and proposes legislation. As the head of government, the chancellor is responsible for translating policies into operational programs. The chancellor has the power to veto budget measures. In a national emergency, the chancellor becomes commander in chief. In short, the chancellor, like the British prime minister, is the linchpin in the system.

The Basic Law contains a provision, called the constructive vote of no confidence, that would seem to make it very difficult to remove a chancellor; however, in this respect the German parliamentary system resembles Britain's. Three of Germany's five chancellors—Konrad Adenauer, Ludwig Eberhardt, and Willy Brandt—resigned between elections when they became liabilities rather than assets to their parties. Similarly, since World War II, no fewer than four Conservative British prime ministers have been persuaded by their party to step down between elections. In both countries, party support, rather than any formal rule, determines whether a head of government stays in office.

The chancellor chooses cabinet members in close consultation with the party's executive committee. Seldom does one of the two major parties win a clear majority in the Bundestag, so it is usually necessary for either the Christian Democratic Union (CDU) or the Social Democratic party (SDP) to enter into a coalition with the small Free Democratic party (FDP). As a consequence, the allocation of cabinet posts typically reflects the need to entice the coalition partner with some key ministerial appointments. For example, Hans-Dietrich Genscher, leader of the FDP, was for many years the Federal Republic's foreign minister, first as the junior partner in a coalition with the SDP under Helmut Schmidt and then, after the FDP broke with the SDP in 1982, in a coalition with the CDU under Helmut Kohl. (Genscher, in poor health, resigned in 1992.)

Almost all cabinet members are also members of the Bundestag and are active in both roles. In contrast to British cabinet members, German ministers are almost always chosen for their expertise in a particular policy area. There are generally about seventeen cabinet members, the most prominent being the ministers of finance, foreign affairs, defense, and interior. Cabinet members participate in decision making, advise the chancellor on policy matters, direct the formulation of policy proposals and legislation within their own departments, and oversee the implementation of policy by their subordinates.

Directly below the chancellor and the cabinet are the parliamentary secretaries (who are members of the Federal legislature) and state secretaries (career civil service employees). The parliamentary secretaries are considered junior ministers—they leave office at the end of the term of the cabinet member they serve. The state secretaries, as professional bureaucrats, provide some continuity from one government to the next—they stay on after cabinet members leave office. The departments tend to be small (in contrast to British departments) because the *Land* governments actually administer most federal programs and enforce federal as well as state laws.

The German Parliament

Unlike Great Britain, Germany lacks a great parliamentary tradition. Bismarck largely ignored the Reichstag (the forerunner of the Bundestag), and during the Weimar period it was ineffectual. Even after 1949, the Bundestag lacked prestige and was treated with a certain disdain by Chancellor Adenauer (who resembled France's authoritarian President Charles de Gaulle in this respect).

The German parliament is bicameral, consisting, as mentioned earlier, of a lower house, the Bundestag, and an upper house, the Bundesrat. The Bundestag, whose members are directly elected, is the primary lawmaking body, although the Bundesrat, as we noted, also plays an important legislative role. Most bills are initiated by the chancellor, but before any bill can become law, the Bundestag must vote its approval. Thus it functions as one of the principal mechanisms in the constitutional system of check and balances. The Basic Law underscores the independence of the Bundestag by stipulating that its members are "not bound by orders and instructions and shall be subject only to their conscience."

In addition to choosing the chancellor, the Bundestag acts as a watchdog over the government. As we have seen, the Bundestag has the power to oust a chancellor at any time with a constructive vote of no confidence. On its own initiative, it can also enact legislation binding on the government, conduct public debates on government policy, investigate government actions, and directly question the chancellor and cabinet members. (The latter can be summoned to appear before the Bundestag, but they cannot be forced to disclose information.)

Voting patterns in the Bundestag reflect a strict party discipline. Parliamentary parties are organized into *Fraktionen* (factions). The *Fraktionen* meet frequently to decide how to vote on upcoming bills and discuss legislative strategy. Indeed, they go so far as to determine the specific responsibility each deputy will assume on each piece of legislation. The assignments and instructions even include the precise arguments that deputies will make. The *Fraktionen* are built into the parliamentary structure: only parties with a large enough block of deputies to form a *Fraktionen* (at least 5 percent of the total membership) can be represented in committees.

In Germany, as in the United States, committees are a principal source of legislative power. Committees generally meet in private, and the opposition has ample opportunity to participate. Most of the nineteen standing committees have identical counterparts in the cabinet; this arrangement facilitates the flow of communications between the government and the Bundestag because cabinet officials are usually deputies in the Bundestag as well. Normally, committees in Germany do not have the kind of investigatory powers found in the U.S. Congress, but the Bundestag can establish special committees of inquiry on the recommendation of one-fourth of the deputies.

The Bundestag elects a presiding officer through a secret ballot. In practice, the majority party actually decides who will be the Bundestag president. There are also three vice-presidents selected from opposition parties. Together with other party leaders, these officials form the Council of Elders, which acts as an advisory board to the president of the Bundestag, schedules debates on pending legislation, and allocates speaking time to the parliamentary parties.

The Bundesrat, or Federal Council, is the main institutional mechanism for adjusting and regulating relations between the *Bund* (federal government) and the *Länder*. It is perhaps the most distinctive feature of the German system. Unlike the relatively powerless British House of Lords, the Bundesrat is a powerful body with exclusive constitutional functions. Directly responsible to the state governments, it has wide-ranging influence on federal policies and procedures.

The sixty-eight members of the Bundesrat are not popularly elected; they are appointed by the various *Land* governments, which have three to six seats each, depending on population. Each *Land* government must vote as a block—a provision that reinforces the federal character of the German parliament.

The Bundestag is constitutionally required to submit the legislation it passes to the Bundesrat. All bills that directly affect the *Länder* must be approved by the Bundesrat to become law; in other words, the Bundesrat can veto such legislation. Other bills do not require its approval but any objections raised by the Bundesrat must be debated in the Bundestag before the bill becomes law. The influence of the Bundesrat over federal policy has increased steadily, giving the *Länder* a role in the political system far exceeding that of the state governments in the United States.

Because the composition of the Bundesrat is not affected by national elections, this house has a special aura of stability. It is also more streamlined and efficient than the lower house because most of its members hold ministerial posts in their respective *Land* governments and can use their own administrative staffs to help them prepare legislation. In general, Bundesrat members tend to have more technical expertise than Bundestag deputies do, and they can be more specialized. Finally, there is little party influence in the Bundesrat. Members are expected to represent the interests of the *Länder* without regard for party preference. The strict party discipline found in the Bundestag is matched by the tight control *Land* governments exercise over their representatives in the Bundesrat. In sum, the Bundesrat gives the German states a powerful weapon to protect themselves against federal encroachment.

The Basic Law divides legislation into three categories: exclusive, concurrent, and framework law. Article 30 lodges state legislative authority firmly in the *Länder,* and Article 70 stipulates that the *Länder* have all legislative powers not expressly conferred on the federal parliament. Exclusive legislative authority, assigned solely to the *Bund* (federal government), is limited to foreign affairs, defense, currency, and trade. Concurrent legislative authority applies in such areas as criminal and civil law, trade and commerce, and public roads. The *Länder* may legislate in these areas so long as the *Bund* has not already done so. (All federal legislation in this category must be approved by the Bundesrat to become law.) Framework legislative authority limits the *Bund* to providing only outline bills, leaving the details up to the *Länder*. This category includes public services, the environment, and regional planning. Although the most important legislation is given to the *Bund,* administration of programs and implementation of policy are left largely in the hands of the *Länder*.

Bills in parliament run a familiar gauntlet: formal introduction, committee review, several readings, debate, and final vote. Measures may be introduced by individual members of the Bundestag, by the government, or by the Bundesrat. Most legislation is drafted by the executive branch. All government bills must be sent to the Bundesrat first, and any changes to a bill must accompany it to the Bundestag. Because the Bundesrat has veto power over all concurrent legislation, the government normally works closely with this body in the drafting stages to avoid potential problems.

After a bill has been introduced, it goes to the Bundestag, where it is debated. Next it is sent to a standing committee, where most of the detail work is done. A committee member is usually assigned to prepare a report on the bill, which then goes back to the full house for further debate. This stage is known as the second reading. A third reading usually follows shortly thereafter, and the measure is voted on. If it passes, it is sent to the Bundesrat.

In the case of legislation introduced by the government, the Bundesrat gets two reviews. If the Bundesrat and the Bundestag do not agree on the form or substance of a particular bill, it goes to a conference committee, as it might in the U.S. Congress. The conference committee has twenty-two members, half from each house of parliament. Differences in language are usually reconciled through this mechanism. Once a bill has been passed by both houses and signed by the president and the chancellor, it becomes law.

Parties and Elections

National elections normally occur every four years in Germany. Two different electoral systems are used to choose the Bundestag's 496 deputies. Half are elected by the "first past the post" system in effect in Great Britain and the United States—plurality vote in single-member districts. This is called the **first vote**. The other half are elected by proportional representation, the **second vote**. In the first vote, the individual candidate is featured; in the second vote, the party is paramount. Thus each voter casts two votes, one for an individual and one for a *Land* list put together by the party. The second vote is crucial because it determines the total number of seats a party receives in each *Land*. The party decides who is at the top of the list and who is at the bottom, a practice that enhances the role and importance of political parties in Germany.

Under the Weimar Republic, the left- and right-wing parties were separated by a yawning ideological chasm that produced the instability that led Germany down the path to totalitarian rule. Today the vast majority of German voters have crowded around the political center, choosing moderation over extremism.

Since 1949, the Federal Republic has had just two major parties, the center-left Social Democratic party (SDP) and the center-right (or conservative) Christian Democratic Union (CDU). The latter has formed a permanent alliance with the Bavarian Christian Social Union (CSU). In addition, the relatively small Free Democratic party (FDP) has shown remarkable staying power and has played a strategic role as the holder of the balance. Because the two major parties are frequently represented almost equally in the Bundestag, the Free Democrats have often controlled the decisive votes; as a result, the FDP's influence has been disproportionate to its size, and it has been a junior partner in most coalition governments.

Although the SDP is a socialist party and the CDU-CSU is a free-enterprise party, both are relatively moderate. Indeed, the two parties shared power from 1966 to 1969 in what was known as the Grand Coalition.

Smaller parties have a better chance of surviving in Germany than in Great Britain because half of the Bundestag is chosen by proportional representation. Even so, the party system was consciously designed to keep the number of parties at a reasonable level and to prevent small extremist groups from disrupting the orderly democratic process. Parties must receive a minimum of 5 percent of the national vote or win seats in a minimum of three electoral districts to gain Bundestag representation.

The most successful fringe party in the Federal Republic has been the Greens, a leftist party that focuses almost exclusively on environmental and antinuclear issues. In the spring of 1987, the Greens led a counterculture coalition in protest against a nationwide census. The ostensible issue was the right to privacy; the real issue was the authority of the state, which the Greens generally regard with fear and loathing.

In the January 1987 elections, a coalition of the CDU-CSU and the FDP won 53.4 percent of the popular vote and 266 (of a possible 496) seats in the Bundestag. The CDU-CSU actually dropped from 48.8 percent of the popular vote in 1983 to 44.3 percent in 1987. The little parties were the big winners: the FDP went from 7.0 percent in 1983 to 9.1 percent; the Greens gained the most, going from just 5.6 percent in 1983 to 8.3 percent. Later in the year, the CDU suffered heavy losses in *Land* elections in Schleswig-Holstein and Bremen. The Greens, however, were hampered by internal wrangling—historically, the curse of left-wing parties in Western Europe and elsewhere.

German Unification

The issue of German unification moved front and center following the dramatic toppling of the Communist regime in East Germany at the end of 1989. The conservative East German Christian Democratic Union, which won a plurality (41 percent) of the votes in March 1990, campaigned on a platform calling for rapid merger of the two German states. With his popularity high and rising, West German Chancellor Helmut Kohl went to East Germany and campaigned for the conservatives and for early unification. On October 3, 1990, the two German states formally merged into a single entity.

Two months later the first free, all-German elections in fifty-eight years were held. The center-right coalition by the ruling Christian Democrats received a strong mandate (almost 55 percent of the popular vote), capturing 398 of 662 Bundestag seats, a clear majority. The Social Democratic party (SDP) garnered 239 seats with only 33.5 percent of the votes. In January 1991, Chancellor Kohl organized a new German cabinet consisting of eleven CDU, four CSU, and five FDP ministers.

Unification added 16 million Germans to the Federal Republic literally overnight. What would be the political implications of suddenly incorporating so many people who had never lived under constitutional democracy or coped with a free-enterprise system? How long would the process take? How much would it cost? How would it be financed? What sort of compromises would be necessary? The answers to these questions are becoming increasingly clear, but the problems associated with making the two states into one and transforming the former East Germany from a police state with a centrally planned economy to a democratic society with a free-market economy remain daunting. The progress made so far and the difficulties being encountered are discussed in Chapter 6.

A Limited Government

Weighing the cumulative effects of the system prescribed by the Basic Law (federalism, the unique organization of the legislature, the carefully structured party system, the independent judiciary, the explicit guarantees of civil liberties), it becomes apparent that one of the main purposes of the Basic Law was to arrange the institutional furniture in postwar Germany to preclude a reincarnation of prewar Germany. Limited government, more than any other facet of constitutional democracy, was central to the drafters of the Basic Law, who deliberately sought to build into the system safeguards against the concentration of power that had caused so much turmoil leading up to the war.

The democratic performance of the Federal Republic of Germany since World War II has indeed been impressive. The experience of Weimar has not been repeated. Though the Weimar Republic was largely undone by severe economic distress, West Germany's rapid postwar recovery and sustained industrial growth since 1949 have frequently been described as an economic miracle. Spurred on by a remarkable economic resurgence and a firm commitment to constitutional government, the present generation of Germans has given democracy a new lease on life in a land where it was once thought to be unworkable. Moreover, West Germany's economic success no doubt spurred East Germans' dissatisfaction with a Communist regime that was unable to match "the other" Germany's performance or come close to providing a comparable standard of living. Germany had been a microcosm of the Cold War for over forty years; the collapse of Communism in East Germany thus symbolized the end of an era in international politics and a new beginning for the German people.

The European Community: An Embryonic State?

Any discussion of contemporary Western Europe would be incomplete without a look at the governing structures of the **European Community (EC)**. Since its inception as the customs union known as the Common Market in 1958, the EC has moved steadily toward economic integration and then economic unification, the abolition of all internal trading boundaries. The movement toward political integration has not kept pace, but there have been significant instances of foreign-policy coordination among EC members in recent years. The EC has also expanded from six to twelve full members. Germany, France, Italy, Belgium, the Netherlands, and Luxembourg, the original members, were later joined by the United Kingdom, Ireland, Denmark, Greece, Portugal, and Spain. It is almost certain that this process of enlargement has not ended. Members of the European Free Trade Association (EFTA)—in particular, Sweden, Finland, Austria, and Switzerland—sought membership in the EC in the early 1990s and appeared likely to be admitted. After 1989, when Communist rule in Eastern Europe gave way to democratization, several new states (Slovakia and the Czech Republic, Poland, and Hungary) were made associate members, a steppingstone to eventual admission as full members. These changes present the EC with new challenges as well as new opportunities.

The EC encompasses three separate legal entities: the European Coal and Steel Community (ECSC), the European Economic Community (EEC or Common Market), and the European Atomic Energy Community (Euratom). It is governed by institutions common to all, including the European Parliament, Council of Ministers, Commission, Court of Justice, and Court of Auditors. The Economic and Social Committee performs an advisory role.

The **EC Council of Ministers** has the final decision-making authority. It is composed of the foreign ministers of the member states, which in practice means that these states have not given up their right of self-determination or sovereignty. The **EC Commission** is the administrative arm. It is accountable to the European Parliament, which can dismiss the Commission by a vote of censure. It initiates proposals but must obtain the prior approval of the Council of Ministers before taking action on any new measures. Parliament shares the power of the purse with the Council of Ministers and has the right to reject the budget—a power it exercised in 1979 and 1984 because it disagreed with the Council's spending priorities.

An "assembly" (named the **European Parliament** in 1962) was envisioned in the original treaties setting up the EC, but the first election of members of the European Parliament (MEPs) did not take place until 1973. For several years delegates were appointed from their national parliaments; MEPs were directly elected for the first time in 1979. In 1984 the second EC direct elections involved 120 million voters in ten countries—60 percent of eligible voters. Turnout varied greatly, ranging from a high of 92 percent in Belgium (where voting is compulsory) to a low of 32 percent in the United Kingdom (where the electorate has always been lukewarm toward the EC).

With the accession to the EC of Greece in 1981 and Spain and Portugal in 1986, the number of MEPs rose from 410 to 518. The largest member states—Germany, France, the United Kingdom, and Italy—have eighty-one members each; the smallest—Denmark, Ireland, and Luxembourg—have sixteen, fifteen, and six, respectively.

The European Parliament is truly European. Its administration is located in

Luxembourg, weeklong plenary sessions take place monthly in Strasbourg, and the eighteen specialized committees normally meet for two weeks each month in Brussels. The proceedings in full sessions and in committees are simultaneously translated into the EC's nine official languages: English, Danish, Dutch, French, German, Greek, Italian, Spanish, and Portuguese.

The members of the European Parliament have represented a broad political spectrum. In the 1980s the largest political groups were the Socialists (165) and the Christian Democrats, or European People's Party (115). Center-right groups and Conservatives held the majority throughout the decade.

In addition to budgetary and economic matters, the special committees deal with a wide range of public policies in such areas as agriculture, energy, transport, and the environment. They also focus on economic relations with nonmember countries, unemployment, women's rights, and consumer protection, among other issues.

Parliament does not have the power to legislate, but in recent years it has become more assertive in dealing with the Commission. In particular, it has applied the powers of delay—effectively a veto—in drafting laws as a means of compelling the Commission to respond to its concerns before proposals go forward for final decision by the Council of Ministers. In 1984 the European Parliament adopted a blueprint for the EC's future organization. This plan for European union sought to enhance the legislative powers of Parliament, streamline decision making, and reduce the ability of the individual member states to impede the progress of the EC. Unsurprisingly, the twelve individual governments considered the plan too radical. Instead, in February 1986 they signed the Single European Act, which called for greater use of majority voting in the Council and a limited increase in Parliament's powers. It also set 1992 as the deadline for the full integration (or unification) of the EC economies.

The act went into effect in 1987 following approval by the national parliaments. The Council of Ministers now adopts most legislation by qualified majority, rather than unanimous, voting. EC members have a total of seventy-six votes, apportioned as follows: Germany, ten; France, ten; Italy, ten; the United Kingdom, ten; Spain, eight; Belgium, five; the Netherlands, five; Greece, five; Portugal, five; Denmark, three; Ireland, three; and Luxembourg, two. It takes fifty-four votes for a qualified majority and twenty-three to block a measure. In practice, this new procedure means that EC decision making has been streamlined—"the equivalent of upgrading the community's motor from steam power to gasoline."[12] Whereas before adoption of the Single European Act any member state could veto any measure, now it takes a minimum of three member states. Six of the seven small states would have to join forces to block a measure. Furthermore, three of the "big four"—Germany, France, Italy, and Great Britain—are needed to defeat a proposal.

Under the new law, Parliament has the right to reject or amend legislation, and the Council of Ministers can override its decisions only by a unanimous vote. Also, the importance of coordinating policy in two salient areas, foreign affairs and environmental protection, was formally recognized, giving higher visibility to Parliament's debates than in the past.

"Nevertheless," notes journalist Stephen Brookes, "Europe still lacks a genuine government; decisions are made through a cumbersome process that might be described as bureaucracy tempered by diplomacy, and national governments are holding firmly to the reins of their sovereignty."[13] Moreover, the executive branch—which, as we have seen, gives the seventeen-member Commission power to propose legislation and the Council of Ministers final authority to approve it—is widely criticized as undemocratic, especially by parties of the left.

In the late 1980s a great debate raged in Europe between the center-right and the left over the future of the EC. The issue was not whether a European union is desirable but rather what kind—one embracing the liberal, free-market policies associated with Margaret Thatcher and Helmut Kohl or one featuring bureaucratic, welfare-state policies typically favored by Socialist parties. The Commission president, Jacques Delors, a former French finance minister, advocated a tight economic unity with a "social dimension," including a "platform of guaranteed social rights" for workers. British Prime Minister Thatcher denounced Delors's "Marxist" vision, declaring in 1988: "We have not successfully rolled back the frontiers of the state in Britain only to see them reimposed at a European level, with a European superstate exercising new dominance from Brussels."[14]

But no amount of eloquence or determination may be enough to prevent the birth of a new technocratic superstate in Europe. Having spurned the Common Market in 1957, Great Britain has always been somewhat isolated within the EC. For a host of historical reasons, the British remain aloof from the Continent and continue to be viewed by other Europeans as less than fully committed to Europe. Economically, London has always objected to the protectionist Common Agricultural Policy (CAP), which places tariffs on agricultural imports and heavily subsidizes European (especially French) farmers. Only the Danes shared British ambivalence toward political unification in the early 1990s.

Elsewhere in the EC, public opinion strongly favored a European union by 1992: an overwhelming majority (75 percent or more) in France, Belgium, Luxembourg, Italy, Spain, Portugal, Greece, and Ireland, a solid majority in Germany and the Netherlands. This widespread acceptance of the idea of a united Europe represented a sea change in popular attitudes and suggested that the EC's economic benefits are eroding the strong nationalistic tendencies that have so long been the hallmark of European politics.

In conclusion, both the political superstructure and the economic foundation for a new European superpower now exist. Will the member states have the political will and popular support to take the final steps toward a united Europe? The obstacles to full-fledged union remain formidable. If Europe is ever ruled by a single political authority, the impetus will come from the economic dynamism of the most successful common market in modern history.

In December 1991 the heads of the twelve EC governments met at Maastricht, a town in the Netherlands, to hammer out the details of an agreement for the final phase of European economic and political integration. This summit meeting was at first billed as a make-or-break effort to achieve a single currency and a federal government. What happened at this conference and how the EC's success has changed the face of Europe—and created new problems for the Continent—will be discussed in the next chapter.

CONCLUSION

At present, the political systems of Western Europe display a remarkable consistency: all are based on the principle of government by consent of the governed, all are ruled by civilians who came to power by free elections based on universal suffrage and the secret ballot, and all protect personal freedoms and civil liberties from infringement by the state. This consistent pattern is no doubt one reason why the West has been able to move further and faster toward economic unity (and perhaps political union) than any region of the world. In Chapter 6 we explore the challenges Western Europe will face in the coming years and assess the future of the European Community as a response to these challenges.

KEY TERMS

constitutional monarchy	two-ballot system
parliamentary democracy	package vote
statutory law	*les grands corps*
member of Parliament (MP)	*les grandes écoles*
House of Commons	prefects
common law	tutelage system
custom	Senate
convention	divided executive
works of authority	*cohabitation*
parliamentary sovereignty	*Länder*
rule of law	Bundesrat
unitary system	Basic Law
fusion of powers	Bundestag
collective ministerial responsibility	chancellor
two-party system	*Fraktionen*
House of Lords	first vote
"first past the post" principle	second vote
corporatist model	European Community (EC)
Fifth Republic	EC Council of Ministers
plebiscite	EC Commission
National Assembly	European Parliament
dual executive	

STUDY QUESTIONS

1. Given a choice between serving as the president of the United States or the prime minister of Great Britain, which job would you prefer, and why?

2. How do the electoral systems of Great Britain, France, and Germany differ, and with what consequences?
3. In comparing and contrasting the constitutional powers of the French president and the British prime minister, what features should be stressed?
4. To what extent is the German political system based on the U.S. model? To what extent is it based on the British model? To what extent is it unique?

SUGGESTED READING

Conradt, David P. *The German Polity.* 5th ed. White Plains, N.Y.: Longman, 1992.

Jacobs, Dan N., et al. *Comparative Politics: Introduction to the Politics of the United Kingdom, France, Germany, and the Soviet Union.* Chatham, N.J.: Chatham House, 1983.

Norton, Philip. *The British Polity.* 2nd ed. White Plains, N.Y.: Longman, 1991.

Rodes, John E. *The Quest for Unity: Modern Germany, 1848–1970.* New York: Holt, 1971.

Safran, William. *The French Polity.* 3rd ed. White Plains, N.Y.: Longman, 1991.

Steiner, Jurg. *European Democracies.* White Plains, N.Y.: Longman, 1986.

Willis, F. Roy. *France, Germany and the New Europe, 1945–1967.* New York: Oxford University Press, 1968.

NOTES

1. Sydney Bailey, *British Parliamentary Democracy,* 3rd ed. (Westport, Conn.: Greenwood Press, 1978), pp. 4–5.
2. Alexander MacLeod, "Britain's Labour Party Faces Watershed Battle," *Christian Science Monitor,* Apr. 15, 1992, p. 1.
3. Bailey, *British Parliamentary Democracy,* p. 131.
4. Punnett, R. M., *British Government and Politics,* 5th ed. (Prospect Heights, Ill.: Waveland Press, 1990), p. 68.
5. See, for example, Craig R. Whitney, "British Race Is Neck and Neck at the Finish," *New York Times,* Apr. 9, 1992, p. A4.
6. "One More Defeat on Long Retreat," *Economist,* May 7, 1988, pp. 51–52.
7. Howard La Franchi, "French Say 'Non' to Traditional Political Parties," *Christian Science Monitor,* Mar. 24, 1992, p. 1.
8. Suzanne Berger, *The French Political System,* 3rd ed. (New York: Random House, 1974), p. 368.
9. Roy Macridis, ed., *Modern Political Systems: Europe,* 6th ed. (Englewood Cliffs, N.J.: Prentice Hall, 1986), p. 120.
10. The term *unification* here is used in preference to *reunification* because the latter term suggests a return to the Germany of Hitler's Third Reich, which would be misleading and provocative.
11. Guido Goldman, *The German Political System* (New York: Random House, 1974), p. 56.
12. Stephen Brookes, "Juggling the Scepter in a Unified Europe," *Insight,* June 19, 1989, p. 9.
13. Ibid., p. 8.
14. Ibid., p. 9.

6

A Common European House?

Europe emerged from World War II exhausted and supine. If the physical destruction was devastating, the psychological damage was nearly as bad. Clearly, the Old World was dead; the Great Powers who had so recently colonized the planet were now reduced to supplicants, and the task of reconstruction was immense.

One nightmare just ended, another loomed. No sooner had the smoke cleared from Europe's battlefields than a new war broke out. The antagonists were not the powers of Europe; the Cold War was a confrontation between the United States and the Soviet Union.

The main battleground, however, was Germany. The Soviet Union, which after the war had seized Eastern Europe and part of Germany, seemed to threaten Western Europe as well. The war-weary United States had quickly demobilized, leaving the Soviet Red Army in a dominant position on the Continent. If Stalin's armies suddenly began to roll westward, who could stop them?

The answer—the United States—created a predicament for Western Europe. It meant that European security now hinged on decisions made outside of Europe and that at the very least, the nations involved had lost not only some of their sovereignty and independence but also a large measure of control over their own destinies.

Moreover, several Western European countries, most notably Italy and France, had strong Communist parties. These parties, closely linked to Moscow, enjoyed wide popularity after the war because they had fought valiantly against fascism. (In France, for example, the Communist party won the largest vote totals in the 1946 elections.) Wherever the Communists gained control of a government, the Soviet Union gained another "satellite"—or so it appeared at the time.

In sum, the war had left the economies of Western Europe shattered and bereft of the financial and human resources needed for reconstruction, and the specter of communism seemed about to envelop the Continent. As the period between the two world wars had demonstrated, fear and despair can predispose societies to political extremism.

Despite its turbulent past, today Western Europe is one of the most prosperous regions of the world with the highest overall quality-of-life ratings (see Tables 6.1 and 6.2). The explanation for this "miracle" has two parts: American economic and security assistance and Western European self-help.

Western Europe's Economic Miracle

Immediately after World War II, the Truman administration made several key decisions regarding the future of Europe. First, it abandoned all isolationist postures and assumed primary responsibility for stimulating economic recovery

Table 6.1   Economic Profile: Western Europe and the United States

	Gross National Product (GNP), 1991 (millions of U.S. dollars)	Real Growth Rate 1980–1991 (percent)	GNP Per Capita, 1991 (U.S. dollars)	GNP Per Capita Growth Rate, 1980–1991 (percent)
European Community	5,973,400			
Germany	1,516,785	2.3	23,650	2.2
France	1,167,749	2.3	20,600	1.8
Italy	1,072,198	2.4	18,580	2.1
United Kingdom	963,696	2.8	16,750	2.6
Ireland	37,738	2.4	10,780	2.2
Belgium	192,370	2.2	19,300	2.1
Netherlands	278,839	2.1	18,560	1.5
Luxembourg	11,761	4.2	31,080	3.8
Denmark	121,695	2.2	23,660	2.1
Spain	486,614	2.3	12,460	2.9
Portugal	58,451	3.2	5,620	2.7
Greece	65,504	1.6	6,230	1.2
European Free Trade Association	833,033			
Sweden	218,934	2.0	25,490	1.7
Norway	102,885	2.5	24,160	2.2
Finland	121,982	2.9	24,400	2.5
Iceland	5,814	2.4	10,780	1.3
Austria	157,528	2.3	20,380	2.1
Switzerland	225,890	2.2	33,510	1.6
United States	5,686,038	3.1	22,560	2.1

Source: Data from the World Bank, *The World Bank Atlas* (Washington, D.C.: International Bank for Reconstruction and Development/The World Bank, 1992). Published by Oxford University Press, Inc., New York.

Table 6.2 Population Size and Quality of Life Indicators: Western Europe and the United States

	Population, 1991 (thousands)	Growth Rate 1980–1991 (percent)	Life Expectancy, 1991 (years)	Infant Mortality Rate (per 1,000 live births)
European Community	345,003	0.0–0.6	75–78	9–15
Germany	79,632	0.1	77	9
France	56,681	0.5	77	9
Italy	57,719	0.2	78	10
United Kingdom	57,536	0.2	76	10
Ireland	3,502	0.2	75	9
Belgium	9,968	0.1	76	11
Netherlands	15,023	0.5	77	9
Luxembourg	378	0.4	75	10
Denmark	5,143	0.0	75	10
Spain	39,045	0.4	76	10
Portugal	10,393	0.6	75	15
Greece	10,083	0.4	77	14
European Free Trade Association	32,574	0.2–1.1	76–78	7–11
Sweden	8,588	0.3	78	7
Norway	4,259	0.4	77	10
Finland	4,999	0.4	76	8
Iceland	258	1.1	78	9
Austria	7,730	0.2	76	10
Switzerland	6,740	0.6	78	8
United States	252,040	0.9	76	11

Source: Data from the World Bank, *The World Bank Atlas* (Washington, D.C.: International Bank for Reconstruction and Development/The World Bank, 1992). Published by Oxford University Press, Inc., New York.

on the Continent. This decision took the form of the European Recovery Program, better known as the **Marshall Plan**, approved by Congress in 1948. Second, it determined on a course of reconciliation rather than retribution toward Germany. Third, it made a long-term commitment to Western European security by creating the **North Atlantic Treaty Organization (NATO)**. This initiative removed any lingering doubts in Europe as to whether the United States would risk war to defend democracy and freedom on the other side of the Atlantic.

Fourth, and perhaps least appreciated at the time, the United States encouraged economic cooperation among the Western European democracies. The first manifestation of this policy was the **Organization of European Economic**

Cooperation (OEEC), set up to administer Marshall Plan aid. The OEEC countries pledged themselves

> to combine their economic strength, to join together to make the fullest collective use of their individual capacities and potentialities, to increase their production, to develop and modernize their industrial and agricultural equipment, reduce progressive barriers to trade amongst themselves, promote full employment and restore or maintain the stability of their economies and general confidence in their national currencies.[1]

In 1961 the Organization for Economic Cooperation and Development (OECD) replaced the OEEC. The twenty-four nation OECD included both EC and EFTA member states, plus the United States, Canada, and Japan.

As things turned out, this lofty rhetoric foretold developments that would transform Western Europe from a blighted region into the world's most dynamic trading bloc.

The OEEC was followed by the creation of the **European Coal and Steel Community (ECSC)** in 1952. The ECSC, which established a framework for sharing strategic resources, set the stage for formation of the **European Economic Community (EEC)** in 1958. The resulting Common Market was a customs union, meaning that the six charter members (France, West Germany, Italy, Belgium, the Netherlands, and Luxembourg) removed tariffs on trade among themselves and set common tariffs on trade with others. This became the nucleus of the larger **European Community (EC)**, which now includes Great Britain, Denmark, Ireland, Spain, Portugal, and Greece.

France, West Germany, and Italy were all undergoing an "economic miracle" during the 1950s. The miracle was not that they recovered but that they did so faster than anybody expected. Within a decade of the war's end, industry was up and running again, granaries were bulging, and roads, railways, and bridges were rebuilt. This rising tide lifted all boats—the resurgence of the bigger nations boosted economic growth in the smaller ones.

But along with prosperity came new problems. As industry became increasingly automated and the work force shifted from manufacturing to the service sector, the challenges facing the governments of the region changed rapidly, and the very pace of change itself became a major challenge. At the same time, the European Community came of age, creating new opportunities for the member nations but also bringing new tensions and necessitating sometimes painful adjustments. And just as Europe appeared to be regaining its historical role as the world's foremost economic engine, new challenges were arising in Asia (see Figure 6.1). A dynamic and potentially dominant China, following Japan's emergence as an economic superpower, served notice that Europe and North America would face formidable economic competition in the coming decades.

We will return to the EC later in this chapter when we assess the prospects for Western Europe, but first we will discuss some problems associated with the post-industrial stage of development in Great Britain, France, and Germany.

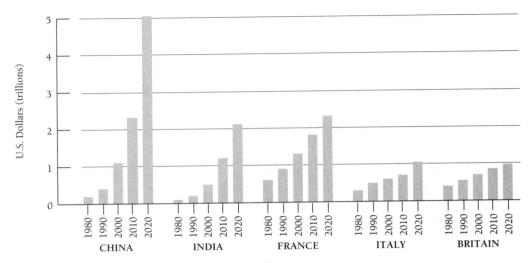

Figure 6.1 Projected gross domestic product for China, India, and certain Western European nations, 1980–2020 (1980 constant U.S. dollars).

Note: Projection for China assumes a 7 percent growth rate 1980–1985 and 8 percent thereafter; for India, 5.5 percent 1980–1985 and 7 percent thereafter; other countries, average annual rates as in 1970–1982.
Source: Economist/International Monetary Fund.

In many respects, the problems these countries are encountering typify the whole region.

The Problems of Postindustrial Society

Students in the United States will relate easily to the concept of a **postindustrial society**. The Industrial Revolution brought a major shift in the economic foundations of both American and European society. The transition from farming to manufacturing entailed a massive demographic shift from rural to urban settings—a shift accompanied by secularization, the breakup of the extended family, and a sharp rise in the need for governmental regulation and intervention (particularly in such areas as public utilities and social services). The problems associated with this "revolution" were offset by major advances in living standards owing to general affluence, political gains by organized labor (such as the right to strike), and consumer-related technological innovation.

Economically, postindustrial society is characterized by a whole collection of shifts: from the manufacturing to the service sector (banking, insurance, advertising, marketing, management, and so on), from domestic to international markets, from a cash-and-carry economy to one based on credit and installment buying, from one-income to two-income families (which means that a very high percentage of adults under age 65 are, or wish to be, gainfully employed), and from a saving culture to a consuming culture. Postindustrialism also brings overdevelopment or **reverse development** (outmigration from cities to suburbs, leaving slums and deteriorating schools, services, and tax bases); these concepts now deserve a place alongside underdevelopment in economics texts.

Overdevelopment is exemplified by the *megalopolis*: concentrations of people and urban sprawl. Such cities as London, Paris, Rome, Milan, Essen, Madrid, and Athens can be considered contemporary Western European megalopolises. The dynamics of economic growth in postindustrial nations lure people to big cities in search of high-paying jobs, professional opportunities, social status, and cultural activities. But as cities become more and more overcrowded, population growth typically outruns the capacity of local government to maintain adequate police and fire protection, sanitation, schools, hospitals, streets, parks, and other amenities.

With overcrowding comes a host of social problems, including traffic congestion, air pollution, crime, juvenile delinquency, drug abuse, high divorce rates, domestic violence, homelessness, and increased stress, which can exacerbate all the other problems. A related issue is immigration, which has generated fears of an unbridled surge of newcomers from the east (the Slavic countries) and the south (North Africa). Legal immigration to the twelve EC countries was estimated at 400,000 persons annually in the early 1990s; another three to four million illegal immigrants were already there.[2] This rapid and unprecedented influx is costly for host governments (many immigrants need health care, housing, education, and other social services), disruptive for communities, and potentially destabilizing. It stands to reason that people are more likely to resent foreigners if they already feel cramped for space or squeezed for jobs.

One reason for the job crunch is that postindustrial societies have failed to solve the economic problems associated with the capitalist business cycle. Since 1970, unemployment rates have varied from a low of less than 1.0 percent of the total labor force (West Germany, 1970) to a high of more than 21.1 percent (Spain, 1985). In the mid-1980s, the United Kingdom, the Netherlands, and France (plus Belgium and Spain) all hit double-digit unemployment (see Table 6.3). Similarly, inflation rates have fluctuated from as low as 2.2 percent to highs of 21.3 (Italy, 1980) and 24.2 percent (United Kingdom, 1975). Germany and the Netherlands have had relatively stable inflation rates, but the United Kingdom, France, and Italy have been on inflation roller coasters (see Table 6.4). These ups and downs tend to erode consumer confidence in the economy and voter confidence in the government. A dilemma that has plagued postindustrial democracies is the teeter-totter effect of disinflation versus full-employment policies: falling unemployment tends to be accompanied by rising inflation, whereas price stabilization (low inflation) is usually associated with rising unemployment.

Politically, postindustrial nations face problems arising from their past economic and technological successes. As society changes, new circumstances give rise to new political forces. For example, the increase in life expectancy (combined with an early retirement option for many employees) has created a powerful new interest group consisting of senior citizens and retirees who are demanding more and better social services. The fact that most households now have two

Table 6.3 Unemployment Rates in the Leading Industrial Democracies, 1970–1990 (percentage of total labor force)

	1970	1975	1980	1985	1990
Sweden	1.5	1.6	2.0	2.8	1.5
Japan	1.1	1.9	2.0	2.6	2.1
Germany	0.8	3.6	2.9	7.2	4.9
United Kingdom	3.0	4.3	6.4	11.2	6.8
United States	4.8	8.3	7.0	7.1	5.4
Netherlands	1.0	5.2	6.0	10.6	7.5
Italy	5.3	5.8	7.5	9.6	10.3
France	2.5	4.0	6.3	10.2	8.9

Sources: OECD Economic Outlook, vol. 48, no. 12 (December 1990) and vol. 51, no. 6 (June 1992).

breadwinners means that even an expanding economy is no guarantee against unemployment (and underemployment). Minorities and first-time workers tend to be hit hardest by joblessness. University-educated people may be forced to take low-paying menial jobs for which they are overqualified. Moreover, immigrants are willing, even eager, to take dirty jobs and work for low wages if it means being able to provide food and shelter for their families.[3] The consequences are disillusionment and resentment.

Threats to the environment also give rise to new policy problems: air and water pollution, noise abatement, chemical and nuclear waste disposal, deforestation, and wildlife conservation are but a few examples. Air polllution is largely an urban scourge—it is caused by emissions from automobiles, mass transit vehicles, and smokestack industries. But the cost of cleaning the air (and of most other environmental ameliorations) must ultimately be borne by all taxpayers and consumers no matter where they happen to live. One of the most fundamental

Table 6.4 Inflation Rates in the Leading Industrial Democracies, 1970–1990 (percent)

	1970	1975	1980	1985	1990
Sweden	10.6	11.7	13.7	7.4	10.5
Japan	7.7	11.8	7.7	2.0	3.1
Germany	3.4	5.9	5.4	2.2	2.7
United Kingdom	6.4	24.2	18.0	6.1	9.5
United States	5.9	9.1	13.5	3.6	5.4
Netherlands	3.7	10.2	6.5	2.2	2.5
Italy	5.0	17.1	21.3	9.2	6.5
France	5.9	11.8	13.3	5.8	3.4

Sources: International Monetary Fund, *Government Finance Statistics Yearbook, 1991* (Washington, D.C.: IMF, 1991), pp. 116–119; *OECD Economic Outlook,* vol. 50, no. 12 (December 1991).

political questions in any society is who gets what, when, and how; an equally fundamental question is who pays what, when, and how.

The situation in Eastern Europe, where the former Communist regimes long operated factories and power plants without regard for the ecological consequences, is much worse than in Western Europe, but given the compact geography of the Continent, there is no way to prevent air and water pollution in the east from spilling over into the west. Estimates of the cleanup costs are staggering. In eastern Germany alone, studies indicated that more than $125 billion would be needed to bring it into line with West German standards.[4] The EC countries are trying to cope by pledging to stabilize carbon-dioxide emissions at 1990 levels by the year 2000. Even such a seemingly modest step is politically controversial, however, because it places potentially unbearable burdens on the least wealthy European countries and may make EC membership for Eastern European countries impossible for years to come.

A fundamental issue facing postindustrial states is defining the role of the state in the economy, the environment, and society. The free-market trend in the West began with the election of Margaret Thatcher's Conservative government in the U.K. in 1979 and was reinforced by the administrations of U.S. President Ronald Reagan and West German Chancellor Helmut Kohl. The political pendulum seemed to be swinging the other way in France, however, where François Mitterrand, a Socialist, was elected president in May 1981 on a pro-labor, anti-business platform. Mitterrand nationalized industrial firms and banks, pushed for wage hikes, and ran up large budget deficits. The results were high inflation, trade deficits, industrial stagnation, and faltering economic growth. Mitterrand then imposed a tough austerity program. In 1986 a center-right coalition won control of the Assembly from the Socialists, obliging Mitterrand to name neo-Gaullist Jacques Chirac as prime minister. Two years later Mitterrand won a second seven-year term as president on a platform that was barely distinguishable from that of the center-right.

The taming of the French Socialists points to one other feature of postindustrial politics: a narrowing of the differences between parties of the right and parties of the left. Extremist parties at both ends of the political spectrum fell by the wayside—at least momentarily. Ideology was downplayed. Government and opposition alike advocated pragmatic solutions to economic and social problems. These trends appeared to reflect a middle-of-the-road popular consensus. In the early 1990s, however, the picture began to change again. The extreme left was discredited by the failure of communism in Europe, but the extreme right was experiencing a revival in France, Germany, and elsewhere.

The Core Countries

The problems faced by Great Britain, France, and Germany are not identical. Nonetheless, many of these problems are present in all three countries, which suggests that they are rooted in certain general conditions rather than circumstances unique or specific to a particular society.

Great Britain

The most persistent policy problem in Great Britain for much of the postwar period has been the disappointing performance of the economy. After World War II, the British people were asked to sacrifice for the future: those with more should sacrifice more. A welfare state would be created with the available resources—that would be society's reward. Marshall Plan funds would be used for capital investment, not current consumption. These policies were widely hailed by outside observers as a shining example of the regenerative powers of democracy. Yet the long-run result was not an economic miracle as occurred in West Germany and Italy but rather economic decay.

So while West Germany and Italy and even France experienced rapid economic recovery, Great Britain stagnated. When OPEC oil prices skyrocketed in the early 1970s, inflation soared in Western Europe. In Great Britain, the annual inflation rate exceeded 20 percent at one point. British voters began wondering whether any government, Conservative or Labour, could revive the economy from its decades-long doldrums. The main bright spot for the British economy in the 1970s was the discovery of oil and gas in the North Sea. By 1980, Great Britain had become basically self-sufficient in energy, whereas France and West Germany continued to be heavily dependent on energy imports. Both of these latter countries began to experience falling growth rates, business slowdowns, declining tax revenues, and rising inflation.

A new economic phenomenon called **stagflation**—stagnating growth accompanied by high inflation—appeared in Great Britain. According to **Keynesian economic theory**, market economies can be expected to go through business cycles of boom and bust. In periods of rapid growth, inflation is a problem (prescribed cure: budget cuts, higher taxes and interest rates); in periods of recession, unemployment is a problem (prescribed cure: deficit spending, lower taxes and interest rates). But in the 1970s the British economy was hit by inflation and recession *at the same time.*

Full employment has been a top priority of British public policy ever since the worldwide depression of the 1930s. Indeed, the jobless rate is a key measure of governmental performance in Great Britain. Starting in the 1970s, however, unemployment inched steadily upward, and by the mid-1980s a record 3.2 million Britons were unemployed. Public opinion polls reinforced the impression that the state of the economy was a potential time bomb for the government.

Yet the British economy bounced back in the 1980s under the free-market policies of Prime Minister Margaret Thatcher's Conservative government. In June 1987, British voters gave the "Iron Lady" a record third consecutive term as prime minister, in part because Conservative economic policies seemed to be working.[5] The official index of leading economic indicators (stock prices, interest rates, housing starts) rose faster during the six months leading up to the election than at any time since the early 1970s.[6] By 1988 the growth rate had climbed to 4.5 percent, but there were storm clouds gathering: the trade imbalance was double that of the previous year, and inflation had crept past 6 percent. Although unemployment dropped to 5.9 percent in 1989 (the lowest in a decade), recession returned in 1990, with inflation approaching double digits and unemployment on the rise. In March 1993 the government of John Major announced a jobs program to counter the 10.5 percent unemployment rate and austerity measures to bring down the $72.5 billion debt (8 percent of GDP). More than a decade of Conservative policies had not cured Britain's economic ills.

Thatcherism Reappraised   In 1979, Thatcher had focused on one fundamental question: What is the proper balance between government intervention and free enterprise? She blamed Britain's sagging economy on the excesses of a cradle-to-grave welfare state in which an ever-expanding public sector encroached on and undercut the private sector. Elect a Conservative government, she vowed, and things will be different.

Under the banner of **Thatcherism**, the Conservatives kept their promise: industry was denationalized, business was given investment incentives, taxes were cut, and welfare spending was curtailed. Coincidentally or not, the British economy did recover.

As for the quality of life, however, the picture was not so rosy. "Amid a revivified economy, Britain's decaying inner cities are the worst blot on eight years of Tory government," proclaimed *The Economist* in 1987.[7] In the 1987 campaign, Thatcher promised to rehabilitate the inner cities, correct chronic housing problems, liberate schools from heavy-handed local controls, and reform local taxes. But some of these problems proved intractable, and at least one of her solutions, the poll tax, provoked popular wrath.

Violence and civil strife in Northern Ireland continued to divert attention, energy, and resources from domestic ills. Militant Irish nationalists, claiming to represent the Roman Catholic minority, have waged a guerrilla war against British rule since the late 1960s. The Provisional Irish Republican Army (IRA) uses terrorist tactics to achieve its objective of separation from Great Britain and union with the Republic of Ireland. Such a union would transform the Protestant majority in Ulster into a minority in Roman Catholic Ireland. Militant Ulster Protestants have also used terrorism against Catholics in Northern Ireland. An end to the bloody deadlock, which had cost nearly three thousand lives by 1990, is nowhere in sight.

Nor is the IRA likely to abandon the struggle. In February 1991, IRA terrorists carried out a mortar attack on 10 Downing Street, the prime minister's official residence, while the cabinet was in session there. Although nobody was hurt, the terrorists had come close to decapitating the British government. Heroic efforts by Peter Brooke, Britain's secretary for Northern Ireland, led to a new round of talks in April and May 1991 among all parties except Sinn Fein, the political wing of the outlawed IRA, but the talks broke down the following July, and Northern Ireland remains a combat zone.

Foreign and defense policy has fueled a good deal of controversy in Great Britain. For many years, other European nations (particularly France) denounced

Great Britain's "special relationship" with the United States. The fact that London chose not to join the Common Market in 1958 underscored the British desire to remain aloof from the Continent. When Britain did apply for membership in the early 1960s, French President Charles de Gaulle vetoed it. Not until de Gaulle was gone from the scene was Great Britain finally admitted, along with Ireland and Denmark, in 1973. But lingering doubts about British loyalties and London's own ambivalence toward the Common Market, reinforced by Margaret Thatcher's personal anti-European stance, continued to obstruct efforts to build bridges (figuratively speaking) across the English Channel. Only under John Major has Great Britain's policy been oriented toward rather than against the European Community.

Public debates have raged over nuclear weapons and defense spending as well. Behind them all lay a fundamental question: What is the proper allocation of resources between national security and domestic programs? The Conservative party emphasized the need for a strong national defense to protect British institutions and national interests. The Labour party stressed domestic programs and argued that a nation's security cannot be measured by the size of its military forces alone. The end of the Cold War and the collapse of the Soviet Union pushed this debate into the background by the time the next parliamentary elections were held in 1992. Ironically, the Labour party had been so badly burned by its radical demand for unilateral disarmament in 1987 that it reversed its position after 1989, reassuring British voters of its commitment to a British nuclear deterrent.

End of an Era: a "Major" Change?   When John Major succeeded Margaret Thatcher in November 1990, he faced two immediate political tests. First, he had to reunite a divided Conservative party after a bruising intraparty battle precipitated by former defense secretary Michael Heseltine's decision to challenge Thatcher for party leadership. Thatcher resigned after Heseltine won enough votes at the Conservative party conference to deny Thatcher a first-round victory. It was then that John Major, chancellor of the exchequer and a Thatcher protégé, and Foreign Secretary Douglas Hurd challenged Heseltine in the second round of balloting. Major was elected as a kind of compromise between Heseltine and Hurd. Thus his first real test was to unite the party.

Major's second test was to show that he could lead the country in rapidly changing times. Major's primary asset in the contest to become head of the party—his image of blandness—was also his greatest potential liability as prime minister. He had to prove that he could be decisive. At first he seemed uncertain whether to continue Thatcher's policies or to chart a new course. With parliamentary elections approaching, the Labour party went on the offensive. Meanwhile, Major was drawing fire from members of his own party. For example, having decided to drop Thatcher's hated poll tax, he wavered on what should take its place, which led to protests from within his own party. But then the government unveiled a new tax plan, devised and presented by Michael Heseltine, whose challenge to Thatcher's leadership had forced her resignation. This signaled Major's first clear break with the Thatcher legacy.

A far bigger surprise came in June 1991, when he informed members of his ruling Conservative party that he would attend the European Community summit at Maastricht and play a constructive role in negotiating a **European Monetary Union (EMU)** treaty. Declaring that "Britain must not be sidelined," Major clearly sided with the pro-EC faction against the antifederalist Bruges Group, headed by Thatcher. Although he did not commit Great Britain to a Europe-wide currency immediately, his acceptance in principle of a monetary union cleared the way for the next giant step toward a unified Europe. This strategy was designed, in Major's words, to prevent Britain from remaining Europe's "odd man out." Perhaps of equal importance to Major's political future was the fact that it laid to rest the charge that he was Margaret Thatcher's puppet.

The British thus entered the final decade of the twentieth century with considerable self-confidence. Despite a nagging recession and persistently high unemployment, Great Britain had emerged from the 1980s with a relatively robust economy. Under Major's leadership, the British had played a key role in the Gulf War against Iraq and were no longer disconnected from the affairs of Europe. One of the most hotly debated issues in the 1992 campaign focused on whether to reform the National Health System, with Labour charging that the Tories wanted to privatize health care. But Major promised not to dismantle the system, and the voters responded positively. That health care was a big issue is significant for two reasons. First, it shows that there are domestic problems in Great Britain, as in every society, that cannot be solved simplistically—the problems are endemic, and the solutions are never final. Second, apart from the ineluctable problem of Northern Ireland, the United Kingdom does not face internal challenges that threaten to overwhelm its political institutions.

France

After World War II, the French adopted an economic strategy that was exactly the opposite of Great Britain's. The working class was made to sacrifice most, while the rich got richer. Marshall Plan aid was used in part for current consumption and indirectly to pay for the Indochina War (which cost more than the Marshall Plan contributed). General de Gaulle rejected the proposal of Prime Minister Pierre Mendes-France to break inflation after the Liberation, so the value of the franc plummeted. Economists in France and abroad wrote the country off. Yet after an initial expansion of the Communist vote in a burst of working-class anger, France eventually did achieve its own economic miracle of sorts, and it is now richer than Britain.

The French postwar economic miracle gave way to a time of troubles in the 1980s. By odd coincidence, France's economic fortunes started to sputter just as the British economy began to crank up. France's difficulties deepened under Socialist economic reforms aimed at enlarging the role of the state and cutting the size of the private sector. France under Mitterrand and Great Britain under Thatcher were moving in opposite directions in the early 1980s.

The Short-lived "Rupture with Capitalism"   In February 1982, the Socialist government nationalized nine major industrial groups and thirty-six banks and lending institutions. (Two failing steel companies had been taken over by the government the previous November.) The nine industrial groups, which employed 760,000 workers in all, represented 20 percent of the French market and 15 percent of France's exports. After the new nationalizations, the public sector accounted for 30 percent of industrial sales and nearly a quarter of the French work force. In addition, the state gained near-total control of France's banking and credit systems. The cost of this expensive **"rupture with capitalism"** was 43 billion francs.

The theory behind the nationalization program was enhancement of the power of the state vis-à-vis the economy—not as an end in itself but as a means to several interrelated ends, including rapid capital formation, economic modernization, and state-managed growth. The plan foundered when the government allowed state-owned enterprises to pursue their own strategies rather than conforming to a central plan. At the same time, the Mitterrand government, anxious to avoid embarrassment, poured money into the newly nationalized industries through budget allocations and loans from state-owned banks. These transfusions depleted the treasury but did not revive the "patients," and one industry after another sank into the rising sea of red ink.

To his credit, President Mitterrand then encouraged state enterprises to seek private investment capital by creating special stock certificates that could be sold on the open market without jeopardizing public ownership. Private capital flowed into public firms in torrents (20 billion francs in 1985). By the 1986 elections, the Socialist government had for all practical purposes abandoned its love affair with *dirigiste* (state-centered) economic policies.

But the consequences of Mitterrand's false start in 1981 could not be swept under the rug. The budget deficit rose from 0.4 percent of GDP when the Socialists took over to 3.0 percent the following year. Inflation remained high in France when it was falling elsewhere in Western Europe, and a sudden trade deficit mushroomed to 94 billion francs in 1982. In the face of these rapidly deteriorating conditions, Mitterrand bit the bullet: in 1983 the government reversed engines and adopted a tough austerity program (called "rigor" by crow-eating Socialist politicians).

The austerity measures involved holding down wages, curbing budget increases, and strictly controlling the money supply. But the response was sluggish. France's growth rate fell below that of most other Western European nations, while inflation stayed high. At the same time, France endured several consecutive "double deficits" (simultaneous budget and trade shortfalls). The chronic trade deficit was particularly troubling because it suggested a loss of French competitiveness in the world market.

To make matters worse, unemployment climbed steadily under Socialist rule. Even a state-mandated job creation program had little effect. If the Socialist party, with its strong commitment to the working class, could not even guarantee jobs for people who wanted to work, the voters were almost certain to punish them at the polls.

From **Cohabitation** *to Crisis of Legitimacy?*   With the economy still in a slump, the Socialists lost the 1986 election to a center-right coalition headed by Jacques Chirac. The French Constitution, with its unique dual executive, was now put to one of its most severe tests: how power could be shared by two leaders with completely different philosophies—an arrangement that came to be called *cohabitation.* Prime Minister Chirac sought to denationalize firms and banks that the Socialists had brought under state control in 1981 and 1982. His more general aim was to deregulate the economy and return the initiative to the private sector.

To no one's surprise, *cohabitation* amounted to little more than treading water until the 1988 presidential election. President Mitterrand campaigned for reelection on a pragmatic, market-oriented platform that closely resembled that of his principal center-right opponent, Prime Minister Chirac. Mitterrand promised voters that there would be no repeat of the failed socialist experiment of 1981—no nationalizations, no new corporate taxes, no quixotic measures like his earlier attempt at shortening the workweek.

Voters believed him, and Mitterrand won a second term with 54 percent of the popular vote. Pollsters predicted that the Socialists would win a clear majority (289 seats) in National Assembly elections the following month, but they were wrong. The center-right parties captured 271 seats to the Socialists' 276, leaving Mitterrand's party thirteen seats short of a majority.

At first glance the results seemed ambiguous, even contradictory. But appearances can be deceiving. According to one interpretation, there was a postindustrial logic at work in these elections. "Forget the razor-close results and confused political maneuvering," advised one close observer. "France wants to be governed from the center."[8] An overwhelming majority of French voters rejected both the extreme-right fascism of Jean-Marie Le Pen's National Front and the extreme-left Marxism of the French Communist party.

> Although they split right down the middle with no party gaining an outright majority, experts say voters do not want renewed right-left dueling. They are instead calling for a bipartisan approach on major issues, a pro-European, pro–Atlantic alliance foreign policy, and a free-market economic policy checked by a strong social system.
>
> This message is spreading not just in France, but through Europe. With nuances, both socialist Spain and conservative Britain promote the virtues of NATO and capitalism. The old ideological battles between a collectivist and individualistic vision of the world slowly is slipping into history's dustbin.[9]

Indeed, it did appear that business was not upset by the prospect of a new Socialist-led government. One piece of evidence: whereas after the Socialist victory in 1981 share values fell so fast that trading had to be suspended, after the 1988 elections the stock market rose.

President Mitterrand's moderation in domestic policy was matched by prudence in foreign policy, including firm support for NATO (in contrast to the Gaullist tradition, which stressed strategic self-reliance and a special role vis-à-vis the two superpowers). At the same time, Mitterrand pursued defense policies long popular in France, bolstering the nation's independent nuclear strike force (the third largest in the world) while promoting strategic and conventional arms reduction in Europe and beyond. Under Mitterrand, France played a leadership role in the European Community as well.

With full economic integration of the EC slated for 1992, President Mitterrand's highest priority was to prepare France for a competitive future, one without the protectionism and state intervention (*dirigisme*) that have been hallmarks of the French economy. It was one of history's ironies that this job fell to a Socialist leader; it was a sign of the times that he seemed to relish the prospect.

Both NATO and the EC have been vital to France as insurance against a resurgence of German nationalism. A Germany militarily dependent on NATO and economically tied to the EC poses little threat to its neighbors. Ingrained fear of Germany might have led to Franco-German tensions in 1989 when the prospect of German unification suddenly seemed possible. But Mitterrand, calm and reassuring in his demeanor, did much to counteract alarmism over this potentially explosive issue. At the end of 1989, Mitterrand's government endorsed the "two plus four" negotiations (involving the two Germanys and the four wartime Allies) that paved the way for German unification in 1990.

Despite the resounding vote for moderate parties and policies, the surprising popularity of right-wing extremist Jean-Marie Le Pen in the 1988 presidential race struck a discordant note. Le Pen, leader of the National Front party, won 14.4 percent of the vote on the first ballot. He campaigned on a nationalistic and racist platform that critics denounced as a new form of fascism. The target of Le Pen's demagoguery was the influx of immigrants from France's former colonies in Africa and Asia; his vehement anti-immigration stance appealed to an odd assortment of conservatives and reactionaries. But the Le Pen phenomenon was not just an aberration. As *The Economist* noted, "The National Front has a mixed ancestry: interwar fascists, wartime collaborators, monarchists, Catholic ultras, Algérie Française diehards, smalltown populists. Yet today's extreme right is also a product of modern France."[10]

The rise of the National Front was a reflection of social and economic troubles facing France in the late 1980s and early 1990s. Unemployment and underemployment aggravated racial and ethnic tensions in French society, as did urban overcrowding, rising crime rates, drug abuse, and traffic congestion. There is likely a connection between the jobless rate and the rise of racial bigotry and xenophobia in France and other Western European countries that can be traced back to this period (see Table 6.5).

The staying power of Le Pen's ultra-right National Front is a source of alarm to the traditional parties of both the left and the right in France. Le Pen's party captured 30 percent of the vote in a municipal election near Paris in March 1990. (Two months later, vandals destroyed tombs at a Jewish cemetery in the

Table 6.5 Immigration and Politics in Western Europe, 1986–1993

Country	Situation
Germany	4.4 million foreigners (just over 7 percent of the population); Frankfurt population 24 percent foreign; influx of several hundred thousand asylum seekers from former Yugoslavia and other Slavic countries in 1991 and 1992; violent attacks on immigrants in the former GDR.
France	9 million immigrants in early 1990s (including children of immigrants); over half the number of foreigners living in France arrived from Africa (mainly North Africa); Le Pen's right-wing National Party has played on rising French xenophobia.
Netherlands	During 1987 Asian refugee wave, 300 of 700 towns refused government requests to accept them; 85 percent of Dutch polled wanted immigration limits set.
Great Britain	Anti-immigration sentiment subsiding; influx of immigrants from former colonies peaked in mid-1970s, declined since.
Italy	Illegal immigrants arriving at rate of 50,000 a year; total approaching 1 million; 100,000 legally registered non-EC immigrants (40,000 from Libya, Tunisia, Morocco, and Ethiopia).

town of Carpentras, signaling an upsurge in anti-Semitism.) But the heaviest blow to the traditional parties—including the Socialists and the center-right RPR and UDF—came in local and regional elections in the spring of 1992 when approximately one-third of the voters cast protest ballots (split about evenly between the National Front on the right and two environmental parties on the left). The RPR and UDF barely outpolled these fringe parties, and the ruling Socialists were embarrassed most of all, garnering only 18 percent of the vote.

Coping with changes both domestically and in Europe presents a major challenge to France in the coming decade. Immigration, especially from North Africa, is changing the character of French society, making it less and less homogenous and creating problems of assimilation. Dealing with these problems is costly in economic and cultural terms; not dealing with them may be even costlier in political terms, as the rise of the ultra-right attests. At the same time, the unification of Germany inevitably raises old fears in France, which lost three wars to Germany between 1871 and 1945. The Franco-German agreement to create a joint army corps separate from NATO reflects France's anxiety over the twin prospects of German resurgence and American retrenchment.

Germany

After World War II, the Allies imposed deflationary policies on West Germany (France rejected them). The Germans in turn imposed austerity and hard work on themselves—in contrast to the British, who fell to taking more and more from the state while giving less and less. Helped in part by the American decision to extend Marshall Plan aid to Germany, the German economy revived very quickly. In short order, the Federal Republic created a welfare state far more lavish than anything in Britain or France. The West Germans came out winners.

In the 1950s, West Germany's economy surged ahead of most of its neighbors' on the Continent (Italy alone kept pace for a time). In the decades that followed, Germany became the standard by which other Western industrial democracies measured their own economic performance. West Germany's extraordinary and sustained record of economic growth would not have been possible without an equally extraordinary record of political stability that lasted through the 1980s.

The Dawn of the Kohl Era   In 1982 the center-right Christian Democratic Union–Christian Socialist Union (CDU-CSU) formed a coalition government with the Free Democrats (FDP), who decided to break a thirteen-year alliance with the left-leaning Social Democrats (SDP). Six months later, German voters gave a solid mandate to Helmut Kohl's conservative government.

The victory of Chancellor Kohl's *Koalition der Mitte* (center coalition) in 1983 followed Germany's worst economic slump since the Great Depression of the 1930s. Many German voters blamed the recession on the generous but expensive welfare-state programs favored by the SDP. Kohl and the Christian Democrats promised to reverse the course with a combination of tax cuts, investment incentives, and budget reductions. Although less drastic, Kohl's approach vaguely resembled "Reaganomics" and the supply-side prescriptions of Britain's Prime Minister Thatcher.

Kohl's economic program produced generally positive results: economic growth stopped declining (growth reached an impressive 3.5 percent in 1986), inflation was brought down to a thirty-four-year low (from over 5 percent in 1982 to 1 percent), and budget deficits were reduced from about $30 billion in the last year of Social Democratic rule to about $8 billion in the 1987 budget. In addition, spending for social welfare programs was curbed significantly.

In this auspicious climate, business and industry rebounded. By mid-1986, German factories were operating at 85 percent of capacity, and in some sectors, including automobiles and machine tools, output could not keep pace with demand. Capital investment perked up as well: after lagging from 1982 to 1984, it increased by 10 percent. Plant modernization, particularly the use of computers and robots, accelerated rapidly. To top it all off, the balance of payments showed a record surplus in 1986. The one low mark on Kohl's report card was unemployment, which remained at 9 percent.

In the 1987 parliamentary elections, West Germans reaffirmed their support for Kohl and his center-right coalition, giving them a combined total of 53.4 percent of the popular vote (44.3 percent for the CDU-CSU and 9.1 percent for the FDP). The vote was not a resounding triumph for Kohl and his party, however; the CDU-CSU lost twenty-one seats, while FDP gained twelve. Of particular concern to conservatives was the fact that the Greens—an antinuclear, environmental party—garnered a million votes more than they had four years earlier.

Environmentalists and peace activists got a boost in West Germany from the Chernobyl nuclear accident in the Ukraine in April 1986. The Greens, trying to capitalize on popular fear, called for Bonn's immediate withdrawal from NATO, unilateral disarmament, and the dismantling of all nuclear power stations in the Federal Republic. Their relatively strong showing in 1987 (forty-two seats in the Bundestag on 8.3 percent of the vote) was still not enough to make them a major force in West German politics. Nonetheless, opinion polls showed that over 80 percent of the voters opposed construction of new nuclear power plants in the country, and nearly half of them saw the Greens as the party best qualified to deal with environmental issues.

It is conceivable that the SDP and the Greens might someday be able to forge a winning center-left coalition. To date, however, the Greens have been hampered by a split between two factions, the Fundamentalists and the Realists. The two groups differ on many matters, including strategy and tactics: the Realists favor coalitions with the SDP, whereas the Fundamentalists oppose any deals with established parties.

Although Germany is an affluent society, the struggle over how wealth and power are (or ought to be) distributed has intensified as a result of German unification. Organized labor has charged that the Kohl government is blatantly partial to business, pointing to a 1986 labor law that tightens the rules on payment of unemployment compensation to striking workers.

A related problem is the growing incidence of poverty amid plenty. Hit especially hard by what Germans call the "new poverty" are the long-term unemployed, divorced women with children, elderly pensioners, and refugees seeking asylum. Some Germans see a relationship between poverty and policy. For example, the percentage of long-term unemployed rose sharply during the 1980s, a trend that feeds into the poverty issue in Germany because under existing rules, the longer an individual is unemployed, the less he or she receives in public assistance.

Unification: Blessing or Curse?   The unemployment issue was greatly exacerbated at the end of the 1980s when the reform movement sweeping Eastern Europe caught fire in the Federal Republic. In a few short weeks, the hard-line regime of Erich Honecker, widely regarded as one of the most repressive figures in the Eastern bloc, was toppled. The fall of communism in East Germany led straightaway to the opening of the intra-German border and made the Berlin Wall, symbol par excellence of the East-West conflict, an anachronism. One consequence of this drama was a surge in unemployment in West Germany.

Germans always longed for a united Germany, but prior to 1989 that seemed a hopeless dream. The Kohl government, like its predecessors, sought close relations with East Germany. The Federal Republic extended loan guarantees worth billions of dollars, encouraged bilateral trade expansion, and concluded the first-ever cultural exchange accord between the two German governments.

In return, the German Democratic Republic allowed more travel to West Germany and, in the late 1980s, let record numbers of East Germans emigrate.

In the fall of 1989, a flood of refugees poured out of the GDR through Hungary, Poland, and Czechoslovakia (where democratic reform movements were either under way or about to burst forth). This mass exodus created a political crisis in East Germany that swiftly ended more than four decades of Communist rule. Democratic elections were held in the spring of 1990; unsurprisingly, the former Communist party was handed a resounding defeat. The expected winner, the left-of-center Social Democrats (SDP), garnered less than 22 percent of the popular vote. Instead, a conservative alliance, the Christian Democratic Union (CDU), won nearly 41 percent. The outcome was widely interpreted as a mandate for unity, in part because West German Chancellor Kohl, an unabashed advocate of rapid unification, had gone to East Germany and campaigned for the CDU. Suddenly, making Germany whole again was at the top of the agenda.

The pace of unification was the primary issue. The CDU on both sides of the border favored a merger "as soon as possible" pursuant to Article 23 of the Basic Law, which allows regions of prewar Germany to join the Federal Republic upon acceptance of the Basic Law. The SDP, however, called for a new constitution. Drafting such a constitution would obviously take time and involve careful negotiations between the two German governments. The timetable for unity was thus a key question. A closely related issue was how much the West would compromise with the East in negotiating the precise terms of unification. For example, would West Germany agree to modernize the Basic Law by including such themes as environmental protection?

Having dreamed of a united Germany for four decades, however, West Germans quickly discovered that the dream had a price tag attached. Absorbing the influx of East Germans and modernizing the GDR's outmoded factories would be expensive. In addition to unemployment, adjustments associated with a quick monetary union (using the West German mark in all German territory) brought the risk of inflation and recession. Inflation, in turn, was likely to drive official interest rates up just as the government was doubling its annual borrowing. Economists predicted that a tax increase of at least 25 billion deutsche marks would also be necessary to cover the costs of aiding East Germany and cushioning the impact of economic reform.[11]

The Federal Republic faces dilemmas in foreign policy as well. The unification issue brought old fears of German megalomania to the surface in both Eastern and Western Europe. In the Soviet Union, Mikhail Gorbachev declared that Moscow would not interfere with East Germany's reform efforts—including movement toward unification—but warned that a united Germany must not be part of NATO. The Kohl government, however, was steadfast in its commitment to the Western alliance. Similarly, Germany's EC partners were concerned about the impact of a German merger on the European Community. Currency analysts predicted:

The potential for a weakened deutsche mark, a West German current-account deficit, and rising inflation and interest rates in Germany will severely strain the European Monetary System, a delicately balanced basket of nine currencies intended to be the basis for a future European Monetary Union.[12]

The question of nuclear weapons is less nettlesome now that the Soviet Union has self-destructed. West Germany pledged never to acquire nuclear weapons when it joined NATO in 1954. But it has allowed the United States to deploy such weapons on its soil. Thus during the Cold War era, West Germany had the worst of both worlds: nucler weapons there were targets for Soviet rockets, but any decision to use these weapons depended on concurrence by a foreign government. New arms control accords following the lifting of the Iron Curtain have resulted in the withdrawal of U.S. nuclear weapons from western Germany; meanwhile, Russia is pledged to remove all former Soviet conventional forces from eastern Germany by the mid-1990s.

The end of the Cold War solved Germany's nuclear dilemma, but not without creating new ones in its place. Most onerous of all, the incorporation of the former East Germany into the Federal Republic will cost the taxpayers of the former West Germany $100 billion. Kohl had promised that he would not raise taxes to pay for German unification. His dilemma was now to raise the revenues to rebuild the former GDR and to pay for the withdrawal of former Soviet troops without fueling inflation. But unless the government recklessly expanded the money supply by printing money, the only options for raising revenue in the short run were austerity measures (cuts in other areas and tough budget restraints) or higher taxes. Both methods were bound to be unpopular and could lead to demands from organized labor for wage hikes to offset higher taxes and fewer benefits. Hence German labor unions in the spring of 1992 asked for a 9.5 percent wage increase to offset higher taxes and inflation (which was running at 4 percent); when Kohl refused to give them even a 5.4 percent raise, they went on strike. Ironically, both the unions and the government were motivated in large part by a fear of inflation, but this fear led them to opposite policy conclusions.[13]

Having embarked on unification, there was no turning back for the Kohl government. But the realities are daunting. For example, East Germany under Communist rule had become an ecological nightmare, and the cleanup costs alone were staggering. In the early 1990s, the states that comprised East Germany, which have 25 percent of the Federal Republic's population and 33 percent of its territory, accounted for only about 7.5 percent of its total output. Closing down inefficient enterprises and modernizing others is essential but cannot be done without causing high unemployment in the former GDR (estimated at 15 percent in 1992, compared to 5 percent in the western part of Germany).

In the meantime, the Federal Republic was struggling to absorb the flood of immigrants from Eastern Europe. Some came as asylum seekers; others were ethnic Germans who could expect immediate citizenship under a policy carried over from the Cold War. In all, some 2.5 million people poured into Germany after 1989, including 775,000 Eastern Europeans of German descent and a large number of refugees (East Germans constituted the majority of new arrivals). This invasion was unsettling to many West Germans—so much so that it opened a debate on the nation's asylum laws and immigration policies. Many obervers attributed the rise of an ultra-right nationalist movement in Germany in the early 1990s to Germans' growing fear that their country would be overwhelmed by a human tidal wave from the east. The neo-Nazis committed a spate of violent crimes against foreigners, especially Turks, in 1991 and 1992—behavior reminiscent of Nazi attacks on German Jews in the late 1930s. Popular indignation both within Germany and from the international community prompted a government crackdown on the far right at the end of 1992.

The European Community

The economic prospects for Western Europe are closely tied to the future of the European Community. Since its founding in 1958, the EC has grown from six to twelve member nations with a combined population of 350 million people. In 1992 all remaining barriers to internal trade were to be removed and the economic unification of the twelve member states—Belgium, Denmark, France, Germany, Great Britain, Greece, Ireland, Italy, Luxembourg, the Netherlands, Portugal, and Spain—was to become a reality. The aim of **Project 1992** was to abolish remaining internal trade barriers, creating five million new jobs and producing $250 billion in savings for EC businesses and consumers. By the end of 1991, two-thirds of the 282 detailed measures required to make this project a reality were in force, but the matters that were not yet decided were the most sensitive ones—social and health policy, taxation, the environment, and state subsidies. Above all, reluctance to take the final steps toward creation of a European Monetary Union clouded the EC's future in the early 1990s, although

Table 6.6   A Single European Currency? The Maastricht Timetable

Date	Significance
September 1992	Earliest date on which negotiations on EC membership for Austria and Sweden could begin.
January 1, 1993	Formal program for the single market to be completed.
January 1, 1994	The European Monetary Institute begins coordinating policy.
June 1994	Election for the next European Parliament.
January 1, 1997	If at least seven members meet the EC's stringent economic criteria, they will adopt a single currency; Britain has the right to opt out at this stage.
January 1, 1999	The single currency, if not yet in force, will be invoked automatically.

Note: All twelve member states signed the treaty, but Great Britain insisted on the right to opt out. The other governments made a legally binding commitment to monetary union by the end of the twentieth century.

the **Maastricht Treaty**, signed in December 1991 (see Table 6.6), appeared to pave the way for a single currency.

The European Community has come a long way since its inception in the 1950s. The nucleus of the original Common Market was the European Coal and Steel Community, proposed by French statesman Robert Schuman. From the standpoint of economic geography, the ECSC's core was the so-called Heavy Industrial Triangle, an area bounded by the regions of the Nord, Ruhr, and Lorraine. According to Geoffrey Parker, there is a "logic of unity" behind the evolution of the EC:

> The countries of the Community originally decided to enter into an economic merger for a variety of reasons, but, particularly in the case of those five of them [France, West Germany, the Netherlands, Belgium, and Luxembourg] which are part of trunk Europe, their motivation was based on a very real geographical unity. The shatter belt of political frontier which extends through its center from the Rhine delta to the Alps coincides only in one place with a linguistic boundary, and frequently divides areas which are physically, economically, and frequently culturally single units. Most basic of all is the essential unity of the Triangle and its associated areas which has been, in the words of the Schuman Declaration, "always prescribed by geography, always prevented by history," and the Community has given this formal expression.[14]

The benefits of economic integration were demonstrated first and foremost in the area of external trade: in 1966 the Common Market overtook the United States to become the world's largest exporter. Total exports to outside countries had risen more than 85 percent in the customs union's first eight years. Four-fifths of these exports were manufactured goods, mostly machinery and transport equipment. (The remainder consisted of food exports.) By 1984 the enlarged EC's share of the world export market had surpassed the United States' share by a wide margin, nearly matching that of Japan, Canada, and the Soviet Union combined.

After the signing of the Single European Act in 1986, the European Community moved toward a historic milestone: economic unification in 1992.

> Physical barriers for shipping goods will be abolished. Technical barriers will end on everything from the contents of food to government procurement. Value-added taxes will be coordinated. Banking, insurance, and capital movements will flow freely. Doctors and other professionals will be able to practice where they please.
>
> It will be a giant step toward an economically united Europe.[15]

The impetus behind this giant step was the same as that behind earlier smaller steps: economic growth. Unifying the market was by itself expected to spur the European Community's GDP by 4.5 to 6.5 percent and to create as many as two million jobs and pare down consumer prices by around 6 percent. Lord Cockfield, vice-president of the EC Commission, characterized it as "the greatest development that has happened since the end of World War II."[16] Little did he know that in 1989 and 1990 another development would push all others into the shadows.

> The coming-apart of Eastern Europe prematurely boosted the coming-together of the western part. First Helmut Kohl, the German chancellor, then François Mitterrand, the French president, were seized by an urge to swaddle Germany in European obligations before the reunited country could develop other instincts. . . .
>
> The result, at least in terms of words on papers, was astonishing. . . . Whereas the Single European Act allowed the Treaty of Rome to work, the Maastricht Treaty grandly sought to redefine what the Community involved.[17]

A unified European "supereconomy" would present unprecedented opportunities for expansion of trade and industry throughout the European Community. If there were no longer any barriers to the movement of goods, labor, or capital, the EC would become one massive and highly lucrative market, an economic leviathan that would dwarf Russia and rival the United States—if it can overcome the chauvinism and cultural particularism that are still prevalent on both sides of the East-West divide.

Assuming that the dream of a unified Europe becomes a reality, there will still be serious challenges ahead for the societies and governments involved. First, not all member states will benefit equally from the union. The countries of the north will benefit more than the countries of the south because of their comparative advantage in manufactured goods. The EC is attempting to deal with this problem in part by doubling its regional development aid (which goes primarily to the southern members) in the years leading up to 1992. But the potential for north-south conflict within the EC will not disappear until intraregional disparities between rich northern members (including Italy, together with France, Germany, Great Britain, the Benelux countries, and Denmark) and poorer southern members (including Spain, Portugal, and Greece) do.

Second, the European Community is not equally popular among all groups *within* the member states. Urban industrial areas have more to gain from economic unification than rural areas do. Most Europeans do not live in cities, where pro-EC sentiment typically runs high. Millions still live in rustic surroundings; their attitudes are conditioned by the relative isolation of villages and provincial towns, and they instinctively distrust both big business and big government. "We risk an increasing polarization in European societies," notes one expert. "There is a large part of society that remains in its little village, insular."[18]

"Personally, I do not feel European at all." This sentiment, candidly expressed by the Communist mayor of a town near Marseilles, France, echoes the sentiment of many people, especially those living outside of the big cities. Moreover, "the European Community is a community of capitals, of the interests of capital cities."[19] This assessment is true enough to color the perceptions of many provincials for whom antibusiness and antigovernment populism always has strong appeal. Claude Cheysson, a former French foreign minister and EC commissioner, warned, "A Europe that would become too much a Europe of the traders and the bankers will give birth to very deep social and cultural reactions."[20]

Cheysson's fears were borne out dramatically in mid-1992, when Danish voters surprised politicians and pollsters by voting against the Maastricht accords. The Danish referendum sent shock waves through the European Community and placed its future in temporary limbo. The fact that Irish voters a few weeks later approved the pact did little to allay the concerns of Europhiles, but it did point to a deep division within the EC between the rich "northern" member states and the not-so-rich "southern" ones (Ireland included).

Danish voters no doubt had various reasons for voting against the Maastricht agreement, but one common complaint in Denmark and other affluent EC countries is that the EC budget has become a mechanism for redistributing wealth from north to south. This is presumably one reason why the Irish voted for Maastricht. The perennial debate over the EC budget raises issues involving equity (or fairness) and reveals the extent to which nationalism continues to compete with regionalism on the Continent. Spain, for example, threatened to block any move toward admission of four EFTA countries (Sweden, Finland, Austria, and Switzerland) without a prior agreement on an EC budget for a five-year period from 1993 to 1998. The debate is over decimal points, but the fractions add up to billions of European Currency Units (ECUs):

> In February [1991] the commission unveiled a plan that would raise the ceiling on EC spending from its current level of 1.2% of the Community's GDP to 1.37% in 1997. That would allow the budget to grow from 66.5 billion ecus ($87 billion) this year to 87.5 billion ecus in 1997 (at current prices, assuming economic growth of 2.5% a year). The bulk of the increase would go on regional aid and a new "cohesion fund" for Spain, Ireland, Portugal and Greece.[21]

Third, the intensified competition that a single, unified market will bring is seen as a boon by most of the EC's biggest companies, but it is threatening to smaller firms and workers who stand to lose their jobs if some of these firms cannot compete.[22] The companies most likely to fail, in many cases, are the family-owned ones. Some have been around for centuries. Their demise could signal the disappearance of a way of life in rural Europe.

The road to a federal Europe has other obstacles. Nationalism and cultural pride are almost impossible to overcome. The British insistence on a clause by which it could postpone participation in a future EMU until 1997 underscored this point. In Germany, long the EC's most enthusiastic backer, sixty economics professors issued a joint criticism of the Maastricht agreement, and the opposition Social Democrats wanted to give the Bundestag the right to back out of the deal later if Germany's legislators were so inclined, thus undermining the EMU's automaticity. A French referendum on the Maastricht Treaty garnered only grudging approval.

The fact that the EC is a collection of democracies does not necessarily facilitate the politics of integration. For example, it took EC members thirteen years to agree on lawn mower noise standards. The difficulties went beyond technical questions such as allowable noise levels: "What actually constitutes a lawn mower and other imponderables kept governments, corporations and gardeners at daggers drawn."[23] If details like these can stir up controversy, imagine what obstacles await the Europhiles who dream of creating a federal Europe!

In 1985 an EC white paper estimated that some three hundred directives were necessary to bring about a unified market. That task would be daunting even without the political complications that inevitably intrude. Attention in the West was riveted on economic restructuring (*perestroika*) in the final days of the Soviet Union. Yet the EC countries face a restructuring hardly less painful, involving

> the merging of companies, the elimination of redundant jobs and the lifting of barriers that protect uncompetitive industries. The force of change will be felt most heavily at the bottom of the pyramid, especially in companies that, because they existed in backwaters, were slower to reduce labor costs and increase investment in mechanization than companies that have been competing internationally for years. In the short run, that means more conflict, more anguish, and perhaps a fatal backlash against the European ideal that the corporate bigwigs have been touting.[24]

Also, the end of the Cold War and the demise of European communism have presented both opportunities and challenges for the EC. The opportunities are suggested by the opening of vast potential markets in Eastern Europe and the former Soviet Union. The challenges are to integrate new member states from the east (especially Poland, Hungary, the Czech Republic, and Slovakia) and to assimilate the flood of immigrants from Eastern Europe and elsewhere for whom a uniting Europe is a new promised land much like the United States has been throughout its history.

Despite the many obstacles, the twelve members of the EC will most likely merge into a single economy by the end of the 1990s. Economic unification will not be easy. Historical precedents do not exist. Indeed, the EC countries are engaged in a pioneering effort, an experiment in international relations on a scale never before attempted anywhere. The trial-and-error method of problem solving, by definition, involves risks. Even so, the prospects for a prosperous new European superstate are so alluring, and the incentives for further unification so powerful, that no problems or risks, however large they may loom, are likely to derail the EC locomotive.

CONCLUSION

Western Europe emerged from the ashes of World War II like a phoenix. The West German "economic miracle" overshadowed the remarkable recovery of the entire western portion of the Continent. The United States played a key role in shaping Europe's postwar destiny by providing generous reconstruction aid (the Marshall Plan); perhaps equally important, the United States encouraged aid recipients to coordinate their recovery efforts. Mechanisms of institutionalized cooperation—the Organization for European Cooperation and Development (OECD), the European Coal and Steel Community (ECSC), the European Atomic Energy Agency (Euratom), and the European Economic Community (EEC)—set the stage for the economic unification planned for 1992—the most spectacular economic integration success story in modern history. Will other regions follow suit? The chapters that follow shed light on this question.

Ironically, Eastern Europe, homogenized by Soviet military might after World War II, came unglued at the very time when integration was bringing Western Europe ever closer together. In Chapter 7 we examine the context of politics in the Slavic world, the Soviet Union, East Central Europe, and the Balkans.

KEY TERMS

Marshall Plan
North Atlantic Treaty Organization (NATO)
Organization of European Economic Cooperation (OEEC)
European Coal and Steel Community (ECSC)
European Economic Community (EEC)
European Community (EC)

postindustrial society
reverse development
stagflation
Keynesian economic theory
Thatcherism
European Monetary Union (EMU)
"rupture with capitalism"
Project 1992
Maastricht Treaty

STUDY QUESTIONS

1. What forms did U.S. assistance to Western Europe take after World War II? What motives, interests, and objectives drove the Truman administration's foreign policy vis-à-vis the Continent during this period?
2. What are the economic characteristics of postindustrial society? What problems developed in Western Europe as a result of postindustrialism? How have the governments in the region dealt with these problems?
3. What is Thatcherism? Is Great Britain better or worse off than it was at the beginning of the 1980s when Margaret Thatcher became prime minister? Is the British economy likely to dominate the Continent in the 1990s?
4. In 1982, the Socialist government led by French President François Mitterrand attempted to revive a sagging economy by nationalizing several industries. What was the theory behind this program? Was it successful? Is France under Socialist rule dismantling its market-based economy? Is the French Socialist party a threat to democracy and free enterprise?

5. Are there limits to growth in Western Europe? Has Germany, the Continent's leading economic power, exhausted its growth potential? Have the other Common Market countries?
6. What is the European Community, who belongs to it, and how does it work? How did it get where it is today, and where is it going? Does it have a bright future, or has it outlived its usefulness?

SUGGESTED READING

Burgess, Michael. *Federalism and European Union: Political Ideas, Influences, and Strategies in the European Community, 1972–1987.* London: Routledge, 1989.
Laurent, Pierre-Henri. "The European Community: Twelve Becoming One." *Current History,* November 1988, pp. 357–360, 394.
Price, Roy. *The Dynamics of European Union.* London: Croom-Helm, 1987.
Yemma, John. "Europe 1992: Setting Sights Boldly on Unity." *Christian Science Monitor,* June 27, 1988.
Yemma, John. "Europe 1992: European States Weigh the Costs of Uniting." *Christian Science Monitor,* June 29, 1988.

NOTES

1. John Paxton, *The Developing Common Market: The Structure of the EEC in Theory and in Practice* (Boulder, Colo.: Westview Press, 1976), p. 7.
2. See Howard La Franchi, "Europe's Immigrants: New Faces in the Old World," *Christian Science Monitor,* Aug. 7, 1991, especially pp. 9 and 16.
3. See Howard La Franchi, "Europe's Demographics Signal New Need for Migrant Labor," *Christian Science Monitor,* Aug. 7, 1991, p. 13.
4. Girard C. Streichen, "Years of Grime and Grunge Will Take Decades to Clean," *Christian Science Monitor,* Apr. 25, 1991, p. 11.
5. Interestingly, Thatcher never received a larger share of the popular vote than U.S. President Bill Clinton did in 1992, yet she was widely perceived as having been given a mandate to impose drastic change, whereas most observers in the United States asserted that Clinton *lacked* a clear mandate—a reflection of differences in political culture, among other factors.
6. *Economist,* June 27, 1987, p. 60.
7. Ibid., p. 57.
8. William Echikson, "French United Despite Divided Parliament," *Christian Science Monitor,* June 14, 1988, p. 1.
9. Ibid.
10. *Economist,* Apr. 30, 1988, p. 46.
11. Terence Roth, "East German Winners in Election Now Seek Fast Monetary Union," *Wall Street Journal,* Mar. 20, 1990, p. 1.
12. Ibid., p. 11.
13. See Patrick Moser, "German Strikers Seek Better Deal," *Christian Science Monitor,* May 8, 1992, p. 8; and Patrick Moser, "Germans Worry Strike Settlement Sends Wrong Message to Metalworkers' Union," *Christian Science Monitor,* May 11, 1992, p. 3.

14. Geoffrey Parker, *An Economic Geography of the Common Market* (New York: Praeger, 1969), p. 127.
15. John Yemma, "'No Going Back' for EC, Biggest Market in the World," *Christian Science Monitor,* May 27, 1988, p. 15.
16. Ibid.
17. "European Community: Into the Void," *Economist,* July 11, 1992, pp. 5–6.
18. Danielle Pletka, "The Supereconomy Stirs in a Web of Self-interest," *Insight,* June 20, 1988, p. 10.
19. Ibid., p. 12.
20. Ibid., p. 17.
21. "Hoping for a Stitch-up," *Economist,* June 20, 1991, pp. 25–26.
22. See, for example, Howard La Franchi, "Small Firms Wary of One-Market Europe," *Christian Science Monitor,* Apr. 11, 1991, p. 10.
23. Pletka, "Supereconomy," p. 15.
24. Ibid., p. 17.

PART III

Russia and Slavic Europe

Russia

Estonia
Latvia
Lithuania
Belarus
Czech. Poland
Moldova
Ukraine
Kazakhstan
Hungary
Rom.
Formerly
Yugo. Bul.
Albania Turkey
Greece
Kyrgyzstan
Azerbaijan
Tajikistan
Armenia Uzbekistan
Georgia Turkmenistan

RUSSIA
_____

Area: 6,592,812 square miles
Population: 149 million
Density per square mile: 23
Languages: Russian, Ukrainian,
Uzbek, Byelorussian, Kazak, Tartar
Literacy rate: 99%
Religions: Eastern (Russian)
Orthodoxy, Roman Catholicism,
Islam, Judaism
Monetary unit: ruble
GNP: (1991) $479.5 billion; $3,220
per capita

CZECHOSLOVAKIA
_____

Area: 49,373 square miles
Population: 15.7 million
Density per square mile: 318
Languages: Czech and Slovak (both
official), Hungarian
Literacy rate: 99%
Religions: Roman Catholicism,
Protestantism
Monetary unit: koruna
GNP: (1991) $38.4 billion; $2,450
per capita

YUGOSLAVIA
_____

Area: 39,000 square miles
Population: 10.3 million
Density per square mile: 264
Languages: Serbo-Croatian, Slovene,
Macedonian, Albanian
Literacy rate: 90%
Religions: Eastern Orthodoxy (50%),
Roman Catholicism (30%), Islam
(9%)
Monetary unit: dinar
GNP: (1991) $70 billion; $2,940 per
capita

7

Slavic Europe:
The Shatter Zone

The October Revolution of 1917 ushered in the most repressive era in the history of modern Russia. The "ten days that shook the world"—the title of John Reed's famous firsthand account of this momentous event—also set in motion a progression toward totalitarian rule that within thirty years would envelop virtually all of the European territories inhabited by Slavic-speaking peoples. Not just Russia and the former czarist imperial lands such as Ukraine and Byelorussia (now known as Belarus), but also Poland, Czechoslovakia, and Bulgaria, fell under the domination of the Soviet Union in the aftermath of World War II. Although Hungary; Romania; the Baltic states of Lithuania, Latvia, and Estonia (annexed by Stalin at the beginning of World War II); and Prussia are not ethnically Slavic, they are located along the predominantly Slavic-speaking regions of East Central Europe and the Balkans. As such, they were critical to Stalin's effort to create a buffer zone against invasion from the west. Among the Slavs, only Yugoslavia—the cobbled-together republic uniting Serbs, Croats, and Slovenes—managed to break away from the Soviet bloc and pursue an independent, albeit Communist, course.

The breathtaking changes in the former Soviet bloc countries, spearheaded by Soviet President Mikhail Gorbachev in the late 1980s, culminated in the collapse of Comunist rule throughout the region. In December 1991, following an abortive coup attempt by hard-liners in Moscow, the Soviet Union self-destructed.

This chapter examines the setting of politics in the eastern half of Europe and traces both the pre-Communist history of the region in broad outline and the Communist era, which now has also passed into history. The end of **Pax Sovietica**—a term once used to describe Moscow's hegemony in Slavic Europe—has ushered in a period of ethnic conflict and generalized instability,

167

which is simply another way of saying that the natural contours of history and political geography, obscured for four decades by the false uniformity imposed by Communist rule, have reappeared.

The Slavic Shatter Zone

On March 5, 1946, Winston Churchill gave an address at Westminster College in Fulton, Missouri, in which he spoke darkly of the danger posed by Soviet communism:

> From Stettin in the Baltic to Trieste in the Adriatic, an iron curtain has descended across the Continent. Behind that line lie all the capitals of the ancient states of Central and Eastern Europe. Warsaw, Berlin, Prague, Vienna, Budapest, Belgrade, Bucharest, and Sofia, all these famous cities and the populations around them lie in what I must call the Soviet sphere, and all are subject in one form or another, not only to Soviet influence but to a very high and, in many cases, increasing measure of control from Moscow.[1]

Whether we regard Churchill's words as alarmist or prophetic, the political geography he traced remained a fact of life for more than forty years.

The region behind that Iron Curtain contained the former Union of Soviet Socialist Republics (USSR), more commonly known as the Soviet Union, plus Bulgaria, Hungary, Poland, Romania, and what were until recently Czechoslovakia, East Germany, and Yugoslavia. **Eastern Europe** (or **Slavic Europe**) today refers to the lands of Central Europe and the Balkans. It encompasses not only the former Soviet republics of Russia, Ukraine, Belarus, and Moldova but also Latvia, Lithuania, and Estonia. The former Soviet republics of Georgia, Armenia, and Azerbaijan, located in a subregion called the Caucasus, are not part of the Slavic world, nor are the former Soviet republics in Central Asia. Tiny Albania has a geographic and political relationship to the Balkans; ethnic Albanians constitute the majority of people living in the Kosovo province of Yugoslavia.

Two-thirds of the peoples of Russia and Eastern Europe are of Slavic origin. Slavs have been the predominant group there since at least the seventh century A.D. They can be divided into three major subgroups: eastern Slavs (Great Russians, Ukrainians, White Russians, and Ruthenians), western Slavs (primarily Poles, Czechs, and Slovaks), and southern Slavs (Serbs, Croats, Slovenes, Montenegrins, and Bulgars).

The Slavic nations are extremely diverse. Cultural and linguistic traditions vary considerably. Christianity spread throughout the region but took different forms: eastern and southern Slavs embraced the Eastern Orthodox rite, while the western Slavs looked to Rome. This explains in part why western Slavs use the Latin alphabet, while eastern and southern Slavs use the Cyrillic.

The non-Slavic groups of Slavic Europe are likewise diverse. The three largest are the Magyars (Hungarians), Moldavians (Romanians), and Germans;

others are Gagauz, Latvians (Letts), Lithuanians, Estonians, Finns, Jews, Tatars, Bashkirs, Chechens, Ingush, Abkhazians, Meshketians, Albanians, and Mongols (Georgians, Armenians, and Ossetians live primarily in the Caucasus and therefore do not belong to Slavic Europe as defined earlier). These groups generally resented Moscow's **Russification** policies of the past and abhor the "pan-Slavic" sentiments often expressed by Russian nationalists. The impact of this non-Slavic presence, particularly in periods of social decay and political instability, is greater than the sum of its parts.

Nor have the mutual antagonisms so common to this region been confined to relations between Slavs and non-Slavs. The "shatter zone" that is Slavic Europe encompasses a bewildering array of historically deep-rooted ethnic conflicts—between Poles and Russians, Russians and Ukrainians, Czechs and Slovaks, Slovaks and Hungarians, Hungarians and Romanians, Hungarians and Serbs, Serbs and Croats, Serbs and Bosnian Muslims, Serbs and Albanians, and so on. Dozens of such enmities persist.

Although the nations of Eastern Europe are diverse in many ways, their fates have been interwoven. Besides linguistic links and the political fortunes (or misfortunes) that have fused them together in one empire or another at different times, in some cases they have shared religious and cultural experiences. Above all, the forces of history and geography have intruded on these nations and shaped a destiny that is uniquely Slavic.

The Influence of Geography

Early in the nineteenth century, France's most famous student of American democracy, Alexis de Tocqueville, predicted that the United States and Russia were apparently "marked out by the will of heaven to sway the destinies of half the globe."[2] Tocqueville anticipated the bipolar world that emerged after 1945 because he understood the importance of geopolitics: the United States and Russia, he observed, would be able to expand over relatively empty landmasses and incorporate or annihilate the indigenous populations, whereas the Europeans would have no choice but to attempt to knock together overseas empires, which for geopolitical and other reasons were much less secure.

For most of the twentieth century, the Soviet Union dominated the map of Eurasia. Occupying more than 8.6 million square miles (one-sixth of the earth's total landmass), it was by far the largest country in the world, more than twice the size of the United States. About 25 percent of the USSR was in Europe.

Accounting for about half of the Soviet Union's total population and slightly more than three-fourths of its territory was Russia proper. Russia's 6.6 million square miles dwarf the United States' 3.6 million, but in terms of population, the situation is reversed: the United States has over 250 million people, Russia only 150 million.

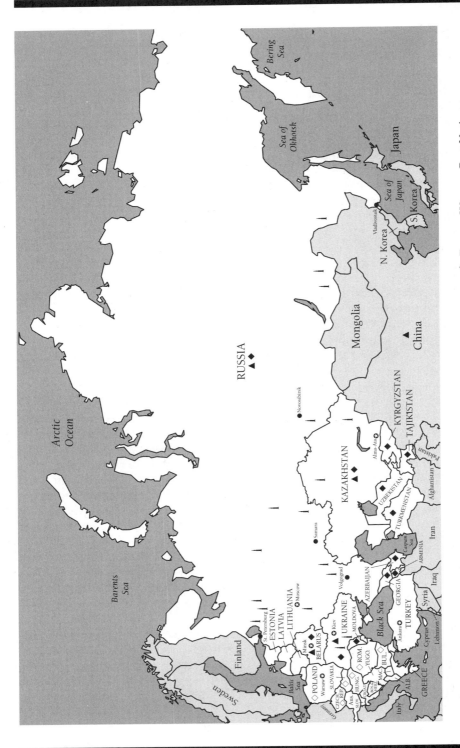

◆ **Republics of the Former Soviet Union:**

Armenia	Kazakhstan	Tajikistan
Azerbaijan	Kyrgyzstan	Turkmenistan
Belarus	Moldova	Ukraine
Georgia	Russia	Uzbekistan

▲ **Nations with Nuclear Weaponry:** Belarus, Kazakhstan, Russia, Ukraine (and China)

Ⅰ Nuclear Missile Bases within Kazakhstan, Russia, and Ukraine

◇ **Former Warsaw Pact Nations:**

Bulgaria	Hungary
Czechoslovakia (now	Poland
Czech Republic and	Romania
Slovakia)	

Russia and the Ukraine

If Eastern Europe was dominated by the Soviet Union, the Soviet Union was in turn dominated by Russia. Geography has played a major role in shaping the political traditions of the Russian people. One authority on Soviet politics has written:

> It is indeed easy to see how Russia's geography has influenced the course of its history. To begin with, Russia's original location on the East European plain contributed directly to many of its important historic events. Being relatively close to Byzantium, for example, influenced Russia's choice of Eastern (Greek) Orthodoxy as its state religion (988). Two and a half centuries later, because of its location, Russia fell prey to the Mongol invasion and remained for several centuries almost completely isolated from Europe, which was then going through the Renaissance and Reformation. A result of this isolation was Russia's lagging behind Europe in technology and industrialization.[3]

Three facts of life determined by geography have been crucial in shaping Russian history and culture. First, Russia lies in the northern latitudes, where it is cold much of the year. Second, it is mostly flat (much like Kansas and Nebraska in the United States) and thus presents no natural barriers to invasion or expansion. Third, it is vast, especially the Siberian wilderness: "The immensity of Russia, the absence of boundaries, was expressed in the structure of the Russian soul . . . the same boundlessness, formlessness, reaching out into infinity, breadth."[4]

Russia has been blessed with an abundance of fertile soil, mineral resources, and mighty rivers. Yet nature's bounties have been yielded grudgingly due to the relatively short growing season and the long, cold winters. The Ukraine, to the south, was the breadbasket of czarist Russia and then of the Soviet empire, but its location on the globe corresponds to that of Ontario, Canada. The storied resilience of the Russian people in the face of adversity no doubt owes much to the rigors of the climate.

Power Vacuum or Empire?

The sheer size of Russia, resulting in a need to protect boundaries thousands of miles long, and the absence of natural barriers, which leaves the nation open to attack from any direction except the north, have contributed to a pervasive sense of insecurity. In the thirteenth century, the Mongols invaded, pillaged, and plundered Kievan Russia. The Mongol yoke was not removed for nearly 250 years.

In the early sixteenth century, danger came from the opposite direction: Poland. The result was another humiliating defeat and another foreign occupation, this time for only three years. In 1709, Sweden attacked, under Charles XII, a military genius. Russia's Peter the Great, soon to become an empire builder in his own right, rose to the challenge. Under his command, the defending Russian forces defeated the Swedes at Poltava in the Ukraine.

A century later, Napoleon invaded Russia and marched all the way to Moscow. The onset of winter was a major factor in forcing his army to retreat. Russia's sheer physical size came into play as well. According to historian Nicholas Riasanovsky, "More soldiers of Napoleon died from hunger and epidemics than from cold, for the supply services, handicapped by enormous distances, insecure lines of communication, and bad planning, failed on the whole to sustain the military effort."[5]

Germany invaded twice in the twentieth century. In World War II, Hitler conquered and occupied much of historic Russia west of the Urals. Kiev was destroyed, Leningrad was besieged for two and a half years, and Moscow came perilously close to falling. Twenty million Soviet citizens died; cities, towns, and villages were reduced to rubble and ash; the foundations of the economy were obliterated.

The same geography that has made Russia vulnerable to invasion and instability has also afforded opportunities for expansion. Thus "when not being invaded, Russia itself was often invading neighboring countries, annexing them, building an empire, and pursuing territorial expansion in the quest for greater physical security."[6] Russian rulers themselves thus created stability problems in peripheral areas by incorporating non-Russian groups into the empire. The czars never achieved full Russification of these groups.

Aside from the quest for security, there were powerful economic and commercial inducements to engage in empire-building, many of them also affected by geography. For example, the desire to gain access to warm-water ports, long a major motif of Russian foreign policy, can be traced directly to Russia's geographic predicament. This drive for trading outlets and the strategic importance of the Bosporus straits (the passage between the Black Sea and the Mediterranean) motivated a push to the south that provoked tension between Russia and the Ottoman Empire (now Turkey) and armed conflict with France and Great Britain in the mid-nineteenth century. Russia's humiliating defeat in the Crimean War (1853–1856) was a classic example of the danger of "imperial overstretch."[7]

Geography has also influenced Russian culture. A famous Russian historian, Vasili Kluchevsky, identified "forest, steppe and river" as "the basic elements of Russian nature" and asserted that they "played an active and unique part in the formation of the life and ideas" of the Russians.[8] Another scholar, Nicholas Berdyaev, argued that "the immensity of Russia" has also left a deep imprint on the culture, society, and general outlook of the Russian people. What is particularly fascinating is the way Berdyaev links geography and politics:

> A difficult problem presents itself ceaselessly to the Russian—the problem of organizing his vast territory. The immensity of Russia, the absence of boundaries, was expressed in the structure of the Russian soul. . . . It might be said that the Russian people fell victim to the immensity of its territory. Form does not come easily, the gift of form is not great among the Russians. Russian historians explain the despotic character of Russian government by this necessary organization of the boundless Russian plain. Kluchevsky, the most distinguished of

Russian historians, said, "The state expands, the people grow sickly." In a certain sense this remains true also of the Soviet-Communist government, under which the interests of the people are sacrificed to the power and organization of the Soviet state.[9]

Geography and environment have not predetermined Russia's history, but these physical factors have undoubtedly conditioned and constrained the development of Russian institutions, traditions, and values. The great constants in Russia's history are environmental in the broadest sense of the word: its vast space and daunting distances; its majestic forests; its smooth, flat plains; and its harsh winter climate.

The Imprint of Recent History

Just as geography influences history, so the legacy of the past, the history of a nation's finest and darkest moments, leaves a deep imprint on political culture. History is relevant to politics for as long as it is remembered (a good example is the Mongol invasion of Russia). Moreover, what is remembered is more important than what actually happened. For example, the Russians and neighboring peoples have very different collective memories of the beginning of World War II. The actual events are much less important, politically speaking, than the prevailing cultural mythology about those events.

Decline of the Romanov Dynasty

When Czar Nicholas II abdicated in 1917 amid the turbulence of war and revolution, he brought to an end three centuries of Romanov rule in Russia. Nicholas and his predecessor, Czar Alexander III, had been obsessed with unifying the multinational empire they inherited. However, unlike Peter the Great (1682–1725), Catherine the Great (1762–1795), Alexander I (1801–1825), or Nicholas I (1825–1855), the last two Romanov rulers were unequal to the challenges they faced.

And challenges sprang up like crocuses in spring. First, there were external threats on two sides: to the west, a united Germany; to the east, Japan. Germany had shown its military prowess in victories against Austria in 1866 and France in 1870. Japan's emergence as a great power caught Russia by surprise. In the Russo-Japanese War of 1904–1905, Japan destroyed Russia's Far Eastern fleet with a surprise attack in the outer harbor of Port Arthur (Lüshun). When Czar Nicholas II ordered the Baltic fleet to sail around the globe to save the day, the Japanese dealt Russia's antique armada another crushing blow in the battle of Tsushima Strait in 1905.

The Far Eastern debacle set the stage for Russia's first revolution. Like the October Revolution twelve years later, the Revolution of 1905 was precipitated by defeat in war. But war alone does not explain the revolutions. The forces of rebellion and violence had been stirring within Russian society for decades before they erupted in 1905. They first appeared in the 1870s, when anarchism and nihilism mixed with populism to produce a homegrown ideology called *narodnichestvo* (the Russian word for populism). The chief ideologues of this movement came to be known as *narodniki;* some of the most prominent were Alexander Herzen, Michael Bakunin, Nicholas Chernyshevsky, Peter Lavrov, and Nicholas Mikhailovsky.

The *narodniki* inspired a group of fanatical revolutionaries, the *Narodnaya Volya* ("People's Will"), who launched an offensive against the government of Alexander II. Members of this group believed that "because of the highly central-ized nature of the Russian state, a few assassinations could do tremendous damage to the regime, as well as provide the requisite political instruction for the educated society and the masses."[10] Alexander II had the misfortune to become their chief target: the ringleaders of *Narodnaya Volya* condemned him to death and began what has been described as an "emperor hunt":

> The Executive Committee of the "Will of the People" included only about thirty men and women. . . . Although the police made every effort to destroy the revolutionaries and although many terrorists perished, the "Will of the People" made one attempt after another to assassinate the emperor. Time and again Alexander II escaped through sheer luck. Many people were killed when the very dining room of his palace was blown up, while at one time the emperor's security official refused to let him leave his suburban residence, except by water![11]

Alexander II was killed in 1881. Several years later, an attempt was also made on the life of Alexander III. The plot failed, but one of the conspirators arrested by the *Okhrana* (the czar's secret police) was Alexander Ilyich Ulyanov, the brother of Vladimir Ilyich Ulyanov, who became known to the world as Lenin. Without Lenin, there would probably not have been an October Revolu-tion; without the October Revolution, there would certainly not have been a Soviet Union.

The Bolsheviks: Vanguard of the Proletariat

Lenin's ideas on revolution were a mixture of Russian populism, anarchism, and Marxism. As a self-styled champion of Russia's oppressed masses, Lenin had a certain kinship with the old *narodniki;* as an advocate of revolutionary violence (though not assassination), he was a soulmate of the anarchists; and as the founder of the Communist Party of the Soviet Union, he was a disciple of Marx.

Lenin split the Russian Social Democratic party in 1903 over the issue of revolution. One faction of the party, the **Mensheviks**, opposed subversion and revolution, arguing that socialism and democracy could be achieved in Russia without violence. The **Bolshevik** faction, led by Lenin, insisted that only a conspiratorial vanguard party, secretly laying the groundwork for all-out revolu-tion, could bring the corrupt czarist order down. Lenin outlined this fundamental tenet in a famous 1902 essay, *What Is to Be Done?*

> The working class exclusively by its own efforts is able to develop only trade union consciousness. . . . Modern social consciousness can be brought to them only from without. . . . [It] can arise only on the basis of profound scientific knowledge. The bearers of science are not the proletariat but the bourgeois intelligentsia. It is out of the heads of members of this stratum that modern socialism originated. . . . Pure and simple trade unionism means the ideological subordination of the workers to the bourgeoisie. . . . Our task is to bring the labor movement under the wing of Social Democracy.

Lest anyone miss the point, Lenin added that "aside from the influence of Social Democracy, there is no conscious activity of the workers."[12]

The working class had become a potent base of power. In the decades leading up to World War I, western Russia had undergone rapid economic growth, thanks to inflows of European capital and to government-promoted industrial development (including state ownership). If the rate of growth had been maintained, and if the Great War had not intervened in August 1914, Russia would have been a major economic power even without a revolution. But Marx's observation that capitalists would be their own gravediggers turned out to be particularly prophetic in the case of Russia, where the growth of a manufacturing sector created centers of large-scale industry in key cities such as Saint Petersburg and Moscow. In these cities, the Bolsheviks found the working class, the **proletariat** that Marx extolled in his writings. This industrial component was the underpinning of the revolution.

Marx and Engels had said that "the emancipation of the working class is the task of the working class itself." Lenin's amendment to this Marxist proposition was to have momentous consequences for Russia and the world. The Communist Party (which Lenin called the "vanguard of the proletariat") would supplant the proletariat as the key to the future. An elite corps of "professional revolutionists" would move front and center on the stage of history; the workers would fade into the background. Here, then, are the seeds of the totalitarian Soviet state sown in the fertile revolutionary soil of a society in decay.

Dress Rehearsal: The February Revolution

In February 1905, twelve years before the Russian autocratic system was toppled, workers staged a peaceful march on the Winter Palace to petition Czar Nicholas II. The unarmed demonstrators were massacred by Russian troops in what came to be known as "Bloody Sunday." A revolution without a vanguard (to use Lenin's term), this event had little real impact on the way Russia was ruled. Although it did lead to some agrarian reforms under Prime Minister Stolypin, the **February Revolution** also triggered a ferocious government assault on political dissent. Well over a thousand revolutionaries and suspected terrorists were sent to the gallows—victims of Stolypin's policy of "pacification."

Were it not for World War I, Lenin's ideas on revolution would not have borne fruit. The defeat of the Russian army at the hands of the invading Germans, like the defeat of the Russian navy by the Japanese a decade earlier, caused a crisis of confidence in the whole czarist system. The extreme hardships, the death and destruction, and the national humiliation associated with Russia's defeat all contributed to the spirit of rebellion.

The popular groundswell against the war was paralleled by a general disintegration of the armed forces in the period leading up to 1917. Alexander Kerensky, a moderate socialist, had tried to lead the nation toward a form of parliamentary democracy, but he foolishly insisted that Russia continue to fight even though the war was tearing the country apart. Lenin seized on this issue, promising "peace, land, and bread" if the Russian masses would heed his revolutionary call.

Why did Kerensky's attempt at democracy fail? Two factors stand out. First, like Weimar Germany, Russia lacked a liberal democratic tradition. This is not to say that Russians have no democratic traditions—for example, historically, the city-states of Kiev and Novgorod were much more pluralistic than Moscow. In addition to a council of *boyars* (merchants and nobles), these medieval cities had *veche* assemblies: when the veche bell tolled, all free male citizens would gather to discuss issues of public interest. But Muscovite rulers later used brutal measures to repress both the *boyars* and the assemblies—this is the darker side of Russia's democratic traditions.

Second, chaos reigned in the Provisional Duma (legislature) in 1917, and discontent was rampant in Russian society. (There is an eerie parallel between Kerensky's difficulties with an unruly Duma and a rebellious public in 1917 and President Boris Yeltsin's current problems with a chaotic Congress of Peoples' Deputies and a Russian people whose patience is wearing thin. We will discuss Yeltsin's prospects in Chapter 9.)

The October Revolution

Lenin, with the help of fellow Bolshevik Leon Trotsky, masterminded the **October Revolution**. Never known for political moderation, Lenin moved quickly to consolidate his power by gutting the elected **soviets** (governing councils), banning or suppressing all opposition groups, and putting Bolsheviks in control of the military, the police, the state administration, and the economy. He also established his own dreaded secret police, the *Cheka*. The *Cheka* imitated the czarist *Okhrana* but went further in perfecting a system of state terrorism that included purges against real or imagined counterrevolutionaries, expropriations of property, and tight control of all mass communications (radio, newspapers, journals, and publishing houses). Thus Lenin and Leninism set the stage for Stalin and Stalinism.

The Bolsheviks faced a variety of challenges during the period of **war communism** (1917–1921). The national government was embroiled in a civil war with the so-called white (anti-Bolshevik) armies supported by the Western Allies. The latter, including the United States, Great Britain, and France, intervened directly, if halfheartedly, on the pretense of recovering war supplies given earlier to the czarist government. The main aim, however, was to assist the "whites" in overthrowing the Bolshevik "reds."

Lenin's government managed to survive the civil war and Allied intervention, but the harsh policies of war communism alienated many former supporters of the October Revolution. In 1921, when sailors (who had played a key role in the revolution) mutinied at Kronstadt, a naval base near Saint Petersburg in the Gulf of Finland, Lenin crushed the rebellion. But the incident apparently made a deep impression on the Bolshevik leader, who subsequently relaxed the stringent measures imposed earlier. The result was the **New Economic Policy (NEP)**, which allowed limited private enterprise, involvement of foreign managers in industry, farming for profit, and considerable literary and artistic freedom.

The Stalin Era: Totalitarianism in Full Swing

To most objective observers, *Stalinism* and *totalitarianism* are synonyms. At the height of the Stalin terror in the mid-1930s, nobody was safe. Nearly all the Party's "old guard"—comrades of Lenin—fell before Stalin's firing squads. Most of the military high command met a similar fate. Guilt by association became the order of the day. Anyone who was connected in any way with the old czarist government—anyone who had ever held a position of responsibility in the economy or been recognized in any professional field (science, education, letters) before the revolution—was purged.

Stalin even invented subversive groups as a pretext for purging whole categories of "enemies." One class of prosperous peasants (*kulaks*) was completely wiped out—either killed or sent into exile in Siberia. Millions more peasants perished in the early 1930s in a famine exacerbated by Stalin's brutal policy of diverting capital from agriculture to industry and confiscating crops to feed city dwellers. Despite the domestic famine, Stalin actually exported grain to the West to earn hard currency during this period.

Why did Stalin wage war against his own society? What did the resulting bloodbath accomplish? Was there a method in his madness?

When Lenin became incapacitated by a stroke in 1922, Stalin knew that a succession struggle was inevitable. On Lenin's death in 1924, Stalin began maneuvering against top Bolshevik leaders. His first victim was Trotsky, whom he condemned for advocating "permanent revolution" (working for the overthrow of bourgeois capitalist governments) and expelled from the Party with the support of Lenin's other lieutenants. Using "salami tactics," he cut the Bolshevik old guard to pieces, cleverly playing one faction against another, denouncing first the leftists, then the rightists, until he had vilified and discredited them all.

By 1928, Stalin had succeeded in turning the obscure position of general secretary of the Communist Party into a vehicle of autocratic power. But achieving personal sway over a weak nation did not satisfy Stalin's lust for power, nor did it assuage his obsessive insecurity. Russia was weak, he reasoned, because it was economically backward. It would never be strong until it industrialized. In the modern age, industrial development is the key to military prowess and national glory: that was the lesson to be learned from Japan, Germany, and the United States. In Stalin's own words: "We are fifty or a hundred years behind the advanced countries. We must make good this lag in ten years. Either we do it or they crush us."[13] But how could the Soviet Union industrialize? It was poor and agrarian. Worse, it was surrounded by hostile capitalist states.

Trotsky's permanent revolution was all wrong, Stalin asserted, because the Soviet Union was all alone in the world. Trying to foment revolution would provoke the nation's enemies and jeopardize the future of the only Socialist state then in existence. Under these unfavorable circumstances, Stalin argued, a policy of "socialism in one country"—a euphemism for his highly nationalistic economic development strategy—made more sense than Trotsky's adventurism.

Stalin's solution was simple but brutal: if the West could not be trusted (or was not willing) to provide the capital for Soviet industry, Stalin would squeeze it out of Soviet society. Given that the Soviet economy was largely agricultural, Stalin's go-it-alone strategy—a policy generally known as **autarky**—meant that the Soviet farmer would have to bear the brunt of the industrialization drive. But Stalin knew that the peasants would resist confiscatory taxes or forced deliveries to the state. So he decided to collectivize agriculture, more for economic expediency than out of ideological conviction. **Collectivization** was Stalin's way of extracting capital from agriculture for investment in industry—collectivization and forced industrialization were two sides of the same coin.

Stalin's economic development strategy also prompted his bloody campaign against the *kulaks*. Because the *kulaks* were the richest farmers, they had the most to lose from collectivization and were therefore the most likely to resist or obstruct. Stalin's "dekulakization" campaign thus appears to have been launched because the hapless *kulaks* were inconvenient (not, as Stalin claimed, because they were capitalist bloodsuckers). Of course, imposing Party control over the majority of the population (the peasantry) was another reason for collectivizing agriculture.

It is no coincidence that the first Five-Year Plan and the collectivization of Soviet agriculture were inaugurated in the same year, 1929.[14] Henceforth Stalin would let nothing (and nobody) get in the way of his crash industrialization program.[15]

Even the Great Terror of the 1930s can be seen as part of Stalin's mad dash for modernization. Millions of citizens were arrested on the flimsiest of pretexts and sent off to labor camps run by the secret police. A major part of the USSR's industrial infrastructure (roads, canals, bridges, railroads, dams, power grids) was built by forced labor. In Siberia, forced labor opened new mines and built new towns. The Moscow subway was built by forced labor.[16]

Forced labor is slave labor. Much of the terror Stalin unleashed in the 1930s was in reality an excuse for enslaving much of the Soviet work force in order to industrialize the nation without having to pay for it. Is this scenario too diabolical to be true? No one familiar with the show trials, in which the old Bolsheviks who had been Lenin's comrades in arms publicly confessed to heinous crimes and denounced themselves as spies and traitors, would doubt Stalin's capacity for cruelty. (After they had confessed, Stalin's rivals were taken out and shot.)

In sum, Stalin created a rigidly centralized system of rule in which state terror was used to mobilize society and enforce strict conformity with his will. He brought the entire economy under a central plan that consistently gave greater priority to industrial development than to agriculture or the production of consumer goods. This dogmatic insistence on the primacy of heavy industry became one of the hallmarks of Stalinist economy policy, not only in the Soviet Union but in Eastern European satellite states as well.

World War II and the Soviet Phoenix

In Egyptian mythology, the phoenix is a beautiful bird that lives for five hundred years before voluntarily consuming itself in flames, only to emerge from the ashes and start a new life cycle. The legendary rebirth of the phoenix is an appropriate metaphor for the Soviet experience in World War II.

On June 22, 1941, Hitler's army invaded the Soviet Union and rolled relentlessly toward Moscow. By October, German forces had encircled the city on three sides at a distance of twenty miles. Although Hitler's troops did not actually enter Moscow, they came much too close for comfort.

Without question, the Soviet Union was the main victim of German aggression in World War II. The Red Army did emerge victorious but, as Isaac Deutscher notes:

> Against this backdrop must be set the price Russia paid for the victory: the seven million dead, officially counted—the losses may in fact have been much larger [twenty million]; the uncounted millions of cripples; the devastation of most cities and towns, and of much of the country-side in European Russia; the destruction of industry, exemplified by the total flooding of the coal-mines of the Donets; the complete homelessness of twenty-five million people, living in caves, trenches, and mud huts, not to speak of the latent homelessness of many more millions of evacuees in the Urals and beyond.[17]

Soviet industry, bought at a terrible human price in the 1930s, lay in shambles. Between 1941 and 1945, Soviet industrial might was cut nearly in half; despite the Stalinist emphasis on steel production, the USSR was producing only about one-eighth as much steel as the United States in 1945. Soviet agriculture, too, had to be rebuilt "almost from scratch."[18]

But for all the death and destruction, the Soviet Union did not disintegrate. On the contrary, the war strengthened Soviet patriotism and made the survivors determined to do whatever was necessary to rebuild the country. West Germany's postwar reconstruction is generally considered an economic miracle. Similar "miracles" occurred in Italy and Japan. What is more remarkable (though less frequently remarked on) is the Soviet economic miracle. Soviet workers, unlike their German, Italian, and Japanese counterparts, had to rebuild without economic aid from the United States.

Most of the Soviet recovery is attributable to two factors: Stalin's draconian system of labor conscription (the war and its aftermath provided a steady flow of fresh recruits to the *gulags,* or labor camps) and a centrally planned economy that permitted all resources and energies to be concentrated on strategic industries (coal, steel, electricity, machine tools, armaments).[19]

By 1950, the Soviet Union had consolidated its hold on Eastern Europe, successfully tested an atomic bomb, and rebuilt much of its heavy industry. Stalin had the largest standing army in Europe (indeed, the largest in the world), and the Soviet Union was less than a decade away from entering the space age. (In 1957, the USSR became the first country to put a satellite—its name was *Sputnik*—into orbit.)

The Cold War Roller Coaster

The Cold War had a major impact on Soviet and Eastern European politics after World War II. The tenor of relations between the United States and the Soviet Union set the limits of East-West cooperation in all areas, including trade, tourism, technology, and cultural exchange. For this reason, we need to look at the general pattern of superpower relations since 1945.

In retrospect, the Cold War began before the Great Patriotic War (as the Soviets call World War II) ended. The Big Three—Churchill, Roosevelt, and Stalin—met several times as the war wound down, at Tehran, in Persia (Iran); Yalta, Ukraine; and Potsdam, Germany. On the surface, these meetings were conducted in a spirit of mutual trust as befits allies in a great and noble cause. Below the surface, mistrust guided the maneuvers of both Stalin and Churchill. Only Roosevelt appears to have entertained illusions about the possibilities for postwar collaboration between the Soviet Union and the West.

President Roosevelt did not live to see the end of World War II or the visible outbreak of the Cold War; he died suddenly in April 1945. His successor, Harry Truman, took a dim view of Stalin from the start. When the United States dropped the atomic bombs on Hiroshima and Nagasaki in August 1945, Truman's desire to stop the Russian advance into Manchuria (northern China) may have been a factor (although defeating Japan without having to invade the main islands was of course the primary consideration).

The United States abruptly cut off aid to the Soviet Union and turned down a Soviet loan request. Stalin then refused to withdraw Soviet troops from northern Iran and reneged on wartime promises to allow free elections in Soviet-occupied Eastern Europe. Instead, Stalin moved to consolidate Soviet control over Poland, East Germany, Romania, Hungary, Bulgaria, and, finally, in early 1948, Czechoslovakia.

Against the backdrop of Stalin's expansionism in Eastern Europe, a great debate unfolded in the Unted States about policy toward the Soviet Union. The Cold War would not emerge clearly until 1948. But a telegram dispatched by George Kennan from the U.S. embassy in Moscow in February 1946 presaged the policy of **containment**, which after 1948 became the cornerstone of the United States' national security strategy for four decades.

Stalin's actions in Poland and Czechoslovakia were particularly alarming to the American public. There was a sizable Polish community in the United States—Chicago at one time boasted the second largest concentration of Polish people in the world (only Warsaw was larger). Stalin had assured Roosevelt that the Soviet Union would respect Polish sovereignty. Czechoslovakia was a special case because it had been a showcase of democracy between the two world wars. In early 1948, leaders of the Czechoslovakian Communist Party, subservient to Stalin, staged a coup—with Stalin's backing and very likely on his orders. In the course of the Communist takeover, President Jan Masaryk, son of the beloved first president of Czechoslovakia, Thomas Masaryk, died under mysterious circumstances—he fell or was thrown from a window. President Truman, capitalizing on the furor created by the latest Soviet land grab, asked Congress to back the multibillion-dollar **Marshall Plan**. Though it was by far the biggest foreign-aid package ever proposed, funding was approved in short order.

The year 1948 also saw the first Berlin crisis. Before World War II, Berlin had been the capital of Germany. After the war, when Germany was divided into zones occupied by each of the victorious Allies, Berlin, located inside the Soviet-occupied eastern zone, was likewise divided. Stalin wanted all of Berlin under East German (Soviet) jurisdiction. He decided to force the issue by blockading Berlin. The United States responded with an airlift that kept West Berlin alive. Stalin was checkmated: either he could shoot down the U.S. supply planes and touch off a new hot war, or he could back off. He backed off.

In 1949, the United States established the **North Atlantic Treaty Organization (NATO)**, the first peacetime U.S. alliance in 150 years. The Soviet Union responded by forming the **Warsaw Pact**. In 1949, two other landmark events occurred: the Soviet Union conducted its first successful atomic bomb test, and the pro-Western government of Chiang Kai-shek was driven off China's mainland onto the island of Taiwan by the forces of Chinese Communist leader Mao Zedong.

Despite a slight thaw following Stalin's death in 1953, the Cold War persisted. The Soviet Union faced major challenges at home and abroad. After Communist Party Secretary Nikita Khrushchev renounced Stalinism in 1956, uprisings against Communist rule occurred in Poland and Hungary. Khrushchev sent troops into Hungary in 1956; the Communist government in Poland weathered the storm without direct Soviet intervention. But the lessons on both sides were clear: for the Eastern European satellites, Moscow would not permit defection from the Warsaw Pact; for Moscow, the price of empire was eternal vigilance.

Between 1958 and 1961, the issue of Berlin heated up again, resulting in an on-again, off-again crisis that culminated in August 1961 in the building of the Berlin Wall to stop the flood of escapees to the West. A year later came a crisis over Soviet offensive missiles stationed in Cuba that brought the two superpowers to the very brink of nuclear war. The confrontation had a sobering effect on both sides. The upshot was the establishment of a telephone "hot line" between the White House and the Kremlin and the Partial Nuclear Test Ban Treaty, signed in July 1963.

But as tensions were stabilizing with the West, they were heating up on the other Soviet flank. In the early 1960s, a rift in relations between the USSR and its erstwhile Communist ally, the People's Republic of China, escalated into a war of words. Throughout the 1960s, the two Communist behemoths traded insults. The spat turned ugly in 1969 when fighting broke out along the border demarcated by the Amur and Ussuri rivers. There were relatively few casualties, but Sino-Soviet relations remained frigid, and Moscow found itself engaged in two cold wars at once.

Even within their own sphere of influence, the Soviets faced challenges. In 1968, Czechoslovakia attempted defiance. With the "Prague spring" came the flowering of a democratization movement ("socialism with a human face"). Led by Alexander Dubček, the Communist regime proposed to open up the political system to opposition parties. Moscow would have no truck with such "bourgeois" heresy. At the order of General Secretary Leonid Brezhnev, Soviet troops rolled into Prague and crushed Dubček's government. Brezhnev justified the intervention on the grounds that socialist states have an obligation to come to the aid of another socialist state threatened by counterrevolution. In other words, once a socialist state, always a socialist state—particularly in Eastern Europe. Elsewhere the so-called **Brezhnev Doctrine** was roundly condemned.

The early 1970s witnessed the opening wedge of a dramatic realignment: the United States and Communist China buried the hatchet after more than two decades of hostility. Moscow looked on in dismay but should not have been surprised: one of the oldest principles of international politics—the enemy of my enemy is my friend—was working to bring these strange bedfellows together.

With relations between Washington and Beijing warming up, the Soviet Union decided it was time to seek accommodation with the United States. In 1972 the two superpowers signed a strategic arms limitation agreement, SALT I. They also moved to improve their trade relations. East-West trade had developed outside the Soviet-American relationship. In the early 1970s, West Germany, under the center-left government of Chancellor Willy Brandt, pursued an independent foreign policy (*Ostpolitik*) that sharply increased trade and other ties between East and West Germany and between Eastern and Western Europe.

Superpower relations in the 1970s were uneven. Progress in strategic arms limitation was not matched in other areas. The decade ended on a discordant note with the Soviet invasion of Afghanistan, a punitive grain embargo imposed on the Soviet Union by the Carter administration, and a boycott of the Moscow Summer Olympics (by the United States, Communist China, Japan, and other nations). The election of Ronald Reagan, a staunch anticommunist, seemed likely to bring a resurgence of the Cold War as the 1980s unfolded.

American distrust of Moscow and a string of Soviet leaders who lacked vision and vigor (due to old age or failing health) prevented progress. The accession of Mikhail Gorbachev in 1985 and Reagan's desire to finish his second term with a flourish broke the standoff. In November 1987, the two superpowers signed a treaty eliminating intermediate-range nuclear forces in Europe. Moscow had made several unilateral concessions in the negotiations. This conciliatory attitude in matters of arms control, combined with Gorbachev's liberal domestic reforms, raised the first prospect of a true thaw in the Cold War.

Stalin's Heirs: From Khrushchev to Gorbachev

Stalin's death in 1953 provoked a succession crisis. Following several years of bitter infighting, Nikita Khrushchev emerged as the winner. He lost little time in distancing himself from the deceased dictator.

At the Twentieth Party Congress in 1956, Khrushchev delivered his famous **Secret Speech**. The four-hour address contained a blockbuster: the pronouncement that Stalin had made serious errors in the 1930s and had committed excesses in the name of building communism. Of course, everyone who heard this shocking "revelation" already knew about the Stalin terror. But prior to Khrushchev's speech, nobody in the Soviet Union dared whisper a word about it.

Khrushchev's **de-Stalinization** drive was his most significant contribution to the development of the Soviet state. Not only did he denounce government by fear and Stalinist terror, but he also emptied the labor camps and dismantled most of the vast camp system (the "gulag archipelago," in Alexander Solzhenitsyn's memorable phrase).

Other attempts at reforming the Stalinist state, however, were destined to fail. In agriculture, Khrushchev launched the **"virgin lands" campaign** under which millions of hectares of land in Kazakhstan and eastern Russia were to be plowed and planted for the first time. It seemed like a good idea at the time, and at first it seemed to be working. But within a decade it turned to disaster as the fragile topsoil was blown away by fierce winds. In the spring of 1963, according to one account:

> Dust clouds hid the sun for several days, irrigation canals were choked, and along some stands of trees drifts of soil more than two meters high were formed. Many towns and villages were covered with dirt, and from thousands of hectares the arable layer was so completely removed by the winds that the underlying bedrock was exposed. Precise data on the damaged areas were not published, but millions of hectares were involved. . . . It will take at least one to two centuries before the arable layer is restored to these areas.[20]

Khrushchev's other attempts at economic and administrative reform were equally ill-fated. In an effort to decentralize the cumbersome state bureaucracy, he abolished most of the Moscow-based economic departments, creating regional economic councils (*sovnarkhozy*) in their place. But this radical reorganization was resisted by officials with a vested interest in preserving the power and status of the center, Moscow. He also introduced a plan for the regular rotation of Party personnel (thus threatening the job security of Party bosses) and tried splitting regional Party committees into agricultural and industrial sectors, again in the name of increased efficiency.

What resulted was confusion and probable sabotage by disgruntled functionaries and administrators. When Khrushchev was ousted in 1964, his successors cited his "hare-brained schemes" as justification. His detractors also accused him of trying to create a "cult of personality" (a Stalinist sin) and thus violating the Leninist principle of collective leadership. Accordingly, Leonid Brezhnev, Khrushchev's successor as general secretary, did not assume the post of premier. (Khrushchev, like Stalin, had simultaneously held the top post in both Party and government.) Alexei Kosygin became the new premier, Nikolai Podgorny the new president. Thus a kind of triumvirate, with Brezhnev as "first among equals," replaced one-man dictatorship for the first time in Soviet history. (Brezhnev ousted Podgorny and assumed the post of president, as well as Party chief, in 1977.)

Brezhnev's long tenure (1964–1982) brought a return to the structures and methods of the Stalinist era (minus state terror). This **neo-Stalinism**, as it is sometimes called, was evident in both cultural and economic policy.

In the economic sphere, the Brezhnev regime briefly toyed with market-oriented reforms, based on the proposals of Soviet economist Evsei Liberman. But the reforms were soon abandoned in favor of a return to the Stalinist system of central planning with its emphasis on quotas, artificial prices, and top-down management.

In the cultural sphere, censorship, which Khrushchev had relaxed in the early 1960s, was restored. In 1968 two writers, Andrei Sinyavsky and Yuli Daniel, were convicted of "anti-Soviet agitation," a political crime under Soviet law that typically carries a penalty of seven years in prison. The trial sent a chill throughout artistic and literary circles in the Soviet Union.

Two events led to the emergence of a human-rights movement in the USSR in the late 1960s: the Israeli victory in the Six-Day War in 1967 and the Soviet invasion of Czechoslovakia in 1968. The first event inspired Soviet Jews to seek permission to emigrate to Israel (or the West); the second focused attention on repressive Soviet policies both at home and abroad and gave rise to protests (even from devout Communists) throughout Eastern and Western Europe. In the Soviet Union, a small but vocal group of dissidents took up the cudgels for liberalization of Soviet politics and culture.

The human-rights movement was given a boost by the Soviet signing of the Helsinki Accords in 1975. Part of the agreement obligated the signatories to respect personal rights and civil liberties. **Détente**, the *rapprochement* between the two superpowers—crowned by SALT I and a new trade pact in the early 1970s—was a major factor. But Soviet-American relations, always tense and tentative, soured in the late 1970s. The Soviet invasion of Afghanistan in 1979 drove relations between Washington and Moscow to their nadir. (The SALT II treaty, which subsequently stalled in the U.S. Senate, was one of the casualties.)

One manifestation of the hardening Soviet attitudes toward both the West and internal liberalization (the two policy tracks tended to move in tandem) was a crackdown on dissent. Several prominent human-rights activists and **refuseniks** (Soviet Jews who have been refused permission to emigrate) were arrested and put on trial. The most famous, Anatoly Shcharansky, was both a human-rights activist and a refusenik, thus symbolizing everything the Brezhnev regime sought to suppress. He was accused not only of anti-Soviet agitation but also of being a spy. The punishment for treason in the Soviet Union was death. Shcharansky was spared, sentenced to thirteen years in a labor colony. (In 1986 he was exchanged for several East German spies and now lives in Israel.)

After 1979, Jewish emigration was reduced to a trickle, and the political climate discouraged manifestations of dissent or nonconformity. The Kremlin's neo-Stalinist social and cultural policies were matched by a strict, orthodox approach to economic problems. The prescribed remedies for inefficiency continued to have one common denominator: overcentralized management within the rigid framework of economic planning. (An in-depth analysis of the Soviet economic malady is presented in Chapters 8 and 9.) In the early 1980s, the ossified Soviet system, like its geriatric leaders, showed clear signs of old age.

The ebb and flow of political repression during the Brezhnev years obscured the steady erosion of central authority. Several forces were causing this growing instability. First, the steel sword of Stalin's totalitarian system had been the secret police, or **KGB**. After Khrushchev's Secret Speech in 1956, the KGB was demoralized, discredited, and partly defanged. Still formidable, it nonetheless ceased to inspire the kind of fear it had in Stalin's day.

That Western visitors were allowed to enter the country and move about specific "open" cities relatively freely, especially after the Soviet-American détente of the early 1970s, was a symptom of the Kremlin's weakening hold on society. At the same time, more Soviet academicians, scientists, and other professionals were permitted to venture abroad. Accompanying this "travel revolution" was a "communications revolution." With the waves of tourists coming to the USSR came Western ideas, clothing, music, magazines, tapes, records, and gadgets. Some young people learned to speak English by approaching Americans (and other English speakers) on the street and striking up a conversation. They would offer their services as unofficial tour guides, asking only for an opportunity to speak English in return.[21]

When Brezhnev died in 1982, he was succeeded by Yuri Andropov, former head of the KGB. Andropov moved quickly to revitalize the Soviet economy, relying primarily on exhortation and admonition; his watchword was discipline. Anyone caught skipping work ("absenteeism"), avoiding work or malingering on the job ("parasitism"), getting drunk or causing a public disturbance ("hooliganism"), dealing on the black market ("speculation"), or engaging in other corrupt practices would be punished to the limits of the law.

Soviet citizens were both optimistic and apprehensive about the new regime. There was widespread recognition that stagnation had set in and that only a strong leader with a clear vision of the future could pull the nation out of its doldrums. But there was also an unspoken fear that Andropov might resurrect the Stalinist police state.

These hopes and fears were for naught, however. Andropov fell ill and died in the spring of 1984. His successor, Konstantin Chernenko, old and frail from the start, died a year later. The Soviet Union had now been without energetic leadership for years. Between 1917 and 1964, three strong leaders—Lenin, Stalin, and Khrushchev—had held sway in the Kremlin. Now, between 1982 and 1985, three men—Brezhnev, Andropov, and Chernenko—had died in office. Something had to be done about the Soviet gerontocracy. Rejuvenation could not be accomplished by aging leaders whose jaded and old-fashioned views precluded initiative and innovation.

Enter Mikhail Gorbachev. Gorbachev was in his fifties when he took over the reins of power—a youngster by Soviet political standards. Gorbachev's reforms are examined in Chapter 9. For now it suffices to note that he moved boldly on the cultural and economic fronts. In the political sphere, he paid lip service to democratization, but the constitutional changes he proposed did not compromise the Communist Party's power monopoly. As the Soviet state passed the half-century mark in 1987, many observers believed that it was on the verge of a new era. In fact, it was approaching its demise.

Ideology and Political Culture

An *ideology* is an official belief system; in the case of Soviet-type Communist states, it was an amalgam of ideas and teachings associated primarily with Marx and Lenin. *Political culture* is broader and encompasses not only ideology but also values, attitudes, myths, fears, prejudices, perceptions, and preferences that permeate and condition the political thoughts and actions of society's members. This distinction was especially crucial in the Soviet bloc countries because the ideology was used as a kind of smoke screen concealing the underlying values that actually motivated political behavior.

Marxism-Leninism: A Secular Religion

During the heyday of communism, volumes were written on Soviet ideology. Now that the Cold War is over and the Soviet Union is defunct, **Marxism-Leninism** has faded into the pages of twentieth-century history. Even so, the moral, economic, and political consequences of decades of communist rule are still very much in evidence throughout the region, as we shall see in Chapter 9. To find the intellectual roots of the ill-fated system Lenin and his successors invented, it is necessary to explore the world of Marxist-Leninist thought.

Marxism is not simply a blueprint for revolution. It combines a philosophy of history with an elaborate theory of social development. Karl Marx claimed to have discovered the laws of sociopolitical evolution. The driving force in history, he believed, is economics, the organization of the means of production. Social and political institutions are seen as mere "superstructure," edifices built on economic foundations defined by relationships of production. Control or ownership of the means of production determines political power, social status, and economic well-being. According to Marx, this iron law of history applies at all times in all places.

Capitalism, in Marx's eyes, is simply a stage in social evolution. Capitalism is a system in which the few ("monopoly capitalists") control the means of production (land, labor, buildings, machines, money) and use this control to exploit the many (who have no choice but to work for meager wages). The **law of capitalist accumulation** operates through fierce dog-eat-dog competition to squeeze out little producers and create opportunities for big ones to get bigger. Darwinian-style survival of the fittest prevails: producers must either "get big or get out" of the market.

Profit is the engine that drives capitalism, according to Marx; even non-Marxist economists agree. But Marx believed that profits are robbery. Under capitalism, workers toil long hours for subsistence wages. The difference between the income their labor generates and the pay they receive for that labor is what Marx called **surplus value** (profit based on exploitation).

As the rich get richer, the poor get poorer. The rich also get fewer, while the ranks of the poor swell as industrialization shifts the economy from rural to urban, from farm to factory. A new underclass, the proletariat, is thus created by a relentless process Marx called the **law of pauperization**. As machines replace human labor, unemployment grows, poverty spreads, and domestic markets shrink. The resulting business recession leads to even greater unemployment and eventually to economic depression. Here, in a nutshell, is the Achilles' heel of the free-market system—the inevitable and recurrent "crisis of capitalism" that will eventually cause its total collapse.

The concept of **alienation** plays a central role in the Marxist theory of revolution. As part of an impersonal wage-labor force, workers are estranged from the means of production. Their labor is owned by someone else. They have no voice in how things are run. Their jobs are monotonous and menial. They take no pride in their work (mass consumption means that quality is less important than quantity, and producers and consumers do not know each other). Workers are cogs in a machine. Thus capitalism is dehumanizing.

The Communist Manifesto opens with these prophetic words: "A spectre is haunting Europe—the spectre of Communism." Marx wrote this pamphlet (with Friedrich Engels) to elucidate his thesis that "the history of all hitherto existing society is the history of class struggle." The final class struggle, between the proletariat and the bourgeoisie, would result in spontaneous revolution and usher in socialism, a system of productive relations characterized by public ownership and a fair, though not equal, distribution of goods ("from each according to his ability, to each according to his work"). In time the state would simply wither away. The ultimate form of society would evolve gradually and naturally from socialism to communism ("from each according to his ability, to each according to his needs"). For Marx, equality was the supreme moral value.

Lenin was less interested in theory than practice. He wanted to make a revolution, not philosophize about history. Marx had called for a **dictatorship of the proletariat** as a temporary measure to forestall counterrevolution. It was an unfortunate turn of phrase: Lenin used it as an excuse to create a dictatorship *over* the proletariat. In addition, as noted, Lenin coined a new term for the Communist Party, exalting it as the **vanguard of the proletariat**. Without the vanguard, the revolution would never get rolling, Lenin argued. In this way, Lenin set the stage for the Party dictatorship that became the hallmark of the Soviet state.

Two other Leninist precepts deserve mention. First, Lenin invented *democratic centralism,* which governed the organization and operation of the Party. As soon as a decision was announced, lower-level discussion within the Party would cease. Decisions on important issues were made behind closed doors at the highest level and were strictly binding on all subordinate levels. Second, Lenin placed a *ban on factionalism* within the Party, meaning that any opposition to the Party line, no matter how loyal, would be suppressed whenever the leadership found it expedient to do so. Also, any Party leader guilty of factionalism risked demotion or expulsion.

Leninism evolved into a state religion. "Despite all the museums of atheism that have taken the place of Russian Orthodox churches throughout the country, the Soviet Union is now less an atheistic country than a Leninist country," wrote one observer just a few years before the collapse of Soviet communism. "Even the most casual visitor to the Soviet Union is overwhelmed by evidence of the religion of Leninism."[22] Every day, thousands of Soviet citizens stood in long lines waiting to file past Lenin's open coffin in a granite mausoleum in Red Square. Pictures, statues, and busts of Lenin were everywhere. Graven images of Lenin set against a background of scarlet to symbolize the Great October Revolution and bathed in a soft halo of light replaced the traditional icons that once adorned special corners in factories and schools.

The Eastern European regimes carried this ideological baggage as well. They continued to pay lip service to Marx and Lenin, but the litany had grown stale. By 1989, when Communist governments in the region toppled like dominoes, Marxism-Leninism had more in common with religious ritual than political reality. (The reasons for the decline of ideology in these nominally Communist societies will be discussed in Chapters 8 and 9.)

Soviet Political Culture: Old Wine, New Wineskins

Understanding other cultures requires a certain ability to suspend our own ingrained values and habits of mind. Failure to do so inevitably leads to misconceptions. To cite one example, a journalist named Hedrick Smith, posted to Moscow in the 1970s, expected to find that most Soviet citizens remembered Stalin with fear and loathing. He was surprised to discover that, on the contrary, "so essential was Stalin to the concept of how Russia should be ruled for many middle-aged and elderly people that they no longer recall their panic at the time of his death."[23] Many ordinary Soviet citizens expressed nostalgia for a strong boss!

Smith's observations comparing Soviet (and especially Russian) attitudes toward authority with Western (in particular, American) views are worth quoting at some length:

> [There is] a fundamental difference between Russians and Americans, who are often moved to seek similarities in their national characters. They may share an openness of spirit but Russians and Americans differ sharply in their attitudes toward power and authority—and not just because of Soviet Communism. Inbred mistrust of authority is an American tradition. We are wary as a people of bigness when it is accompanied by unchecked power—Big Business, Big Labor, big anything. . . .
>
> Not so the Russians. Bigness and power are admired almost without qualification. Size inspires awe—huge Kremlins, cannons, churchbells under the czars; huge dams, missiles, atom smashers under the Communists. Marxism-Leninism has provided a rationale for large-scale production and concentrated power in the hands of Party leaders and central planners. But six centuries of authoritarian rule from Ivan the Great and Ivan the Terrible forward had made Russians monarchists in their bones long before Lenin and Stalin came along. . . .
>
> So much has been inherited from the past that a Russian takes for granted elements of political despotism that are instantly an affront to a Westerner. History has conditioned Russians differently. The cruel tyranny of Stalin was prefigured by the bloody reign of Ivan the Terrible in the 16th century and the iron rule of Nicholas I in the 19th century. Peter the Great, celebrated for opening Russia to the West and introducing a more modern Army and state administration, is well known abroad for having also improved the efficiency of authoritarian controls, some of which survive today. It was Peter who set up the first political police administration and who officially instituted censorship and the practice of issuing internal passports to keep Russians from traveling away from their permanent homes without special permission.[24]

The easy assumption that the virtues of democracy are as obvious to Russians as they are to Americans turns out to be a delusion. For reasons deeply rooted in their history, Russians tend to value security more than freedom (which, prior to the Gorbachev reform campaign, they had never known); at the same time, they often fear disorder more than tyranny.[25]

Part of the Russian aversion to overt forms of disobedience can probably be explained by their history of draconian rule, the resulting absence of democracy, and a natural fear of the unknown. People accustomed to stern discipline are bound to feel insecure and perhaps disoriented when that discipline is reduced or removed. Of course, not all Soviet citizens feared freedom or equated democracy with disorder, but most probably did.

Russians deal with embarrassing facts by hiding them. Western observers are often struck by the Russian penchant for *pokazukha,* putting up a false front. The practice of deliberately disguising unpleasant realities is a time-honored and highly perfected tradition in Russia. One of the most famous examples occurred in the eighteenth century when a prince named Potemkin erected fake villages along the route used by Catherine the Great to impress her with the wealth of his region. The "Potemkin trick" was used extensively by the Communists—for example, the Soviet travel agency, Intourist, packaged special tours of showcase cities just for foreigners, provided guides (who did double duty as chaperones), and kept visitors' schedules so jam-packed with excursions, museums, ballet performances, and the like that there was no time to poke around and explore the darker side of Soviet life.

Russians have long believed that Western nations view them as crude and uncultured. "You like to laugh at our misfortunes" is a common sentiment Russians express toward Americans. (Like many other misperceptions we entertain about each other, this one contains a kernel of truth.) The deep-rooted Russian inferiority complex—manifested, for example, in the proclivity of Russian schoolteachers to challenge American visitors to impromptu poetry-reciting contests—was reinforced by Soviet propaganda during the Cold War. The upshot was a kind of reflexive Soviet patriotism that popped up even in nonthreatening interpersonal encounters with the West. Such reactions may strike Westerners as inappropriate, but they are a natural reflection of a deep-seated Russian sense of inferiority vis-à-vis the West.

Patriotism is a universal emotion, but the "blood and soil" Russian variety startles many Western visitors. During the Communist era, "Soviet" patriotism was really Russian patriotism with a thin Bolshevik veneer. Signs of patriotism were everywhere; some were transparently contrived by the regime for foreign consumption, but many were spontaneous and heartfelt. Hedrick Smith quoted a young Soviet economist: "We learned from our history that to survive, we must band together." Smith also noted that Suvorov, the great Russian military commander who defeated both Frederick the Great and Napoleon, used to say, "*Pust khuzhe, da nashe*" ("Let it be worse, but let it be ours").[26]

This attitude is akin to "My country, right or wrong," something the Russians call *kvasnoi patriotizm*. Smith explained it this way:

> Like so many essentials of Russian life, the phrase does not readily lend itself to translation, for one has to know that kvas is a fermented peasant drink made from water dripped through burnt bread. Kvas has a malty flavor, and cheap kvas can be like cold coffee—bitter, the color of muddy water, with grounds at the bottom. In cities all over Russia, white-coated women serve up glass mugs of kvas from large, saffron-colored, mobile metal kegs in the summertime. Foreigners usually pass up a second mug, but Russians swear by it, and peasants produce their own home brew of kvas. So kvas patriotism represents the earthy peasantry: an intensely Russian brand of patriotism.[27]

The impact of communism on Russian political culture was (and still is) evident in a phenomenon called *blat*—a generic term for the pervasive corruption, cheating, and dishonesty that permeated everyday life in the USSR. *Blat* assumed myriad forms: theft of state property, bribery, embezzlement, moonlighting, dealing on the black market. It involved bending, evading, or breaking the rules in all sorts of subtle and not-so-subtle ways. Almost everybody did it, largely out of necessity, because consumer goods and services were always scarce (and therefore precious) and because prices fixed by the state did not reflect their true (market) value. Thus the distortions introduced into the Soviet economy by the system of central planning—in particular, the emphasis on heavy industry and defense production at the expense of consumer needs—created a morally ambiguous climate in which widespread dishonesty and underhandedness were rewarded (and tacitly accepted) while honesty and integrity appeared foolish. Moreover, the rigidities of central planning made it expedient for plant managers, too, to cheat, lie, and falsify records on a vast scale, including the use of illegal go-betweens to obtain essential materials on the black market, in a never-ending struggle to fulfill monthly production quotas.

Public morality in the USSR reflected the collectivism that lay at the core of Marxist ethics. This moral propensity contrasted sharply with the individualism so prevalent in countries like France and the United States. In the Soviet Union, the paramount importance of the *kollektif* was rarely questioned. Schoolchildren were taught to place group rights above individual rights and to take responsibility for the performance and conduct of their classmates. Similarly, teachers generally held parents responsible for the attitudes and actions of their children in school. Adults were even expected to take responsibility for the conduct of other adults—especially family members, neighbors, and coworkers—to an extent that was startling and alien to Westerners.

Eastern Europe before 1945

The nations of Eastern Europe have historical roots, but the present states emerged as sovereign entities only in the modern age, after centuries of foreign rule. Hungary regained internal independence in 1867 with the establishment of the dual monarchy (the emperor of Austria was also Hungary's king). Romania became independent in 1878, Bulgaria in 1908, and Albania in 1912. Czechoslovakia and Yugoslavia emerged as independent states only after World War I and dissolved shortly after the demise of the Soviet Union. Poland was reconstituted as a sovereign state after the war; Russia, Prussia, and Austria had dismantled it in a series of "partitions" more than a century earlier.

East Germany was a special case. Stalin formed the German Democratic Republic (GDR) from the portion of Germany occupied by Soviet troops after the defeat of Hitler's Third Reich in 1945; it had never aspired to a separate existence, always considering itself part of a single German nation.

Before World War I, four great empires dominated Eastern Europe, all located on the periphery of the region and only one, Russia, anchored in a Slavic culture. By the mid-nineteenth century, the Russian empire encompassed all of the Ukraine, part of Poland, and Bessarabia (now part of Moldova). The German and Austrian empires partitioned and ruled Poland from the end of the eighteenth century until 1918. Austria's domain included the territories of what are now the Czech Republic, Slovakia, Hungary, Slovenia, and Croatia from the fifteenth century until its defeat and dissolution in World War I. The Ottoman Empire

(Turkey) ruled the present-day Balkan nations of Bulgaria, Romania, Bosnia, Yugoslavia, Macedonia, and Albania.

The most important distinction, politically, is between the Eastern European countries once ruled by Austria and Germany and those ruled by the Ottoman Turks. Most of the former were greatly influenced by Western Europe and made important contributions to the high culture of the West (consider, for example, the impact on classical music of Czech composers such as Dvořak, Smetana, and Janáček or the Polish composer Chopin). The Balkans developed in relative isolation from the West, and hence the cultural contributions of its peoples are generally less widely known outside the region.

Although all Eastern European countries had limited autonomy, the northern-tier Slavic nations generally experienced less oppression and abuse than their neighbors to the south, who endured religious persecution and heavy taxation while benefiting from little or no economic and political development well into the twentieth century.

In the turbulent period between World War I and World War II (1918–1939), many Eastern European governments had a democratic veneer, but only Czechoslovakia was a true democracy. Other nations in the region lacked experience in democratic self-government. Many also lacked moderate leadership and faced enormous economic and social problems. Anti-Semitism and extreme nationalism were prevalent throughout the region, as were divisions over religion, social reform, and national aspirations. The leaders of Hungary, Romania, and Bulgaria saw the Nazi totalitarian model as a solution to their desperate domestic circumstances. (All three countries later joined the Hitler-led Axis.) Widespread hostility to both Russia and communism also reinforced this perverse inclination to embrace Nazi Germany.

All of the nations of Eastern Europe lost their independence in World War II. Poland, Czechoslovakia, and Yugoslavia were conquered by Nazi Germany (but in Yugoslavia, Tito's Partisans waged a ferocious guerrilla war against the Germans).

In 1939, Hitler and Stalin signed a nonaggression pact under which they split Poland. Two years later, Hitler tore up the agreement, overran Poland, and attacked the Soviet Union. Later, when Stalin turned the tide, the advancing Red Army waited on the eastern bank of the Vistula River while German troops crushed the Polish underground. (The Polish government in exile had called for the Warsaw uprising in the belief that it would hasten the defeat of the Germans; rather than helping the Polish fighters, Stalin kept his army on the sidelines.) In due time, Soviet troops crossed the Vistula and pursued Hitler's retreating forces into Germany. Thus in an ironic twist, Hitler ended up giving the USSR a golden opportunity to dispatch Soviet troops into Poland. After the war, the Red Army occupied Poland and ensured Soviet domination of that country until 1989.

The story of Poland is tragic but not without precedent. In 1772, Prussia and Russia annexed major portions of Polish territory in the First Partition of Poland. According to Ivan Volgyes, "Poland then tried to re-create its former greatness by reforming the obsolete workings of its government." In the Second Partition in 1793, Poland was further reduced. "Even though the Poles, under the brilliant general Tadeusz Kosciuszko, fought valiantly against partition, the dream of Polish independence was brutally crushed by the invading Prussian and Russian armies." The Third Partition, involving the Austrians, in 1795 marked "the end of Poland as a political entity, as a state."[28]

Hungary, Romania, and Bulgaria were first seduced and then subjugated by Hitler. As accomplices of Nazi Germany, they could expect little sympathy from the Allies after the war. (This point is often underemphasized in historical treatments of this period.) Thus the postwar Soviet land grab in Eastern Europe was actually facilitated by the very nations that eventually fell victim to Stalin's megalomania.

One of the most important consequences of World War II was the unification of Eastern Europe into a military and political bloc under the Warsaw Pact, led by the Soviet Union. Thus one Slavic nation, Russia, the nucleus of the USSR, succeeded in bringing Eastern Europe's Slavic peoples under a single political authority for the first time in history. But in so doing, Stalin made the same mistake the czars had made in earlier centuries: he overextended the empire.

Eastern Europe under Soviet Tutelage

The Soviet grip on Eastern Europe was probably never as firm as it appeared to the West, as periodic revolts in Poland and attempted defections by Hungary and Czechoslovakia revealed. In addition, the "captive nations" resisted Soviet rule in a number of subtle ways. In the first place, most people seldom paid more than lip service to the official ideology. It was the subject of jokes and sarcasm in private, even as it was treated with mock reverence in public. In the second place, an undercurrent of anti-Communist (anti-Russian) sentiment bubbled just beneath the surface throughout Eastern Europe. The extent of this rejection of the Communist ideology was dramatically revealed in 1989, as one Communist government after another simply abandoned the ship of state.

According to one scholar, "The failure of the Soviet Union to Russify the area and convert the population to its brand of 'Marxism-Leninism' should not overshadow the enormous moral, spiritual, and cultural damage inflicted upon the East European nations." The Soviet model was "superimposed on natural diversity," and no aspect of life was left untouched:

> The extent of damages and the degree of recovery naturally vary from country to country, but in all of them deep-rooted feelings of having been robbed and degraded by an alien superpower are still very live issues. Indeed it is hardly an exaggeration to say that nationalism constitutes the heart of the challenge to Soviet domination and that external and internal emancipation from the Soviet Union is the central theme of East European political life.[29]

Remarkably, these words were written two decades before the great "emancipation" of which they spoke came to pass.

Widespread anti-Sovietism was reinforced by another universal element in Eastern Europe: ethnic particularism, or nationalism. Each group is highly conscious of its heritage. When the Soviet Union interfered (or worse, intervened) in the internal affairs of the various countries, it stirred strong nationalistic impulses. Moscow's heavy-handed treatment of its satellites in Eastern Europe helped heterogeneous states like Czechoslovakia and Yugoslavia overcome ethnic tensions within their own societies. The dissolution of these states following the Soviet withdrawal from Eastern Europe strongly supports this conclusion.

In the absence of Pax Sovietica, nationalism is again playing a major role in Eastern Europe, both within and between states. Historic rivalries were submerged but never dissolved by ideology or alliance ties. Even during the heyday of the Cold War, these rivalries occasionally came to the fore:

> Witness, for example, the glee with which the East Germans and Poles intervened in Czechoslovakia in 1968, the pressures for military intervention in Poland in 1981 expressed by the East Germans and Czechoslovaks, or the problems between Hungary, on the one hand, and Czechoslovakia and Romania, on the other, regarding the presence of significant Magyar minorities in the latter two states.[30]

One commonality that may have helped ease the pain of adjustment to the Stalinist system after World War II is the tradition of authoritarianism that pervades most of Slavic Europe. The fact that of all the nations of Eastern Europe, only Czechoslovakia has ever tried democracy with any degree of success has taken on new relevance with the collapse of communism in the region.

In retrospect, the underlying problem throughout the Soviet bloc was more spiritual than material, more psychological than economic. What ultimately determines the success or failure of a society or an economy (especially one endowed with the natural resources and population base necessary for sustained growth and prosperity) is the heart and soul of a nation, the intangible factors that account for the vigor and vitality of a country. Japan, for example, achieved its postwar economic miracle even without the natural resources that would seem to be a prerequisite.

Chiang Kai-shek, the pro-West leader of Nationalist China, once described Communism as a disease of the heart. In the 1980s, the Communist leaders of the Soviet Union and Eastern Europe were forced to confront the fact that Chiang might have been right. As the events of 1989–1991 were to show, the disease was ultimately to prove fatal.

CONCLUSION

Slavic Europe has developed along quite different lines from Western Europe. Powerful intellectual and cultural movements such as the Renaissance and Reformation never penetrated much of Eastern Europe; it remains a Slavic world. The history of the region bears scant evidence of fraternal ties among Slavic nations beyond ethnolinguistic similarities. On the contrary, outbreaks of ethnic conflict have been quite common except during the period of Soviet domination. The Soviet Union ruled most of the Slavic world for four decades after World War II; Russia, in turn, dominated the Soviet Union. All of the nations of Eastern Europe have almost always been dominated by an imperial power—Russia, Germany, Austria-Hungary, the Ottoman Turks. In 1989, one Communist regime after another fell in a wave of popular discontent and brought an end to the period of Pax Sovietica—stability enforced by Soviet military might. In December 1991, the Soviet Union itself collapsed following an abortive coup by hardliners. In the next chapter, we turn our attention to the new political institutions now being put to the test in the former Soviet Union and Eastern Europe.

KEY TERMS

Pax Sovietica
Eastern Europe
Slavic Europe
Russification
Mensheviks
Bolsheviks
proletariat
February Revolution
October Revolution
soviets
war communism
New Economic Policy (NEP)
Stalinism
autarky
collectivization
containment
Marshall Plan
North Atlantic Treaty Organization (NATO)

Warsaw Pact
Brezhnev Doctrine
Secret Speech
de-Stalinization
"virgin lands" campaign
neo-Stalinism
détente
refuseniks
KGB
Marxism-Leninism
law of capitalist accumulation
surplus value
law of pauperization
alienation
The Communist Manifesto
dictatorship of the proletariat
vanguard of the proletariat
blat

STUDY QUESTIONS

1. How did geography influence the Soviet Union's history, political traditions, economy, and political culture (its attitudes, beliefs, myths, prejudices, hopes, fears, and the like)?

2. What impact did the Cold War have on East-West relations in such areas as arms control, trade, investment, and conflict management?

3. What, if anything, is distinctive about the geography and cultures of Eastern Europe? How have these factors influenced the region's history? Has a sense

of Slavic solidarity been present throughout the region in modern times, or is today's nationalism more particularistic?

4. What were the main tenets of Soviet ideology? How did both Lenin and Stalin bend Marx's ideas to fit the political circumstances that each faced?

5. What were the most significant developments in the Soviet Union after Stalin's death in 1953? What reforms are associated with Nikita Khrushchev? With Leonid Brezhnev?

SUGGESTED READING

Berdyaev, Nicholas. *The Origin of Russian Communism.* Ann Arbor: University of Michigan Press, 1960.

Conquest, Robert. *The Harvest of Sorrow: Soviet Collectivization and the Terror-Famine.* New York: Oxford University Press, 1987.

Conquest, Robert. *V. I. Lenin.* New York: Viking Penguin, 1972.

Crankshaw, Edward. *Khrushchev: A Career.* New York: Viking Penguin, 1966.

Halle, Louis J. *The Cold War as History.* New York: HarperCollins, 1991.

Lendvai, Paul. *Eagles in Cobwebs: Nationalism and Communism in the Balkans.* Garden City, N.Y.: Anchor/Doubleday, 1969.

Mackenzie, David, and Curran, Michael W. *A History of Russia and the Soviet Union.* 3rd ed. Belmont, Calif.: Wadsworth, 1987.

Palmer, Alan. *The Lands Between: A History of East-Central Europe since the Congress of Vienna.* New York: Macmillan, 1970.

Riasanovsky, Nicholas V. *A History of Russia.* 4th ed. New York: Oxford University Press, 1977.

Rothschild, Joseph. *Return to Diversity: A Political History of East Central Europe since World War II.* New York: Oxford University Press, 1989.

Smith, Hedrick. *The Russians.* New York: Ballantine, 1984.

Ulam, Adam B. *Stalin.* Boston: Beacon Press, 1989.

NOTES

1. Louis J. Halle, *The Cold War as History* (New York: HarperCollins, 1991), pp. 103–104.
2. Alexis de Tocqueville, *Democracy in America* (New York: Knopf, 1945), p. 452.
3. Vadim Medish, *The Soviet Union* (Englewood Cliffs, N.J.: Prentice Hall, 1987), p. 23.
4. Nicholas Berdyaev, *The Origin of Russian Communism* (Ann Arbor: University of Michigan Press, 1960), p. 9.
5. Nicholas V. Riasanovsky, *A History of Russia,* 4th ed. (New York: Oxford University Press, 1977), p. 347.
6. Medish, *Soviet Union,* p. 22.
7. See, for example, Paul Kennedy, *The Rise and Fall of the Great Powers* (New York: Vintage Books, 1987), pp. 70–77.
8. Medish, *Soviet Union,* pp. 22–23.
9. Berdyaev, *Origin of Russian Communism,* pp. 8–9.

10. Riasanovsky, *History of Russia,* p. 425.
11. Ibid., p. 426.
12. Robert Conquest, *V. I. Lenin* (New York: Viking Penguin, 1972), p. 32.
13. Isaac Deutscher, *Stalin: A Political Biography* (New York: Vintage Books, 1960), p. 550.
14. In the Stalinist tradition, five-year plans were documents that set forth general economic goals. These plans, drawn up at five-year intervals, provided the framework for the annual plans that prescribed detailed production targets (quotas) for each industrial and agricultural enterprise.
15. See, for example, Robert Conquest, *The Harvest of Sorrow: Soviet Collectivization and the Terror-Famine* (New York: Oxford University Press, 1987); and Adam B. Ulam, *Stalin* (Boston: Beacon Press, 1989).
16. See Edward Crankshaw, *Khrushchev: A Career* (New York: Viking Penguin, 1966).
17. Deutscher, *Stalin,* pp. 550–551.
18. Alexander Werth, *Russia at War, 1941–1945* (New York: Avon, 1964), pp. 904–906.
19. On the question of forced labor, one eyewitness estimates that at least a million Russian refugees were "perfidiously returned by Allied authorities into Soviet hands" in 1946 and 1947. The same writer records many other instances of mass arrests and banishment to the gulags during this period. See Alexander Solzhenitsyn, *The Gulag Archipelago, 1918–1956* (New York: Harper & Row, 1973), p. 85.
20. Roy A. Medvedev and Zhores A. Medvedev, *Khrushchev: The Years in Power* (New York: Norton, 1978), p. 121.
21. See J. Philip Rogers, *The Future of European Security* (New York: St. Martin's Press, 1993.
22. Stanley Meisler, "For Kremlin Rulers, Lenin Is Only God," *Los Angeles Times,* Oct. 25, 1987.
23. Hedrick Smith, *The Russians* (New York: Ballantine, 1984), p. 332.
24. Ibid.
25. See David K. Shipler, *Russia: Broken Idols, Solemn Dreams* (New York: Viking Penguin, 1983), p. 200.
26. Smith, *Russians,* pp. 410–411.
27. Ibid., p. 411.
28. Ivan Volgyes, *Politics in Eastern Europe* (Homewood, Ill.: Dorsey Press, 1986), pp. 29–30.
29. Paul Lendvai, *Eagles in Cobwebs: Nationalism and Communism in the Balkans* (Garden City, N.Y.: Anchor/Doubleday, 1969), p. 15.
30. Volgyes, *Politics in Eastern Europe,* p. 297.

8

New Order, Old Disorders

Although later Soviet regimes were not identical to the one Lenin and Stalin built after 1918, many of the elements of both Leninism and Stalinism survived several post-Stalin reform campaigns and, even in a time of radical restructuring, continued to influence political patterns and practices in the USSR and Eastern Europe. After 1985, the policies and practices associated with Mikhail Gorbachev's "new thinking"—including *glasnost* (openness), *perestroika* (restructuring), and *demokratizatsiia* (political pluralism)—led first to the relaxation of police state controls on society and then, at the end of 1991, to the breakup of the Soviet Union.

The tidal wave of popular uprisings that rolled across Eastern Europe in 1989 swept away Communist regimes in Poland, Hungary, East Germany, Czechoslovakia, and Romania. (Communist governments in Bulgaria and Albania soon fell by the wayside as well.) In East Central Europe, new leaders with popular mandates moved rapidly to democratize the political processes and reorient domestic and foreign policies. But the pace of change in Poland, Czechoslovakia, and Hungary was not matched in the Balkans (Romania, Bulgaria, and Yugoslavia). In the former Soviet Union, the old order was replaced by a new disorder. As a consequence, the East-West conflict quickly faded from the vernacular of European politics, but the Slavic world found itself dividing into parts going in different directions at different speeds.

New political systems cannot be implemented overnight, nor can ruined economies be easily restored. Given the obstacles to the integration of Eastern and Western Europe and the distinctive historical, ethnic, and cultural experiences of the various Slavic nations, it is still appropriate to consider the former Soviet Union, East Central Europe, and the Balkans a distinct region separated from Western Europe by a socioeconomic chasm in addition to ethnolinguistic differences. Furthermore, Westernization will continue to be impeded by the lingering effects of Sovietization (Soviet-imposed Communist rule). Many of the problems facing Slavic Europe in the 1990s (which will be the focus of Chapter 9) are the product of dogmatic Communist policies that emanated from Moscow and that were imitated by its satellites in Eastern Europe for more than four decades.

From World War II until the watershed events of 1989, Moscow sought to impose the Soviet model of "scientific socialism" on its client states in Eastern Europe. That model shaped the region's approach to politics, government, and economy.

The Communist Party-State

The 1977 Soviet Constitution proclaimed the Communist Party the "leading and guiding force of Soviet society and the nucleus of its political system." This Party monopoly, the keystone in the arch of Communist rule, was renounced in February 1990 at a historic meeting of the Central Committee. With the collapse of Soviet power in December 1991, the Communist Party of the Soviet Union (CPSU) was cast into the dustbin of history, but since 1918 it had been the sole repository of legitimate authority in the Soviet Union and throughout Slavic Europe.

For seven decades after the October Revolution of 1917, the CPSU was an all-pervasive presence in Soviet society. Its tentacles reached deeply into four structures that implemented Communist Party policy: the state bureaucracy, the secret police (KGB), the economy (a kind of giant corporation), and the military.

The principle of the Party's leading role was rooted in Leninist ideology, which stresses the surpassing importance of the Party as the "vanguard of the proletariat." Karl Marx used the word *proletariat* to designate the oppressed working class, which, he theorized, would eventually seize power in a revolutionary takeover. Lenin believed that leadership—in the form of the Communist Party—was necessary to galvanize the masses into revolutionary action. These two seminal ideas—that revolution is the path to working-class power and that the Communist Party is the necessary catalyst—are basic tenets of Marxism-Leninism. No Soviet leader before Gorbachev had dared (or cared) to renounce them.

Party Organization

Centralization of power and authority was the hallmark of the Soviet political system. Imagine a huge pyramid. At the apex of this structure was the Politburo and the central party apparatus, including the Secretariat and the Central Committee; in the middle were the regional Party organizations; closer to the base were the local Party organizations; and at the very bottom were the primary Party organizations (PPOs).

How Regimes Stay in Power

All political regimes must choose from among a limited set of strategies, means, and methods to stay in power. These include **force**, **co-optation**, and **socialization**.

Force

Stalin relied heavily on coercion and intimidation, epitomized by the Great Terror of the 1930s. His predecessors, the czars, also relied on force, but to a lesser degree; his successors, beginning with Khrushchev, curbed the use of force and in so doing set the stage for an eventual popular revolt.

Co-optation

Just as the czars tried to co-opt the Russian Orthodox Church and the nobility (*boyars*), Stalin's successors sought to co-opt the military, the Communist Party functionaries, the secret police, and even the artists and intellectuals.

Socialization

Socialization aims at instilling a popular belief in the legitimacy of the government. There are two types of legitimacy. **Functional legitimacy** means that the people believe the government capable of both governing and providing life's necessities. For functional legitimacy to be effective as a means of control, all the government must do is persuade the people that as bad as the situation might be, they are better off with this regime than without it. From 1921 to perhaps the mid-1970s, a majority of the Soviet people did believe the Marxist-Leninist propaganda that at some point in the not-too-distant future they would be better off under this system than they were under czarism or would be under capitalism. **Moral legitimacy** is the inculcation of a specific ideology. Given the long-suffering acquiescence of the Russian people to the conditions they faced both in the czarist era and later under communism, something more than functional legitimacy was obviously at work. There were, of course, periodic revolts in Russian history, but what is surprising is that there were not more incidents of civil unrest. The Russian people's belief that revolt was immoral probably accounts for part of the explanation. The cult of personality created around the czar, reinforced by the Russian Orthodox religion, served this purpose admirably well. (Marx's observation that religion is the "opiate of the masses" fits the Russian experience.) As heir to the czars, Stalin also created a cult of personality (but reinforced by ideology rather than religion). The yearning of the Russian people for a "strong boss" reflects the traditional reliance of Russian (and Soviet) regimes on moral legitimacy. To this day, many Russians believe that Russia can only be governed by a hugely powerful and autocratic state.

Politburo

In theory, the **Politburo** was elected by the Party Central Committee; in practice, Politburo members were co-opted (chosen in secret by the voting members of the Politburo itself). Politburo leaders thus constituted a self-perpetuating oligarchy, consisting of eleven to fifteen full (voting) members and six to eight candidate (nonvoting) members. This elite group enjoyed a monopoly of decision-making power in the Soviet Union and its Eastern European client states. Moreover, it handpicked the Central Committee, one of two bodies to which it was theoretically accountable (the other being the Party Congress).

General Secretary

The Soviet Union was much like a huge corporation with the **general secretary** playing the dual role of chairman of the board and chief executive officer. There was a crucial difference, of course: the board of directors of the USSR, Inc., unlike General Motors or IBM, was not subject to any higher authority.

Although the office of general secretary was the paramount position in the Soviet system, it was not mentioned in the Party statutes, the Constitution, or Soviet textbooks. The general secretary, no matter what his limitations, was always glorified in the Soviet press as "heroic" but "modest." For example, during the Brezhnev years, Leonid Brezhnev's portrait was everywhere, and posters and banners quoting his speeches adorned walls and bulletin boards throughout the country. (See Table 8.1).

Secretariat and Party Apparatus

The general secretary was so named by virtue of his formal position as "first among equals" (and presiding officer) in the **Secretariat**, which was the executive committee of the CPSU. In some cases, Party secretaries (usually ten or so) were also members of the Politburo; joint membership in the Politburo and the Secretariat indicated that a particular leader was firmly entrenched in the inner circle of power. Major policy initiatives were unlikely without consensus within this group.

The Secretariat ran the Party. Each secretary headed a department within the Central Committee apparatus. The Politburo, for its part, held supreme political power and thus controlled the Secretariat as well as every other aspect of the political system. The overlapping composition of these two party organs virtually ensured that they would never clash.

The nerve center of the CPSU was the Party *apparat* (apparatus). The *apparat* was really the tip of an iceberg: beneath it lurked a huge Party bureaucracy that paralleled (and duplicated) the vast state bureaucracy Stalin set up to control

Table 8.1   Soviet Leaders, from Lenin to Gorbachev

	Years in Power
V. I. Lenin*	1917–1924
Josef Stalin*	1922–1953
Nikita S. Khrushchev	1953–1964
Leonid I. Brezhnev	1964–1982
Yuri V. Andropov	1982–1984
Konstantin U. Chernenko	1984–1985
Mikhail S. Gorbachev†	1985–1991

All top Soviet leaders, whatever specific title(s) they may have preferred or position(s) they may have held, presided over the Politburo.

* As chairman of the Council of Peoples' Commissars, Lenin was the de facto head of the party and the government; although Stalin was named general secretary of the party in 1922, he was unable to assert unquestioned control over the party until after Lenin's death in 1924.

† In 1989, the office of chairman of the presidium of the Supreme Soviet was strengthened and renamed "chairman of the Supreme Soviet." Gorbachev was elected to this new office and served until the Congress of Peoples' Deputies created the executive presidency in March 1990. The office of chairman of the Supreme Soviet remained, but its executive and ceremonial functions were transferred to the executive presidency.

Soviet society, defend the motherland, administer a wide array of welfare programs, and manage the centrally planned Soviet economy. Its main functions were to act as a watchdog for the Party leadership, to supervise the state bureaucracy, and to guard against the emergence of independent power bases from which "enemies of the people" might obstruct or oppose Party-endorsed policy.

Certain politically sensitive functions were hidden in this structure. For example, personnel matters, such as high-level promotions, were handled by the "Organization Party Work" department—a rather innocuous name for a body with the power to make and break careers. By the same token, the department that acted as Party watchdog over the military—ensuring, for example, that any coup plotting or disloyalty would be quickly detected—was known as the "Main Political Administration."

Central Committee

In theory, the Politburo and Secretariat were elected by a Party assembly known as the **Central Committee**, which was in turn elected by a much larger elective assembly, the **Party Congress**. In reality, these elections were rigged: there was only one candidate for each position, preselected by Party committees. Voting was little more than a ritual.

Central Committee membership was a status symbol, a sign of success not only in the Party but also in the arts, sciences, technology, diplomacy, mass media, economy, and armed services. Membership was a form of recognition, as well as a measure of political influence. The size of the Central Committee was an indication of the elite social status its members enjoyed—there were fewer than five hundred members (around three hundred full members, the rest candidate members).

The Central Committee was, in theory, the Party's supreme decision-making body. In practice, however, it merely rubber-stamped Politburo policies. It thus played a useful role in legitimizing the Politburo.

Party Congress

Before 1990, Party elections were cut and dry. Delegates (about five thousand in all) were handpicked from all over the Soviet Union. When a Party Congress was called, delegates gathered in Moscow where, amid great pomp and ceremony, they listened to boring speeches by an assortment of "heroic" workers and long-winded Party leaders. Eventually the speechmaking would end (congresses usually lasted about ten days) and the delegates would go home, but not before they voted unanimously to adopt the new Party program—a blueprint or outline of things to come.

Regional and Local Party Organizations

Below the central Party apparatus in Moscow were several levels that mirrored the territorial subdivisions of the state bureaucracy. These included the rural and urban district (*raion*), the city (*gorod*) or autonomous area (*okrug*), the

The *Nomenklatura* System

There were no upstarts in Soviet politics. The only way to the top was to begin at the bottom. Party bosses had at least one thing in common: they had all paid their dues, all persevered for decades, all made the long, slow climb from one rung of the Party bureaucracy to the next. As a consequence, Soviet leaders, with few exceptions, emerged dull and colorless. Indeed, they had all been acculturated within an often arcane environment that demanded abject loyalty and frowned on efforts by individual Party members to curry popular favor or establish a public personality.

How did a Party member become a Party boss? The answer can be found in the *nomenklatura* system, under which lists of positions controlled by the Party were drawn up. Party approval was required before an incumbent in any position could be removed or replaced. Not all coveted positions were filled by Communists, but Party members held most of the prestigious (and highest-paying) supervisory jobs in the Soviet Union.

This does not mean that the Politburo or Secretariat directly controlled all important appointments. One scholar argued that the emergence of a *nomenklatura class* actually limited the power of the central bodies. Most personnel decisions were controlled by district and local PPOs, and the Politburo rarely interfered at these levels. The cronyism that characterized this self-perpetuating system acted as a barrier to promotion of bureaucrats who were younger, more energetic, and perhaps less jaded in their views. For this reason, the Soviet Union became a gerontocracy, ruled by the aged.

One other consequence of this system was to create deeply entrenched local and regional Party elites that, ironically, were to prove much more difficult to oust from power than the national Party leadership after the August 1991 coup attempt.

province (*oblast*) or territory (*krai*), and the union republic. At the very bottom of the Party pyramid were the **primary Party organizations (PPOs)**. Every Party member, without exception, belonged to a PPO. Normally set up at places of employment, a Party cell had to have at least three members to be recognized as a PPO. Several million workers served in leadership roles as members of PPO committees and bureaus or as PPO secretaries. Most PPOs were relatively small: 40 percent had fifteen or fewer members and 80 percent had fewer than fifty members in the 1980s. Only several hundred of the more than 425,000 PPOs had a thousand or more members. In theory, all PPOs were supposed to hold general meetings at least once a month; in practice, this rule was widely ignored.

Party Membership

The Party rules set strict admission standards and rather elaborate rites of initiation. Anyone 25 years of age or older was eligible to join the Party. Applications had to be supported by recommendations from at least three Party members of five or more years' standing who had known the applicant for at least one year. Party members presumably did not give out recommendations lightly: the Party rules indicated clearly that members making recommendations could be held responsible for the character and conduct of the persons they endorsed. Initiates were placed on probation for one year as candidate members before they gained full membership.

Principles of Operation

Lenin established the doctrine of **democratic centralism** as the set of operational principles governing the CPSU. The Party had its own constitution (or "rules"), which enshrined four basic principles: election of all executive Party organizations, the obligation of lower organizations to abide by the decisions of higher ones, strict Party discipline and subordination of the minority to the majority, and periodic reporting to members and to higher Party bodies. In practice, the second rule overshadowed the others. Strict obedience and rigid discipline were enforced from above: party elections were rigged, majorities were produced on command, and accountability was a one-way street. In the Soviet system, bosses ruled their bureaucratic fiefdoms like medieval lords.

Reinforcing this hierarchical pattern was a long-standing Leninist ban on factionalism. The preamble to the Party rules did not equivocate on this point:

> Ideological and organizational unity, monolithic cohesion of its ranks, and a high degree of conscious discipline on the part of all Communists are an inviolable law of the CPSU. All manifestations of factionalism and group activity are incompatible with Marxist-Leninist principles and with Party membership.[1]

Finally, the CPSU rules incorporated a kind of confessional obligation called "criticism and self-criticism" requiring Party members to keep an eye on one another and to admit to their own shortcomings. Watching and confessing were integral to the ethics of Party membership.

USSR, Inc.: The Proprietary State

If the Communist Party monopolized political power in the Soviet Union, the state was the mechanism for monopolizing economic power. The Party set policies and made rules, and the state implemented those policies and enforced those rules. The Soviet system thus featured a symbiotic relationship between the Party and the state. And because the government owned and operated *all* farms and factories, it was a proprietary state, exercising its authority primarily through the Council of Ministers.

Council of Ministers

The **Council of Ministers** was the Soviet counterpart to the cabinet in a Western parliamentary or presidential system. Nominally elected by the Supreme Soviet, the Council of Ministers was the executive arm of the Politburo for the state bureaucracy (much as the Secretariat was the Party executive). The head of the Council of Ministers was the premier (analogous to a prime minister in British-style parliamentary systems).

Throughout most of Soviet history, the position of premier was a highly coveted post in the Soviet government, second only to that of general secretary.

Stalin held both top posts simultaneously, as did Khrushchev at the time of his ouster in 1964.

The premier was both head of the Council of Ministers and a member of the Politburo. Usually several other ministers held Politburo seats as well. This overlapping membership ensured continuous communication between the two governing bodies and minimized the likelihood of serious friction of policy conflict. It also blurred the boundary between the Party and the state at the pinnacle of the political system.

The resemblance between the Council of Ministers and Western-style cabinets was misleading. For example, the British cabinet, headed by the prime minister, *is* the government; other than Parliament itself, no supreme body instructs the cabinet. In the Soviet Union, however, the Council of Ministers took orders from the Politburo. According to the Constitution, it was "the highest executive and administative organ" of the USSR. Note the absence of any reference to a "guiding" or "leading" (decision-making) role, which was reserved for the highest Party organs.

Size was another major difference. The Council of Ministers, unlike cabinets in parliamentary systems, was huge, with more than one hundred members. Because this body was so unwieldy, the true executive functions of the government were carried out by a much smaller group of about fifteen members known as the Presidium, consisting of the chairman (premier), first deputy chairman, and other deputy chairmen.

There were two main reasons for the immense size of the Council of Ministers: the vastness of the Soviet empire and the large number of economic ministries necessitated by the system of central planning. In addition to the usual ministries such as foreign affairs, defense, and justice, there were more than sixty economic ministries covering everything from coal production to chemicals and automobiles.

Federalism, Soviet Style

From its inception, the Soviet Union had a federal structure. The nation was broken down into political-administrative subdivisions known as **union republics** (also called *Soviet socialist republics,* or *SSRs*), **autonomous republics** (*autonomous Soviet socialist republics,* or *ASSRs*), autonomous provinces, and autonomous districts. Despite their names, these entities were *not* autonomous; they were politically subservient to Moscow.

Under Article 72 of the Soviet constitution, union republics had the right "freely to secede from the USSR." But Article 75 contradicted this provision by declaring that the USSR "is a single territory and comprises the territories of the union republics" and that "the sovereignty of the USSR extends throughout its territory." Which in truth prevailed? This was not answered until the Baltic states and then other republics began agitating for greater autonomy in 1989. The winner turned out to be Article 72.

Federal units in the USSR reflected the predominant ethnic or nationality group in the various republics (Ukrainians in the Ukraine, Georgians in Georgia, and so on). The ASSRs represented concentrations of nationalities ("national minorities") within union republics, including the Buryats and the Kalmuks in the Far East, the Yakuts in northern Siberia, the Tatars five hundred miles east of Moscow, the Komi (related to the Lapps of Scandinavia), and the Karelians in the border zone with Finland.

The administrative structures in the union republics and autonomous republics were a mirror image of the setup on the federal level. Each republic had its own constitution, presidium, and council of ministers nominally chosen by an "elected" supreme soviet, or legislature. Each republic also had administrative counterparts for the myriad departments, agencies, and state committees that made up the state Council of Ministers.

Supreme Soviet: Not So Supreme

In the 1980s, the neon signs above some factories still proclaimed, "The soviets plus electrification equals communism." This may not be a stirring slogan to Western ears, but it is one of Lenin's best-known lines. Had the original blueprints been followed, the *soviet* aspect of the Soviet Union would have been the key to the system; as it turned out, it was little more than a museum piece.

The word *soviet* in Russian means "council"; its verb form means "to advise." Soviets played a key role in Lenin's prerevolutionary promise to establish a workers' democracy following a Bolshevik takeover. The idea was to base governmental power on elected councils (*soviets*) of peasants, workers, and soldiers. Hence the new government would derive its authority and legitimacy from grassroots organizations among the proletariat.

This talk of a workers' democracy made good propaganda, but Lenin quickly jettisoned the idea once he and his Bolshevik party seized power. He continued to pay lip service to the soviets, even putting *soviet* in the country's new name. But the real power passed to the Bolshevik party (later renamed the Communist Party of the Soviet Union).

Until 1988, the highest legislative body in the Soviet Union was the **Supreme Soviet**. It functioned like a parliamentary system; its fifteen hundred members were elected to two chambers of equal size, the Soviet of Nationalities and the Soviet of the Union. The Supreme Soviet chose the Council of Ministers, which implemented the laws it passed. The same pattern was replicated on lower levels all the way down to local soviets.

Elections to the Supreme Soviet and the fifty thousand soviets at the republic, provincial, and local levels were held with a good deal of fanfare. Everyone was required by law to vote; supposedly, 99.99 percent of all eligible voters cast ballots in national elections. (According to official figures, one election in the Turkmen SSR was almost perfect: only one voter out of 1.5 million failed to vote!)

Gorbachev's "Democratization" Campaign

Any type of reform is risky in a country accustomed to repressive rule. Pushing for political change threatens the power and privilege of the rulers and their minions. By 1990, Mikhail Gorbachev's democratization campaign had gone farther than most Western experts had earlier thought possible. Although he certainly never intended to dismantle the whole system, he did take dramatic steps to reconstitute the Soviet parliament and to allow the first truly meaningful elections in Soviet history, at the same time breaking the Communist Party's monopoly and permitting a modicum of pluralism.

Gorbachev had apparently decided that a greater measure of popular participation was the price the Party had to pay to get the country out of its economic doldrums. His reforms involved converting the Supreme Soviet into the 2,250-member **Congress of Peoples' Deputies**, which would elect a smaller, full-time parliament and a president. The president would assume the power previously exercised by the Communist Party leader. (Gorbachev already held both positions.)

Another part of the plan shifted power away from Party committees to local governing bodies (soviets). When the promised multicandidate elections were held in the spring of 1989, an open process of nominating candidates for national as well as local soviets was allowed for the first time. Public nominating meetings were organized. The popular response was enthusiastic, and the meetings, at times, were raucous. Given its superior organization, resources, and experience, the CPSU was able to get most of its candidates nominated. But in many electoral districts, non-Communist candidates were also nominated. Although the Communists won a majority of the seats, many independents also won. Moreover, some highly placed Communist officials were defeated. And such outspoken opposition figures as Andrei Sakharov and Boris Yeltsin (who had been removed as Moscow Party chief for criticizing Gorbachev) were elected handily. Yeltsin, running as an at-large candidate for all of Moscow, won by a landslide.

The congressional election was followed by a second election within the Congress to determine the membership of the smaller Supreme Soviet. Yeltsin was not elected to the Supreme Soviet, but such a hue and cry arose that he was quietly given a seat. Thanks to Gorbachev, popular opinion had become an important factor in the political process.

Incipient pluralism was also evident even at the federal level in Moscow. Two non-Communists were put on the Council of Ministers, and a parliamentary faction known as the interregional group, made up of four hundred to five hundred radical deputies, emerged as the formal opposition. This group had its own agenda, including a demand to end the Communist Party's monopoly on power by abolishing the article of the constitution that guaranteed the Communist Party's "leading and guiding" role in Soviet society. Popular support for the Party was indeed eroding. In the first half of 1989, for example, party membership fell by 600,000, and an opinion poll found that only 4 percent of Party members believed the moral authority of CPSU was still high; 50 percent said it was low, and one member out of three felt that the Party was incapable of reform.[2]

Precisely what Gorbachev meant by "democratization" was always a mystery. He made it clear from the outset that Western-style democracy was not what he had in mind. At a Party conference in June 1988, he denounced attempts to "use democratic rights for undemocratic purposes." As examples, he mentioned efforts aimed at "redrawing boundaries" or "setting up opposition parties."[3] Gorbachev's failure to detail his intentions was apparently a calculated ambiguity—a fatal miscalculation that hastened the death of Soviet socialism and the empire he was trying to save.

Stalin's Legacy: Dysfunctional Economies

In the closing decades of the twentieth century, the rulers of Slavic Europe's Communist countries had to ask whether state planning was appropriate for industrially developed socialist nations. The specter of a moribund workers' state had haunted the Soviet Union and its Warsaw Pact allies at least since the early 1960s. As noted in Chapter 7, Nikita Khrushchev launched a series of ill-starred reforms in industry and agriculture (as well as a radical reorganization of the Party-state machinery) before he was ousted in 1964. Later in the decade, Hungary experimented with market-style reforms, and Czechoslovakia tried to introduce multiparty democracy. In the Soviet Union, Premier Alexei Kosygin tried to restart the stalled reform effort. In so doing, he was guided by the theoretical writings of Soviet economist Evsei Liberman.

The **Liberman reforms** were designed to decentralize economic decision making. Managers were to be given considerable discretion in making microeconomic production and investment decisions. Enterprises were even to be charged interest on the capital they used. Given more latitude, "managers were expected to take risks, innovate, reduce costs, and thereby increase the sales and profits of their enterprises."[4]

Had Libermanism triumphed, Soviet managers would have had to operate a lot like Western entrepreneurs. But the embryonic reform movement was quickly aborted by the entrenched Party-state bureaucracy, at whose expense the reforms would have come. In retrospect, the failure of the reforms in the 1960s sealed the fate of the Soviet Union and its satellites in Eastern Europe.

Marxism versus the Marketplace

According to the Soviet constitution, the nation's economy was "based on the Socialist ownership of all the means of production," including the land. Two forms of socialist ownership were recognized in the USSR: state ownership and collective or cooperative ownership. The former was considered a higher form because it encompassed the entire society, whereas the latter was a lower form because it was limited to relatively few people. This distinction was clearly evident in agriculture, which was divided into collective farms (*kolkhozy*) and state farms (*sovkhozy*). Collective farms were technically owned by the farmers themselves, whereas state farms were owned by society at large and run by the government, which gave them preferential treatment (more funds, better equipment). State farms were huge, averaging some 92,500 acres—five or six times the size of the average collective farm. They were operated like an assembly line in an industrial enterprise and were managed by professionals trained in such fields as agronomy, animal husbandry, and horticulture. State farmers, like industrial workers, were specialized by function and were paid an hourly wage. Thus the Soviet government sought to industrialize agriculture.

The state also owned all industrial enterprises, public utilities, banks, transportation systems, and mass-communication facilities, as well as most retail outlets and repair shops. One result of this system of ownership was that nearly every employed person (approximately 85 percent of the work force) worked for the state. The other 15 percent belonged to cooperatives or collectives, which, though not state-owned, were tightly controlled by the state.

This employment monopoly gave the state enormous control over the individual. Furthermore, a so-called antiparasite law made it a crime *not* to work. If you were fired for any reason (including unauthorized political activity), where could you go to find another job? The employer who dismissed you from one job could bar you from another and at the same time put you on the wrong side of the law—a kind of "double jeopardy" that very effectively kept Soviet workers in line.

The Concept of Central Planning

For Marxist true believers, capitalism is to be abhorred because it leads to exploitation of the many by the few. But capitalism is just another name for the economics of the marketplace. So if an alternative to the evils of capitalism were to be found, according to Communist orthodoxy, an alternative to the marketplace must also be found. In the Soviet Union, that alternative was central planning.

The concept of **central planning** is simple enough: decide what society needs, put the people to work, and distribute material benefits fairly. (Initially, distribution is according to the value of each person's work; eventually, under full communism, the formula would be "from each according to his abilities, to each according to his needs.") Nobody owns anything but transportable personal possessions (clothing, furniture, books).

Prices are set by the state; they do not fluctuate in response to the market forces of supply and demand, as under capitalism. The Soviet economy—the largest ever to adopt this system—was thus planned and managed from the top, whereas a market economy is driven from the bottom, by consumers.

The State Planning Committee (Gosplan) had primary responsibility for charting the course of the Soviet economy but had to coordinate its work with a number of other bureaucratic entities, including the State Committee on Prices, the State Bank (Gosbank), the Ministry of Finance, the State Committee on Material and Technical Supplies (Gossnab), and nearly fifty central ministries (as well as 750 in the fifteen union republics) that ran the various industries.

The complicated planning process involved both long-range (five-year) and short-range (one-year) plans. These plans set production growth targets for the various sectors of the economy, which were then translated into output quotas for individual enterprises. The short-range plan contained the growth targets for the whole economy for the current year. This general blueprint was then broken down by the various ministries into monthly plans with quotas for every factory, plant, enterprise, and association in the Soviet Union. The plan always reflected the political priorities of the top leadership in the interlocking directorates of the Politburo, the Secretariat, and the Council of Ministers.

Such detailed economic planning would be daunting under any circumstances. To keep factories humming and assembly lines moving, it is necessary to determine in advance how many parts, in what exact sizes, would be needed to turn out the quota of, say, tractors at a given plant; how many train cars, trucks, or barges would be needed to deliver the right quantities of iron and steel and other components on schedule; how much energy would be needed to run the plant during different times of the year; and on and on. Innumerable calculations must be made for every single item manufactured or processed.

Under the Stalinist system of economic management, the state planning mechanism made 83 million supply and demand calculations each year and set prices on 200,000 industrial and consumer items.[5] Obviously, if material allocations were miscalculated or if suppliers' and producers' timetables were not synchronized or if a key transportation pipeline got disrupted or clogged, the system would break down. Indeed, bottlenecks were one of several generic problems that plagued Soviet central planning. Rare attempts to link producers, suppliers, and consumers more directly failed miserably.

Problems of Planning

The absence of market mechanisms was at the root of many, if not most, Soviet economic problems. Take performance indicators as an example. Output quotas (rather than the profits that drive capitalism) were used to measure success in the Soviet economy. Every factory was expected to fulfill its quota every month. If a factory overfulfilled its quota for the year, its workers and managers were rewarded with pay bonuses. Underfulfillment blocked promotions for plant managers and dashed workers' hopes for a year-end windfall. Thus the primary objective of every plant manager was not to improve efficiency but rather to overfulfill the quotas by a small margin (overfulfilling by large margins would lead to higher quotas the next year, thus creating new pressures).

Plan fulfillment became an all-consuming end. To achieve it, plant managers typically hoarded supplies and deliberately inflated labor requirements to provide a cushion in the event that vital materials were not delivered on time or speeding up production should become necessary to meet the monthly quota. These widespread practices caused planning distortions and supply bottlenecks.

Moreover, as performance indicators, quotas themselves were problematic. Imagine that a factory produced nails. Nails of all sizes, weights, and types were needed, but there was always a dilemma: if the quota was based on gross weight, the manager had an incentive to produce big, heavy nails rather than small, lightweight ones, but if the quota was based on quantity, the manager would produce lots of little nails.

Another economic fact of life in the USSR was low labor productivity, due mostly to the paucity of incentives. Workers were all paid about the same no matter how much or how little they produced. Everyone was guaranteed a job, and rarely did anyone get fired (except for political reasons). In short, the system did little to encourage efficiency.

The collapse of communism was primarily the result of economic failure. Stalin imposed this inefficient system on all the satellite states of Slavic Europe after World War II. Many of the problems these countries face today are rooted in the economic deformities caused by central planning.

The Soviet Economy before the Crash

Gorbachev inherited an economy that had been declining steadily for at least two decades (see Table 8.2). By the mid-1980s, Soviet economic growth had fallen to less than 2 percent a year, about half what it had been a decade earlier. One out of every nine industrial enterprises and nearly a third of the farms were losing money, and such essentials as food, housing, medical treatment, and transportation were being subsidized to the tune of about 75 billion rubles per year.

At about 1 percent a year, growth in food production was barely keeping pace with population growth, and despite the heavy investment in agriculture (some 600 billion rubles over twenty years), the Soviet Union continued to spend billions to import meat and grain. Even so, the supply of meat and butter was so far short of demand nearly three years after Gorbachev's rise to power that rationing remained in force in many provincial cities: as little as 1 kilogram (2.2 pounds) of meat and sausage and 200 grams (less than a quarter pound) of butter for each adult per month![6]

Investment priorities in agriculture, ironically, reflected terrible planning.

Table 8.2 The Shrinking Soviet Economy, 1961–1985 (annual average percent growth in net material product)

	1961–1965	1966–1970	1971–1975	1976–1980	1981–1985
Official Soviet statistics	6.5	7.8	5.7	4.3	3.2
CIA (GNP)	4.8	4.9	3.0	1.9	1.8

Source: Anders Aslund, *Gorbachev's Struggle for Economic Reform* (Ithaca: Cornell University Press, 1991), p. 17.

Farm-to-market roads and facilities for storage, processing, packaging, and retailing were woefully neglected. As much as 30 percent of Soviet farm output—including a quantity of grain equal to what the government was buying on the world market—spoiled or was eaten by rodents. In 1987 an estimated 60 percent of the potato crop rotted in the fields when heavy rains disrupted the harvest.

General living standards were abysmal compared with those in the industrial democracies of the West. Housing was always in short supply. One-fifth of the people in cities lived in communal apartments, sharing bathrooms and kitchens with other families.

The most critical problem was the technology gap, which widened in the 1970s and 1980s as the computer revolution, like the Renaissance and the Reformation centuries earlier, eluded the East as it transformed the West. The consequence, in Gorbachev's own words, was to create "precrisis conditions" that forced the USSR to change the way it worked in order to ward off decline and decay. Soviet economists conceded shortly before dissolution of the USSR that "no more than about 10% of the country's industrial production measures up to world standards of quality and technological advancement."[7]

Perestroika: Making a Virtue of Necessity

The conventional wisdom within the Soviet bloc long held that Moscow was the model for the other socialist countries; a small country like Hungary could not assume this role. But with the advent of Gorbachev's "new thinking," the Soviet Union showed a willingness to learn from the experience of other socialist states, especially Yugoslavia, Hungary, and the People's Republic of China (PRC).

At a Communist Party conclave in early 1986, Gorbachev endorsed calls for a radical restructuring of Soviet society (perestroika). Later in the year, the official gazette of the Supreme Soviet published a list of thirty-eight measures to be implemented before the end of 1990; the new laws' concerns ranged from voting and plebiscites to economic incentives, pricing, the press, governmental reorganization, and the activities of the KGB. In November, the Supreme Soviet approved a law allowing citizens to moonlight for extra cash (many of them had been doing so illegally for decades). Finally, in January 1987, the Communist Party's Central Committee gave its imprimatur to Gorbachev's reform package.

The moonlighting law, which took effect in the spring of 1987, was the first to ease the ban on free enterprise since Lenin's short-lived New Economic Policy in 1921. Any Soviet citizen could now ask local authorities for permission to start what would amount to a small business. However, the Kremlin warned that it was not sanctioning "free-enterprise activities." Its ostensible aim was to tap the energies of Soviet citizens who were not in the work force, including housewives, pensioners, invalids, and students.

The service sector of the economy was woefully underdeveloped; the moonlighting law was an attempt to alleviate that situation. Moreover, it represented a first tentative step toward recognition of individuals' economic rights by a regime long hostile to the idea of private property. But jealousy proved to be a problem, for many Russians resent entrepreneurs who make a lot of money. This is an excellent example of how Marxist ideology can get in the way of economic reforms.

The main instrument of *perestroika* was the 1987 Law on Soviet Enterprise, which mandated three major changes by 1990. First, about 37,000 industrial enterprises were slated for managerial decentralization, meaning that they were to operate on a strict profit-or-loss basis rather than depending on state financial support.

Second, some state firms were permitted to deal directly with foreign companies rather than working through a bureaucratic maze of ministries and foreign-trade monopolies. The law also allowed a small number of Soviet enterprises to negotiate joint ventures with Western firms, which could hold up to 49 percent of the equity. Many such joint-venture agreements were signed, but few bore fruit. One obstacle was the difficulty foreign companies had repatriating profits (the ruble was not convertible). Another was bureaucratic inefficiency.

Third, the law increased the autonomy of the nation's 49,000 collective and state farms. For the first time in fifty years, collective farms were encouraged to organize into "family brigades" (apparently inspired by the highly successful Chinese moves to reprivatize agriculture in the early 1980s). Moreover, farmers were allowed to lease land from the state for fifty years or more, retain profits in return for paying taxes, and pass their holdings on to their children.

In 1988 the Law on Cooperative Enterprises permitted individuals to produce and sell consumer goods for a profit at free-market prices. By the end of 1988, some fifty thousand new businesses were operating—a burgeoning private sector that employed about two million citizens. Although these new cooperatives produced consumer goods of better quality than those made by state-run enterprises, shoppers complained that their prices were prohibitively high. The cooperatives in turn complained that the government policies (including high taxes) made it impossible to lower prices.

Gorbachev promised to decentralize the Soviet economy by changing the regulations governing external trade. About seventy industrial enterprises and twenty governmental departments were empowered to make deals with foreign firms. (Previously, all international commerce was conducted through a state monopoly.) Moreover, these enterprises and departments were to be allowed to retain some of their profits.

The Perils of *Perestroika*

Gorbachev's dilemma was acute. On the one hand, Stalinist central planning had the great advantage of giving the state total control over the economy. As a result, the command economies of the Soviet bloc generally experienced very low inflation (see Table 8.3). Only in the 1980s did this begin to change significantly in certain countries; until the late 1980s, price stability was a given in the Soviet Union, East Germany, Czechoslovakia, and Romania. However,

Table 8.3 Inflation Rates in the Centrally Planned Economies of the Warsaw Pact, 1970–1990 (percent per annum)

	1970	1975	1980	1985	1990
USSR	0.0	0.1	0.1	1.0	10.0
Bulgaria	−0.4	0.3	14.0	1.7	64.0
Czechoslovakia	1.7	0.7	2.9	2.3	10.0
East Germany	−0.3	0.2	0.5	0.0	−3.0
Hungary	1.3	3.8	9.3	7.0	28.3
Poland	1.2	2.3	9.4	15.1	584.7
Romania	0.4	0.2	1.5	−0.4	4.7

Sources: Domenico Mario Nuti, "Perestroika," *Economic Policy,* October 1988, p. 369; Vienna Institute for Comparative Economic Studies, ed., *Comecon Data, 1988* (London: Macmillan, 1989), p. 157; Vienna Institute for Comparative Economic Studies, ed., *Comecon Data, 1990* (London: Macmillan, 1991), p. 159.

growth rates slowed perceptibly between 1951 and 1988 (see Table 8.4), not only in the Soviet Union but also in the other Comecon states. This downward trend in the face of dynamic market economies in Western Europe, Asia, and North America forced Gorbachev's hand.

But Gorbachev proved unequal to the task. His halting economic reforms failed miserably. *Perestroika* turned out to be a series of halfway measures that had the effect of disrupting the centrally planned economy without laying the foundations for a true market economy.

At the end of the 1980s, Soviet economic indicators were bleak. During the first half of 1989, for example, productivity rose a mere 2.7 percent, according to official Soviet figures. Against a backdrop of unprecedented inflation and

Table 8.4 Real Gross Domestic Product Growth Rates in the Centrally Planned Economies of the Warsaw Pact, 1951–1988 (annual average percent growth in GDP at constant prices)

	1951–1973	1974–1982	1983–1988
USSR	5.0	2.1	1.9
Bulgaria	6.1	2.4	1.4
Czechoslovakia	3.8	1.8	1.8
East Germany	4.6	2.6	2.1
Hungary	4.0	1.9	1.4
Poland	4.8	0.5	4.2
Romania	5.9	3.7	2.9

Sources: International Monetary Fund, *World Economic Outlook, 1990* (Washington, D.C.: IMF, 1990), p. 65; International Monetary Fund, *International Financial Statistics Yearbook, 1991* (Washington, D.C.: IMF, 1991), pp. 160–163; Organization for Economic Cooperation and Development, *The World Economy in the 20th Century* (Paris: OECD, 1989), p. 36.

all-too-familiar empty shelves, Soviet consumers complained bitterly that the shortages were worse than at any time since World War II. And yet the nation was running a foreign-trade deficit.

The extent of consumer deprivation in the Soviet Union was long treated as a state secret. Comparisons in Soviet publications between the standard of living in the United States and in the USSR typically stressed the seamy side of life in America and the superior social benefits—subsidized housing, cheap and efficient public transportation, socialized medicine—offered by the Soviet state. This myth was exposed in 1989 when a Soviet scholar named Zaychenko published an article in the journal of the prestigious Institute of USA-Canada Studies showing that living standards in the United States were far ahead of those in the Soviet Union in virtually all areas of comparison. Looking at everything from nutrition and medical care to housing and transportation, Zaychenko challenged the official propaganda. He asserted, for example, that "the cost of housing in our country is 41 percent higher" than in the United States and that the means of transportation are ten times greater in the United States than in the USSR. He calculated that the average Soviet worker toils ten to twelve times as long as an American to buy a kilo of meat and ten to fifteen times as long to buy a dozen eggs. More daringly, Zaychenko observed that "in the last 80 years the difference in the economic accessibility of foods in the US and the USSR has become particularly pronounced." He also cited other quality-of-life indicators, such as the availability of desirable consumer goods; the number of shopping centers, restaurants, and telephones; and even government outlays for education. In all areas, he said, the Soviet Union trailed far behind. Zaychenko's message was unmistakable: "Let's face it, comrades, under Communism the East-West gap has grown steadily."

The Zaychenko article pointed to Gorbachev's greatest challenge: to reverse the trends that threatened to relegate the Soviet Union to the status of a second-rate power. There was also a more immediate threat: political instability in the form of labor unrest, food riots, and other economically motivated protests. Gorbachev's reforms were a double-edged sword: they were necessary to get the economy moving, but they raised expectations and increased public awareness of social and economic ills that were once cloaked in secrecy.

Glasnost: Building a Civic Culture

Perestroika was overshadowed in the late 1980s by *glasnost* ("openness") and democratization, which eased some of the political controls that were so tight under Communist Party rule. Even before the landmark political reforms of 1989–1990, Gorbachev had allowed greater public candor. This new freedom of expression was an integral part of Gorbachev's strategy for economic revitalization, but it carried considerable risks.

Gorbachev apparently realized that "to unleash the latent human potential necessary to make national restructuring a success, each citizen must undergo a personal *perestroika*."[8] That would necessitate a fundamental change in the social psychology of a nation unaccustomed to personal freedom or individual initiative, encumbered by a moribund ideology, and inhibited by centuries of political and religious oppression. There was a "cultural fear of spontaneity here dating back to the czars, a tendency to see Western-style individual freedom as the first, inevitable step toward anarchy."[9] Breaking this pattern without breaking up the political system was the challenge. Far from abandoning the system, Gorbachev hoped to breathe new life into it.

Glasnost was thus a kind of grand experiment in behavioral engineering. Soviet society became a giant laboratory for testing new forms of cultural expression and political activity. Writers and books long banished—among them Boris Pasternak (*Dr. Zhivago*), Vasily Grossman (*Life and Fate*), and Yevgeny Zamyatin (*We*)—were "rehabilitated." The poetry of Joseph Brodsky, the Nobel laureate who spent eighteen months in a Soviet labor camp for "social parasitism," appeared in *Novy Mir* (*New World*), a popular Soviet magazine, in 1988. Many films and documentaries that had been blocked by the censors for decades were cleared for Soviet audiences in 1987 and 1988. Even such American films as *Platoon, Amadeus,* and *One Flew over the Cuckoo's Nest* began appearing in Soviet movie theaters.[10]

The Soviet press also enjoyed a new openness, publishing articles on such previously taboo subjects as prostitution, drug abuse, homosexuality, and even the misuse of psychiatry to punish dissidents. Embarrassing statistics on infant mortality and life expectancy, withheld for years by Soviet authorities, were again made available. Negative news—crime statistics, industrial accidents, traffic mishaps, official corruption—began to transfigure the Soviet mass media: the old formula combining Pollyanna and propaganda gave way to accuracy, honesty, and realism.

Potentially the greatest challenge to the Kremlin's authority spawned by *glasnost* was the proliferation of informal groups with no connection to Party or state. Many of these involved activities with no political overtones, such as chess, rock music, or soccer. But some were less innocuous:

- A Moscow group called Memorial urged the government to build a monument and information center in honor of Stalin's victims.
- Green World in Leningrad (now Saint Petersburg) opposed on environmental grounds a government flood-control project to dam a part of the Gulf of Finland.
- Press Club Glasnost, comprised mainly of former political prisoners, monitored human rights and the progress of *glasnost*.[11]
- The Moscow Jewish Association was created as "an umbrella and support organization" for Soviet Jews. It was allowed to hold a rally in 1987 to honor the victims of the German massacre at Babi Yar but was nonetheless denounced in the Soviet news media as a "Zionist conspiracy."[12]

Many informal groups circulated uncensored newsletters that were openly published, distributed, and discussed. Unofficial tabloids reported objectively on events the official press either ignored or slanted. Certain official publications, such as the *Moscow News* and *Ogonyok,* also began demonstrating extraordinary editorial independence.[13]

Glasnost and Soviet Public Opinion

Westerners tended to assume that Gorbachev's reforms were popular in the Soviet Union. The reality was not so simple. Given their history of political oppression, the peoples of the USSR had good reason to be skeptical of government, pessimistic about progress, wary of reforms, and indifferent to democracy. In fact, their fear of anarchy was probably much more intense than any yearning for the individual liberties enjoyed in the West.[14] "Their history," wrote David Shipler,

> as they repeatedly remind a foreigner, is replete with illustrations that their authority cannot be eroded only a little but is swept away completely when weakened and overwhelmed. . . . And in the milieu of Russia's upheaval and chaos, revolutions have been made.[15]

There are also pragmatic reasons why the people were cynical about reforms. Reformers in the Soviet Union had always failed. Furthermore, the surface changes associated with *glasnost* "failed to bring any substantial change in the everyday life of people or the functioning of the system."[16] On the contrary, the first effects of *perestroika* were to bring a cut in pay for many workers, price increases for food and other state-subsidized essentials, and the disturbing possibility of unemployment. Suddenly the great advantage of state-centered socialism—security—gave way to a new and nagging sense of precariousness.

Given the premium that Russians placed on security—for historical reasons—and their indifference or even hostility toward liberty, it is a small wonder that *perestroika* was greeted with less than wild enthusiasm. To succeed in revitalizing the Soviet economy, Gorbachev had to revitalize Soviet society; to succeed in revitalizing society, he had to overcome widespread fear that radical reforms would only mean longer food lines and emptier shelves. And little has changed since Gorbachev's departure: Yeltsin faces precisely the same challenge in Russia today.

Bureaucratic Opposition

Even more than the general public, the nation's eighteen million bureaucrats had little to gain and much to lose under the Gorbachev reforms. As part of the planned restructuring, half of these functionaries would lose their jobs as ministries consolidated and streamlined.

Party bureaucrats also felt threatened. The Party's power was inseparable from its watchdog function in all areas of Soviet life—social, cultural, political, economic, and military. The pervasiveness of the surveillance system nurtured and maintained by the Party since 1917 was suggested in this sardonic (and thoroughly Russian) condensation of the Soviet constitution: "Whatever is not forbidden is compulsory."[17]

The "National Question"

Former U.S. National Security Adviser Zbigniew Brzezinski called it "the Achilles' heel of the Soviet system"—the ethnic diversity of the Soviet state, which encompassed eleven time zones, one-sixth of the earth's surface, 120 official languages, and over a hundred separate nationalities. Russians constituted a bare majority (52.4 percent) of the total Soviet population at the time the union came apart.

For decades, expressions of cultural and linguistic particularism were suppressed by the Russian-dominated and highly centralized Soviet government. To some degree, contempt for ethnic traditions was an outgrowth of Marxist-Leninist ideology and of the need to fuse a multinational empire into a unified state. The ideology became a convenient (though not very satisfactory) substitute for the various cultures.

In the Baltic states, Latvians, Estonians, and Lithuanians looked back nostalgically to the period before World War II, when they were self-governing. In the Transcaucasus, Azerbaijanis, Georgians, and Armenians retained a strong sense of national identity. In the Ukraine, with a population nearly equal to that of France or Great Britain, nationalism and separatism were reinforced by a rich cultural legacy, a history that predates the Muscovite era, and a long-standing resentment of Russian dominance. Finally, in Soviet Central Asia, Turkmen, Kirghiz, Uzbek, Kazakh, and Tajik nationalities continued to observe their own customs and practices, despite Soviet efforts to "modernize" them; all except the Tajiks speak Turkic languages, and all are Muslim.

Gorbachev was reminded of the power of ethnic nationalism in early 1987 when violence broke out in Kazakhstan after he replaced its regional Party chief, a Kazakh, with an ethnic Russian. But manifestations of militant nationalism and internal turmoil were most prevalent in the Baltic states and the Transcaucasus.

In 1988, long-standing ethnic tensions between Armenians and Azeris (the indigenous population of Azerbaijan) were brought sharply into focus when Armenian activists demanded the transfer of the Armenian enclave of Nagorno-Karabakh from predominantly Muslim Azerbaijan to Armenia. In February, rioting broke out in the Azerbaijani city of Sumgait, where Armenians and Azeris had previously lived together in harmony. When the rampage was over, thirty-two people were dead.[18] Huge demonstrations in Yerevan, the capital of Armenia, culminated in a strike that paralyzed the city in mid-June. Mass demonstrations and bloody rioting erupted repeatedly until in early 1990, Gorbachev sent Soviet troops to Azerbaijan to restore order.

The Transcaucasus was not the only region where nationalism posed a problem for Gorbachev. Mass demonstrations rocked the Baltic states in the summer of 1988, when thousands of Latvians demonstrated in Riga, the capital, to mark the anniversary of mass deportations from Latvia under Stalin. Asserting that Latvians were threatened with becoming "a minority within their ethnographic borders," Latvian leaders urged that Lettish be made the primary language of the Latvian republic and asked that local authorities be allowed to limit the influx of Russians, who comprised about 33 percent of Latvia's population.

In Estonia, authorities set a precedent by permitting the creation of the first large-scale political group outside the Communist Party. The new organization, the People's Front of Estonia, was reported to have "mushroomed" to forty thousand members in less than two months. Its platform combined support for Gorbachev's reforms with calls for greater political and economic independence for Estonia.[19]

In August 1988, mass demonstrations were held in the capitals of all three Baltic republics to mark the anniversary of the infamous 1939 Nazi-Soviet pact that led to the Baltic states' forced incorporation into the USSR. Some of the marchers demanded independence from Moscow, and speakers repudiated the official Soviet version of history, which claimed that the Baltic states joined the Soviet Union of their own free will. In Vilnius, the capital of Lithuania, 100,000 people, one-sixth of the city's population, turned out.

Soviet central authority quickly unraveled in the Baltics. The Estonian press for the first time published the secret protocols of the Nazi-Soviet deal; the protocols, which Moscow had refused to acknowledge, belied the Soviet claim that the Baltic states entered the union by choice.

Estonia's Communist Party agreed to legalize the national colors of the Estonian flag (an emotionally charged issue) and to switch to Estonian time (one hour behind Moscow). It also agreed to consider demands that Estonian (rather than Russian) be the official language of the republic and that a separate and distinct Estonian citizenship be established.[20] Estonians managed to get Gorbachev to endorse an extraordinary plan for the republic's economic autonomy as well. The plan called for cutting Estonia's links to the central ministries in Moscow and instituting market reforms in industry and agriculture. Given the fact that only 10 percent of Estonia's industry was locally controlled, this plan added a new wrinkle to restructuring—one with far-reaching implications for the future of the union.

In November 1988, the Estonian parliament unanimously rejected Gorbachev's proposed changes in the Soviet constitution, claiming that these reforms would further restrict the rights of individual Soviet republics. Instead, the Estonian chamber voted to amend the Estonian constitution so as to allow Estonia to exempt itself from Soviet legislation.

Developments in Lithuania were hardly less alarming as viewed from the Kremlin. The Lithuanian reform movement held a national convention in late October. Boasting a membership of 180,000 in grass-roots organizations throughout Lithuania, the movement (known locally as Sajudis) was already nearly as large as the Lithuanian Communist Party. The October meeting produced demands for sweeping reforms aimed at national autonomy and democratization.[21] However, Latvia and Lithuania backed away from confrontation in November when their leaders decided not to follow Estonia's lead.

The Baltic states became increasingly adamant in demanding independence from Moscow in 1989. In August, Estonia's supreme soviet passed transparently anti-Russian legislation setting residence requirements of two years for voting and five years for holding local elective office. Later that month, Lithuania's supreme soviet declared the 1940 Soviet annexation of Lithuania illegal. Huge demonstrations took place in the Baltics throughout the fall; at one point, as many as a million people formed a human chain four hundred miles long stretching from the Estonian capital, Tallinn, through the Latvian capital, Riga, to the Lithuanian capital, Vilnius.

In December 1989, the Lithuanian supreme soviet raised the ante by voting overwhelmingly to abolish the Communist Party monopoly in Lithuania and to legalize opposition parties. Next the Lithuanian Communist Party declared itself independent of the Party leadership in Moscow. Finally, the head of the Lithuanian Communist Party, Algirdas Brazauskas, called for "an independent democratic Lithuanian state."

Gorbachev viewed this action with alarm and warned that it would "sow discord, bloodshed, and death." The crisis turned into confrontation in the early months of 1990 when Lithuania formally declared its independence and Estonia followed suit. In January 1991, Gorbachev acquiesced in a bloody storming of television facilities in Vilnius by Soviet security forces. Following the crackdown, Lithuania's fate, and that of the other Baltic republics, remained unclear until the collapse of Soviet power following the abortive coup in August 1991 suddenly threw the door to independence wide open.

The August Coup: Prelude and Aftermath

The rebellious mood of the republics posed a danger to the survival of Gorbachev's reform movement and ultimately to the union. The other danger lurking in the background was the faltering economy. Gross national product, increasing by 2 percent in 1988, began shrinking in 1990 and plunged sharply in 1991.

That same year, the Soviet budget deficit escalated to $33.5 billion, almost 30 percent of GNP (by comparison, the U.S. deficit that year accounted for roughly 5 percent of GNP). The causes of this deficit were readily apparent: Soviet food subsidies alone amounted to one-tenth of GNP, and Soviet oil commanded only 2.5 percent of the world market price. At the same time, inflation was running at about 3 percent a *week* (other estimates put it as high as 250 percent per year). Soviet printing presses were stamping out ruble notes around the clock.[22]

The Soviet debt to the West hovered around $70 billion. (The largest creditor was Germany, owed $20 billion.) The head of the Soviet central bank estimated that the USSR lost $15 billion in 1991 because Western banks pulled back due to the unstable domestic situation. Soviet officials calculated that the government would need $200 billion in foreign loans over the long haul to turn the economy around. In the short term, the Soviets needed $10 billion in financial aid, $3 billion of it urgently. By some estimates, Moscow was more than $60 billion behind in payments to creditors abroad.[23]

Gorbachev's failure to revive the economy had two immediate consequences. First, it brought further hardships to long-suffering Soviet consumers who, thanks to *glasnost,* now had a voice. In 1990 and 1991, Gorbachev faced growing public hostility to *perestroika;* as his popularity plummeted, the danger of a coup by hard-liners rose commensurately. Second, Gorbachev's vacillation on the conversion to a free-market economy damaged his prestige in the West. The combination of disaffection at home and disillusionment abroad made Gorbachev vulnerable. His carefully cultivated public image had been his greatest political asset; now that image was badly tarnished.

But it was the unresolved nationalities problem that provoked the **August coup.** In April 1991, Gorbachev convened a conference at which he concluded a compact with the nine participating republics, granting them internal autonomy under a proposed new constitution that would establish the "Union of Soviet Sovereign [rather than Socialist] Republics." Gorbachev was to meet with the nine republics to sign the new union compact on August 20; Kremlin hard-liners tried to preempt this action by staging a coup on August 18.

There had been hints that a coup was in the offing. In December, former Foreign Minister Eduard Shevardnadze had resigned, warning that the country was drifting into dictatorship. In June, Prime Minister Valentin Pavlov had attempted a "parliamentary coup"—a surprise move in the Supreme Soviet to pare down Gorbachev's presidential powers. Finally, on August 16, Alexander Yakovlev, one of Gorbachev's closest confidants and a leading reformer, resigned from the Communist Party and warned that a coup was imminent. Gorbachev's failure to heed these warnings dealt the fatal blow to his prestige and credibility. By contrast, Boris Yeltsin, the democratically elected president of Russia (and Gorbachev's chief rival), emerged from the crisis a hero. With Gorbachev in captivity, Yeltsin bravely rallied the nation, at one point climbing onto a tank to read a ringing proclamation of defiance against the would-be destroyers of Russia's nascent democracy.

The coup quickly fell apart. Ironically, it accelerated the processes of national decay. With the now politically bankrupt Gorbachev standing alone against the republics, the dissolution of the Soviet Union was only a matter of time. The end came in a mere four months. By then efforts to make alternative arrangements linking the former Soviet republics had already been undertaken. There was talk of an economic community or perhaps a "commonwealth," but it was not clear what either would entail or even which republics would participate. The Baltic states opted out, leaving the twelve remaining republics to engage in what proved to be very difficult negotiations. These talks eventually led to the creation of the **Commonwealth of Independent States (CIS)** with headquarters in Minsk, the capital of Belarus. But the CIS was built on political sand and quickly began to crack at its foundations. That left the moribund Soviet Union without even a shadow of its former self; in its place there were now fifteen sovereign republics facing an uncertain future—alone.

East Central Europe and the Balkans: From Stalinism to Pluralism

From 1945 to 1989, Eastern Europe consisted of nine sovereign nations: Albania, Bulgaria, Czechoslovakia, East Germany, Hungary, Poland, Romania, Yugoslavia, and the USSR. After World War II, the Red Army occupied all of them except Albania and Yugoslavia. By 1948, Stalin had imposed the Soviet model everywhere; in Yugoslavia, Marshal Tito rebuffed Stalin but in many ways imitated Stalinism. Monolithic rule prevailed until an avalanche of popular demands for democratization and socioeconomic reforms swept it away in 1989 and 1990—and more than doubled the roster of nations.

Stalin insisted that the governments of the "outer empire" in Eastern Europe be modeled on his own: dictatorship by the Communist Party, a government apparatus democratic in appearance but highly centralized and hierarchical, a socialist command economy in which patterns of production and consumption reflect political priorities rather than market forces, and a foreign policy based on fraternal relations with other Communist states. All this changed dramatically after the deluge of 1989.

Slavic Europe during the Cold War

Throughout Slavic Europe, the Communist Party dominated politics. In some cases, other political parties existed (for example, in Poland and Hungary), but they were permitted primarily to hide the fact that the Party was all-powerful.

Party organization in Eastern Europe mirrored Soviet practice. The size of Party membership in each country was kept at 6 to 12 percent of the total population, ensuring that the Party remained an elite organization. Elitism was apparently necessary for Party morale, political recruitment, ideological integrity, and internal discipline.

Communist Parties in Eastern Europe also imitated the Soviet insistence on political and intellectual conformity. Like the CPSU, they were intolerant of dissent and used censorship, surveillance, intimidation, coercion, and incessant propaganda to suppress freedom of artistic and literary expression, as well as political free speech.

The Hierarchical State

Government structures in the Eastern European nations differed superficially from the Soviet model, but in all of them, executive authority was centralized, and the state apparatus was subservient to the Party.

The heads of state in Czechoslovakia and Romania were presidents who in theory were chosen by the legislature but in practice were co-opted by the top Party bosses. Poland, East Germany, Bulgaria, and Hungary had a collective chief executive called a state council. Yugoslavia, too, had a collective presidency. Only in Romania was the presidency a position of great power: from 1967 to 1989,

Nicolae Ceauşescu was both president and Party chief (Brezhnev, Andropov, Chernenko, and Gorbachev in the Soviet Union likewise held both posts).

In these countries, as in the Soviet Union, responsibility for day-to-day administration rested with the premier and a council of ministers who were handpicked by the Party leadership. Rubber-stamping was the primary function of Eastern European parliaments, much as the Supreme Soviet legitimized Politburo decisions in the Kremlin.

Central Planning

Following World War II, Moscow imposed on Eastern Europe not only Stalinist political structures and methods but also Stalinist economic practices. Hence the entire region simultaneously embarked on the adventure of central planning, nationalization of industry, and collectivization of agriculture. Only in Poland did stiff peasant resistance keep most land in private hands.

In organization and operation, the command economies of Eastern Europe became copies of the Soviet economy. Developmentally, however, they lagged behind even the Soviet Union (and fell farther and farther behind the Western European economies). Moscow was content to buy raw materials from these countries and sell manufactured goods back to them. But this arrangement understandably made the Eastern European satellites feel exploited. So long as they continued to provide grist for the mill of Soviet industry, they would remain industrially dependent and backward. Furthermore, Soviet manufactures were relatively expensive, and the quality was generally poor.

The main problem with central planning, however, was that as the years passed, it became clear that the system was not working. First Hungary and then other countries began experimenting with market mechanisms. These experiments were cautious and highly controlled, but they suggested that the Stalinist model was a major impediment to economic growth and technological progress.

The Crumbling of the "Outer Empire"

Although several Eastern European states had begun to display a measure of independence from Moscow in economic matters before 1989, there had been no corresponding movement for political independence. Undoubtedly, Eastern Europeans remembered all too well the Soviet invasion of Hungary in 1956 and Czechoslovakia in 1968, as well as Soviet pressures on the Polish government to crack down on dissent in 1956 and again in 1980 and 1981.

The bitter lessons of Hungary, Czechoslovakia, and Poland were that Moscow would not allow any Eastern European member state to withdraw from the Warsaw Pact; Imre Nagy of Hungary tried and failed. Nor would Moscow allow genuine opposition parties to be formed. The government of Czechoslovakia under Alexander Dubček vowed to move in this direction, jeopardizing the Party's monopoly on power. Dubček's heresy led to the Soviet invasion and the enunciation of the **Brezhnev Doctrine**, asserting that Moscow and its allies have a right to intervene in Eastern Europe to defend socialism. Finally, Moscow would not tolerate independent power centers (such as the Solidarity trade-union movement in Poland in the early 1980s) that threatened or challenged the Party's monopoly on power. Under the Brezhnev Doctrine, the Soviet Army stood ready to intervene against such "counterrevolution," if necessary. As the events of 1989 demonstrated, this Pax Sovietica was the only glue holding the "socialist commonwealth" together.

The Revolutions of 1989

The year 1989 was a turning point in the long struggle between two irreconcilable ideologies—communism and capitalism—and Eastern Europe was the stage on which the drama was acted out. The year began with steps toward free elections in Poland and Hungary; it ended with the ouster of Erich Honecker in East Germany, the subsequent opening of the intra-German border (and the dismantling of the Berlin Wall), the resignation of the Communist leadership in Czechoslovakia, and the overthrow of Ceauşescu in Romania.

During 1989, Poland and Hungary introduced a series of political reforms aimed at democratization. In Poland, the independent trade union Solidarity, banned for eight years, was relegalized. The government allowed relatively free elections to a newly constituted parliament in June. Solidarity was allowed to contest all the seats for the Senate (upper house) and won an overwhelming majority in that body (92 percent). It also won all 161 seats it was allowed to contest in the 460-seat Sejm (lower house). Although the Communists (PUWP) enjoyed a guaranteed majority in the Sejm (nearly two-thirds of the seats), the June elections were a ringing mandate for Lech Walesa's opposition Solidarity "party." In August, the Polish parliament confirmed Tadeusz Mazowiecki as the first non-Communist prime minister in a Soviet bloc country.

The Hungarian parliament voted to allow freedom of association and assembly in January 1989, and the following month the Hungarian Socialist Workers' Party (HSWP), more commonly known as the Hungarian Communist Party, approved formation of independent political parties. Hungary thus became the first Eastern European state since the Stalinist takeover to relinquish the Communist Party's monopoly position and embrace a competitive multiparty system. In May, Hungary dismantled the barbed-wire fence separating it from neutral Austria.

The pace of change accelerated in the fall when the Hungarian government announced that it would allow East Germans on holiday in Hungary to emigrate to the West and reestablished diplomatic relations with Israel (suspended at the time of the Six-Day War in 1967). Next came a series of measures institutionalizing a multiparty system, a unicameral legislature, and free elections in 1990. In early October, delegates to a special congress of the HSWP changed the party's name to the Hungarian Socialist Party, enlarged the ruling presidium from four to twenty-four members, and renounced Marxism in favor of democratic socialism. The congress also voted to divest the party of property holdings, disband the Workers' Militia (the party's praetorian guard), and disestablish party cells in factories. In mid-October, the Hungarian National Assembly voted to make ninety-four changes in the constitution—deleting all references to the "leading role" of the Communist Party, allowing independent political parties, establishing a separation of powers, codifying civil and human rights, and changing the country's official name from the People's Republic of Hungary to the Republic of Hungary. The Assembly also formally legalized opposition parties and disbanded the Workers' Militia.

On November 26, 1989, voters in a national referendum opted for parliamentary rather than popular election of the president. The outcome was widely viewed as a victory for the liberal Alliance of Free Democrats and a setback for Imre Poszgay, the most outspoken "liberal" within the ruling circle. Poszgay was the first Communist leader in Eastern Europe to advocate a multiparty system and competitive elections.

By the end of the year, Hungary's Communist Party leaders had set the stage for a peaceful transfer of power to a noncommunist government. (Again, Poszgay had been the first Communist leader to say unequivocally that the Communist Party ought to relinquish power if it failed to win in free and fair elections.) Voters went to the polls in March and April 1990. No fewer than eighteen political parties contested the elections. As a result, no single party won a clear majority, but the newly enfranchised electorate gave two noncommunist groupings, the conservative Democratic Forum and the liberal Alliance of Free Democrats, strong endorsements (24.9 percent and 19.7 percent, respectively). The independent Smallholders party, which had won the last free elections in Hungary back in 1945, came in third. The parties of the left were the big losers.

The movement toward multiparty democracy proceeded rather quietly in Poland and Hungary. Not so in East Germany, Czechoslovakia, and Romania, where Communist regimes toppled in rapid succession. These events were interrelated. The crisis in the German Democratic Republic began with the flight of East Germans, vacationing in Hungary, to West Germany. Soon East Germans were clamoring for freedom to emigrate, freedom of speech, freedom of assembly—in a word, for freedom. Some fled through Poland; others sought refuge in the West German embassy in Prague, Czechoslovakia. Spectacular mass demonstrations occurred in Leipzig, East Berlin, and other East German cities throughout the fall of 1989. Under intense popular pressure and increasingly isolated (even Gorbachev offered no support), the Communist Party leadership replaced its hard-line chief, Erich Honecker, with Egon Krenz, who proved unable to slow the popular groundswell. Only Hans Modrow, one of the few East German Communists reputed to be a "liberal," had any credibility.

In an effort to placate a society now in open revolt, the Krenz regime gave the Czech government permission to allow thousands of East Germans in Czechoslovakia to go west. With the pressure mounting, the beleaguered GDR government lifted emigration restrictions and opened the intra-German border.

For the first time since 1961, East Germans were allowed to travel freely to West Germany.

The Berlin Wall came tumbling down. Berliners from both sides of the city, divided since 1961, celebrated day and night atop the wall. People came from all over the world to celebrate with them, and millions more joined the party via satellite television. German youths danced and sang, laughed and cried. Strangers embraced. For anyone who had grown up during the Cold War, it was an unforgettable scene.

In short order, the Krenz government resigned, and an interim cabinet headed by Hans Modrow set about preparing the country for free elections. East German voters went to the polls in March 1990 and gave the conservative Christian Democrats a mandate to rule. The Social Democrats came in a distant second. The Communist Party, renamed the SED, suffered a humiliating defeat. What is more, East Germans had endorsed an early merger of the two German states—the key plank in the Christian Democrats' platform. Indeed, West German Chancellor Helmut Kohl had campaigned in East Germany for unification, and the process was completed faster than most observers expected, on October 3.

In neighboring Czechoslovakia, the conservative Communist government of Milos Jakes steadfastly resisted major economic and political reforms until it was swept away by popular discontent in late 1989. In an amazing role reversal, Vaclav Havel, a dissident writer who had been jailed earlier in the year, accepted the presidency in December after aging hard-liner Gustav Husak resigned. Havel's chief rival for that position was Alexander Dubček, the fallen hero of the 1968 Prague Spring uprising. One of Husak's last official acts as president was to name a new cabinet in which most of the twenty-one members were non-Communists.

Although the new prime minister, Marian Calfa, was a Communist, it was Havel, the conscience of the nation, who was hailed both at home and abroad as the hero of the "velvet revolution." As the leader of a coalition of opposition groups called Civic Forum, Havel played a key role in negotiating the terms on which Czechoslovakia's beleaguered Communists would relinquish power. At the beginning of 1989, Havel was a playwright and a pariah; at the end, he was the president. Havel's personal triumph in 1989 was rich in symbolism for the region as a whole: democracy, too, had been rehabilitated.

Romania was the last domino to fall. It had had the most repressive regime in Eastern Europe. For Nicolae Ceaușescu, governing the country was a family affair; he practiced nepotism shamelessly and lived in royal splendor. His opulent lifestyle contrasted sharply with the impoverished conditions afflicting the Romanian people. Even electricity was rationed, and most apartments in Romania were dark and cold all winter.

In December 1989, Ceaușescu's security forces staged a bloody crackdown against demonstrators in Timisoara and Bucharest. The army, refusing orders to fire on civilians, fought a series of battles with the security police, who remained loyal to Ceaușescu. The army captured Ceaușescu in flight, staged a perfunctory trial, and executed the hated dictator and his wife. Later, mass graves containing the bodies of hundreds of demonstrators were discovered in Timisoara.

Romania's new leaders—so-called reform Communists—set up the Council of National Reconciliation to run the country until free elections could be held. Critics denounced the new government for including former members of Ceaușescu's inner circle and for operating too much like the old government.

In the string of elections held in Eastern Europe in the first half of 1990, voters rejected not only the Communists but also other parties of the left and center-left (most notably the Social Democrats). *The Economist* noted: "In one country after another, 'reform communism' proved empty. Once the Soviet veto on change was withdrawn, there was suddenly no stopping point halfway. Communist power collapsed."[24] The surprising popularity of center-right parties touting free enterprise pointed to the main reason why Communist power toppled in Eastern Europe: the disappointing performance of economies saddled with the Stalinist system of central planning. But rising expectations associated with market reforms put the new leaders under the gun, for failure to produce results could be politically destabilizing. Fragile democratic reforms might be the first casualties.

Case Studies: Czechoslovakia and Yugoslavia

Slavic Europe encompasses the former Soviet Union west of the Urals, East Central Europe, and the Balkans. We have already examined the USSR in this chapter; now we will focus on Czechoslovakia (recognized as the Czech and Slovak Federal Republic—or CSFR—between 1990 and 1992) in East Central Europe and Yugoslavia in the Balkans.

Poland and Hungary are also strong candidates for special consideration in this section. Both are examples of relatively homogenous societies in this region. Hungary is not Slavic—a fact that helps underscore the point that there are many important non-Slavic groups in Slavic Europe. Poland is enduring the transition problems experienced by all the former Communist states and illustrates the fact that even in the absence of ethnic conflict, the challenges of economic and political liberalization are daunting. At the same time, many of the issues discussed here—privatization, restructuring, inflation, unemployment, currency convertibility, foreign investment, and external trade—are common to all former Communist states.

Czechoslovakia

Czechoslovakia is located in East Central Europe, bordered by Poland, Germany, Austria, Hungary, and Ukraine. The Czechs are widely considered to be the most Western-oriented people in Slavic Europe. Dr. Thomas G. Masaryk (1850–1937), Czechoslovakia's principal founder, was both a product of this tradition and its perpetuator.

Masaryk's Democratic Experiment   Czechoslovakia came into being after World War I. Established as an independent republic in 1918, it was the only functioning democracy in Slavic Europe during the interwar period. Masaryk succeeded in melding the two parts of the country—Bohemia and Moravia, the Czech lands to the west, and Slovakia in the east—into a single state under a constitution that provided for a freely elected parliament that in turn elected the president. Appropriately enough, Masaryk became Czechoslovakia's first and most beloved president. He was perfect for the job: his father was a Slovak, his mother a Moravian, and his wife an American! A philosopher and teacher by profession, he was an extraordinary leader who displayed both wisdom and moral courage throughout his long life.

Carved out of the Austro-Hungarian Empire, Czechoslovakia was a hybrid state from the beginning. The Czech lands were part of Austria before World War I, and Slovakia was part of Hungary. The Czechs were more numerous than the Slovaks (by almost two to one), more Western, and industrially more advanced. Although their languages are Slavic and very similar, Czechs use the Roman alphabet, Slovaks the Cyrillic. So even at its founding, the political institutions of Czechoslovakia had to bridge economic, cultural, ethnic, and geographic divides.

Totalitarianism Right and Left   Czechoslovakia's golden age of democracy ended in 1938 following the infamous appeasement of Hitler by British Prime Minister Neville Chamberlain at Munich. Chamberlain conceded the Sudetenland, a part of Czechoslovakia inhabited by three million ethnic Germans, to Hitler in return for the Nazi leader's false promise of peace. The Nazi occupation lasted from 1939 to 1945 and helped set the stage for a new kind of totalitarian dictatorship by brutalizing the society and introducing police state methods into a country that had been governed by good and decent leaders committed to constitutionalism and the rule of law.

After World War II, the fate of Czechoslovakia was in the hands of the Soviet Union due to the fact that the Soviet army had played the largest role in liberating the country from Nazi rule. The Communists staged a coup in February 1948, ousting President Eduard Beneš and establishing the Communist People's Republic (changed to Socialist Republic in 1960). Subservient to Moscow from its inception, Communist Czechoslovakia became a federal system in 1969 following the Prague Spring uprising, a popular uprising against Communist rule put down by invading Soviet forces the previous year. Until the "velvet revolution" at the end of 1989, Czechoslovakia had a reputation as one of the most rigidly Communist states in the Soviet bloc.

The Velvet Revolution   At the end of 1989, after the Soviet-installed regimes in Poland, Hungary, and East Germany had fallen, Czechoslovakia also rose up against its Communist rulers. The leaders of the revolt were moderates who opposed violence (hence the name "velvet revolution"). They rallied around a dissident playwright named Vaclav Havel. Modest and soft-spoken, Havel had

CONTRAST and COMPARISON

Poland

Unlike the former states of Czechoslovakia and Yugoslavia, Poland is a largely homogenous Slavic society; its population of 38,363,000 is 99 percent Polish. In contrast to the Czech Republic, which has a mixed Protestant-Catholic religious tradition and is now a largely secular society, and the former Yugoslavia, which had large Catholic, Eastern Orthodox, and Muslim populations, Poland remains 95 percent Roman Catholic. A Polish pope (the first ever) and the Polish Catholic church's outspoken opposition to Communist rule gave the church great credibility in Poland, although there has been friction between the Vatican and the Polish government since 1990, especially on the issue of abortion.

Poland discarded Communist rule quickly in 1989 and adopted a democratic constitution, but it discovered that it was easier to destroy the old order than to create a new one. The coalition that Solidarity had forged in the 1980s broke apart (as did its counterparts—Sajudis in Lithuania and Civic Form/Public against Violence in Czechoslovakia). Its political party system is among the most badly fragmented in Eastern Europe—in the October 1991 general election, sixty-seven parties participated, and twenty-nine actually won seats in the parliament. The largest party gained only 14 percent of the seats. Unstable government is the inevitable upshot: Poland had three governments in 1992 and changed privatization ministers five times between 1990 and March 1993. Poland's experience has been mirrored elsewhere in the region.

Economically, Poland set the pace for privatization with its "shock therapy"—radical, rapid market reforms. The result was to bring great hardship at first as the society endured the pain of adjustment. But by the end of 1992, the therapy had started to work. Polish GDP was expected to rise by 3 to 4 percent in 1993 (after falling by over 30 percent in 1990–1992). Some analysts attribute Poland's success in getting back on the road to recovery to its privatization policies. For example, industrial growth in the third quarter of 1992 rose 7.7 percent compared to the same quarter in 1991. Of this growth, state-firm output accounted for only 1.1 percent, whereas private output rose 25 percent. Poland has privatized the fastest of all former Communist nations: private firms accounted for over 40 percent of GDP in Poland and nearly 60 percent of the labor force by the beginning of 1993.

been a human-rights activist and had spent time in jail as a prisoner of conscience. Other popular leaders included Jiri Dienstbier and Alexander Dubček, a Slovak who had been a central figure in the ill-fated attempt to introduce a multiparty system free of police state controls ("socialism with a human face") in the late 1960s.

That earlier episode ironically helped seal the fate of Czechoslovakia's ruling Communists. Having crushed the 1968 reform movement and conducted widespread purges of reformers (ultimately affecting half a million Party members) from 1969 to 1971, they could not easily jump on the reform bandwagon in the late 1980s. Thus in March 1987, President Gustav Husak warned that "no one is forcing Soviet ideas on Czechoslovakia." When Husak was replaced as Party leader in December 1987, Gorbachev publicly urged his successor, Milos Jakes, to proceed with the "democratization of public and political life." Gorbachev's *perestroika* campaign had put Czechoslovakia's Communist leaders on the defensive.

An Inherited Constitution   The new short-lived Czech and Slovak Federal Republic (CSFR), which came into being in 1990, inherited a cumbersome constitution adopted in the 1960s. At a meeting with the leaders of Civic Forum, a short-lived opposition party hastily created to negotiate the transition to democratic rule in late November 1989, the tottering dictatorship agreed to delete all references to the Communist Party's "leading role" and a few other provisions. For the most part, however, the government after 1989 continued to operate within the preexisting constitutional structure. (A new constitution was being drafted, but it turned into a race against the clock as the two halves of the CSFR started splitting apart in 1991.) The big difference, of course, was that the Communist rulers treated the constitution as an ornament, whereas the new democratic leaders were obliged to take it seriously.

The system set up by the inherited constitution created a division of powers between the federal government on the one hand and the two national governments on the other. It established Prague as the capital of the Czech Republic and Bratislava as the seat of government in the Slovak Republic. Each of the component republics was given separate political institutions, including a National Council (or legislature) and an executive (prime minister and cabinet), to operate concurrently with the federal government in Prague.

The bicameral Federal Assembly, consisting of the Chamber of Nations and the Chamber of the People, was the highest organ of state power (although in practice, of course, the Communist Party enjoyed a de facto power monopoly until 1989). The Federal Assembly elected a president (under the Communists this was *pro forma*), who in turn appointed a head of government and cabinet. Hence Czechoslovakia had both a head of state (the president) and a head of government (the prime minister), an arrangement common elsewhere in Europe. The Federal Assembly chose the Supreme Court judges, and the National Councils chose judges for regional and district courts.

The federal structure was more complicated than the unitary systems of Western Europe, but it was necessary due to the ethnic makeup of Czechoslovakia. The federation's political problems after 1989 were to some degree attributable to procedural difficulties built into the inherited constitution.

The Constitutional Trap   Under Czechoslovakia's original 1918 constitution, the president was elected by a three-fifths majority in the Federal Assembly. This stringent majoritarian requirement was no doubt adopted to ensure that the president would have a clear mandate and could therefore speak with moral authority. It was not a problem in 1918: Thomas Masaryk was the unchallenged leader of the country. (He was elected to a seven-year term and exempted from the constitutional ban against self-succession.) But the three-fifths majority rule was a potential problem in the future. A fragmented Federal Assembly might not be able to agree on a worthy candidate, which could lead either to a constitutional crisis or the election of a weak compromise candidate. In some circumstances, it might even result in the election of a demagogue. (How this rule came back to haunt the CSFR in the summer of 1992 is discussed in Chapter 9.)

The inherited constitution also prescribed legislative procedures that made it relatively easy for opposition parties in a fragmented parliament to block legislation and in general play an obstructionist role. Both legislative chambers had to approve legislation before it could become law—not an unreasonable rule. The 150 seats in the Chamber of the People were allocated in proportion to population (the Czech Republic had 101 seats, the Slovak Republic 49); the 150 seats in the Chamber of Nations were split equally between the two republics. The Chamber of Nations also voted in a peculiar way: the two parts vote *separately*. Legislation had to be approved not only in both chambers but also in both parts of the Chamber of Nations. Hence a relatively small opposition (as few as thirty-eight members) in one part of this chamber could block all government policy and federal legislation, which meant that the will of the majority in the Federal Assembly could be thwarted by one-eighth of its delegates. Moreover, certain actions (such as election of a president) required a three-fifths majority in both houses of the Federal Assembly. In this case, it took not only 180 votes total for approval but also forty-five members in both parts of the Chamber of Nations: thirty-one members (10 percent of the whole body plus one) could kill a measure.

Finally, the existence of the two National Councils created an institutionalized tug-of-war between three governments of more or less equal weight (although the political balance shifted decisively against the federal government in 1992). In such a compact country (about 15 million people inhabiting a territory the size of New York State), it was an open invitation to a schism between the federal government in Prague and the Slovak National Council in Bratislava. Intended by the Communist regime to give the appearance of autonomy to Czechs and Slovaks, it had the effect of magnifying the points of contention between the two parts of the country once the Communists were gone.

A discussion of the problems and prospects for the CSFR is beyond the scope of the present chapter. For now it is enough to note that the CSFR in the early 1990s was headed for a breakup and that this process was aided and abetted by certain improvident features of an inherited constitution.

Yugoslavia

The Balkans have proved to be a particularly unstable subregion of Europe in the twentieth century. In this area, Yugoslavia had long been considered the country most likely to disintegrate. That it stayed together for more than four decades after World War II was due largely to the leadership skills of one man, Josip Broz Tito.

Tito's Fragile State   The largely Slavic population of Yugoslavia consisted of eight primary ethnic groups speaking one of four languages (Serbo-Croat, Macedonian, Slovenian, and Albanian) and comprising three distinct religious communities (Eastern Orthodox, Roman Catholic, and Muslim; see Table 8.5).

After World War II, Marshal Tito, the popular leader of the Communist-inspired Partisans who fought valiantly against the Axis powers, created one of

Table 8.5 Composition of the Population of Prebreakup Yugoslavia

Ethnic Group	Share of Population (percent)	Religion
Serbs	37	Eastern Orthodox
Croats	20	Roman Catholic
Bosnian Muslims	9	Muslim
Slovenes	8	Roman Catholic
Albanians	8	Muslim
Macedonians	6	Eastern Orthodox
Montenegrins	3	Eastern Orthodox
Hungarians	2	Roman Catholic

the most complex political and economic systems anywhere in the world. This complexity was a reflection of the fragile ethnic and historical basis for the Yugoslav state, which had come into being after World War I. Tito himself was the glue that held the country together. After his death in 1980, the country began to come apart. Before the violent breakup in 1991–1992 there were six constituent republics and two autonomous provinces (see Table 8.6), each with its own governmental apparatus (presidency, prime minister and cabinet, indirectly elected assembly, and judiciary).

Between East and West   Tito's decision to break with Stalin in 1948 was a watershed in the history of world communism. It ensured that Moscow would use its control over the rest of Eastern Europe to try to isolate Belgrade and force Tito out. This left Tito little choice but to turn to the West for trade and aid.

But how could Tito, a fervent Communist, expect a sympathetic hearing in the industrial democracies, particularly the United States? Communism and capitalism are antithetical, and Europe in 1948 was feeling the chill of the Cold

Table 8.6 Prebreakup Yugoslavia

Republic or Province (Capital)	Area (square miles)	Population
Republics		
Bosnia-Herzegovina (Sarajevo)	19,741	4,116,439
Croatia (Zagreb)	21,829	4,578,109
Macedonia (Skopje)	9,928	1,913,571
Montenegro (Titograd)	5,333	583,475
Serbia (Belgrade)	21,609	5,666,060
Slovenia (Ljubljana)	7,819	1,883,764
Autonomous Provinces		
Kosovo (Pristina)	4,203	1,584,558
Vojvodina (Novi Sad)	8,303	2,028,239

War. Tito's solution was to complicate the picture enough so that the leaders of the "free" (non-Communist) world could deal with Yugoslavia without seeming to be consorting with the enemy.

In addition, Tito no doubt wanted to show the Soviets that he could find a way between communism and capitalism that would be a model for the newly emerging nations of Africa and Asia. Indeed, Tito established himself as an early leader of the nonaligned movement—Third World nations that sought to avoid choosing sides in the East-West conflict and to redefine global issues along North-South lines.

Reforming Workplace and Marketplace   Tito's reforms were aimed at decentralizing decision-making authority—the antithesis of the highly centralized Stalinist system. One of the first and most dramatic steps in this direction was the introduction of **workers' self-management.** The idea was to give the workers control over production (and hence responsibility for it) via freely elected workers' councils and management boards. Even the enterprise manager was to be elected by the workers.

Workers' self-management, Tito reasoned, would remove one major obstacle to labor productivity: worker alienation. On the positive side, workers would take greater pride in their work, leading to improved quality of goods; they would better understand the problems of management and thus avoid unreasonable demands and expectations, and they would develop a greater loyalty to the collective—both the enterprise and their coworkers.

Within this system evolved **indicative planning** to set overall targets for the various sectors of the economy. These targets were guidelines, not obligatory goals. In agriculture too the state relinquished direct control: collectivization was halted, and most farmland was reprivatized in the 1950s.

In the 1960s, the Yugoslav leadership gave greater autonomy to plant managers and further reduced the role of central administrators. As in the West, prices were set by market forces of supply and demand, and profitability became the test of efficiency. A state planning agency remained active in Belgrade, but production targets were set at the republic level and coordinated by the federal agency. Under the impact of these reforms, Yugoslavia developed the most consumer-oriented economy in Eastern Europe.

How well did these reforms work? The results were mixed. While Tito was alive, the economy remained healthy, but in the 1980s a number of chronic problems emerged, including mounting external debt, a falling standard of living, and rising unemployment. In addition, despite workers' self-management, low productivity caused prices to climb, and energy costs were high. And even harder times lay ahead.

Federalism, Yes; Democracy, No   Economic reforms in Yugoslavia were accompanied by changes in the formal structures of the government. These changes were designed to create the appearance of decentralized, democratic republicanism.

Under Tito, it did not matter much who held what official position. As founder and chief architect of the nation, Tito called the shots, and no one expected otherwise. This extraordinary consensus enabled Tito to experiment with various forms of political power sharing without having to relinquish any personal power. He designed an elaborate set of institutions that shrouded the dominant role of the Yugoslav Communist Party (officially the League of Yugoslav Communists) in the trappings of federalism and democracy. Under this unique system, Yugoslavia had a rotating collective chief executive that consisted of nine persons, one from each of the six republics and the two autonomous provinces, and one ex officio member representing the Communist Party. The Federal Assembly elected a chairman to a one-year term. Under a special constitutional provision, Tito served as president until his death in 1980. The system was therefore never really tested during Tito's lifetime.

The thirty-three-member Federal Executive Council (the cabinet) was the functional equivalent of the Council of Ministers in the USSR. The collective presidency nominated a member of the bicameral Federal Assembly to be president of the Federal Executive Council, and the Assembly then voted confirmation. The Yugoslav premier was thus chosen in a manner similar to that of many parliamentary democracies. The council was responsible for the government's day-to-day operations.

The Federal Assembly was a bicameral legislature made up of the Federal Chamber and the Chamber of Republics and Provinces. The electoral process was Byzantine in its complexity, but during Tito's lifetime it mattered little because elections were stage-managed (and all candidates were screened) by a Communist front organization called the Socialist Alliance of Working People of Yugoslavia (SSRNJ). Ultimately, delegates to the Federal Chamber were chosen by local assemblies and to the Chamber of Republics and Provinces by the assemblies of the republics and provinces.

The basic unit of local government, the *commune,* had considerable administrative authority and some autonomy in matters not expressly delegated to the federal government, the constituent republics, or the autonomous provinces. Government at this level involved extensive citizen participation. One student of Yugoslav politics reported in 1977:

> The communes have become key local units that have several primary concerns. One of these is economic, including planning, investments, internal trade, and supervision over economic enterprises. Another concern is municipal services, such as water supply, sewers, streets, and public utilities. A third comprises the area of "social management," that is, citizen control over public utilities.[25]

Administration of municipal services and public utilities is certainly relevant to the quality of life, but such matters are trivial compared to the momentous issues that confront whole societies and nations. The Communist Party did not relinquish its right to address those issues.

The Party Vanguard   Thus despite the elaborate façade of federalism and democracy, political power remained a Communist Party monopoly to the end. Other political parties were banned, and dissent was kept to a minimum. Marxist-

Leninist dogma pervaded the press, the arts, and propaganda. In the final analysis, Yugoslavia, though not in the Soviet sphere, was nevertheless a Communist state not too different from the Soviet model.

Nearly a decade after Yugoslavia split with the Soviet Union, Milovan Djilas, Tito's former comrade in arms and perhaps the most famous inside critic of Soviet-style communism in the postwar period, published a book called *The New Class*. (Djilas was in prison at the time for expressing the ideas contained in the book.) "The greatest illusion," he wrote, "was that industrialization and collectivization in the USSR, and destruction of capitalist ownership, would result in a classless society." Instead, he argued, a "new class" emerged in place of the old one:

> The roots of the new class were implanted in a special party of the Bolshevik type. Lenin was right in his view that his party was an exception in the history of human society, although he did not suspect that it would be the beginning of a new class. . . .
>
> This is not to say that the new party and the new class are identical. The party, however, is the core of that class, and its base. . . . The new class may be said to be made up of those who have special privileges and economic preference because of the administrative monopoly they hold.[26]

Nonetheless, thanks to Tito, the Yugoslav Communist Party had a stronger bias toward collective leadership than its Soviet counterpart.

Thus Tito balanced regional and ethnic interests in the top party organs much as he did in the collective presidency and the Federal Executive Council. This system may have ensured representation of the major parts of Yugoslavia's diverse multiethnic society, but it did not constitute a participatory democracy. Nor could such a façade resist, once the iron hand of Tito was gone, the centuries-old resentments of those various ethnic groups.

CONCLUSION

The Soviet state developed an elaborate set of highly centralized political institutions. The Communist Party apparatus was the organizational backbone of this Stalinist system. The will of this monolithic party was carried out by an all-encompassing state bureaucracy. Political dissent was suppressed by the secret police (KGB), which operated outside of the normal legal framework of Soviet society during Stalin's long reign of terror. This system mellowed after Stalin's death in 1953 but continued to be inhospitable to open dissent until Gorbachev's accession to power in 1985. By that time, the Soviet economy had stagnated. Gorbachev called for new thinking and launched a series of bold economic and political reforms. His own indecision; resistance from vested interests within the party, state bureaucracy, secret police, and military; and the sheer magnitude of the tasks combined to bring the reforms to grief. The "outer empire" came unraveled in 1989; the "inner empire" disintegrated in 1991 after an abortive coup by hard-liners. In Chapter 9, we explore the problems of transition facing Russia and the other newly independent republics of the former Soviet Union and Eastern Europe.

KEY TERMS

glasnost

perestroika

demokratisatsiia

force

co-optation

socialization

functional legitimacy

moral legitimacy

centralization

Politburo

general secretary

Secretariat

apparat

Central Committee

Party Congress

nomenklatura

primary Party organizations (PPOs)

democratic centralism

Council of Ministers

union republics

autonomous republics

Supreme Soviet

Congress of Peoples' Deputies

Liberman reforms

central planning

August coup

Commonwealth of Independent States (CIS)

Brezhnev Doctrine

workers' self-management

indicative planning

STUDY QUESTIONS

1. Why did the founders of the Soviet state opt for federalism, and what does the term mean in the Soviet context? How has federalism been affected by Gorbachev's reforms? (Hint: Focus on the role of the new Soviet legislature.) How have recent events threatened to reshape the Soviet federal system?

2. What is the traditional relationship between ideology and economics in Soviet-type systems? What leader most left his imprint on the Soviet economy? (Identify specific ideas and institutions associated with this leader.) What are the comparative advantages and disadvantages of central planning (versus market economies)?

3. What were the major structural elements and operating principles of the Soviet system in the pre-Gorbachev era?

4. How and why did Mikhail Gorbachev attempt to reform the Soviet system, and what were the consequences?

5. How can the collapse of the Soviet system be explained? What were the key internal factors that undermined the Soviet state? Could anybody or anything have saved it?

6. In what sense is 1989 a watershed in the political history of Eastern Europe? What were the major events of that year, and how have those events transformed the region's politics?

SUGGESTED READING

Aslund, Anders. *Gorbachev's Struggle for Economic Reform*. Ithaca, N.Y.: Cornell University Press, 1991.

Banac, Ivo, ed. *Eastern Europe in Revolution*. Ithaca, N.Y.: Cornell University Press, 1992.

Bialer, Seweryn. *The Soviet Paradox: External Expansion and Internal Decline*. New York: Knopf, 1986.

Doder, Dusko, and Branson, Louise. *Gorbachev: Heretic in the Kremlin*. New York: Viking Penguin, 1991.

Goldman, Marshall I. *Gorbachev's Challenge: Economic Reform in the Age of High Technology*. New York: Norton, 1987.

Goldman, Marshall I. *What Went Wrong with Perestroika*. New York: Norton, 1991.

Gorbachev, Mikhail. *Perestroika: New Thinking for Our Country and the World*. San Bernardino, Calif.: Borgo Press, 1991.

Havel, Vaclav. *Vaclav Havel, or Living in Truth*. London: Faber & Faber, 1986.

Laquer, Walter. *The Long Road to Freedom: Russia and Glasnost*. New York: Macmillan, 1990.

Lovenduski, Joni, and Jean Woodall. *Politics and Society in Eastern Europe*. Bloomington: Indiana University Press, 1988.

Rothschild, Joseph. *Return to Diversity: A Political History of East Central Europe since World War II*. New York: Oxford University Press, 1989.

Smith, Gordon B. *Soviet Politics: Continuity and Contradiction*. New York: St. Martin's Press, 1987.

Starr, Richard F. *Communist Regimes in Eastern Europe*. 5th ed. Stanford, Calif.: Hoover Institution Press, 1988.

Vozlensky, Michael. *Nomenklatura: The Soviet Ruling Class*. Garden City, N.Y.: Doubleday, 1984.

NOTES

1. Gordon B. Smith, *Soviet Politics: Continuity and Contradictions* (New York: St. Martin's Press, 1987), p. 365.
2. *Economist,* Dec. 16, 1989, p. 48.
3. Paul Quinn-Judge, "Gorbachev Presses for a Rollback of Party's Power," *Christian Science Monitor,* June 29, 1988, p. 1.
4. Stanley Rothman and George W. Breslauer, *Soviet Politics and Society* (St. Paul, Minn.: West, 1978), p. 242; see also E. G. Liberman, *Economic Methods and Effectiveness of Production* (White Plains, N.Y.: International Arts and Sciences Press, 1971).
5. Robert Gillete, "Perestroika: Bold Shift in Economy," *Los Angeles Times,* Oct. 27, 1987.
6. Ibid.
7. Ibid.
8. Dan Fisher and William J. Eaton, "Rumbles of Change Stir Soviet Union," *Los Angeles Times,* Oct. 25, 1987.
9. Ibid.
10. Dan Fisher, "Glasnost: Soviets Try to Open Up," *Los Angeles Times,* Oct. 29, 1987.
11. See Alex Goldfarb, "Testing Glasnost: An Exile Visits His Homeland," *New York Times Magazine,* Dec. 6, 1987, pp. 47ff.

12. Ibid.
13. See Dan Fisher, "Editor on Cutting Edge of Glasnost Sees 'Chance for My Generation,'" *Los Angeles Times,* Oct. 29, 1987.
14. See Hedrick Smith, *The Russians* (New York: Ballantine, 1984), pp. 320–362; and David Shipler, *Russia* (New York: Viking Penguin, 1983), pp. 301–346.
15. Shipler, *Russia,* p. 326.
16. Goldfarb, "Testing Glasnost," p. 49.
17. Shipler, *Russia,* p. 324.
18. Bill Keller, "Riots' Legacy of Distrust Quietly Stalks a Soviet City," *New York Times,* Aug. 31, 1989, p. 1.
19. Bill Keller, "Setting Precedent, Estonia Allows a Non-Communist Front to Form," *New York Times,* June 21, 1988, p. 1.
20. "Estonians Protest Soviet Nazi Pact and Press for Autonomy," *Christian Science Monitor,* Aug. 23, 1988, p. 7.
21. See, for example, Philip Taubman, "Moscow's Baltic Torn," *New York Times,* Oct. 25, 1988, p. 1.
22. Paul Hofheinz, "Let's Do Business," *Fortune,* Sept. 23, 1991, p. 62; Amy Kaslow, "Swedish Adviser Says Soviet Republics, West Are Squandering Chance to Solve Problems," *Christian Science Monitor,* Oct. 23, 1991, p. 1; Gerald F. Seib and Alan Murray, "IMF Effort to Reform Soviet Economy Runs Many Daunting Risks," *Wall Street Journal,* Oct. 15, 1991, p. 1.
23. Ibid.
24. *Economist,* March 24, 1990, p. 21.
25. Richard F. Starr, *Communist Regimes in Eastern Europe,* 5th ed. (Stanford, Calif.: Hoover Institution Press, 1988), p. 194.
26. Milovan Djilas, *The New Class* (New York: Praeger, 1957), pp. 37–40.

9

Transition or Regression?

Economically, Slavic Europe has lagged far behind Western Europe throughout modern history. In recent times, however, the gap has become a chasm. Indeed, in 1991, the West German economy *alone* was much larger than the combined economies of the entire Slavic world (see Tables 9.1 and 9.2).

The impediments were the Stalinist system of central planning, a domestic climate generally inhospitable to technological innovation and foreign investment, and a lingering Cold War rivalry that barred Soviet bloc countries from full participation in the global economy. After 1989, the leaders of Poland, Hungary, and Czechoslovakia moved quickly to replace the police state organs that undergirded Communist rule for four decades. The movement toward a free-market economy was now unhampered by ideological strictures or the threat of Soviet intervention. In Poland, the government boldly adopted a strategy called **shock therapy**—austerity measures (budget cuts, wage restraints, reduced state subsidies), an end to price controls, and rapid privatization of the economy. In Czechoslovakia, an alternative strategy aimed at a less jarring—but no less complete—transition to a free market.

In the Balkans, however, the pace of change was much slower and the ghost of totalitarianism lingered longer. Any hope of a peaceful evolution toward a new order was shattered by the bloody civil war in Yugoslavia, where tens of thousands of people were killed and millions more left homeless. To some observers, it seemed like the country might end as it had begun—with a major war sparked by ethnic hatred in Bosnia-Herzegovina. "It is one of the accidental symmetries of history that ethnic tensions in southern Europe have been the alpha and omega of the 20th century," wrote one commentator.[1] Elsewhere in the Balkans, Romania sank deeper into a political and economic morass, while Bulgaria engaged in cautious reforms and withdrew into an isolationist shell.

The danger that instability in one country would spill over into neighboring countries, possibly causing cross-border conflicts, could not be discounted.

239

Table 9.1 Economic Profile: Slavic Europe and Preunification West Germany

	Gross National Product, 1991 (millions of U.S. dollars)	Real Growth Rate, 1980–1991 (percent)	Per Capita GNP, 1991 (U.S. dollars)	Per Capita GNP Growth Rate, 1980–1991 (percent)
West Germany	1,516,785	2.3	23,650	2.2
Slavic Europe	897,408			
Belarus	32,131	4.0	3,110	3.3
Bulgaria	16,316	1.7	1,840	1.7
Czechoslovakia	38,427	0.7	2,450	0.4
Hungary	28,244	0.5	2,690	0.7
Moldova	9,529	2.7	2,170	1.8
Poland	70,640	1.2	1,830	0.5
Romania	31,079	0.3	1,340	−0.1
Russia	479,546	2.0	3,220	1.3
Ukraine	121,458	2.7	2,340	2.3
Yugoslavia	70,038	−0.7	2,940*	−1.4

* 1990. *Source:* World Bank, *The World Bank Atlas* (Washington, D.C.: World Bank, 1992).

Massive population movements—refugees, asylum seekers, and immigrants in search of jobs—posed an ever-present threat. For example, in Hungary, where unemployment (unknown under Communist rule before 1989) was reaching 40 percent in some areas, as many as 40,000 Yugoslav war refugees, plus countless illegal immigrants from Romania and the former Soviet Union, had flowed in by the spring of 1992.[2]

Table 9.2 Population Size and Quality-of-Life Indicators: Slavic Europe

	Population, 1991 (millions)	Population Growth Rate, 1980–1991 (percent)	Life Expectancy, 1991 (years)	Infant Mortality Rate (per thousand live births)
Belarus	10.3	0.6	73	15
Bulgaria	8.8	0.0	73	16
Czechoslovakia	15.7	0.3	72	14
Hungary	10.5	−0.2	71	19
Moldova	4.4	0.9	69	23
Poland	38.3	0.7	71	20
Romania	23.3	0.4	70	28
Russia	148.9	0.7	72	20
Ukraine	51.0	0.4	73	16
Yugoslavia	23.7	0.7	72	28

Source: World Bank, *The World Bank Atlas* (Washington, D.C.: World Bank, 1992).

There were many ironies in these circumstances. The Balkan tensions that sparked World War I were blamed on outside forces. For centuries, the Balkan nations wanted to get the Great Powers (later the two superpowers) out. In the past, these nations had important strategic interests in southern Europe, but times were changing. In the early 1990s, outsiders (especially the United States, the European Community, and Russia), interested mainly in stability, were reluctant to intervene in Yugoslavia's civil war even after reports of atrocities and human-rights violations (especially by the Serbs) in Bosnia-Herzegovina were reported in the press and condemned by the United Nations.

The Western powers were particularly anxious not to do anything that might provoke the Russians into intervening on the side of the Serbs (as they did in World War I). As long as Yeltsin remained in power, that was highly unlikely. But in the chaos and uncertainty that enveloped Russia, one danger was that Russian commanders might intervene without consulting Yeltsin or even that Russian nationalists (including neo-Communists and elements in the security forces) would oust Yeltsin from power.

Clearly, democracy has not been a panacea for Slavic Europe. In fact, it brought to the surface ethnic tensions forcibly suppressed during more than four decades of Communist rule after World War II. In the process, it opened a Pandora's box in economically distressed societies, thus creating the danger that demagogues parading as patriots and populists would seek to ride to power on a rising crest of nationalism, fed by public fear, anger, and despair.

The turmoil resulting from the collapse of the Soviet imperium in Slavic Europe occasioned an intellectual debate over the pros and cons of the **hegemonic stability theory**. This theory holds that stability in Eastern Europe and the Balkans, as well as in the former Soviet Union itself, was purely a function of Moscow's hegemony (dominance) in the region. When Mikhail Gorbachev pulled the props from under the structures that his predecessors had built (the Warsaw Pact, Comecon), the whole thing collapsed like a house of cards. Subscribers to this theory tend to be pessimistic about the long-term prospects for peace in the region.

The consequences of the Soviet withdrawal are obvious, but cause and effect are much more difficult to establish. For example, Yugoslavia was never under Soviet domination and might well have disintegrated even if the Cold War had not ended. Nor is it a foregone conclusion that the conflict there will spill over. Significantly, Czechoslovakia went through a bloodless breakup very different from Yugoslavia's violent one. Moreover, the Slavic nations are not alone in fighting wars with neighboring states—witness the innumerable conflicts in Western Europe following the emergence of the nation-state system in the sixteenth century. And it is quite possible that a stable order will emerge in Slavic Europe after all. Everywhere but Poland, the winnowing effect of elections has narrowed the number of viable political parties (see Table 9.3) and thus reduced the danger of parliamentary fragmentation and governmental paralysis. Given the long period of enforced conformity and constraint they have just gone through, it is not surprising that the former Socialist countries are having some

Table 9.3 Elections and Parties: The Winnowing Effect

Country	Election Date	Number of Parties in Prior Election	Number of Parties in the Parliament
Bulgaria	October 13, 1991	37	5
Czech Republic	June 5, 1992	21	6
Hungary	March 26, 1990	45	7
Poland	October 27, 1991	67	29
Romania	September 27, 1992	7	7*
Slovakia	June 5, 1992	5	5

* Excludes 13 seats for national minorities

difficulty containing pent-up collective emotions, coping with newfound liberties, and reaching consensus on the best solutions to the problems that are the legacy of Communist rule.

Russia under Yeltsin

The problems detailed in Chapter 8 did not evaporate with the passing of the Soviet Union. Nor did the prospects for Russia or the other former Soviet republics suddenly improve. Post-Soviet Russia remained a multiethnic Eurasian empire stretching from the Gulf of Finland to the Sea of Japan. By itself, it still boasted roughly two-thirds of the total land area of the Soviet Union (6.6 million square miles) and one-half of its population (150 million).

Although the great majority of Russia's population (over 82 percent) consists of ethnic Russians, many ethnic minorities (including Tatars, Ukrainians, Chuvash, Germans, and Poles) live there as well. Under the old Bolshevik structure (which remains in place), Russia comprises twenty constituent republics representing relatively large ethnic groups and a plethora of smaller administrative entities.*

The virus of nationalism also infected some of these hitherto submerged minorities, especially in Tatarstan (Tatars constitute 3.6 percent of Russia's population) and the Chechen-Ingush autonomous republic, where a bid for independence in November 1991 triggered a crisis. When Yeltsin decreed a state of emergency in the rebel area and dispatched special Interior Ministry troops to enforce it, a majority in the Russian parliament refused to back it and called instead for negotiations under parliamentary auspices. The opponents of this action charged that it was no different from Gorbachev's failed attempts to settle ethnic conflicts by force, while defenders warned that if Yeltsin failed to act

* In all, the Russian Federation had eighty-eight parts in mid-1993: twenty national republics, six territories, forty-nine regions, two federal cities (Moscow and Saint Petersburg), ten autonomous areas, and one autonomous region.

decisively, Russia would suffer the same fate as the disintegrating Soviet Union. The issue split the **Democratic Russia** movement, a pillar of Yeltsin's political support. "In the ensuing uproar," wrote one reporter, "the Russian government backed down, leaving an uneasy truce in which the Chechen government issues statements as if it were independent and the Russian government ignores them."[3] This unresolved armed rebellion was the first reminder that the new Russia would face many of the same problems that had undone the old Soviet order.

Another was not long in coming. In March 1992, despite pleas and warnings from Moscow, Tatars voted yes in a referendum on independence for Tatarstan (see box). The Russian Constitutional Court and parliament invalidated the vote on technical grounds (the wording of the referendum proposed that Tatarstan become a "subject of international law"). Yeltsin had used carrot-and-stick tactics to no avail, pledging "civilized dialogue" but also citing a "limit that should not be exceeded in any case or under any circumstances—the unity of Russia." Neither the Tatars nor the Chechen were intimidated, and both disputes continued to smoulder. (There was also a religious dimension—both groups are Muslim.)

These internal difficulties were overshadowed by disputes between Russia and other former Soviet republics in 1992. The dispute with Ukraine over the disposition of the Black Sea fleet was potentially the most dangerous. Other flash points were Georgia, where the South Ossetians wanted to secede to join Russia, and Moldova, where ethnic Russians were fighting native Romanians in a Russian-majority enclave in the Dnestr region. After Russian Vice President Alexander Rutskoi accused the Georgians and Moldovans of genocide, a Russian army intervened. Hundreds of people were reportedly killed.

The decaying economy was the other immediate threat to the stability of the Russian Federation. On November 1, 1991, the Russian parliament gave Yeltsin emergency powers to implement a Polish-style shock therapy approach to economic reform. But the Russian president, despite praise from the West, soon encountered the same sort of obstacles that had confounded Gorbachev's reform efforts.

A Country Called Tatarstan?

Tatarstan is the designated homeland of the Tatars, the Muslim Turkic descendants of invaders who swept across Russia in the thirteenth century. The oil-rich republic, roughly the size of West Virginia, is located in the Volga region, on the territory of the former Kazan khanate, which was conquered by Russia in the sixteenth century. Its population of 3.6 million is 48 percent Tatar and 43 percent Russian. In addition to pumping about 30 million tons of oil a year, it is a major industrial center whose economy equals that of the three former Baltic republics of the Soviet Union combined.

Source: Daniel Sneider, "Yeltsin Struggles to Keep Russian Federation Intact," *Christian Science Monitor,* Mar. 25, 1992, p. 1.

In January 1991, the Russian government freed most prices and tried to implement an austerity program. These moves pleased key Western governments and helped clear the way for Russia's admission to full membership in the International Monetary Fund (IMF). They also prompted the IMF, in concert with the United States, Canada, Great Britain, France, Germany, and Japan, to pledge financial aid totaling $24 billion to ease Russia's transition to democracy.

In April 1992, a conservative backlash in the Russian Congress of Peoples' Deputies threatened to stop the government's reform juggernaut dead in its tracks. The opposition's tactics were to strip Yeltsin of the extraordinary powers granted earlier by the parliament. Yeltsin, who was acting as both president and prime minister, promised to give up the latter post in return for an extension of his special presidential authority. But the congress said *nyet* and demanded instead that he relinquish this authority within three months. At the same time, it passed measures to cushion the shock of radical reforms, thus placing itself on a collision course with the austerity-minded Yeltsin government. Yeltsin's cabinet responded by publicly threatening to resign unless the congress rescinded these acts. Ominously, this political drama was being played out against a backdrop of hyperinflation (over 400 percent in 1992).[4]

Yeltsin tried to blunt this assault on his reforms first by removing Yegor Gaidar, the architect of the reform program, from his post as finance minister (but keeping him on as deputy prime minister) and then compromising with the opposition. Without backing away from the radical reform in principle, Yeltsin made concessions to conservatives in the congress. Perhaps most important (and disappointing to Western financiers) were his decisions to loosen monetary controls and delay oil price rises in mid-1991, rather than let oil prices float freely on the domestic market.

Like the other new leaders of Slavic Europe, Yeltsin was hampered by the political institutions left over from the days of Communist rule. The Russian Congress of Peoples' Deputies that convened on April 6, 1992, was particularly obstructionist. Not only was it unwieldy in size (over one thousand members), but it was elected in 1990, when the Communists were still in power. As a

Russia's Political Parties

The Russian parliament is organized into political blocs and parties. A bloc known as Democratic Russia, which supported Boris Yeltsin, fell apart in 1992. A number of organized groups have since emerged.

In the center is *Civic Union,* an opposition bloc that favors gradual market reforms. It comprises two main parties, the *Democratic Party of Russia,* led by Nikolai Travkin, and the *People's Party of Free Russia,* led by Alexander Rutskoi. It also includes the *League of Entrepreneurs,* an organization headed by Arkady Volsky representing the industrial managers and directors of state and collective farms.

On the left are *Democratic Choice,* a coalition of at least forty groups, and *New Russia,* another democratic bloc. These groups favor fast-track reforms.

On the right, opposing reforms and longing for a return to the past, is the *National Salvation Front,* a coalition of extreme Russian nationalists and Communist supporters.

result, it was still dominated by Communists and other conservative die-hards. Hard-core liberal reformers, including Democratic Russia and smaller parties, numbered only slightly more than three hundred. In addition, a new opposition party, Civic Union, was formed in the summer of 1992. Headed by three leading political figures—including Russian Vice President Alexander Rutskoi; Arkady Volsky, chairman of Russia's largest business organization; and Nikolai Travkin, leader of Russia's biggest and best-organized political organization—this embryonic party posed a new challenge to Yeltsin's leadership.

Between Democracy and Dictatorship

In March 1993, the Russian parliament voted to strip Yeltsin of his power to issue decrees, an act that led directly to a dangerous political and constitutional crisis. By this time, Yeltsin's popularity had eroded: in one Russian poll, only 36 percent of the respondents approved of his performance. In addition to this challenge to his legitimacy as Russia's foremost democratic leader, Yeltsin faced four other challenges, involving the economy, the constitution, the party system, and the federal structure of the nation.

The Economic Challenge

In 1992, the economy continued its tailspin, incomes and output plummeted, inflation soared, and the government was powerless to reverse the trends. Meanwhile, in the eyes of many law-abiding Russians, only profiteers and criminals were prospering. Overall, gross domestic product fell by more than 20 percent in 1992. That Russia's industrial slump since 1990 was smaller than elsewhere in Slavic Europe was little consolation to people waiting in long, cold lines for sugar, flour, and other staples.

In part because of reckless monetary policies, the country was teetering on the brink of hyperinflation. Massive government subsidies to failing state enterprises had been financed by a flood of freshly printed rubles. In the third quarter of 1992 alone, the central bank printed over 2 trillion rubles. The stock of money rose nearly 600 percent, from 700 billion rubles at the beginning of the year to 4 trillion rubles by October 1. (Only a few years earlier, a dollar was worth considerably less than one ruble at the official exchange rate; in 1992 a dollar would buy around 450 rubles.)

In November 1992, the annualized inflation rate reached 1,350 percent—eight times higher than in August. Overall, prices rose by some 2,000 percent in 1992. The 10,000-ruble privatization vouchers issued by the government had become practically worthless; many Russians sold them to speculators for a fraction of their face value.

Russia was also running up large trade deficits and foreign debts. The amount owed Germany alone stood at about $32 billion. Russia received roughly $20 billion in debt relief and credits from the West in 1992. None of this largesse helped the Yeltsin-Gaidar government stop the economic nosedive.

Russian nationalists found it humiliating for Moscow—still a nuclear super-power, after all—to be financially dependent on the West. Small wonder that Yeltsin was no longer a hero to most Russians. Not one Eastern European leader—not Gorbachev in the Soviet Union, not Lech Walesa in Poland, not even Vaclav Havel in Czechoslovakia—succeeded in maintaining a national consensus during the transition from Communist rule to democracy.

The Constitutional Challenge

The constitutional crisis facing Russia nearly came to a head in December 1992 when Yeltsin's emergency powers expired. These powers, granted by the parliament in 1991, enabled Yeltsin to push reforms by decree. After frantic maneuvering by both Yeltsin and the parliamentary opposition, Yeltsin threatened to call a referendum (a threat he carried out a few months later), and his opponents agreed to a murky compromise that settled nothing but temporarily extended Yeltsin's decree powers. Under the pre-existing constitution, some experts say, the president's hands were tied. The prime minister, not the president, was in charge of the day-to-day management of the government. The president nominated the prime minister, but the parliament could reject that choice. Although this is a common practice in parliamentary democracies, the absence of an established party system made it more problematic in Russia.

Similarly, the president could veto a law, but his veto could be overridden by a simple majority (the U.S. Congress needs a two-thirds majority). If he declared martial law, he had to obtain approval by the Supreme Soviet within twenty-four hours. Finally, he could not dissolve the Supreme Soviet (as Gorbachev could).

In sum, the old constitution subordinated the president to the Supreme Soviet and its parent body, the Congress of Peoples' Deputies. This may or may not have been a good thing, but it did create problems for a president who was trying to lead the country in troubled times.

In the spring of 1993, Yeltsin took a gamble and called for a national referendum that would put the question of a new constitution to the Russian people. Yeltsin won the gamble, and in June 1993, a constitutional assembly was convened to approve a preliminary draft that closely followed Yeltsin's proposals. Article One of the proposed constitution declared Russia as a "democratic, law-governed, secular state whose highest values are the individual and his dignity and unalienable rights to freedoms." The Yeltsin constitution would invest the power to issue federal laws to a two-chamber parliament (called the Federal Assembly), comprising the Federal Council and the State Duma. But it nonetheless would allow the president and the government to issue decrees and directives.

In certain respects, the proposed constitution resembles the constitution of the French Fifth Republic. Hence, the Russian president could have extensive emergency powers that parallel those of the French president. Similarly, if the Federal Assembly rejects the president's first and second choices for prime minister, the president could dissolve the Federal Assembly and call new elections.

There are still issues that will not be easily resolved by any constitutional formula: Does the chairman of the Central Bank, the State Duma, or the government control monetary policy? How much autonomy should the Russian Federation's many regions be given?

Generating enough consensus to adopt a new constitution was a major achievement for President Yeltsin; breathing life into the new political structure and creating a new political culture capable of sustaining this structure will be an even greater challenge.

The Party System Challenge

Yeltsin has had to deal with a confusing array of opposition groups and frequently shifting parliamentary coalitions. Even the largest political parties have a narrow popular base, and none has strong national identity. Party discipline is minimal; deputies tend to be highly independent. The result is a chaotic legislative body and an alienated electorate. (The voters give Russia's parliament abysmal marks.)

Facing fractious opposition, Yeltsin has no party to stand behind him. Democratic Russia, the coalition that had backed his presidency, dissolved in 1992, and Yeltsin thereafter made no move to create his own.

The Federal Challenge

The federal challenge was hinted at earlier. Although the majority of the nation's population is Russian, the Russian Federation remains a multiethnic empire: some 27 million non-Russians live in its twenty constituent republics. The distinction between *Russkye* (ethnic Russians) and *Rossianie* (citizens of Russia) in the vernacular reflects this diversity. When the parliament proposed calling the country just plain *Russia,* objections were raised on the grounds that this name refers only to the *Russkye*—the *Rossianie* would have been left out. This may seem like an abstruse point to outsiders, but the ethnic wars in the former Yugoslavia serve as a reminder that in this part of the world, such matters are anything but academic.

That Yeltsin was not the knight in shining armor that the West had hoped for was disappointing, but the decay at the core of Russia's new political order was a matter of grave concern. When Gorbachev fell from grace and the failed coup fractured the Soviet state, Yeltsin was there to pick up the pieces, and Russia was there to inherit the Soviet Union's nuclear weapons. But if Yeltsin falters and the fragile Russian Federation comes unglued, who will take his place? Will anyone be able to put the country back together again? And what will become of those nuclear weapons?

Russia without Yeltsin?

No one can predict what is in store for Russia if Yeltsin is ousted in a coup, defeated in an election, or if he simply decides to step down. But we can suggest some scenarios for a Russia without Yeltsin.

In the event of a coup, it seems likely that key elements within the military and the police (including the successor to the KGB, known as the Federal Security Agency) would have to be involved. If so, that would give the military a strong voice in a new government. Such a government could be expected to favor social discipline and political stability, as well as policies likely to enhance Russia's prestige in the world (including formidable military forces) and possibly a firmer hand in relations with the former Soviet republics. This does not mean that a more politically assertive senior military class would necessarily favor confrontation with the United States or a revival of the Cold War. Nor does it mean that the military would encourage adventurist or interventionist policies with regard to Russia's neighbors. However, the possibility of military action as in Serbia (say, to reclaim Russian-inhabited territories on Russia's periphery) cannot be ruled out.

A second scenario involves the possibility of a popular uprising fueled by economic privations and political paralysis. Such a groundswell might well be exploited by extreme Russian nationalists nostalgic for the past. Elements from the old Communist Party apparatus, the industrial-managerial class, and the security forces might join forces with blood-and-soil Russian patriots who yearn for the Russia of the czars and the Orthodox religion. This scenario is worrisome because it might propel a new government onto a militaristic course, set the stage for a bloody attempt to reconstitute the historic Russian empire, and lead to confrontation with the West.

A third scenario would involve the deterioration of political authority at the center as a prelude to the breakup of the Russian Federation. As noted earlier, the federation comprises dozens of republics and regions, many of them populated by non-Russian ethnic groups that seek self-determination. Dissolution is perhaps the worst-case scenario in that thousands of nuclear weapons are scattered around Russia, and it is anybody's guess in whose hands they might end up. The dangers of nuclear war inherent in such a situation—along with the possibilities for nuclear blackmail, nuclear accidents, and the illicit transfer of nuclear technology or even weapons to such countries as North Korea, Iran, Iraq, and Libya—are frightening indeed.

The breakup of the Soviet Union brought a new urgency to the debate over nuclear proliferation and accidental nuclear war, but the fact that Russia was there to serve as the natural heir to the Soviet nuclear arsenal mitigated the dangers. If Russia were to break up, there would be no natural heir, and the world might be facing a nuclear nightmare.

East Central Europe and the Balkans

Many of the problems plaguing the former Soviet Union are also present elsewhere in Slavic Europe. The economic dilemmas and dislocations associated with making the transition from central planning to the free market are regionwide. And the ethnic animosities suppressed by police state controls prior to 1989 have resurfaced in the Balkans and in parts of what was the USSR.

Balkan Conflicts: Containment or Spillover?

The overarching question in the Balkans is whether conflict in the former Yugoslavia, centered in Bosnia-Herzegovina in 1992–1993, could be contained. The immediate danger was a spin-off conflict in Macedonia or the Albanian-majority Kosovo region of Serbia. Beyond that, there was the larger question of "Greater Serbia" and Serbia's Balkan neighbors. Would Bulgaria, Romania, Hungary, Albania, Greece, and Turkey stand by if Serbia attempted to incorporate more territories of the former Yugoslavia into Greater Serbia? For example, 500,000 Hungarians live in the Vojvodina region of Serbia, 600,000 in Slovakia, and as many as two million in Romania. Some two million Albanians live in Kosovo and another 427,000 in Macedonia.

Given the explosive mixture of ethnic politics and balance-of-power logic in the region, Romania would probably side with Serbia in a war between Serbia and Hungary because both Romania and Serbia have a "Hungarian problem." In a civil war between Serbs and Albanians in Kosovo, Albania and Macedonia would oppose the Serbs. Not only the adjacent states but also Slavic states elsewhere in the region could become embroiled if a spillover occurs. As noted, there is a large ethnic Hungarian minority in Slovakia; there are also 120,000 ethnic Slovaks in Hungary. In addition, 600,000 ethnic Poles live in Belarus, 250,000 in Lithuania, and 300,000 in Ukraine. And Russian minorities number in the millions in the Baltic states, Ukraine, the Transcaucasus, and other former Soviet republics. In one instance, the 550,000-strong Russian minority in Moldova tried to split off and create a separate republic.

At least four factors exacerbate these centrifugal forces: hypernationalism and "Slavic unity," mass population movements and ethnically illogical borders, alliances, and geographic necessity. The Russian sympathy for Serbia in the Bosnian civil war is an example of the first factor. The second factor arises because of the large number of refugees from political violence (first in Romania and now in the former Yugoslavia) and because of the lack of correspondence between borders and ethnic groups in **East Central Europe**—Poland, the Czech Republic, Slovakia, and Hungary—and the Balkans. The third and fourth factors are interrelated. Alliances in the region are determined by geopolitics; if the conflict in Yugoslavia spills over, the result might be a kind of "catalytic war" into which other Slavic nations (including Russia) could be drawn in. Western nations might also be drawn in, as happened in World War I.

Three factors might ameliorate the tendency toward a larger regional war. First, the interests of the European Community, Japan, and the United States have converged to prevent a widening war, and these states possess overwhelming military and economic might, especially when operating in concert, as the 1991 Persian Gulf War demonstrated. Second, modern-day alliances are much more fluid than under the web of mutual-defense treaties that set off a chain reaction following the assassination of Archduke Ferdinand in Sarajevo, precipitating World War I. Third, and perhaps most important, cultural attitudes in Western Europe have matured. The members of the European Community understand much better now than they did before World War I that the fate of Europe is indivisible and that the two halves of Europe must be bridged if the Continent is to have a stable and prosperous future.

A key consideration for the former Communist states of East Central Europe is whether and when they will be invited to join the European Community (and on what terms). We turn our attention now to this vital "crossroads" between the European Community and the former Soviet Union.

East Central Europe: Economic Revival?

Poland, Hungary, the Czech Republic, and Slovakia want to join the European Community. For this to happen, they must meet several tests—a democratic test, a free-market test, and a regional-stability test. If they can govern by constitutional means, establish open free-market economies, and avoid the kinds of ethnic conflicts that have torn the former Yugoslavia asunder, the EC will probably admit them. If they have not done these things, the EC will almost certainly keep them out. The prospect of entering the European Community is a major incentive for these countries to work for change and stability simultaneously; it may also help governments facing vociferous opposition parties to encourage pragmatism and moderation rather than ideological posturing and confrontation.

Democracy is still fragile in Eastern Europe. Czechoslovakia split apart—albeit without violence—in 1992, but the Czech and Slovak governments both

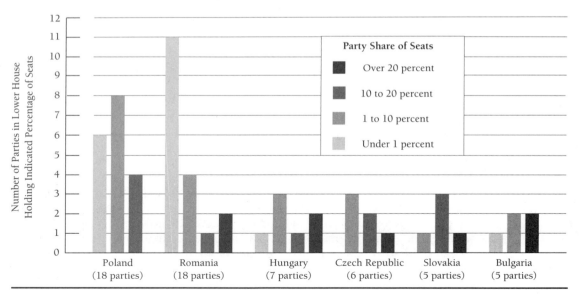

Figure 9.1   Party representation in the lower house of parliament is fragmented throughout East Central Europe.

remain committed to liberal reforms. The relatively homogeneous societies of Poland and Hungary are in no danger of breakup, but they too display signs of political immaturity—shaky institutions, weak civic cultures, and badly fragmented party systems (see Figure 9.1). On the plus side, however, all have abolished the communist system, moved to create a free press, extended civil liberties widely, and held free parliamentary elections. And the seeming chaos in the parliaments has not produced chaotic government. Even in Poland, despite frequent changes of prime ministers and cabinets, economic policy has been strikingly consistent.

The period 1990–1992 witnessed a sharp drop in industrial production throughout the region. Other persistent problems included inflation, high unemployment, and large budget deficits. For example, Hungary's unemployment was forecast to reach 20 percent in 1993, and its budget deficit was projected at 11 percent of GDP in 1993 (compared to 7 percent in 1992). Poland's budget deficit was 5 percent of GDP in 1992, and the parliament wanted to double it in 1993.

Despite these nagging problems, Poland, Hungary, the Czech Republic, and Slovakia have taken significant steps toward the free market (see Figure 9.2). Moreover, all four economies showed signs of economic revitalization. One bright spot is the success these countries have had in liquidating the old, inefficient, outmoded, and uncompetitive state-owned industries that dominated their economies prior to 1989. The steep three-year decline in industrial output between 1990 and 1992 reflects this painful but necessary adjustment. (Economists agree that these industries wasted energy, produced inferior goods, and caused environmental pollution.)

Although direct foreign investment in the region rose from $2.3 billion in 1990 to $11 billion in 1992, this was still well under 10 percent of the GDP of

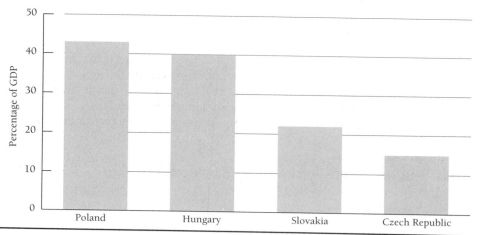

Figure 9.2 Where the wealth comes from: private sector as a percentage of GDP, 1992.
Source: National Statistical Offices.

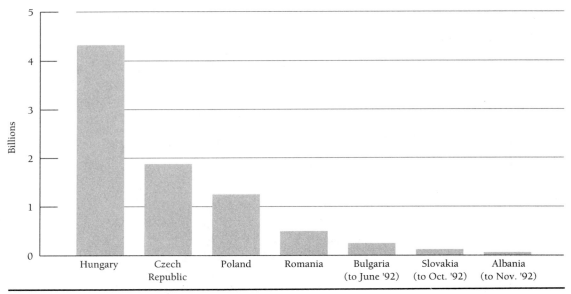

Figure 9.3   Foreign direct investment flows, 1991–1992 (cumulative total).
Source: OECD.

these nations. The caution of Western and Japanese investors in entering these markets has been a major source of frustration for leaders in Poland and the Czech Republic in particular. Hungary has fared the best, attracting roughly half of all foreign investment in the region (see Figure 9.3).

Fear of instability continues to impede private foreign investment, and Western preoccupation with Russia has resulted in the diversion of most public loans and grants to the former Soviet Union. This situation is not likely to change. Nor are the depressed economies of the old Soviet empire attractive potential markets. (During the Cold War, Comecon had taken 70 to 80 percent of many countries' exports.) What this means is that the countries of East Central Europe and the Balkans cannot expect much external help and will not be able to rely on export-driven economic growth (the Japanese model), at least in the short term. But the reward for patience and hard work in the medium term could be full membership in the world's largest trading bloc.

Case Studies: Yugoslavia and Czechoslovakia

Yugoslavia

Yugoslavia was the first Communist state in Eastern Europe to experiment with market-oriented reforms. The Yugoslav experience suggests that halfhearted market reforms do not work and may be worse than no reforms at all.

The Failure of Self-management   Yugoslavia broke with Moscow in 1948 and looked westward for friendship and assistance. Recall that it was the only Eastern European state not occupied by Stalin's armies in World War II, having had the good fortune not to share a border with the Soviet Union.

Yugoslavia's pioneering efforts to decentralize administration and to institute workers' self-management, as well as its welcoming approach to trade with the West, were widely admired.[5] The workers' councils were the cornerstone of Yugoslavia's "socialist democracy" from 1950, when Tito promised "factories to the workers" as the first step toward repudiating the Stalinist model. The councils were intended to ensure democratic self-management at the enterprise level in order to avoid the stultifying effects of Party-state control.

But in the 1950s, reality failed to catch up with the rhetoric of self-management, and in the 1960s, reformers made repeated attempts at economic liberalization. They sought "to end arbitrary political intervention in the economy in order to allow the market to work freely."[6] Self-management finally came of age in the 1970s, by which time Yugoslav workers did, at least in theory, manage the means of production and make decisions on product distribution. The social and political significance of this system was once described as follows:

> Within Yugoslavia, self-management provides the foundation for the "democratization of social life" and the "construction of a political system" that expresses the plurality of interests in society and allows contradictions inherent in such a society "to be resolved democratically by dialogue and consultations." . . . Self-management affects almost every facet of Yugoslav life.[7]

Up to 1989, Yugoslavia was the most innovative state in Eastern Europe. Yet its experimentation with market-oriented, pseudodemocratic reforms failed to revitalize its lethargic economy or solve its political problems. The attempt to combine a free-market economy (including free emigration and free trade) with socialism and a one-party state foundered. Efforts to close unprofitable factories threatened workers with unemployment even as soaring inflation reduced purchasing power. Austerity measures, including price increases and a wage freeze, implemented in 1987 led to widespread strikes.

Social unrest, spurred by ethnic tensions, was nothing new in Yugoslavia. The rivalry between Serbs and Croats was legendary. But in the 1980s, conflict between Serbs and Yugoslavia's Albanians broke out. In 1981, thousands of young Albanians demonstrated in the Serbian province of Kosovo, chanting anti-Yugoslav slogans and demanding political emancipation from Serbia. Such subnational particularism was never far below the surface in Yugoslavia, but the upheaval in Kosovo also had economic causes: Yugoslavia had piled up a $20.5 billion foreign debt, inflation was running at 40 percent per year, and unemployment was hitting double digits.[8]

Yugoslavia's economic outlook remained bleak throughout the decade, although it did reduce its foreign debt (thanks to trade surpluses in the mid-1980s) and in 1986 achieved a respectable 3.5 percent growth rate. But evidence of remaining structural problems was easy to find: inflation rose above 90 percent, unemployment reached 15 percent, and state control of the economy was increasing.[9]

Almost predictably in this economic climate, ethnic strains reached crisis levels. Milovan Djilas, Yugoslavia's most famous dissident, aptly summed up the situation: "We now face a choice. Either we go forward, become freer and join the rest of Europe, or we will fall backward and become the underdeveloped state we were before World War II."[10] Little did he realize that Yugoslavia was about to fall back even further, to the time before it was ever a unified state.

Yugoslavia's Violent Breakup   Ever-increasing economic problems, including hyperinflation (more than 1,000 percent for a time in 1989–1990), accelerated Yugoslavia's disintegration. On July 2, 1990, democratically elected governments in Slovenia and Macedonia declared their independence ("full sovereignty") within Yugoslavia, and Croatia approved constitutional changes having basically the same effect. On the same day, a majority of Serbs approved a referendum on a new constitution that made the formerly autonomous provinces of Kosovo and Vojvodina parts of Greater Serbia (in violation of the federal constitution). Meanwhile, the Kosovo assembly approved a measure making Kosovo a sovereign republic within Yugoslavia. Serbia then dissolved the Kosovo legislature.

Serbia, Montenegro, and Bosnia-Herzegovina held multiparty elections in November and December (following the example of the other Yugoslav republics and the rest of Slavic Europe). Former Communists won by landslides in Serbia and Montenegro but lost decisively in Bosnia-Herzegovina. Ethnic tensions were thus reinforced by a political and ideological rift between the Serbs and Montenegrins on the one hand and the rest of the crumbling Yugoslav federation on the other. (A similar phenomenon occurred in Czechoslovakia in 1992, with the Czechs being led by free-market enthusiasts and the Slovaks by a leftist politician who opposed rapid privatization.) The Serbian government further exacerbated the situation by issuing, without National Bank approval, $1.4 billion in new money to ease its own financial straits. Branded as "stealing from the other republics," this action triggered the beginning of the end for the Yugoslav federation.

In January 1991, Croatia and Slovenia concluded a mutual-defense pact. The freely elected Slovene assembly then voted to secede (in phases) from the federation. In the chain reaction of events that followed, a predominantly Serbian-populated region of Croatia known as Krajina voted to secede from Croatia. In March, Serbia's president, Slobodan Milosevic, the only popularly elected Communist leader in Slavic Europe, used his control of Serbia, Montenegro, Vojvodina, and Kosovo to immobilize the federal collective presidency, thereby provoking a constitutional crisis. The wild card in this confrontation was the national army, outwardly an instrument of the federation but at its core a Serbian force. The army balked, and Milosevic was forced to negotiate with the presidents of the other five republics. Although the resulting talks produced a formula for keeping the country together (all parties agreeing not to seek international recognition), Croatia declared its independence at the end of May; one month later, the parliaments of both Croatia and Slovenia approved declarations of independence and sovereignty.

Following skirmishes with the Yugoslav national army, the two rebel republics and the federal government backed away from the brink, but sporadic fighting continued, and the army threatened "decisive military action" unless Slovenia agreed to an unconditional cease-fire. A three-month truce brokered in July by an EC team of foreign ministers quickly broke down.

A bitter civil war ensued, but the epicenter of the conflict was at first in Croatia rather than Slovenia. (Serbia and Slovenia do not share a border; Serbia and Croatia do.) The fighting brought extensive loss of life and damage to Croatia; when the smoke cleared, Serbia had detached Krajina from Croatia. Many towns and cities, including Vukovar and Dubrovnik, had endured heavy bombing and artillery attacks by the Yugoslav (Serbian) armed forces. International mediation and a United Nations peacekeeping force brought a cease-fire but not a settlement. The conflict was simply uncontainable. Suppressing hostilities in Croatia only shifted the focus of the fighting to a different battleground, Bosnia-Herzegovina. Like a rupturing balloon, pressing on one bulge only caused another to pop out somewhere else.

In Bosnia-Herzegovina the tragedy was compounded by the fact that Bosnian Muslims, although numerically the largest ethnic group there, were caught in the crossfire between Serbs and Croats. After months of bloody fighting and a particularly brutal artillery assault on Sarajevo, the capital, Serbs (31 percent of Bosnia's population) controlled 65 percent of the territory and Croats (17 percent of the population) about 30 percent. That left the Muslim population (44 percent of the total) with only 5 percent of the territory. Some well-informed observers feared that the upshot of the war would be to divide Bosnia between Serbia and Croatia, leaving the Bosnian Muslims a nation without a state. Worse, it was not entirely clear who was doing what to whom. The Yugoslav army made a pretense of neutrality, but it was widely reported that the army was supplying Serbian guerrillas with arms and ammunition. Although Yugoslav forces were withdrawing from Slovenia, Croatia, and Macedonia in April 1992, the army was reluctant to withdraw from Bosnia-Herzegovina because 65 percent of its arms industry and installations were concentrated there.

The war in Bosnia worsened in 1992 and 1993. Reports of **ethnic cleansing**—the systematic deportation or slaughter of Muslims by Bosnian Serbs, allegedly with the covert support of Belgrade—caused outrage in the West and led to calls for economic sanctions, no-fly zones, and even military intervention, especially in the United States. As stories of atrocities (concentration camps reminiscent of the Holocaust and the systematic rape of Muslim women) piled up, pressures built for effective measures to punish the Serbs, who nonetheless remained defiant in the face of growing diplomatic isolation.

Former U.S. Secretary of State Cyrus Vance and former British Foreign Secretary David Owen, representing the United Nations and the European Community, respectively, attempted to broker a cease-fire based on a proposed division of Bosnia into ten autonomous regions, some controlled by Serbs, some by Croats, and some by Bosnian Muslims, all supervised by a United Nations peacekeeping force.

But the warring sides rejected this plan, and the Bosnian Serbs continued their relentless ethnic cleansing in the widening areas under Serb military control. Fears that Macedonia and Kosovo would be the next battlegrounds added to the sense of alarm in the international community.

Czechoslovakia

Like Yugoslavia, Czechoslovakia was buffeted by irreconcilable ethnic differences in the early 1990s. But unlike the warring groups in Yugoslavia, the Czechs and the Slovaks were able to avoid violence.

A Bittersweet Legacy   The big question after Czechoslovakia restructured itself as the Czech and Slovak Federative Republic (CSFR) in 1992 was whether Prague would continue to be the capital of both republics or whether Bratislava would become the capital of an independent Slovak state. Slovakia's populist leader, Vladimir Meciar, whose party emerged from the June 1992 national elections as the dominant force in Slovakian politics, rode a crest of nationalism. His confrontational stance toward Prague was widely perceived, especially by Czechs, as intended to provoke a split.

Before 1989, Czechoslovakia and East Germany had been the two most rigidly Stalinist states in the Soviet bloc. They also had the healthiest economies in the Communist world. In the early 1990s, about one-half of the Czechoslovak labor force was employed in industry, producing machinery and machine tools, chemical products, textiles, and glassware. The principal crops were wheat, potatoes, barley (a prime ingredient in beer, for which the Czechs were famous), and sugar beets. Czechoslovakia had been a net exporter of food since the early 1970s.

By 1980, economic tremors prompted the government to call for greater efficiency, cuts in subsidies to state enterprises, the gearing of wages to productivity, and advances in quality control to boost Czechoslovak imports to the West. But economic performance during the 1980s resembled a roller coaster ride.

Economic figures do not tell the whole story, however. Anyone who had spent a few days in Moscow or Leningrad (Saint Petersburg) and then visited Prague could see the sharp contrast in living standards. In Prague, unlike Moscow, one did not see people waiting in long lines, sometimes for hours, to buy food and other necessities. Nor did one see empty shops or bare shelves. Quite the contrary. Czechoslovaks generally dressed well, shopped without difficulty, and could even afford a few luxuries. Most Czechoslovak families owned an automobile (typically a domestically built Skoda), whereas most Russians could only dream of having a private car. And the national health system in Czechoslovakia was much better than in the Soviet Union.

In sum, if the Czechoslovak economy was not vibrant in the 1980s, neither was it bleak. To the extent that economic factors contributed to public disenchantment with communism, it would probably have been due to the fact that the Western-oriented Czechoslovaks tended to use the West rather than the East as a yardstick for comparison. The fact that Czechoslovakia shared a border with prosperous West Germany might well have been a contributing factor. (The low living standards of East Germans in comparison to those of West Germans were the primary cause of the popular groundswell against the hard-line Honecker government in the GDR in 1989.) Also relevant is the famous **J curve theory**, which holds that the greatest danger of mass revolt occurs not during progressively worsening conditions, as one might expect, but rather when steadily *improving* conditions are followed by a leveling off or a downturn. As living standards improve, there is a natural surge of rising expectations, and if those expectations are not met, disappointment may be manifested in the spirit of rebellion.

Amicable Divorce   The Czech and Slovak republics formally split into two separate states at the end of 1992, peacefully but not painlessly. For many Czechs and Slovaks, the divorce was unwanted. Polls showed that a majority in both republics opposed it. There were many wrenching issues to resolve, including how to divide Czechoslovakia's assets and liabilities (including military facilities and weapons, foreign reserves, the external debt, and foreign embassies); what to do about the flag, anthem, and other important symbols of the former nation; and whether or not to create a customs union or retain a common currency.

The separation caused dislocations on both sides of the new border, but it hit Slovakia harder. The former federal statistical office estimated the cost to Slovakia at 38 billion crowns (14 percent of GDP) in 1993 alone in lost transfer payments and budget subsidies from the Czech side.

Despite the disruptive effects of the imminent breakup, Czechoslovakia's GDP stabilized in 1992 and began rising again. Amazingly, the Czech Republic accomplished "the world's first mass-privatization scheme" during this period.[11] It seems likely that the Czech economy will revive faster than the Slovak economy. But there remains the nagging question as to whether the breakup will replace one viable medium-sized country with two smaller ones that will have to struggle to survive.

The viability question depends in no small part on when and if the Czech Republic and Slovakia, along with Poland and Hungary, are admitted to the European Community. In December 1992, the EC committed itself for the first time to letting these four states in, but it did not set a timetable for membership. The EC governments cite five reasons for the delay: there is a danger of east-west mass migration; key EC industries (particularly textiles, footwear, coal, and steel) would be threatened by competition from low-cost producers in the east; Central Europe is not ready; EC institutions, set up when there were only six members, are already strained to the breaking point by the difficulties of running a greatly expanded community of twelve, and adding several more members would render it that much more cumbersome; and it would cost the EC an additional $6 to $10 billion in regional equity payments and agricultural

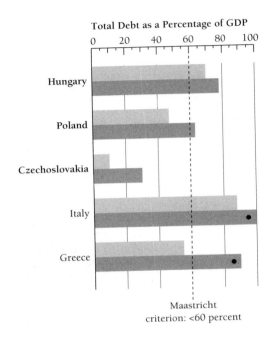

Total Debt as a Percentage of GDP

Hungary
Poland
Czechoslovakia
Italy
Greece

Maastricht
criterion: <60 percent

Longterm Interest Rates (percent)

Poland
Hungary
Czech Republic
Slovakia
Greece
Italy

Maastricht
criterion: <10.6 percent

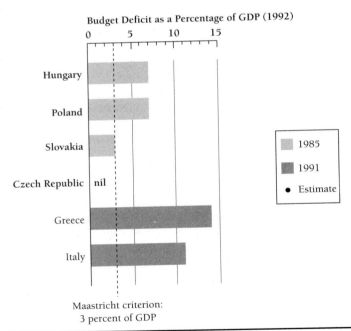

Budget Deficit as a Percentage of GDP (1992)

Hungary
Poland
Slovakia
Czech Republic   nil
Greece
Italy

1985
1991
● Estimate

Maastricht criterion:
3 percent of GDP

Figure 9.4   Economic and financial fitness of select East Central European nations.

Source: World Bank, EBRD, PlanEcon, OECD, Morgan Stanley.

subsidies. The validity of these arguments can be debated; for example, by the EC's own standards of economic and financial fitness, the East Central Europeans are better suited for membership right now than some of the EC's current members. (See Figure 9.4.) But in the final analysis, it comes down to a political decision that will be made in Brussels, not in Prague or Bratislava.

CONCLUSION

The former Communist states of Europe are going through a difficult transition period from central planning and police state controls to market economies and multiparty democracy. In Russia, as elsewhere in the former Soviet Union, this process has been tumultuous, and the outcome remains indeterminate. In East Central Europe, the reforms have progressed rapidly but not always smoothly. Poland, Hungary, the Czech Republic, and Slovakia are all implementing ambitious privatization schemes and have all held free democratic elections. Reforms have proceeded more slowly in Bulgaria and Romania. The former Yugoslavia has been torn asunder by ethnic conflict and civil war. There is a danger that the war there will spill over or spark a wider war. The problem of ethnic conflict is not confined to the Balkans. Czechoslovakia split into two separate republics at the end of 1992. Ethnic conflict threatens peace and stability in many regions of the former Soviet Union as well.

KEY TERMS

shock therapy	East Central Europe
hegemonic stability theory	ethnic cleansing
Democratic Russia	J curve theory

STUDY QUESTIONS

1. What were the principal challenges facing Russian President Boris Yeltsin in 1992 and 1993?
2. What sort of political opposition did Yeltsin encounter in his efforts to reform Russia? What was the source of this opposition?
3. What stake does the United States have in Russia's reform movement?
4. What are the most urgent problems facing the new popularly elected governments of Eastern Europe? What are the prospects for economic revival in the short run? What dangers loom?
5. What are the causes of the conflict in the former Yugoslavia? How great is the danger of a spillover? Are the Balkans more susceptible to strife than other areas? If so, why?
6. Contrast Czechoslovakia's breakup with Yugoslavia's. What factors led to the

split between Czechs and Slovaks? How important were the institutional anomalies left over from the Communist era? What are the prospects for the Czech Republic on its own? For the Slovak Republic?

7. What general problems of transition do all the former Soviet bloc states face? What are the prospects for this region? How much of a difference would joining the European Community really make to these countries? Do you think that will happen soon? Why or why not?

SUGGESTED READING

Aganbegyan, Abel. *The Economic Challenge of Perestroika.* Bloomington: Indiana University Press, 1988.

Bialer, Seweryn, ed. *Politics, Society, and Nationality inside Gorbachev's Russia.* Boulder, Colo.: Westview Press, 1989.

Bremmer, Ian, and Taras, Ray, eds. *Nations and Politics in the Soviet Successor States.* New York: Cambridge University Press, 1992.

Brzezinski, Zbigniew. *The Grand Failure: The Birth and Death of Communism in the Twentieth Century.* New York: Macmillan, 1990.

Goldman, Marshall. *Gorbachev's Challenge: Economic Reform in the Age of High Technology.* New York: Norton, 1987.

Hough, Jerry F. *Opening Up the Soviet Economy.* Washington, D.C.: Brookings Institution, 1988.

Morrison, John. *Boris Yeltsin: From Bolshevik to Democrat.* New York: NAL-Dutton, 1991.

Rothschild, Joseph. *Return to Diversity: A Political History of East Central Europe since World War II.* New York: Oxford University Press, 1989.

Taylor, Trevor, ed. *The Collapse of the Soviet Empire.* Washington, D.C.: Brookings Institution, 1992.

Tismaneanu, Vladimir. *The Crisis of Marxist Ideology in Eastern Europe.* New York: Routledge, 1988.

NOTES

1. George D. Moffett III, "To Begin and Close the Century, Ethnic Strife in Southern Europe," *Christian Science Monitor,* Nov. 8, 1991, p. 1.
2. Ken Kasriel, "Rights Abuses Alleged in Hungary," *Christian Science Monitor,* May 14, 1992, p. 5.
3. Daniel Sneider, "Yeltsin Struggles to Keep Russian Federation Intact," *Christian Science Monitor,* Mar. 25, 1992, p. 1.
4. Fred Coleman, "Could Stalinism Return to Russia?" *Newsweek,* July 13, 1992, p. 23.
5. See Bogdan Denitch, "The Relevance of Yugoslav Self-management," in *Comparative Communism: The Soviet, Chinese, and Yugoslav Models,* Gary K. Bertsch and Thomas W. Ganschow, eds. (New York: Freeman, 1976), pp. 268–279.
6. April Carter, *Democratic Reform in Yugoslavia: The Changing Role of the Party* (Princeton, N.J.: Princeton University Press, 1982), p. 5.

7. Wayne S. Vucinich, "Major Trends in Eastern Europe," in *Eastern Europe in the 1980s,* Stephen Fischer Galati, ed. (Boulder, Colo.: Westview Press, 1981), p. 5.
8. Darko Bekič, "Yugoslavia's System in Crisis: Internal View," *Problems of Communism,* Nov.–Dec. 1985, p. 71.
9. Jackson Diehl, "Yugoslavia's New Leader Has Yet to Take Hold," *Washington Post,* Dec. 8, 1986, p. A17.
10. William Echikson, "Top Dissident Now Free to Go Abroad: Yugoslavia 'Faces a Choice,'" *Christian Science Monitor,* Jan. 22, 1987, p. 12.
11. "Survey of Eastern Europe," *Economist,* Mar. 13, 1993, p. 9.

PART IV

The Middle East

Mediterranean Sea

Lebanon

Syria

Israel

Iraq

Iran

Gaza Strip — West Bank

Suez Canal

Jordan

Kuwait

Persian Gulf

Iraq–Saudi Arabia
Neutral Zone

Egypt

Red Sea

Saudi Arabia

Qatar

United Arab Emirates

Gulf of Oman

Oman

Arabian Sea

Yemen

Gulf of Aden

ISRAEL

Area: 7,847 square miles
Population: 4.9 million
Density per square mile: 624
Languages: Hebrew, Arabic, English
Literacy rate: 88%
Religions: Judaism (83%), Islam (13%)
Monetary unit: shekel
GNP: (1991) $59 billion; $11,330 per capita

EGYPT

Area: 386,659 square miles
Population: 53 million
Density per square mile: 137
Languages: Arabic (official); English and French often understood
Literacy rate: 44%
Religions: Islam (94%; mostly Sunni), Coptic Christian and others (6%)
Monetary unit: Egyptian pound
GNP: (1991) $33 billion; $610 per capita

SAUDI ARABIA

Area: 829,995 square miles
Population: 15.5 million
Density per square mile: 19
Languages: Arabic
Literacy rate: 62%
Religions: Islam
Monetary unit: Saudi riyal
GNP: (1991) $105 billion; $7,070 per capita

10

Religion and Nationalism

In the mass media and in diplomatic parlance, the Middle East is also called both the "Near East" and the "Arab world." The three names are often used interchangeably. Generally, however, the **Middle East** encompasses all the Arabic-speaking countries from Morocco in the westernmost corner of North Africa to Iran, whose neighbors to the east are the Asian nations of Afghanistan and Pakistan. The only non-Arab nations in the region are Turkey, Iran, and Israel (where Palestinian Arabs make up roughly 18 percent of the population).

The "Arab core" has about 85 million people who share a culture based on religion (Islam), language (Arabic), and memories of colonial rule. Despite this common heritage, conflict among the Arab states has been as prominent a feature of their relations as cooperation.

The Middle East can be subdivided in several ways. For example, the countries of North Africa—Morocco, Algeria, Tunisia, Libya, Sudan, and Egypt—make up the region known as the **Maghreb**. Israel, Lebanon, Jordan, Syria, Iraq, Saudi Arabia, Yemen, and the Persian Gulf ministates are often referred to as the **Near East**. Turkey and Iran (along with Afghanistan) form the **Northern Belt** (or **Northern Tier**).

North Africa is separated from the rest of the African continent by a vast desert, the **Sahara**, and the Near East is separated from North Africa by the Red Sea. Language separates the Arabic-speaking Near Eastern states from the Northern Belt states (Turkish is spoken in Turkey, Farsi in Iran, and Pushtun in Afghanistan).

The **Fertile Crescent** consists of Iraq, Syria, Lebanon, Israel, Jordan, and Egypt. The Red Sea region—the vast, arid, and thinly populated **Arabian peninsula**—contains the world's richest oil reserves. Saudia Arabia occupies most of the peninsula; its neighbors are sheikdoms (some tiny) that, like Saudi Arabia, depend on oil exports for their livelihood. The surrounding waters and the forbidding desert isolate Saudi society from the rest of the world—even from the Arab world. Consequently, the Saudi monarchy has not been influenced by Europe, and its lands were never effectively colonized.

Egypt, a cradle of civilization, is sustained by the world's longest river, the Nile. Among Egypt's many natural assets are the lush Nile delta, where three crops a year can be produced; an abundant supply of water; and a propitious location astride a great commercial route. However, Cairo, the capital, is one of the most overcrowded cities in the world, and Egypt is the only Arab country in which the population explosion has become a pressing problem. Yet despite its general poverty, Egypt is one of the most economically advanced countries in the Arab world.

Geostrategic Considerations

The term *Middle East* is appropriate: the area it describes is located at the crossroads of Europe, Africa, and Asia. The strategic importance of the region derives in part from its proximity to international waterways and "chokepoints" such as the Turkish Straits, the Suez Canal, and the Strait of Hormuz. During the nineteenth century, the "Near East question" was essentially "a rivalry on the part of the big powers for control of the Turkish Straits until the Isthmus of Suez was pierced by a canal in the latter part of the century."[1] Furthermore:

> The economic significance of these waterways is obvious. Since time immemorial the Turkish Straits have been a vital trade route between the Black Sea shores and the Mediterranean. The prosperity of many a Mediterranean state, such as Genoa or Greece, has been largely dependent upon its ability to trade with the Black Sea hinterland. And, conversely, the Straits have played an increasingly important role in the foreign trade of Russia ever since the latter obtained an outlet to the Black Sea. The commercial significance of the opening of the Suez Canal, which replaced the old Cape route, is so obvious that it does not require elaboration.[2]

The military importance of the Middle East's waterways was amply demonstrated in World War II. Germany and Italy launched various offensives toward Egypt in an effort to seize the Suez Canal; the British, in turn, tenaciously defended the canal. Meanwhile, Allied efforts to get arms and equipment to the Soviet Union were hampered when Turkey closed the straits. Even in peacetime, "control of these waterways may prove decisive so far as the political independence of Turkey and the diplomatic alignment of Egypt are concerned."[3]

Outside powers have long cast a covetous eye on the Middle East. As dominant naval forces in different eras, Great Britain and the United States have both sought preeminence in the region, and after World War II, the United States and the Soviet Union engaged in intense rivalry there. The USSR made inroads in the 1950s and 1960s, especially in Algeria, Egypt, and Syria. Soviet influence declined dramatically in the 1970s but was partly restored after 1985 by Mikhail Gorbachev. Both superpowers sought a secure grip on the eastern Mediterranean that would guarantee access to the Suez Canal and to Middle Eastern oil. Forty percent of Western Europe's oil and 90 percent of Japan's come from the Middle East (see Figure 10.1)—a fact that tipped the balance of interest toward the West.

Surrounded by the waters of the Mediterranean, the Red Sea, the Arabian Sea, and the Persian Gulf, much of the Middle East has been vulnerably exposed. It is more accessible by sea than by land—another reason why the West, with its superior naval and merchant marine fleets, has succeeded at gaining a foothold in the region.

Birthplace of Three Great Religions

Geography is not all that makes the Middle East so pivotal. This region is the cradle of three great monotheistic religious traditions: Judaism, Christianity, and Islam. All three have spanned the globe, but the region remains the center of the newest of the three, **Islam**, which has 850 million adherents from Morocco to Malaysia, Indonesia (90 percent Muslim), and the Philippines. The Middle East holds the holiest places of Islam, above all Mecca, Saudi Arabia, birthplace of the Muslim faith. The Dome of the Rock in Jerusalem is another important Muslim shrine. Thus Jerusalem, site of the Hebrews' original tabernacle and of Jesus' crucifixion, is regarded as a holy city by believers in all three faiths.

Islam and the culture that grew up around it have permeated the Arab world, including the countries of the periphery—Turkey (98 percent Muslim) and Iran (95 percent Shiite, a major Muslim sect). Although Islam has spread beyond the Middle East proper, it is first and foremost the religion of the Arabs:

> In many ways, the Arab world today is a religious empire. It encompasses eighteen countries and 4.6 million square miles, an area 25 percent larger than the United States. The largest country, Sudan, is more than three times the size of Texas; the smallest, Bahrain, would fit neatly inside the boundaries of New York City. Except for a small, aged generation of Jews and a relative handful of Christians—religious minorities have not fared well in the Middle East—94 percent of the people are Muslim.[4]

For the faithful, Islam is more than a religion; it is a way of life. Its scripture, the **Koran**, covers politics, law, and social behavior and even sets forth procedures for divorce, loans, and wills.[5]

Judaism and Christianity have even deeper roots in the Middle East. Like Muslims, Jews and Christians consider Jerusalem the holiest of holy places, and both view Palestine, in which Israel is located, as the Holy Land. It is the setting for the action in the Old Testament and encompasses biblical Judea and Samaria (on the West Bank of the Jordan River), which Israel has occupied since its

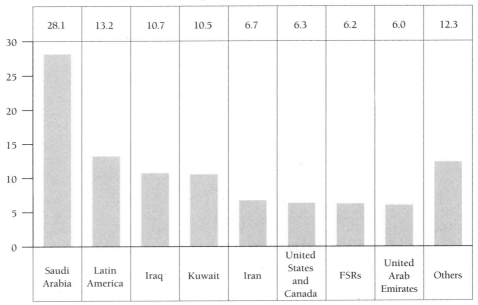

Share of World Petroleum Reserves (percent)

Saudi Arabia	Latin America	Iraq	Kuwait	Iran	United States and Canada	FSRs	United Arab Emirates	Others
28.1	13.2	10.7	10.5	6.7	6.3	6.2	6.0	12.3

Other major reserves are found in Libya, China, and the North Sea.

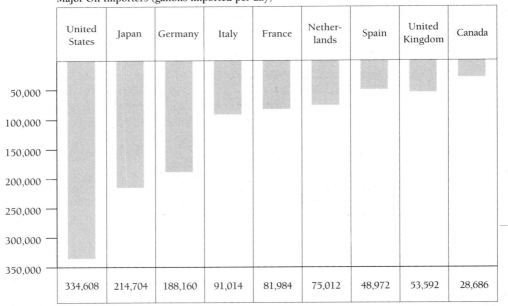

Major Oil Importers (gallons imported per day)

United States	Japan	Germany	Italy	France	Nether-lands	Spain	United Kingdom	Canada
334,608	214,704	188,160	91,014	81,984	75,012	48,972	53,592	28,686

Figure 10.1 World petroleum reserves and major petroleum importers, 1990.

Sources: Adapted from John Rourke, *International Politics on the World Stage,* 3rd ed. (Guilford, Conn.: Dushkin, 1991), p. 246, and updated with data from the CIA (1991); OAPEC *Monthly Bulletin,* October 1991; *World Almanac* (1992).

1967 victory over Egypt and Syria. It is also the setting for the New Testament; such places as Bethlehem, Nazareth, and Galilee are in Palestine. Jews everywhere see Israel as the embodiment of the long-awaited Zionist state, a refuge from political and religious persecution. Because Jews and Christians share the Old Testament and because the West is steeped in the Judeo-Christian tradition, Islam and Arabs seem more arcane and exotic to Westerners than the two older religions and their adherents.

Religion has played a central role in the Middle East conflict. Arabs (especially Palestinians) and Jews have fought for control of land that both claim as their own. In truth, the conflict is about territory more than religion, but religious issues have inflamed passions on both sides. Religion played an even more direct role in the Iranian Revolution and in the subsequent war between Iran and Iraq, which pitted Arab against Persian and Shiite against Sunni (the two main branches of Islam).

Judaism and Christianity

Judaism and Christianity have common origins. Both are monotheistic, and both regard books of the Old Testament as sacred texts. **Judaism** traces its origins to a Sumerian named Abraham, his son Isaac, and Isaac's son Jacob. Jacob took his own sons (including Judah, after whom the faith is named) to Egypt. According to legend and biblical history, Moses led the Hebrews out of Egypt and through the wilderness to the Promised Land (modern Israel). The religion of the Hebrews became monotheistic by the acceptance of Yahweh, the god of the patriarchs, Abraham, Isaac, and Jacob, as the one true God. This monotheism was symbolized by a covenant between Yahweh and Abraham, confirmed by the rite of circumcision and reiterated to Moses on Mount Sinai when the Ten Commandments were handed down from on high, according to Jewish and Christian teachings.

The foundations of Judaism are contained in the Pentateuch, or Torah (first five books of the Old Testament), and in the Talmud, the collected decisions and opinions of the **rabbis** (scholars) concerning civil and religious law. After thousands of years as a monolithic religious community, Jews in the late nineteenth century began to divide into several branches, the two most prominent being Orthodox and Reform. Judaism has an elaborate set of rites and religious holidays that differ from those of Christianity, and its places of worship are called synagogues (not churches or cathedrals, as in Christianity, or mosques, as in Islam).

Christianity is an offshoot of Judaism. It dates back nearly two thousand years to the birth of **Jesus Christ**, an event that has since become the great divide in world history, separating time into B.C. ("Before Christ") and A.D. (*anno Domini,* Latin for "in the year of our Lord").* According to Christian teaching,

---

* To avoid this Christian bias, the designations C.E. ("Common Era") and B.C.E. ("Before the Common Era") are sometimes used instead of A.D. and B.C., respectively.

Jesus is the Son of God, born of a virgin, Mary, through a miracle known as the Immaculate Conception. As an adult, Jesus roamed Palestine, at the time a Roman province, to preach. His teachings are recorded in the New Testament, written primarily by twelve early believers, known as apostles. Jesus was executed for heresy by crucifixion, a typical Roman punishment.

Judaism and Christianity differ sharply on whether or not Jesus was the Christ—the Messiah prophesied in the Old Testament. From that, many doctrinal differences flow. For example, Christians believe that Jesus died on the cross to save sinners from eternal damnation (hence the idea of Jesus as Savior); Jews believe that forgiveness of sins depends on one's willingness to repent and do good deeds.

Tensions between Christians and Jews have been most apparent in Europe. In the Middle East, the religious differences that have led to extremism, zealotry, and terrorist violence have involved Zionism on the one hand and Arab nationalism (or Islamic fundamentalism) on the other.

Islam

Historically, in the Middle East, Christians and Muslims have clashed far more extensively than Muslims and Jews. The hostility reached its zenith in the Crusades, three centuries of Christian expeditions intended to wrest the Holy Land from the Muslims. Islam dates back to the seventh century A.D., when **Muhammad**, a merchant from Mecca, received revelations from God through the angel Gabriel, according to Muslim belief. Mecca was a trading center to which the Arabian nomads of the time would make pilgrimages to worship their various deities (more than two hundred of them). Muhammad taught that only one god, **Allah**, was the true God and that Allah spoke through him. Thus Muhammad was merely a messenger, the Prophet of Islam. His revelations, passed along to his followers over a period of twenty-two years (A.D. 610–632), constituted the Way (*Sharia* in Arabic) and are recorded in the sacred text of Islam, the Koran.

Islam's five basic tenets, the Five Pillars, can be summarized as follows:

1. The confession of faith: "I testify that there is no God but God, and Muhammad is the Messenger of God."
2. Prayer five times daily, facing in the direction of Mecca, the holy city
3. Fasting during the daylight hours in the month of Ramadan (the time of Muhammad's revelations)
4. Almsgiving (at least 2.5 percent of one's income) to the community for relief of the poor
5. Pilgrimage to Mecca at least once in one's lifetime

Muslims have much in common with Jews and Christians—belief in one God, in the power of prayer, and in an ethic of compassion. They believe that God revealed himself to many prophets before Muhammad, including Abraham,

Moses, and Jesus. But Muslims do not accept Christian beliefs in the divinity of Jesus (that Jesus was God), the Resurrection (that Jesus rose from the dead), or the Trinity (that God consists of God, Jesus, and the Holy Spirit responsible for the Immaculate Conception). Judaism and Islam have much in common, including strict dietary rules and reliance on an authoritative body of scholarship to interpret divine law.

Muhammad was not only a religious figure but also a powerful political leader. Forced to flee Mecca (his escape is called the *Hegira*), he went to Medina and there established a power base from which he came to rule Arabia. Muhammad mixed politics and religion and created a kind of **theocracy**—a pattern still discernible in some parts of the Middle East (especially Iran).

Muslims consider Muhammad's life a model. His decisions and revelations constitute the *Sunna* ("Beaten Path"). Muhammad did not have an heir apparent. Although most of his followers favored an elective *caliph* ("successor"), some believed that Muhammad had intended his cousin Ali to assume leadership. This minority was adamant that only someone of the same bloodline could succeed Muhammad. These **Shiite** ("sectarian") purists thus originated as the partisans of Ali. The majority Muslims are known as **Sunnis**, followers of the *Sunna*.

Sunni versus Shiite

Thus the division between Sunni and Shiite is almost as old as Islam itself. About 90 percent of all Muslims are Sunni; most of the rest are Shiite, and most Shiites are Iranian. The split in the seventh century was a bloody affair. Ali was eventually elected caliph, only to be murdered; one of his sons was poisoned; another was ambushed and killed on the orders of Ali's rival, who established his own dynastic rule. Through it all, the Shiite Muslims, though outwardly obedient, never changed their beliefs.

Shiite Muslims generally recognize a line of twelve direct descendants of Muhammad as Islam's spiritual leaders (**imams**). Most Shiites believe that the twelfth imam is alive but invisible and that he will reveal himself on the Day of Judgment. Until the "hidden imam" reappears, the religious leaders (**mullahs**) have the right and duty to interpret God's will and guide Shiite true believers in the Way. Thus the Shiite tradition gives religious leaders (like the late Ayatollah Khomeini in Iran) more power over Shiite Muslims than Sunni religious leaders have over Sunni Muslims.

The barbarism exhibited by both sides in the Iran-Iraq War of the 1980s was motivated partly by opposing nationalisms and partly by Arab-Persian enmity. It was also a reflection of Islam's religious schism and the mutual suspicions it has spawned. A majority of Iraqis are Shiite Muslims (55 percent), but the Sunni minority (40 percent) is politically dominant; Saddam Hussein, Iraq's Sunni ruler, feared the spread of Khomeini-style Islamic revolutionary fervor in Iraq and believed that Khomeini was out to conquer Iraq for Shiite Islam. The two leaders loathed each other. This example demonstrates the difficulty of disentangling religious, political, and even personal factors in the conflicts that have rocked the Middle East since World War II.

Jihad and Islamic Fundamentalism

The concept of *jihad* is now well-known to Westerners, who equate it with holy war and terrorism. One meaning of the word *is* "holy war," but it can also mean "sacred struggle" or simply a personal "striving" to carry out God's will. In its violent form, *jihad* can be directed against external or internal enemies. The assassins of Egyptian President Anwar al-Sadat claimed at their trial that they had acted out of religious principle, insisting that Egyptian law was at odds with Islamic law and that Sadat's 1979 peace treaty with Israel betrayed the Palestinians, whose cause concerns Muslims everywhere. Similarly, Muslim militants who seized the Great Mosque in Mecca in 1979 did so in the name of God—in their view, the secular Saudi monarchy was illegitimate and only halfheartedly Islamic.

Although the West has come to associate *jihad* primarily with the Shiites of Iran, Sunni Muslims also embrace the concept. For example, the **Muslim Brotherhood** is a militant Sunni secret society that seeks to establish a single universal Islamic state. It has been especially active in Syria, where it is the main opposition to the Alawi Shiite minority rule of President Hafez al-Assad. It has assassinated Alawi officials and committed other violent acts.

The concept of *jihad* behind certain terrorist acts in the Middle East is the one stressing individual striving to carry out God's will. For example, in early July 1989, a Palestinian seized the steering wheel of a crowded bus in Israel and caused it to plunge into a deep ravine, killing and injuring civilians. Witnesses heard the terrorist shout, "Allahu Akbar," the battle cry of the *intifada* (the Palestinian uprising in the occupied territories). Islamic tradition is inextricably intertwined with Palestinian nationalism, of course. On the other side, a militant *Jewish* minority called Hamas also justifies acts of violence on religious grounds, but here too, tradition and extreme nationalism are inseparable.

The Shiite tradition admires martyrdom, a trait traced all the way back to the murder of Ali's son. Consequently, some terrorist attacks have been carried out by Shiites on suicide missions. Similar motives led Iranian children to walk through minefields ahead of soldiers during the war against Iraq: the Ayatollah Khomeini assured them that martyrdom in the *jihad* against Iraq would give them immediate entry to heaven.

The Challenges of Modernity

Many conflicts in the Middle East are rooted in religious and ethnic animosity, but the state of war that has characterized the politics of the region since the late 1940s is perpetuated by another equally divisive issue: How should Arabs and Muslims respond to the challenges of modernity? Should they embrace

Western ideas of individual rights and democracy? The secularized and bureaucratic state? Modern science and technology?

Based in part on the responses of their leaders and ruling elites, Arab states can be characterized as either moderate and "traditional" or radical and "revolutionary". Thus, for example, Egypt under Nasser (1954–1970) chose the radical course by following the path of Arab nationalism, non-Marxist socialism, and a secularism that denied any special role for Islam in political life. In contrast, the ruling dynasty of Saudi Arabia chose the traditional path of hereditary monarchy, fidelity to Islamic law, and rejection of Western-style modernization. Syria, Iraq, Algeria, and Libya are among the Arab states that followed the Egyptian model. Jordan, Morocco, and the Perisan Gulf sheikdoms have chosen the traditional path—all are moderate regimes that respect Islamic law, spurn revolutionary doctrines (including Islamic fundamentalism), and show little enthusiasm for an Arab superstate.

Iran illustrates the fury generated by these alternative responses to the West. Iran's modernizing elite, led by the Shah, Muhammad Reza Pahlavi (1941–1979), hastened the pace of change. The Shah accepted massive military aid and economic investment from the West (especially America), attempted to remake Iranian society along Western lines, reduced the role of the imams, and vigorously pursued a pro-West foreign policy. Reaction came in 1979, when the exiled Ayatollah Ruhollah Khomeini led an uprising that toppled the Shah and forced him to flee Iran, leaving a power vacuum that fanatical followers of the Ayatollah hastened to fill. The revolutionary government arrested opponents (many of whom it executed) and imposed a harsh regime based on strict observance of Islamic law. Iran then became embroiled in a bloody war with Iraq, which raged throughout the 1980s. Perhaps more than any other country in the Middle East, Iran epitomizes the conflicts that can be provoked by Western intrusion into Islamic societies.

Another way of differentiating the modern, secular societies of the Middle East from the traditional, religious ones is according to customs, lifestyles, and religious observance. Measured by such indicators as industrialization or state of technological advancement, Iran and Saudi Arabia are just as modern as Iraq, Syria, and Egypt—perhaps even ahead of them. Oddly enough, some of the most vigorous resistance to modernity can be found in Israel, the most modern society in the Middle East. Extreme Jewish religious sects, like many Islamic fundamentalists, take a dim view of the contemporary world, including modern technology.

A Brief History of the Middle East

The Arab world's Golden Age dates back to the seventh century, when Muhammad founded Islam. His successors, the caliphs, conquered new territories and welded disparate tribes into a single state inspired by Islam. The tide of Arab conquest rolled over Iraq, Persia (Iran), Syria, Egypt, Cyprus, and North Africa.

In 711 the Arabs surged into Spain, and six years later they nearly seized Constantinople (Istanbul).

At its fullest extent, the Arab empire extended from the Pyrenees to India. In contrast to the Western stereotype of Islam as a militant, prosyletizing creed (reinforced by the Ayatollah Khomeini and his followers after 1979), Arab rulers showed considerable religious tolerance, permitting conquered peoples who chose not to convert to Islam to practice their own religions under certain civil arrangements. Arabs everywhere established themselves as the ruling aristocracy and absorbed the flourishing cultures of Persia, Syria, and Egypt. Arabic became the dominant language of a brilliant new culture.

The Arab empire was doomed to be short-lived, however; it expanded too fast and soon burned itself out. It was torn apart by such internal forces as sectionalism and schism, still apparent in the Arab world today. One fundamental weakness was the lack of an accepted rule of succession to the caliphate. One dynasty moved the seat of government to Damascus; the next, to Baghdad. By the ninth century, the empire had become a commonwealth of independent and often contentious states. Attacks from external enemies hastened its disintegration after the eleventh century.

Thus the Arabs created a flourishing Islamic civilization that was concurrent with the Christian medieval period in Europe. Arab culture made significant contributions to world literature, philosophy, historiography, art, and science, as well as to religious-law disputation.[6] Pride in this former grandeur may in part explain Islam's resistance to the West.

The Ottoman Intrusion

For hundreds of years before World War I, the history of the Middle East was dominated by the Ottoman Empire and European colonialism. By the late fifteenth century, the Black Sea had become a "Turkish lake," and the tentacles of the empire reached into three continents. Yet the Ottomans had to contend with "the involvement of practically every great European power in its foreign and domestic affairs in the course of the last three hundred years."[7] Under Suleiman I, the Magnificent (1520–1566), the Ottoman Turks expanded their domain well into the Balkans, Armenia, and Mesopotamia (Iraq). A formidable navy allowed Suleiman to conquer Aden and the southeastern coast of Arabia and to project his power into the Mediterranean and Adriatic seas and North Africa. It was quite a performance:

> At the time of Suleiman's death the Ottoman Empire stretched from the Danube to the Persian Gulf and from the Ukrainian steppes to the Tropic of Cancer in upper Egypt. It included the mastery of the great trade routes of the Mediterranean, of the Black and Red seas, and of parts of the Indian Ocean. It had an estimated population of fifty million as against some four million in England and embraced some twenty races and nationalities.[8]

The Ottoman Empire declined toward the end of the seventeenth century following a failed attempt to defeat Austria and conquer Vienna in 1683. After that, Russia pushed southward toward the Near East, and the British established a toehold in Egypt. France, too, under Napoleon Bonaparte, made a play for the Land of the Nile at the end of the eighteenth century, without success.

European Colonialism

Imperialism characterized the second half of the nineteenth century, when the major powers of Europe scrambled for colonial territories in Africa and Asia. The Middle East was not spared. The French were interested in the area before the British, mainly because France looked on the Ottoman Turks as natural allies against their archrival, Austria. But as imperial Russia encroached on the periphery of the Middle East in the second half of the eighteenth century, British interest in the region grew.

Napoleon's misadventure in Egypt drew British attention even more strongly. As the preeminent naval and mercantile power in the eighteenth and nineteenth centuries, Great Britain was anxious to control strategic waterways and choke-points, including the Strait of Gibraltar, the Turkish Straits, the isthmus of Suez, the Bab el-Mandeb, and the Strait of Hormuz. Furthermore, the waterways of the Middle East were the shortest route to India, the "Jewel of the British Empire." It thus became "an axiom of British foreign policy to uphold the independence and integrity of the Ottoman Empire, in order to prevent the undue strengthening of Russia and to protect the imperial life line."[9]

Despite British goodwill, the Ottoman Empire continued to decline in the nineteenth century, and Russia was the main beneficiary. Britain (allied with France) and Russia came to blows in the Crimean War (1854–1856), after Russia and France quarreled over control of the holy sites in Palestine. The British won the war, and thus Russian encroachment was effectively stopped, but Western imperialism continued to erode Ottoman rule in the Near East until displacing it entirely after World War I.

The two main rivals for colonial control in the Middle East were Great Britain and France. The French were able to annex large territories in North Africa, directly across the Mediterranean from France's southern coast, taking Algeria (1830), Tunisia (1883), and Morocco (1906–1912). France also had formal ties to the Levant (Syria and Lebanon). The British gained the upper hand in Egypt—where France again tried to gain a foothold but failed—and in Palestine. Meanwhile, on the eve of World War I, Germany made inroads into the Ottoman Empire, and Italy managed to obtain control of Libya.

Persia (Iran) was an object of Russian imperialist aims in the nineteenth century, but Great Britain safeguarded its independence:

> Britain's Persian policy was dictated primarily by her concern for India, and Persia was to be an independent buffer state or neutral zone between the Indian and Russian empires. Britain sought unimpeded commercial opportunity in Persia, and to this extent she was interested in exercising moderate influence in the area. She was unwilling, however, to assume direct imperial responsibilities similar to those in India. It was, therefore, in her interest to see Persia relatively strong and capable of withstanding Russian pressure. It was largely due to this

British policy that Persia succeeded in maintaining her independence instead of falling under Russian domination.[10]

An Arab Awakening?

No account of modern Middle Eastern history would be complete without reference to what has been called the "Arab awakening."[11] One reaction to foreign subjugation by both Ottomans and Europeans was the articulation of Arab nationalism. The rhetorical basis for Arab unity is rooted in this history, as is reaction to the establishment of Israel (in which, to Arabs, the West was an accomplice); this history has led Arabs to adopt the Palestinian cause as their own.

Because Egypt is prominent in the Middle East today and because its experience as a Western dependent in many ways typifies that of other Arab countries, it might serve to link the legacy of foreign domination with the persistent urge to create a single Arab superstate. Foreign domination of Egypt dates from the Persian conquest in 525 B.C. Then came the Greeks (Alexander the Great), the Romans, the Byzantines, and, in the seventh century, the Arabs, who introduced Islam and the Arabic language. Large numbers of nomadic Arabs settled in the Nile valley under the rule of the caliphs. In the tenth century, a Shiite group split with the Sunnis, and in the desert south of Alexandria, the ancient capital, they established a new capital, al-Qahira ("City of War"—modern Cairo).

The Ottoman Turks annexed Egypt in the sixteenth century. The Ottoman overlords permitted the Mamluks, former slaves or war prisoners converted to Islam, to administer the area in return for occasional tribute and taxes. The leaders eventually became slaveholders themselves, formed a military aristocracy, and, as powerful warlords, fought for supremacy. Thus the Ottoman Empire encompassed Egypt but never penetrated its society and culture the way the Arabs had under the caliphate.

Egypt emerged virtually autonomous under a powerful and visionary Albanian officer, Muhammad Ali, who ruled from the Ottoman garrison at Cairo. Appointed governor by the sultan in 1805, Ali eased Egypt into the modern world. His successors, called *khedives* ("viceroys"), were nominally under the Ottoman sultan but ruled as autocrats in their own right.

The Suez Canal was opened in 1869 under Khedive Ismail. The British were keenly interested in the opening of the canal, not least because it provided a shortcut to India. An attempted military coup against the khedive in 1882 precipitated a British intervention and formation of a "protectorate," which interrupted Egypt's movement toward independence.

The British protectorate lasted until 1922, by which time an Egyptian national movement advocating an Islamic revival as a means of resisting the incursions of European imperialism had emerged. During World War I, Great Britain promised Egypt's leaders that it would back independence after the war but subsequently reneged on the grounds that the Egyptians were not ready for self-rule.

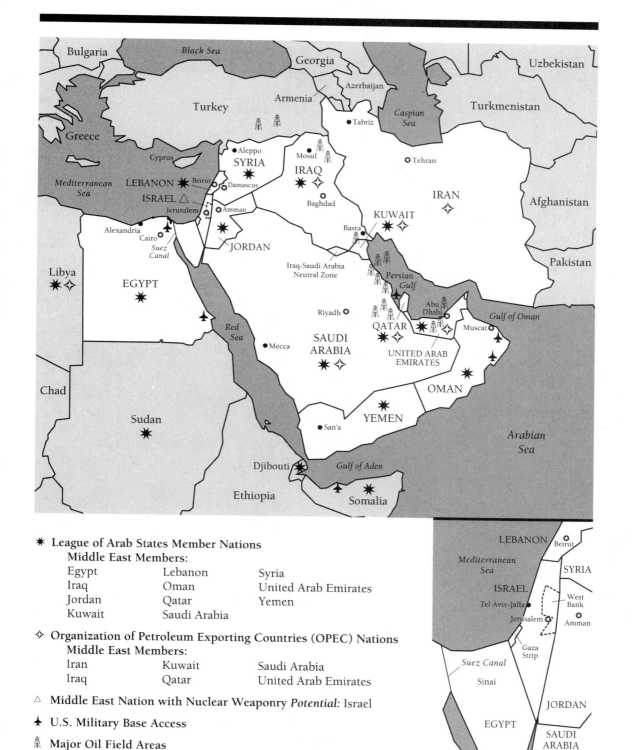

* **League of Arab States Member Nations**
  Middle East Members:

Egypt	Lebanon	Syria
Iraq	Oman	United Arab Emirates
Jordan	Qatar	Yemen
Kuwait	Saudi Arabia	

◇ **Organization of Petroleum Exporting Countries (OPEC) Nations**
  Middle East Members:

Iran	Kuwait	Saudi Arabia
Iraq	Qatar	United Arab Emirates

△ **Middle East Nation with Nuclear Weaponry *Potential*: Israel**

✈ **U.S. Military Base Access**

🛢 **Major Oil Field Areas**

Kemal Atatürk: The Middle East's First Modernizer

The first modernizing movement in the Middle East occurred in Turkey early in the twentieth century. The glory days of the Ottoman Empire had passed, and the part of the Balkans still ruled by Turkey was embroiled in incessant ethnic conflict. Because of these troubles, Turkey was often called the "sick man of Europe." The "Young Turks" were a group of politicians and patriots who dreamed of revitalizing Turkey. Many of them had studied in Western universities and sought to transform Turkey into a modern, secular society resembling the most progressive European countries. They embraced education, science, and technology as the keys to success. At the same time, they were impressed by the integrating and mobilizing power of militant, patriotic nationalism in Greece, Serbia, Bulgaria, and Romania. The Young Turks staged a coup d'état on July 23, 1908, and established a constitutional monarchy, but in triumph they eventually turned against all of the liberal principles enunciated by the Young Turk movement. In World War I, the Young Turks sided with Germany. Having fought on the losing side, the Turkish empire was dismembered after the war. This experience aroused strong nationalistic sentiment among Turks. Mustafa Kemal Atatürk, leader of the Nationalist party, harnessed this sentiment. In 1923, the Republic of Turkey was established, and Kemal Atatürk became its first president, a post he retained until 1938. Kemal Atatürk, a gifted leader bent on modernizing his country, propelled Turkey into the twentieth century.

A nationalist party, the Wafd, led the fight against British colonialism until Britain formally ended its protectorate. Egypt was given nominal independence under a new king, Faud, but London continued to control Egypt's foreign policy, armed forces, and some internal affairs.

This brief historical overview necessarily omits a great deal, but it sets the stage to examine the recent history of three key Middle Eastern countries: Israel, Egypt, and Saudi Arabia.

Case Studies: Israel, Egypt, and Saudi Arabia

Westerners, especially Americans, often entertain negative images of the Arabs. Ignorance and prejudice are to blame:

> Once Jews, blacks and other minorities were subjected to similar degradation; today only Arabs and homosexuals are still fair game for media bashing. The Arabs, I think, are singled out primarily because, unlike most other peoples of the developing world, they have resisted assimilating Western ways or capitulating to Western values. Thus they are seen as a threat and, armed with oil and the ability to make war or peace with Israel, are thought to be in a position to translate that threat into actions that affect the industrialized world.[12]

Whatever its basis, prejudice against Arabs often evokes images of sheiks and harems and nomadic bedouins with towels on their heads roaming the scorched desert, riding camels, living in tents, and so on. It is a short step to portraying Arabs as barbaric and cruel, treacherous and warlike, fanatical and feudalistic (particularly in their attitudes toward women). Although most Americans are aware that the Middle East has nurtured many advanced civilizations (Egyptian, Sumerian, Babylonian, Assyrian), many remain ignorant of Arabic culture and are indifferent or unsympathetic to Arab concerns.

Western prejudice against Middle Easterners includes a long history of anti-Semitism as well. Hatred of Jews reached a fever pitch in Nazi Germany, of course, but anti-Semitism has also been a recurring element in American life. Extremist groups like the Ku Klux Klan and the American Nazi party have embraced virulently anti-Semitic doctrines.

Besides breeding suspicion and hostility, prejudiced stereotypes can affect policy. Some critics contend that U.S. policymakers have shown a systematic bias against the Arabs in the Arab-Israeli conflicts of the post–World War II period, while others maintain that State Department career officials have for decades been consistently pro-Arab. Without expecting or even trying to resolve this question, let us examine the politics of the region as impartially and objectively as possible.

Israel

Proclaimed a Jewish state on May 14, 1948, Israel was founded under extreme duress. On that date, the British mandate over the territory of Palestine, established after World War I under the auspices of the League of Nations, formally expired.

At its inception, Israel was a small country, approximately the size of New Jersey, surrounded by hostile Arab neighbors—Lebanon to the north, Syria and Jordan to the east, and Egypt to the west. Only the Mediterranean Sea prevented Israel from being completely encircled by enemies. The fact that many charter members of the new Zionist state, including some of its leaders, were survivors of the Holocaust reinforced the fierce determination that marked the Jewish struggle for Palestine.

Nothing has made a deeper imprint on the Israeli psyche than the nation's precarious geography. As a consequence of its exposure to attack on all sides, and given the sizable Palestinian population within its borders, Israel's political life has been permeated by security considerations. Before the 1967 Six-Day War, Israel shared a jagged 50-mile border with Lebanon, a 48-mile border with Syria, and a meandering 335-mile border with Jordan. Israel's frontier with Egypt in the blistering Sinai desert provided a buffer, but even that did not prevent the two nations from fighting three wars in seventeen years (1956, 1967, and 1973). From north to south, Israel was 280 miles long; east to west, it measured nowhere more than 70 miles—its narrow waist, just north of Tel Aviv, was a spare 12 miles wide, and in the south, a mere 9 miles separated Israel's port of Eilat and Jordan's port of Aqaba.

The close proximity of Israel to its Arab neighbors is especially threatening in the age of air power. Flying time from Cairo, Amman, or Damascus to Tel

Aviv or Jerusalem is measured in minutes, scant warning time in an attack. Israel's neighbors, for their part, feel vulnerable to Israeli attack and, since 1967, fear Israeli expansionism. In the Six-Day War, Israel trebled its territory, adding about twenty thousand square miles by occupying the Sinai (returned to Egypt under the 1979 peace treaty); the Gaza Strip (taken from Egypt); the West Bank, including East Jerusalem (from Jordan); and the Golan Heights (from Syria).

The new Middle East map seemed to make Israel secure at last. But the **Occupied Territories** were inhabited primarily by Arabs, meaning that Israel now had a major *internal* Palestinian problem. Including the West Bank and the Gaza Strip, Israel presently has a Palestinian population of about 1.5 million (out of a total of about five million). And the seizure of Arab lands made future conflict inevitable. To appreciate the situation, it is necessary to consider Israel's origins.

The Idea of Israel   Israel was established as a Jewish state following a bitter and bloody struggle with the native Arab population, the Palestinians. The state of Israel was the culmination of **Zionism**, a Jewish national movement dating from the late nineteenth century.[13] Jews had dreamed of being reunited in the Promised Land since their flight from Palestine, known as the **Diaspora**, after a failed rebellion against Roman rule in A.D. 70. The fact that Jews had been isolated and persecuted in their adopted lands no doubt helped sustain the dream. For example, although Jews in Eastern Europe and Russia were legally emancipated by the late nineteenth century, they continued to be subjected to anti-Semitism, pogroms (massacres), and cultural isolation. Between 1882 and 1914, several million European Jews emigrated to the United States and tens of thousands went to Palestine, which was still part of the Ottoman Empire.

In 1896, a young Viennese journalist named Theodore Herzl published a pamphlet titled *Der Judenstaat* ("The Jewish State"), advocating the creation of a self-governing community for the Jews. The next year, he convened the First World Zionist Congress in Basel, Switzerland. The delegates declared that the goal of Zionism was to create a "home for the Jewish People in Palestine to be secured by public law" and created the World Zionist Organization to pursue this aim.

Herzl died in 1904, the same year in which Chaim Weizmann, a Zionist and a brilliant chemist, emigrated from Russia to Great Britain. Weizmann's scientific discoveries contributed to the Allied war effort and 'gave him access to British political elites. He used these connections to persuade the British government to back the cause of a Jewish homeland in Palestine. On November 2, 1917, Lord Balfour, the British foreign secretary, declared that Great Britain favored "the establishment in Palestine of a national home for the Jewish people" and pledged to "facilitate the achievement of this object, it being clearly understood that nothing shall be done which may prejudice the civil and religious rights of the existing non-Jewish communities in Palestine or the rights and political status enjoyed by Jews in any other country."

When the British replaced the Ottoman Turks in Palestine after World

War I (Palestine became a British mandate in 1923 under the League of Nations), they were in a position to make good on this promise. The mandate expressly provided for a Jewish home in Palestine, incorporating the Balfour Declaration into its text almost verbatim. It also authorized Jewish immigration into Palestine and began to lay the groundwork for a future Jewish state. It divided Palestine, designating the territory east of the Jordan River the "Transjordan." In the truncated Palestine that remained, the British had intended to set up the promised Jewish homeland. But the native Palestinian Arabs had other ideas.

Between the two world wars, Jews immigrated to Palestine in great numbers. Some were in search of the Promised Land; others, especially from the Soviet Union and Central Europe, were fleeing oppression and persecution. On the eve of World War II, the exodus from Europe turned into a flood as Jews sought refuge from the intolerable conditions created by the Nazis.

In Palestine, a different tempest was stirring. The native Arabs rioted and revolted against the British, culminating in the Arab Rebellion of 1937. The influx of Jews alarmed and dismayed the Arabs, who attacked both mandate authorities and immigrants. The enmities formed in this crucible have fanned the flames of violence in the Middle East to the present day.

The War for Palestine   The Palestinian Arabs' attacks on Jews in the 1930s were answered in the 1940s with Jewish terrorist acts by such groups as *Irgun* and the Stern Gang. Jewish militants of this period included at least two future prime ministers, Menachem Begin and Yitzhak Shamir. The British could not find a solution that was acceptable to both sides, and their vacillation pushed the level of frustration ever higher. The British were committed to the idea of a Jewish state but seemed to envision a federation in which Jews and Palestinian Arabs would participate equally.

World War II gave a new impetus to Zionism. Yet just when so many displaced persons wanted to go, the British government halted Jewish immigration into Palestine. This resulted in highly publicized scenes of refugees on ships being turned away and stories about illegal landings of immigrants. Critics maintain that the ban on immigration was the chief reason Zionist leaders pushed so hard for a Jewish state at that time. And of course, the Nazis' genocidal intentions for the Jews further steeled the resolve of Zionist leaders to win the struggle for Palestine. The Palestinian Arabs, however, were equally determined to resist.

The British finally brought the issue before the United Nations, which approved a plan to partition Palestine into an Arab state and a Jewish state. It also stipulated that Jerusalem was to become an international city. The Arab states rejected this plan and warned that "any attempt by the Jews or any other power or group of powers to establish a Jewish state in Arab territory is an act of oppression which will be resisted in self-defense by force."[14] The Zionists, however, accepted the plan. The proclamation of the state of Israel cited the UN resolution as its authority. Thus, paradoxically, Palestinian Arabs had been offered a much larger state than they may someday obtain on the West Bank, but they turned the offer down. Had the Arab side accepted the UN resolution, Israel might still be a small enclave in an Arabic Palestine.

Ironically, the UN's attempt to resolve the Palestinian problem peacefully precipitated the first Arab-Israeli war, which did not reach full intensity until after the British had left and the Jewish state was proclaimed. The war lasted about eight months. When the smoke cleared, tiny Israel had prevailed over the armies of Egypt, Transjordan, Syria, Lebanon, and Iraq; it now occupied 30 percent more territory than the UN had contemplated. But it left a bitter legacy:

> The war drove nearly one million Arabs out of their homes. This flight was partly due to the fear of Jewish reprisals and partly to the urgings of Arab political leaders to evacuate probable battle areas. The refugees fled to the surrounding Arab countries or to the Arab-occupied parts of Palestine. In the spring of 1949 the number of Arab displaced persons eligible for relief was officially estimated at 940,000. At the beginning of the war there were 1,320,000 Arabs and 640,000 Jews in Palestine. The establishment of Israel resulted in the displacement of nearly 70 percent of the Arab population, which the Israeli government refused to readmit.[15]

Israel Ascendant and Besieged, 1949–1973   David Ben-Gurion led Israel through the crucial early years, serving as both prime minister and defense minister. (Weizmann was the nation's first president.) In the 1950s, the Israeli government was made up of coalitions dominated by Ben-Gurion's socialist Mapai party. Under the Declaration of Independence and the Law of Return, Israel welcomed Jewish immigrants with open arms. The population of Israel, around 900,000 in 1948, nearly doubled by 1955. Jews came from all parts of Europe and the Middle East, an influx that created serious tensions within the new state. For example, the **Sephardic** or Oriental Jews, of Spanish, Portuguese, and Middle Eastern background, had a completely different culture from that of **Ashkenazic** or European Jews (from Central and Eastern Europe). By the mid-1950s, more than half of Israel's population consisted of Sephardim, but Ashkenazim continued to dominate politics and business.

The war for Palestine led to a reshuffling of the population of the Middle East. Palestinian Arabs fled to surrounding Arab states, while Oriental Jews flocked to Israel. The 300,000 or so Palestinian Arabs who remained in Israel became second-class citizens. They were deprived of much of their land, denied freedom of movement and economic opportunities, and shut out of the government.

The treatment of Arabs in Israel was only one grievance of the Arab states. After the war, Israel refused to relinquish the territories in Palestine occupied by its army, arguing that the Arab states had invalidated the UN resolution on Palestine by invading Israel on May 15, 1948. Israel also spurned the UN stipulation that "the refugees wishing to return to their homes and live at peace with their neighbors should be permitted to do so at the earliest practicable date, and that compensation should be paid for the property of those choosing not to return." Though Israel's stand may appear harsh, remember that the new nation was greatly outnumbered and faced constant threats from the Arab states, all of which refused to recognize Israel's right to exist.

During the period leading up to the 1956 Suez Crisis (which was really the second Arab-Israeli war), terrorist acts were perpetrated by both sides. Ben-Gurion advocated a policy of retaliation; his trusted lieutenant, Moshe Sharett, who served as prime minister during Ben-Gurion's brief retirement from politics (1953–1955), advocated a policy of accommodation. Sharett spoke Arabic and understood Arab culture, which may explain why he believed peace possible. Ben-Gurion's school of thought has prevailed in Israeli politics for most of the years since 1955; Golda Meir, Moshe Dayan, Menachem Begin, and Yitzhak Shamir were all devoted advocates. But the Sharett school has not died; hard-liners and moderates continue to debate how best to deal with Arab discontent.

As Israel's position hardened, so did that of the Arabs, especially in Egypt. In 1956, Egyptian President Nasser nationalized the British-operated Suez Canal. Viewing this as one more in a series of provocations, Israel attacked, with British and French backing. America, however, condemned Israel's action (ironically placing the United States on the same side as the Soviet Union). Although the Israelis won on the battlefield, the superpowers in effect came to Egypt's rescue by creating the United Nations Emergency Force to act as a buffer.

The UN peacekeepers did their job, but from the Arab standpoint, the Suez Crisis had added insult to injury. Egypt felt humiliated. Between 1956 and 1967, when the next war was fought, an arms race occurred in the Middle East, with the United States supplying Israel and the Soviet Union supplying Egypt. When Egypt attacked in 1967, Israel was ready. Indeed, it took the Israelis less than a week to score one of the most impressive military victories of modern times. Having defeated both Egypt and Syria in this Six-Day War, Israel seized and occupied territory from both those countries and from Jordan: Sinai, the West Bank, Gaza, and the Golan Heights.

There would be other wars: the Yom Kippur War in 1973, the 1983 war in Lebanon, and the Palestinian *intifada* ("uprising") of 1989–1991. These events will be discussed in Chapter 11.

Egypt

Egypt is located in the northeastern corner of Africa. The Sinai peninsula, an uninhabitable wasteland, links it to the Near East. Fully 96 percent of Egypt is desert. The vast majority of the nation's 55 million people are concentrated in a narrow strip along the Nile River, virtually the only area in the country conducive to farming and settlement. Cairo, the capital, teems with thirteen million people. Rapid population growth has spurred urbanization, and today almost half of Egypt's population lives in increasingly crowded urban areas.

Egypt is a Muslim nation—93 percent of its people are Sunni Muslims (the remaining 7 percent are Coptic Christians). Egypt has played a key leadership role in the Arab world since the mid-1950s, particularly under President Nasser (1954–1970). The nation's sparse natural resources are offset by more human resources—teachers, doctors, nurses, engineers, agronomists—than any other Arab country. Egypt has supplied much of the Arab world with professionals, specialists, and skilled workers of all kinds.

The Nile River is Egypt's greatest natural resource. Its waters sustain the dense urban population as well as the vital agricultural sector. Without irrigation, Egypt would be forced to import most of its food; instead, the rural economy employs over 40 percent of the labor force and produces crops for export (especially cotton), even though only 4 percent of the land is fit for cultivation.

In its modern form, Egypt is a young country, having gained full independence only after World War II. But it has had a glorious history as a distinctive civilization since ancient times; indeed, its Golden Age preceded Rome's by thousands of years.

As noted earlier, Egypt has been coveted and dominated by various foreign powers at different times. The isthmus of Suez—and later the canal built through it—was long an essential link between Europe and Asia, and control of it gave Egypt strategic importance. This was underscored in the war in North Africa in 1941–1943 when the Axis powers (Germany and Italy) tried to take Egypt but failed.

Although Suez is no longer as vital as it once was, Egypt is still in a pivotal position, given its proximity to Israel. Before President Sadat's decision to sign a separate peace with Israel, Egypt was the leader of the Arab world. After the treaty, as Egypt's stance changed from confrontation to mediation (see Chapter 11), its stature as standard-bearer for the Arab cause slipped.

The Egyptian Revolution   The Egyptian national movement, a reaction to Ottoman rule and subsequent European colonialism, was energized and agitated by developments in Palestine. In 1952, popular unrest precipitated a military coup, planned by a secret organization calling itself the Society of Free Officers. The Free Officers persuaded King Farouk to abdicate and set up the Revolutionary Command Council (RCC)—in effect, a military junta—at first led by Major General Mohammed Naguib.

But the power behind the scenes was a young lieutenant colonel named Gamal Abdel Nasser, who soon emerged as the junta's leader. In 1954, he deposed Naguib and became president and prime minister. Nasser ruled as a popular autocrat (he was "elected" president overwhelmingly in 1956) and created a cult of personality. During the Nasser era, Egypt became a leader not only in the Middle East but also in the Third World. Along with Nehru of India and Tito of Yugoslavia, Nasser was one of the founders of the so-called **nonaligned movement**.

The Egyptian revolution had three major aspects. It was first and foremost a nationalist affair. Egyptians wanted to be free of foreign interference for the first time in thousands of years. Second, it was a socialist revolution: Nasser was anticommunist (he outlawed and persecuted the Egyptian Communist party), but he was also anticapitalist and anti-imperialist. He railed against everything associated with European (particularly British) domination. This posturing against the West was immensely popular in Egypt at the time. Third, the revolution embraced the goal of Arab unity, or **pan-Arabism**. Nasser recognized that so long as the Arab world was fragmented, Arabs could not win the struggle against imperialism and Zionism.

The Egyptian revolution and its leader's role in it, known as **Nasserism**, became a model for many other developing countries, especially in the Middle East and Africa. Nasser never made himself a general. He chose the civilian title of president but retained his military position and appeared in uniform at national celebrations. Though a dictator, Nasser staged periodic elections to demonstrate his popularity and thus his legitimacy. His example was followed in Algeria, Libya, Syria, and Iraq. In Libya, for example, Colonel Muammar al-Qaddafi, having led a 1969 coup that ousted the king, established an authoritarian regime based on Islam, socialism, and personal charisma. Like Nasser, Qaddafi also had visions of a pan-Arab superstate and tried to unite Libya with neighboring Tunisia and Algeria. He also emulated Nasser in forging close ties with the Soviet Union and launching vitriolic propaganda against Israel and the United States.

Though committed to Egypt's modernization and economic development, Nasser's preoccupation was foreign affairs, and above all, Israel. As noted, the Suez Crisis in 1956 was triggered by Nasser's decision to nationalize the canal. Only U.S. diplomatic intervention saved Egypt from humiliation at the hands of Israel. Despite its claim of a moral victory, Egypt had suffered a crushing defeat.

To develop Egypt's economy, Nasser sought whatever assistance he could find. When the United States refused to help finance the Aswan Dam project, he turned to the Soviet Union. Moscow not only helped build the dam but also supplied military equipment and advisers to train the Egyptian army.

The Six-Day War in 1967 was the nadir of Nasser's political life. Israel invaded Egypt in a preemptive attack after Nasser asked the United Nations Emergency Force to withdraw; Egypt's defenses were demolished in a matter of days. For the next few years, hostilities continued to smolder, and Nasser once again had to turn to the Soviet Union to rebuild his shattered military.

Nasser's Legacy and His Successors   Nasser died in 1970, before he could redeem himself. Though he had made an indelible mark on Egypt and the Middle East, he also left a legacy of defeat. In internal politics, he had never trusted political parties and had outlawed even the venerable Wafd, which had been so instrumental in resisting the British after World War I. He created instead the Arab Socialist Union (ASU), his own political organization, a one-party monopoly.

Vice President Anwar al-Sadat succeeded Nasser and quickly made his own mark. In 1972, he surprised the world by ordering fifteen thousand Soviet advisers to leave Egypt because he believed that dependency on a single outside power raised the specter of a new form of colonialism. On October 6, 1973, Sadat again surprised everyone by launching an attack against Israel on Yom

Kippur, the holiest day on the Jewish calendar. The Egyptian army crossed the Suez Canal and broke through Israel's forward defenses in the occupied Sinai, but Israel quickly recovered and counterattacked, retaking all of the territory it had lost and more. As in 1956 and 1967, only outside intervention stopped the Israelis from marching all the way to Cairo. Nonetheless, Sadat claimed a moral victory. The Egyptian army had proved, he said, that Arabs could fight with modern arms and that Israel was not invincible.

In 1977, Sadat made another unexpected foreign-policy move when he addressed the Israeli parliament (the Knesset), breaking not only precedent but also the logjam in Egyptian-Israeli relations. There followed a meeting at Camp David, Maryland, where U.S. President Jimmy Carter brokered an agreement embodied in the 1979 peace treaty. In the so-called **Camp David Accords**, Israel agreed to give the Sinai back to Egypt in return for Egypt's recognizing Israel's right to exist. Israel may appear to have given away more than it got, but it was in truth Sadat who went out on a limb. Egypt thus became the first Arab state to recognize Israel. Throughout the Arab world, Sadat was denounced as a traitor to the Arab cause.

Sadat's actions also rankled Arab nationalists and Islamic fundamentalists in his own country. The fact that he was awarded the Nobel Peace Prize (jointly with Menachem Begin) meant little to his compatriots; to many Egyptians, the peace treaty was a sellout, and Sadat had betrayed a sacred trust. On October 6, 1981—eight years to the day after his fateful Yom Kippur invasion—Sadat was assassinated by domestic Islamic extremists. Vice President Hosni Mubarak, another strongman with a military background, succeeded him and has ruled Egypt uneventfully ever since.

Like Nasser, Sadat left an ambiguous legacy. On the one hand, having once made war on Israel, he had taken a bold and historic step toward peace in the Middle East. On the other hand, he had alienated the Egyptian people and made his country a pariah in the Arab world. In internal politics, he had continued in Nasser's footsteps, ruling with personal flair and a firm hand. Though attentive to the trappings of democracy, Sadat was no less authoritarian than Nasser. He often displayed an imperious contempt for public opinion, as when he pursued the extremely unpopular economic policy of *infitah* ("opening"); designed to attract foreign investment and spur an economic miracle, the policy succeeded only in making a few Egyptians very rich, including members of Sadat's family.

In the eyes of the West, Sadat is the great Arab leader of the postwar period. But to Egyptians and most other Arabs, Nasser is still the paragon of political virtue. Of course, the political culture of the West is very different from that of the Middle East, and Arab and Western perceptions and values are rarely identical. By Western measures, Nasser was a failure: Egypt lost two wars to Israel during his tenure, and the Egyptian economy stalled and stagnated. But Nasser understood the intangible elements of success in the Egyptian context—the yearning for independence, the desire to recapture past glory, the resentment of outside interference, the need to fight the "enemy" (almost as an end in itself). For better understanding between and among nations, it is not necessary (or possible)

Iran

Geographically, Iran is part of the Middle East, but in many ways it stands out as a unique society in the region; most Iranians are Persians, not Arabs; the vast majority of Iran's population are Shiite Muslims (most Arabs belong to the far more numerous Sunni branch of Islam); as a militant theocratic state, Iran is politically and ideologically distinct from all other governments in the Middle East; and Iran's historical development has diverged sharply from that of the Arab world.

Iran was once the core of the ancient Persian Empire. Dating back to the eleventh century B.C., the empire's vast territory encompassed many ethnic groups. Persians, who speak Farsi rather than Arabic, constitute about 63 percent of Iran's current population. The Arab minority in Iran are Sunni Muslims.

Despite its ethnic and religious diversity, Iranian society is held together by strong cultural bonds. Language, the Shiite sense of community, and a fervent nationalism reinforced by the glories of Persia's past all contribute to Iran's remarkable social cohesion.

Invading Arabs introduced Islam into Persia in the seventh century. The Arab rulers were Sunni Muslims who regarded the Shiites as subversive. To escape Sunni persecution, the Shiites adopted a practice called *taqiya* ("concealment"), hiding their beliefs.

In 1502, the Safavids won control of Persia. The first Safavid ruler, Shah Ismail, proclaimed Shiism the state religion and invited all Shiites to move to Persia.

Iran's modern borders were defined in the nineteenth century by treaties with Great Britain, Russia, and the Ottoman Turks who ruled Persia for several centuries. The foundations of a modern educational system were laid, and a small intellectual elite developed among the children of the aristocracy. These became the nucleus of a future opposition to the Shah, whose dealings with foreigners was, they believed, bankrupting the country. The Shiite holy men (mullahs) agreed, and to this day they oppose all Western intrusions into Iranian life. This attitude erupted in the Constitutional Revolt of 1905, a dress rehearsal for the Iranian Revolution of 1979.

After World War I, Iran had no government for a time. Russian and British forces partitioned the country. A clever military commander named Reza Khan to set up a new ruling Pahlavi dynasty. Reza Shah Pahlavi was a visionary leader who ruled with an iron fist. Following the example of Kemal Atatürk in Turkey, he set about modernizing and secularizing Iranian society. He abolished traditional dress, including the veil and the fez, and brooked no criticism from the mullahs. Resentful of British interference, Reza Shah favored Germany. In 1941, the British and the Russians occupied Iran. After the war, Reza Shah abdicated in favor of his son and went into exile.

When the new Shah, Mohammed Reza Pahlavi, ascended to the Peacock Throne, he was only 22 years old. The young Shah resumed the modernizing policies of his father. In 1962, he announced the White Revolution, a six-point program that included land reform, nationalization of industry, voting rights for women, profit sharing for workers, and a literacy campaign in rural areas. This modernization plan was unpopular among landowners and religious leaders, but the only critic who dared to speak out was the Ayatollah Ruhollah Khomeini, Iran's leading religious scholar. Thus began a vendetta between the Shah and the Ayatollah that continued until 1979, when Khomeini, exiled for many years, returned in triumph.

In the 1960s and 1970s, Iran became a repressive police state. The hated SAVAK (secret police) maintained an elaborate network of informers, and Iranian jails teemed with the Shah's presumed enemies. But the Iranian economy surged, lubricated by oil profits. The Shah sought and received the most advanced U.S. arms, including combat aircraft. To outsiders his regime seemed impervious to the political instability that plagued much of the Middle East.

But in 1977 and 1978, the situation deteriorated into violence and revolution. Had the Shah acted swiftly and decisively, he surely had enough force to crush the opposition. However, he did not order a crackdown and the crisis snowballed. In January 1979, the Shah and his family fled Iran, and his archrival Khomeini returned to establish the world's strictest Islamic state.

to see eye to eye with each other; what is essential is to be able to see the world from perspectives other than one's own.

Saudi Arabia

Traditional monarchies are an oddity in the modern world, but they are not nearly so old-fashioned in the Middle East as they would be in Europe or North America. After World War II, most of the self-rule in the Middle East was done by kings. Many of these monarchs were deposed in the 1950s and 1960s; the last in the region to fall was King Idris of Libya in 1969. (In nearby Ethiopia, Emperor Haile Selassie stayed in power until 1974.)

Monarchs have survived in Jordan and Morocco, but in both cases they have promoted modernization and made concessions to political pluralism. By contrast, old-style monarchies in Saudi Arabia and the Persian Gulf sheikdoms have been impervious to political change from within. The Iranian Revolution is the obvious exception, but Iran is not an Arab country, and the Shah had created a modern dictatorship quite different from the conservative monarchies of Arabia.

Saudi Arabia is an anomaly in the modern world. Nonetheless, because of its great oil wealth and its powerful air force, it is an important player in Middle Eastern politics.

Situated on a great arid peninsula surrounded by the Red Sea, the Arabian Sea, and the Persian Gulf, Saudi Arabia is isolated and insulated geographically, culturally, and politically. Nearly three-fourths of its population of seventeen million live in urban areas—an unusually high figure for the Middle East—primarily because only 1 percent of the land is arable. So immense and uninhabitable is the Arabian desert that no defined boundaries separate Saudi Arabia from its neighbors on the Arabian peninsula.

Beneath the barren desert, however, lies a gold mine—of "black gold." Saudi Arabia's crude oil reserves are the largest in the world—between 165 and 170 billion barrels. The Saudis demonstrated their capacity to affect the regional and global balance of power in the 1970s, when they spearheaded an oil embargo following the 1973 Middle East war.

The Wahhabi Tradition   Saudi Arabia combines antiquity with youth. The modern Saudi state dates back only to the eighteenth century. At that time, Muhammad ibn-Saud, the ambitious leader of a nomadic tribe, sought the moral support of Abd al-Wahhab, an important religious scholar who lived near the village of Riyadh. The Saudi leader promised to protect Wahhab (whose opponents wanted him dead) in exchange for Allah's blessing. Thus was born the **Wahhabi movement**, an Islamic crusade based on an alliance between two powerful leaders, one secular and one Sunni.

Saudi kings institutionalized the Wahhabi tradition based on the strict moral code practiced by the Prophet Muhammad in Mecca and Medina (both located in Saudi Arabia). This code remains the basis for Saudi law and social behavior. Indeed, the Ministry of Public Morals Enforcement is one of the most important cabinet portfolios; its police patrol the streets, making certain that women wear veils at all times, that there is no eating or drinking by daylight during the month of Ramadan, and that Saudi society remains free of alcohol and drugs. By Western standards, the ancient Islamic strictures seem particularly oppressive for women (who are not even allowed to drive cars). Religious leaders play a strong role in setting public policy; for example, because they consider motion pictures evil, Saudi Arabia has no movie theaters.

A Family Affair   The father of the Saudi state is Abd al-Aziz ibn-Saud. He grew up in exile in Kuwait, where his father had fled in the 1890s after the Rashidis, a rival tribe, seized Riyadh. In 1902, ibn-Saud and a small band of followers made their way across the desert, scaled the village's walls at night, and surprised the sleepy-eyed Rashidi rulers at daybreak. The people of Riyadh rallied behind the future Saudi king and drove the Rashidis out of town.

For the next thirty years, ibn-Saud tried to regain the Saudis' ancestral lands. He eventually succeeded, using both diplomatic and military skills, and in 1932, he aptly named the state *Saudi Arabia*—it was *his* country, and it still is. The Saudi clan owns and operates it. Today, the Saudi royal family "counts more than 5,000 princes and princesses among its numbers, each of whom occupies a privileged position."[16] Thus there is a prince or princess for every two thousand commoners.

As we shall see subsequently, Saudi Arabia is an odd mixture of the old and the new. It combines antediluvian social mores with the most modern technology that money can buy.

CONCLUSION

More than in any other region of the world, the history of the Middle East has been dominated by religion. Judaism, Christianity, and Islam all have their roots there, and the cultures of the region are strongly influenced by the aesthetics and ethics associated with these religions. In the past century, religious differences have been exacerbated by rising nationalism. Today, conflicts that appear to be religious are more often the result of rival nationalisms. Political systems in this area are authoritarian and in many cases repressive, and the foreign policies of several powerful players in the region at times reflect a militancy and an uncompromising spirit often associated with religious zealotry. Chapter 11 will look more closely at the forms of government found in the Middle East today.

KEY TERMS

Middle East	Shiite
Maghreb	Sunni
Near East	imam
Northern Belt (Northern Tier)	mullah
North Africa	*jihad*
Sahara	Muslim Brotherhood
Fertile Crescent	*intifada*
Arabian peninsula	Occupied Territories
Islam	Zionism
Koran	Diaspora
Judaism	Sephardic
rabbi	Ashkenazic
Christianity	nonaligned movement
Jesus Christ	pan-Arabism
Muhammad	Nasserism
Allah	Camp David Accords
theocracy	Wahhabi movement

STUDY QUESTIONS

1. What are the major religions of the Middle East, and in what ways has religion shaped the region's history and culture?
2. Why do Muslims, Christians, and Jews all view Jerusalem as the Holy City? Has this common element in all three religious traditions contributed to greater mutual understanding, or has it done the opposite?
3. What inspired the Iranian Revolution? In what sense (if any) was the revolution the cause of the Iran-Iraq War?
4. What role did colonialism and foreign intrusion play in setting the stage for Middle East conflict? When and how did colonialism end in the region?
5. How have international relationships in the Middle East evolved since World War II? How many instances of war and revolution can you cite? How many successful efforts at peacekeeping and conflict resolution?

SUGGESTED READING

Bligh, Alexander. *From Prince to King: Royal Succession in the House of Saud in the Twentieth Century.* New York: New York University Press, 1984.

Cooper, Mark N. *The Transformation of Egypt.* Baltimore: Johns Hopkins University Press, 1982.

Eickelman, Dale P. *The Middle East.* 2nd ed. Englewood Cliffs, N.J.: Prentice Hall, 1989.

Lamb, David. *The Arabs: Journeys beyond the Mirage.* New York: Random House, 1988.

Lenczowski, George. *The Middle East in World Affairs.* Ithaca, N.Y.: Cornell University Press, 1980.

Mackey, Sandra. *The Saudis: Inside the Desert Kingdom.* New York: NAL-Dutton, 1990.

Marsot, Afaf L. *Egypt in the Reign of Muhammad Ali.* Cambridge: Cambridge University Press, 1984.

Mattehedeh, Roy. *The Mantle of the Prophet: Religion and Politics in Iran.* New York: Simon & Schuster, 1985.

O'Brien, Conor C. *The Siege: The Saga of Israel and Zionism.* New York: Simon & Schuster, 1987.

Pryce-Jones, David. *The Closed Circle: An Interpretation of the Arabs.* New York: Harper, 1991.

Sivan, Emmanual. *Radical Islam: Medieval Theology and Modern Politics.* New Haven, Conn.: Yale University Press, 1990.

Viorst, Milton. *Sands of Sorrow: Israel's Journey from Independence.* New York: Harper, 1987.

NOTES

1. George Lenczowski, *The Middle East in World Affairs* (Ithaca, N.Y.: Cornell University Press, 1980), p. 694.
2. Ibid.
3. Ibid.
4. David Lamb, *The Arabs: Journeys beyond the Mirage* (New York: Random House, 1988), p. 7.
5. Ibid., p. 15.
6. Bernard Lewis, *The Arabs in History* (New York: Harper, 1966), pp. 131–143.
7. Lenczowski, *Middle East in World Affairs,* p. 27.
8. Ibid.
9. Ibid., p. 35.
10. Ibid., p. 46.
11. See George Antonius, *The Arab Awakening* (New York: Putnam, 1965).
12. Lamb, *Arabs,* p. 15.
13. For a concise discussion of the origins and evolution of Zionism, see "Zionism Now," *Economist,* July 11, 1992, p. 21.
14. Arab Higher Committee of Palestine, Feb. 6, 1948; quoted in Lenczowski, *Middle East in World Affairs,* p. 405.
15. Lenczowksi, *Middle East in World Affairs,* p. 410.
16. Monte Palmer, *Dilemmas of Political Development* (Itasca, Ill.: Peacock, 1989), p. 314.

11

Monarchies, Dictatorships, and a Garrison State

Political institutions in the Middle East may vary, but authoritarian patterns are the rule. Authoritarianism is etched into Arab history and political culture—witness the survival of traditional monarchies in Arabia and more modern versions in Jordan and Morocco. (Half a century ago, most Arab nations were monarchies.)

Political traditions in the Middle East are also characterized by extremism and violence, implicit in the concept of *jihad,* or holy war. The militancy and zeal that Westerners associate with the region's politics are rooted in religion; Islam has a history of conflict, conquest, and conversion going back some thirteen centuries (see Chapter 10).

These turbulent spirits and combative energies are not always directed against outsiders, as the Iraqi invasion of Kuwait in August 1990 attested. Xenophobia is no greater among Arabs than among other groups. Like other peoples, Arabs are intensely nationalistic, and sometimes, like the nations of Europe, they have fought among themselves over religious or other differences. This history of internecine warfare is captured in the following passage:

> The very first anecdote usually told to students of the Middle East is the story of the scorpion and the frog that one day find themselves on a riverbank. The scorpion asks the frog to carry him across to the other shore.
>
> "Don't be ridiculous," answers the frog. "If I let you on my back, you'll sting me."
>
> But the scorpion points out that he cannot swim and if he were to sting the frog in midriver, "we both would drown."
>
> So the frog, persuaded by the logic of the argument, allows the scorpion

to climb on his back, and they set out into the river. When they reach the middle, however, the scorpion stings the frog, and the paralyzed amphibian starts to sink beneath the water. "Why did you do that?" he croaks. "Now we'll both die."

"Oh, well"—the scorpion sighs, shrugging his carapace—"after all, this is the Middle East."[1]

A certain turbulence has been evident in domestic politics throughout the region as well. This may explain why fallen monarchs have typically been replaced by strongmen or "popular tyrants." As Barry Rubin has observed:

> The contemporary Middle East is a stronghold of modern dictators, men whose energy, cleverness, and ruthlessness have enabled them to master their countries. Muammar al-Qaddafi in Libya, Khomeini in Iran, Hussein in Iraq, and Hafez al-Assad in Syria constructed populist, repressive regimes able to tame some of the world's most turbulent and violent political systems. To stay atop the tiger, they must have an ideology acceptable to their cultures, a party and mass organizations furnishing a wide base of supporters, and an energetic secret policy to break up antigovernment conspiracies.[2]

Rubin points out that Middle East dictators "must also dominate the economy and control the army" and contends that they are, if anything, "more ambitious" than their counterparts in other Third World regions in that they "claim to have discovered a proper ethical and political system for the entire region or even the whole world."[3]

The Logic of Arab Politics

There is a notion in the West, reinforced by the behavior of such leaders as Qaddafi, Khomeini, and Saddam Hussein, that Arabs are irrational and that chaos is their natural condition. On the contrary, most Arab rulers are rational—"they act in accordance with domestic and regional needs, rather than behave as the West might think proper." At the same time, however, these rulers "face very exacting demands from Islam and Arab nationalism and are simultaneously manipulators and prisoners of the power symbols of these politics."[4] For example, anti-Zionism is a powerful unifier, but it also locks governments into positions that make seeking peace with Israel untenable. (That is why Arab leaders accused President Sadat of betrayal when Egypt signed its peace treaty with Israel in 1979.)

In the 1930s, Arab nationalism began to eclipse Islam as a force shaping Arabs' identities and aspirations. This movement, which stressed Arab unity, was fueled by two external forces: European imperialism and Zionism. Before World War I, the main motive for unity was anti-imperialism; as Jews flowed into Palestine between the wars, that sentiment merged with anti-Zionism; and after the Palestine War of 1948–1949, the primary motive was hatred of Israel.

But Arab unity is like the weather: easy to talk about but impossible to control. Many attempts have been made to merge Arab nations—Nasser was always trying, and Qaddafi has tried as well. All efforts have failed. One reason why Israel has survived as an independent state despite being isolated and outnumbered is that the Arab states have so often been preoccupied by quarrels among themselves. Even the Palestinians, with a passionate cause to unite them, have fought each other, and groups have broken away from the **Palestine Liberation Organization (PLO)**, thus splintering and weakening the Palestinian movement.

Moreover, the bickering sometimes bursts into open hostilities. Iraq's forcible seizure of Kuwait is a case in point; the Lebanese civil war is another. Tense situations have also arisen between Iraq and Syria, Syria and Jordan, Egypt and Libya, Libya and Tunisia, Libya and Chad, and the PLO and Syria. In the Iran-Iraq War, Algeria and Syria backed Persian Iran against Arab Iraq (Saudi Arabia and Jordan, among others, supported Iraq). And in the Persian Gulf War of 1992, most Arab states, including Syria, sided with the anti-Iraq coalition led by the United States.

Sadat's decision to make peace with Israel led to Egypt's expulsion from the Arab League. This illustrates one major verity of Middle Eastern politics: Arab states all agree that Israel is the enemy, but they have never been able to agree on strategy. Some are radical, "rejectionist" states (Iraq, Libya, Syria); others are more moderate (Egypt, Jordan, Saudi Arabia). Even the moderates, however, distrust and detest Israel.

The Arithmetic of Instability

The turbulence that plagued Arab politics in the 1950s and 1960s, when the new nationalist regimes were struggling to consolidate their newfound power, can be demonstrated with a few statistics. During the three decades following the Egyptian revolution, no fewer than fifty-five *unscheduled* transfers of power occurred in Arab nations (see Figure 11.1), including coups, revolutions, and assassinations. Arab states outside the Persian Gulf experienced two dozen coups during the 1950s and 1960s. Syria averaged one coup about every two years.

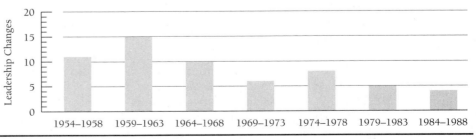

Figure 11.1 Unscheduled leadership changes in the Middle East, 1954–1988.

Iraq had coups in 1958, 1963, and 1968. A coup in Libya in 1969 brought Qaddafi to power. The number of such events declined in the 1970s and 1980s, suggesting that Arab leaders had learned techniques for staying in power, and the internal politics of most Arab nations stabilized considerably. (The assassination of Sadat, however, is a reminder that political violence is an ever-present possibility.)

In sum, coups and rumors of coups dominated Middle East politics in the 1950s and 1960s. The military took charge in one Arab country after another. Where the military did not take charge, an anachronistic form of authoritarianism—hereditary monarchy—remained in force. Jordan, Morocco, Saudi Arabia, and the oil-rich Persian Gulf sheikdoms of Bahrain, Kuwait, Qatar, Oman, and the United Arab Emirates are cases in point. Western-style democracy made inroads only in Israel, where it does not fully extend to the Arab population.

Modern Arab Regimes

The new military regimes of the 1950s and 1960s stressed nationalism, pan-Arabism, and socialism. They denounced imperialism, capitalism, and, above all, Zionism. Egypt, Algeria, Syria, Iraq, and the PLO all looked to the Soviet Union for economic and military aid; after 1969, Libya and South Yemen did too (the latter became a Soviet client state in the 1970s). The reason these regimes all embraced the Soviet Union had little to do with ideology (indeed, they typically persecuted their own Communists) and much to do with *Realpolitik*. The United States supported the old order and Israel, while the USSR backed modern dictatorships and was cool toward Israel.

Once in power, the strongmen combined Arab traditions with modern authoritarian techniques. Nasser set the standard for using symbols, propaganda, and charisma to manipulate the masses. He has since been emulated by Assad (Syria), Saddam Hussein (Iraq), Qaddafi (Libya), and others. But Arab rulers have given autocratic tactics and methods a new wrinkle. For example, the leader's inner circle is typically reinforced with friends, relatives, and others who have special ties to the leader. In Syria, the ruling clique consists mainly of members of Assad's Alawite Muslim minority. In Iraq, most of the ruling elite come from the Sunni Muslim minority, especially from villages around Tikrit. In Libya, Qaddafi relies on loyal confederates from his own clan and home territory.

As military officers who themselves plotted against previous rulers, the new populist dictators know well the danger of coups and have figured out how to prevent them. Typically, they purge any officers who have ties to the old regime or to competing parties, factions, interests, or ideologies. They also tightly control military promotions and rotate or transfer officers so that no one can count on the loyalty of a given unit. Trusted officers are placed in key positions, thus giving the military a stake in the success of the regime and shared responsibility for any failures. Finally, multiple intelligence networks are created, not only to stamp out dissent but also to have each keep an eye on the others.

In modern Arab dictatorships, a single party is at the center of a web of mass organizations (for workers, youths, students, teachers, women, peasants, and so on). The party is an extension of the leader, who uses it to control the society and reward the faithful, in part through patronage appointments in the bureaucracy, schools, mass organizations, industry, and the armed forces. Examples are the Baath party in Syria and Iraq, the Islamic Republican party in Iran, and the people's committees in Libya.

We turn now to our case studies. Israel is the only true multiparty democracy in the Middle East. Egypt, an authoritarian state with one dominant party and a few minor parties, is more typical of modern quasi-democratic Arab regimes. Saudi Arabia is a traditional monarchy, one of the few still in existence.

Case Studies: Israel, Egypt, and Saudi Arabia

Israel and Egypt have been at the center of the Middle East conflict for nearly half a century. Three major wars—in 1956, 1967, and 1973—were fought primarily between these two countries. In fact, Egypt's claim to leadership of the Arab world was based mainly on its belligerency toward Israel. After Egypt signed the 1979 peace treaty with Israel, the political face of the Middle East *as a region* changed drastically, but the internal politics of the Arab states remained largely unaffected.

Israel

In the garrison state of Israel, the peace treaty was a major event, but it was offset by the rise of Khomeini's Islamic fundamentalism, which posed a new threat to the stability of the region. An outpouring of extremism in the Middle East was directed against the United States and, of course, Israel. But despite the pervasive siege mentality in Israel, the state has functioned as a parliamentary democracy since its stormy beginnings in 1948. The inhabitants of the Occupied Territories, however, have not enjoyed the same civil liberties as people who live within the official boundaries of Israel.

Israel's multiparty system is unique in the Middle East. Perhaps owing to the nation's endemic insecurity, Israel has no written constitution—such a document might complicate matters when, for example, martial-law measures are deemed necessary. Statutory laws define basic rights, election procedures, voting qualifications, military service obligations, and the like. The Law of Return (see Chapter 10) is unique: it provides that any Jew has the right to immigrate to Israel and become an Israeli citizen at any time. In effect, Jews living in other countries have dual citizenship. In this sense, Israel is a true Jewish homeland.

A Parliamentary System   Israel's government is similar to the British parliamentary system. The **Knesset** (parliament) consists of 120 members elected to four-year terms by proportional representation. The party with the most seats in the Knesset (or the one that can form a majority coalition) chooses a prime minister and a cabinet to run the government. The prime minister is accountable to the Knesset and can be forced to resign by a vote of no confidence. Instead of a British-style figurehead monarch, Israel has a ceremonial president.

For the first thirty years, David Ben-Gurion's Mapai (Labour) party dominated Israeli politics. But the Labour party rarely had a clear majority (the proportional representation system has encouraged party proliferation), so unstable coalition governments have been the rule.

After the Yom Kippur War in 1973, the **Labour party** was challenged by opposition hard-liners including the **Likud party**, who charged that Israel had suffered heavy casualties because the Labour government of Prime Minister Golda Meir had been caught with its guard down. Labour's economic policies were also called into question after runaway inflation forced the government to adopt an unpopular austerity program. In 1977, the right-wing Likud won more seats than Labour, the Menachem Begin, a veteran of the struggle for Israeli statehood, became prime minister. But because Likud lacked a clear majority, Begin had to make concessions to smaller parties in order to form a governing coalition.

The "Separate Peace" with Egypt   Ironically, it was the hard-liners' victory that made the peace treaty with Egypt possible. In Israel, as in the United States, a conservative leader is often able to act more boldly in foreign policy than a liberal one, whose patriotism might be more easily questioned. (Hence it was Richard Nixon, the crusading Cold Warrior, who initiated rapprochement with the People's Republic of China and signed the first Strategic Arms Limitation Treaty with the Soviet Union.) Begin, an unabashed Zionist, succeeded where all predecessors had failed: Egypt, the nation that had spearheaded the campaign to "drive the Israelis into the sea," agreed to recognize Israel's right to exist within secure and defensible borders. In return, Israel agreed to return the occupied Sinai to Egypt.

As noted in Chapter 10, winning the 1978 Nobel Peace Prize, with Begin, did not enhance Sadat's popularity at home. But it did make Begin a hero in Israel. The national euphoria helped him and Likud win reelection in 1981.

The Invasion of Lebanon   Celebration soon gave way to anguish when Israel invaded Lebanon the following year. The Likud-led coalition was starting to unravel in 1981; after the invasion, during which Lebanese Christians committed atrocities against civilians in Palestinian refugee camps while Israeli military guards apparently turned a blind eye, Begin survived a no-confidence motion in the Knesset by a single vote. The invasion caused a furor in Israel and elsewhere because it appeared to violate Israel's own precept that the only justification for war is self-defense. Though initially provoked by PLO cross-border raids from Palestinian bases in southern Lebanon, the Israeli army pressed northward. In June 1982, it encircled Beirut and then called in the Israeli air force. The strategy was to drive the PLO out of Lebanon. Massive bombing achieved that goal—at an enormous political cost.

Thus Israel won the battle but not the war. Prime Minister Begin found himself in the middle of a political maelstrom. Depressed by the turn of events in Lebanon and the death of his wife, Begin retired in 1983. There was still peace with Egypt, but now Israel itself was deeply divided. Even the military was split: some high-ranking officers resigned their commissions, and many soldiers refused to fight. Meanwhile, the high cost of the war strained the economy and added to growing domestic unrest. Finally, the Arabs had a new *cause célèbre,* and opinion turned sharply against Israel, even in the West.

The Government of National Unity   The economic and political repercussions of the Lebanon invasion made it necessary to seek a new popular mandate. But the 1984 elections were ambiguous: Labour won the most votes but failed to win a majority of the seats in the Knesset. Both Labour and Likud scrambled to form a coalition government, but neither succeeded. These two odd bedfellows then worked out a so-called government of national unity—the first in Israeli history. The two parties agreed to alternate in power, with the leader of the Labour party serving as prime minister for two years and then handing over the government to the Likud leader. Under this arrangement, Labour's Shimon Peres became prime minister in September 1984 and was succeeded by Likud's Yitzhak Shamir in October 1986.

The 1988 Elections and the Extreme Center   The attempt at a national unity government was not entirely successful. In the 1988 elections, both Labour on the left and Likud on the right lost votes to religious parties in the center that were willing to side with either side in exchange for certain concessions on religious issues. Orthodox parties and leaders seek legislation imposing religious restrictions on Jews, funding for religious schools, and draft exemption for rabbinical students.

The trend toward polarization and fragmentation was clear in 1988. Labour won the largest number of votes, "but only a nationalist bloc could act as an effective pivot of a viable coalition."[5] The upshot was that Likud's Shamir "was able to form a viable government on the basis of another national unity coalition with Labour; his alternative, partnership with the religious and the non-religious right, was abandoned because of the preconditions of the religious right."[6]

As the 1980s drew to a close, consensus seemed more remote than ever. Professor Avner Yaniv of Haifa University summed up the situation as follows:

> More than anything else, the country needed a clear electoral decision that would facilitate a strong government. But the number of parties and the lists [slates of candidates] in the campaign indicated that this was not to be. Almost 30 lists obtained enough signatories to qualify. The total number of eligible voters was 2,840,000. The necessary minimum for a Knesset seat was thus little more than 23,000 valid votes. Half the lists that obtained enough signatures to qualify therefore stood a reasonable chance of winning enough votes to claim a seat in the next Knesset.

Thus, in addition to Labour and Likud, the two broadly based contenders for national leadership, there were more than 20 single-issue lists standing for anything from the expulsion of the Arab population of the West Bank and Gaza to the drastic reduction of the income tax, the establishment of Orthodox Judaism as the law of the land, the rights of senior citizens, and Israel's recognition of the PLO.[7]

The 1992 elections brought a stunning victory for the Labour party led by Yitzhak Rabin, but it was not enough to give Labour clear sailing in the Knesset. With forty-four seats (seventeen short of a majority), Rabin was forced to seek coalition partners among the smaller parties.[8] We will take a closer look at the makeup of the new Labour-led government and consider Israel's major problems and prospects in the 1990s, including the implications of the historic Israeli-PLO accord, in Chapter 12. The problem of a fragmented electorate has not surfaced in Egypt, where one party continues to dominate the political scene.

Egypt

Modern Egypt's founding father, Gamal Abdel Nasser, created a one-party state in the 1950s. Nasser outlawed the Wafd party, despite its heroic role in the struggle for Egyptian independence. Having survived an assassination attempt by the Muslim Brotherhood in the mid-1950s, he retaliated by breaking up the organization, ignoring its popular appeal (membership was estimated at around two million). He also outlawed the Egyptian Communist party, despite his close ties with the Soviet Union. The **Arab Socialist Union (ASU)** became the sole embodiment of Nasser's will—all opposition was outlawed, disbanded, or driven underground. A populist dictator par excellence, Nasser's subliminal message to the masses was always, "He who is not with *me* is against *you*."

Sadat's "Liberal" Dictatorship   After Nasser's death in 1970, his personalistic one-party dictatorship was continued under President Sadat, with certain cosmetic changes. For example, Sadat abolished the ASU and allowed several new parties to organize. In the meantime, the power elite of the defunct ASU formed the National Democratic Front, headed by Sadat. Many observers found Sadat even more autocratic than Nasser.

In fairness, Sadat took a number of significant steps to broaden human rights in Egypt. According to George Lenczowski:

> Sadat . . . launched a thorough policy of "de-Nasserization" in virtually every field of public policy. In the domestic political process Sadat inaugurated an era of liberalism that contrasted with the police methods used in the last years of Nasser's presidency. Egyptians found travel abroad easier than it had been. Citizens began to move and to express their opinions with much greater freedom. Censorship over the Egyptian press was formally removed, and editorials espousing various points of view began to appear. . . . On his part, President Sadat did not cease to castigate what he called the old centers of power, composed of influential dignitaries in the intelligence and ASU organizations, who, according to him, exercised arbitrary power and were guilty of many abuses.[9]

Despite movement toward pluralism within the ruling party, the Egyptian National Assembly was little more than a debating society and a mere rubber stamp—Sadat's lip service and outward show of respect notwithstanding. This hypocrisy galled many Egyptians, especially the educated. Nasser, they reasoned, made no bones about his authoritarian style, but Sadat pretends to be a democrat. The extensiveness of this cynical view became apparent in October 1981, when Sadat's assassination seemed to cause greater consternation in the West than in Egypt.

Nasser without Nasserism? Egypt under Mubarak   Vice President Hosni Mubarak succeeded Sadat. Under Mubarak, several other political parties have been legalized. In 1984, the first multiparty elections since 1952 were held, with no surprises: Mubarak, running unopposed, was reelected to a full six-year term as president, and the ruling **National Democratic party** won nearly three-fourths of the seats in the National Assembly. The elections appeared to be free and open, but the rule requiring that a party receive at least 8 percent of the popular vote to be awarded any seats in the legislature made it difficult for new parties to make their mark. Only the New Wafd party was able to qualify.

In 1987, four opposition parties contested the Assembly elections. The **New Democratic party** won by a landslide (with 70 percent of the popular vote), but 17 percent of the electorate voted for a coalition consisting of two socialist parties and members of the Muslim Brotherhood (running as independents). The New Wafd party gained ground as well, garnering nearly 11 percent of the vote. A prominent newspaper editor in Cairo proclaimed, "The one-man system is over"—wishful thinking, perhaps, but a sign of changing times.[10]

The Challenge of Islamic Fundamentalism   The rise of **Islamic fundamentalism** challenged Egypt's single-party system for two reasons. First, Nasser had led a secular and nationalist revolution; bent on modernization, he was contemptuous of Islamic law and tradition.[11] Sadat was no less confrontational in dealing with Islamic fanaticism. Thus Egypt was a natural target for groups ranging from the Muslim Brotherhood, which Nasser had crushed, to followers of the Ayatollah Khomeini, who viewed Sadat as a traitor.

Second, Sadat had made peace with the enemy, Israel. This move was risky because it offended both Arab nationalists and Islamic zealots. The group that assassinated Sadat fit both descriptions.

Mubarak's strategy for dealing with Islamic tumult has been subtle:

> By gradually shifting its posture toward the religious opposition from indiscriminate confrontation to selective accommodation, the Mubarak government has . . . isolated and discredited the extremist fringes of the Islamic movement, allowing the state security forces to hunt down and crush remaining pockets of armed resistance. It has [also] allowed the . . . moderate mainstream of the Islamic movement to compete more openly in the political system and in the economy. Several groups that Sadat claimed were trying to tear the country apart have already developed a strong interest in expanding Egypt's multiparty capitalism.[12]

Iran: The Theocratic State

The Shah and the Ayatollah went through the revolving door at the same time but in opposite directions. Khomeini's return in 1979 occasioned a tumultuous national celebration and led directly to the formation of the Islamic Republic of Iran.

Khomeini set about creating a *theocracy*, a government guided by holy men, in Iran's case based on a strict interpretation of the Koran. Islamic law would be the law of the land. Religious leaders would serve in the **Majlis** (parliament) and play an active role in the political life of the nation. The Council of Guardians was created to act as a kind of supreme court, using the Koran, not the constitution, as the ultimate arbiter. Many of Iran's eighty thousand clerics became local political agents of the Islamic Republican party (IRP). Ultimate authority became vested in a "supreme legal guide," the Ayatollah, responsible only to God.

The first years of Khomeini's rule were chaotic. One outrageous incident was the seizure of the U.S. embassy in Tehran in November 1979. Fifty-two Americans were held hostage until January 1981. This unprecedented act made no sense except by the twisted logic of Khomeini's fanatical followers, for whom America was the "Great Satan." To many Iranians, however, the long history of collusion between the United States and the Shah made a *jihad* against America seem right. Nonetheless, it left Iran diplomatically isolated.

Internally, Khomeini launched a reign of terror; thousands of enemies of the Islamic state—intellectuals, former officials, military officers, and political figures—were arrested, tried, and executed. A series of bombings killed some Khomeini confederates, including the newly elected president (Khomeini had dismissed the first president). In retaliation, Khomeini crushed his political opponents.

In the midst of this instability, Iraq had invaded Iran. In one of the bloodiest wars of attrition in modern history, the conflict drained the economies of both countries and caused appalling carnage and suffering. It disrupted oil supply lines and for seven years held the entire region under the threat of a wider war. Suddenly, Khomeini announced that he had decided to accept a cease-fire with Iraq. The regime had painted itself into a corner: it could not continue the war without powerful foreign friends, which it lacked, and it could not quit the war without victory, which it could not achieve. The war and the revolution were thus linked. Some observers believed that the survival of the Islamic Republic depended on who won the war.

When the fighting stopped in 1988, there was no clear winner or loser. Iran had come close to defeating Iraq on several occasions despite being vastly outgunned, but it had dissipated its energies and had sacrificed thousands of its young men in a war that ended in stalemate.

Within a year of the war's end, the Ayatollah died, leaving a bitter legacy. He had inspired the nation to shed the Western influences that in the minds of his followers had eroded the Islamic essence of Iran's proud and ancient culture. But in doing so, he had presided over a pariah state that was identified with terrorism abroad and human rights violations at home.

Nor did Khomeini's successors change Iran's militant image or alter the course of its domestic and foreign policies. Ironically, Iran was one of the few countries that opposed the U.S.-led, UN-sponsored coalition military strike against Iraq following the Iraqi invasion of Kuwait in 1990. This turnabout—involving moral and political support for a leader, Saddam Hussein, who had previously been Iran's archenemy—clearly demonstrated that the Iranian leadership viewed the West as an even greater evil than Saddam. This position also differentiated Iran's leaders from the majority of Arab leaders who denounced Saddam's methods and repudiated his policies.

Iran's success in rebuilding its petroleum industries and armed forces after its prolonged war with Iraq; its refusal to condemn acts of aggression and international terrorism; and its efforts to acquire a nuclear capability have all contributed to a renewed sense of alarm. Although President Clinton continued the Bush administration policy of forcing Iraq to comply with strict UN-imposed directives (such as "no-fly zones" and bans on various kinds of advanced arms technology and materials), the United States and its Western allies came to view Iran as a far greater future threat to peace and stability in the Persian Gulf than a defeated and largely isolated Iraq.

In sum, Mubarak has made concessions both to democracy and to Islam. Although his democratic reforms have been largely symbolic, they uphold the principle of pluralism as embodied in competing parties and free elections with meaningful choices. He continues to fit the model of a quasi-civilian strongman (like Nasser and Sadat, he earned his spurs as a high-ranking military officer). Egypt remains a highly centralized, one-party authoritarian state with a populist president who claims to personify the spirit of the nation. In Nasser's case, the claim was justified; in Sadat's case, it was not. Mubarak probably falls somewhere between the two. He seems to be highly respected and has restored trust in the government, but he has not attained exalted status.

We will defer an evaluation of Egypt's prospects for peace, political stability, and economic development to the next chapter. Suffice it to say that Egyptian government has weathered four turbulent decades nearly intact. Changes that have been made are more in the nature of fine-tuning than restructuring. On the one hand, the survival of the system demonstrates that it has been congruent with Egyptian political culture; on the other, the changes in the nation, the region, and the world since the early 1950s raise the question of how much longer the present system can continue to function.

Saudi Arabia

Saudi Arabia is the richest and most powerful monarchy in the world. Its political and social system remains rigidly traditional, despite the modern architecture of its capital, Riyadh. Saudi Arabia is a paradoxical society where the sight of a Mercedes Benz or the sound of jet fighters overhead is common but the sight of a Saudi woman without a veil or the sound of Western rock music would cause a sensation. Socially and politically, Saudi Arabia has not changed much since ibn-Saud succeeded in reclaiming Saudi territories in the early 1930s (see Chapter 10).

Absolutism and Populism   Ibn-Saud's major aim was to build a durable political order under a traditional monarchy. The basis for the Saudi system was to be the Wahhabi interpretation of Islamic law; there was thus no need for a written constitution. Political parties and any kind of organized dissent or opposition were prohibited.

But ibn-Saud was not the aloof patriarch one might imagine. In fact, he added a democratic touch to his regal duties. Every day he held a *majlis* (public assembly) in Riyadh at which any citizen could express a grievance, ask a favor, or present a petition. His subjects often addressed him by his given name, Abd al-Aziz. Ironically, the Saudi people, in the region's strictest society, had far easier access to their ruler than people in any other country in the Middle East.

Where Kings Reign and Princes Rule   When ibn-Saud died in 1953, he was succeeded by Crown Prince Saud, his eldest son. Saud was ill-suited to rule, and soon the country was on the verge of bankruptcy. The royal circle feared a coup, possibly instigated by radical Arab nationalist regimes in the region (perhaps Egypt or Syria), whose leaders disdained traditional monarchies. The senior princes decided that Saud should step aside in favor of his politically adept younger brother, Faisal. In 1964, Saud abdicated.

Thus the power of the Saudi king is not as absolute as it might appear. Senior princes are regularly consulted on policy matters. Important decisions are apparently made by consensus, but the process is shrouded in secrecy: laws and policies are issued by fiat, and no reasons are ever given publicly (to do so would suggest that royal authority is dependent on popular approval). Archaic as this system might seem to Westerners, it has proved surprisingly durable in a region where political turmoil is the norm.

King Faisal's Reforms   King Faisal (1964–1975) was a forward-looking ruler who modernized Saudi society as far as possible within the confines of strict Islamic culture. For example, Faisal introduced education for girls and drew up the first development plan for the nation. He also played an active and generally constructive role in regional politics, mediating in the Yemen civil war and taking a relatively moderate stance on negotiations with Israel. But it was under Faisal that Saudi Arabia and its partners in OPEC imposed the 1973 oil embargo on the West, demonstrating the Arab world's ability to disrupt the global economy. The embargo frustrated the industrial democracies and caused strains between the United States and its NATO allies (plus Japan), all heavily dependent on Persian Gulf oil. Faisal was more anticommunist than anti-Zionist; he equated communism with revolution, and he did not regard Israel as a threat to the Saudi monarchy. The best evidence of this was his close and cordial relationship with the United States. Faisal was assassinated by a disgruntled member of the royal family in 1975. He was succeeded by Khalid, who abdicated in favor of Faud in 1982.

An Iranian Threat?   Ironically, Islamic radicalism has threatened the Saudi monarchy more than communism or any other secular doctrine. Threats have come from both Sunnis and Shiites. In November 1979, fanatical Sunni Muslims seized the **Great Mosque** in Mecca. Saudi security forces quashed the uprising, but only after a battle that left many dead on both sides. The incident sent shock waves through Riyadh and beyond. Its timing—the Iranian revolution was in full swing, and followers of the Ayatollah Khomeini had seized the American embassy a few weeks earlier—gave reason to suspect that Iran was involved (it was not). The Saudis feared that the Ayatollah was unleashing a tempest in the Middle East. Islamic revivalism was catching fire; it had spilled over from the Shiites to ultra-rightists in the Sunni camp.

The Saudi government responded with a two-pronged policy: more funds were directed to the minority Shiite community in Saudi Arabia, and the Saudis sought accommodation with Iran. This policy worked until the summer of 1987, when Iranian pilgrims to Mecca turned violent. Panic ensued, and blood flowed. Khomeini angrily called for the overthrow of the Saudi monarchy, and the Saudis expelled the Iranian ambassador. But the political regime showed no signs of cracking.

The Midas Touch   One key to the stability of the Saudi system is its wealth. As Monte Palmer points out:

> Saudi Arabia and the oil sheikhdoms are unique. They can pursue a policy of buying political support by distributing the vast wealth derived from their oil reserves. At the present time, there is enough wealth to support both massive royal families in luxury and a reasonable distribution of the state's wealth to the masses. Indeed, a trade-off exists in which the citizens of the state can prosper economically but are denied political rights. Few states, however, can afford this luxury.[13]

In the 1970s, when oil hit a peak of $34 a barrel (it had sold for $3 a barrel before the 1973 embargo), the bonanza benefited the Saudis most of all. They were awash in oil revenues and had more money than they dared to invest in domestic economic development:

> The Saudi leaders are, with some justification, wary of any type of economic growth that would lead to the emergence of labor unions, political parties, and other political manifestations likely to threaten the regime. Accordingly, the Saudi government has pursued a careful policy of gradual growth. Policies of income distribution are favored over industrial capacity. Education is free, and many students are paid for attending school. Health care and housing are also subsidized by the state. In most instances, to be a Saudi citizen is to live well. Limited industrialization has been initiated by the government and operates under strict government supervision. Labor unions, strikes, political parties, a free press, and similar institutions are strictly forbidden. This is not to say that the Saudi elite is opposed to economic growth. It is, however, opposed to economic growth that poses a threat to the political regime. If one or the other must be sacrificed, it will most surely be economic growth.[14]

The outbreak of the war between Iran and Iraq was another windfall for the monarchy. As world oil production plunged, the Saudis took up the slack, raising their output to over ten million barrels a day. The economic boom transformed Saudi society. Gleaming high-rises sprang up; shops were filled with imported goods; oil refineries, petrochemical plants, steel mills, cement works, and related industries sprouted almost overnight in settlements that for centuries had changed very little. And along with industrial development came new schools and hospitals, airports and seaports, roads and power plants.

But the oil boom of the 1970s led to an oil glut in the early 1980s. Saudi Arabia was able to weather this storm far better than oil-producing debtor nations such as Nigeria, Mexico, and Venezuela, but the reversal of fortunes unsettled the Saudis, who were unaccustomed to belt-tightening.

Saudi Arabia's oil wealth is a mixed blessing in another sense. With such a valuable asset and a small population, the Saudis have every reason to be on their guard. Many much larger nations envy Riyadh's riches, as the Iraqi threat to the Saudi oil fields during the Persian Gulf crisis made clear. As a result, Saudi Arabia devotes about one-third of government spending to defense—a financial drain even for the wealthy Saudis. So when menaced by Saddam Hussein in 1990, Riyadh invited U.S. troops to defend the Arabian peninsula. This was a daring move in that the U.S. military presence, while bolstering Saudi defenses, risked undermining the Saudi government by accentuating its vulnerability. Furthermore, when the United Nations mounted the effort to remove the Iraqi invaders from Kuwait, many Arabs were apprehensive about having on their soil military forces from pro-Israeli Western governments, especially the United States. The coalition's surprisingly swift military victory over Iraq in 1991 and the rapid withdrawal of Western forces from Saudi territory laid these considerations to rest, but the sense of precariousness remained.

CONCLUSION

The political systems of the Middle East are authoritarian and range from personalistic military or civilian dictatorships to hereditary monarchies. Most of the monarchies are found on the Arabian peninsula and are blessed with large oil reserves. Jordan and Morocco are two traditional monarchies in the Arab world without the advantage of oil riches. Israel is the only parliamentary democracy in the Middle East, but a two-tiered system has evolved: Jewish citizens enjoy broad civil and political rights that are denied to Palestinian Arabs in the Occupied Territories. Egypt now has the trappings of a Western-style multiparty democracy but retains many of the elements of a civilian dictatorship. Saudi Arabia continues to be ruled by traditional monarchy, the House of Saud. Iran is a notable exception in the Middle East—not only is its population not predominantly Arab, but also its leaders are fundamentalist Shiites (most Arab Muslims are Sunnis), and its government is militantly theocratic. Chapter 12 explores the problems and prospects for the region in general and for Israel, Egypt, and Saudi Arabia in particular. It also considers several "hot spots" that cloud the prospects for peace and stability in the Middle East.

KEY TERMS

Palestine Liberation Organization (PLO)
Knesset
Labour party
Likud party
Arab Socialist Union (ASU)

National Democratic party
New Democratic party
Islamic fundamentalism
Majlis
Great Mosque

STUDY QUESTIONS

1. What forms of government are most prevalent in the Middle East? How have governments typically changed in the past?
2. How is Egypt ruled? Has the Egyptian political system changed much since the overthrow of the monarchy? Since the death of Nasser? If so, what are the significant changes?
3. How is Israel ruled? Is it a theocracy? A democracy? A police state? What are the salient characteristics of Israeli politics? What issues dominate the political scene? Which party or parties control the Knesset and the government? Why?
4. How is Saudi Arabia ruled? What is the basis of legitimacy in the Saudi system? What role does religion play? What threats (internal or external) most concern the rulers?
5. How is Iran ruled? Why was the Ayatollah Khomeini so powerful? How did Khomeini's ideas about Islamic law and ethics shape Iranian politics, and with what consequences? Is Iran changing again now?

SUGGESTED READING

Ansari, Hamied. *Egypt: The Stalled Society.* Binghamton: State University of New York, 1986.

Bakhash, Shaul. *The Reign of the Ayatollahs: Iran and the Islamic Revolution.* Rev. ed. San Bernardino, Calif.: Borgo Press, 1991.

Bianchi, Robert. "Islam and Democracy in Egypt." *Current History,* February 1989.

Chafets, Ze'ev. *Hard Hats and Holy Men: Inside the New Israel.* New York: Morrow, 1987.

Cudsi, A. S., and Dessouki, Ali, eds. *Islam and Power.* Baltimore: Johns Hopkins University Press, 1981.

Dekmejian, R. Hrair. *Islam in Revolution: Fundamentalism in the Arab World.* Syracuse, N.Y.: Syracuse University, 1985.

Fuller, Graham E. "War and Revolution in Iran." *Current History,* February 1989.

Palmer, Monte. *Dilemmas of Political Development.* Itasca, Ill.: Peacock, 1989.

Rubin, Barry. *Modern Dictators: Third World Coup Makers, Strongmen, and Populist Tyrants.* New York: NAL-Dutton, 1988.

Springborg, Robert. *Mubarak's Egypt: Fragmentation of the Political Order.* Boulder, Colo.: Westview Press, 1989.

Yaniv, Avner. "Israel Comes of Age." *Current History,* February 1989.

al-Yassini, Ayman. *Religion and State in the Kingdom of Saudi Arabia.* Boulder, Colo.: Westview Press, 1985.

NOTES

1. Barry Rubin, *Modern Dictators: Third World Coup Makers, Strongmen, and Populist Tyrants* (New York: NAL-Dutton, 1988), p. 201.
2. Ibid., p. 200.

3. Ibid.
4. Ibid., p. 202.
5. Avner Yaniv, "Israel Comes of Age," *Current History,* February 1989, p. 102.
6. Ibid.
7. Ibid.
8. See "Bargaining Time for Rabin," *Newsweek,* July 13, 1992, p. 26.
9. George Lenczowski, *The Middle East in World Affairs* (Ithaca, N.Y.: Cornell University Press, 1980), p. 562.
10. Jane Friedman, "Egyptian Elections Marred by Opposition's Allegations of Fraud," *Christian Science Monitor,* Apr. 7, 1987, p. 13.
11. See Robert Bianchi, "Islam and Democracy in Egypt," *Current History,* February 1989.
12. Ibid., p. 94.
13. Monte Palmer, *Dilemmas of Political Development* (Itasca, Ill.: Peacock, 1989), p. 314.
14. Ibid.

12

Beyond the Arab-Israeli Conflict?

The Middle East is a region of paradoxes. Its sun-baked deserts and withering heat disguise the richest oil reserves in the world. Arab nations share a religion, a language, and a cause (Palestine), yet unity has evaded them. Arab culture is permeated by the strict moral codes of Islam, yet the region's history has been one of conflicts, crusades, and cruelties. Modern Arab nationalism is a reaction against Western capitalism and imperialism, yet Marxism has made few inroads, and Communist parties are outlawed nearly everywhere.

The problems of the region are evident from various statistical indicators of demographic and economic trends and measures of the quality of life (see Table 12.1). The population of the Middle East, 267 million in 1991, was expected to double in twenty-three years thanks to high fertility rates (due to low literacy and poor employment prospects for women) and a sharp drop in the death rate (due to better sanitation and more widely available health care). An important characteristic of the rapidly growing Arab population of the Middle East is its youth: four out of ten people are under age 15. Urban over-crowding is also a potential problem: three-quarters of the region's population already live in cities. Cairo and Tehran teem with thirteen million inhabitants each.

The region has not experienced the economic awakening that occurred in such newly industrialized countries as South Korea and Taiwan (see Table 12.2). Growth rates in most Arab countries have been very slow, especially considering their small economic base. More important, per capita growth rates have actually been negative in many Arab countries, meaning that the population is increasing

Table 12.1 Demographics and Development: Selected Middle Eastern States and South Korea

	Population in 1991 (millions)	Average Annual Growth Rate, 1980–1991 (percent)	Fertility Rate (births per woman)	Life Expectancy at Birth in 1991	Mortality Rate (per thousand live births)	Illiteracy Rate (percent)	Women as Percentage of Labor Force
Egypt	53.1	2.4	3.9	61	98	52	10
Israel	4.9	1.9	2.8	76	12	12*	34
Saudi Arabia	15.4	4.6	7.0	65	77	38	8
Turkey	57.2	2.3	3.4	67	74	19	34
Iran	57.8	3.6	6.2	63	110	46	18
Syria	12.8	3.6	6.5	66	58	36	18
Algeria	25.8	3.0	4.9	66	84	43	10
South Korea	43.2	1.1	1.8	71	20	<5	34

* Among Arabs in the Occupied Territories, rate is 30 percent.

Sources: Data from the World Bank, *The World Bank Atlas* (Washington, D.C.: World International Bank for Reconstruction and Development/The World Bank, 1992). Published by Oxford University Press, Inc., New York; *World Almanac and Book of Facts, 1992* (New York: Pharos Books, 1991).

faster than the economy's ability to support it—a dangerous omen for future prosperity.

The prospects for the region are intertwined with the problems of war and peace, as evident in Lebanon and in the West Bank and the Gaza Strip. It became alarmingly apparent in 1990 when the Iraqi army invaded and occupied Kuwait, precipitating a crisis that engulfed the region in yet another war.

Table 12.2 Economics of Selected Middle Eastern States and South Korea

	Gross National Product (GNP), 1991 (billions of U.S. dollars)	Average Annual GNP Growth Rate, 1980–1991 (percent)	Per Capita GNP, 1991 (U.S. dollars)	Average Annual Per Capita Growth Rate, 1980–1991 (percent)	Share of Gross Domestic Product, 1991 (percent)		
					Agriculture	Exports	Investment
Egypt	33	4.5	610	2.0	18	30	20
Israel	59	3.7	11,330	1.8	6	28	23
Saudi Arabia	105	0.4	7,070*	−4.2	7	46	17
Turkey	103	5.4	1,820	2.9	18	19	22
Iran	127	2.5	2,320	−1.1	21	22	21
Syria	14	1.4	1,110	−2.1	28	27	14
Algeria	52.2	2.1	2,330	−0.8	13	29	31
South Korea	274.5	10.0	6,340	8.8	8	29	39

* 1990.

Source: Data from the World Bank, *The World Bank Atlas* (Washington, D.C.: World International Bank for Reconstruction and Development/The World Bank, 1992). Published by Oxford University Press, Inc., New York.

There is not one "Middle East conflict" but many; the most enduring, however, has been the conflict between Israel and the Arab world. We turn first to this complex and multifaceted problem.

The so-called **Palestinian question** and the apparent breakthrough in Israeli-Palestinian relations in the fall of 1993 receive special attention in this chapter because the future of the Middle East hinges on its solution. We also examine how superpower rivalry contributed to the region's problems and how peace between Israel and Egypt has soothed them somewhat. Finally, we look at Lebanon as a tragic metaphor for the Middle East and the emergence of Iraq as a challenger of the region's status quo.

The Arab-Israeli Conflict

The "**Middle East conflict**" is semantic shorthand referring to the de facto state of war—the permanent crisis—between the Arab nations and Israel. The conflict involves a long series of contentions rooted in the Palestinian dispute. In essence, the problem is that Palestine is now called Israel. Palestinian Arabs lived there before the 1948 war for Israeli independence (see Chapter 10). Most of the Jews who make up the majority of Israel's population are "returned Jews" whose ancestors fled Palestine in ancient times and lost physical contact with the place. The concept of the Promised Land thus became a powerful abstraction, kept alive in the Diaspora by religious symbols and sacred texts that through the centuries have connected Jews everywhere in a community of believers that transcends the boundaries of politics and geography.

For the Arabs who had lived there for at least three thousand years, Palestine was no abstraction. To the Zionists of Europe, it was a homeland, but for the Palestinians, it was *home*. They had been born there; it was family, friends, life. Most of all, it was the piece of earth they possessed—had it not always been so? Most Zionist leaders were Europeans; to the Palestinians, they were interlopers, and Zionism was just another form of imperialism.

Jewish determination to make the abstraction of the Promised Land real was steeled in the 1930s and 1940s; the genocide of the Holocaust made a Jewish homeland not merely desirable but imperative. Jews had tolerated persecution in Europe for centuries, but the atrocity of Hitler's "final solution" made it clear that they would be truly secure only in a land of their own.

These brief comments reveal the deep tragedy of the Palestinian dispute: both sides believe they are fighting for their national survival. For both, it is a life-and-death struggle, and "their leaders have been willing to use any means, including terrorism."[1]

American journalist and author David Lamb has aptly called Palestine "the twice-promised land." His book *The Arabs* sums up the issue succinctly:

> In the midst of the Beirut siege, when Israel was pounding the hell out of the Palestinians, Bill Barret, the Middle East correspondent for the *Dallas Times Herald*, received a telex at the Commodore Hotel from his editor in Texas. The

message, which was in effect a request for a story, read: "Who are these Palestinian people, and why don't they just go home?"

Whether intended or not, there was brilliance in that telex. In twelve words, the editor had cut to the marrow. He had boiled the most complex of Middle East issues into the simplest of terms—land. The Palestinians couldn't go home because they had no home. Their land had been promised by the British after World War I to two peoples, the Jews of Europe and the Arabs of the Middle East. When it came time to fulfill that promise, the former got a state, the latter got dispossessed. And neither has known a day of true peace since.[2]

The Palestinian Arabs

An estimated 5.5 million Palestinian Arabs live in the Middle East. Nearly 700,000 live in Israel proper, and another 1.7 million are in the Israeli-controlled West Bank and Gaza Strip. Thus if Israel were to annex the Occupied Territories outright, it would have an Arab minority of some 2.4 million (compared to roughly 3.5 million Jews). The rest of the Palestinian Arabs live for the most part in neighboring Arab states (see Table 12.3). Some are still in refugee camps dating from the 1948 war.

The Palestinian Arabs are, "as a people, the most literate, industrious and best-educated Arabs in the Middle East."[3] Most Palestinian children attend primary school, and more of them go on to higher education than any other Arab group. Furthermore:

> They are middle class and politically conservative . . . . secular and less conservative than other Arabs. (About 12 percent of the Palestinians are Christian.) They wear Western-style clothes, have only one wife and speak English. They run newspapers in Jordan, banks in Lebanon, the civil service in Kuwait, construction companies in the United Arab Emirates. Within their ranks are poets

Table 12.3   Where the Palestinian Arabs Live

Country or Region	Population (thousands)
Jordan	1,700
West Bank	1,100
Gaza Strip	620
Israel	690
Lebanon	330
Syria	300
Kuwait	100
Other Gulf states	293
United States	150
Other Arab states	102
Other	175
Total	5,560

Source: Institute for Palestine Studies.

in Syria, millionaire traders in Saudi Arabia, insurance brokers in London, importers in Los Angeles and professors at leading universities in the United States and Europe.[4]

In Israel, Arabs face many obstacles and do not enjoy equal opportunities, despite equal rights in theory. David Shipler, *New York Times* bureau chief in Jerusalem from 1979 to 1984, gives a glimpse of this double standard:

> A drive down a country road between a Jewish and an Arab town is a journey between privilege and neglect. In the Arab villages, there are no public swimming pools, no neat parks, and often no sewage systems. The narrow streets are sometimes unpaved, often surfaced poorly, and pitted with potholes. Schools have little science equipment, much scarred and broken furniture, and so many pupils that some classes have to be held in rented rooms. In many areas, the government has confiscated land in such tight rings around the villages, and has barred the issuance of building permits for new houses, that the communities have no place in which to expand. Arabs frequently build without necessary permission, thereby risking their future if authorities should decide to have the illegal houses demolished.[5]

Roots of the *Intifada*

The Palestinian issue was exacerbated when Israel seized the West Bank and Gaza Strip after the 1967 war. This action created a new category of Palestinian Arabs: those living in Israeli-occupied Arab territory. Unlike Arabs within Israel's pre-1967 boundaries, these Palestinians have no legal rights. No consensus has been reached on what to do with the Occupied Territories. The "hawks" insist that Israel must retain control of the West Bank and Gaza for security reasons; the "doves" contend that the lands will ultimately have to be given up as part of a larger Middle East peace plan. The Rabin government that came to power in the summer of 1992 adopted a position midway between the hawks and the doves.

One of the most controversial issues involves the Israeli policy of establishing settlements in the Occupied Territories. In 1967, the Labour government established the first Jewish settlements in the West Bank to defend Israel's new eastern border with Jordan. Between 1976 and 1977, without official approval, the ultra-right **Gush Emunim** ("Bloc of the Faithful") set up a number of settlements. The Begin government (1977–1983) shared Gush Emunim's enthusiasm for "the integrity of the whole Land of Israel," and Ariel Sharon, in charge of the policy, called the settlements "the strongest answer to the establishment of a second Palestinian state" (the first, according to Israel's hawks, being Jordan, with more than one-third of all Palestinian refugees). Begin said that Israel was "creating facts"—meaning that settlements in the Occupied Territories would in effect colonize them. In this way, Israel laid claim to more than half of the West Bank by the mid-1980s, and the number of Jewish settlers had quadrupled from 10,000 at the time of the Camp David Accords (1977) to 42,500. By 1992, following the influx of Soviet Jews, the number had grown to more than 147,000 in the West Bank, Gaza Strip, and Golan Heights, making settlers a potent special-interest group in Israeli politics (see Figures 12.1 and 12.2). The settlers tend to be vehemently opposed to any return of the Occupied Territories, and some even threaten armed resistance if the Israeli army should ever withdraw under a future peace pact.

Terrorism in the West Bank became a daily fact of life. Both Arabs and Jews were victims as well as perpetrators of violence ranging from rock throwing to car bombings to stabbings and shootings. The Israeli army deported Arab suspects and often dynamited their homes. Palestinian Arabs accused of terrorist acts could be detained indefinitely and were tried by military courts without counsel or the right of appeal. Jewish suspects were not prosecuted or were given light sentences.

Censorship was imposed on Arab newspapers in the West Bank, and Arab universities, originally set up under the Israeli occupation, were periodically shut down for disseminating "hostile" or "nationalist" ideas. The situation continued to deteriorate until in December 1987 it erupted in the *intifada,* the Palestinian uprising, first in Gaza and then in the West Bank. Frequent clashes occurred between Israeli security forces and Palestinian youths, armed with little more than sticks and stones:

> For the first time, the Palestinians showed both a willingness to die for their cause and a significant degree of self-restraint. . . . [Israeli] soldiers were

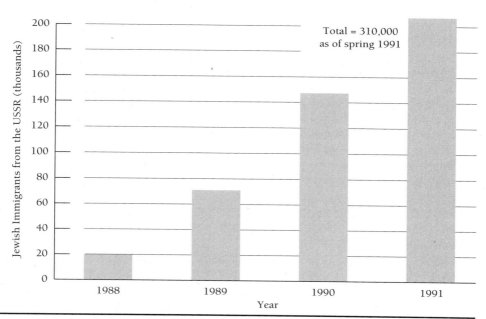

Figure 12.1   Soviet Jewish emigration to Israel, 1988–1991.

Source: Adapted from data presented in Benjamin Cohen, "Israel's Expansion through Emigration," *Middle East Policy,* vol. 1, no. 2 (1992), pp. 120–135.

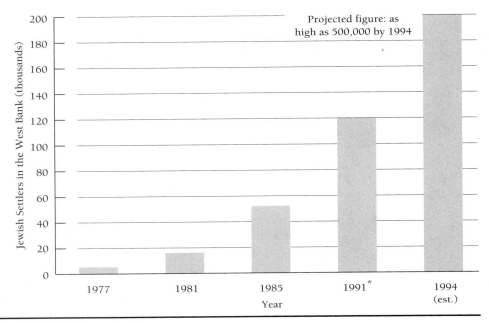

Figure 12.2   Jewish settlers in the West Bank, 1977–1994.

* Excludes 130,000 settlers in annexed East Jerusalem.

Source: Adapted from data presented in Benjamin Cohen, "Israel's Expansion through Emigration," *Middle East Policy,* vol. 1, no. 2 (1992), pp. 120–135.

ordered to avoid fatalities and instead to resort to a tactic of ferocious beatings. When this policy led to a worldwide uproar it was abandoned, and the world press was soon barred from access to the territories. The Israeli emphasis then shifted to a combination of curfews, searches, spot raids, covert penetration of Palestinian groups and unidentified sabotage, economic pressures, [and] the exile and (reportedly) assassination of political leaders by undercover elite troops.[6]

The *intifada* posed a dual threat to Israel. First, it might spark another war with Israel's neighbors. Second, it eroded Israel's support in the United States and Western Europe, where public opinion was becoming increasingly critical of Prime Minister Shamir and his Likud-led government.

It is only fair to mention that hundreds of Arabs have been killed by fellow Arabs in the *intifada.* Whereas Jews who favor immediate peace are free to demonstrate in Israel, Arabs who take that position in the Occupied Territories are frequently killed by their more militant confreres.

In May 1990, a disgruntled Israeli soldier turned a machine gun on some Palestinians at a bus stop, killing seven of them. Prime Minister Shamir called it "a shocking act of madness." Israel's enemies falsely claimed that the gunman was acting on orders from the Shamir government, but all the evidence indicated otherwise. Nonetheless, this tragic incident further inflamed Arab passions.

The Superpower Rivalry

Although conflict is endemic in the Middle East, outside powers—especially the United States and the former Soviet Union—have had a hand in aggravating it. Cold War rivalry between East and West had a negative impact in at least three ways.

First, the superpowers viewed the region as an arena in which to pursue competitive goals. U.S. aims were always to maintain access to Middle East oil for itself and its NATO allies (plus Japan) and to protect oil supply lines. Washington sought stability above all and backed Israel (and moderate Arab regimes) to the point of alienating more conservative Arab states. For its part, the Soviet Union had always viewed Iran and Turkey as within its sphere of influence and jealously guarded its position in the Black Sea area. Protecting its access to the Mediterranean through the Bosporus and Dardanelles straits was also a vital Soviet objective. In the mid-1960s, the Soviet navy acquired a global reach and began to challenge the United States in the Persian Gulf and the Indian Ocean. The Kremlin backed Arab states whose intention was to "drive the Israelis into the sea." To Moscow, Israel was a bastion of American power and influence in the Middle East; to Washington, radical Arab leaders such as Libya's Qaddafi and Syria's Assad were troublemaking sponsors of terrorism.

A second effect of superpower rivalry was the introduction of vast sophisticated arsenals into the region. The United States gave or sold billions of dollars' worth of arms to Israel, Saudi Arabia, Jordan, and Iran (under the Shah) and has supplied Egypt with substantial aid since 1979. The Soviet Union provided weapons and aid to Egypt (until 1973), Syria, Libya, and Algeria, among others; it also supplied weapons to Iraq and to both sides in the Persian Gulf War. Other powers have been involved too: France sent arms to Iraq, and the People's Republic of China sold missiles to Iran. Examples of arms trafficking in the region are easy to come by.

A third negative effect was that superpower politics actually impeded peace negotiations. The Soviet Union insisted on an international peace conference, while the United States backed Israel's position that no such conference could be held until the Arab states recognized Israel's right to secure, defensible borders.

With the collapse of the Soviet Union in December 1991, the situation changed radically. Gone was the superpower jousting that kept regional rivals flush with military and economic aid from Washington and Moscow. With but one world power left—and the increasing effectiveness of broad-based international coalitions under the auspices of the UN—things in the Middle East were certain to change.

The Missing Peace

The 1979 peace treaty between Egypt and Israel was hailed as a major step toward lasting peace in the Middle East. In accordance with the treaty, Egypt recognized Israel, Israel returned the Sinai to Egypt, and the two nations exchanged ambassadors. The United States underwrote the agreement, making generous new commitments of military and economic aid to both signatories. Relations between these former foes have remained cool but correct. One crucial item was missing, however: resolution of the Palestinian issue.

As provided in the treaty, Egypt and Israel began talks in May 1979 aimed at bringing "full autonomy" to the West Bank and Gaza. The intent was to complete arrangements for free elections in the Occupied Territories and to define the powers of a Palestinian "self-governing authority" within a year. But the talks foundered on such issues as security, land, water, Jewish settlements, and Jerusalem. The issue of Jerusalem was the most emotionally charged.* On July 30, 1980, the Knesset declared Jerusalem the undivided capital of Israel, even though the Arabs and the United Nations both consider East Jerusalem occupied Arab territory.

There the matter had rested until September 1993. Little progress was possible on any aspect of the Palestinian question throughout the 1980s. Frustrations built on all sides. One sticking point was the status of the Palestine Liberation Organization (PLO). Israel refused to engage in talks with any Palestinian delegation that included PLO representation, while most Palestinian Arabs continued to look to the PLO for leadership. The Occupied Territories gradually became tinderboxes ready to ignite. The result was the *intifada* that was started in 1987.

In December 1988, the PLO, led by Yasser Arafat, made what purported to be a peace initiative of its own; it renounced terrorism and implicitly recognized Israel's right to exist. In return, the United States established low-level contacts with the PLO. The Israeli government then announced a plan for elections in the Occupied Territories, but Prime Minister Shamir's hard-line pledges about the peace process put the election plan in doubt. Shamir continued to place obstacles in the path of peace talks—Israel would talk only with non-PLO Palestinian leaders, the Arabs in Jerusalem could not take part in proposed West Bank elections, the *intifada* would have to stop before talks could start, and so on. Palestinian leaders were also unyielding: they would accept nothing short of an Israeli withdrawal from the Occupied Territories and a return to the pre-1967 borders (permitting the West Bank and the Gaza Strip to form a new Palestinian state). The Rabin government made overtures in the summer of 1992, promising to stop subsidizing "political" settlements (but not "security" settlements) in the West Bank and Gaza. Whether this new distinction was a sign that Rabin would show greater flexibility in future negotiations or whether the Palestinians would accept this distinction as a valid premise in future peace

---

* During the 1948 war, the Jews asked that Jerusalem be declared an open city in which there would be no combat. The Jordanians disregarded that request; they surrounded a Jewish quarter of the city, inhabited primarily by old people, and cut off all food and water. The UN made no protest, despite the fact that it had already decided to internationalize the city. The Jordanians expelled all Jews from the Old City, destroyed Hadassah Hospital, and shut down the Hebrew University. Jordanian soldiers destroyed synagogues and used Jewish cemeteries as latrines. Jewish worshipers were forbidden to approach the Western Wall, their holiest site for prayer. Thus the emotionality of the issue of Jerusalem went far beyond its historical significance.

talks remained to be seen. The talks that got under way shortly thereafter soon deadlocked—or so it seemed.

A New Dawn? The Israeli-PLO Accord

In September 1993, Prime Minister Yitzhak Rabin of Israel and Yasir Arafat, Chairman of the Palestine Liberation Organization (PLO), stunned the world by signing an historic agreement aimed at resolving the decades-long conflict between Jews and Arabs over the rightful ownership of Palestine. Although Norway had acted as the intermediary for the two sides, the ceremony was held on the lawn of the White House in Washington, D.C. With President Bill Clinton looking on, Rabin and Arafat shook hands after signing the agreement: perhaps the most important handshake—and undoubtedly the most famous—in recent history.

Widely hailed as historic, the accord provided for mutual recognition and limited Palestinian autonomy in the Gaza Strip and the city of Jericho in the West Bank (part of Jordan before the Six-Day War in 1967). Most important, it set a timetable for the two sides to negotiate the details of a plan that would transfer governmental power to Palestinians in Gaza and the West Bank in stages over a five-year period.

Nettlesome questions dampened the mood of the signing ceremony from the start. Would Arafat be able to guarantee a stop to terrorist acts against Israel? According to Thomas Friedman, a Pulitzer prize-winning journalist and expert on the Middle East, "only after the PLO proves it can live with Israelis might it be allowed to live entirely without them."[7]

From 1967 to 1993, Israel controlled all aspects of public life in the occupied territories, "and not simply in military terms, but also in functional ones: from education textbooks, to the number of oranges that a Gaza farmer can export, to taxation, tourism, and even permission to dig for archeological artifacts."[8] Meron Benvenisti, an Israeli historian, explained the apprehensions of many Israelis:

> For us to finally recognize Arafat from the outside is one thing. . . . I can say hello to him on the street. But that is not all. Now he is coming into my house. We are going to share some of the rooms. And he needs space, and that is going to be the difficulty at all levels. Because we are not just talking about physical space. We are talking about everything. It is much more complicated than the peace treaty with Egypt. There, space was being divided. Here it is being shared.[9]

Not surprisingly, the accord was greeted with rejoicing in some quarters and bitter denunciations in others. Opponents on both sides vowed to block progress toward a final Israeli-Palestinian settlement. On the Palestinian side there were public threats to assassinate Arafat. Hamas, a radical Islamic group which rivals the PLO for popular support in the occupied territories, vowed to intensify its struggle for Palestinian national rights. This struggle had taken a heavy death toll by the fall of 1993—more than 1,900 Palestinians and 146 Israelis. It was clear that unless the *intifada* could be abruptly halted, the Israeli-PLO accord would have little chance of succeeding. Even among moderate Palestinians, there was a fear that Arafat's gambit might open the door for other Arab governments to normalize relations with Israel and leave the Palestinians empty-handed.

On the Israeli side, the leader of the conservative Likud faction, Benjamin Netanyahu, declared that the PLO did not want peace and promised that a Likud government would abrogate the treaty. Thus, formidable obstacles to a lasting peace in the Middle East remain.

These obstacles, however, in no way diminish the bright prospects that are likely to follow if the gamble both sides have taken does succeed. For Israel, there is now the possibility of a future without war clouds on the horizon—something Israeli citizens have never known. Beyond the psychological benefits of peace, Israel stands to gain a great deal economically if it can break out of the isolation it has endured under a longstanding Arab boycott. Even the possibility of a Middle East common market, with Israel and its Arab neighbors as equal partners, cannot be ruled out. Finally, military, political, and economic realignments could result. If Syria and Jordan make peace with Israel, it is *possible* that a powerful and well-financed coalition of moderate Arab states plus Israel might (with U.S. backing) pursue a regional containment policy against Iran, Iraq, and Libya.

For the Palestinians, the potential benefits are also great. First, there is the prospect of regaining a homeland. Second, massive infusions of economic aid from abroad can be expected. Third, Palestinians in the occupied territories will gain new political rights. Fourth, the PLO has gained international legitimacy and can now represent the Palestinian cause in a way that it could not do before the signing of the accord.

Will the obstacles to peace prove to be greater than the incentives for peace? If recent Middle East history is any guide, it would be prudent to expect setbacks. Even so, the steps already taken suggest the winds of change that buffeted Eastern Europe in 1989 were blowing across the Middle East in 1993.

A New Israel?

Israel has come far since 1948. It has not only survived among hostile neighbors but has also won several wars and, as a result, now has more secure and defensible borders. The peace treaty with Egypt greatly reduced the threat of a two-front war, and it seems unlikely that other Arab states would attack without Egypt's involvement. But in the Middle East, crisis is chronic—in the Occupied Territories, in southern Lebanon, and in the minds of Arab leaders in Libya, Syria, Iraq, and the PLO. The 1982 invasion of Lebanon haunted many Israelis who had never doubted the moral basis of Israel's foreign policy or its justification for military action. A seige mentality—resulting from five wars in four decades, the *intifada,* and the constant threat of terrorism—hangs heavily in the air. In Israel, there is no peace.

Nor is there prosperity. After twenty-five years of impressive achievements, Israel's economy began to sputter during the **OPEC oil embargo** in 1973. Israel's small size and limited natural resources make it vulnerable to economic pressures and reprisals. After the embargo, which led to worldwide recession and inflation, Israeli GNP growth rates dropped to zero (from an average of 9 percent a year between 1950 and 1976—comparable to rates in Japan, South Korea, and Taiwan). Inflation and trade deficits plagued Israel in the 1980s, reflecting an increased dependency on foreign oil after returning the Sinai wells to Egypt, rising defense spending, and deregulation of the economy after 1977.

The Specter of Hyperinflation

Between 1980 and 1984, inflation ran over 100 percent annually. In 1985, it skyrocketed to 800 percent and forced the national unity government, then headed by Shimon Peres, to declare a three-month state of emergency. Peres ordered an 18.8 percent devaluation of the shekel, a temporary wage-price freeze, a $360 million cut in subsidies, a 3 percent pay cut for civil servants, and increased income taxes (already the highest in the world). Thousands of government workers were cut from the public payroll (previous Labour governments had created a huge bureaucracy that employed two out of three Israelis).

Inflation forced the government to keep the shekel artificially high, and exports suffered. The economy bounced back in 1987, but economic growth was halved the following year. Belt-tightening continued through the late 1980s, and everyday life was a struggle for most Israelis. It was difficult to make ends meet, there was little time for relaxation, and the nation was sullen and polarized. People sensed that economic prosperity was slipping away, maybe forever. With this new pessimism came a brain drain as talented young people left Israel for opportunities abroad. And if young people were leaving, would Jews from other nations want to come to Israel? Or would they, like so many Soviet Jews, choose to go to the United States instead?

The Arab Boycott and Other Burdens

A widespread Arab boycott of companies that do business with Israel has also hurt the Israeli economy. It has led large multinational corporations wishing to trade with the oil-rich Arab states to avoid Israel. In recent years, the boycott has weakened, but it still constrains Israeli economic progress.

The largest budgetary drains on Israel are defense, immigration costs, the bureaucracy, and, until recently, financing settlements in the Occupied Territories. In the early 1990s, Israel's economic growth rate was higher than that in the United States, but unemployment remained high because of the great influx of immigrants. As a welfare state (social programs equal one-third of GNP each year) with high defense outlays (about one-fourth of the budget), Israel operates on a deficit. This is alleviated by four sources of funds: donations from abroad (especially Jews in the United States), reparations from Germany for World War II, foreign aid (mainly from the United States), and borrowing from foreign banks. In the mid-1980s, Israel's foreign debt reached $24 billion, equal to the nation's GNP, and interest totaled $4 billion.

Sources of Vitality

In the bigger Middle East picture, Israel is economically more advanced than most Arab states that have greater natural resources. In agriculture, Israel has "made the desert bloom" through sophisticated technology and by diverting water from the Jordan River. More than half its farmland is irrigated, and the nation has nearly achieved food self-sufficiency. Israeli kibbutzim (communes) also deserve some credit for this impressive agricultural record. But agriculture represents only about 6 percent of GNP and cannot ensure prosperity by itself.

Israel's manufacturing sector is mostly small-scale, except for its aircraft industry. The cabinet scuttled a major jet fighter project in 1987 by a one-vote margin. Cancellation meant the loss of several hundred jobs, but it was argued that expanding such industries as electronics and microprocessing would create new jobs and ease unemployment.

In the eyes of some observers, Israeli society showed clear signs of dramatic and far-reaching changes in the early 1990s. First, despite its myriad problems, Israel is undergoing a transformation from "a spartan, socialist, isolated and highly militarized country into a modern consumer society suffused by Western secular culture."[10] Israelis are now more affluent, consumer-conscious, and individualistic and less willing to make personal sacrifices in the name of national security or the general good. Israel has thus come of age as a consumer society.

Second, the end of the Cold War brought a diplomatic windfall, even before the 1993 agreement with the PLO, and gave Israel "a place in the world it never enjoyed before."[11] In a period of four years, thirty-five countries, including Russia and China, recognized Israel. In the last half of the 1980s, its foreign trade nearly doubled, and travel abroad by Israelis rose 66 percent between 1985 and 1992.

Third, the lines of communication with the outside world suddenly opened for "once-insular communal Israel." As Jackson Diehl notes, "In 1967, there was no television in the country. Today, almost all Israeli homes have television sets and 60 percent have access to 40 channels of cable offering news and programming from across Europe, the United States and the Middle East."[12]

Finally, about 400,000 immigrants from the former Soviet Union had settled in Israel by mid-1992. These new arrivals account for about 10 percent of Israel's population and reinforce the larger society's tendencies toward secularization, economic modernization, and individual values. In the early 1990s, polls consistently found that huge majorities of Israelis wanted the peace process to go forward and favored major reforms in the fragmented political system and state-dominated economy.

A Fresh Start? The 1992 Elections

In the summer of 1992, Yitzhak Rabin's Labour party won control of the Knesset but failed to win a majority of seats. Forced to seek coalition partners to form a government Rabin's stragegy was to strike a balance between right and left. He thus brought into the coalition the dovish Meretz party and the hawkish Tsomet party. At the top of Rabin's agenda was the issue of settlements and settlers. As noted earlier, Rabin said he would favor only "security" settlements in the future, not "political" ones. But the distinction was unclear. According to one estimate, 60 percent of the West Bank and Gaza, as well as all of Arab East Jerusalem (home to 140,000 Jews), would fall within Rabin's definition of "security." Even Rabin's promise to stop new settlements was greeted less than enthusiastically by Palestinian leaders: What was to become of the 16,500 housing units under construction at the time?

Several other major issues were connected with the security question. One was defensible borders. Rabin declared that "Tel Aviv must be defended from the Jordan Valley and not from Emmanuel," a West Bank settlement. Another issue was the Palestinians. Reconciliation between Jews and Arabs continues to hinge on the disposition of the Occupied Territories, but Rabin will be constrained both by the opposition Likud party and by the right-wing faction in his own coalition.

A third issue was U.S. loan guarantees. The Bush administration had held back $10 billion in loan guarantees in 1991 and 1992 to pressure Israel into taking a more conciliatory approach to negotiations with the Palestinians.

A fourth issue involved ultra-Orthodox Jews. Rabin said he would examine whether to continue the policy of allowing thousands of students at Jewish parochial schools to be exempted from army duty; two ultra-Orthodox parties were adamantly opposed to any change in this practice, while some other small parties insisted that it must be changed.

One issue over which there has been little dissent until recently is immigration. The inflow of immigrants slowed by nearly 70 percent after 1991 due primarily to the failure of Israel's state-controlled socialist economy to provide new jobs. High unemployment, close to 12 percent in mid-1992, makes it difficult for Israel to absorb new immigrants, but limiting immigration is out of the question under the Law of Return.

Clearly, the end of the Cold War has hastened change in Israeli society. Although external threats remain, internal economic and social issues now overshadow the security question. The results of the 1992 elections confirmed that most Israelis want peace and prosperity but no longer believed that either could be achieved so long as Israel remains in a state of war with Arabs (including

Palestinians). The Rabin government's decision in 1993 to make peace with the PLO must be seen against this backdrop.

Egypt: Subsidized Stability

Egypt's economy remains precarious. Agriculture is the most important sector, accounting for 30 percent of national income, but arable land is limited, and population growth (averaging 2.4 percent a year during the 1980s) tends to cancel out any gains. Cotton and sugar cane are the main crops. Increases in output in the 1980s were accomplished through better irrigation thanks to the High Aswan Dam, expansion of land devoted to cash crops, and improved planting methods. But the dam has not boosted the economy as much as Egyptians had hoped. The goal was to offset population growth and achieve a measure of food self-sufficiency by reclaiming vast tracts of desert with the abundant waters of the Nile. However, costs have been much higher than expected, and a prolonged drought has imperiled Egypt's water supply. In 1987, Lake Nasser reached its lowest level, and there was not enough water to run the Aswan power station, which supplies 20 percent of Egypt's energy.

Trade, Aid, and Investment

Egypt has sizable reserves of oil and natural gas, and new oil discoveries have been made in the Western Desert and the Gulf of Suez. The nation also earns foreign currency from Suez Canal tolls and user fees, tourism, and remittances from roughly four million Egyptians working abroad (especially in Saudi Arabia and other Persian Gulf states). U.S. foreign aid—billions of dollars annually—has helped a great deal.

President Mubarak's government has sought to reduce dependency on imported goods by encouraging expansion of manufacturing, especially of consumer goods. Incentives include tax exemptions and refunds of customs duties on imported machinery. Foreign investors have shown interest in setting up assembly plants in Egypt to take advantage of the abundant labor supply.

The 1979 peace treaty with Israel has been a mixed blessing for Egypt. Other Arab nations ostracized Cairo for a decade, and the treaty caused political tremors inside Egypt as well, culminating in the assassination of President Sadat. From an economic standpoint, however, the treaty has paid off. It has brought billions in U.S. aid and has created cordial relations with the West, which encourages tourism. (The pyramids are among the world's most famous attractions.) Finally, the treaty has diminished the risk for foreign investors, who fear political instability.

Subsidies and Social Stability

Public subsidies are a way of life in Egypt. For example, the government pays high prices to producers of food staples and keeps consumer prices low. That makes both groups happy, but it diverts resources into consumption rather than investment. Similarly, Egypt built a massive bureaucracy under Nasser and Sadat to create jobs for educated youths who otherwise had few career opportunities. The government pursues such policies for at least two reasons. First, as previously noted, Nasserism was and is a socialist philosophy that blends populism and nationalism. Second, subsidies and jobs mollify the people despite lagging economic development. They are a kind of bribe to encourage each side to overlook the other's shortcomings.

President Mubarak is making an effort to get the economy moving, to wean Egyptians from their addiction to subsidies, and to create real jobs by starting new industries. In November 1986, he fired his entire cabinet and assembled a new team of highly qualified technocrats. Egyptian business leaders and foreign investors had confidence in the new cabinet. Egypt's outlook remains neither bright nor bleak. There are signs of progress and reasons for optimism. But prosperity will come slowly, if at all.

The Middle East Tinderbox

As a crossroads between Europe and Asia, the Middle East has long had great strategic importance. After World War II, the region became the focus of intense East-West rivalry due to its huge oil reserves, essential to the industrial economies of Western Europe, Japan, and the United States.

But the Middle East is also home to some of the world's most volatile societies, militaristic states, and reactionary governments. Lebanon is an example of a volatile society, Iraq under Saddam Hussein stands out as a militaristic state, and Iran's theocratic form of government is among the most reactionary in modern history. All three societies have been flashpoints in the recent past and could destabilize the region in various ways in the future.

Lebanon

Lebanon is a once-lovely little country on the Mediterranean Sea. Its narrow coastal plain contains Beirut, the capital, just a few miles east of which rises the rugged Lebanon mountain range. Beyond lies the fertile Bekaa Valley, where most of the country's wheat is grown. Farther east, a second range of snow-capped mountains separates Lebanon from Syria.

Origins of Modern Lebanon   The Lebanon Mountains, nucleus of the modern Lebanese state, have been a natural buffer against frequent invaders en route to some other object of imperial conquest. If Lebanon's misfortune was that it happened to be on the way to other places, its main advantage was its seaports, which gave Syria, Jordan, and other inland areas access to Europe via the Mediterranean.

Lebanon's origins as a nation-state can be traced to the sixteenth century. The Ottoman Turks, who conquered most of the Near East at that time, left the

Lebanon Mountain region in the hands of powerful local **Maronite Christian** and **Druze** families that built the modern state. Both Maronite dominance and the fragmented nature of Lebanese society date from this early period.

The Lebanese Mosaic   Thus Lebanon has always been a social and political mosaic. Its religions include twenty-one Christian and five Islamic sects; Maronite Christians, Druze, and Sunni and Shiite Muslims are the most prominent. Equally diverse is the feudal social system in which families and clans form intricate networks. Each is headed by a *zaim* ("boss"). Zaims had private armies, and family feuds were often violent. Social rivalries were reinforced by religious animosities.

A particularly bitter rivalry developed between Maronites and Druze, and in 1860, a bloody civil war broke out between them. The British and French intervened after the Druze massacred twelve thousand Christians and drove another hundred thousand from their homes in a single month. After World War I, Lebanon was made a French mandate. Maronite leaders persuaded France to create a separate Lebanese state in 1920 (rather than combining Lebanon and Syria, as France had originally intended). The borders of the nation that emerged extended far beyond the Lebanon Mountains, thereby setting the stage for Lebanon's current predicament, for it included large populations of Sunni and Shiite Muslims.

The National Pact   Lebanon emerged from World War II an independent but disunified nation. The political system was based on a preexisting constitution that favored the Maronites. An unwritten rule ensured that the president would always be a Maronite. More important, in 1943, Maronite and Sunni leaders had formed the **National Pact**, whereby the Christians foreswore alliances with nations outside the region and the Muslims agreed not to seek a merger with the Arab world. It was further agreed that the six-to-five ratio of Christian to Muslim representatives in the legislature would extend to all public offices. (Historically, Christians have outnumbered Muslims in Lebanon, but the Muslim communities have grown faster in the postwar years due to an influx of refugees and higher birthrates.)

Lebanese society is thus a loose confederation of religious communities and patron-client networks. But except for a civil-war "dress rehearsal" in 1958, these groups coexisted in relative peace in a political system that always teetered on the brink of anarchy, undergirded by a bargain struck during World War II and sealed with a handshake—the National Pact was never even put in writing.

Perhaps one reason why this precarious arrangement worked as well and as long as it did was that economic prosperity gave everyone a stake in political stability. Per capita incomes rose steadily between 1950 and 1974; petroleum-poor Lebanon compared favorably in this regard with some of the oil-producing Arab nations. Its flourishing economy was a monument to free enterprise. Basic social and even financial services were provided by extended families rather than by the state. Fortunes were made in real estate and construction. Millions of tourists flocked to Lebanon, attracted by its mild climate, scenic mountains, and sandy beaches. Foreign banks and corporations set up Middle East headquarters in Lebanon because of its location, educated labor force, absence of government regulation, and communications and transportation links. Most of all, they were attracted to Lebanon because it was an island of stability in a sea of turmoil.

The Civil War   The illusion of tranquillity was shattered in 1975, when a ferocious civil war broke out—sparked, ironically, by the presence of a non-Lebanese group, the Palestinians. Many Palestinian war refugees had fled to Lebanon after 1948 and were absorbed into Lebanese society, working in such fields as business, banking, journalism, and higher education. But a second wave of Palestinian refugees, arriving after the 1967 war, ended up in refugee camps. They were stateless, without a homeland; lacking passports, they could not go anywhere else.

When the PLO was expelled from Jordan in the early 1970s, it moved its headquarters to Beirut, and the refugee camps in Lebanon became PLO strongholds. Then the PLO began launching raids against Israel from southern Lebanon, and Israel retaliated. Step by step, Lebanon was drawn into the Middle East conflict. Tensions between Christians and Muslims exploded into civil war after a bus filled with Palestinians was attacked by a group connected to the militant Maronite Phalange party.

The civil war brought to the surface the many conflicting interests and aspirations that had been contained for thirty years by the National Pact. Maronites wanted to rid Lebanon of Palestinians; Sunni Muslims wanted full equality with Christians; Shiite Muslims and Druze wanted a larger voice in government.

A cease-fire was arranged in 1976, and the Arab League asked Syria to enforce it. Syria had always had a special interest in Lebanon, which is vital to its trade and communications with the outside world. Israel also had a special interest in Lebanon, particularly after the PLO began launching attacks from the south of the country. Israel responded by seizing control of the area.

Thus what had begun as a civil war sparked by the presence of Palestinians as the result of the larger Middle East conflict soon developed into a multifaceted confrontation directly involving Syria and Israel and indirectly entangling the other Arab nations, the superpowers, and ultimately United Nations peacekeepers. But no force could keep the peace in a jigsaw country that had fallen apart. Feuding Lebanese factions fought relentlessly, and blood flowed. Some 300,000 Lebanese fled to northern cities from the Israeli-occupied south, and cosmopolitan Beirut became an urban battleground.

The Israeli Invasion   By 1982, the continuing turmoil had become intolerable, and Israel decided to force the issue. In June, the Israeli army invaded Lebanon, surrounded Beirut, and drove the PLO guerrillas out of Lebanon. Maronite Christians and Shiite Muslims in south Lebanon hailed the PLO exodus but chafed under the Israeli presence. Furthermore, many PLO guerrillas slipped back into the country or established new camps under Syrian protection in the Bekaa Valley. Israel's control of Beirut gave the Phalange an excuse to take revenge against Palestinians, who were defenseless without the PLO. In September 1983, Phalangists entered two refugee camps in West Beirut and massacred hundreds of people, mostly women and children, in cold blood. The incident outraged public opinion and sent shock waves through Israel's government, whose apparent complicity stunned the world. Shortly thereafter, Prime Minister Begin resigned.

Even after the Israeli invasion, Lebanon remained fractured by fratricidal warfare. Different parts of the country and of Beirut were controlled by different factions. Syria ruled the Bekaa Valley, and Israel held southern Lebanon. Phalange leader Bashir Gemayel was elected to head a "government of national reconciliation" that in reality lacked both legitimacy or authority, never had national scope, and could not hope to effect reconciliation. Gemayel's reputation for ruthlessness had earned him a raft of enemies, and before he could be sworn in, he was assassinated by a bomb that destroyed Phalange headquarters. Parliament then elected his older brother, Amin Gemayel. Israeli troops left Lebanon in June 1985 but retained a "security zone" in the south to guard against future attacks.

Ironically, Israel's invasion of Lebanon may have paved the way for Iran's inroads there:

> The effects of the Iranian Revolution combined with the aftermath of the Camp David Accords and Egyptian-Israeli peace treaty to give rise to an unprecedented alliance between Syria and Iran. Iran's new access to Lebanon through Syria effectively shortened the distance between Iran and Lebanon. The alliance also diminished Syria's resentment over Iranian influence in Lebanon, especially after the Israeli invasion. The invasion, which was prompted in part by the Iranian Revolution, provided a unique opportunity for the Khomeini ideological crusade against the "twin evils" of America and Israel. . . .
>
> The invasion presented an extraordinary opportunity for the Iranian revolutionaries to try to export their Islamic revolution to Lebanon. The ideological appeal of the Khomeini regime could have found no more fertile soil in which to flourish than in the sense of victimhood festering among the [Shiite] masses in Lebanon.[13]

Middle East Metaphor   Lebanon has become a metaphor for the Middle East. It has been immersed in violence—assassinations, vendettas, bombings, and reprisals—ever since the civil war. Foreign intervention has only exacerbated and complicated an already impossible situation. Besides old rivalries between Christian Phalangists and Sunni Muslims, new ones have arisen, like that between Shiite Muslims and the PLO. Radical Shiite groups such as **Amal**, **Hezbollah**, and **Islamic Jihad**—some linked to Iran—have carried out kidnappings and other acts of violence, while cease-fires and endless conferences have led nowhere.

Israel's departure from Lebanon left Syria in the unenviable position of being "an external power, enjoying partial hegemony and struggling with the tasks of keeping public order, effecting political reform, reconciling the diverse interests of its allies and . . . advancing its own interests."[14] Syrian attempts to end the deadlock proved fruitless. In February 1987, Syria sent seven thousand soldiers to Beirut in another effort to bring safety and stability to the battle-scarred city.

As soon as the Iran-Iraq War ended, President Saddam Hussein's thoughts turned to revenge against other enemies, including Syria. Lebanon had become a convenient, all-purpose battlefield for the pursuit of regional rivalries:

> Beyond an intensification of the propaganda warfare, Iraq's determination to penalize Syria has already been translated into actual policies in Lebanon. Iraq provided Syria's main Lebanese adversary, the Lebanese Forces, with new weapons and financial aid with a view to encouraging the Maronite militia to stand up to Syrian pressure. . . . Iraq intends to return to the Lebanese arena from which it was practically absent during the last eight years [during the Iran-Iraq War].[15]

Lebanon is thus a cauldron in which the region's many rivalries and hatreds boil. Here is a short list of ingredients: Syria versus the PLO; Christian Phalange versus Sunni Muslims; Syria versus Israel; Israel versus the PLO; Syria versus the pro-Iranian Hezbollah (Shiite Muslims); and Lebanese Forces (Christians) versus Syria. In this stew, the Lebanese Forces have at times cooperated with the PLO and Hezbollah against Syria's Assad, whom many Maronites now view as the main threat to Lebanon's independence as well as their own privileged position.[16]

In September 1988, Amin Gemayel stepped down as president, and political stalemate prevented the Lebanese parliament from choosing a successor. Two prime ministers, a Maronite and a Sunni, were eventually named, but no president. General Michel Aoun, commander of the Christian army, claimed to be the head of the legitimate government, but the Sunni prime minister set up a rival government. Syria imposed a land blockade on Aoun's forces in March 1989, and four months later, it added a sea blockade, charging that Iraq had given Aoun Soviet-made missiles.

A new president was finally elected toward the end of 1989, but was assassinated in a car-bomb explosion in November of that same year. The subsequent election of Elias Hrawi as president failed to stabilize the situation. Indeed, at the beginning of the 1990s Lebanon was locked in "a permanent though low-profile conflict involving Lebanese, Syrians, Iranians, Palestinians, Israelis, and United Nations forces."[17]

Lebanon remains nominally independent but faces serious questions about how long the fiction of a Lebanese government can survive. As far back as 1966, an American scholar had a premonition about the country: "Lebanon is too conspicuous and successful an example of political democracy and economic liberalism to be tolerated in a region that has turned its back on both systems."[18] Indeed, all the conflicts of the Middle East have converged on this once idyllic oasis.

Iraq

Historically known as **Mesopotamia** ("the land between the rivers"), Iraq is situated in the Tigris-Euphrates valley. Rich in oil reserves but lacking easy access to strategic waterways, Iraq is an almost entirely landlocked country larger than California. The population of around 21 million is largely Muslim. Shiite Muslims comprise a slight majority, but the ruling Baath party, under the iron-fisted control of President Saddam Hussein since 1979, is Sunni-dominated. (The Shiites predominate in neighboring Iran.) Women constitute only 25 percent of the paid labor force and 30 percent of the professionals in education and health care but nearly half of all agricultural workers. The number of women delegates to the National Assembly rose from fourteen to eighty in 1984 (32 percent). Women in Iraq have equal rights in divorce, land ownership, and suffrage, reflecting a liberal interpretation of Islamic law.

The 1958 Coup   Iraq was a traditional monarchy until 1958, when the king was overthrown and murdered in a military coup. The coup makers set up the Revolutionary Command Council (RCC), a military dictatorship. For two decades, Iraq was ruled by the military, using the **Baath Socialist party** as a fig leaf of legitimacy. Several subsequent coups changed the faces but not the character of Iraq's political leadership. Force, not law, ruled; intrigue and murder were rampant. Occasional elections were held, but they were carefully stage-managed: no candidates could run on party tickets, and Baath candidates always won solid majorities. Moreover, only Baath was allowed to operate within the military and security apparatus.

At its founding, Baath rejected Western values and influence, stressing ideological themes that sounded Marxist (socialism, anti-imperialism, anticapitalism), with an Arab twist; it naturally gravitated toward the Soviet Union. In 1967, Baghdad broke diplomatic relations with Washington following the Six-Day War in which Israel soundly defeated Egypt and occupied the Sinai, the West Bank, the Gaza Strip, and the Golan Heights.

The Ascent of Saddam Hussein   The RCC gave Iraqi Communists a minor role in the government until Saddam Hussein assumed dictatorial powers in 1979. Thereafter, Saddam waged war against all real and imagined internal opposition, including Communists, Kurds, and Shiites. Iraq invaded Iran's Khuzistan province in 1980, repudiating a "reconciliation" treaty signed in 1975 and igniting a war that lasted for eight years. The Iran-Iraq War proved enormously costly in lives and treasure for both sides. Before this conflict, the Iraqi government had been engaged in an internal war against the Kurds; Iran's policy of aiding the Kurdish rebellion in Iraq was one reason for Saddam's decision to invade Khuzistan. Another reason was Iraq's desire to gain control of the lower Tigris and Euphrates waterway, the Shatt-al-Arab, which formed its border with Iran to the Persian Gulf. After fighting to a stalemate, the war was called off in 1988, although a formal peace pact was not signed until two years later.

The Invasion of Kuwait   In August 1990, Saddam Hussein ordered his army into Kuwait, catching Iraq's neighbors and the rest of the world by surprise. Tactically, the invasion was brilliant: in mere hours, Iraq seized control of the country and forced the emir to flee. In one fell swoop, Saddam grabbed an extremely valuable parcel of the Middle East, enlarging the considerable oil reserves already under his control and serving notice that Iraq had arrived as a great power in the region.

For years, Saddam Hussein had been reputed to entertain nuclear and expansionist ambitions. That was one reason why Israel had bombed Iraq's nuclear reactor near Baghdad in 1981—a humiliation that Saddam and many of his Arab admirers would never forget. For eight years, Iraq fought fiercely against Iran, using chemical weapons and ballistic missiles. By 1990, Baghdad boasted a million-man army equipped with thousands of Soviet-supplied tanks and missiles captured from Iran. The military takeover of Kuwait was thus the culmination of a drive for hegemony that had been under way for many years.

The forced annexation of Kuwait was a shock, but the greater danger was that Saddam's real aim was to take the Saudi oil fields. To deter such a move, the United States sent a massive force to the Persian Gulf—the largest U.S. military deployment since the Vietnam War. But the United States was not alone in condemning Iraq. Voting for a total embargo against Iraq, the United Nations Security Council expressed the consensus of the international community that Baghdad's aggression against Kuwait could not go unpunished. Despite the involvement of the international community, it was above all the military might of the United States that confronted Iraq. In no small measure, the future of the Middle East—the regional balance of power—hinged on the outcome of this confrontation.

When Saddam refused to withdraw his forces by January 15, 1991, the deadline set by the Security Council, a U.S.-led international coalition launched a fierce air offensive followed by a land invasion deep into Iraq. By the end of February, Kuwait City had been liberated, and Iraq's much-feared armed forces had been vanquished. What is more, the nation's economy had been demolished: airports, military installations, laboratories, warehouses, power plants, communications systems, bridges, roads, and virtually everything related to Iraq's warmaking capacity was destroyed or badly damaged.

Saddam Is Still a Threat?   Despite the humiliating defeat, Saddam remained in power. Both the Kurds in the north and the Shiites in the south rebelled against the central government, but Saddam suppressed these uprisings—with the tacit consent of the outside world. The dismemberment of Iraq, it was feared, would destabilize the notoriously volatile region. Moreover, Iraq's neighbors—Syria, Iran, and Turkey—also had Kurdish minorities. If the Kurds succeeded in creating a rump Kurdish state, how long would it be before a new Kurdistan government would seek to extend its control over adjacent lands inhabited by kin? And in the south, a breakaway Shiite enclave might threaten the domestic tranquillity of Saudi Arabia, a strategic pillar supporting Western interests in the Persian Gulf.

Although it was never a publicly stated objective, the coalition partners made no secret of the fact that they wanted Saddam out of the picture. For his part, Saddam tried to resist the UN's harsh peace terms, which included extensive inspections of Iraq's research facilities.

Iran

Although Iraq was the common enemy at the beginning of the decade, the threat from Iran did not go away. Saddam unintentionally did his archrivals in Tehran a favor by diverting attention from Iran's attempts to reassert its role as a major force in the Persian Gulf.

After the Ayatollah   The turmoil of the Islamic Republic's first decade obscured the fact that Iran's prerevolutionary political institutions were left largely intact. New parallel structures such as the Council of Guardians and the Revolutionary Guard were simply grafted onto the old system. As time passed, the Majlis came to play an increasingly prominent role, and the 1985 presidential election, albeit not the free-for-all such elections often are in the West, was nonetheless contested by opposition candidates. (Even so, a former prime minister who spoke out against the war with Iraq was not allowed to run.) Ali Khaminei was elected to a second term in 1985, and four years later he was named to succeed the Ayatollah Khomeini as Iran's supreme leader.

Ten years of revolution and war had made a shambles of the Iranian economy. The war with Iraq had cost an estimated $250 million a month. Unemployment had more than doubled, inflation had risen steadily, and the national budget was strained beyond its limits. Agriculture was disrupted by the revolutionary upheaval, but a more settled political environment and a bumper crop in 1985 cut food imports sharply. Besides saving $500 million in foreign-exchange outlays, this greatly improved the nation's self-sufficiency.

The war's damage to Iran's economy resulted mostly from reduced oil sales. The United States and its NATO allies boycotted Iranian oil during the hostage crisis, and some of Iran's other customers refused to pay the steep prices set by the new government ($37 a barrel, compared with $17 a year earlier). Iran's best customer, Japan, sought alternative supplies. Worst of all, Iraq bombed Iranian oil fields, refineries, and ports, crippling Iran's oil infrastructure and cutting its export capacity by one-third.

Iran Resurgent?   Through the turbulent 1980s, the Islamic Republic somehow managed to stay afloat and even to keep some oil flowing. Toward the end of the decade, Iran began to break out of its diplomatic isolation as well, signing natural-gas agreements with the Soviet Union, for example. Shortly after Khomeini's death on June 4, 1989, Hashemi Rafsanjani, the Majlis speaker, even suggested that the United States should help in freeing Iranian hostages held in Lebanon, implying that Iran might be willing to reciprocate.

The passing of Khomeini permitted less strident voices to emerge, and pragmatists like Rafsanjani and Khaminei soon prevailed over the radicals. According to one observer, "Ideology will surely remain a factor in Islamic Iran's foreign policy . . . [but] Iran's pressing economic and social ills demand that its international environment be 'normalized,' a fact working against the most xenophobic of the remaining radicals."[19]

A comparison between Iran under Khomeini and the People's Republic of China under Mao Zedong is tempting. China enjoyed its greatest economic successes after the passing of Mao, who was indispensable in overthrowing the old order but disastrous as the architect of a new one. The same might be said of Khomeini. If the new leaders can set the Islamic Republic on a steady, pragmatic course, Iran has a bright future. The nation has great natural resources and an energetic people. The task now is to channel those assets to achieve national reconstruction and international reconciliation.

CONCLUSION

There is not one Middle East conflict but many. Similarly, the Arab-Israeli conflict is multifaceted. Throughout the 1980s, war ravaged Iran and Iraq, and there have been sporadic tensions or confrontations between Syria and Iraq, Egypt and Libya, Libya and Tunisia, Morocco and Algeria, and others. In 1992, most of the Arab states joined a U.S.-led coalition in a war against a fellow Arab state, Iraq, after the Iraqi army invaded Kuwait. All this strife has been a financial drain on virtually all the countries in the region. The oil-rich states of the Persian Gulf can afford to spend large sums on defense, but many Arab states, including Egypt, can divert funds to military adventures only by neglecting pressing domestic needs. Israeli society has also felt the stresses and strains of heavy defense expenditures. Yet the Middle East is not the only region where war and revolution have destabilized governments, torn the social fabric, and savaged economies. In Part V, we will see that Asia has also endured great violence in the past century.

KEY TERMS

Palestinian question	National Pact
Middle East Conflict	Amal
Gush Emunim	Hezbullah
Intifada	Islamic Jihad
OPEC oil embargo	Mesopotamia
Maronite Christians	Baath Socialist party
Druze	

STUDY QUESTIONS

1. In what sense is the Middle East a region of paradoxes?
2. What are historical sources and contemporary manifestations of Arab-Israeli enmity? Why has peace between these two groups been so elusive?
3. What was the *intifada?* How did it start, and why?
4. What do Palestinians want? What do Israelis want? Who is right, and who is wrong, in your opinion?
5. How and why did Egypt and Israel sign a peace treaty in the late 1970s, what were the terms of the treaty, and where do relations between these two former foes stand at present? Will Egypt and Israel continue to live in peace? (Analyze the situation from the standpoint of both countries.)
6. Is Israel an economic success or not? Is it better off, about the same, or worse off than it was twenty-five years ago? What are its most pressing economic and social problems now?
7. Is Egypt's economy still developing, or has it stalled? What are Egypt's major obstacles?
8. In what sense is Lebanon a metaphor for the Middle East? Can Lebanon be saved, or is it too late? (Give reasons for your opinion.)

SUGGESTED READING

Farah, Tawfic E. *Pan-Arabism and Arab Nationalism: The Continuing Debate.* Boulder, Colo.: Westview Press, 1987.

Luciani, Giacomo, and Salambe, Ghassan, eds. *The Politics of Arab Integration* London: Croom-Helm, 1988.

Quandt, William B., ed. *The Middle East: Ten Years after Camp David.* Washington, D.C.: Brookings Institution, 1988.

Smith, Charles D. *Palestine and the Arab-Israeli Conflict.* 2nd ed. New York: St. Martin's Press, 1991.

Yehoshafat, Harkabi. *Israel's Fateful Hour.* New York: Harper, 1988.

NOTES

1. David Lamb, *The Arabs: Journeys beyond the Mirage* (New York: Random House, 1988), p. 200.
2. Ibid., p. 199.
3. Ibid., p. 201.
4. Ibid.
5. David Shipler, *Arab and Jew: Wounded Spirits in a Promised Land* (New York: Viking Penguin, 1987), pp. 443–444.
6. Avner Yanev, "Israel Comes of Age," *Current History,* February 1989, p. 101.
7. Thomas L. Friedman, "Dividing a Homeland," *New York Times,* Sept. 15, 1993, p. 1.
8. Ibid.

9. Ibid.

10. Jackson Diehl, "New Mall in Israel Gives Better Clues than Old Politics," *International Herald Tribune,* June 9, 1992, p. 1.

11. Ibid.

12. Ibid.

13. R. K. Ramazani, *Revolutionary Iran* (Baltimore: Johns Hopkins University Press, 1986), p. 175.

14. Itamar Rabinovich, "Syria and Lebanon in 1988," *Current History,* February 1989, p. 80.

15. Ibid., pp. 77–78.

16. Ibid., p. 103.

17. Itamar Rabinovich, "Paralysis in Lebanon," *Current History,* February 1990, p. 73.

18. Charles Issawi, "Economic Development and Political Liberalism in Lebanon," in *Politics in Lebanon,* Leonard Binder, ed. (New York: Wiley, 1966), pp. 80–81.

19. W. Scott Harrop, "Iran's Foreign Policy Realists Take Charge," *Christian Science Monitor,* June 21, 1989, p. 19.

PART V

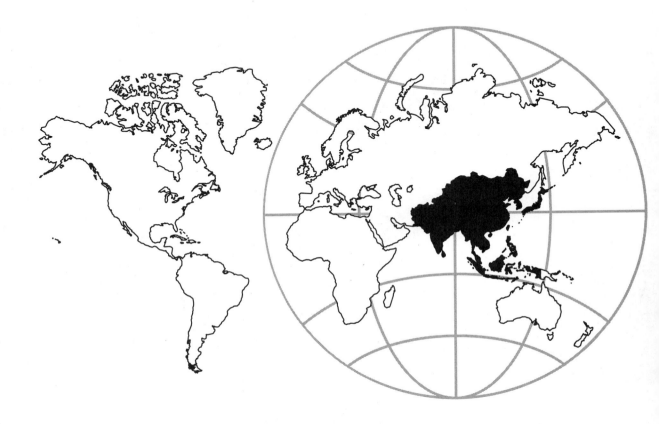

Asia

CHINA

Area: 3,691,521 square miles
Population: 1.1 billion
Density per square mile: 298
Languages: Chinese (Mandarin, Cantonese, local dialects)
Literacy rate: 73%
Religions: Confucianism, Buddhism, Taoism, Islam
Monetary unit: yuan
GNP: (1991) $424 billion; $370 per capita

JAPAN

Area: 145,856 square miles
Population: 124 million
Density per square mile: 850
Languages: Japanese
Literacy rate: 99%
Religions: Buddhism, Shintoism
Monetary unit: yen
GNP: (1991) $3.3 trillion; $26,920 per capita

INDIA

Area: 1,266,595 square miles
Population: 865 million
Density per square mile: 683
Languages: Hindi (official), English (official associate)
Literacy rate: 48%
Religions: Hindu (83%), Islam (11%), Christianity (3%)
Monetary unit: rupee
GNP: (1991) $284.7 billion; $330 per capita

13

Civilizations and Empires

Think of Asia as a sleeping giant. First of all, it is immense—it accounts for 30 percent of the earth's landmass and is home to 60 percent of the earth's inhabitants. But it is demographics rather than geography that makes Asia a colossus. Wealth in the world is grossly maldistributed, most of it concentrated outside of Asia. But several nations, led by Japan, are in the process of redressing the global economic balance in Asia's favor. According to some prognosticators, the giant is awakening. The twenty-first century may well belong to Asia.

Of the six regions explored in this book, Asia is the most difficult to treat as a unit because of its diversity. Geographically, the Asian continent extends from the Mediterranean Sea and the Ural Mountains in the west to the Pacific Ocean in the east. Thus it encompasses most of the countries of the Middle East (see Part IV) and more than half of the former republics of the Soviet Union (see Part III). In the remainder of Asia, on the basis of history, geography, culture, and language, we can identify five overlapping subregions: **East Asia** (primarily mainland China), **South Asia** (India, Afghanistan, Pakistan, Bangladesh, and Sri Lanka), **Northeast Asia** (the two Koreas, northern China, and the Russian Far East), **Southeast Asia** (Vietnam, Laos, Cambodia, Thailand, Burma, Malaysia, and Indonesia), and the **Pacific Rim** (Japan, Taiwan, and the Philippines, plus the South Pacific island regions of Polynesia, Micronesia, and Melanesia).

These nations range in size from mainland China and India, with a combined population of nearly two billion (about 40 percent of all people in the world) to tiny Brunei, with a population of 240,000.

Although these disparate nations defy easy generalization, certain patterns are distinctive to Asia or large parts of it. First, until the middle of the twentieth

337

century, no nation in Asia had experienced democratic rule. None had any indigenous democratic or republican institutions. There was no tradition of "natural rights." Authoritarianism, in most cases dynastic, was the basis of all politics.

The archetypal Asian political system was that of Imperial China, long described by Western historians as **oriental despotism** and generally thought to be a pattern repeated, with local variations, throughout Asia. In reality, there were any number of oriental despotisms, just as there were a variety of African and European despotisms. Nevertheless, it is true that China, Korea, Japan, Vietnam, Cambodia, and India all had hereditary autocratic rulers who governed through centralized administrative systems embedded in hierarchical societies. Moreover, these rulers were the products of advanced civilizations with complex writing systems, scholars and scribes, monumental architecture and public works (especially roads and irrigation systems), and impressive religious and philosophical traditions.

To survey Asian politics, we will feature three countries, selected on the basis of their size and importance and on their representativeness of regional patterns. We must of course take account of China, known today as the People's Republic of China (PRC). China's large and industrious population, technological ingenuity, cultural prowess, and imposing geopolitical traits have long thrust it onto Asia's center stage. Japan, democratically governed and economically ascendant, is Asia's greatest success story in the post–World War II period. It is tempting to view Japan as an exception to the trends and patterns of political and economic development in the rest of Asia. Until recently, Japan seemed economically and politically to belong more to the West than to the East. Indeed, the **Trilateral Commission**, a private foreign-policy interest group founded by David Rockefeller in 1973, consists of representatives from the United States, the European Community, and Japan. But today, Japan is no longer an isolated example of Western technology in an Asian setting: South Korea, Taiwan, Hong Kong, and Singapore have become important producers of high-tech exports, and even mainland China has begun moving toward an export-oriented model of development.

Finally, India, the second most populous nation in the world, is the dominant power in South Asia. Though newly in possession of nuclear weapons, India faces daunting problems related to overpopulation, regional and communal strife, vulnerability to natural catastrophe, pervasive poverty, uneven growth, and excessive regulation of the economy.

Physical Environment and Population

Stereotypes of Asia often revolve around size and scale—teeming masses of people and vast deserts, mountain ranges, rivers, and jungles. These images are part imagination and part truth. In area and population, Asia *is* gigantic. It is nearly twice the size of North America, the second-largest continent. And as noted, three-fifths of all people on earth live in Asia (two-thirds of them in China and India).

Environment

Because of its huge size, Asia has climates of every kind, from the frozen tundra of Siberia to the steamy jungles of Indochina and the tropical lowlands of Indonesia. In between lie temperate zones, which encompass northern China, Korea, Japan, and Taiwan; a massive desert in western China and the semiarid plains of Central Asia; the high plateaus and snowy, craggy wilderness of Tibet, Bhutan, and Nepal; and the huge subcontinent of South Asia, with the Great Indian Desert in the northwest and the semitropical Deccan peninsula in the south.

The topography, too, offers great variety—forbidding mountain ranges, fertile river valleys, coastal lowlands, and flowing plains. Much of Asia's deep interior is inhabited either sparsely or not at all. In fact, Asia supports well over half of the world's people, but much of the surface area is mountain, desert, or jungle terrain that makes human habitation difficult. For example, mainland China has more than one-fifth of the world's population, yet two-thirds of its territory is uninhabitable.

We might expect an abundance of natural resources in so large and diverse a territory, but Asia is not particularly well endowed in this respect. Only mainland China, Indonesia, and Brunei produce oil, in modest amounts. (Indonesia's reserves are estimated at about 9 billion barrels, about one-third of Venezuela's reserves and a small fraction of Saudi Arabia's.) Japan, the richest nation in Asia, imports all of its petroleum. Malaysia produces 35 percent of the world's tin and rubber, and Indonesia also exports various raw materials. In general, however, no Asian nation has extraordinary mineral resources.

Human beings are Asia's most abundant resource. Japan has proved that human resources are more vital to economic growth and development than natural resources. Although burgeoning population has been a liability for many Asian nations, South Korea, Taiwan, Hong Kong, Singapore, and the PRC have harnessed their human potential and made impressive economic gains. By contrast, India and Indonesia have failed to do so, and nations like Bangladesh, Burma, Vietnam, Laos, and Cambodia remain among the most economically stagnant in the world.

Population

Extraordinary efforts to control the population explosion in the People's Republic of China brought the rate of increase down to 0.8 percent a year by the mid-1980s, though it has risen since. In India, however, such efforts have been desultory, and the annual growth rate there remains 2.1 percent (see Table 13.1). Other populous Asian nations also face demographic pressures, especially Indonesia (1.8 percent), Bangladesh (2.3 percent), Vietnam (2.5 percent), Malaysia (2.6 percent), and Pakistan (3.1 percent). The most highly developed Asian nations have the lowest population growth rates: Japan (0.5 percent), followed by South Korea (1.1 percent). Fertility rates (births per woman) also range widely, from 1.6 in Japan to 5.7 in Pakistan.

Overall, the fastest-growing population in the world is in Africa, not Asia. (Kenya's natural rate of increase in 1989 was a staggering 4.1 percent.) But the population *base* is so large in Asia that even moderate growth will keep the trendlines climbing rapidly well into the twenty-first century. Statistical projections for Asia are truly alarming. The region's population in 1990 was estimated at 3.057 billion (the last two decimal digits alone represent a population larger than that of France or Great Britain), and during the 1990s, the population will grow by about 486 million, to 3.543 billion. By 2020, Asia's population is projected to reach 4.466 billion—equivalent to the population of the whole world in 1980.

We will explore the disparities in economic development and income distribution in Asia in Chapter 15; here we are interested mainly in the links between population dynamics and development. Japan, one of the wealthiest countries in the world, continues to be in a class by itself in Asia; South Korea, Taiwan, Hong Kong, and Singapore have followed in Japan's footsteps. Communist China has experienced an "economic miracle" since the late 1970s. A few other countries, including India, Malaysia, and Thailand, have made significant gains. The rest lag behind; indeed, Bangladesh and Burma are among the poorest countries in the world. The close interrelationship between demographic factors and eco-

Table 13.1 Demographic Facts for Selected Asian States

	Population, 1991 (millions)	Annual Growth Rate, 1980–1991 (percent)	Fertility Rate (births per woman)
Bangladesh	108.8	2.3	4.4
China	1,150.1	1.5	2.4
India	865.0	2.1	3.8
Indonesia	181.4	1.8	3.0
Japan	124.0	0.5	1.6
Malaysia	18.3	2.6	3.7
Pakistan	115.6	3.1	5.7
Singapore	3.0	2.1	1.9
South Korea	43.2	1.1	1.8
Thailand	56.7	1.8	2.4

Source: Data from the World Bank, *The World Bank Atlas* (Washington, D.C.: World International Bank for Reconstruction and Development/The World Bank, 1992). Published by Oxford University Press, Inc., New York.

nomic development is suggested by stark differences in key quality-of-life indicators (see Table 13.2).

These figures indicate the dimensions of the challenge Asia faces. Even Japan, with its booming economy, has a demographic quality-of-life problem related to **overdevelopment**: its population is stable, but 124 million Japanese are now living in a country smaller than California. In the late 1980s, fully 35 percent of Japan's population lived on 1 percent of the land. The Tokyo-Yokohama metropolitan area had a population of more than 25 million in the mid-1980s; the Osaka-Kobe-Kyoto area, 13.6 million. If projections hold, Tokyo-Yokohama will reach 30 million and Osaka-Kobe-Kyoto 20 million by the year 2000. The prospect of social unrest, political instability, and a deteriorating quality of life looms large unless Japan can find ways to soften the socioeconomic impact of this urban population growth.

Economic Development: The Three Faces of Asia

Levels of economic development vary widely from one part of Asia to the next (see Table 13.3). Japan has one of the most highly developed economies in the world. On the basis of gross national product (GNP), only the United States ranks above Japan. In qualitative terms, Japan's dynamic high-tech multinational corporations, its strong currency, its thriving financial institutions, its huge trade surpluses, and its status as a major creditor nation all make it an economic superpower.

Table 13.2 Development Profile of Selected Asian States

	Life Expectancy at Birth, 1991 (years)	Mortality Rate (per thousand live births)	Illiteracy Rate (percent)	Female Labor Force (percentage of total)
Bangladesh	52	148	65	7
China	70	33	27	43
India	59	115	52	25
Indonesia	62	78	23	31
Japan	79	6	<5	38
Malaysia	70	19	22	35
Pakistan	56	146	65	13
Singapore	75	8	<5	32
South Korea	71	20	<5	34
Thailand	66	31	7	44

Source: Data from the World Bank, *The World Bank Atlas* (Washington, D.C.: World International Bank for Reconstruction and Development/The World Bank, 1992). Published by Oxford University Press, Inc., New York.

Table 13.3 Indicators of Economic Dynamism for Selected Asian States, 1991

	Percentage of Gross Domestic Product		
	Agriculture	Exports	Investment
Bangladesh	35	9	12
China	27	20	36
India	32	9	21
Indonesia	19	27	35
Japan	3	11	33
Malaysia	20*	81	36
Pakistan	26	16	18
Singapore	0	185	37
South Korea	8	29	39
Thailand	12	38	39

* The range for Malaysia is 10 to 19 percent in the north and 20 to 29 percent in the south.

Source: Data from the World Bank, *The World Bank Atlas* (Washington, D.C.: World International Bank for Reconstruction and Development/The World Bank, 1992). Published by Oxford University Press, Inc., New York.

Following in Japan's footsteps were Asia's "four little dragons"—South Korea, Taiwan, Hong Kong, and Singapore. They have adopted strategies patterned on the Japanese model: accelerated industrialization, export promotion, and heavy protectionism. All four nations, like Japan, are now mass-consumption societies and exporters of high-tech manufactures as well as other, more traditional goods. Besides exporting motor vehicles and electronic equipment, Japan has become a major international financial market. South Korea also exports cars, and both South Korea and Taiwan produce many other consumer products that compete directly with Japanese exports. By the early 1990s, South Korea's per capita income had climbed above $6,300, Singapore's stood at $12,890, and Japan's soared to $26,920 (see Table 13.4).

Elsewhere in Asia, countries undertaking basic economic development (road building, mining, steelmaking, electric power generation, and so on) have all they can do to keep pace with population growth. The poorest Asian nations have abysmal annual per capita income levels: in Bangladesh, it is only $220; in Cambodia, Vietnam, and Burma, even lower.

Economic statistics do not necessarily give an accurate picture of conditions. For example, Sri Lanka and the Indian state of Kerala have a low per capita GNP by Western standards, and the number of people living in poverty is still rising, but other indicators—infant mortality, life expectancy, literacy, nutrition, and employment—have shown significant gains.[1] These may be more meaningful measures of development than financially based Western standards.

Some experts argue that the greatest need in poverty-stricken developing countries is for more and better jobs. How, they ask, can overpopulated, under-

Table 13.4 Economic Profile of Selected Asian States

	Gross National Product (GNP), 1991 (millions of U.S. dollars)	GNP Growth Rate, 1980–1991 (percent)	Per Capita GNP, 1991 (U.S. dollars)	Annual Per Capita Growth Rates, 1980–1991 (percent)
Bangladesh	23,449	4.2	220	1.9
China	424,012	9.4	370	7.8
India	284,668	5.5	330	3.3
Indonesia	111,409	5.8	610	3.9
Japan	3,337,191	4.3	26,920	3.7
Malaysia	45,787	5.6	2,490	2.9
Pakistan	46,725	6.5	400	3.2
Singapore	39,249	7.1	12,890	4.9
South Korea	274,464	10.0	6,340	8.8
Thailand	89,548	7.8	1,580	5.9

Source: Data from the World Bank, *The World Bank Atlas* (Washington, D.C.: World International Bank for Reconstruction and Development/The World Bank, 1992). Published by Oxford University Press, Inc., New York.

capitalized nations advance unless they can put their most abundant resource, their people, to work? And how can they create good jobs without capital and without markets, both domestic and foreign? Finally, how can they afford to produce for domestic consumption unless people have incomes that let them translate needs into demand? A large population creates the *potential* for demand-driven economic growth, but only if the majority of people have purchasing power.

Thus from the standpoint of political economy, Asia presents three faces to the world: one is affluent and technologically sophisticated, another is impoverished and tradition-bound, and a third is in transition.

Historical and Cultural Patterns

Asia provided the setting for several ancient civilizations. For millennia, empires flourished in China, India, and Indochina. An urban civilization with an as yet undeciphered writing system evolved in the Indus valley and may have been ruled as a single empire between 3000 and 2500 B.C. It had geometric cities with underground sewers and huge granaries. Bronze was used, and graphic arts were highly developed. This early civilization was overrun by Aryan invaders from the north around 1750 B.C. The latter spoke an Indo-European language from which the modern languages of Pakistan, North India, and Bangladesh descend. An Aryan civilization spread from the west as far as the Ganges valley by 500 B.C.

Regarding the dissemination of culture, Asia is to some extent analogous to Europe. Just as the cultures of Western Europe were in many cases heavily influenced by the Greek and Roman civilizations, many of the cultures of Asia were influenced by the Chinese and Indian civilizations. And just as Russia was insulated by physical, cultural, and linguistic barriers from European intellectual and spiritual movements (such as the Renaissance and the Reformation), India was cut off from Chinese influence by the world's highest mountain range, the Himalayas.

China's cultural and political influence explains some of the similarities among Asian nations. For example, the imprint of the Chinese writing system is clearly evident in the written languages of Vietnam, Korea, and Japan. **Confucianism** (an ethical system emphasizing the family and respect for authority) spread well beyond the borders of Imperial China. The Chinese system of centralized administration was imitated by Japan, Korea, and the Vietnamese kingdom in Indochina which gradually displaced the great Khmer Empire (600–1300). Indeed, China dominated the Vietnamese culturally and politically for a thousand years.

The religions of Asia also show cultural influences. India was the cradle of a number of religions, including two of Asia's three great religious traditions, Buddhism and Hinduism. Buddhism spread from India to China and from there to Japan. It also found its way to Southeast Asia. Hinduism spread across India to Sri Lanka, Malaysia, and Indonesia. Islam, the continent's third great religion, is prevalent in much of South and Southeast Asia; in fact, more of the world's Muslims live in Afghanistan, Pakistan, India, Bangladesh, Malaysia, and Indonesia than in the Middle East.

Cultural grandeur is common throughout Asia. In every part of the region, magnificent shrines, temples, palaces, and gardens bear witness to the greatness of bygone ages. These architectural remnants are reminders that many Asian societies have a history of economic prosperity and political stability.

The past reveals striking political patterns. First, **empire-building** has been a dominant motif throughout Asia for well over 2,000 years. Early examples include the Asoka Empire in India (250 B.C.), followed by the great Mogul Empire. In China, the Han Empire prospered around 200 B.C.—the first of many dynastic empires that dominated East and Southeast Asia until the second half of the nineteenth century. In Indochina, the Khmer Empire (1000–1250) controlled vast territories and built the monumental Angkor Wat temple center (1113–1150). Japan was first united under the House of Yamato sometime between the second and fourth centuries A.D. From the late sixteenth century until the Meiji Restoration (1868), Japan was ruled as one nation by the Tokugawa shogunate. In World War II, the Japanese attempted to establish an Asian empire that would have included Korea, China, Taiwan, Vietnam, Laos, Cambodia, Malaysia, Indonesia, and the Philippines. Imperialism is thus a major motif in Asian history.

Second, Asia's indigenous political institutions and traditions are rooted in **dynastic authoritarianism**. Its characteristics include the concentration of power in a single potentate who claims to rule by divine authority. In Japan, the emperor was worshiped as a god; in China, autocrats ruled with the Mandate of Heaven; the Khmer rulers were Hindu god-kings; and the Mogul emperors of India based their legitimacy on the teachings of Islam. Dynastic rule is an integral element in this pattern, and the great empires of Asia were assembled and administered by royal families. Power was passed from one male heir to the next (in the absence of a male heir, empresses did occasionally ascend to the throne). This pattern of rule varied somewhat from place to place and from time to time. For example, in China, a merit-based civil service system was established, and in Japan, administrative positions were reserved for the feudal nobility.

Labor regimentation for large-scale construction projects was another characteristic of dynastic authoritarianism. The flood control and irrigation systems of China and Vietnam, the ancient Angkor Wat temple center in Cambodia, and the famous Taj Mahal in India are examples of the use of conscript labor to build on a grand scale. Centralized administration for political control, law enforcement, and tax collection was also typical of Asian autocracy. For example, during the eighteenth century, the golden age of the Qing (Manchu) dynasty, a cadre of only twenty thousand civil servants governed a population of 300 million. (At lower levels, officials depended on the cooperation of local landowners and on the greed of nonofficial functionaries to get things done.) Finally, advanced methods of food production, epitomized by the Chinese system of permanent agriculture, allowed Asia to sustain relatively large populations in premodern times.

None of these characteristics—religion-based authoritarianism, centralized administration, labor regimentation, and advanced agriculture—was unique to Asia. Yet the pattern of highly centralized authoritarian rule reinforced by effective administrative control radiating to the periphery of the political system made it possible to mobilize peasants for massive public-works projects. This pattern was typical of Asian rule until recent times; it was even used, with some modifications, by the Maoist regime in mainland China until the mid-1970s.

A third facet of Asia's traditional political culture is the prevalence of **patron-client relations**. Such sociopolitical arrangements are informal, affective (based on friendship or familiarity), and particularistic (excluding all but kinfolk or members of some in-group) rather than formal, cognitive, and universalistic. In other words, Asian society has traditionally preferred personal relationships based on mutual trust and loyalty over organizational ties based on abstract values. The natural setting for patron-client relations is the village, whereas the city is the natural setting for impersonal, formalistic ties such as political parties, civic associations, and trade unions.

Higher levels of economic development are generally associated with greater urbanization, and vice versa. Thus we might expect patron-client networks to be eroded by the social changes that accompany modernization. The case of Japan, however, casts doubt on this proposition. As we shall see in Chapter 14, the Japanese have assimilated traditional patterns of patron-client relations into the democratic process, resulting in a distinctive "patron-client democracy."[2] They have managed to combine Western form with Japanese substance.

Finally, **colonialism** and **neocolonialism** directly affected nearly every Asian nation. (*Neocolonialism* refers to the economic domination and alleged exploitation of former colonies by industrially developed nations such as the United States, France, and Great Britain.) Historically, Asian colonization of other Asians antedated the arrival of European powers in the region. In the nineteenth century, Europe established its dominance throughout much of Asia. India was among the first nations to be colonized; China was the last (and even then incompletely). Japan escaped domination by a European power. It did so by adapting to the Western challenge. As already noted, Japan's genius was to absorb Western technology and imitate Western institutions while keeping the essence of its own culture intact.

The British colonized present-day India, Pakistan, Sri Lanka, Burma, Singapore, Malaysia, and Hong Kong. The Dutch colonized Indonesia, and the Portuguese, Goa, Timor, and Macao. The French colonized present-day Vietnam, Cambodia, and Laos. (Thailand was never colonized; Korea was controlled first by China and then by Japan.)

The effects of colonization are still debated. Some scholars stress the benefits that it brought to the colonies; others maintain that the burdens far outweighed any benefits. One school argues that the cumulative effects of colonialism have been to impede economic development in the Third World by creating a deleterious dependency:

> Dependency theorists point out that during the nineteenth-century industrialization of the West, there were no already developed nations whose economic power could effectively control or manipulate the paths of development. . . . Japan, the one Asian nation that successfully industrialized in the late nineteenth century, did so by first fighting off Western imperialism and by prohibiting foreign investment from coming into Japan; in current jargon, it "delinked" itself from the world capitalist system in order to independently develop its economy from internal sources and under leadership of a native entrepreneurial class. Only then did Japan join the European powers in imperialist exploitation of China and Southeast Asia.[3]

Other observers argue the opposite—that the nations of Africa and Asia that have developed most rapidly did so by absorbing Western capital and technology, developing export-oriented industries, and aggressively entering overseas markets. In this view, nations that responded to colonialism by withdrawing into a protectionist shell and pursuing a strategy of economic self-reliance fared the worst.

Asians do not wax nostalgic about colonial days. Regardless of the effects on economic development, the political effect of colonialism was to impose a degrading foreign dominance on proud, once relatively independent and even powerful nations.

Decolonization also left an indelible imprint. The nations and governments of the Asian subcontinent took form in the struggle to emerge from European domination. For example, after the British left, India and Pakistan separated along religious lines. Pakistan originally consisted of two ethnically and linguistically dissimilar territories on opposite sides of India, separated by nearly one thousand miles. When East Pakistan demanded autonomy in 1970, West Pakistan refused. There ensued a bloody war in which India—West Pakistan's archrival—became deeply involved. East Pakistan ultimately won independence as the new nation of Bangladesh, but the Indo-Pakistani conflict, an unintended consequence of the way in which the subcontinent was decolonized, smolders even today.

Bangladesh was not the first breakaway nation in Asia. In 1965, Singapore quit the newly formed Confederation of Malaysia (which united the former British colonies of Malaya, Sarawak, and Sabah, or North Borneo). Admirably, Singapore's independence was achieved without bloodshed. More recently, several groups in India have sought unsuccessfully to secede, at considerable cost in human lives.

The political division of Indochina was another legacy of decolonization. The French did not leave Vietnam gracefully. Communist leader Ho Chi Minh led the nation in a war for independence that ended with the French defeat at Dien Bien Phu in 1954. At the Geneva Peace Conference later that year, Vietnam was divided temporarily into North and South, with the understanding that national elections would occur within two years. The Western powers reneged on the agreement when it became obvious that Ho Chi Minh and his Communist party would win. The resulting civil war escalated into an international conflict that raged on for two decades. It finally ended in 1975, with North Vietnam unifying the nation militarily and colonizing Laos and Cambodia as well.

Clearly, colonialism and decolonization have left scars in Asia, especially in the subcontinent and Indochina. Decolonization accentuated the artificiality of cultural and ethnic bonds in most Asian nation-states, and conflicts inevitably followed independence. Since 1945, wars have pitted Indians against Pakistanis, North Koreans against South Koreans, Vietnamese against Cambodians, and Chinese against Russians, Vietnamese, and Indians. To some extent, these wars can be attributed to actions taken (or not taken) by Western powers during the hasty decolonization process. Politically and psychologically, the colonial experience will continue to affect Asian politics for years to come.

In sum, a survey of Asian history reveals a tradition of empire-building; a pattern of centralized, bureaucratic, authoritarian rule; an intricate web of patron-client ties; and a struggle to overcome the detrimental effects of colonialism, decolonization, and neocolonialism. None of these elements by itself is uniquely Asian. The combination of the four, however, has produced a distinctive Asian political culture. Furthermore, despite the cyclical rhythms of Asian social and political history, most of Asia has exhibited extraordinary resilience and continuity from ancient times to the present; as we shall see, parts of Asia, led by Japan, have also shown remarkable adaptability in the modern era.

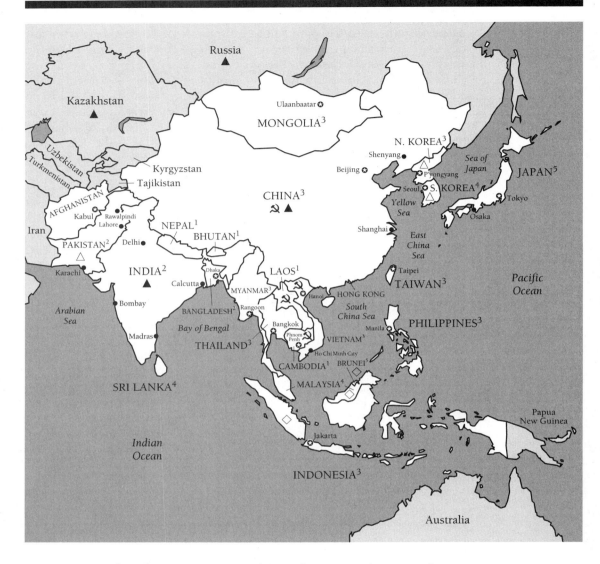

◇ **Association of Southeast Asian Nations (ASEAN):** Brunei, Indonesia, Malaysia

☭ **Communist Government Nations:** Cambodia, China, Laos, Vietnam

▲ **Nations with Nuclear Weaponry:** China, India (Kazakhstan and Russia)

△ **Nations with Nuclear Weaponry** *Potential:* North Korea, South Korea, Pakistan

Number of Deaths of Children under 5 Years (per thousand live births):
   [1] More than 150
   [2] 91–150
   [3] 31–90
   [4] 11–30
   [5] 10 or less

Case Studies: China, Japan, and India

Geography, physical environment, resources, levels of economic development, and history vary greatly among the three countries examined here. Each is distinctive, and yet each shares features with other parts of Asia.

China

In area, the People's Republic of China is the third-largest country in the world, after Russia and Canada. It is the largest nation wholly in Asia and has an area of 3.7 million square miles, including Tibet and Taiwan, both of which it claims as provinces. The mainland's long coastline extends from the mouth of the Yalu River in the northeast to the Gulf of Tonkin in the south. The PRC's total perimeter measures over seventeen thousand miles; its boundary with Russia alone is 3,500 miles long.

Topographically, China consists of lowlands in the east, comprising 20 percent of the total territory and 90 percent of its population, and mountains and plateaus in the west. From the eastern seaboard, the land rises to plateaus in central China and Mongolia; beyond these lie the high plateaus of Tibet and the great mountain ranges, most notably the Kunluns and the Himalayas. China has several great rivers that flow eastward toward the Pacific. These include the Amur in the north, the Yellow (China's second longest), and the Yangtze in the south (the longest). Northern China is in a major earthquake zone; in July 1976, a tremor measuring 8.2 on the Richter scale hit the city Tangshan, ninety miles east of Beijing, killing an estimated 650,000 people.

Most of mainland China lies in the temperate zone, but the country's climates vary greatly with the topography. Northern areas have colder winters and shorter summers than southern areas. Rains are heaviest in the south and southeast, ranging from eighty inches a year in Guangzhou (Canton) to about twenty-five inches a year in the north and northeast. In the Gobi Desert of the northwest, rainfall averages only about four inches a year.

Natural Resources and Population   The PRC is well endowed with natural resources, including oil reserves of nearly 20 billion barrels, iron, coal, lead, and a variety of other minerals (tungsten, antimony, mercury, manganese, molybdenum, potash, phosphates, and tin). The great rivers make hydroelectric power abundant. China is a major producer and exporter of silk and has achieved food self-sufficiency, even though only 11 percent of the land is arable.

China's population surpassed the billion mark in the early 1980s. If current projections hold, China will have over 1.2 billion people at the turn of the twenty-first century—twice the number of a half century earlier. Nonetheless, China's birthrate has dropped dramatically, to about twenty-one per thousand women in the early 1980s, down from nearly forty per thousand at midcentury. These figures reflect a major effort on the part of the government to stabilize China's population.

United Nations estimates of the age structure in China suggest that fully one-third of the population is 14 or under. This large youthful segment, combined with the elderly, means that working adults (roughly 60 percent of the population) must support a growing number of dependents, either directly or through tax-supported government programs. China is one of the few countries in the world where males outnumber females; the traditional preference for male babies has led to female infanticide.

Population is distributed unevenly in the PRC. Much of the mainland is too high, too hot and dry, or otherwise too rugged and barren to support large numbers of people. As a result, 94 percent of the population is crowded onto about 45 percent of the land, mostly in eastern and southeastern China. About 70 percent of mainland China's people live in a dozen densely populated provinces (Anhui, Fujian, Guangdong, Hebei, Henan, Hubei, Hunan, Jiangsu, Liaoning, Shandong, Sichuan, and Yunnan) and three cities (Beijing, Shanghai, and Tianjin).

The largest ethnic group by far is the Han (94 percent of the total population), who predominate in the densely populated parts of China but remain a minority in Inner Mongolia and Tibet. Fifty-five recognized ethnic minorities make up the remaining 6 percent. These minorities have an importance disproportionate to their numbers because they are located in strategically sensitive zones around the country's periphery.

Various Chinese dialects are spoken, but Mandarin is the official language. Written Chinese is a highly refined form of calligraphy; it consists of thousands of *ideographs*—characters that represent concepts as well as words. There is no Chinese alphabet.

China's Heritage   Modern China traces its origins back to Xia (Hsia)* dynasty (about 2200–1700 B.C.). The Shang dynasty (1766–1122 B.C.) ruled the Yellow River valley for several centuries and left records cast in bronze or inscribed on tortoise shell and bone. Historians believe the Shang were conquered by the Western Zhou (Chou) dynasty (1122–771 B.C.), which established a flourishing feudal agricultural society. In 771 B.C., the Western Zhou abandoned their capital at Xi'an (Sian) and founded a new capital farther east at Luoyang (Loyang). This new Eastern Zhou dynasty (770–249 B.C.) produced the great Chinese philosophers Kongfuzi (K'ung Fu-tzu, known to the West as Confucius) and Laozi (Lao-tzu). This Golden Age in China overlapped with the Golden Age of Greece.

Between 475 and 221 B.C., the great Qin (Ch'in) dynasty emerged. Shi Huangdi (Shih Huang-ti), the first Qin emperor, ended the feudal fragmentation of China, organizing it into a system of prefectures and counties under central control. During his reign (221–210 B.C.), work was begun on the Great Wall as a defense against nomadic Mongolian tribes. Under the Qin, the Chinese

---

* The system for transliterating Chinese into English was changed in the 1950s. We use the modern spellings but give the traditional versions in parentheses.

developed an elaborate irrigation system in the fertile Yellow River valley and began cultivation in the Yangtze valley. Supported by a system of intensive farming, China's population grew to an estimated forty million.

The Qin were displaced by the Han dynasty (206 B.C.–A.D. 220), followed by three kingdoms (Wei, Shu, and Wu). From the fourth century on, a succession of northern and southern dynasties ruled China. The empire was reunited under the Sui (589–618) and Tang (618–907) dynasties. Under the Tang, especially Emperor Taizong (T'ai Tsung, 627–649), China reached its zenith as the cultural and commercial center of Asia. Poetry and painting also flourished, particularly under Emperor Xuanzong (Hsüan Tsung).

A period of partition under the Five Dynasties (907–960) was followed by the Song (Sung) dynasty (960–1279), which is notable for its achievements in literature, philosophy, and science. The Song rulers saw the invention of movable type, gunpowder, and the magnetic compass. Beginning in the twelfth century, Mongol and Tatar tribes forced the Chinese to abandon their capital and move it to a new, safer site. In the thirteenth century, the Mongols under Genghis Khan (Temujin, about 1162–1227) subjugated all of China. The Great Canal, begun under the Sui and Tang dynasties, was completed during the reign of Kublai Khan (1279–1294), the first ruler of the Mongols' Yuan dynasty (1280–1368). No doubt impressed by Chinese culture and technology, the Mongols accommodated to the ways of China rather than attempting to displace or destroy them.

After nearly a century of foreign rule and domestic turmoil, the Mongols were supplanted by the native Chinese Ming dynasty (1368–1644). During the reign of Yongluo (Yung-Lo, or Ch'eng Tsu, 1403–1424), the heyday of the Ming dynasty, the capital was moved to Beijing (Peking, or Peiping). It was during the Ming that Europe discovered China: the Portuguese arrived in 1516, followed by the Spanish in 1557, the Dutch in 1606, and the English in 1637.

The Ming dynasty was overthrown in 1644 by invaders from the northeast, the Manchus, who established the last imperial dynasty, the Qing (Ch'ing, 1644–1911). The Manchus proved effective administrators as well as warriors. Like the Mongols, the Manchu conquerors adopted Chinese culture, laws, and administration. At its peak, their dominion extended to all of China proper, plus Manchuria, Mongolia, Tibet, Taiwan, and Turkestan—a far-flung empire of 300 million people.

Remote, self-sufficient, and aloof, China was not penetrated by Europeans until the nineteenth century. Until the 1840s, only one Chinese port, Guangzhou (Canton), was open to foreign merchants, and trade was tightly restricted. British demands for more trade and Chinese anger over illegal opium imports from British-controlled India led to the **Opium War** (1839–1842), which China lost. The **Treaty of Nanjing** (1842) forced China to open five major seaports and to cede Hong Kong to Great Britain. At midcentury, the prolonged and bloody Taiping Rebellion, aimed at overthrowing the Manchus, reduced southern China to ruins. A second war with Britain (1856–1860), joined by France, opened another major port to foreign trade. From this point forward, the empire was supine, and a series of "unequal treaties" resulted in territorial losses to Russia and Japan. (After the Sino-Japanese War of 1894–1895, Japan annexed Korea.) In 1898, Britain, France, and Germany all "leased" major ports in Shandong (Shantung), the concessionary terms dictated by the Europeans. In 1900, the **Boxer Rebellion**, a xenophobic uprising, was crushed by the joint intervention of British, French, German, American, Russian, and Japanese troops. China's humiliation was complete, but its nightmare was far from over.

A plan to relinquish control of a Chinese-owned railway to European interests in 1911 precipitated the downfall of the Manchu dynasty. Following a brief period of republican rule under Sun Yat-sen, a strongman named Yuan Shikai took power. Yuan died in 1916, whereupon warlords ruled in Beijing. Meanwhile, Sun Yat-sen, having consolidated his Nationalist party (**Kuomintang**), set up a government in the south at Guangzhou. China endured four decades of domestic turmoil until the Chinese Communist takeover unified and pacified the country in 1949.

The Chinese Civil War   Although the Beijing regime joined the Allies in World War I, it was not rewarded at the Versailles Peace Conference. The powers refused to accede to Chinese demands for an end to all foreign "extraterritorial" privileges. (Some foreign rights were abolished at the Washington Naval Conference in 1922; also, Japan and Great Britain agreed to evacuate the Shandong peninsula.)

Following Sun Yat-sen's death, Chiang Kai-shek, the party's new leader, succeeded in unifying part of the country. The Kuomintang was founded on Western democratic principles, but it evolved into an instrument of Chiang's dictatorial power. In 1927, he tried to destroy the Chinese Communist party; its remnants fled to southern Jiangxi Province and set up a rural "soviet," gaining valuable experience in governing. Following repeated Nationalist attacks, the Communists again took flight, embarking on their arduous and now legendary **Long March** during 1934 and 1935. Moving north and gaining recruits along the way, they eventually arrived in Shaanxi Province and, now under the firm leadership of Mao Zedong (Mao Tse-tung), set up headquarters at Yenan.

Japan's military leaders watched with keen interest as the Chinese civil war dragged on. In 1931, Japan occupied Manchuria, China's industrial heartland. (Recall that Japan had won control over neighboring Korea before the turn of the century, following a war with China.) The Japanese kept up the pressure in northern China, and in July 1937, war broke out. The hostilities merged into World War II, and Japan soon occupied much of the mainland. Chiang, forced to abandon the Nationalist capital at Nanjing, took his government to the southwestern hinterland, beyond the reach of Japan's armies. Meanwhile, Mao's guerrilla forces stood their ground in the northwest and fought the Japanese invaders to a stalemate.

Time was on Mao's side: in 1945, a defeated Japan was occupied by American forces under General Douglas MacArthur and forced to evacuate China. The United States became the new nemesis of the Chinese Communists. After Japan's departure, the Chinese civil war had resumed with fury. Despite massive U.S. support, the Nationalists could not mount an offensive, and in 1949, the Communists won a near-total victory. Chiang Kai-shek took refuge on the island of Formosa (Taiwan), where he set up a rival regime and pressed an increasingly feeble claim that his was the legitimate government of all China. Meanwhile, on October 1, 1949, the Chinese Communists proclaimed the People's Republic of China and made Beijing its capital.

Japan

The Japanese archipelago is located off the eastern coast of the Asian continent and has a total area of 145,851 square miles, about the size of California. Japan is divided into five districts: Honshu, Hokkaido, Kyushu, Shikoku, and Okinawa. Each consists of one main island and many smaller surrounding islands. The principal district is Honshu, which is in turn divided into five administrative units.

Like Great Britain, Japan is an island nation near a large continental land-mass. But Japan is geophysically very different from the British Isles. Consisting of the peaks of a vast, mostly submerged mountain range in the Pacific Ocean, much of Japan's terrain—over 70 percent—is steep and rugged. Twenty-five mountains rise ten thousand feet or more; the highest is the majestic Mount Fuji, at 12,388 feet. Of Japan's nearly two hundred volcanoes, thirty are still active. Earthquakes are also a constant threat. One of the world's worst recorded natural disasters was the Kanto earthquake of 1923, when Tokyo and Yokohama were devastated and more than 140,000 persons perished.

At first glance, Japan appears to suffer from severe natural disadvantages. Most of its land is unsuitable for cultivation, and its mineral resources are negligible. Only about 29 percent of the terrain is flat, and these plains lie mostly along the seacoast, where Japan's population is concentrated. Thus urban development and agriculture compete intensely for the same scarce real estate.

The climate varies from north to south, but most of the nation is fairly humid and gets abundant rainfall. Two major ocean currents—a warm one from the south and a cold one from the north—affect weather patterns. Typhoon season runs from May through October, and several storms sweep through the islands each year. Environmental pollution related to the large and concentrated population threatens Japan's ecological balance.

With 124 million people, Japan ranks seventh among the world's most populous nations; it is fifth in terms of population density, with about 856 people per square mile. In terms of density per unit of arable land, however, Japan ranks first, with about eight persons per acre. As noted, the population is very unevenly distributed. Four out of five Japanese live on the island of Honshu; only 5 percent live on Hokkaido.

Japan's Homogeneity   In terms of culture, language, and ethnicity, Japan is one of the world's most homogeneous nations. The spoken language is unique to Japan, but the written language was borrowed from the Chinese. Japan's religions are Buddhism and **Shinto**. The former originated in India and migrated eastward; the latter is a native religion involving worship of natural spirits that developed under the influence of Chinese Confucianism and eventually grew into an instrument of Japanese nationalism. After the Meiji Restoration in the nineteenth century, Shinto became the state religion. It was taught in the schools, and all Japanese were required to belong to a state Shinto shrine. State religion was abolished after Japan's defeat in World War II, but Shintoism remains an integral element of Japanese culture.

Buddhism is often considered Japan's most important religion. It was introduced from China and Korea in the sixth century and spread rapidly throughout the country. Its influence can be seen in the fine arts and in many social institutions. Japan's temples and gardens, its unique tea ceremony, and such arts as flower arranging (*ikebana*) are all derived from Zen Buddhism.

Confucianism has also been significant in shaping Japanese religious, cultural, and social institutions. For example, one offshoot of Confucianism, a cult known as Soka Gakkai, controlled the third-strongest political party in Japan (Komeito) until a 1970 law required the strict separation of politics and religion.

The Origins of Modern Japan   Mythology holds that Japan's emperors descend from the sun goddess and that Emperor Jimmu Tenno ruled all of Japan in 660 B.C., but there is no evidence of this legendary empire. The present emperor is a direct descendant of the House of Yamato, which established hegemony over Japan during the first centuries A.D. Contacts with mainland China in the fifth century led to wholesale cultural borrowing: the Japanese imitated or adopted the Chinese industrial arts, script, medical texts, and calendar; they even embraced Buddhism. Japanese rulers also copied China's political administration, with one notable exception: they did not adopt the Chinese merit system, preferring to apportion power on the basis of heredity. The imperial capital was established in 784 at Kyoto, where it remained until 1868.

During the twelfth century, powerful military clans arose outside the capital. Yoritomo, leader of the Minamoto clan, set up a military regime at Kamakura in 1192 and forced the emperor to recognize him as the **shogun**. Thus began the famed Japanese **shogunate**, a feudal form of government based on hereditary land ownership, vassalage, and military prowess that prevailed for seven hundred years. The emperor remained as a figurehead; political power was held by the dominant military clan.

Isolated from Asia by the Sea of Japan, the nation developed a strong military tradition, as rival feudal lords (*daimyo*) kept the nation in a nearly continuous state of civil war until the sixteenth century. The Japanese professional warrior (*samurai*) class developed during this era. At the same time, Japan's first contact with Europe occurred: Portuguese traders arrived in southern Japan in 1543, followed six years later by Saint Francis Xavier, who introduced Christianity. Spanish and Dutch traders were not far behind.

Civil warfare finally ended in 1590, when Hideyoshi Toyotomi, a peasant who rose to supreme power, pacified and unified the country. He was followed by another great clan leader, Ieyasu Tokugawa, who was appointed shogun in 1603 and consolidated the **Tokugawa shogunate**, which ruled Japan until 1868. The Tokugawas moved the capital to Edo (modern Tokyo), closed Japan to all foreigners except Chinese and Dutch traders (who were restricted to Nagasaki), and banned Christianity. Under Tokugawa rule, Japan enjoyed 250 years of unaccustomed peace and internal order. With domestic tranquillity came the flowering of culture.

Opening to the World   Japan's insularity ended abruptly with the arrival of Commodore Matthew C. Perry and his fleet of "black ships" in 1853. The following year, Perry extracted a treaty of peace and friendship between Japan and the United States, and similar treaties soon followed with Russia, Great Britain, and the Netherlands under Japan's new **open-door policy**. The forced opening of Japan to foreigners led to a decade of turmoil. In 1868, *samurai* from several southern clans forced the Tokugawa shogun to abdicate and restored the emperor, Meiji, to power. With the **Meiji Restoration**, Japan embarked on a modernization drive that brought it to a position of preeminence in Asia by the end of the nineteenth century.

Spurred on by a new elite of modernizing *samurai,* Japan industrialized rapidly. It also abolished feudalism, establishing a modern army and navy, universal military conscription, and compulsory education. State-led economic development based on imported technology propelled Japan toward the twentieth century. In 1889, a new constitution set up a bicameral legislature, the Diet. The reforms created a parliamentary system in theory but not in practice: the new civilian cabinet, headed by a prime minister, was made responsible only to the emperor.

Japan's ascendancy was signaled by spectacular victories over China (1895) and Russia (1904–1905). As a result, Japan began to acquire the elements of an Asian empire, including the island of Formosa (Taiwan), part of Sakhalin Island, and railway and port rights in Manchuria. China also recognized Korea's independence; this led to a Japanese protectorate in 1910.

Though not a major participant in World War I, Japan was one of the five chief powers at the treaty signing in Versailles, and at the 1922 Washington Naval Conference, it was recognized as the third-ranked naval power in the world. The economy advanced rapidly in the 1920s, and Japan was transformed from an agricultural to an industrial nation. Japanese industry was organized into huge combines (*zaibatsu*) controlled by the families of *samurai* who had spearheaded modernization fifty years earlier. In 1925, universal male suffrage introduced democracy, and political parties arose for the first time. But when Emperor Hirohito ascended the throne the following year, the military seized the initiative and swept the political parties aside; in 1931, still acting independently of the government, the Japanese army invaded Manchuria. Japan had embarked on a course of military adventurism and empire-building that would end in the atomic tragedy of Hiroshima and Nagasaki fourteen years later.

Japan's Bid for Hegemony in Asia   On the eve of World War II, Japan entered into a military pact (the infamous Axis alliance) with Germany and Italy. The goal of Japan's militarists was to conquer all of Asia and create a Japan-ruled "coprosperity sphere." Viewing the formidable United States Navy as the only obstacle to this aim, Japan decided to launch a surprise attack on the American Pacific naval fleet at Pearl Harbor, Hawaii, on December 7, 1941; simultaneously, the Japanese attacked American forces in the Philippines and British forces in Hong Kong and Malaya.

The attack on Pearl Harbor was a preemptive strike, designed to deliver a knockout blow to the U.S. Seventh Fleet. The United States was caught utterly off guard. At Hawaii, five battleships and three cruisers were sunk or severely damaged, three other battleships sustained some damage, many smaller vessels were sunk or crippled, and 177 aircraft were destroyed on the ground. The casualties were shocking: 2,343 dead, 876 missing, and 1,272 injured.

The attack on Pearl Harbor aroused American indignation like nothing before and cleared all domestic political hurdles to America's entry into the war in both Asia and Europe. In time, it was America's great economic capacity (see Tables 13.5 and 13.6) and the fact that the territory of the continental United States was not subjected to any direct attacks during the war that turned the tide decisively in the Pacific (as well as in the European theater).[4] The war's Armageddon-like end in August 1945 found Japan totally defeated, exhausted, and demoralized. Japan was now at the mercy of the United States—specifically of General Douglas MacArthur, commander in chief of U.S. forces in the Pacific.

The iron-willed general compelled the Japanese to abandon emperor worship (which American leaders associated with Japanese ultranationalism), renounce war, and draft a new liberal democratic constitution. Japan was quickly trans-

Table 13.5 Aircraft Production of the Powers, 1939–1945

	1939	1940	1941	1942	1943	1944	1945
United States	5,856	12,804	26,277	47,836	85,898	96,318	49,761
USSR	10,382	10,565	15,735	25,436	34,900	40,300	20,900
Great Britain	7,940	15,049	20,094	23,672	26,263	26,461	12,070
British Commonwealth	250	1,100	2,600	4,575	4,700	4,575	2,075
Total Allies	24,428	39,518	64,706	101,519	151,761	167,654	84,806
Germany	8,295	10,247	11,776	15,409	24,807	39,807	7,540
Japan	4,467	4,768	5,088	8,861	16,693	28,180	11,066
Italy	1,800	1,800	2,400	2,400	1,600	—	—
Total Axis	14,562	16,815	19,264	26,670	43,100	67,987	18,606

Source: Paul Kennedy, *The Rise and Fall of the Great Powers* (New York: Vintage Books, 1987), tab. 34, p. 354.

Table 13.6 Armaments Production of the Powers, 1940–1943 (billions of 1944 U.S. dollars)

	1940	1941	1943
Great Britain	3.5	6.5	11.1
USSR	− 5.0	8.5	13.9
United States	− 1.5	4.5	37.5
Total of Allied combatants	3.5	19.5	62.5
Germany	6.0	6.0	13.8
Japan	− 1.0	2.0	4.5
Italy	0.75	1.0	—
Total of Axis combatants	6.75	9.0	18.3

Source: Paul Kennedy, *The Rise and Fall of the Great Powers* (New York: Vintage Books, 1987), tab. 35, p. 355.

formed from America's all-time Asian nemesis into America's number-one Asian partner.

India

The Republic of India is the world's most populous democracy and the second-largest country wholly in Asia (only China is bigger). About one-third the size of the United States, India's territory encompasses most of the Asian subcontinent, which it shares with Pakistan, Nepal, Bhutan, and Bangladesh.

The southern half of India is bounded by the Bay of Bengal to the east, the Indian Ocean to the south, and the Arabian Sea to the west. In the north, the Himalayan Mountains effectively insulate India, climatically and politically, from the rest of Asia. India shares borders with Pakistan to the northwest; China, Nepal, and Bhutan to the north; and Burma and Bangladesh in the east. Between the northern mountains and the southern peninsula lies a fertile lowland. In addition, there is a slender coastal plain along the Arabian Sea and a wider one along the Bay of Bengal. These five surface features—the mountains, the Ganges floodplain, the peninsula, and the two coastal plains—have shaped India's economic and political history for thousands of years.

India's spectrum of climate types range from the arid Rajasthan Desert in the west to the rain-drenched Khasi Hills of Assam in the east, from winter snowfalls in the northern mountains and the Kashmir valley to scorching spring dust storms in the Deccan Plateau to the south. Monsoon winds govern the weather patterns, dividing the year into four seasons: rainy (southwest monsoon, June to September), moist (retreating monsoon, October and November), dry and cool (northeast monsoon, December to March), and hot (no monsoon, April and May).

India is not particularly rich in minerals but does possess sizable deposits of iron, coal, bauxite, manganese, mica, salt, and gypsum. Oil reserves are small (about 3.7 billion barrels) but significant. As in China, India's huge population is its most abundant natural resource and presents both problems for the present and potential for the future.

A Mosaic of People, Language, and Religion   Some 865 million people were living in India in 1991, an average of 682 people per square mile. The population had stabilized at around 250 million in the 1920s, but over the next seventy years it more than tripled, due primarily to the death rate falling much faster than the birthrate. The death rate has plummeted thanks to improvements in health care, nutrition, and sanitation. Birthrates tend to fall more slowly, but India's was slashed by one-third in the 1970s through an aggressive program of family planning, contraception, and sterilization. Nonetheless, the natural rate of increase (crude birthrate minus crude death rate) is around 17.2 per thousand, and the compounded population growth rate remains high at 2.1 percent a year; in absolute numbers, India's annual population increase is the largest in the world, exceeding even the PRC's.

The age structure in India, as in all societies with rapidly growing populations, is skewed toward youth. More than 40 percent of the population is 14 years of age or younger, while only 3 percent is 65 or older. Thus 57 percent of the population has to support hundreds of millions who are too young or too old to work. The challenge of providing jobs for millions of new workers every year strains the nation's political, economic, and social systems.

Despite nuclear power plants and modern steel mills, India remains a traditional society in many ways. Three-fourths of the population is rural, living in nearly 600,000 villages with fewer than ten thousand residents (78 percent have a population of less than one thousand). When observers contemplate rural life in Third World countries, they often think of India, where a person can be born, live, and die in the same village and never travel beyond the horizon.

India's tremendous cultural, religious, and ethnic diversity is perhaps its most striking feature. Ethnically, India is one of the most complex societies in the world. Linguistically, it is one of the most prolific, boasting 1,652 different languages and dialects. Officially, there are 211 distinct languages; sixteen are recognized by the constitution. About 90 percent of the population speaks at least one of these sixteen languages.

The two principal native languages are Hindi and Urdu. Hindi is spoken by 50 percent of the population (mostly Hindus), and Urdu is the primary language of India's huge minority Muslim population. Hindi is written like Sanskrit, whereas Urdu is written in Arabic-Persian script and contains many Arabic and Persian words. Other northern Indo-Aryan languages include Assamese, Bengali, Gujarati, Kashmiri, Marathi, Oriya, Punjabi, Rajasthani, Sanskrit, and Sindhi. In the south, the languages are of Dravidian origin; examples include Telugu, Tamil, Kannada, and Malayalam. English is the language of government, diplomacy, education, science, communications, and industry.

Language has played a major role in determining India's internal boundaries, and efforts by the central government to make Hindi the national language have met with resistance. In some cases, linguistic differences have magnified cultural and religious rivalries. Punjab is a case in point. Punjabi-speaking leaders (mostly Sikhs) demanded that the province be divided in two. The result was the creation of Haryana, the part of the former state inhabited primarily by Hindi-speaking people. (The "new" Punjab is, of course, the part inhabited by Punjabi-speaking people.) Many such examples of the interaction of linguistics and politics could be cited.

India is the birthplace of several religions, including Hinduism and Buddhism. **Hinduism** can be traced back to 1500 B.C. The Buddha taught in the fifth century B.C., around the time that **Jainism**, another distinctively Indian religion, appeared. **Sikhism**, a monotheistic Hindu sect founded in the fifteenth century, is the dominant religion in Punjab. Originally an effort to reconcile Muslim and Hindu doctrine, Sikhism evolved into a militant sect that violently opposes Islam.

Fully 83 percent of India's population is Hindu; about 11 percent is Muslim. Though Hinduism is clearly preponderant, India's Muslim community is the third largest in the world, after Indonesia's and Pakistan's. Buddhism has died out in India—there are actually more Christians (4 percent) than Buddhists (3 percent). Religion-based violence—between Hindus and Muslims, Sikhs and Muslims, Sikhs and Hindus, and so forth—has been a recurring problem since India's independence in 1947. Indeed, religious differences led to the creation of Pakistan, and tensions still remain unresolved.

India's **caste system** is prescribed by Hinduism but proscribed by Indian law. A clearer case of conflict between sacred and secular values would be difficult to find. Every Hindu baby is born into one of four castes, or classes—*Brahman* (priests and scholars), *Kshatriya* (warriors and rulers), *Vaisya* (artisans, shopkeepers, farmers), and *Sudra* (farm laborers and menial workers)—or is an outcast, or "untouchable." These castes are in turn divided into as many as three thousand subcastes (*jatis*) based on occupation, geographic location, and other factors. The Indian constitution abolished discrimination based on caste (especially untouchability), but the caste system is so deeply ingrained in India's culture that outlawing it has had little effect.

India's Heritage: Splendor amid Poverty   The Indus valley is one of the oldest continuously inhabited regions in the world. It was civilized long before the Aryans (Hindus) began invading from the northwest in 2400 B.C. For centuries thereafter, small states and larger kingdoms came and went in various parts of the subcontinent as a steady procession of would-be conquerors struggled for power. Over this long period, enduring patterns of village and family life evolved, as did the caste system.

When Alexander the Great invaded in 326 B.C., the region already had a population of thirty million, two-thirds of whom lived in the Ganges Basin. A new Aryan dynasty followed under Chandragupta, who subdued most of northern India and established the Maurya Empire; his successor, the great Asoka (273–232 B.C.), unified all of India. Asoka converted to Buddhism, and his rule brought outstanding administrative, legal, and cultural achievements. Many of India's most impressive ancient Buddhist *stupas* (shrines), pillars, and temples date from this time. After Asoka, invaders from the northwest again overran India, and the empire disintegrated into separate kingdoms again. Caste Hinduism now prevailed over Buddhism, which almost completely vanished from the land of its origin.

Although Brahmanic states had been present in peninsular India for a long time, genuine Hindu kingdoms first appeared there after the fourth century, and Hindu Rajput princes did not reach the height of their power until 700 or later. Descendants of these rulers retained power and influence until well after the British arrived in the seventeenth century. Magnificent Hindu structures dating from long before the time of Christ can be found throughout the peninsula, and many of them are still places of worship.

The Hindu epoch was followed by a long period of Muslim rule no less glorious or grandiose. Muslim invaders began streaming through the northeast mountain passes in the eighth century; in the early eleventh century, Mahmud of Ghazni led seventeen forays into Hindustan over the course of three decades. The first Muslim sultan (king) of Delhi held sway in the thirteenth century, and Muslim power reached its pinnacle under the Moguls during the sixteenth century. Babur, who invaded Punjab in 1526, was the first Mogul despot to proclaim himself emperor of India, a title he thought he had earned by defeating the Afghan sultan of Delhi. Babur's grandson, Akbar (1556–1605), ruled the Ganges Basin and became the first Muslim emperor to attempt to create a national state through alliances with Hindu kings. Art and literature flourished under Akbar, though the emperor himself was illiterate. Akbar's successors were no less illustrious. Two of them, Shah Jahan and Aurangzeb, were especially renowned and left legacies of splendid palaces, fortresses, mausoleums, and gardens. The Taj Mahal epitomizes the grandeur of the great Mogul rulers, but it is only one of many dazzling works of architecture from this period. Under the despotic rule of Aurangzeb (1658–1707), the frontiers of the Mogul Empire were pushed to new limits, but the emperor's repressive policies prompted armed revolts, and the empire fell into decline.

In the eighteenth century, one form of alien rule replaced another as the British reduced India to a colony through the agency of the **British East India Company**. (The company itself was brought under British government control in 1784; the first British governor-general was appointed in 1786.) When the Indian army revolted in the **Sepoy Mutiny** (1857–1859), which has been called "the most dramatic event in nineteenth-century India," the British crown abolished the powers of the East India Company and assumed direct control of India in 1858. Long the object of imperialistic designs, India was the "crown jewel" of the British Empire until independence was achieved in 1947.

CONCLUSION

There is no single Asian civilization; indeed, there are a great many distinctive civilizations in Asia, the largest being the Chinese, the Indian, and the Japanese. Except for Islam, which spread across much of South and Southeast Asia from the Middle East, the civilizations and cultures from Arabia westward to the Pacific are essentially homegrown. They did interact with and influence one another, but they borrowed virtually nothing from non-Asian societies before the Western intrusions of the mid-nineteenth century. In Chapter 14, we will examine the political systems of Asia, again focusing on China, Japan, and India.

KEY TERMS

East Asia
South Asia
Northeast Asia
Southeast Asia
Pacific Rim
"oriental despotism"
Trilateral Commission
overdevelopment
Confucianism
empire-building
dynastic authoritarianism
patron-client relations
colonialism
neocolonialism
Opium War
Treaty of Nanjing
Boxer Rebellion

Kuomintang
Long March
Shinto
Buddhism
shogun
shogunate
daimyo
samurai
Tokugawa shogunate
open-door policy
Meiji Restoration
Hinduism
Jainism
Sikhism
caste system
British East India Company
Sepoy Mutiny

STUDY QUESTIONS

1. To what extent is China a victim of circumstances, such as scarcity of natural resources, overpopulation, unfortunate geography, and a harsh environment?
2. How has geography influenced Japan's cultural and political development? What features of contemporary Japanese society can be traced to Japan's unusual physical environment (topography, land scarcity, resources, climate)?
3. What are the salient characteristics of Indian society and culture, and how do such factors as ethnicity, religion, and language constrain or facilitate the political process?

4. How do the historical experiences of China, Japan, and India compare in terms of (a) empire-building, (b) forms and methods of rule, (c) foreign intrusion, and (d) sociocultural unity or diversity?

SUGGESTED READING

Embree, Ainslie T. *India's Search for National Identity.* 2nd ed. New York: Knopf, 1988.

Fairbanks, John K. *The United States and China.* 4th enlarged ed. Cambridge, Mass.: Harvard University Press, 1983.

Hinton, William. *Fanshen: A Documentary of Revolution in a Chinese Village.* New York: Random House, 1968.

Isaacs, Harold R. *Scratches on Our Minds: American Images of China and India.* Westport, Conn.: Greenwood Press, 1973.

Li, Chien-nung. *The Political History of China, 1840–1928.* Stanford, Calif.: Stanford University Press, 1956.

Reischauer, Edwin O. *Japan: The Story of a Nation.* 4th ed. New York: Knopf, 1991.

Schram, Stuart. *Mao Tse-tung.* New York: Viking Penguin, 1966.

Schurmann, Franz. *Ideology and Organization in Communist China.* Berkeley: University of California Press, 1968.

Snow, Edgar. *Red Star over China.* Rev. ed. New York: Grove Press, 1989.

Spear, Percival. *India: A Modern History.* Ann Arbor: University of Michigan Press, 1961.

Steinberg, David J., ed. *In Search of Southeast Asia: A Modern History.* Rev. ed. Honolulu: University of Hawaii Press, 1987.

Wolpert, Stanley A. *A New History of India.* 3rd ed. New York: Oxford University Press, 1989.

NOTES

1. Rushworth M. Kidder, "The North-South Affluence Gap," *Christian Science Monitor,* July 25, 1988, p. B7.

2. See Nobutaka Ike, *Japanese Politics: Patron-Client Democracy* (New York: Knopf, 1972).

3. John Nagle, *Political System Performance in Three Worlds* (Chicago: Nelson-Hall, 1985), p. 230.

4. See Paul Kennedy, *The Rise and Fall of the Great Powers* (New York: Vintage Books, 1987), pp. 347–357.

14

Change and Continuity

Asia's political traditions are authoritarian. Old-fashioned autocratic rule has largely disappeared, surviving only in the hereditary monarchies of Nepal, Bhutan, and Brunei. Nonetheless, most Asian governments remain authoritarian; the precise form, however, varies from country to country.

Constitutional democracy has also made significant inroads. Although clear-cut cases of popular rule are few, two of Asia's three major powers—India and Japan—are thriving democracies. Sri Lanki and the Philippines are also democratic republics. Prosperous Singapore is a parliamentary democracy in form, but one figure, Prime Minister Lee Kuan Yew, has long dominated the political system. South Korea has moved cautiously toward constitutional rule. Taiwan has continued under one-party rule, making only symbolic gestures toward a truly representative form of government.

In the early 1990s, five Asian nations were ruled by Communists: the People's Republic of China, North Korea, Vietnam, Cambodia, and Laos. The end of the Cold War had led to the liquidation of Communist rule in the former Soviet republics and Afghanistan and a transitional regime in Cambodia. Communism remains strong only in China—where it affects roughly one-fourth of the world's population.

Other Asian nations, especially in South and Southeast Asia, display a variety of authoritarian political structures. Indonesia is ruled by a military strongman, General Suharto, who has been in power since the overthrow of Sukarno in 1965. Malaysia is governed by a hybrid system involving elements of federalism, parliamentary democracy, and traditional monarchy. Thailand's government—in theory, a constitutional monarchy— is difficult to categorize. The military has always played a very active role in governing, but civilians have typically occupied formal positions of power and the political system normally functions as a parliamentary democracy. To illustrate this fact, in February 1991, the military staged a bloodless coup against the democratically elected prime minister, but then allowed a civilian successor to be chosen. Burma was ruled by a military strongman named Ne Win for twenty-six years. When he stepped down in 1988, General Saw Maung, a close associate, seized power. In 1990, free multiparty elections were held for the first time in decades. The main opposition party won, but the military refused to step aside, resorting instead to a brutal crackdown. Burma's name was changed to Myanmar in 1989.

Pakistan has mixed authoritarian practices with democratic promises since the nation's founding in 1947. A 1977 coup made Pakistan a military dictatorship under General Mohammad Zia ul-Haq. Zia dismissed the prime minister and dissolved the parliament in May 1988, promising "free, fair, and independent elections," but political repression continued. In August, Zia died in a suspicious airplane crash, and Benazir Bhutto—the popular daughter of former president Zulfikar Ali Bhutto, who had been executed by Zia in 1979—was elected, becoming the first woman prime minister in Pakistan's history. Ms. Bhutto's tenure in office was short-lived. She was replaced by Nawaz Sharif amid controversy and signs of deepening political disorder. Political disarray continues to plague Pakistan. In the summer of 1993 President Gulam Ishaq Khan sacked Prime Minister Sharif, but the Pakistan Supreme Court reinstated Sharif. This instability at the top prompted speculation that the military might be tempted to intervene as it had on several past occasions.

The Impact of War and Revolution

Today's Asian governments came about through war and revolution. Politically speaking, World War II was the most important event in modern Asian history. Japan's attempt to unite nearly all of East and Southeast Asia under a new Greater East Asian empire ended in defeat at the hands of the U.S. military.

Japan's constitution, in effect since 1947, was prepared under the watchful eye of General Douglas MacArthur, U.S. proconsul in Japan after World War II and the architect of Japanese democracy. Thus Japan's current political system was imposed from outside, a consequence of losing the war. Because the Japanese constitution was based on Western principles and imposed by the United States, Japan became part of America's postwar military-strategic system in the western Pacific. This meant that Japan would provide bases for U.S. forces, that the United States would be Japan's chief trading partner, and that Japan would never again threaten its neighbors or fall prey to extremism (indeed, the constitution prohibited two alleged causes of Japanese aggression, military forces and emperor worship).

World War II also put mainland China on the road to communism. When Japan invaded and occupied much of China in the 1930s and early 1940s, the Chinese Nationalist government of Generalissimo Chiang Kai-shek was discredited; only Mao Zedong's Communist guerrilla forces had any success against the Japanese. After Japan's withdrawal, Mao's forces continued to wage war, now against the Nationalist government rather than the Japanese. This civil war lasted until 1949, when Mao's Communists drove Chiang's Nationalists (the Kuomintang) off the mainland. Chiang took his rump government to the island of Formosa (Taiwan), where his successors continue to monopolize political power. Mao took over China, setting up the highly authoritarian Communist state currently in place.

India's present political system is the result of a largely nonviolent national independence movement led by Mahatma Gandhi. Gandhi's strategy of nonviolent resistance (or civil disobedience) was highly successful, but World War II played a role as well: the British were too weary and preoccupied with domestic reconstruction after the war to resist Indian demands for self-rule. In fact, Great Britain dismantled nearly all its colonial empire after the war. In Asia, Pakistan obtained independence when India did, in 1947; Burma and Ceylon (Sri Lanka), in 1948; and Malaya (now part of Malaysia), in 1957.

The creation of a parliamentary-style democracy in India reflects the strong British influence. At the same time, however, India's extreme diversity made democracy as essential as it was difficult; the only other option capable of holding the nation together would be a highly centralized police state. Thus by establishing popular self-rule, the founders of independent India made a virtue of necessity.

Pakistan was an afterthought in the British rush to decolonize. When Muslim chieftains—led by Mohammad Ali Jinnah, head of the Muslim League—objected to becoming part of a Hindu-dominated independent India, the British took the course of least resistance and allowed Pakistan to become a separate dominion (actually two separate states, West Pakistan and East Pakistan—now Bangladesh). Much of the conflict that has plagued the subcontinent since independence derives from the national boundaries drawn in 1947.

War and revolution were closely related to the decolonization process elsewhere in Asia as well. Despite the urgent tasks of reconstruction at home, the French clung tenaciously to their colonial possessions in Indochina. The Vietnamese, led by Ho Chi Minh, waged a protracted "war of national liberation" against France (emulating Mao's guerrilla strategy and tactics) and emerged victorious in 1954. It took another long struggle—this one against the U.S.-backed Saigon-based regime in the south—and two more decades to reunite Vietnam under Communist rule. The Hanoi government quickly consolidated its control in the south and in 1979 invaded and conquered Cambodia, ousting the bloody, pro-Chinese dictatorship of Pol Pot.

After World War II, Korea was also divided into north and south sections along the 38th parallel (line of latitude). This temporary expedient became permanent after the **Korean War** (1950–1953) ended in a draw. North Korea, the territory controlled by Soviet troops in August 1945, was set up as a Communist state under the personal dictatorship of Kim Il Sung. South Korea became a pro-American, anticommunist military dictatorship thinly disguised as a democracy. Following widespread protests and rioting in 1987, military strongman Chun Doo Hwan agreed to permit direct popular election of the next president. Roh Tae Woo, a civilian who had strongly criticized Chun's government, was elected. But the military held veto power over policy formulation, and mass demonstrations, often violent, kept the country on the brink of civil war. Although reunification is the declared intention of both Korean governments, the prospects for it remain very dim.

Indonesia and Thailand are unusual, for different reasons. Indonesia was the only major Dutch colony in Asia. The Japanese occupied Indonesia in World War II; after they left, a war of independence ensued, much as in Indochina. When the Netherlands quit the fight in December 1949, Sukarno, who spearheaded Indonesia's liberation struggle, took over the reins of government and ruled as a dictator until his overthrow in 1965. The leader of that coup, General Suharto, has dominated Indonesian politics ever since.

Thailand (Siam) was never colonized. Although Japan occupied it in 1941, after the war Thailand returned to self-government. During the Vietnam War, Thailand placed a major air base at the United States' disposal, and the nation has generally pursued a pro-Western foreign policy.

Patterns and Trends

There is no specifically Asian model of democracy. Although the governments of Japan and India are patterned after the British parliamentary system, they both deviate from it in important ways. For example, the British two-party system has no counterpart in Asia. As we shall see, Japan's ruling Liberal Democratic party has dominated Japanese politics and government since the mid-1950s; similarly, India's Congress party—now known as Congress I—has ruled India almost continuously since independence. Thus rule by a single party, rather than alternation in power by two or more parties, seems to be one aspect of Asian democracy.

If there is no Asian model of democracy, neither is there an Asian model of authoritarianism. There is no modern form of oriental despotism. Most authoritarian governments in Asia today have at least a patina of popular rule and use a mixture of modern and traditional methods to stay in power (modern methods include control of the mass media, public education, and welfare-state benefits; traditional methods involve political patronage, corruption, and police-state repression).

The most common form of government is **military dictatorship**, as in Pakistan and South Korea before 1988, Burma, and Bangladesh. Taiwan and Indonesia are civil authoritarian regimes set up by military strongmen (Generalissimo Chiang Kai-shek and General Suharto, respectively); the military continues to dominate politics in both countries. Regimes of this type, quite common in the Third World, might be termed "**civilitary**" **rule**, a hybrid in which the leader is a civilian president but the military has a primary role in government.

A second pattern is Marxist-Leninist government, as in the PRC, Vietnam, Cambodia, Laos, and North Korea. And some regimes are best described as mixed democratic-authoritarian (including South Korea since 1988, Malaysia, Singapore, and Thailand during the 1980s).

Since the 1970s, there has been a gradual trend in Asia toward democratization and greater respect for human rights. This has been evident in a variety of settings, including the PRC, the Philippines, and South Korea. Exceptions can be found, of course, and trends can be reversed. Nor is it certain that democracies will proliferate around the region, for Western-style democracy and the Asian patron-client tradition are a strange, if not wholly incompatible, pair.

In terms of political economy, Asian nations have been moving away from central planning and state intervention and toward greater reliance on market forces. This trend is not simply a move in the direction of *laissez faire* economics, however. Rather, it involves an alliance between the state and private enterprise for the purpose of coordinating public and private investment, attracting foreign capital, and developing overseas markets. Japan's success has been influential, and similar arrangements have produced impressive results in South Korea, Taiwan, Hong Kong, and Singapore.

Case Studies: China, Japan, and India

World War II unleashed forces that transformed the political map of Asia. Within two years of the war's end, India became independent, and Pakistan sprang into being as its rival. Within four years, the U.S.-backed Nationalist government of Chiang Kai-shek was driven off the Chinese mainland by the **People's Liberation Army (PLA)** of Mao Zedong. A democratic constitution was imposed on demilitarized Japan. All across Asia, European power was receding, and the two superpowers—the United States and the Soviet Union—filled the power vacuum.

The United States established a massive military presence in Japan and the Philippines, and Mao's Communist forces controlled all of China, though they were isolated and needed foreign assistance. Stalin waited until the Chinese civil war was over and then offered economic aid to Mao in return for allegiance. In Korea, as mentioned earlier, a Soviet-installed Communist government ruled north of the 38th parallel, while a U.S.-backed anticommunist regime ruled in the south. This uneasy arrangement exploded in the Korean War (1950–1953) after North Korea invaded South Korea. (The United Nations condemned the North Korean invasion and voted to intervene on the side of South Korea.)

The French tried to hold on in Indochina, and a slow war of liberation dragged on until Ho Chi Minh's knockout blow in the 1954 battle of Dien Bien Phu. Both superpowers sought a toehold in South Asia, but India's great postindependence leader, Prime Minister Jawaharlal Nehru (1947–1964), chose a policy of **nonalignment**—friendly relations with both, obligations to neither.

Thus Asia was an arena of superpower competition after World War II. At the same time, the nations of Asia had aspirations of their own—in many cases, such basic questions as who would govern and how remained unresolved.

The Rebirth of China

After 1949, the Maoist regime quickly consolidated power and launched an aggressive program of industrialization and collectivization, getting significant, though limited, economic aid from the Soviet Union. In 1957, Mao proclaimed the **Hundred Flowers movement**, an invitation to the country's professionals and intellectuals to criticize the political system. This unprecedented thaw was followed by an antirightist campaign against those who had previously attacked the system! The tumult was a prelude to the **Great Leap Forward**, one of history's most ambitious experiments in social transformation.

In the Great Leap, launched in 1958, Mao attempted to catapult China into full communism, ahead even of the Soviet Union. Khrushchev had denounced the "crimes of Stalin" in his Secret Speech at the Twentieth Party Conference in 1956. His daring move had led directly to unrest in Eastern Europe, particularly in Hungary and Poland. Mao observed these events with chagrin, and he concluded that the Soviet Union had strayed from the revolutionary path. Communist China, he vowed, would show the way. The Great Leap was an effort to do that.

Although Mao claimed to be a good Marxist-Leninist, he added his own twist, much as Lenin had done. But **Maoism** stood Marx on his head. Mao asserted that human will could overcome all material obstacles, and he placed leadership above economics as the driving force in society. In Marxist terms, Mao considered the superstructures—a revolutionary party, inspired leadership, a mass-mobilizing ideology—more important than the economic base. The Great Leap Forward was designed to prove that revolutionary will had the power to reshape society. Thus Maoism was the antithesis of Stalinism: Mao sought to harness the "hurricane force" of the people and thus prevent a privileged elite from evolving.

Mao's experiment in mass mobilization turned out to be a great leap backward rather than forward. It enlisted some seventy million peasants in a bizarre undertaking that, among other things, involved a futile attempt to produce steel from backyard furnaces. Meanwhile, the fields remained unattended, even though agriculture had been reorganized into huge communes where all work was performed by groups and every aspect of private life was collectivized. Life in the communes was regimented to the point of being militarized; for example, food was prepared in communal kitchens, meals were eaten in mess halls, and men and women slept in segregated barracks.

The scale of impending disaster was not immediately apparent as overzealous cadres, eager to please Chairman Mao, vied with each other by falsifying production figures. Once the dimensions of the debacle became clear, leadership split between utopians (Mao's supporters), who stressed social and moral perfection, and pragmatists, who favored economic efficiency. When the defense minister,

Marshal Peng Dehuai, denounced the Great Leap Forward, Mao had him replaced with Marshal Lin Biao, who extolled the virtues of "**Mao Zedong thought.**" Lin even urged that a "people's army" be trained to perform domestic revolutionary tasks, rather than a Soviet-style army led by professional officers and trained solely for combat.

Although the infighting was concealed, the dire consequences of the Great Leap Forward became increasingly obvious as the PRC plunged into an economic abyss. The period from 1960 to 1962 was known as the "three bitter years," as production dropped sharply and famine stalked the countryside. Chairman Mao retreated from daily management of domestic affairs, which were now handled by Liu Shaoqi, Deng Xiaoping, and Zhou Enlai. Between 1962 and 1966, this trio spearheaded the PRC's economic and political recovery while Mao concentrated on foreign affairs and conducted ideological warfare against the Soviet Union.

The Cultural Revolution   In 1966, Mao reasserted his leadership by launching the **Great Proletarian Cultural Revolution**, an even stranger campaign than the Great Leap Forward. Mao was apparently troubled by the decline in revolutionary élan among party cadres, the masses, and especially youth. He believed that the only way to keep the revolution alive was to infuse the next generation of leaders with the kind of revolutionary spirit that had sustained the Communist revolutionaries through the Long March and the years of struggle with the Kuomintang. The only way young people could learn the meaning of revolution was to experience it firsthand; otherwise, Mao feared, they would become complacent and elitist. What was needed was a new revolution, created by Mao himself to purify the party ranks and educate the next generation.

Mao's shock troops were the **Red Guards**, mostly high school and university students inspired by a little red book containing the "thoughts of Chairman Mao." The Red Guards regarded this pocket-size publication as their catechism and Mao as their hero. Directed by a group of zealots later condemned as the **Gang of Four**, the Red Guards stormed the bastions of authority, waving the book in the faces of their teachers as they dragged them into the streets, hung insulting signs around their necks, and paraded them for the masses to ridicule.

At first, intellectuals bore the brunt of the Red Guards' fury, but soon others in authority, including party and state officials, came under scrutiny. At the height of the Cultural Revolution, no one who had ever held a position of authority was safe from the rampaging students. In the meantime, Mao purged the party leadership, including Liu Shaoqi (once designated as his successor) and Deng Xiaoping (secretary general of the Central Committee since 1954). Few senior leaders survived the Cultural Revolution unscathed. Mao's aim was to remove entrenched elites who had "taken the capitalist road." The Cultural Revolution thus set the party against itself and ushered in a decade of infighting and polarization.

Having destroyed the party and state machinery, Mao turned to the only organization still intact, the **People's Liberation Army** (**PLA**). As early as 1967, he had denounced two key leaders of the Cultural Revolution. By 1968, the Red

Guards had divided into factions engaged in armed struggles against each other. Having unleashed a tempest, Mao had little choice but to ask the army to restore order, and the PLA thus became the dominant force in the new "three-way revolutionary committees" (party cadres who had escaped the purge, the masses, and the army). The Red Guards, having fallen from grace, were sent to work in the fields alongside millions of educated young Chinese conscripted earlier.

By 1969, the country lay in ruins. The entire educational system had shut down, the party was demolished, factories were operating languidly or not at all, food production and distribution were disrupted, and it was unclear who was in charge. As many as two million people may have died. Mao now called for a reconstruction of the party. As a border war broke out between the PRC and the Soviet Union along the Amur and Ussuri rivers in the northeast, the Ninth Party Congress met and elected a new Central Committee dominated by the army. In addition, a new constitution was announced; among other things, it named Lin Biao, the PLA's leader, as Mao's heir apparent.

Rather than clarifying the situation, the Ninth Party Congress led to another prolonged power struggle. The principal antagonists were Lin Biao; Mao's wife, Jiang Qing (one of the Gang of Four); Deng Xiaoping; and Zhou Enlai (a brilliant politician and the sole moderate who remained in Mao's inner circle). In 1971, Lin allegedly tried to stage a coup that involved an attempt to kill Mao. In the official version, Lin died in a plane crash as he tried to flee the country. After Lin's death, the role of the PLA was diminished, and two factions fought for the next five years. On one side were the pragmatists, led by Zhou Enlai and Deng Xiaoping; on the other were the radicals, led by Jiang Qing (presumably with the aging Mao's blessing).

Zhou died in January 1976, leaving Deng without a shield from attack by radical Maoists. In April, rioters in Beijing's Tiananmen Square expressed sympathy for Zhou and, by extension, Deng. Although the incident was evidently spontaneous, Deng was condemned as the instigator and was stripped of his official posts. Hua Guofeng, a little-known former minister of public security, was named premier and first vice-chairman. Mao died in September 1976, setting the stage for a showdown between Mao's widow and Hua. When Jiang Qing and her Gang of Four associates tried to oust Hua, he had them arrested, tried, and imprisoned. The Cultural Revolution was finally history.

China after Mao

The two preeminent Chinese leaders, Mao Zedong and Zhou Enlai, both died in 1976. Mao's death removed a major ideological roadblock to economic reform in the PRC; Zhou's death removed a major pragmatic influence in Chinese politics. In the past, when Communist China was plunged into chaos, Mao was always the "trigger" and Zhou was always there to pick up the pieces. After 1976, both the destabilizing force of Mao and the restabilizing presence of Zhou were suddenly gone. The outcome of the bitter power struggle between the radical Maoists (led by the so-called Gang of Four) and more moderate elements was far from certain. There was no telling what the departure of these two giants foreshadowed for China and the world.

The Third Plenum: Practice over Theory   Hua Guofeng assumed the top two posts in the party and the state, but he and his cohorts were relative newcomers who owed their rise to the Cultural Revolution. By the spring of 1977, Deng Xiaoping had returned to center stage, and a low-key power struggle ensued between Deng and Hua, who retreated into the sanctuary of "Mao Zedong thought." In sharp contrast, Deng stressed practice over theory, expressing his view in a now-famous metaphor: it does not matter whether the cat is black or white, he said, as long as it catches mice. The tug-of-war between Hua and Deng was only the latest expression of what had become a perpetual battle between two conflicting tendencies within the Chinese Communist party.

The culmination came in 1978 at the **Third Plenum** of the Central Commit-tee, when Deng and his "practice group" emerged the clear winners. The plenum sharply criticized the "whateverist faction" that slavishly mouthed Maoist slo-gans, stamped out the last vestiges of the Cultural Revolution, and adopted the formula of "emancipating the mind" by making "practice the sole criterion of truth." The Third Plenum was thus a watershed in the history of the PRC: from then on, practical policies that could be measured by economic results were given priority over revolutionary actions that lacked focus or attainable aims.

Before and immediately after the Third Plenum, a movement for democracy took place. Perhaps to underscore the break with the legacy of the Cultural Revolution, party leaders relaxed restrictions on free expression. Public debate and open criticism of the government, past and present, suddenly appeared. Huge posters bearing democratic slogans, displayed on Democracy Wall in the center of Beijing, attracted much attention. At first this popular agitation was useful to the reform-minded Deng, but soon it became a threat to the regime and provoked a crackdown. Deng subsequently issued four guidelines for political discussion, stressing the primacy of the socialist road, the dictatorship of the proletariat, the vanguard party under the banner of Marxism-Leninism, and "Mao Zedong thought."

The Third Plenum had nonetheless produced important changes in leader-ship and policy. Two rising young stars, Hu Yaobang and Zhao Ziyang, were made full members of the Politburo. The history of the party was now revised, and some distortions of the past were corrected. Mao was still presented in a positive light, but he was criticized for creating a cult of personality and for leftist tendencies in his last twenty years. The Cultural Revolution was denounced as a prime example of Mao's reliance on theory over practice, but schemers such as the Lin Biao faction and the Gang of Four were blamed for the worst excesses. The Gang of Four was tried and sentenced to life in prison. (Jiang Qing and Zhang Qunqiao were sentenced to death, but this was commuted to life imprison-ment. Lesser figures were shown no such clemency.)

How China Is Ruled   After Mao's death, personal rule was replaced by institutionalized rule, but the institutions look and function much as they were intended to since the founding of the regime in 1949.

Although the 1982 constitution is the nation's fifth since 1949, formal government structures continue to be based on the Stalinist model—dual hierarchy of party and state organs radiating from the center outward and downward through regional levels to local units of administration and supervision. In theory, at least, the party formulates and coordinates policy, and the state bureaucracy implements it. (The ubiquitous local party committee monitors the implementation of party policy.) Under the principle of **dual rule**, adopted in 1956, state organs are responsible both to the next-higher level of state administration and to the party organization on the same level. In practice, this has meant that managers at any given level must serve two masters. This stultifying setup tends to stifle initiative and to demoralize the very bureaucrats whose efforts are essential to success.

Communist China's approach to administration is a legacy of the long civil war, when necessity required that the functions of party, state, and army be fused into an efficient instrument of mass mobilization. This tradition of **guerrilla administration** is reflected in a peculiar blend of civil and military functions, on the one hand, and party and state functions, on the other—one of the trademarks of Chinese communism. This blurring has always been discernible, but it was taken to new extremes during the Cultural Revolution, when party and state organizations from the provincial level down were dissolved and replaced by so-called revolutionary committees representing the PLA, "revolutionary mass organizations," and "revolutionary state and party cadres." Separate party organizations were reestablished in 1971, but state administration remained in the hands of revolutionary committees until 1979. The 1980s gave a new impetus to the separation of party and state.

The party is the supreme repository of institutional power in Communist China. It was built on the Leninist principle of democratic centralism (see Chapter 8) and patterned after the Communist Party of the Soviet Union. In theory, the highest-level policymaking body is the **National Party Congress**, which normally convenes every five years to elect the **Central Committee** of roughly 350 members (only 60 percent of whom can vote). The Central Committee in turn elects the **Politburo**, which has around twenty members. Unlike its former Soviet counterpart, the Chinese Politburo is not the most powerful decision-making body; this distinction is reserved for the **Standing Committee**, an inner circle of six or seven leaders who set economic priorities, formulate defense and foreign policies, and direct the pursuit of these priorities and policies. The **Secretariat**, which administers the party's daily affairs, is chosen by the Central Committee.

The **general secretary**, as head of the Secretariat, is the highest-ranking party official. (The position of chairman, preeminent in Mao's day, was abolished in the early 1980s.) China's top leader does not necessarily hold any particular title. Deng Xiaoping, for example, was clearly the most powerful figure in the PRC after 1978, but during much of the 1980s he did not hold a high formal position in either the party or the state. He was, however, chairman of the powerful Central Military Commission, set up by the 1982 constitution to supervise the armed forces.

The **State Council** is the chief executive organ of government. It is headed by the *premier*, who is theoretically appointed by the *president* with the approval of the **National People's Congress (NPC)**. The president, as chief of state, performs such formal duties as promulgating laws and decrees, ratifying treaties, appointing members of the State Council, and receiving foreign diplomats. The president serves a maximum of two five-year terms and is assisted by a vice-president, who becomes president if that position is vacated.

The premier heads the State Council (or government) and is assisted by a secretary general and two or three vice-premiers (reduced from thirteen in 1982). The State Council comprises the heads of forty-one ministries, commissions, and agencies (reduced from ninety-three in 1982). The State Council drafts laws for approval by the NPC, supervises the state bureaucracy, devises economic plans, and constructs national budgets. (Under the 1982 constitution, the PLA falls under the control of the State Council; it had reported directly to the Politburo.)

The 1982 constitution declared the National People's Congress "the highest organ of state power," but in reality it is a rubber stamp for the ruling organs of the party and the state. Its members are elected by provincial people's congresses and units of the PLA. The term of office is normally five years, and the NPC is supposed to convene once a year. (Because of the upheaval of the Cultural Revolution, the NPC did not meet from 1965 to 1975.) As a deliberative body with roughly three thousand members, the NPC is unwieldy; moreover, it meets for only a few days at a time. Hence it is largely symbolic. When the NPC is not in session, its duties are performed by the Standing Committee; with approximately 150 members, the committee is much better suited to act than the NPC itself. In theory, it possesses several important legislative, judicial, and executive powers, including the right to nullify laws it deems unconstitutional. Nevertheless, its functions appear to overlap with those of the State Council, and its actual role in the governing process is ambiguous.

The PRC does not have an independent judiciary. Since the late 1970s, however, there has been renewed emphasis on *socialist legality*, a policy that fits the attempt to foster stability, creativity, and productivity. After a short period of liberalization in 1978, the government clamped down on dissent in 1979 and 1980. The 1982 constitution devotes twenty-four articles to the "fundamental rights and duties of citizens," including freedom of speech, assembly, religion, and privacy. However, Article 51 introduces a caveat: the exercise of citizens' rights "may not infringe on the interests of the state, of society, and of the collective." Thus true liberty in the PRC remains elusive.

The Four Modernizations: China's Economic Reforms   Reform in the PRC has had little to do with political change. Rather, it has been focused on the **Four Modernizations**—of agriculture, industry, science and technology, and national defense. The most impressive early results came in agriculture. Between 1979 and 1981, the rural economy was completely converted from collectivized production to family farming. Long a net importer of food, feed, and fiber, the PRC quickly became a net exporter of grain and cotton.

The present farm system operates on a few simple principles. Land ownership is public rather than private, but peasants lease the farmland for fifteen years or more. Beyond a certain quota that must be delivered to the state each year, peasants are free to grow anything they wish. Many specialize in various agricultural services and participate in profit-making peripheral enterprises. Peasant incomes doubled in just a few years under this ersatz free-enterprise system. And as the rural economy became more diversified and more specialized, the proportion of the population directly dependent on agriculture (roughly 80 percent in the late 1970s) began to decline.

These impressive gains were not initially matched in the industrial sectors. Economic reforms in industry were introduced more cautiously. At first, industrial managers were allowed to market only a small amount of the output that exceeded their targets; the rest continued to go to the state. The main emphasis in this first phase was on the redress of sectoral imbalances between agriculture and industry and between heavy industry and light industry while allocating more resources to consumption and less to accumulation.

In October 1984, new arrangements were designed to decentralize industrial decision making—in effect, to dismantle the system of central planning. In all but a few strategic industries, taxation replaced quotas as the means of giving the state its due. Managers were, in theory, granted more discretion in making production, marketing, and investment decisions. Instructions from above were to be replaced by guidelines, and plan fulfillment was to be replaced by profit. The state would not withdraw entirely but would seek to control the operation of the market.

The most delicate and most difficult adjustments involved prices and wages. Under central planning, great distortions occurred. Prices reflected the government's priorities rather than the realities of the marketplace. Wages were set by the state, and labor had no means of organizing to improve pay, benefits, working conditions, or other concerns. Switching to a system in which prices and wages respond to market forces is bound to be destabilizing, both economically and politically. The state must relinquish some control over the economy; at the same time, workers' hopes for higher wages and a better life can lead to rising expectations that, if unmet, can provoke civil unrest. Thus in a previously controlled society, even purely economic reforms are politically risky.

The consequences of reduced control were evident in several reform-related problems. For example, enterprises and local governments tended to overspend on construction projects. Left to their own devices, managers did not introduce new technologies as rapidly as the central leadership had hoped. Other, older problems could not be solved by economic reforms. For example, energy shortages and an outmoded transportation system continued to hamper industrial production. Unused plant capacity and supply bottlenecks were the telltale signs of these two flaws in the economic infrastructure. Even so, China's industrial output grew considerably after 1978, and China's leaders set the optimistic goal of quadrupling the nation's GDP by the year 2000. This optimism still seems warranted.

Political Reconstruction   China's economic reforms were accompanied by legal and administrative reforms aimed at normalizing politics. Many new laws, decrees, and regulations were enacted, including the Criminal Law and the Law of Criminal Procedure. The civil rights protected under the 1982 constitution, however, are vitiated by law against "disruption of the socialist system." Nonetheless, the PRC's present political and legal systems have lasted longer than any others in its history.

In February 1980, the Secretariat of the Central Committee was resuscitated with Hu Yaobang as the new secretary general. Hu and Zhao Ziyang were elected to the powerful Standing Committee of the Politburo. Daily affairs of government are handled by the Secretariat and by the senior officials of the State Council. At the insistence of Deng Xiaoping, lifelong tenure for top party leaders was abolished. Equally important, the party was enjoined to take a hands-off approach to state administration, that is, to stop interfering in executive management. This reflected the new emphasis on pragmatism and professionalism in economic matters.

Hua Guofeng was gradually eased out between 1980 and 1982. In April 1980, he was replaced as premier by Zhao; a year later, he was replaced as party chairman by Hu and as chairman of the military affairs committee by Deng. In September 1982, Hua was removed from the Politburo. These changes confirmed the ascendency of the moderates, especially Deng.

As part of a purge of Maoist remnants, the position of chairman was abolished in 1982, and the office of president was restored. In June 1983, Li Xiannian was elected president by the NPC. The normalization of Chinese politics was complete.

Major changes in party leadership occurred in September 1985 when the party held its first national conference in four decades. Ten elder members of the Politburo retired at this time, making room for six new younger ones. In addition, five new members were appointed to the Secretariat, and ninety-one (fifty-six full members and thirty-five alternates) were added to the Central Committee. Sixty-four of these new recruits were relatively young—their average age was 50. These changes represented a victory for Deng, who wanted to rejuvenate and professionalize the top leadership as part of his plan to modernize the economy.

The Twelfth Central Committee Plenum, held in September 1986, sought to bring party ideology into line with the new pragmatism. One resolution adopted at this meeting called for greater freedom of expression. It also reaffirmed the open door in foreign policy, especially in trade and investment. Finally, it defended the reforms against attacks by conservative critics within the old guard.

During this period, Deng also restructured, streamlined, depoliticized, and professionalized the army; retired older officers; and made promotion dependent on merit (in particular, outstanding performance in military academies). The armed forces were cut by 25 percent (one million men), and military regions were reduced from thirteen to seven. Above all, Deng and his confederates redefined the army's mission to exclude domestic functions; the military was now clearly focused on national defense. China's government was thus reclaimed in full by Deng Xiaoping and the new civilian leadership.

Political Reform: The Limits of Change   By early 1986, at least part of the PRC's leadership had apparently decided that continued economic revitalization, especially in urban industrial sectors, was impossible without some sort of political restructuring. During the first nine months of 1986, articles appeared in the Chinese press advocating greater autonomy for plant managers in decisions regarding consumption, production, and research—precisely the areas that the party had reserved for itself. Moving in this direction would thus diminish the powers of the party. Some advocates of liberalization went even further, maintaining that China's rapid transition from feudalism to socialism had bypassed the capitalist stage altogether. Consequently, according to this view, China lacked the capital accumulation that normally occurred during the capitalist stage; the only way to make up for this deficiency was to extend the open-door policy further—allow greater competition, give more play to market forces, even create a stock exchange to facilitate the raising of venture capital.

In 1987, an ideological struggle erupted within the party leadership, precipitated by massive demonstrations the previous December by students demanding democracy and Western-style freedoms. In one camp were the reformers, presumably led by Deng Xiaoping and Zhao Ziyang; in the other were the conservative old guard, led by such party stalwarts as Peng Zhen, Li Xiannian, and Chen Yun. Because Deng had expressed his intention to retire after the Thirteenth National Congress scheduled for fall 1987, the leadership struggle was in effect a succession crisis; the future direction of the country was at stake.

In January 1987, Premier Hu Yaobang, a Deng protégé, was forced to resign, following self-criticism in which he took the blame for the student uprisings. He confessed to having allowed "bourgeois liberalization" (officially defined as "the negation of the socialist system in favor of capitalism") to pollute the political environment. It was clear that Hu was the scapegoat, that he had in fact been faithful to Deng's wishes. Nonetheless, Deng, wily veteran of many battles, managed to survive this challenge unscathed. That also ensured the survival of his economic reforms.

The Chinese leadership remained divided over the pace and scope of reform. The Thirteenth Party Congress, held in October 1987, brought a further rejuvenation of the PRC's leadership, as aging members of the top party organs bowed out to make room for a new generation of leaders. Seven new members were added to the Politburo. Among the five members of the Politburo's prestigious Standing Committee, only General Secretary Zhao Ziyang was a carryover from the previous ruling group. Perhaps the preoccupation with this changing of the guard explains why no major policy initiatives were undertaken.

Beijing's leading reformer, the purged Hu Yaobang, died on April 15, 1989, while attempting a political comeback. Hu's death triggered student demonstrations that led directly to yet another struggle for power within the PRC's top leadership. Subjected to a thinly veiled attack in the official *People's Daily* for engineering a "planned conspiracy," the reform-minded Zhao Ziyang publicly defended the students as "well intentioned and patriotic." In the end, Zhao himself was purged, and the hard-liners once again gained the upper hand—but not before the bloodiest crackdown since the Cultural Revolution, a massacre in Beijing's Tiananmen Square, brought death to several thousand demonstrators and dashed all hopes for the triumph of liberal reforms. The tragedy of Tiananmen and its aftermath are discussed in Chapter 15.

Reforms, Beijing-Style: Why There Is No Chinese Gorbachev   The Chinese leadership watched the drama unfolding in the Soviet Union closely and critically. Gorbachev's promises of economic reform had almost certainly been inspired by the Chinese example. But he made economic reform secondary to rapid political and cultural liberalization. By Beijing's lights, Gorbachev thus put the cart before the horse: he created the conditions for political dissent without first attacking the underlying economic causes of growing social unrest. The social fabric of the Soviet Union quickly unraveled, and the once-impregnable fortress of the Bolshevik party-state collapsed.

In stark contrast to the failed Gorbachev strategy, China's reforms have been confined to the economic realm. Measures such as decollectivization of agriculture, liberalization of foreign trade, and encouragement of free enterprise have not been accompanied by parallel reforms in the cultural and political spheres. China's approach to reform may thus be less gratifying to Westerners, but it appears to be succeeding spectacularly.

Japan: Land of the Rising Sun

As noted in Chapter 13, Japan had little experience with democracy before the 1940s. Its history and culture were in many ways antithetical to Western democratic ideas. Today, a half century after its crushing defeat in World War II, Japan is a shining example of democracy and capitalism in Asia. At the same time, its politics and government reflect Japan's unique cultural heritage.

The 1947 Constitution   The United States was in a commanding position in Japan after World War II. The 1947 constitution, still essentially unchanged, embodied U.S. resolve never to permit a resurgence of Japanese militarism. The American influence on the Japanese constitution is especially apparent in its preamble:

> We, the Japanese people, acting through our duly elected representatives in
> the National Diet, determined that we shall secure for ourselves and our posterity
> the fruits of peaceful cooperation with all nations and the blessings of liberty
> throughout this land, and resolved that never again shall we be visited with
> the horrors of war through the action of government, do proclaim that sovereign

power resides with the people and do firmly establish this Constitution. . . . Government is a sacred trust of the people, the authority for which is derived from the people, the powers of which are exercised by representatives of the people, and the benefits of which are enjoyed by the people.

The framers of the 1947 constitution sought to construct an elaborate system of representative government for Japan. In addition to a wide range of civil liberties, the constitution guarantees the right of citizens to an equal education and the right of workers to organize and engage in collective bargaining.

Article 9 explicitly renounces war and pledges that "land, sea, and air forces, as well as other war potential, will never be maintained," although self-defensive forces are permitted. Japan has taken this pledge seriously; until recently, it spent less than 1 percent of its GNP on defense. Ironically, this has given the Japanese a competitive edge in world trade: with the United States assuming the security burden, Tokyo has been free to concentrate on industrial development.

The role and mission of the self-defensive forces became the focus of political controversy in 1992, when the Liberal Democratic party, under pressure from other governments (especially the United States), moved to allow Japanese forces to be deployed outside Japan. Although these forces were to be restricted to humanitarian missions, the opposition charged that *any* dispatch of Japanese soldiers to foreign soil would be a violation of Japan's constitution.

Government by Consensus   Japan has a parliamentary form of government. The emperor is nominally the chief of state, but his duties are strictly ceremonial. The real chief executive is the prime minister, who is chosen by the majority party in the **Diet** (parliament). In theory a powerful figure, the prime minister must mediate among various factions in the majority party to function effectively. The prime minister has the constitutional power to choose and dismiss the twenty or so cabinet ministers. Only civilians may serve in the cabinet (to prevent a recurrence of militarism), and a majority of members, including the prime minister, must hold Diet seats.

The cabinet prepares and submits the annual budget to the Diet, formulates domestic and foreign policies, manages the bureaucracy, negotiates treaties, and reports to the Diet on national and international affairs. In short, the cabinet heads the executive branch of the government. As in Great Britain, the principle of collective responsibility is observed—all cabinet members are jointly responsible for all policies and decisions of the government. In keeping with Japanese tradition, decisions are usually made by consensus; taking a formal vote, especially in the intimacy of a small group, is alien to Japan's political culture. Personal bonds of mutual trust play a major role in virtually all social, political, and even economic transactions. By the same token, the legalism so prevalent in Western constitutional democracies is almost entirely lacking in Japan.

The authors of the constitution intended to place supreme power in Japan's bicameral Diet. This legislature is divided into the House of Representatives (511 members serving four-year terms) and the House of Councillors (252 members serving six-year terms). Members of each house are elected by universal suffrage from multimember districts in which voters make only one selection from a list of candidates from various political parties (often five or more). Smaller parties, such as the Clean Government party and the Communist party, can obtain seats in the Diet quite easily; for example, in a four-member district, a candidate can win by coming in fourth.

In such an electoral system, the distribution of votes is crucial. If the dominant **Liberal Democatic party (LDP)** puts up candidates for all the seats in a given district and one candidate attracts most of the votes cast for the LDP in that district, strong candidates from smaller parties have a good chance of securing seats. (Small parties may thus choose to run but a single candidate in order to make every vote count.)

The constitution declared that popular sovereignty was to be expressed through the Diet, the only institution empowered to make laws. Whereas the prime minister and cabinet had been answerable to the emperor, they were now responsible to the Diet, "the highest organ of state power."

Thus the Japanese parliamentary system closely resembles the British system. For example, the lower house of the Diet can force a government to resign through a vote of no confidence. (Alternatively, the cabinet can dissolve the lower house and call for new elections following a no-confidence vote.) But appearances are sometimes deceiving, for the Japanese have adapted Western institutions to their own political culture. The result is a unique system that combines democratic politics and market economics with traditional Japanese political hierarchy, economic conglomeration, and social discipline.

The distinction between formal (constitutional) powers and informal (real) power is crucial to understanding any political system, and Japan is no exception. Although formal power is vested in the Diet by the constitution, the country is actually run by a triad consisting of top bureaucrats, corporate leaders, and LDP chiefs.

Japan's Ruling Party and Its Rivals   The Liberal Democratic party has dominated Japanese politics since 1945, making Japan a **one-party-dominant system**. Although numerous smaller parties have appeared, they have usually been ineffectual. The Socialist party has come closest to challenging the LDP, but its role has been confined to parliamentary opposition.

The governing of Japan has fallen exclusively to the LDP. In a constitutional democracy, such success usually indicates that the government is identified with progressive economic and social policies and that the society is prosperous. Such is the case in Japan. After the war, the conservatives implemented the reforms imposed by General MacArthur and skillfully minimized discontinuities with the past. As the party in power, the LDP "controlled a considerable amount of patronage and had the advantage when seeking the support of economic and professional interest groups." It could count on a majority of the rural vote and had access to the resources of the business community. It was also "on intimate terms with the bureaucracy."[1] But these advantages would not have been enough to keep the LDP in power had the party not taken one additional step: in the mid-1950s, it began building a national organization with mass membership—"a surprisingly difficult thing to do in Japan where, on the local scene, groups based on personal loyalties, often around one individual, were more acceptable than branch units of a national party."[2]

In short, the LDP has succeeded by co-opting much of the opposition, satisfying a multiplicity of interests, and seeking broad popular appeal rather than ideological purity. The LDP is thus a classic catch-all party: instead of depending on a particular social class, it draws support from a wide range of interest groups.

The internal power structure of the LDP becomes especially crucial during biennial party conferences, at which the party elects its president, who in turn becomes the prime minister by virtue of leading the majority party. Thus Japan's chief executive is elected by a political party. This method may seem undemocratic, but Japanese voters do have an opportunity to choose a new majority party at least every four years. (Elections have actually occurred more frequently—every two years, on average.) Moreover, LDP conferences are nothing like the staged and orchestrated party conclaves held in Communist China or the former Soviet Union. In Japan, the outcome of presidential balloting is the result of intense bargaining by factions, each of which has its own leader, its own constituencies, and its own policies.

As noted in Chapter 13, Japan has retained some elements of its patron-client system. Before World War II, Japan had been ruled by powerful heads of factions and cliques who built and maintained power bases by dispensing personal favors and rewards. This aspect of the political system has endured, in less pronounced form. Perhaps the most important vehicle for perpetuating Japan's patron-client tradition has been the LDP itself.

Because the LDP held power for four decades and because it still embraces an assortment of political interests, powerful factional leaders have emerged within the party organization. They "feed" their factions with money and influence obtained through personal support groups known as *koenkai*. As the political fortunes of party leaders rise and fall, the faction leaders act as power brokers, deciding who will become prime minister and which cabinet post will go to whom. By contemporary Western standards, this system may seem neither open nor democratic, but by Japanese standards, it is remarkably Americanized. Even so, the "paradox of Japan's being an open society made up of closed components" continues to set Japanese democracy apart from its counterparts in the West.[3]

Despite LDP dominance, Japanese voters have not lacked party choices. In addition to the Socialists (JSP), there are the Democratic Socialists (DSP) and the Communists (JCP). There is also the Clean Government party (Komeito), which is the political offshoot of the Value Creation Society (Soka Gakkai), one of Japan's recently established religious sects. (A ruling by the Japanese Supreme Court barring religious sponsorship of political parties forced the Komeito to sever its formal ties with Soka Gakkai, but the public continues to identify the party with the religion that spawned it.) In addition, several new political parties sprang up in the early 1990s after a series of political scandals involving top LDP leaders badly tarnished the party's image.

Following the collapse of the Miyazawa government in 1993, the LDP lost its legislative majority for the first time in forty years. This reversal led to the formation of a seven-party coalition government (see Chapter 15). Japan's new government is headed by Morihiro Hosokawa whose upstart Japan New party captured a mere thirty-five parliamentary seats. The LDP, now in opposition to the new government, nonetheless remains the largest party in parliament. Its closest rival, the Social Democratic party, claimed only seventy seats.

In national elections, the LDP normally wins 46 to 48 percent of the popular vote: prior to 1993, it had never fallen below 42 percent. The Socialists (now called the Social Democratic party) usually capture about 20 percent, and other minor parties typically win 10 percent or less. Again, the 1993 election was an exception: several new parties garnered enough votes to win a combined total of more than one hundred seats in the Diet. (The precedent-breaking election of 1993 and its consequences will be discussed in greater detail in Chapter 15.)

The electoral mechanism tends to magnify the LDP's plurality enough to give it a clear majority in the Diet, partly through a Japanese-style **gerrymandering**—manipulating district boundaries so as to favor farmers, who traditionally support the LDP. Now that the LDP's rivals are in power it is likely that *they* will endeavor to redraw the electoral districts.

Stability and Prosperity   Despite occasional riots, demonstrations, and even violent outbursts in the Diet, Japan's democratic government has been remarkably stable. This is all the more impressive considering that Japan's political traditions before 1947 were authoritarian. Economics has played a key role, for Japan's economic revival after World War II was little short of miraculous.

Close cooperation between political and business elites was one major reason for the Japanese postwar prosperity, but a drive to penetrate overseas markets and massive infusions of American aid during the Korean War were also crucial. Within two decades, the alliance of government, business, and labor that became a Japanese trademark produced huge advances in industry and technology. Today Japan is an economic superpower, second only to the United States—this despite "the loss of 52 percent of Japan's prewar territories, the return of 5,000,000 persons to a country about the size of California, the loss of 80 percent of Japan's shipping, and the destruction of one-fifth of her industrial plants and many of her great cities."[4] In the 1980s, the success of the Japanese market economy was clearly apparent in Japan's massive multibillion-dollar trade surpluses with the United States, which absorbs more than one-third of Japan's exports.

Japan's political and economic success, like that of Germany, indicates that self-government that is adapted to suit specific national circumstances can work in a variety of social and cultural contexts. India, too, illustrates that representative democracy can work even in a country that is ethnically diverse, overpopulated, and impoverished.

India: Democracy amid Diversity

Although a democracy like Japan, India is beset by chronic economic problems. The country seems ill-prepared for democracy:

> I have the impression that when we talk so confidently of liberty, we are unaware of the awful servitudes that are created by the ancient enemies of mankind: the servitude of poverty when means are so small that there is literally no choice at all; the servitude of ignorance when there are no perspectives to which the mind can open because there is no education . . . ; the servitude of ill-health which means that the expectation of life is almost too short to allow for any experience of freedom. . . .[5]

Such doubts about the appropriateness of democracy for the Third World seem especially germane to India, that nation of 865 million people encompassing a bewildering array of cultures, languages, religions, and ethnic identities.

India's Drive for Independence   India's quest for self-rule can be traced back to the nineteenth century. Great Britain had originally ruled India indirectly, through Indian intermediaries and allies, but in the process it introduced various institutions that the British found useful, including property laws and notions about the nature and functions of government. Indians chosen for minor posts in colonial administration were first sent to England to receive a "proper classical education." Familiarity with Western ideas of equality, liberty, social justice, and representative democracy spread among India's English-speaking elites—merchants, landlords, public officials, doctors, lawyers, teachers—whose common interests transcended caste, religion, or region. After 1885, they began to meet annually in a conference called the **Indian National Congress**, the seed from which the independence movement would spring.

The British yielded power in India gradually and reluctantly. World War I strained Britain's resources, and London conceded that it would be necessary to transfer power (but not sovereignty) to Indian hands. Beginning in 1919, the National Congress, led by Mahatma Gandhi, conducted nationwide campaigns of **civil disobedience** (*satyagraha*), or passive resistance to British rule. Periods of confrontation (1919–1922, 1929–1932, 1942) alternated with periods of Congress participation, first in a power-sharing arrangement known as *dyarchy* and, after 1935, in provincial self-government.

The last thirty years of British rule saw the National Congress grow steadily in stature and strength, evolving into a major force in Indian politics—at once a mass movement, a political party, and an alternative government.

The rise of the Congress, however, created a schism between Hindus and Muslims; the latter came to regard the Congress as just as dangerous to Muslim interests as the British themselves. Bloody communal riots occurred in the 1940s. When the British quit India after World War II, they chose the easy way out by partitioning the subcontinent along religious lines.

The most contentious issue involved the future of Jammu and Kashmir. Located between India and Pakistan, Kashmir was partitioned between them in 1947, but both claimed the entire territory. Kashmir was ruled locally by a

Hindu maharaja, but the population was predominantly Muslim and sought union with Pakistan; the maharaja favored merger with India. Hostilities erupted almost immediately. It was the first of three major wars between India and Pakistan (1947, 1965, and 1971). Inside India, too, communal violence between Hindus and Muslims has been a recurring problem.

The Indian Constitution   Although India gained independence from Great Britain in 1947, it took nearly three years to complete the new constitution. India's diverse society and sprawling geography necessitated not only a federal model but also the specific delineation of how power would be parceled out. The resultant constitution was a long and intricate document, containing not one list of powers but three: the **Union List**, enumerating powers of the central government; the **State List**, reserving certain powers to the provincial government; and the **Concurrent List**, spelling out the powers to be shared by both.

The division of power is laid out in painstaking detail. The Union List contains ninety-seven items covering national defense, the armed forces, atomic energy, foreign affairs, transportation, communications, banking, currency, insurance, regulation of industry and mining, income taxes, customs duties, and other areas. Enumerated in the State List are sixty-six items of primarily local interest: legal administration, public health and sanitation, education, agriculture, forests, fisheries, burials, duties on alcohol, and a variety of taxes (especially land taxes). The Concurrent List contains forty-seven items that fall into gray areas: marriage and divorce, contracts, bankruptcy, civil suits, trade unions, social security, labor welfare, price controls, and so on. States may pass their own laws dealing with these matters, but the constitution stipulates that national law always prevails over state law.

Federalism: Overcoming Language Barriers   The Indian federal system divides the country into twenty-three states and eight union territories. It strongly favors the central government to counterbalance the centrifugal tendencies inherent in India's cultural and linguistic diversity.

Because language had at times been a source of civil strife, India's states were deliberately drawn along linguistic lines. The Indian Federal Union was reorganized in 1956; the number of states was reduced, and all but two of the new states were based on regional language patterns. English, a vestige of the colonial past, has remained the language of privilege and power. Although the 1949 Constitutional Assembly specified that Hindi would become the national language after 1965, regional opposition was so violent that this timetable had to be abandoned. Rather than one national language, India has adopted a three-language formula: schoolchildren learn to read and write in their native tongue but also study English and Hindi.

The Central Government   India's independence leaders were well aware of the dangers inherent in the nation's cultural diversity, so they designed a highly centralized democratic system in federal form.

The powers of the central government are epitomized by elaborate constitutional provisions covering states of emergencies. A national state of emergency can be declared in cases of imminent war or revolution. (Under this provision, Prime Minister Indira Gandhi, facing a challenge to her political authority, suspended the constitution in 1975 and assumed dictatorial powers for a period of nineteen months.) In addition, through a special declaration of emergency, the central government can take over any state that is threatened with a breakdown of law and order. Finally, if a state becomes financially insolvent, the central government can declare an economic emergency and can step in to run state affairs until the situation is under control.

The legislature, called the **Federal Parliament**, is divided into two houses. The upper house, known as the **Council of the States** (*rajya sabha*), has considerable legislative power, except in budget matters, where it has only the power to delay. Far more powerful is the **House of the People** (*lok sabha*), modeled after the British House of Commons. An interesting aspect of the lower house is that it reserves a certain number of seats for groups that were victims of past discrimination, including former untouchables (outcasts).

As in other parliamentary systems, India's executive is divided. The president, or chief of state, is chosen by an electoral college made up of officials from the Federal Parliament and state assemblies. The prime minister, the head of government who appoints the cabinet, directs policy formulation, and represents the nation abroad, is elected by the majority party or coalition in the House of the People. Except for two brief spells, the prime minister has always been the head of the **Congress party**, the dominant party since independence.

The Judiciary, Civil Liberties, and Social Rights   India has an independent judiciary that acts as a bulwark against official abuses of human rights. However, during periods of "presidential rule," civil liberties have been suspended, and political opponents have been arrested and jailed. The most notorious use of these emergency powers occurred in the mid-1970s when Indira Gandhi ruled as a virtual dictator for nineteen months. These powers have been used often by the central government when instability in a particular state has led to a breakdown of law and order. But ordinarily, India's citizens enjoy freedom of speech, the press, assembly, religion, and so on.

Of particular interest is a section of the constitution that sets forth basic "social" rights (as opposed to the more familiar civil rights). These can be found in the "directives," of which Article 39 is a prominent part. It stipulates:

> The State shall, in particular, direct its policy towards securing
> a. that the citizens, men and women equally, have the right to an adequate means of livelihood;
> b. that the ownership and control of the material resources of the community are so distributed as best to subserve the common good;
> c. that the operation of the economic system does not result in the concentration of wealth and means of production to the common detriment;
> d. that there is equal pay for equal work for both men and women;

   e. that the health and strength of workers, men and women, and the tender age of children are not abused and that citizens are not forced by economic necessity to enter avocations unsuited to their age or strength.

India's One-Party-Dominant System   Before it broke up in the late 1960s, the Congress party encompassed a variety of interests and was supported by middle- and upper-class nationalists as well as by many members of traditionally lower castes. With the disintegration of the party and the emergence of Indira Gandhi as the eventual successor to her father, Jawaharlal Nehru (1889–1964), a major political realignment appeared likely. What actually happened, however, is that one preeminent party merely replaced another, and the basic power structure in India did not change.

   A new national party emerged from the old Congress coalition—Prime Minister Gandhi's **New Congress party**, later renamed the **Congress I** (for "Indira"), which was essentially a reincarnation of the one-party-dominant system under Gandhi's personal tutelage. Against fragmented and ineffectual opposition, she was able to remain in power despite growing disenchantment with her methods and policies.

   When Gandhi declared the state of emergency in 1975, she had many opposition leaders arrested. At the end of martial law in 1977, new elections were announced, and the revitalized opposition parties formed an umbrella organization, led by Morarji Desai, known as the **Janata party**. This loose-knit coalition won a parliamentary majority and formed a government, but its fragile unity was predicated on little else than hostility toward Gandhi. Lacking consensus or a coherent program, the coalition lasted only two years. As India's foreign and domestic problems mounted, the need for a strong leader became more and more apparent; in the 1980 parliamentary elections, the Congress I won an overwhelming victory (albeit with only 42 percent of the popular vote) and again fashioned a coalition that enabled Gandhi to form a government. The Janata party faded into oblivion, and the other parties once again became part of a fragmented and ineffectual opposition.

Communal Violence: India's "Low-Intensity" Civil War   Gandhi's return to power was plagued with misfortune, turmoil, and tragedy. First, her son Sanjay, who won a seat in the *lok sabha* in 1980, was killed in an airplane crash. Then a resurgence of caste and communal violence threatened Indian society as religious and regional separatism racked the federal structure. In Assam and northeast India, hatred of Bengalis and immigrants was expressed in murders, bombings, strikes, and civil disobedience. Hundreds of lives were lost in 1982 and 1983. When Prime Minister Gandhi tried to hold new elections rather than prolong presidential rule, the violence escalated, and New Delhi was forced to make concessions to the militants. Violence also broke out in Kashmir during another election.

   The bloodiest outbreaks, however, occurred in Punjab, where a Sikh secessionist movement had been brewing for several years. At first, the secessionists represented a small minority, but Punjabis became polarized as hundreds of people, most of them Hindu, were killed by terrorists. Hindus pressured the central government to intervene. The climax came after an extremist Sikh leader, Jarnail Singh Bhindranwale, turned the Golden Temple of Amritsar into a terrorist stronghold. The Indian army stormed the citadel, killing Bhindranwale and hundreds of his backers and damaging sacred buildings. An army blockade and curfew followed. Sikh troops mutinied in various parts of India, but the ultimate act of retribution occurred when Sikh members of Indira Gandhi's personal guard assassinated her.

Gandhi's martyrdom came when her popularity was at low ebb, but Congress I and the country rallied around her surviving son, Rajiv, who had entered politics after his younger brother's untimely death in 1980. In the elections of December 1984, Congress I won a landslide victory, capturing all but 19 of the 508 seats contested.

Rajiv Gandhi won early respect for his conciliatory gestures both at home and abroad. But the success of the Congress I party at the national level was not matched by similar success in state elections. These defeats undermined Rajiv's credibility, as did continuing communal violence and a resurgence of Sikh separatism. In the summer of 1987, Sikh militants launched a new terrorist offensive. Such intractable problems, plus charges of high-level corruption within the government, a personally damaging conflict over constitutional issues with the outgoing president, and a series of cabinet resignations, raised doubts about the fate of India's democracy.

This point deserves special emphasis. Indian society has not become secularized, despite the efforts of such great Indian leaders as Gandhi and Nehru. The importance of secularization in the context of a multicultural society like India has little to do with religious piety and much to do with political stability. The contrast here between India, on the one hand, and Japan or China, on the other, is stark, as we will see in Chapter 15. For now, suffice it to say that India's continuing social and political instability, caused above all by its communal divisions, is a major obstacle to domestic tranquillity. Without civil order, there is virtually no chance that India will be able to solve its pressing economic problems or compete with other up-and-coming Asian nations.

The Indian Synthesis   India has traditionally been ruled by charismatic leaders. The great Mahatma Gandhi was the first in a succession of dominant Congress figures. After him, both the party and the nation came to be dominated by a new dynasty. Nehru ruled from 1947 to 1964; Indira Gandhi, his daughter, from 1966 to 1977 and 1980 to 1984. When she was assassinated and her son Rajiv succeeded her, the tradition of dynastic rule appeared to have returned in a new guise, adapted to the structures and processes of constitutional democracy. This ability to synthesize foreign and indigenous elements into a new political order is a striking feature of contemporary Asian politics visible in Japan and China as well as in India.

The presence of firm leadership throughout the postwar period was undoubtedly the key to India's success with democracy. In late 1989, political scandals and social unrest forced Rajiv Gandhi to step down. His successor, V. P. Singh, when confronted with continuing Sikh terror in Punjab, resorted to emergency rule—the same policy for which he had criticized Gandhi—and the situation in Kashmir threatened to burst into flames. Singh's government fell under the strain.

Rajiv Gandhi was assassinated in May 1991 while campaigning to regain his position as prime minister. In the absence of a leader of great stature capable of healing the nation's social and political wounds, the prospects for stability in India are bleak. Can India survive as an integrated nation-state? We explore this question in the next chapter.

CONCLUSION

The political traditions of Asia are distinct from those of Europe and the Middle East. Although both the Asian and Arab political traditions and systems have been predominantly authoritarian, many Asian societies display a greater propensity to assimilate and adapt certain features of Western society (such as secularization and the emergence of a large middle class) and Western political economics (including market economies, liberal trade policies, mass consumption, techno-logical innovation, free elections, and parliamentary democracy). India is a notable exception because it has not become secular nor, as we shall see in the next chapter, is it becoming a mass-consumption society (in contrast to its even more populous neighbor, China). Also, Asia displays a greater maldistribution of wealth than any other region in the world. That pattern, and its implications for the future of Asian nations, is the focus of Chapter 15.

KEY TERMS

Korean War
military dictatorship
"civilitary" rule
People's Liberation Army (PLA)
nonalignment
Hundred Flowers movement
Great Leap Forward
Maoism
"Mao Zedong thought"
Great Proletarian Cultural Revolution
Red Guards
Gang of Four
Third Plenum
dual rule

guerrilla administration
National Party Congress
Central Committee
Politburo
Standing Committee
Secretariat
general secretary
State Council
National People's Congress (NPC)
Four Modernizations
Diet
Liberal Democratic party
one-party-dominant system
koenkai

gerrymandering
Indian National Congress
civil disobedience
Union List
State List
Concurrent List

Federal Parliament
Council of the States
House of the People
Congress party
New Congress (Congress I) party
Janata party

STUDY QUESTIONS

1. What effects did the outcome of World War II have on political systems in China, Japan, and India?
2. What was China's Great Leap Forward? Was the Cultural Revolution a second "great leap," or was it qualitatively different? Why did Mao believe it was necessary to launch periodic revolutions from above? Is Maoism dead, or does the ghost of Mao continue to haunt the PRC?
3. How is the People's Republic of China governed? What, if anything, changed after Mao's death?
4. How does Japan's political system work? How is it similar to Western parliamentary government? How is it different?
5. Given the multiethnic nature of Indian society, how can India function as a parliamentary democracy? What features of other political systems did India borrow? What features are unique to India?

SUGGESTED READING

Chang, David Wen-wei. *China under Deng Xiaoping: Political and Economic Reform.* New York: St. Martin's Press, 1991.

Hardgrave, Robert L., Jr., and Kochanek, Stanley A. *India: Government and Politics of a Developing Nation.* 4th ed. Orlando, Fla.: Harcourt, 1986.

Hrebenar, Ronald J. *The Japanese Party System: From One-Party Rule to Coalition Government.* 2nd ed. Boulder, Colo.: Westview Press, 1992.

Kohli, Atul, ed. *India's Democracy: An Analysis of Changing State-Society Relations.* Princeton, N.J.: Princeton University Press, 1990.

Lieberthal, Kenneth J., and Oksenberg, Michel. *Policymaking in China: Leaders, Structures, and Processes.* Princeton, N.J.: Princeton University Press, 1990.

Manor, James. "India: State and Society Diverge." *Current History,* December 1989.

Pye, Lucian W. *The Spirit of Chinese Politics.* 2nd ed. Cambridge, Mass.: Harvard University Press, 1992.

Reischauer, Edwin O. *Japan: The Story of a Nation.* 4th ed. New York: Knopf, 1991.

Richardson, Bradley M., and Flanagan, Scott C. *Politics in Japan.* Glenview, Ill.: Scott, Foresman, 1987.

NOTES

1. Franz Michael and George Taylor, *The Far East in the Modern World* (New York: Holt, 1964), p. 607.
2. Ibid.
3. Robert H. Scalapino and Junnosuki Masumi, *Parties and Politics in Contemporary Japan* (Berkeley: University of California Press, 1962), p. 153.
4. Franz Michael and George Taylor, *The Far East in the Modern World* (New York: Holt, 1964), p. 603.
5. Barbara Ward, *The Rich Nations and the Poor Nations* (New York: Norton, 1962), pp. 158–159.

15

A Regional Economic Miracle in the Making?

As the twentieth century wanes, Asia stands at a crossroads between past and future, tradition and modernity, nationalism and regionalism. Today's world offers little choice but to modernize or retreat into self-defeating isolationism. The question is not *whether* to change but *how*. A key issue for many Asian nations is how to manage change so that the economy grows and society prospers without eroding moral, spiritual, cultural, and aesthetic values.

Economic Differences among Asian Nations

In terms of economic development, one of Asia's most striking features is its variety. Apart from Japan, which is in a class by itself, Asian nations can be grouped into several categories: **newly industrialized countries (NICs)**; **newly exporting countries (NECs)**; **Marxist-Leninist countries (MLCs)**, in which central planning has been substituted for market forces; and **less developed countries (LDCs)**. Many LDCs face serious problems arising from food shortages, land and resource scarcity, natural disasters, and the like. South Asia is home to several of these nations—including India, Pakistan, and Bangladesh—in which meeting basic human needs absorbs virtually all available resources. For lack of a better term, we will call these nations **basic-needs countries (BNCs)**.

As noted in earlier chapters, no classification scheme is perfect. Some countries fit into more than one category. For example, Vietnam is both an MLC and a BNC; India is both an NIC and a BNC; Indonesia is both an NEC and a

BNC. These distinctions illustrate the diversity of developmental stages and strategies found throughout Asia. They also call attention to the possible relationship between strategies and stages of development.

The Wealth of (Some) Nations

The richest nation in Asia is Japan. Its GNP ranks second in the world (surpassed only by that of the United States), and the Japanese economy is the most dynamic among industrially developed nations (see Table 15.1). In fact, its very success has been a major source of friction between Japan and its trading partners, especially the United States.[1]

Nor is Japan the only prosperous country in Asia. South Korea, Taiwan, Hong Kong, Singapore, and now the People's Republic of China have all shown remarkable economic vitality (see Table 15.2). These NICs are not only emulating Japan but also exporting to Japan. They are producing a variety of consumer goods at lower costs than the Japanese. This "import invasion" poses a challenge to Japan, potentially as formidable as Japan's challenge to the United States since the 1960s.

Until quite recently, Taiwan's economic miracle contrasted sharply with the troubled economic history of mainland China since 1949, when the revolution catapulted the Chinese Communist party to power. In the 1980s, the economy of tiny Taiwan was ten times richer than that of the giant on the mainland. Taiwan bustles with economic activity of all kinds. Per capita GNP is about $5,000, and consumer durable goods are available at affordable prices. Taiwan's economy has absorbed new technology like a sponge; the result is prosperity built on a foundation of massive exports. Taiwan is the world's twelfth-largest trader, and the fifth-largest trading partner with the United States. In 1988, its foreign-exchange reserves were more than $75 billion.[2] As we shall see, the PRC

Table 15.1 Comparison of Seven Leading Economies (percent per annum)

	Gross National Product (GNP) Real Growth, 1980–1991	Real GNP Growth Per Capita, 1980–1991
United States	3.1	2.1
Canada	3.1	2.1
Japan	4.3	3.7
Germany	2.3	2.2
France	2.3	1.8
Italy	2.4	2.1
Great Britain	2.8	2.6

Source: Data from the World Bank, *The World Bank Atlas* (Washington, D.C.: World International Bank for Reconstruction and Development/The World Bank, 1992). Published by Oxford University Press, Inc., New York.

Table 15.2 Growth in Four of Japan's Asian Challengers (percent per annum)

	1970–1983	1980–1991	Per Capita, 1980–1991
China	7.8	9.4	7.8
Hong Kong	8.7	6.9	5.4
South Korea	7.1	10.0	8.8
Singapore	8.9	7.1	4.9

Source: Data from the World Bank, *The World Bank Atlas* (Washington, D.C.: World International Bank for Reconstruction and Development/The World Bank, 1992). Published by Oxford University Press, Inc., New York.

on the mainland now seems to be replicating Taiwan's economic miracle, in the face of far greater obstacles.

Just as Japan has set an example for Asia's NICs, they in turn have set an example for other Asian nations. Indonesia, the Philippines, and Thailand have all improved their external trade position vis-à-vis Japan, particularly in agricultural and fishery products. Between 1984 and 1986, this export surge halved the annual combined trade deficit among the members of the **Association of Southeast Asian Nations** (**ASEAN**; members are Indonesia, Malaysia, the Philippines, Thailand, and Singapore). These states (and a few others) are being called "newly exporting countries" because their economic prospects are so closely tied to exports. If Japan's model works as well elsewhere in Asia as it has in South Korea, Taiwan, Hong Kong, Singapore, and the PRC, today's NECs may reasonably aspire to become tomorrow's NICs.

The Marxist-Leninist states in Asia are North Korea, the PRC, Vietnam, Laos, and Cambodia. Vietnam dominates Indochina politically, but its overall economic performance has been dismal. The PRC has shifted from a near total reliance on central planning to an approximation of free-market conditions, especially in the agricultural sector; indeed, the vast nation has achieved food self-sufficiency thanks to market-oriented economic reforms instituted since 1979. North Korea remains an unreconstructed Stalinist state with a largely autarkic economy; until the PRC's recent economic resurgence, it was probably the most economically viable Marxist-Leninist state in Asia.

The BNCs include India, Pakistan, Bangladesh, and Burma. Their per capita incomes are among the lowest in Asia (and in the Third World generally), and their population growth rates are among the highest.

The Population Bomb

As noted in Chapter 13, the population explosion has been a pattern throughout Asia and one of the chief obstacles to net gains in economic growth (annual GNP growth minus population growth).

In Pakistan, for example, annual population growth rate averaged more than 3 percent in the 1980s, while the GNP per capita was a mere $400. For the situation to have improved significantly, Pakistan's economy would have had to grow at a much faster rate than 3 percent a year if registered during this period. However, the average annual per capita growth rate for South Asia as a whole in the period 1980–1991 was quite low, ranging from 3.3 percent in India to an abysmal 1.9 percent in Bangladesh. In India, the picture is still rather bleak. At 2.1 percent, India's annual population growth rate is lower than Pakistan's, but India's population base is eight times larger. At current rates, the population of the two nations will double to two billion in about twenty-five years.

Myanmar and Bangladesh are even poorer. GNP per capita is around $220, and population growth rates are high. To make matters worse, Burma was racked by severe domestic turmoil in the late 1980s, and Bangladesh was hit by floods that left millions homeless, cost countless lives, overwhelmed relief efforts, and reduced the nation's chronically stagnant economy to ruins.

The population explosion in Asia has been smaller than in sub-Saharan Africa and Central America, where population growth rates have long exceeded 3 percent. Nevertheless, Asia's growth is spectacular when compared to Europe's, which averaged a mere 0.3 percent in the 1980s. To understand the implications of these statistics, consider the time it takes to double the population at a constant growth rate. At 0.5 percent annually, it takes 139 years; at 1 percent, it takes 70 years; at 2 percent, it takes 35 years; and at 3 percent, it takes a mere 23 years.

The Poverty Trap

Other demographic characteristics also have important implications for Asia's future. There are generally more males than females in Asian society (the opposite is true in industrially developed nations). The reasons reflect culture as well as economic factors: deaths due to frequent pregnancies, poor female hygiene and health care, and a tendency to prefer male babies. Some of these problems arise from poverty; others are related to the lower social status of women in many LDCs.

In societies with rapidly growing populations, the age composition changes dramatically. As the number of babies born each year rises and the infant mortality rate drops, the population gets younger. In most Asian societies, children under 15 years old account for at least 40 percent of the total population. The comparable figures for the industrial democracies are 22.3 percent for Europe, 22.6 percent for North America, and 23.6 percent for Japan. The implications for LDCs are enormous. First, more health care services are required, for both childbearing women and their infants. A large proportion of the very young in Asia suffer from malnutrition, a problem that is likely to worsen as the number of infants increases. Survivors will constitute the future labor force; because malnutrition at an early age affects physical and mental development, it also has an impact on later productivity and health care needs. As preschool populations grow, governments have to increase educational expenditures, diverting resources from development projects that could improve the standard of living.

Second, the larger the proportion of children, the greater the burden on productive adults. This notion can be expressed as a **dependency ratio**: number of dependents (under age 14 and over age 65) in relation to the economically active population (between 15 and 64). Dependency ratios are generally higher in Asia than elsewhere (with the exception of Japan). In addition, high unemployment typically hits young adults hardest. When unemployed young adults (15 to 24 years old) are factored in, the dependency ratio worsens considerably.

Third, the prospects for the vast majority of Asia's youth (outside Japan and the NICs) are dim. Adolescents and young adults are typically rebellious, and students everywhere are loath to accept the status quo, even if it is favorable. Education without opportunity can be dangerous, especially for societies that are beset by problems that they lack the resources to address. Will Asian youth accept this plight? Or will frustration boil over—as it already has in Communist China, Myanmar, and South Korea—thus further impeding economic growth and development? How can Asia's overpopulated and underdeveloped nations escape this poverty trap?

Finally, the demographic conundrum affects all of Asia's nations, rich and poor. Dependency ratios come into play at both ends of the age spectrum. As life expectancy increases and the birthrate comes down, the proportion of elderly pensioners also rises. This problem is only beginning to have an impact in most of Asia, but it is already being felt in Japan, which is one of the fastest-aging countries in the world. In the future, however, it is the PRC, with its billion-plus population despite its policy of promoting one-child families, that faces the heaviest burden in Asia as the birthrate drops and life expectancy climbs.

The Dilemmas of Development

Economic development and population control pose major challenges for most of Asia. Both encompass a host of interrelated problems. For example, if unchecked population growth affects future economic prospects, underdevelopment also puts obstacles in the path of population control. Education is one essential ingredient in any formula for reducing the birthrate. It is no coincidence that societies with low birthrates also have high literacy rates. By the same token, affluent societies whose governments can afford to provide a wide range of social services, including pensions and medical care for the aged, typically have lower birthrates. In contrast, the poor and needy in developing countries cannot rely on government to provide for them in their old age; having a large family is the only form of "social security" available. Hence what appears to be irresponsible behavior for society as a whole may be entirely rational behavior for individuals.

Large families also make sense in societies where wage-earning jobs are few and farming or running a small business is a family affair. Children, especially males, ensure that the head of the household will have help with the arduous labor needed to eke out a living in an agrarian society where plots are too small and capital is too scarce to permit the use of modern farm machinery.

This incentive to have large families will not change unless most Asians become wage earners—they must be able to get jobs for fair wages and benefits that are taken for granted in industrial nations. "Developing Asia" is still predominantly agrarian: roughly 70 percent of the total population is engaged in subsistence farming, and many of the rest survive by working, often on a seasonal basis, for subsistence wages. They earn barely enough to stay alive and have no money for anything but the bare necessities; they have no savings and little or no security.

The developing countries of Asia account for more than half of the world's population but only 10 percent of its wealth and production, and their share is actually shrinking. Gunnar Myrdal, a renowned Swedish economist, titled his book on Asian economic development problems *Asian Drama: An Inquiry into the Poverty of Nations*. In it, he pointed out starkly that Asia has the worst poverty in the world. United Nations statistics support this conclusion: several of the world's least developed countries (including Afghanistan, Bangladesh, Laos, and Nepal) can be found in Asia.

In Asia as elsewhere, endemic poverty translates into massive unemployment. No one knows for certain how many of Asia's working-age adults are actually unemployed (most official figures greatly understate the problem), but the figure is probably in the range of 15 to 20 percent. Worse still, **underemployment** is much higher than unemployment in most of developing Asia.* In reality, perhaps half of the working-age population needs jobs.

Whatever their relative levels of economic development, Asian nations face the challenge of continuing to modernize, of integrating traditional methods of production with new technologies, and of adapting to regional and global competition without losing their cultural identities and spiritual values. In other words, Asia must learn to *manage* change rather than be swept along by it. Change is inevitable; its pace and direction will either be dictated by chance or be molded by conscious choice.

Lacking such choice in public policies, Asia may or may not reap the benefits of modernization, but it will definitely experience most of the burdens: pollution, traffic congestion, overcrowding, escalating crime rates, and the other ills of most advanced industrial societies. Less obvious is the moral and spiritual erosion that accompanies modernization as the family gives way to the cult of the individual, as values and virtues are reduced to materialism, and as affluence leads not to leisure but rather to a rat race in which keeping up replaces happiness as a goal.

Japan is a case in point. Affluent and admired, many Japanese now seek the spiritual and cultural values that they subordinated in the climb up the economic

---

* Underemployment exists when people are overqualified for the jobs they are doing or when they can get only part-time or seasonal work.

ladder. Although Japan is an Asian society, it has responded to the challenges of modernization with extraordinary resourcefulness and ingenuity; it has adapted to a changing world much more rapidly than its Asian neighbors. It is in a class by itself—in Asia and beyond.

Case Studies: China, Japan, and India

Among Asia's giants, China stands out because its immensity and geographical position place it centerstage in the region. Recent economic gains strengthen Beijing's claim to a central role in regional affairs. By contrast, Japan's claim to regional leadership rests almost exclusively on its economic prowess. For centuries, Japan existed in splendid isolation, separated and insulated from the Asian mainland, in contrast to Korea and Vietnam which were under the cultural and, at times, political influence of neighboring China. Today, Japan boasts the most dynamic developed economy in the world. As we shall see, many of Japan's most pressing political problems relate directly or indirectly to its spectacular economic success.

India is another story. Japan and China, despite their glaring differences, have several competitive advantages in common, including highly stable societies and cultures that are conducive to entrepreneurship. India enjoys neither the stability nor the economic vitality associated with the kind of entrepreneurial cultures found in Japan and China. Despite its competitive disadvantages (for example, linguistic, cultural, and religious barriers to internal consensus, communication, and commerce), India has managed to function as a democratic society and has made slow but steady economic progress.

The puzzle of Chinese politics has never been solved, often making it difficult to predict or explain twists and turns in Beijing's domestic or foreign policies. This generalization is particularly appropriate relative to the new market-oriented economic policies that are rapidly changing the face of Chinese society.

Communist China: Maoism or the Marketplace?

Noted China scholar A. Doak Barnett assessed China in the mid-1980s:

> A decade has passed since the death of Mao Zedong. During these years, China has embarked on a course of reform that Deng Xiaoping has called a "new revolution" and Premier Zhao Ziyang asserts represents "an extensive, profound and sustained transformation" of the country's economic structure. In a 180-degree change of direction from Mao's last years, the Chinese have moved rapidly from ideological dogmatism toward eclectic pragmatism, from extreme totalitarianism toward liberalized authoritarianism, from a command economy toward "market socialism," and from autarkic isolationism toward international interdependence. These trends signal a major new stage in China's long march toward modernization.[3]

Beijing's Roller-Coaster Reforms   In the late 1970s, Deng Xiaoping launched a program of market-oriented reforms. These prefigured Mikhail Gorbachev's much-touted restructuring campaign (*perestroika*) in the USSR and may have inspired it. The original intent was to decentralize economic decision making and allow the market forces to determine prices, profits, and investments. But the drive for marketplace efficiency turned into a roller-coaster ride that ended in disaster.

The PRC's shift toward market principles was most dramatic in agriculture, where average annual productivity more than quadrupled during the early 1980s, compared with the previous quarter century. The average annual increase in agricultural output was over 8 percent, and rural per capita income rose nearly 14 percent. This success resulted primarily from one factor: the decision to allow private farming. Peasants now manage their own land, decide what to plant, and sell only a portion of their crops to the state. They dispose of their net produce, after taxes, in any way they choose. Moreover, individual households have a guaranteed land tenure of at least fifteen years. Legal ownership is key to generating investment, but Chinese culture has never given it as much importance as the West. The success of the market reforms in agriculture are the best (and only) insurance Chinese peasants have that the Communist party will not recollectivize.

Of far-reaching importance is the land-use policy that separates public ownership of land from the private right to use it. Once a farmer has obtained the right to use land, the state cannot take it away. Furthermore, land-use rights are transferable, meaning that they can be kept in the family. In an effort to curb the loss of farmland (about 400,000 hectares a year in the mid-1980s), fees are now charged for nonfarming purposes. In urban areas, the sale of land-use rights is

> a vehicle by means of which local government can raise investment funds; at the same time it has created a real estate market in which long-term leases can be bought and sold, mortgaged and passed from generation to generation. In December 1987, the right of use for 8,580 square meters of land was publicly auctioned for Y5.25 million (about $1.4 million) in Shenzhen. Since then, sales of land rights have been conducted in Shanghai and several other major cities.[4]

In industry, decentralization and a shift from bureaucratic strangulation to economic regulation was to be the cornerstone of the PRC's reform efforts. The number of major industrial products subject to central planning was to be halved, from 120 to 60. For a time, Beijing claimed that by the end of the Seventh Plan (1986–1990), the number would be reduced to "a few vital commodities," but the pace of industrial-sector reforms slackened after a student revolt in December 1986 and a short-lived campaign against "bourgeois liberalization." Later, in June 1989, the Tiananmen Square episode prompted a purge of market-minded reformers.

Although central planning has remained the rule in heavy industry, China's leaders talk about giving managers greater decision-making authority and stronger incentives for efficiency. The regime's plan to switch enterprises over to a sink-or-swim system of financial and managerial autonomy by 1990, on hold for most of 1987, was reactivated after the Thirteenth Party Congress in October of that year.

In 1988, the Beijing regime's vacillations over (and ambivalence toward) market reforms reached new heights. On the one hand, the leadership unveiled a comprehensive package of new market-oriented reforms, including an enterprise law aimed at giving managers greater autonomy. On the other, it reimposed economic controls intended to curtail the role of the free market and local decision making. The government also froze the prices of basic foods, agricultural supplies, and raw materials; curbed the proliferation of private traders; and cut back capital spending by localities. If the reasons for the retrenchment in 1987 were primarily political, in 1988 they were primarily economic. The annual rate of inflation was running at about 50 percent, causing widespread discontent. At the same time, the new flush of capitalism was leading to corruption involving officials at all levels.[5]

Despite major gains, the PRC in the late 1980s was still among the poorest nations in the world in terms of per capita gross national product, as Zhao himself noted publicly. Three-quarters of China's teeming population was rural and used hand tools rather than machines to make a living. Illiteracy remained high, affecting one-fourth of the population. And the disparity between rising expectations and disappointing results threatened the stability of the system and eroded the credibility of the reforms themselves. Finally, the crushing of student protest in Tiananmen Square in 1989 was a reminder of the perils of reform in a society based on coercion. Given the highly centralized nature of China's political system, everything depends on the qualities of China's leaders. The ouster of Zhao Ziyang cast a shadow over the future of reforms in the PRC.

Zhao's progressive policies were reason enough for hard-liners to purge him at the first opportunity, but the persistent economic problems also contributed. In the fall of 1988, a shift in power away from Zhao Ziyang in favor of more cautious reformers like Prime Minister Li Peng and Politburo economist Yao Yilin was reported in the Western press.[6] That shift turned out to be a harbinger of repression and retrenchment.

Massacre in Tiananmen Square   The stage was set for the **Tiananmen Square massacre** in May 1989, when 100,000 students and workers staged a march in Beijing to demand democratic reforms. Protests continued throughout the month of May and coincided with a visit to Beijing by Soviet leader Mikhail Gorbachev—the first Chinese-Soviet summit in three decades. As the protest movement gathered momentum, demonstrations were mounted in at least twenty other cities, and Beijing declared martial law—to little avail.

Army troops entered Beijing with tanks and armored personnel carriers on June 3. They brutally attacked the demonstrators—now a million strong—in Tiananmen Square, outside the Great Hall of the People, crushing the revolt, killing and injuring thousands of demonstrators, and arresting many more.

Security forces later rounded up as many as ten thousand dissenters, and at least thirty-one were tried and executed. The bloody crackdown was all too reminiscent of the awful days of totalitarian rule.

Economic reforms were stalled for a time by the political fallout from the Tiananmen episode, but they were not scuttled. The economic growth rate slumped to 4 percent in 1989 (down from double-digit gains in 1983–1988). But the economy had recovered by 1992, when the overall growth rate was again expected to reach at least 10 percent. Deng Xiaoping, the aging author of China's restructuring program, won a major victory over Li Peng and other hard-liners in the summer of 1992. Believing that slower growth would help ensure social stability and continued Communist party rule, Li advocated holding growth to 6 percent. But Deng wanted to go for broke, aiming for 10 percent annual growth after inflation for the rest of the decade.

> If that happens, China will have grown faster in the 22 years after Mr. Deng began his reforms in 1978 than the economies of either Japan or Taiwan did at their peak (1950–1973), and only a little slower than South Korea's between 1965–1988.
> This ambitious goal is not immodest. With its 35%-plus savings rates, constantly growing workforce and furiously expanding non-state businesses, China's economy could lope along for years at 10% without working up a sweat.[7]

Nonetheless, there were danger signs (including excessive bank lending and a rapidly expanding money supply) that inflation would again take off. China was still saddled with too many inefficient state firms—"the main obstacle to China becoming the greatest economic miracle ever."[8]

China's Half-Open Door to the West   As part of the reform effort, Beijing adopted an open-door policy under which the PRC more than doubled its foreign trade (primarily with the West) during the Sixth Plan (1981–1986). Under Deng's pragmatic guidance, the PRC reversed its long-standing ban on foreign loans and direct foreign investment and began eagerly seeking both. By the end of 1985, Beijing had borrowed more than $10 billion from abroad.

The decision to seek direct foreign investment—absolutely taboo when Mao was alive—was even more remarkable. Deng's most controversial and innovative step was the creation in the 1970s of **special economic zones (SEZs)**, which were intended not only to attract foreign capital but also to stimulate exports and improve access to modern technologies and management methods. Although obstacles to foreign companies remained formidable, the new policy had attracted over $5 billion worth of investment by 1985.

In 1986, Beijing took several steps to lure more capital into the country, including incentives such as preferential tax treatment, priority access to supplies at guaranteed prices, and loans for export-oriented or technologically advanced projects. But these new measures did not remove the bureaucratic obstacles, legal impediments, distorted prices, and political uncertainties, and foreign investment fell short of expectations. According to one expert, "Japanese business-men do not regard China as a particularly attractive investment site (particularly when Hong Kong and other Asian NIC opportunities are taken into account)."[9]

Beijing also hoped to attract capital from Taiwan and even set up an SEZ in Guangdong province to accommodate it. So far, Taiwanese firms have invested little in mainland China, but if the two Chinese governments move toward rapprochement, Taiwanese investment could rise sharply.

In the absence of massive infusions of foreign investment, the PRC's best hope for prosperity is boosting exports. Japan's economic growth in the 1970s was export-driven, and the Japanese example probably played a role in inducing the PRC to adopt an export-oriented open-door policy after Mao's death. As a result, the PRC's two-way foreign trade totaled $82.7 billion in 1987, more than twice what it was in 1980. Meanwhile, the number of organizations permitted to engage in foreign trade had grown from sixteen to more than twelve hundred by mid-1988.

The PRC's attempt to generate export-led growth in the 1980s met with only limited success, however. At the peak of the reform campaign, only about 6 percent of the total labor force was employed in exporting industries, and exports accounted for about 15 percent of national output (compared to 55 percent in Taiwan and 37 percent in South Korea).[10] China's trade balance was also a problem. For example, between 1985 and 1987, its trade deficit totaled more than $30 billion. Along with rising inflation, the trade shortfall undermined economic reform.

For a time in the 1980s, Beijing's foreign economic policy fluctuated between market-oriented policies and central planning. In 1984, when reform was encouraged, fourteen cities were opened to foreign trade and investment; shortly after, however, opponents of reform succeeded in reducing the number. Trade liberalization resurfaced in 1987 and 1988, only to be put on hold again the following year. Two factors worked against reforms: inflation and political instability. Inflation jeopardized price reform (the core of any move toward a market economy), and the student-led democracy movement threatened the core of the political system, the legitimacy of the Communist party's power monopoly.

Despite the ups and downs of the 1980s, a legal framework to regulate foreign commerce gradually emerged. Laws covering joint ventures, contracts, land-use rights, taxes, copyrights, patents, and SEZs were promulgated. In 1986, Beijing applied for membership in the General Agreement on Tariffs and Trade (GATT).

Beijing became a major arms supplier in the 1980s. Weapons sales in 1987 amounted to roughly $2 billion, making the PRC the fourth-largest arms supplier to the Third World (behind the Soviet Union, the United States, and France). China sold $5.3 billion worth of arms between 1983 and 1986—an amount that loomed large in the PRC's trade statistics, for it represented a jump of 167 percent over the previous three-year period.

Although China's principal trading partners are Asian, Western Europe and the United States have accounted for significant shares in recent years. From

1979 to 1986, China's two-way trade was apportioned as follows: Japan, 24.9 percent; Western Europe, 22.6 percent; Hong Kong, 21.5 percent; the United States, 11.8 percent; all others, 19.2 percent. It is noteworthy that just two Asian nations, Japan and Hong Kong, accounted for nearly half of China's trade.

The figures fail to reveal some noteworthy trends. First, Soviet trade had been reviving in the 1980s; whether prospects will remain encouraging in the post-USSR years is still uncertain. Second, trade with South Korea and Taiwan began to climb sharply in the late 1980s. Third, the PRC has gradually shifted away from being an exporter of primary products. Beijing has begun to register substantial trade surpluses (nearly $9 billion in 1990, $10 billion in 1992).

Despite these positive signs, China's foreign trade remains modest compared to that of Japan, South Korea, or Taiwan. For instance, in 1987, the two-way trade of both Taiwan ($87.5 billion) and South Korea ($83.4 billion) exceeded the PRC ($82.7 billion) *in absolute terms.* One scholar sums up China's predicament this way:

> If Chinese exports are to lead Chinese economic development, they will have to compete with the other export-oriented economies of the Pacific, economies in which skillful exploitation of world technology trends is a key factor. For instance, Taiwan is now the world's third largest producer of personal computers (PC's), after the United States and Japan, and South Korea is number four.[11]

The Dragon Stirs: A Chinese Economic Miracle?   "China's economic performance has brought about one of the biggest improvements in human welfare anywhere at any time."[12] Thus begins a 1992 survey of China in *The Economist*, a highly respected British weekly magazine. This assertion is particularly astonishing given the fact that China's leaders, as we have noted, took the economy on a roller-coaster ride in the 1980s. What *are* the facts?

Between 1978, when China first launched its economic reform program, and 1992, the Chinese economy grew at an average rate of almost 9 percent a year. At that rate, it will be four times bigger in 1994 than it was in 1978—and eight times bigger by the year 2002! China will then have replicated the economic miracles of Japan, Taiwan, and South Korea.

Some 800 million Chinese, roughly 75 percent of the population, still live on the land. During the early post-Mao period, grain output grew by a third in six years, cotton almost trebled, oil-bearing crops more than doubled, and other agricultural products boomed. Farm incomes increased threefold in eight years. Even more astounding, the numbers of people living in absolute poverty in China dropped from an estimated 200 to 270 million in 1978 to 100 million by 1985.

The transformation of China has surpassed anything Mao Zedong achieved in his lifetime. Rural China depended on agriculture for 70 percent of its income in 1978, while industry accounted for only 20 percent; in the early 1990s, farming and industry were almost equal in importance (about 45 percent each). At the same time, private firms and foreign-owned firms have sprouted alongside state enterprises. State-owned firms accounted for nearly four-fifths of all industrial output in 1978 and three-fifths of all nonagricultural employment; those figures had dropped to about 50 percent and 40 percent, respectively, by the end of 1992.

By various measures, Chinese consumers have experienced an unprecedented leap in general living standards—a surge in the availability of everything from seafood, meat, and poultry to color television sets, washing machines, and refrigerators. Despite a burgeoning population of 1.2 billion, China has managed to move into the ranks of the world's "middleweight" economies.

Despite this impressive economic performance, China will continue to face an enormous population challenge in the coming decades. Although growth of 8 or 9 percent is in itself quite remarkable, the fact remains that China's economy must grow rapidly if it is to absorb an expected additional 180 million people by the end of the 1990s. But if China's economy continues to grow as fast as it has been growing since the late 1970s, it will be the biggest economy on earth in just twenty years.

Changing of the Guard?   At the Communist party's Fourteenth Congress in Beijing in October 1992, General Secretary Jiang Zemin reaffirmed the government's intent to push on with economic reform. About half of the party's Central Committee was replaced with younger, more technocratic members, many of whom are likely to represent the provinces rather than the center. Some changes were made in the Politburo as well, but there continued to be a rough balance of power between conservatives and reformers.

Key changes in the Standing Committee, the most important decision-making body, however, suggested that the reformers had gained the upper hand. Two hard-line allies of Chen Yun (like Deng one of the last veterans of the Long March in the top leadership) were sacked. At least two of the three new members were thought to back economic reform, especially Zhu Rongju, the former mayor of Shanghai and a protégé of Deng. Zhu was placed in charge of economic policy.

What will happen after Deng, the "godfather" of Chinese politics, dies is anybody's guess. There is no reason to believe that Deng's successor will succeed. Indeed, several of his heirs apparent have fallen by the wayside. Deng's death could well occasion an intense power struggle in Beijing.

Will China break up in the manner of the Soviet Union? That is highly unlikely. China is by no means homogeneous, but it is not the ethnic crazy quilt that was the USSR. Also, the Communist party is a powerful and pervasive force in Chinese society. Its popularity is rooted not in ideology but rather in China's economic success and the material benefits that the vast majority of the Chinese people are now enjoying (in stark contrast to the former Soviet peoples).

Japan: The Perils of Success

It may seem as though Japan has no serious economic or social problems—at least when compared with the rest of Asia. But Japan's very success has created problems. A few of these are essentially internal; most are primarily external.

And even the problems that seem domestic have an international dimension because Japan's economy is so thoroughly enmeshed with the global economy.

Asia's First "Miracle"   Japan's economic miracle began in the mid-1950s. From then until the oil crisis of 1973–1974, Japan did not rely heavily on exports to sustain its accelerating economic growth; on the contrary, an expanding domestic market energized Japan's economy. Exports rose rapidly, but so did imports of raw materials and fossil fuels.

The oil crisis brought dramatic changes. Japan's annual economic growth rate fell from 10 percent to 4 or 5 percent annually, which led automatically to a reduction in imports. The energy crisis also led to conservation efforts. At the same time, leaders of government and business—always closely linked in Japan—began looking to foreign markets as a way to cope with sluggish domestic demand.

Other trends also pushed Japan toward an export orientation in the 1970s and 1980s. For example, Japan's steel, shipbuilding, manufacturing, synthetic textile, motor vehicle, petrochemical, and home appliance industries—once the engines of Japanese economic growth—became depressed. Foreign competition, especially from Asian NICs, contributed to the slump in heavy industry. Many Japanese consumers opted to save rather than spend. Japan turned increasingly to high-technology industries for the export market. The economy renewed its surge (see Figure 15.1).

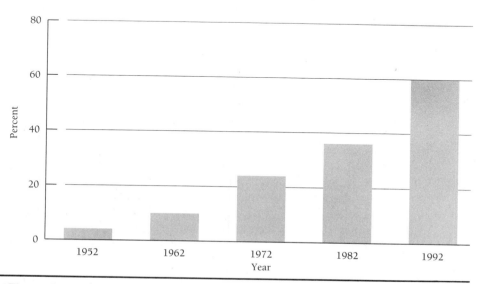

Figure 15.1 Japan's gross domestic product (GDP), as a percentage of the United States'.

By 1980, Japan had become the largest automobile producer in the world, overtaking the United States, Japan's leading trade partner. In 1988, the United States absorbed some 34 percent of Japan's exports, while Japan took only 22 percent of U.S. exports. This gap has been reflected in huge trade imbalances between the United States and Japan. For example, the U.S. trade deficit (or Japan's trade *surplus*) was expected to top $50 billion by the end of 1993. Japan's success in penetrating the American automobile and consumer electronics markets elicited calls in the United States for protectionist measures against "unfair" Japanese trading practices.

Equilibrium and Fairness   According to Robert S. Ozaki:

> Japan, with the second largest economy in the world, has become a nation that exports too much and imports too little, much to the dismay and frustration of deficit-prone countries, especially the United States. Enormous trade surpluses, instead of being spent in Japan, have found their way abroad as capital investments. For 1986, Japan's trade surplus was $102 billion, of which $52 was charged to the United States, and the net capital outflow from Japan amounted to $144 billion. In contrast, in the same year, the United States ran a trade deficit of $134 billion and absorbed a $57 billion net capital inflow from abroad. In 1985, Japan became the world's largest creditor nation, while the United States, the richest country on earth, became the world's largest debtor nation, with net external liabilities of $107 billion.[13]

Ozaki and others argued that Japan had become a major source of "disequilibrium," not just for the United States but in the world economy as a whole. "Translated into an obligation on the part of Japan," Ozaki wrote, "this means that Japan is expected to alter the internal properties and structure of its economy fundamentally to make it an equilibrating (rather than disequilibrating) force . . . commensurate with its weight and strength in the world." Given the nexus between Japan's prosperity and global economic stability, Ozaki believes that "it has become imperative that Japan 'internationalize' its economy to a far higher degree than it has already achieved."[14]

Japan's critics cite the need for a wide range of internal economic reforms. First, deregulate the banking system and money markets to end Japan's policy of low interest rates and thus attract overseas assets back into the country. Second, put an end to agricultural protectionism (especially for rice). Third, break up state-supported monopoly arrangements in the distribution system, which make it extremely difficult for foreign manufacturers to penetrate Japanese markets even without tariffs, import quotas, and other barriers. Fourth, actively combat the unfair trade practices of enterprise groups that discriminate against foreign firms. Fifth, do away with closed bidding for government contracts, which traditionally go almost exclusively to a handful of Japanese construction firms. Finally, tighten the interpretation of Japan's antimonopoly laws, thus further opening Japan's economy to free-market forces and foreign competition.

Japan was also urged to institute tight-money policies (to push up interest rates and thus keep capital at home) and to implement expansionary fiscal policies, including tax cuts (to encourage imports and absorb more domestic production internally, thereby reducing exports). Instead, Japan did just the opposite, while the United States pursued "Reaganomics"—the very mix of policies that Japan should have been putting into effect!

For both economic and political reasons, Japan faces pressure from the international community to make major policy adjustments that may require sacrifices. For example, developing nations have amassed foreign debts totaling $1.3 trillion, while Japan has become the world's leading creditor nation. It is inevitable that governments and international agencies will look to Japan for leadership, loans, and debt relief, much as the world once looked to the United States as benefactor and backbone of the international monetary system.

Moreover, Japan's affluence raises expectations of free-flowing foreign aid. Japan recognizes this fact, and in recent years, Japanese public and private assistance to developing countries has burgeoned. Most Japanese foreign aid goes to Asian countries.

There has been a growing chorus of criticism, led by the United States, of Japan's purportedly unfair trade practices in recent years. For example, the United States has demanded that Japan lift its strict quotas on beef and citrus fruit, and rice-producing countries want Japan to abandon the **protectionism** that has long prevented foreign rice (and other foodstuffs) from entering the Japanese market. "Tariff rates are roughly equal to those of other industrial nations," but in many instances, "they are spiked with special tariffs in industries that are considered vulnerable to foreign competition."[15]

The Japanese are also adept at devising **nontariff barriers** (**NTBs**). For example, the 20 percent tariff on foreign cigarettes is only the tip of the protectionist iceberg. Imported tobacco products may be sold by only 10 percent of Japan's 250,000 tobacconists, and importers are allowed to advertise only in English-language publications. Such NTBs are common in Japan.

Restrictions like these are especially upsetting to foreign competitors because Japan has been so aggressive in developing overseas markets for its own exports. According to David Brock:

> Examples of the dynamics of the Japanese trade thrust are by now the stuff of legend among foreign competitors. The Ministry of Finance backs industries in which it perceives high demand by directing the allocation of development funds to private companies through the banks it controls. Support originally went to textiles, then switched to automobiles, steel, electronics, semiconductors, and now to financial services. To do this, the Japan Development Bank draws on Post Office savings accounts, which, thanks to an exemption from taxes and generous interest rates, have grown to a sum greater than the assets of the 10 largest American money center banks combined. (Japanese law forbids any private bank to pay a higher rate on savings than the Post Office.)[16]

During the early years of Japan's export push, the Ministry of Finance also waived taxes on up to 80 percent of a company's export earnings; depreciation allowances pegged to export earnings were later substituted for tax exemptions, but the net effect was the same. At the same time, the **Ministry of International**

Trade and Industry (**MITI**), charged with promoting the nation's export industries, "targets countries and market to be penetrated" and "can also bring together large producers into one company to achieve economies of scale—a practice U.S. antitrust law would prohibit." Finally, the Japanese "are willing to go to extreme lengths, subsidizing vulnerable items in foreign markets by raising domestic prices and shielding home markets."[17]

Japan Bashing: Who Threatens Whom?   Accurate or not, this view of Japanese economic policies is widely held. Even Japan's admirers in the West express alarm at the Japanese challenge. For example, in 1988, Norman Cousins, former editor of the *Saturday Review,* published an article arguing that Japan, not the Soviet Union, posed "the greatest single threat to American capitalism."[18]

If Japan's diplomatic relations with important allies and trading partners are strained, if the international economy founders, or if nations in jeopardy blame Japan, the consequences could be dire for Japan as one of the most export-dependent nations on earth. The source of Japan's economic vitality is also the source of its greatest vulnerability.

Nowhere is this vulnerability more evident than in the area of energy. Japan has imported virtually all of its fossil fuels since the early 1950s. Before the 1973 oil crisis, Japan's rapid economic growth was fueled by "the relatively stable postwar petroleum regime, managed by the large oil firms and protected by American diplomatic and military strength."[19] Since 1973, Japan has tried to reduce its dependency on imported oil by conserving energy and diversifying its sources, but imported oil still supplies 60 percent of Japan's energy needs, and 70 percent of this oil comes from the Persian Gulf. Two trends—the oil glut and the appreciation of the yen—alleviated the immediate problem in the 1980s, but energy security remains an unresolved issue in Japan, one that critics believe must be faced head-on.

Island of Stability   Politically, Japan does not face the kind of instability that plagues many Asian governments. Like the Imperial Chinese whose statecraft they imitated, the Japanese have an extraordinary record as institution builders. "They invent or borrow from others, adapt, refine, but never so rigidly that the rules obstruct rather than facilitate the achievement of their objectives."[20]

This extensive institutionalization makes Japanese politics stable, even predictable. The postwar predominance of the Liberal Democratic party appears likely to continue, even though opposition parties are protected by law and national elections are free and fair. The choice of Noboru Takeshita to succeed Yasuhiro Nakasone as LDP president and prime minister in the fall of 1987 came as no great surprise to people familiar with Japanese politics. Recall that the party president is chosen by bargaining among faction leaders in the Diet, not by the party rank and file or by individual Diet members. Typically, the winner is the faction leader with the best record (measured by cabinet, Diet, and party posts held). In elevating LDP Secretary General Takeshita to the party presidency, ensuring his election as prime minister, the LDP followed the unwritten rules of tradition and precedent.

Similarly, Takeshita's cabinet was selected in accordance with well-established unwritten rules whereby posts are distributed according to factional strength, seniority, and other criteria. As a result, the integrity of the process of forming a cabinet was reaffirmed, and the cohesion of the party, despite its factional substructure, was maintained. Policy considerations do not seem to play a major role in the distribution of cabinet posts—perhaps reflecting the extent to which policymaking has been institutionalized and depoliticized.

Takeshita, however, was politically damaged by a bribery scandal involving confidential information provided by a business services conglomerate. Takeshita and other business and political leaders reaped windfall profits from the purchase of privately held shares in Cosmos, a real estate subsidiary, before the stocks were offered to the public. This insider trading scandal led eventually to the resignation of forty-three politicians and businessmen. It also led to Takeshita's decision to step down as prime minister in April 1989. The LDP suffered electoral reversals in mid-1989, making a poor showing in Tokyo municipal balloting and losing its majority in the House of Councillors. Takeshita's successor, Sosuke Uno, was in office for only a few months when revelations of adultery forced him to resign. Under the leadership of Toshiki Kaifu, the LDP rebounded, winning the elections to the lower house in February 1990, albeit with a reduced majority. Kaifu named a new cabinet comprised of individuals without any skeletons in the closet: only the foreign and finance ministers were carry-overs from the previous government. His advocacy of electoral reform and honest government, however, ruffled powerful figures in his own party, and in October 1991, Kaifu was replaced by Kiichi Miyazawa.

Kaifu's housecleaning nevertheless paid off in the 1992 elections to the upper house: with half the 252 seats up for grabs, the LDP won 54 percent (68 seats) and was well positioned to regain an upper-house majority in 1995. But voter turnout was only about 47 percent, the lowest ever for a Senate election.

The disappointing voter turnout for the 1992 Senate elelction was symptomatic of a spreading disillusionment within Japanese society. The Japanese people work long hours for wages that afford them, at best, a modest lifestyle in an environment of astronomically high prices for housing and other basic essentials. Recognizing this problem and its implications for the future of his ruling party, Prime Minister Miyazawa came to office in 1991 promising an improved standard of living for the Japanese people. "It's been said we Japanese live in rabbit hutches, and, unfortunately it's true," he mused.[21] Among other things, Miyazawa promised to bring down the cost of a home in Tokyo from eight times the annual salary of a worker to five. He also promised to reduce the average employee workload from 2,100 hours a year to 1,800 hours. (The average workload in Germany, for example, is 1,600 hours.) These promises, however, turned out to be too little, too late.

In the watershed 1993 parliamentary election, the LDP—widely blamed for the unrelieved rigors of daily life and damaged by the scandals and defections that brought the Miyazawa government down—won 223 seats; twenty-eight short of a clear majority. Although the LDP claimed fifty-two fewer seats than it won in the 1990 election, it captured all but four of the seats left to it after prominent faction leaders split with the LDP and created two new parties, the Japan Renewal party led by Tsutomu Hata and the New Harbinger party. The Japan New party also drew votes away from the LDP.

Like the LDP, all three new parties occupy the political center. Individually, they were unable to cut into the LDP's traditional popular support base (the biggest loser in 1993 was the Social Democratic party, not the LDP). Jointly, the new parties did what no other opposition party or alliance had been able to do in four decades: oust the LDP from power (see Table 15.3).

The new prime minister, Morihiro Hosokawa, heads the Japan New party, which he founded in 1992. The New party won only thirty-five seats, but without New party support neither the LDP nor Hata's Renewal party (the biggest winner in the 1993 elections) could form a government. In the end, Hosokawa emerged as the consensus choice of a multifaceted coalition comprising centrist, center-left, and leftist parties.

Japan's Perilous Fortune   Japan faced several major challenges in the early 1990s. Extreme scarcity of land had produced runaway real estate inflation in metropolitan areas, making urgent the need for an effective land-use policy. (One idea was to construct office complexes underground.) Many Japanese have come to regard Tokyo, with its high-rise landscape, as a "concrete desert."

In 1991 and 1992, Japan's economic bubble burst. Real estate and stock values plummeted. The stock market fell to a six-year low in the summer of 1992, at only 40 percent of its December 1989 peak. The pace of bankruptcies by the first half of 1992 had doubled to the highest since the oil shocks of the early 1970s. And some 1.6 million Japanese were out of work, a bad omen in a society unaccustomed to layoffs.

One problem was the tax structure. Income taxes claimed as much as 80 percent of the gross personal income of the wealthiest Japanese. High taxes and

Table 15.3 Japan's Parliamentary Election Results, 1990 and 1993 (lower house seats won)

	February 1990	July 1993
Liberal Democratic party	275	223
Social Democratic party	136	70
Japan Renewal party*	—	55
Clean Government party	45	51
Japan New party*	—	35
Democratic Socialist party	14	15
Japan Communist party	16	15
New Party Harbinger*	—	13
Others	26	34

* New opposition groups.

Source: Data presented in "The First Glint of a New Japan," *Economist,* July 24, 1993, p. 33.

the collapse of private-sector investment (which accounted for 60 percent of growth in better times) slowed economic growth to an estimated 2 percent (well below the expected 3.5 percent increase). In an effort to revive the economy, the government lowered interest rates repeatedly in the early 1990s and in the fall of 1992 introduced a panoply of stimulatory measures, including tax cuts, investment grants, and public-works projects.

Strains in Japan's relations with the United States over the long-standing trade imbalance continued as well. Beginning in the 1980s, the U.S. trade deficit with Japan reached levels that were politically and economically unsustainable. Japan's share of the U.S. automobile market, for example, exceeded 20 percent, which led to protests from American automakers. Allegations in 1987 of **dumping** (selling goods below cost in foreign markets) prompted the Reagan administration, following a unanimous resolution in the U.S. Congress, to approve a 100 percent tariff on Japanese electronic goods. The European Community also retaliated against alleged Japanese dumping at this time. The friction between Japan and its major trading partners, particularly the United States, has continued in the 1990s.

Japan has much to lose and little to gain from a trade war. Economically, the United States is far and away the most important overseas market for Japan.

Nor can Japan afford to rest on its economic achievements. The Asian NICs are nipping at Japan's heels, the European Community is moving toward economic unification, and the United States and Canada, the world's largest trading partners, have entered into a free-trade pact that Mexico may soon be invited to join. Japan could thus find access to major foreign markets increasingly difficult. The trend toward regionalization of trade would imply that Japan's best interest lies in promoting economic cooperation in Asia. Any such policy, however, would require long-range planning and coordination.

Too Much of a Good Thing   Ironically, the stability of the Japanese political system, long a major asset, could become a liability if the entrenched forces of business and government obstruct needed policy changes. Significantly, the leader of the new coalition government, Prime Minister Hosokawa, "came to power promising to overhaul an electoral system that encourages corruption and to introduce stringent fund-raising laws and ban or phase out corporate contributions."[22] If economic reform was still a "hot button" in China, political reform was just as hot in Japan in the early 1990s.

Japan has little choice but to redefine its role in Asia and the world. As it does so, it will be walking through a political minefield. For example, clamor in the United States over the cost of maintaining U.S. forces in the western Pacific has been growing. Critics ask why the United States should continue to foot the bill for Japan's defense while Japan runs up a massive trade surplus with the United States. In response to such pressures, Tokyo has increased military spending, but the U.S. security umbrella remains in place.

Japan has the potential to be a military as well as an economic superpower, a fact which makes the rise of Japanese nationalism in recent years especially noteworthy. In 1989, this trend was accentuated by the passing of Emperor Hirohito, whose reign of more than sixty years encompassed the rise of Japanese militarism in the 1930s, the achievement of Japanese supremacy in Asia during World War II, Japan's abject defeat in the wake of the cataclysms at Hiroshima and Nagasaki, the adoption of Western-style democratic rule during the U.S. occupation, and the resurgence of Japan as an economic colossus after the mid-1950s. The outpouring of affection for the emperor—the most important symbol of Japan's political heritage—demonstrated that the majority of Japanese people remain emotionally attached to traditional values.

In the wake of the Persian Gulf War, the question of whether or not Japanese military forces ought to participate in future United Nations peacekeeping operations was hotly debated in Japan. (Japan had contributed money and transport planes to the war effort but not troops.) In 1992, a controversial bill was passed allowing future Japanese governments to dispatch self-defensive forces abroad for humanitarian purposes. Thus for Japan, the stigma of World War II lingers in Asia much as it does for Germany in Europe, making such issues as defense spending, troop commitments, and military capabilities extremely sensitive.

India: Development or Disintegration?

That India can be so poor and yet remain a relatively stable democracy is a marvel that rivals even the magnificent Taj Mahal. The durability of democracy attests to the coercive power of India's central government, to the resolution of strong leaders like Jawaharlal Nehru and Indira Gandhi to preserve the union, and to the success of a single national political party in integrating the nation's extremely diverse society. Finally, Indian democracy has survived despite a burgeoning population that would strain any nation's resources.

India's development record has been checkered. The economy has grown 3.0 to 3.5 percent annually, well below targets but above the dismal 1 percent growth rate during the first half of the twentieth century. When population growth (2.1 percent) is taken into account, per capita gains have been only slightly above 1 percent a year—a sluggish pace that has nonetheless raised per capita GNP by a third since 1947. The many causes of India's plight include "inadequate demand, poor economic management, a decline in public-sector investment, high capital-output ratios, an increasingly hostile global economic environment, overregulation, high cost production, low productivity, and rapid population growth."[23]

Mixed Results   A striking feature of India's development experience has been its failure to achieve a steady pattern of high growth. The golden decade of development, from 1956 to 1966, has not been matched since. India remains a very poor country with a per capita GNP of $330, one of the lowest levels in the world. Recent trends have been somewhat encouraging, with an average overall growth rate of 5.5 percent a year between 1980 and 1991, but the economy's performance continued to fluctuate widely, ranging from 3.6 percent to 7.6 percent during one five-year period (1980–1985).

Although nearly 80 percent of India's population is rural, India has more industrial infrastructure than most developing countries. Coal production has increased fourfold, steel production is up to 11 million tons a year, and domestic oil production increased from 28 percent of total consumption in the 1960s to about 70 percent in the 1980s. India's major basic industries besides coal mining and electricity generation are producing steel, cement, and chemicals, including fertilizers needed to grow wheat, rice, and other grains. By the 1980s, India was producing a wide array of industrial and capital goods, from traditional textiles to heavy machinery and transport equipment. Much of India's heavy industry is in the public sector. There is also a diversity of light (consumer) industries. Indians who have the money can buy a wide variety of domestically made consumer goods. The growth and diversification of the industrial economy in the 1980s made India a potential NIC. But these gains have done relatively little to alleviate India's economic and social problems.

The Poor Majority   The persistence of widespread poverty continues to challenge the Indian government and mar its record. Income distribution is very uneven. Millions of people earn just enough to stave off starvation. Estimates of the number of Indians living in poverty seem to be stabilizing at around 40 percent, but the absolute numbers of course continue to rise.

Human Resources or Wasted Assets?   One tragic irony of underdevelopment in a populous country like India is that so much of the nation's most abundant resource—people—is wasted:

> One of India's most serious problems is unemployment. Unemployment increased from 3.5 million in 1961 to an estimated 20.6 million in 1978 (16.5 million rural; 4.1 million urban). The 1980s has seen an increase rather than a decrease in these unemployment levels. The number of unemployed grows yearly at an accelerating rate, for each year a larger number of young people enter a labor market that is not expanding fast enough to absorb them. Among the unemployed are increasing numbers of university-educated men and women, often highly trained engineers and technicians, who are unable to find work in an industrial sector that continues to operate substantially below capacity. The urban unrest generated by deepening unemployment, especially among the young, is compounded by the deteriorating economic position of the lower middle classes.[24]

Underemployment is even more prevalent than unemployment. Because social services are largely unavailable in India, people need paid employment to survive. But demand for full-time jobs far exceeds supply. In rural India, between 5 and 10 percent of adult males may be unemployed, but another 15 to 20 percent are underemployed.

Sick Industries   The problems of unemployment are exacerbated by India's many "sick industries." The state owns and operates such capital-intensive industries as steel and mining, and most industrial expansion is financed by state-owned banks. The state also tightly regulates the private sector. As a result, in 1986, India had "an astonishing 130,600 money-losing concerns" that the government would not allow to close down "for fear of increasing unemployment."[25] The contrast between this picture and the vibrant economies of Japan and the "four little dragons" suggests that India will have to restructure its economy or fall further behind in the region.

Despite socialist slogans, official policies perpetuate fundamental inequities and sustain the caste-sanctioned structure of inequality in India. The nation's considerable economic achievements "have not been secured without social costs, as evidenced in the wide regional and individual disparities in income." At the same time, changes accompanying economic development—most notably, improvements in education, transportation, and communication—have "brought a new awareness of poverty to the Indian masses and a sensitivity to the widening gap that separates them from the rich."[26]

Neither Beggar nor Basket Case   External assistance remains essential if India is to avoid catastrophe, but in recent years, U.S. foreign aid, which has amounted to more than $12 billion since 1947, has been cut. Although its role has declined as India's economy has grown, foreign aid still financed 20 to 30 percent of the Indian government's economic development projects in the late 1980s.[27] In addition, "India's vulnerability to the flux of the world market, to the erection of trade barriers against its manufactured goods, and to monetary revaluations imposes overwhelming constraints on its development capacity."[28]

This vulnerability is underscored by India's relatively large external debt, which topped $70 billion in the early 1990s. The government requires billions of dollars in IMF loans to cover the principal and interest payments each year. At one point, Delhi sold twenty tons of confiscated black-market gold in order to meet these payments, a move "akin to selling the family jewels," in the eyes of some Indians.[29]

Thus despite considerable progress, India still has far to go to improve the lives of the majority of its citizens. Individual well-being depends on sustained (and accelerated) economic growth accompanied by a falling birthrate. Both parts of this equation continue to present problems, and there are no simple solutions.

Too Many Wild Parties   India's economic problems are exacerbated by a fragile and fragmented party system reflecting deep divisions within Indian society and a political ethos that places a low value on party loyalty. The original Congress party split in 1969 and again in 1978. Breakaway elements and opposition parties tried to come together in 1975 and again in the late 1980s, but both of these coalitions soon fell apart. Kaleidoscopic changes of party affiliation by Indian politicians led in 1985 to an extraordinary constitutional amendment dubbed the "antidefection bill," the aim of which was to disqualify members of parliament (and state legislatures) who switched party allegiance. But in politics, as in law, there are often loopholes: when V. P. Singh organized the People's Front in October 1987 after his break with Rajiv Gandhi, he characterized it as a "nonparty political forum."

Singh was later instrumental in the formation of the National Front (NF), a coalition of odd groups including Singh's *Janata Dal,* the Communist Party of India (CPI), and the Communist Party of India—Marxist (CPI-M). The National Front failed to outpoll the Congress I in 1989 but managed to form a coalition government with the support of the Hindu fundamentalist Bharatiya Janata party (BJP). That government, like the anti-Gandhi Janata coalition of the late 1970s, proved too unstable to rule. In June 1991, Congress I returned to power as the senior partner in an alliance that captured 239 of 545 *lok sabha* (lower house) seats. In the months leading up to this election, India had a caretaker government under Chandra Shekhar because no party or coalition in parliament could muster a majority.

The assassination of Rajiv Gandhi during the election campaign appeared to dash any hope that India would have a strong national leader in the near future. The choice of P. V. Narasimha Rao to succeed Gandhi was widely viewed as a compromise, even a stopgap measure. But in his first year as prime minister, Rao surprised many skeptics by strengthening the position of his Congress I party in the *lok sabha* and installing an elected government in violence-torn Punjab. He also moved to institute free-market reforms and improve relations with the United States.[30]

Communalism against Community   In addition to poverty, inequality, and a fragmented party system, India continues to be plagued by **communalism** and **regionalism**. Violence between Hindus and Muslims breaks out regularly; hundreds of incidents are reported each year. Tensions boiled over in 1984, when Hindu-Muslim rioting occurred throughout the year in Hyderabad, and in Bombay an alleged insult to Muhammad touched off the worst communal fighting since partition. In December 1992, a Hindu mob destroyed an ancient Muslim mosque in the northern Indian town of Ayodhya. The ensuing riots and violence prompted Prime Minister Rao to dismiss the governments in four states run by the Hindu-nationalist BJP. New elections in these states were scheduled but could be postponed if communal passions do not cool down.

Tensions between Sikhs and Hindus also run high. Following Prime Minister Indira Gandhi's assassination by two Sikh security guards, anti-Sikh riots in New Delhi and elsewhere left 2,717 people dead. Sikh **separatism** has been simmering in Punjab, India's wealthiest state. Sikhs constitute about half the population, but the balance is shifting against them as entrepreneurial Sikhs move out and Punjab's flourishing agriculture draws Hindu laborers in. As a result, the Sikhs have felt an increasing need to protect their culture, religion, and language.

Violence in Punjab escalated in 1984. As noted in Chapter 14, a militant

Sikh leader converted the Golden Temple at Amritsar into a terrorist sanctuary. Soon murders were occurring regularly, and a military reaction became inevitable. The assault on the temple lasted three days and left as many as a thousand people dead. Bitterness over this incident led directly to the assassination of Indira Gandhi and subsequent bloody reprisals by Hindus against Sikhs. The spiral of conflict continues and the underlying issues remain largely unresolved. Indeed, such festering animosities pose perhaps the greatest threat to India's long-term political stability.

Separatism is a problem elsewhere in India as well. In the geographically isolated and strategically vulnerable northeast, rebels have mounted an insurrection since 1947. Tribalism and secessionism combine to produce an extraordinarily volatile situation in the states and territories of this region. Attempts by New Delhi to placate the various tribal and secessionist groups—for example, by creating the states of Nagaland in 1963 and Mizoram in 1972—have not succeeded.

In Assam, foreigners are the issue. The immigration of Bengalis from neighboring Bangladesh has alarmed the Assamese, who fear becoming a minority in their own state (as indeed they may already be). Religion is a factor too: the Bengalis are Muslim; the Assamese, Hindu. The northeast is not wealthy, like Punjab, and has long felt neglected by New Delhi. The slogan "Assam is not India's colony" indicates how economic grievances combine with ethnic concerns in the bubbling cauldron that is India.

A Tough Neighborhood   Conflict between India and Pakistan continues to smolder over the issue of Kashmir. Mutual mistrust has exacerbated the problems in Punjab, where India frequently accuses Pakistan of trying to stir up trouble. India and Pakistan have fought three wars since partition—1947, 1965, and 1971. Communalism is again a factor: Pakistan is a Muslim nation, whereas India is 88 percent Hindu. But the territorial dispute over Kashmir is most worrisome in that India has now successfully tested an atomic bomb, and Pakistan is trying to build one. Is the conflict over Kashmir really worth a nuclear confrontation?

India has a history of troubled relations with other neighboring states, too. From 1959 to 1962, it fought a major border war with China. More recently, India faced off against Sri Lanka over the latter's handling of an insurgency by Tamils. India also sent troops to thwart a coup in the Maldives and has feuded with Nepal over its relations with China. Tensions with neighboring Bangladesh continue to mount as illegal Bengali immigrants flood into India.

India is widely viewed as the bully of the neighborhood and as a potential threat to the regional balance. Pakistan alone can act as a military counterweight to India on the subcontinent. Herein lies the paradox: India is too strong to live comfortably with its neighbors and too weak to compete in the larger global community.

To survive as a constitutional democracy, India will need an international support system for many years to come. India's most famous modern poet,

Rabindranath Tagore (1861–1941), summed up the situation as clearly as anyone:

> Power has to be made secure not only against power, but against weakness; for there lies the peril of its losing balance. The weak are as great a danger for the strong as quicksand for an elephant. . . . The people who grow accustomed to wield absolute power over others are apt to forget that by so doing they generate an unseen force which some day rends that power to pieces.[31]

CONCLUSIONS

Compared with other regions, Asia has experienced remarkably uneven rates of development, with some countries ranking among the fastest-growing economies in the world and others continuing to be among the poorest. The success of Japan, South Korea, Taiwan, Hong Kong, Singapore, and, most recently, the People's Republic of China may spur similar successes elsewhere in the region. Leading candidates to join the ranks of the NICs are Thailand, Malaysia, and Indonesia. Rapid population growth clouds the prospects for much of the region, but the success of the PRC in raising living standards for the majority of China's people and drastically reducing the numbers living in absolute poverty suggests that the demographic obstacles to social progress need not be insuperable. China's economic miracle holds out hope not only for other overpopulated and impoverished nations of Asia but also for sub-Saharan Africa, to which we turn next.

KEY TERMS

newly industrialized countries (NICs)
newly exporting countries (NECs)
Marxist-Leninist countries (MLCs)
less developed countries (LDCs)
basic-needs countries (BNCs)
Association of Southeast Asian Nations (ASEAN)
dependency ratio
underemployment
Tiananmen Square massacre

special economic zones (SEZs)
protectionism
nontariff barriers (NTBs)
Ministry of International Trade and Industry (MITI)
dumping
communalism
regionalism
separatism

STUDY QUESTIONS

1. Have Japan, China, and India dealt successfully with the problem of managing change so that the economy grows and society prospers without eroding the values that define what it means to be Japanese, Chinese, or Indian?

2. How and why has Japan achieved such spectacular economic success? What is the link between Japanese politics and economics? Can the Japanese model of political economy be copied? Why or why not?

3. In what ways do China and India face similar challenges in building a modern, competitive economy? In what ways do their challenges differ? How has each responded to their challenges? Which country, in your opinion, has the better chance of succeeding, and why?

4. If political instability should threaten Japan, China, or India, what forms might it assume, what might cause it, and what might it mean for the society where it occurs? For the region? (Analyze the situation in each country separately, and then compare their prospects.)

SUGGESTED READING

Chang, David Wen-wei. *China under Deng Xiaoping: Political and Economic Reform.* New York: St. Martin's Press, 1991.

Frankenstein, John. "Chinese Foreign Trade in the 1980s." *Current History,* September 1988.

Fukui, Haruhiro. "Japan's Takeshita at the Helm." *Current History,* April 1988.

Hardgrave, Robert L., Jr., and Kochanek, Stanley A. *India: Government and Politics of a Developing Nation.* 4th ed. Orlando, Fla.: Harcourt, 1986.

Harding, Harry. *China's Second Revolution: Reform after Mao.* Washington, D.C.: Brookings Institution, 1987.

Manor, James. "India: State and Society Diverge." *Current History,* December 1989.

Nathan, Andrew J. *Chinese Democracy.* Berkeley: University of California Press, 1986.

Ozaki, Robert S. *Human Capitalism: The Japanese Enterprise System as World Model.* New York: Viking Penguin, 1992.

Ozaki, Robert S. "The Japanese Economy Internationalized." *Current History,* April 1988.

Perkins, Dwight A. *China: Asia's Next Economic Giant?* Seattle: University of Washington Press, 1989.

NOTES

1. See Robert S. Ozaki, "The Japanese Economy Internationalized," *Current History,* April 1988, pp. 157–160, 178.

2. John Hughes, "Taiwan's Miracle," *Christian Science Monitor,* July 22, 1988, p. 12.

3. A. Doak Barnett, "Ten Years after Mao," *Foreign Affairs,* vol. 65, no. 1 (Summer 1986), p. 37.

4. David Wen-wei Chang, *China under Deng Xiaoping: Political and Economic Reform* (New York: St. Martin's Press, 1991), p. 254.

5. Edward A. Gargan, "China Reigning In Economy's Shift to a Free Market," *New York Times,* Oct. 17, 1988, p. 1.

6. Ibid.

7. "China Goes for Broke," *Economist,* July 25, 1992, p. 53.

8. Ibid.

9. John Frankenstein, "Chinese Foreign Trade in the 1980s," *Current History,* Sept. 1988, p. 274.
10. See Harry Harding, *China's Second Revolution: Reform after Mao* (Washington, D.C.: Brookings Institution, 1987).
11. Frankenstein, "Chinese Foreign Trade," p. 258.
12. "When China Wakes," *Economist,* Nov. 28, 1992.
13. Ozaki, "Japanese Economy Internationalized," p. 157.
14. Ibid., p. 158.
15. David Brock, "Fortress of Mercantilism Still Wary of Competitors," *Insight,* July 18, 1988, p. 17.
16. Ibid.
17. Ibid.
18. Norman Cousins, "Japan Is the Real 'Threat' to the U.S.," *Christian Science Monitor,* Feb. 25, 1988, p. 14.
19. G. John Ikenberry, "The Irony of State Strength: Comparative Responses to the Oil Shocks in the 1970s," *International Organization,* vol. 40, no. 1 (Winter 1986), p. 105.
20. Haruhiro Fukui, "Japan's Takeshita at the Helm," *Current History,* April 1988, pp. 173–175, 185–186.
21. "The Test for the LDP," *Economist,* July 25, 1992, p. 17.
22. "No More Payoffs, Japan Executive Vow," *International Herald Tribune,* August 17, 1993, p. 2.
23. Robert J. Hardgrave, Jr., and Stanley A. Kochanek, *India: Government and Politics of a Developing Nation,* 4th ed. (Orlando, Fla.: Harcourt, 1986), p. 329.
24. Ibid., p. 328.
25. Julia Leung, "China Is Pursuing Bold Experiments in Property Sales," *Asian Wall Street Journal,* Mar. 7, 1988, p. 1.
26. Ibid.
27. Stephen R. Weisman, "U.S. in India: Less Aid, Less Influence," *New York Times,* Apr. 21, 1988, p. 4.
28. Hardgrave and Kochanek, *India,* p. 361.
29. Sheila Tefft, "Economic Woes Besiege India," *Christian Science Monitor,* June 4, 1991, p. 5; Sheila Tefft, "India Deals with Economic Crisis," *Christian Science Monitor,* July 3, 1991, p. 7.
30. See Cameron Barr, "India's Prime Minister Gains Ground despite Nation's Poor Economic Prospects," *Christian Science Monitor,* Mar. 24, 1992, p. 5; and Cameron Barr, "India Takes Lead in Warming U.S. Relations," *Christian Science Monitor,* Mar. 2, 1991, p. 3; see also Sheila Tefft, "India Pursues Free-Market Reform," *Christian Science Monitor,* Oct. 30, 1991, p. 7.
31. Rabindranath Tagore, in *Aspects of Our Foreign Policy: From Speeches and Writings of Indira Gandhi,* All-India Congress Committee, ed. (New Delhi: All-India Congress Committee, 1973), p. 72.

PART VI

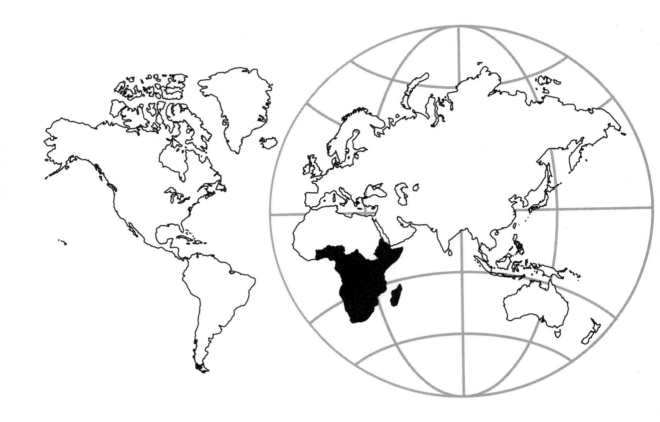

Sub-Saharan
Africa

Togo
Benin
Ghana
Nigeria
Cameroon
Central African Republic
Djibouti
Ethiopia
Somalia
Equatorial Guinea
Gabon
Congo
Uganda
Kenya
Rwanda
Zaire
Burundi
Tanzania
Angola
Malawi
Zambia
Mozambique
Zimbabwe
Namibia
Botswana
Swaziland
Lesotho
South Africa
Madagascar

KENYA

Area: 266 square miles
Population: 25 million
Density per square mile: 94
Languages: Swahili (official),
English, several others among 40
ethnic groups
Literacy rate: 69%
Religions: Protestantism, Roman
Catholicism, Islam
Monetary unit: shilling
GNP: (1991) $8.5 billion; $340 per
capita

NIGERIA

Area: 356,667 square miles
Population: 119 million
Density per square mile: 334
Languages: English (official), Hausa,
Yoruba, Ibo
Literacy rate: 51%
Religions: Islam (50%) in north,
Christianity (40%) in south
Monetary unit: naira
GNP: (1991) $34 billion; $290 per
capita

SOUTH AFRICA

Area: 472,359 square miles
Population: 37 million
Density per square mile: 78
Languages: English, Afrikaans,
Xhosa, Zulu, other tribal languages
Literacy rate: 99% (whites), 50%
(blacks)
Religions: Christianity (majority),
Islam
Monetary unit: rand
GNP: (1991) $100 billion; $2,530 per
capita

16

The Legacy of Colonialism

Sub-Saharan Africa shares a continent with some of the Arab nations of the Middle East (see Part IV): Egypt, Libya, Tunisia, Algeria, and Morocco. The rest of the continent is sometimes divided into East Africa, West Africa, and Southern Africa.

In all, sub-Saharan Africa comprises forty-eight separate and independent nation-states. Most are artificial creations, a legacy of colonialism. The borders—drawn by the great powers of Europe for their own convenience—in some cases arbitrarily divide ethnic groups between two or more states; in other cases, they combine several ethnic groups into a single state.

The very idea of the nation-state is foreign to Africans; indeed, Western students of Africa can easily be misled by their own concept of "country." In Africa, a country is not necessarily an aggregation of people whose primary allegiance is to a single state. Rather, it is a state or government recognized by other states or governments as having a legitimate claim to rule a certain territory and population, even though its native inhabitants may reject that claim or view it with indifference.

Land, People, and Politics

A major geographic feature of **sub-Saharan Africa** is its relationship to the world's largest desert, the Sahara. Some 3.3 million square miles in area and three thousand miles long, the Sahara stretches from the east coast to the west coast of the continent, forming a formidable natural barrier between the Arab world to the north and Black Africa to the south.

South of this vast desert are found five great rivers—the Nile, the Congo, the Niger, the Zambesi, and the Orange. Together they flow a total distance of 12,500 miles and boast a basin area of 4.1 million square miles. These mighty

421

rivers played a significant role in political and cultural patterns before the colonial era, for centuries serving both as natural boundaries and as barriers against foreign intrusion. Ironically, during the nineteenth century, the same waterways were important conduits for Africa's colonization by European powers.

The ancient Greeks, who claimed the first European contact with this part of the world, called the region Ethiopia ("land of the burned faces"). During the eighteenth century, European explorers and geographers dubbed sub-Saharan Africa the "Dark Continent," admitting their ignorance of the cultures and geography of the region. (It is ironic that the term *dark* was ever applied to such a sun-drenched part of the world!) This ignorance of Africa is all the more surprising in light of archaeological evidence that sub-Saharan Africa may have been the birthplace of *Homo sapiens* and thus the cradle of the first human civilization.[1]

Africa's Cultural Kaleidoscope

Sub-Saharan Africa hosts a great diversity of cultures and environments that have shaped its traditions and institutions. The region comprises 9.4 million square miles, or 80 percent of Africa's landmass, and more than 70 percent of the continent's population. With a total of forty-eight sovereign states, sub-Saharan Africa accounts for roughly one-third of the votes in the United Nations General Assembly. (Although African nations do not always vote as a bloc in the UN, they do tend to see eye to eye on issues such as apartheid in South Africa, reform of the international economic order, and decolonization.)

Sub-Saharan Africa is a mosaic of ethnic groups and cultures—most experts set the total number at more than a thousand. Ethnic composition ranges from essentially homogeneous countries (such as Botswana, Lesotho, Seychelles, and Swaziland) to extremely heterogeneous ones (Cameroon and Chad each have 200 groups, Tanzania has 130, and Zaire has 80). Most sub-Saharan countries have two to five ethnic groups, and this diversity is matched by a great diversity of religions and languages. The resulting sociocultural fragmentation is compounded by the presence of non-African religions (Islam and Christianity) and languages (English, French, Spanish, Portuguese, and Afrikaans, derived from Dutch).

The countries of sub-Saharan Africa vary tremendously in size. They range from tiny Seychelles (145 square miles in the Indian Ocean) to the huge Sudan (967,500 square miles), nearly four times the size of Texas. The smallest five countries contain only 2,054 square miles; in contrast, the largest five countries comprise 2,857,656 square miles.

Territorial size, however, in Africa as elsewhere, does not necessarily reflect population size. Nigeria, for example, with less than 4 percent of the region's land, holds nearly 25 percent of its population. Sudan, three times the size of Nigeria, has less than 4 percent of the region's population. Nigeria's population density is about ten times Sudan's.

Geography has had an especially profound influence on national development in sub-Saharan Africa. Some countries are landlocked, while others have long seacoasts. Proximity to oceans (or distance from them) often determined exposure to foreign intruders. The countries blessed with nearness to the oceans were at the same time cursed by being the first to be colonized. They were also often the last to gain their independence, in part because their harbors and ports made them strategically valuable.

The countries of West Africa along the Atlantic coast are generally richer in mineral wealth than the highlands of the interior, where agriculture and livestock form the basis of local economies. Location, size, population, topography, and natural resources have shaped relations among the states in the region. For example, Mali, Mauritania, Nigeria, and other nations of West Africa called for economic and military solidarity against South Africa during the heyday of apartheid, while Malawi, Mozambique, and Botswana, aware of the costs of antagonizing their powerful neighbor, were more cautious and conciliatory. By the same token, South Africa has long enjoyed generally good relations with the West, for it offers major seaports, vast mineral wealth, and access to some of the world's most important maritime and naval routes.

The Aftershocks of Independence

Patterns of government and politics vary throughout sub-Saharan Africa, but there are common threads. For example, upon achieving independence, the nations of the region sought to adapt the forms of government that the colonial powers had established earlier. But the grafting of foreign models onto African cultures and the neglect of African traditions led to neither peace nor stability. Since independence, almost all the states in the region have experienced political violence, including assassinations, massacres, coups and coup attempts, revolts, insurgencies, and civil wars. To many experts, this chronic instability can be ascribed to the artificial boundaries drawn by the European powers. Nearly two-thirds of the states in the region are today under military regimes, and most of the civilian governments, whatever their specific form, display strong authoritarian tendencies. This predominance of dictatorship and one-party rule has given the region a deceptive monolithic veneer. It is too little understood in the West that Black Africa had a political history before the Europeans arrived. There were empires and dynasties in West Africa and South Africa and monarchies in East Africa. Thus large-scale political organization is not simply a colonial artifact. What colonialism did was wipe out virtually all traces of preexisting political institutions in sub-Saharan Africa, much as the Spanish did in Latin America (Chapter 19).

Foreign Intrusion and Conquest

In the culture and history of African politics, nothing has been more significant than European imperialism. What explains the origins and patterns of colonial rule in Africa? Why were the Europeans able to conquer this vast region in so short a time? Geography and ethnic rivalries were two key factors. So was the state of the various civilizations at the time. It is important to remember that African history did not begin with the arrival of the Europeans.

Africa's Neglected Precolonial History

Basil Davidson has written:

> For most of Africa, the effective time-span of history, insofar as it can now be understood, reaches back over about two millennia, and is divided from prehistory—along a line that is always faint and sometimes arbitrary—by the development of iron-working and cultivation, as early populations dispersed and spread through the plains, hills and forests south of the Sahara. . . .
>
> It is the Negroes, evolving a thousand languages and cultural variants over the past several thousand years, who have been responsible for the peopling of Africa with most of its modern inhabitants. Almost certainly they were dominant among the Late Stone Age pastoralists of the Saharan regions before the area began to become dessicated around 2000 BC; thus they formed or helped to form the early populations of Pharaonic Egypt and other peripheral areas along the Nile.[2]

The long history of Africa's social and political evolution cannot be recounted in detail here; only its contours can be traced. Civilization is always cumulative, a process of accretion spanning many centuries, at once differentiating and ordering human existence. One of the principal aims of society is to enable communities to cope with nature. This interaction of invention and environment, however, is only part of the story. The interaction of self-contained social groups—often with different rituals, languages, and customs—is equally important. As our case studies later in this chapter will illustrate, ethnic particularism and interethnic conflict have often gone hand in hand in Africa.

The Colonial Legacy

The geography of Africa—its size, surface features, climate, resources, and strategic importance—gave rise to a paradox: athough physically remote from the principal power centers of Europe, North America, and East Asia, Africa is surrounded by water and thus can be reached easily via the maritime "highways" between the continents.

For centuries, Africa was viewed by outsiders with curiosity, awe, and greed. Before the modern era, however, foreign intrusions were hindered by geography. The regularity of Africa's coastlines put the perimeter within reach, but the interior was largely impenetrable due to the rugged terrains, tall mountains, hot and rainy seasons, unnavigable rivers, swamps, jungles, tropical rain forests, and the vast and forbidding Sahara. No other continent had such effective natural defenses.

By the second century A.D., Arab merchant caravans were moving along the coast of the Sahara and East Africa, and various crusades in the seventh century spread Islam among Africans along the trans-Saharan trade route. The Romans had gained a foothold on the Mediterranean coast of Africa as early as the second century B.C., but further European encounters with Africa were minimal and sporadic for nearly two thousand years. Thus while the Africans of the interior were adapting to their environment—cultivating land, herding cattle, inventing implements, building societies and kingdoms—coastal African societies were trading goods and establishing ties with foreign traders, explorers, and missionaries. In this manner, coastal Africans themselves helped Europeans explore and eventually colonize the African interior by befriending the foreigners, serving as their guides and interpreters, protecting them from hostile interior inhabitants, repairing their ships, and giving them food and shelter. In the final analysis, the geography that had deterred foreign intruders could not prevent gradual encroachment by the European powers with the natives as their helpmates.

European explorers began sailing along Africa's coasts around 1450. Portugal, under the stewardship of Prince Henry the Navigator, sponsored many seafaring expeditions. Bartolomeu Dias rounded Cape Horn (the southern tip of Africa) in 1488, and in 1497, Vasco da Gama became the first European to reach India by this route. The Portuguese successes attracted other European naval powers. Propelled by the new mercantilist ideology, the balance of influence in Africa shifted from Arabs to Europeans, setting the stage for the later arrival of Christian missionaries seeking converts, even in Muslim-dominated areas. A host of other highly destabilizing changes accompanied the European influx.

From 1795 to 1930, European geographers and missionaries took it as their duty to explore the African interior and to map and settle the continent. Europeans flocked to Africa in the second half of the nineteenth century in search of riches and adventure. Missionaries came to fulfill the "Great Commission," Christendom's solemn duty to save African souls (the "white man's burden," in Rudyard Kipling's famous phrase). These activities ultimately led to Europe's colonial domination over African cultures and politics and helped create some of the continent's most intractable problems.

By the mid-nineteenth century, Europeans had established colonies and were vying for hegemony. Their push for overseas territories was propelled in part by the Industrial Revolution and the need for cheap labor, raw materials, and new markets. In 1884, this "scramble for Africa" culminated in the **Conference of Berlin** (1884–1885), at which the European powers divided up Africa. By the end of the century, nearly all of Africa was under European colonial rule.[3] By 1914, only Ethiopia and Liberia remained self-governing. Although the colonial empires gradually broke up after World War II, most of southern Africa remained under white minority rule for decades.

Cultural Overlays

As prominent Africanist Ali Mazrui has pointed out, most of Africa has a **triple heritage**—African, Islamic, and Western.[4] These overlapping traditions are manifested most clearly in the prevalence of externally derived religions and languages in Africa. Most educated Africans, like Mazrui, are likely to speak three languages—an ethnic language, a national language, and Arabic or a European language.

Religion and Politics

Islam is the majority religion in fourteen sub-Saharan countries and virtually the only one in Mali, Somalia, Mauritania, and Djibouti. Large Muslim communities can be found in many others, including Nigeria and Ethiopia. Christianity is the main religion in eighteen countries.

In recent years, the Islamic nations have exhibited greater religious activism than the predominantly Christian ones. No doubt this phenomenon is related to Arab militancy regarding the Palestinian question and to other turbulent events in the Middle East, including the Iranian Revolution, which replaced the secular Western-oriented regime of the Shah with a fundamentalist Islamic theocracy. This event provoked a sharp increase in Islamic religious fervor not only in the Arab world but also in certain African countries. For example, more Muslims made pilgrimages to Mecca from Nigeria (which is 50 percent Muslim) than from any other country in the early 1980s,[5] and five of Nigeria's seven heads of state since independence have been Muslims. Moreover, the influence of Islam transcends national politics in Africa: nineteen of the forty-five members of the Islamic Conference are from sub-Saharan Africa.

Some scholars question whether Africans who embrace Christianity are as devout as their Muslim counterparts.[6] Studies have shown that although European and American missionaries were the most aggressive in evangelizing, they did not teach their religion within the context of local African traditions. **Mission Christianity**, according to John Mbiti, isolated new members from their roots without grounding itself in their culture. Moreover, to most converts, the mission Christians, as role models, were often indistinguishable from other Europeans whose lifestyle was identical. Then, too, some locals converted to Christianity for opportunistic reasons, such as gaining employment in mission projects or wanting to appear "modern." Indeed, a self-conscious preference for modernity set Africans who were educated in mission schools apart from most other Africans, at least until quite recently.

Thus the mission legacy produced new elites, but some of those elites rejected the philosophy of the missions, which discouraged higher education and secular pursuits in politics or the sciences. Some mission students, including Jomo Kenyatta, the "George Washington of Kenya," even came to resent the missions: "When the Europeans first came to Africa, they told us to shut our eyes and say amen."

Kenyatta was a gifted public speaker, thanks in part to his mission background. As W. H. Taylor noted in a study of Nigeria, the missions succeeded most in teaching such things as interpersonal relations and verbal self-expression.[7] And even if the missionaries avoided politics, their students often applied religious lessons to political and social analysis and used their verbal skills to persuade and politicize people. This may explain why so many of Africa's most illustrious independence leaders had an early affiliation with mission Christianity.

Traditional religions continue to predominate in fourteen sub-Saharan countries. These religions are sometimes lumped together under the name of **animism**. Unlike Christianity and Islam, which are monotheistic, indigenous African religions espouse a multiplicity of divinities and spirits. Thus for the Oromos of Ethiopia, Abdari represents a universal deity in whom all spirits and nature are unified and in whose name ancestral gods and natural divinities are called on to perform miracles and fulfill needs. The Yoruba of Nigeria have Ashe or Arisa, the god of all power who can make all things happen. The Yoruba can also call on seventeen hundred other divinities and spirits for specific needs and occasions.[8] That traditional religions continue to thrive in many parts of the region must not be ignored by African leaders, who themselves are likely to be Muslim or Christian.

The Language of Politics

The linguistic legacy of colonialism in African political culture is no less striking than the impact of imported religions. Non-African languages have both united and divided the societies of Black Africa. Thus if the classification of a country as Anglophone (English-speaking), Francophone (French-speaking), or Lusophone (Portuguese-speaking) has provided a sense of group identity, it also points to one of the nation's most intransigent problems: deciding which language should be the official one. Some Africanists ascribe the failure of efforts to launch a pan-African movement to the absence of a common language used throughout the region.

English or French is used in business or official matters in most sub-Saharan countries. Portuguese is spoken officially in five countries, Spanish, Italian, German, and Dutch (Afrikaans) in others. Despite the spread of Islam, which is the religion of about 250 million Africans, Arabic is not widely spoken anywhere in sub-Saharan Africa; it is a minority tongue in Somalia, Ethiopia, Eritrea, Djibouti, and Sudan.

To capture the kaleidoscopic character of African societies, some scholars talk about "**Africanity**":

> Those with a superficial knowledge of black Africa see it as a monolithic culture in which everyone lives, feels and thinks alike . . . [but] those who know it really well detect beneath the diversity a large cultural unity. . . . The cultural unity of the diverse African people—the sum of all the component parts that give the various societies of traditional Africa their common characteristics—is known as "Africanity."[9]

This diversity gives rise to some contradictions. In a number of sub-Saharan countries, conflict born in cultural pluralism and social rifts has led to bloody rebellions and massacres. In some countries (Senegal, Tanzania, Zambia), statesmanship has contained ethnolinguistic tensions. But where group affinity is stronger than national identity (as in Angola, Burundi, Ethiopia, Nigeria, Sudan, Somalia, and Uganda), ethnic and religious tensions have erupted in full-scale civil wars.

Where imported or imposed cultural differences have generated conflict, indigenous religions and languages have sometimes ameliorated civil strife. In fact, African leaders who recognize the unifying force of indigenous culture may politicize local traditions to gain legitimacy or to galvanize popular support for particular policies.

Deprivation and Militarization

Some experts view the prevalence of civil strife in sub-Saharan Africa as a legacy of foreign intrusion and domination. Deprivation and militarization are two prominent features of this legacy.

From their earliest contacts with Africa, Europeans typically found nothing cultural that engaged their interest. They did, however, see resources they coveted: ivory, gold, and diamonds; lush and productive land; and people they could exploit. Systematically, they deprived the Africans of their dignity, their land, and their natural riches and denied them the fundamental right to self-determination. On their own soil, Africans were obliged to learn foreign languages, take foreign names, and worship foreign deities. Many suffered a loss of self-esteem and experienced self-doubt. Some resolved their "identity crisis" by fully assimilating foreign norms and values; others, by rejecting foreign ways. During most of the twentieth century, the societies of sub-Saharan Africa were torn by conflicts between **rejectionists**, demanding political independence and national liberation, and **assimilationists**, accepting of foreign domination.[10]

Even the religions that were brought to Africa have contributed to hostilities. In a book titled *Things Fall Apart*, Nigerian novelist Chinua Achebe illustrated how mission Christianity created tension among the Africans when the converts denigrated the unconverted as "pagans" and the unconverted maligned the converts as traitors who fraternized with foreign gods. In the same vein, Jomo Kenyatta, in *Facing Mount Kenya*, explained how colonial religions disrupted Kikuyu sociopolitical institutions. During colonization and the later struggle for independence, some Africans fought on the side of the Europeans with whom they shared religion, employment, and social status. To combat the factionalizing effects of alien religions, many postcolonial leaders persecuted local converts, shut down mission operations, and restricted missionaries to teaching only government-approved subjects.

In the postindependence period, sub-Saharan Africa has struggled to overcome the lingering effects of economic and military domination, known as **neocolonialism**. The economic legacy of colonialism limited Africa to producing raw materials for Europe and consuming finished products imported from overseas, often with borrowed capital or foreign aid. For all its long association with

Europe, sub-Saharan Africa's average per capita gross domestic product was only a paltry $450 at the end of the 1980s. All of Africa accounts for only 1 percent of world industrial output, yet the continent still supplies significant amounts of raw materials to the industrial world. To describe this relative deprivation another way, the sub-Saharan countries, which account for about one-third of the UN's membership, together cannot afford to contribute even 1 percent of the UN budget.

Militarization is another legacy of foreign domination. Sub-Saharan countries, despite widespread poverty, spend huge sums of money importing military hardware from former colonial powers. Not only do such arms purchases divert foreign-exchange earnings and domestic revenues from indigenous economic development, but they also nurture militarism among national groups.[11]

The legacies of colonialism have provoked and prolonged conflicts among sub-Saharan countries. The long duration of wars for independence—nearly two decades in Angola, Mozambique, and Zimbabwe—is attributable in part to foreign influences. When Angola finally won independence from Portugal in 1974, the Soviet-backed Popular Movement for the Liberation of Angola (MPLA) seized power in most of the country, touching off a civil war. The Soviets used Cuban troops as a proxy army to defend the Marxist regime, while the United States and South Africa backed Joseph Savimbi's guerrilla forces (known as UNITA—the National Front for the Total Liberation of Angola).[12] South Africa sent troops across the southern Angola-Namibia border in June 1981, killing three hundred people and occupying several towns. South African forces withdrew the following September, but the war raged on until the late 1980s. Following a peace agreement and free elections, fighting again broke out in 1993 (see Chapter 18).

The independence struggle has given way to civil war in other places as well. In Mozambique, an insurgency during the 1980s took many lives and left a wake of economic devastation. Struggles for majority rule in South Africa and for independence in Namibia—both against the same white minority regime—continued for more than two generations.

Indigenous Problems

Foreign intrusions cannot be blamed for all the socioeconomic problems of sub-Saharan Africa. Internal causes include mismanagement of resources, natural calamities (especially drought), and the absence of a spirit of compromise and civic responsibility that transcends group animosities.

During the 1960s, sub-Saharan Africa enjoyed an average annual economic growth rate of 3.4 percent; that deteriorated to 0.5 percent in the 1970s and plunged to −2.4 percent in the 1980s.[13] African leaders have raised expectations, but their promises remain unfulfilled.[14]

National unity in many countries is obstructed by military coups, border conflicts, abuses of human rights, hordes of refugees victimized by famine and

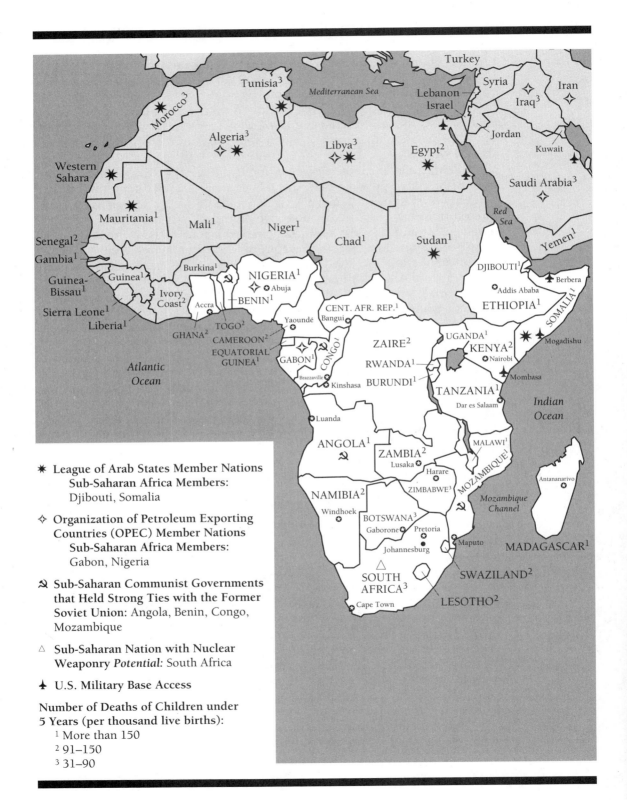

Turkey

Tunisia[3]

Mediterranean Sea

Lebanon
Israel

Syria

Iran
Iraq[3]

Morocco[3]

Algeria[3]

Libya[3]

Egypt[2]

Jordan

Kuwait

Western
Sahara

*Red
Sea*

Saudi Arabia[3]

Mauritania[1]

Mali[1]

Niger[1]

Chad[1]

Sudan[1]

Yemen[1]

Senegal[2]
Gambia[1]

Burkina[1]

NIGERIA[1]

DJIBOUTI[1]

Berbera

Guinea-
Bissau[1]

Guinea[1]

Abuja

Addis Ababa

Ivory
Coast[2]

Accra

BENIN[1]

CENT. AFR. REP.[1]

ETHIOPIA[1]

Sierra Leone[1]
Liberia[1]

GHANA[2]

TOGO[2]
CAMEROON[2]

Yaoundé

Bangui

UGANDA[1]

SOMALIA[1]

Mogadishu

*Atlantic
Ocean*

EQUATORIAL
GUINEA[1]

GABON[1]

ZAIRE[2]

KENYA[2]

Nairobi

RWANDA[1]

CONGO

Brazzaville

Kinshasa

BURUNDI[1]

TANZANIA[1]

Mombasa

Dar es Salaam

*Indian
Ocean*

Luanda

ANGOLA[1]

ZAMBIA[2]

MALAWI[1]

Lusaka

Antananarivo

NAMIBIA[2]

Harare

ZIMBABWE[3]

MOZAMBIQUE[1]

*Mozambique
Channel*

Windhoek

BOTSWANA[3]

Gaborone

Pretoria

Johannesburg

Maputo

MADAGASCAR[1]

SWAZILAND[2]

SOUTH
AFRICA[3]

LESOTHO[2]

Cape Town

✱ **League of Arab States Member Nations**
Sub-Saharan Africa Members:
Djibouti, Somalia

✧ **Organization of Petroleum Exporting**
Countries (OPEC) Member Nations
Sub-Saharan Africa Members:
Gabon, Nigeria

☭ **Sub-Saharan Communist Governments**
that Held Strong Ties with the Former
Soviet Union: Angola, Benin, Congo,
Mozambique

△ **Sub-Saharan Nation with Nuclear**
Weaponry *Potential:* South Africa

✈ **U.S. Military Base Access**

Number of Deaths of Children under
5 Years (per thousand live births):
[1] More than 150
[2] 91–150
[3] 31–90

violence, and a continuing brain drain.[15] In Uganda alone, hundreds of thousands lost their lives under the bloodthirsty regimes of Idi Amin and Milton Obote. One tragic consequence of continual turmoil in sub-Saharan Africa is the fact that in the late 1980s there were roughly five million African refugees (more than six times as many as in 1960). And in the early 1990s, famine decimated Ethiopia, Sudan, and Somalia.

One of the most intractable problems is the population explosion. The rate of population growth for the region as a whole is about 3 percent, the highest in the world. At this rate, sub-Saharan Africa, which had a population of about 385 million in 1985, will have 600 million people by the year 2000, and another 18 million babies will be born in that year alone.[16]

The region will thus be squeezed in a deadly vise as the population gets younger and the carrying capacity of the land gets ever more fragile. Estimates are that by the year 2000, 80 percent of Ethiopia's population will be under age 40 and more than half of all Kenyans will be age 30 or under.[17] In both nations, most of the population will consist of school-age youths who will represent a burden on society and government in terms of food, shelter, education, and job opportunities. This demographic time bomb means the political systems of sub-Saharan Africa, many of them already unstable, will come under even greater stress.

Case Studies: Kenya, Nigeria, and South Africa

Kenya is a former British colony and potentially a leader in East Africa. Nigeria, also a former British colony, is potentially a leader in West Africa. South Africa, the most powerful nation south of the Sahara, is ruled by a white minority government under an oppressive system of racial discrimination known as *apartheid*. As such, it is an anachronism, a vestige of European colonialism.

Kenya

During the European scramble for Africa in the late nineteenth century, Kenya fell under British colonial rule, which ended in 1963. Although Kenya is a large country (nearly the size of Texas), its northern three-fifths is arid. The English language and the Anglican church made a lasting imprint on the nation, but Kenya's recent history is also a product of tradition, geography, and other factors. Swahili is the main indigenous language. Over two-thirds of the population is Christian (38 percent Protestant, 28 percent Roman Catholic). The remainder are Muslim (6 percent) or embrace a traditional native religion.

A Multiethnic Society   Kenya has the multiethnic character of many sub-Saharan nations. With a total population of about 25 million, Kenyan society is composed of some forty ethnic groups, including the Kikuyu, Luo, Luhya, Kelenjin, and Kamba, along with Asians, Arabs, and Europeans.

Kenya has the highest population growth rate in the world (4.1 percent per year in 1989), and over half the population is 14 years of age or younger. This demographic trend has overwhelmed the country's steady but unspectacular economic growth. With a per capita income of less than $400, Kenya has struggled to meet the many challenges of economic and political development since independence. Between 1965 and 1985, Kenya's per capita economic growth amounted to a mere 1.9 percent per year. Income is maldistributed: 10 percent of the population receives nearly half the national income.

Contacts with Foreigners   The Arabs, the first foreign arrivals, sailed down the east coast in the seventh century. Although they made forays into the interior in search of slaves, ivory, gold, and iron, their primary interest was controlling trade routes, and they built city-states along the coast of modern Kenya, Tanzania, and Mozambique. Much later, around 1500, the Portuguese forcibly displaced the Arabs, only to be ousted by them again in the seventeenth century. The Arab sheikdom of Oman controlled the Kenyan coast until the British took control in the late nineteenth century. Although the Arab influence was of longer standing, the British influence may well prove longer-lasting. Before the twentieth century, foreign influence was generally confined to coastal areas—a pattern observable elsewhere in Africa as well.

Kenya became a British crown colony in 1920. In World War II, joint British-Kenyan forces launched a successful offensive against Italian positions in Ethiopia and Somalia. After the war, a nationalist movement emerged.

During the colonial period, native Kenyans relied on trade unions to express their political interests.[18] As part of this tradition, the **Kenya African Union (KAU)** was founded in 1944. Destined to become Kenya's largest mass organization, with 100,000 members, the KAU played an active role in the independence struggle. In the late 1940s, a charismatic Kikuyu leader named Jomo Kenyatta spearheaded Kenya's drive for independence from Great Britain.

The Mau Mau Rebellion   Early in 1952, the Mau Mau, a secret society bent on expelling all whites from Kenya and purifying Black Africans, launched a campaign of terror against Europeans and Africans who were friendly to them. The Mau Mau were mainly Kikuyu, the largest of Kenya's ethnic groups and the dominant force north of Nairobi, the capital. In October, the colonial government proclaimed a state of emergency, and the British sent troops. A bloody guerrilla war ensued. Over 10,000 Mau Mau were killed, and some 2,200 were captured. The Mau Mau themselves killed an estimated 2,800 people.

Until the **Mau Mau Rebellion** (1952–1956), violence was rare in Kenyan politics. Though the Mau Mau guerrilla movement took far more Kenyan than British lives, it demonstrated the Kenyan desire to be free of colonial domination and the inevitability of independence. London responded to the Mau Mau challenge in several ways. First, it launched a military campaign that resulted in heavy casualties. Second, it arrested KAU members, charged them with participating in the Mau Mau movement, and sentenced them to long jail terms. Jomo Kenyatta, who had been president of the KAU since 1947, was imprisoned for seven years

(1954–1961). Third, colonial authorities made a conciliatory gesture, allowing eight Kenyan representatives to serve in the colonial parliament, the Legislative Council, including Oginga Odinga, Tom Mboya, Ronald Ngala, and Daniel arap Moi, all members of the KAU who later became national leaders in independent Kenya.

The Mau Mau uprising faded after the capture of several of its leaders, but the violence underscored the strength of nationalist feelings in Kenya. The British arranged for elections to the Legislative Council in March 1957, granting a limited African franchise based on educational qualifications. The eight Africans who were elected refused to serve, demanding instead a universal franchise and free primary education for all.

KANU, Kenyatta, and an Independent Kenya   In 1960, the KAU was reconstituted as a full-fledged political party, the **Kenyan African National Union (KANU)**. At this time, the realities of multiethnic politics in Kenya became painfully apparent. KANU membership was dominated by the Kikuyu and Luo ethnic groups. Fearing that such an alliance would ignore the interests of their own ethnic groups, Ronald Ngala and Daniel arap Moi left KANU and formed the Kenyan African Democratic Union (KADU).

In February 1961, the British allowed a general election to be held within the framework of a parliamentary system. KANU and KADU contested the election, and KANU won a parliamentary majority. KANU leadership decided to delay the choice of a party president until Kenyatta was released from prison in October 1961. As chief of the majority party, Kenyatta became Kenya's first prime minister upon independence in 1963. (In 1964, Kenya proclaimed itself a republic, with Kenyatta as president.) In the euphoria of the moment, KADU was voluntarily dissolved, and most of its members joined KANU.

After independence, the government made an effort to replace ethnic particularism with Kenyan nationalism. As part of this effort, Kenyatta moved away from party pluralism, which only exacerbated ethnic rivalries. Culturally, Swahili was championed over English. Kenyatta himself downplayed and criticized English as a colonial language and spoke it sparingly. He coined the slogan Kenya na KANU ("Kenya and KANU") to emphasize national unity and the fact that all ethnic and other groups in Kenyan society were encompassed in a single political party.

A major threat to Kenya's political stability was the ethnic clash between the Kikuyu, led by Kenyatta, and the Luo, led by Mboya and Odinga. The first Kenyatta government was based on a delicately balanced coalition in which the Luo and other ethnic leaders were given key roles in the government. The arrangement soon broke down, however, and Odinga split from KANU in 1966, forming his own party, the Kenyan People's Union (KPU).

The assassination of Mboya in 1969 led to an outbreak of ethnic violence after a Kikuyu was charged with the crime and executed. Kenyatta then banned Odinga's party. In the elections that year, KANU was rebuffed by the voters, although Kenyatta, the only candidate for president, was reelected. Concluding that a competitive multiparty arrangement would not work, Kenyatta moved to establish a one-party system with a strong executive. (Some of Kenyatta's critics considered him a virtual dictator.)

Despite persistent instability, Kenyatta remained president until his death in 1978. As we will see in Chapter 17, his successor, Daniel arap Moi, followed in Kenyatta's footsteps, ruling with a firm hand and at times resorting to repressive measures.

Nigeria

A nation with great potential and great problems, Nigeria holds one-fifth of Africa's total population on only 3 percent of its land. The climate is tropical, and the terrain spreads through two main zones, savanna and rain forest. There are mangrove swamps in the extreme south, especially in the delta of the Niger River, and highlands in the east.

The interplay of geography, environment, and economic development in Nigeria can be exemplified by the problem of the tsetse fly, for which science has as yet no solution. Where the tsetse fly thrives, cattle and horses cannot survive. This has far-reaching implications for agriculture and transportation and hence for the diet and living standards of Nigerians. As one noted Africanist has written:

> Equally important are the implications for conquest: the tsetse fly and forest stopped invading cavalry as man could not. These hills and mountains provided refuge; so too did the swamps and creeks far to the south, which must have been as unfathomable to African outsiders as they were to the succession of European explorers trying to solve the great geographical mystery of the Niger.[19]

A Cultural Crucible   Nigeria's geographic diversity is matched by ethnic and cultural diversity. Nearly four hundred languages are spoken, testimony to the cultural richness and deep-rooted identity of the nation's many subgroups.

Over centuries, a variety of political systems evolved, including states, confederations, and empires. Some polities were localized and relatively democratic (though far less institutionalized than modern democracies). Most developed without foreign intrusions until the nineteenth century. Northern traders crossed the Sahara during the tenth century and introduced Islam. European traders did not appear until the sixteenth century and then did not venture beyond the Niger delta for another two hundred years. Only in the late nineteenth century was the full impact of British expansionism felt.

British Colonial Rule   The British drew the boundaries of the country that came to be called Nigeria after 1914. They were latecomers and made the mistake of trying to impose uniform administrative and political structures throughout the territory. But what worked in the north did not work in the south. The decision to divide the country initially into only two parts, northern and southern, now

West Africa: The Great Race

Toward the end of the nineteenth century, especially following the 1884–1885 Conference of Berlin, the European powers engaged in a mad scramble for colonial territories. France had lost a war to Prussia (Germany), and was not about to lose out in the struggle for overseas possessions.

France's great advantage over Germany and others in this race was geostrategic. With direct access to both the Atlantic Ocean and the Mediterranean Sea, France was able to knock together an impressive empire both in North Africa (Algeria and Tunisia) and in West Africa (the present nations of Senegal, Mauritania, Mali, Niger, Chad, Guinea, Côte d'Ivoire, Burkina Faso, Togo, Benin, Cameroon, Gabon, Congo, and the Central African Republic).

French West Africa was considered an integral part of France, and its residents were French citizens. In time, an African elite educated in France emerged.

Although France's colonies outnumbered those of Britain, France's main imperialist rival, the British grabbed most of the "prize territories" (from a strategic or geopolitical standpoint, at least)—Nigeria in West Africa, South Africa and Rhodesia in the south, and Kenya in East Africa.

After World War II, the United States and the Soviet Union emerged as superpowers, with continental rather than overseas empires. The former European powers' Asian colonies, having been occupied by Japan during the war, now quickly became independent (French Indochina was one exception). It was obvious that the African colonial empires would also break up. The French and British governments (but not the Portuguese or the Belgians) helped clear a path to independence. But just as they held on too long in Indochina, the French clung tenaciously to Algeria in North Africa. Only a bloody and prolonged war of national liberation gained Algeria its independence in 1962.

In West Africa, the story was quite different: France's colonies became independent states through a peaceful process of transition that was completed by 1960, when most were admitted to the United Nations.

The cultures and politics of West Africa vary widely. Some, including Senegal, Côte d'Ivoire (Ivory Coast), and Gabon, have been relatively stable societies whose governments respect individual rights most of the time; others, such as the Central African Republic, have endured episodes of extremely repressive rule.

Economically, West Africa is among the world's poorest regions, with a 1991 per capita GNP of under $700. Unlike Asia, the range is not very wide. With the exception of Gabon's annual per capita GNP of $3,780, countries in West Africa are extremely poor with annual per capita GNP levels below $1,000. The actual figures range from Cameroon's annual per capita GNP of $940 to Sierra Leone's paltry $210. The demographic picture is also alarming. Population growth rates are extremely high throughout the area (an astronomical 3.8 percent in Senegal for example), and life expectancy is exceedingly low: a mere 42 years in Sierra Leone—the lowest in the world, where 245 out of 1,000 children die before the age of 5 and nearly 80 percent of the population is illiterate. These figures are higher than the regional norm in which the mortality rate for children age 5 is generally in the range of 100 to 200 deaths per 1,000 births, and the illiteracy rate is over 50 percent in nearly all of West Africa: over 60 percent in the majority of these countries. The illiteracy rate in Ghana and Gabon is slightly under 40 percent.

seems a major blunder. This north-south division reinforced a psychological split: British-educated southerners who lived in the coastal areas believed themselves more fit to rule than Islamic and supposedly insular northerners, who were widely scorned in the south.

The trauma that the Great Depression of the 1930s wrought on Europe's economies had repercussions in the colonies as well. Nigeria was a source of export revenue for beleaguered Britain, a fact that intensified Nigerians' desire to cast off British rule. Even so, Nigeria did not become independent until 1960.

World War II was the catalyst for decolonization throughout Asia and Africa. Before the British left Nigeria, they divided it into three regions (splitting the south into east and west). Each region was dominated by a distinct ethnolinguistic group: the Hausa in the north, the Yoruba in the west, and the Ibo in the east. In 1967, the government, then under military control, replaced the regions with twelve states.

The Politics of Particularism

The three major ethnic groups—Ibo, Yoruba, and Hausa—have dominated Nigerian politics, and the most popular and most charismatic political figures have usually been identified with one of them. (Other sizable groups are the Nupe, Edo, Ijaw, Tiv, Fulani, and Kanuri.) The Ibo, Yoruba, and Hausa each advanced a political party, resulting in a three-party system.

During the 1950s, when independence was being negotiated, there were two main sources of domestic tensions: the north-south split and the resentment of minority groups against the majority in each of Nigeria's administrative subdivisions. Violence erupted at times and smoldered even in periods of apparent tranquillity.

In Nigeria, as elsewhere, the British did not foresee the issues of ethnic politics that they had helped create and consequently did little to resolve them. As a result, within a few years after the British left, Nigeria was convulsed by one of the bloodiest civil wars in modern African history, precipitated when the Ibo declared an independent republic, Biafra, and attempted to secede. One vital political lesson to be drawn from Nigeria's turbulent past is that a multiparty system in an ethnically fragmented society—particularly when that society faces enormous economic challenges—is likely to be unworkable.

Nigeria's political experience since independence will be detailed in Chapter 17. Briefly, at its inception, Nigeria was hailed by outsiders, especially the British, as a "model of democracy." But that was not to last. The first government after independence, elected in the first nationwide elections, was a coalition whose stability was threatened from the start. After a succession of political crises, the military in January 1966 staged a coup—the first in a series—and assumed power. Ever since, democracy was vied with dictatorship; the latter has prevailed most of the time.

South Africa

Nowhere has the colonial legacy been more tenacious and invidious than in South Africa. **Afrikaners**—the dominant white minority of Dutch descent—claim that when their ancestors arrived in the seventeenth century, the southern tip of Africa was largely uninhabited. They claim to have been the first to settle it.

The Roots of Apartheid   In truth, when the Dutch East India Company set out to establish a way station at the Cape of Good Hope in 1652, the expeditionary force of two hundred men encountered an indigenous group called the Khoikhoi, whom they enslaved. The Khoikhoi (called Hottentots by whites) were eventually wiped out by smallpox, and the Dutch colonialists then imported slaves from the East Indies and Madagascar. The resulting racial mixture of Khoikhoi, Dutch, Malay, and others produced the group now known as the **Cape Coloured**, who in time were classified by the Afrikaners as a distinct inferior group. (Coloured are not to be confused with blacks, the majority group ranked below the Coloured in the apartheid system.)

The **Boers**, Dutch farmers who immigrated to what is now South Africa, pushed outward from the Cape Colony. Many Boers settled only long enough to exhaust the soil and then moved on. As they penetrated into the interior, they encountered another indigenous group, the San. The Boers shot the San, whom they called Bushmen and disdainfully regarded as savages and thieves.

The Kaffir Wars   The Boers met no serious challenge from the indigenous Africans until the late eighteenth century. As Dutch settlers moved northward along the Indian Ocean coast, Africans were moving south to escape population pressure, tribal wars, and British slave raids. In the ensuing **Kaffir Wars**, which lasted over a century, the Boers subdued the Africans, with great loss of life on both sides.

Reverberations from the Napoleonic Wars in Europe were felt as far away as South Africa. When France occupied the Netherlands in 1795, the Dutch asked the British to take over the Cape and keep the French out. The British obliged but then decided to stay; in 1814, the Netherlands ceded South Africa to Great Britain, thereby legitimizing what was plainly a *fait accompli*.

The Great Trek   The Dutch in the Netherlands could adjust to the loss of South Africa more easily than the Boers. The British takeover turned the tables: now it was the Afrikaners who were forced to live under rules made by "foreigners." For example, the British insisted that everyone be equal before the law, regardless of color or creed, and in 1834, to the dismay of many Boers, slavery was abolished. Two years later, the Boers, convinced that the British were out to destroy their way of life, began the **Great Trek**. Between 1836 and 1838, about twelve thousand Dutch farmers and their families headed out in search of new frontiers. Afrikaners venerate these stouthearted forebears much as Americans honor the pioneers. As on the American frontier, these *voortrekkers* set out in caravans, endured tremendous hardships, and occasionally fought battles with natives, drawing their wagons into a circle called a *laager*. One ill-fated group vanished without a trace. When Zulus massacred 570 Boer settlers in 1838, the Boers retaliated by killing three thousand Zulus. In general, the *voortrekkers* dealt with Africans just as the pioneers dealt with Native Americans: they used persuasion, force, and fraud to push the native inhabitants off the land. The very idea of owning land was alien to Africans, as it was to most Native Americans.

The *voortrekkers'* destination was the fertile Natal region, on the Indian Ocean coast. But in 1843, the British annexed Natal, outraging the Boers and prompting them to undertake yet another great trek. This time they moved inland and established two small republics, the Transvaal and the Orange Free State. Again ensconced in their own enclaves, the Boers coexisted with the British, uneasily but peacefully, until 1867, when diamonds were discovered in the Transvaal.

The Boer War   The discovery of diamonds drew the British into the Transvaal; the flow became a flood when gold was discovered there in 1886. So many British *uitlanders* rushed into the Transvaal that they soon outnumbered Afrikaners two to one. The Transvaal government, headed by Paul Kruger, attempted to undercut the British by disenfranchising them—a favorite Boer tactic.

The British in the Cape Colony cast a covetous eye at the Transvaal and the Orange Free State. Sir Cecil Rhodes, founder of Rhodesia (and of the Rhodes scholarships to Oxford), conspired with the British high commissioner, Alfred Milner, to provoke Kruger into declaring war; their goal was to annex the Boer republics.

The ensuing **Boer War** (1899–1902) was bitter and bloody. The Boers fought valiantly; the British resorted to drastic measures, including what today would be considered human rights abuses (such as putting Boer women and children in concentration camps, where an estimated 26,000 of them died of typhus). When the Boers finally sued for peace in 1902, the British had won the war but lost the territory: guilt-ridden and dispirited, London extended full political rights to the defeated Boers, who eventually converted their numerical advantage over the British into full control of the republics.

Ascent of the Afrikaners   The British allowed the Boers of the Transvaal and the Orange Free State to govern themselves, which ushered in a brief era of goodwill. In 1910, the Boer-run colonies were yoked to Natal and Cape Province in a new nation-state, the Union of South Africa. World War I produced new strains on British-Afrikaner relations: although South Africa's foreign policy was dictated by Great Britain, many Afrikaners were sympathetic to the Germans, and the German colony of South-West Africa (now Namibia) was right next door. When the British pressured the South African government to join an invasion of South-West Africa, many Afrikaners were opposed; Pretoria participated anyway. Many Afrikaners similarly opposed South Africa's entry into World War II.

Anti-British sentiment also had economic causes. The British dominated South African industry and commerce, whereas the Afrikaners were primarily farmers. When the Depression disrupted world trade and precipitated a collapse in farm prices, many Afrikaners, now desperate, streamed to the cities in search of jobs. Against this backdrop, they became mobilized and radicalized. They set about creating the infrastructure of a new Afrikaner state and society—cultural associations, schools and universities, insurance companies, and political parties.

The **National party** was founded in 1914 as the vehicle of Afrikaner self-assertion. At first, the party was moderate and conciliatory toward the British, but in the 1930s, under the leadership of Daniel Malan, it became a militant instrument of Afrikaner nationalism. The doctrine of white supremacy—the cornerstone of apartheid—was thus solidified in the worldwide depression between the wars. Thus the South African system originated in the same turbulent era as Nazi Germany, Fascist Italy, and other extreme right-wing regimes and movements founded on notions of racial superiority.

The Nationalists did not simply build a party; they launched a movement. With patience and persistence, they spread their ideology of white supremacy, using the poignant image of wagons huddled in the *laager*: anyone who resisted indoctrination into the movement was breaking the circle and aiding the enemy. In 1948, the National party won the general election—what Afrikaners had lost by the bullet they had now recaptured by the ballot. Spurred by their tragic history, the Afrikaners now dug in, building a fortress state prepared to meet all challenges with force.

CONCLUSION

Politics and government in sub-Saharan Africa are conditioned by such factors as geography, ethnic and cultural diversity, and especially colonialism. This part of Africa is separated from North Africa and the Arab world by a natural barrier (the Sahara) and by language, race, culture, and history. Economically, much of sub-Saharan Africa is extremely poor. But if the image of Africa as a wonderland of exotic jungles, wild animals, and primitive tribes is a Hollywood creation, the other familiar image of poverty, drought, and famine gives the false impression that Africa is a wasteland. Indeed, some countries in the region are scenes of great human misery, but others are not so blighted. In reality, sub-Saharan Africa is a region where, due in part to the legacy of colonialism, good government and political stability have been elusive. We will take a closer look at patterns of politics in sub-Saharan Africa in the next chapter.

KEY TERMS

sub-Saharan Africa
Conference of Berlin
triple heritage
mission Christianity
animism
"Africanity"
rejectionists
assimilationists
neocolonialism
Kenya African Union (KAU)

Mau Mau Rebellion
Kenyan African National Union (KANU)
Afrikaners
Cape Coloured
Boers
Kaffir Wars
Great Trek
voortrekkers
Boer War
National party

STUDY QUESTIONS

1. How has geography influenced economic and political development in sub-Saharan Africa?
2. What role did colonialism play in shaping African politics?
3. How does the historical and cultural context of politics differ between Kenya and Nigeria? Are there any striking similarities?
4. Compare the experience of the Boers (Afrikaners) with that of early pioneers in the United States. What is the relevance of this history to the current situation in South Africa?

SUGGESTED READING

Davidson, Basil. *Africa: History of a Continent.* New York: Macmillan, 1972.

Davidson, Basil. *Africa South of the Sahara.* 17th ed. Lanham, Md.: Europa Publications, 1988.

Fanon, Frantz. *The Wretched of the Earth.* Constance Farrington, trans. New York: Grove Press, 1988.

Mazrui, Ali A. *The Africans.* Boston: Little, Brown, 1986.

Mbiti, John S. *African Religions and Philosophy.* London: Heinemann, 1990.

NOTES

1. See, for example, Alan Walker and Mark Teaford, "The Hunt for Proconsul," *Scientific American,* January 1989, pp. 76–82.
2. Basil Davidson, *Africa South of the Sahara,* 17th ed. (Lanham, Md.: Europa Publications, 1988), p. 4.
3. See, for example, Frantz Fanon, *Black Skin, White Mask,* C. Van Markman, trans. (New York: Grove Press, 1967); T. Walker Walbank, *Contemporary Africa: A Continent in Transition* (New York: Van Nostrand, 1956), pp. 107–110; and Basil Davidson, *Africa: History of a Continent* (New York: Macmillan, 1972), pp. 275–293.
4. Ali A. Mazrui, *The Africans* (Boston: Little, Brown, 1986); for an opposing viewpoint, see Hailu Habtu, "The Fallacy of the Triple Heritage Thesis: A Critique," *Issue,* vol. 13, no. 1 (1984), pp. 26–29.
5. Ali A. Mazrui, "The Semitic Impact on Black Africa: Arab and Jewish Cultural Influences," *Issue,* vol. 13, no. 1 (1984), pp. 3–8.
6. See, for example, John S. Mbiti, *African Religions and Philosophy* (London: Heinemann, 1990), pp. 75–91.
7. W. H. Taylor, "Missionary Education Reconsidered: The Nigerian Case," *African Affairs,* vol. 83, no. 331 (1984), pp. 189–205.
8. Mbiti, *African Religions and Philosophy,* pp. 75–91.
9. Georges Balandier and Jacques Marquet, eds., *The Dictionary of Black African Civilization* (New York: Amiel, 1974), p. 3; see also Jacques Marquet, *Africanity: The Cultural Union of Black Africa* (New York: Oxford University Press, 1972).

10. See Fanon, *Black Skin, White Mask*, and Frantz Fanon, *The Wretched of the Earth*, Constance Farrington, trans. (New York: Grove Press, 1988).

11. See, for example, John D. Rusk, "Warfare and Human Rights in Angola and Mozambique," *Africa Today*, vol. 34, no. 4 (1987), pp. 33–44.

12. See, for example, John Stockwell, *In Search of Enemies* (New York: Norton, 1978).

13. World Bank, *World Development Report, 1987* (New York: Oxford University Press, 1987), p. 171.

14. Peter Robbs, "Privatization in Africa," *Development International*, March-April 1987, pp. 27–30; Salim Lone, "Africa Moving Rapidly on Reforms," *Africa Recovery*, vol. 1, no. 1 (1987), pp. 14–17.

15. K. Matthews, "The OAU and the Political Economy of Human Rights in Africa," *Africa Today*, vol. 34, nos. 1–2 (1987), pp. 85–96; see also special series in *Issue*, vol. 9, no. 14 (1979), and *Issue*, vol. 12, nos. 1–2 (1982).

16. Robert Pear interview with Jonathan Moore, U.S. coordinator for refugee affairs, "The World's Debt to 12 Million Refugees," *New York Times*, Aug. 21, 1988, p. E3.

17. World Bank, *World Development Report, 1987*, p. 17.

18. See Bethwell A. Ogot, *Historical Dictionary of Kenya* (London: Scarecrow Press, 1981).

19. Jean Herskovitz, *Power and Democracy in Africa*, Headline Series No. 257 (Washington, D.C.: Foreign Policy Association, 1982), p. 8.

17

Endemic Authoritarianism?

In the eighteenth century, a Swedish civil servant named C. B. Wadstrom became fascinated with Africa as a result of reading and hearing about it from Europeans who had been there. His curiosity got the best of him: in 1787, at the time when Hamilton, Madison, and the other founders of America were meeting in Philadelphia to forge a constitution and a new nation, Wadstrom set sail for Africa. For a year he traveled around that continent, making observations on what he called the "character and disposition" of the inhabitants (much as Alexis de Tocqueville would do in America a half century later).

What Wadstrom learned about Africans was contrary to what he had read about them in the works of his European contemporaries. Rather than stereotypical primitives and savages, he found Africans possessed of many civil and cultural virtues. After returning to Europe, he wrote a series of essays about Africa based on his firsthand experiences. For example, Wadstrom said of Africans that "their understandings have not been nearly so much cultivated as those of the Europeans; but their passions, both defensive and social, are much stronger."[1] Tendentious though Wadstrom's conclusions may be, he did engage in the kind of field research vital to any comparative study of politics. Today's scholars face similar problems in studying foreign societies: what questions to ask, what issues to observe, what comparisons to make, and what conclusions to derive.

Clashing interests and festering issues are the stuff of politics in sub-Saharan Africa, as elsewhere, and they shape political patterns. As we examine the political structures of sub-Saharan Africa, remember that the nation-states of this region are almost all newcomers, having gained independence only since World War II. We will focus on two principal issues—political unity and economic self-reliance—because they provide essential background for understanding contemporary Africa.

Independence and Its Aftermath

As noted in Chapter 16, the political systems of contemporary sub-Saharan Africa were formed in the crucible of colonialism and, later, in the process of decolonization. For more than seventy years after the Conference of Berlin that parceled out Africa among the European powers, all of sub-Saharan Africa, with the exception of Ethiopia and Liberia, was under colonial rule. In most cases, this meant either direct foreign rule or **trusteeship**, somewhere between sovereignty and subjugation.

Divide and Rule: The Conquest of Africa

In some countries, nationalist guerrillas attempted to resist European colonizers, but such efforts proved futile.[2] The balance of power favored the Europeans, who had professional armies and superior weapons and were adept at using a divide-and-conquer strategy, playing off rival ethnic groups against each other and hiring African mercenaries to fight rebellious African nationalists.

Long-standing ethnic rivalries in Africa made it relatively easy for the colonial powers to pit African against African. In addition, the rich European intruders had the wherewithal to entice segments of the native population into alliances. Human frailties are not confined to any one culture; the complicity of Africans in their own subjugation testifies to this. The interethnic conflicts and violence associated with European colonialism in Africa set the stage for the internal instability so prevalent in the region today.

World War II ushered in a new epoch in the history of sub-Saharan Africa. The international system collapsed, and the nations of the world realigned. The Cold War (and anticommunism) was now the West's obsession. World opinion turned against colonialism: what had been a status symbol at the turn of the century became an anachronism. The United Nations Charter enshrined the principles of self-determination and noninterference, and this gave the African struggle a new moral impetus.

End of the Colonial Era

The cracks in the edifice of colonialism became increasingly apparent. Among the new factors in world politics was the spontaneous blossoming of **national liberation movements** throughout the colonized world (later called the **Third World**). The economic and political costs of maintaining overseas empires for war-torn European nations preoccupied with their own recovery and reconstruction were now prohibitive. The three former Great Powers of Europe—Great Britain, France, and Germany—were replaced by two superpowers, the United States and the Soviet Union. The Eurocentric balance of power itself was replaced by a global balance in which the Western European nations, once colonial overlords, were no longer even autonomous or self-reliant.

In this new world, Africans found ready allies among emerging socialist revolutionary states such as Cuba, China, and the Soviet Union. The radical anticapitalist and anti-imperialist ideology of these states struck a responsive chord among Africans, for whom capitalism and imperialism had meant exploitation. When Europeans conscripted Africans to fight in World War II, they did not realize that they were also preparing colonial peoples for armed resistance against their oppressors.[3] Meanwhile, the United Nations provided a new forum for all nations seeking liberation, and Articles 1 and 2 of its charter obligated member states to support the cause of self-determination everywhere.

Sudan became the first sub-Saharan country to obtain independence (1956), followed by Ghana (1957) and Guinea (1958). In 1960, seventeen new sub-Saharan nations gained independence, bringing the total to twenty-two; by the end of 1965, the number had climbed to thirty. African nationalists deserve some of the credit for pushing the pace of **decolonization**, but larger historical forces also played a crucial supporting role.

The momentum of decolonization, which seemed so irresistible in the beginning, was thwarted south of the equator. The Portuguese clung tenaciously to Angola and Mozambique; protracted civil wars had to be fought there and in Namibia (formerly ruled by South Africa) before these nations won independence.

Elsewhere, however, the colonial powers bowed out gracefully, even too quickly. The relatively benign process of independence in French and British colonial Africa did not necessitate armed resistance. Ironically, the fact that political separation was not marked by a sharp break in preestablished relations tended to perpetuate a colonial mentality in postindependent Black Africa. This may explain why weak governments and internal fragmentation afflict so many countries in the region today.

Development and Self-Reliance

A fundamental choice for the newly independent states of sub-Saharan Africa was whether to adopt the Soviet model of central planning and collective farming, the Western free-market model, or a composite African model based on local traditions and methods. A fourth alternative was to design a new model tailored to fit Africa. Meeting the challenge of economic and political development necessitated a series of interconnected policy decisions about strategies, resources, and procedures.

Most African nations chose neither the Soviet model nor Western-style capitalism—both models, though starkly different, were European. Emerging from the experiences of colonialism, war, and the relatively peaceful struggle for independence, they opted for a model based on self-affirmation and self-reliance. They wanted to be masters of their destiny. They stressed cooperative social values and relations in which the members of society work and produce for the good of the whole and the state acts as the agent of society, protecting and promoting the freedom and well-being of the individual. Debates over policy, both domestic and foreign, were almost always undertaken within the context of shared assumptions about the need for socialist self-reliance.

African Socialism

Self-reliance, as discussed here, is part of an ideology known as **African socialism**, which draws on the traditional system of the extended family, the members of which are expected to work for the common good and share benefits and burdens equally.[4] African socialism has been espoused by such prominent leaders as Kwame Nkrumah and Léopold Senghor in West Africa and Julius Nyerere, Tom Mboya, Oginga Odinga, and Kenneth Kaunda in East Africa. All recognize the imperatives of material progress but place human development above capital accumulation; in short, social well-being takes precedence over industrial growth.

For Nkrumah, the starting point was affirmation of the African personality, enriched by Africa's traditions and its heritage of cultural pluralism, including Islamic and Christian values. He put it this way:

> With true independence regained, however, a new harmony needs to be forged, a harmony that will allow the combined presence of traditional Africa, Islamic Africa and Euro-Christian Africa, so that this presence is in tune with the original humanist principles underlying African society. Our society is not the old society, but a new society enlarged by Islamic and Euro-Christian influences. A new emergent ideology is therefore required, an ideology . . . which will not abandon the original humanist principles of Africa.
>
> Such a philosophical statement . . . will give the theoretical basis for an ideology whose aim shall be to contain the African experience of Islamic and Euro-Christian presence as well as the experience of the traditional African society, and, by gestation, employ them for the harmonious growth and development of that society.[5]

Léopold Senghor of Senegal struck a similar chord in arguing that the African outlook is humanist and that Africa must build on this foundation. He used the concept of what he called **negritude** to encompass the cultural values of blacks everywhere. He expanded the idea of an African personality to include all actions and principles necessary to enhance the cultural development of people who have been deprived of identity and self-esteem by the inhuman experiences of slavery or colonialism.[6]

For Julius Nyerere, the essential ingredient of self-reliance was more social and political than psychological. It was intimately tied to the broadening of human freedom:

> If the purpose of development is the greater freedom and well-being of the people, it cannot result from force. . . . By orders, or even by slavery, you can build pyramids and magnificent roads, you can achieve expanded acreages of cultivation, and increases in the quantity of goods produced in your factories.

All these things, and many more, can be achieved through the use of force; but none of them results in the development of people.[7]

The method of self-reliant development envisaged by Nyerere is cooperation between society and state, but starting with the smallest unit, the individual: "To maintain our independence and our people's freedom, we ought to be self-reliant in every possible way and avoid depending upon other countries for assistance."[8]

As president of Tanzania, Nyerere devoted himself to thinking, speaking, and writing about self-reliance and socialism in the African context. Like Ghandi and Mao, Nyerere stressed the necessity of a national work ethic and moral character. He asserted that true development comes from indigenous resources—the land and the people (both abundant in Tanzania)—not from capital and technology (both scarce, not only in Tanzania but throughout sub-Saharan Africa). In 1967, Tanzania issued the **Arusha Declaration**, a socialist program of development known as *ujamaa,* or "familyhood."[9]

The expression of African socialism began introspectively in Kenya. Tom Mboya and Oginga Odinga defined what self-reliance and socialism came to mean there. Athough they differed on the details, they agreed that Kenya's economic development should be based on indigenous resources and values. Mboya wrote:

> When I talk of "African Socialism," I refer to those proved codes of conduct in the African societies which have, over the ages, conferred dignity on our people and afforded them security regardless of their station in life. I refer to universal charity which characterized our societies and I refer to the African's thought processes and cosmological ideas which regard man, not as a social means, but as an end and entity in the society.[10]

Another advocate of socialist self-reliance for Africa was Kenneth Kaunda, former president of Zambia. Kaunda's humanist approach to economic development contrasted sharply with Western capitalist views, which stress the profit motive, or self-interest. "I have a passionate belief in the worth and possibilities of man," Kaunda once confessed, "and I expect him someday to achieve a perfection."[11]

Kaunda's vision may seem idealistic and naive to Western observers, but it is an authentic expression of African values, which tend to be group-oriented rather than individualistic and are not tied to Western logic and pragmatism. Kaunda is not a utopian dreamer; on the contrary, he emphasizes the work ethic and the need to modernize. The way to prove one's worth, he says, is with "a spade or a sickle."[12]

In the following passage, Kaunda synthesized hard work, humanism, and modernity into a philosophy of African economic development:

> Modern Africa is no place for the uncommitted. Life here demands cool nerves, perpetual optimism and great faith in human possibilities. Those who live with their bags mentally packed are of all men the most miserable. They are like hypochondriacs, taking their temperature and feeling their pulse every hour to

see whether they are still fit. They are blind to the positive aspects of independence. They do not notice the immense nerve and dedication of our people—their gritted-teeth determination to make Zambia great—because they are utterly preoccupied with the search for cracks in the foundation. They magnify every isolated incident into a full-blown calamity. Every loose stone heralds an avalanche, every gust of wind a tornado. They wish to feast upon the fruits of our prosperity but will slink off at the first sign of adversity.[13]

Neither Communism nor Capitalism

In sum, Africans have embraced a world view that is neither communist nor capitalist, neither revolutionary nor conservative. Rather, it reflects Africa's cultural diversity and unique historical experience. One scholar noted that Africa has

> one continent, Africa; two permanent [geographic parts], the Arab North and black South; three religious systems, African traditional religions, Christianity and Islam; four dominant international languages, English, French, Arabic and Portuguese; five external hegemonic systems competing for influence or profit within Africa, Western Europe, North America, the Soviet bloc, China and Japan; six political traditions partly fed by those five hegemonic systems and partly in opposition to those systems, liberal capitalism, socialism, nationalism, conservative traditionalism, militarism, and pan-Africanism; [and] seven combat traditions, the warrior tradition, the jihad, passive resistance, guerrilla warfare, revolutionary terrorism, modern conventional warfare, and prospects for a nuclear option first in South Africa and later elsewhere in Africa.[14]

In this mosaic of social, cultural, and historical diversity can be seen the need for an African synthesis. As we have noted, the principal elements of this have been self-reliance, socialism, and pan-Africanism (this last has remained a distant ideal). Self-reliant socialism, in the African context, is predicated on the values of social equality and harmony and has provided a conceptual framework for development strategies and policies. It may seem as though self-reliance and African unity are contradictory aims, but the African notion of self-reliance does not imply autarky at all. On the contrary, most African leaders advocate equitable interdependence. (What they mean by "equitable" will be discussed in the next chapter.)

Political Patterns in Sub-Saharan Africa

As noted throughout this book, politics and government are conditioned by geography, history, culture, and the physical environment. Into this contextual tapestry the sub-Saharan countries have woven a variety of political patterns, including military dictatorship, civilian authoritarianism, and the rare constitutional democracy. Note that the institutional patterns of most governments in the region do not fit readily into a neat separation-of-powers framework. Instead, the primary functions of government typically overlap more than they do in most Western countries.

Christian Potholm has developed a useful classification of African political systems. He identifies two basic regime types, polyarchic and authoritarian. He subdivides the **polyarchies** (representative democracies) into single-party and multiparty forms and the authoritarian regimes into civilian oligarchies and military praetorian forms.[15] Potholm distinguishes one form from another by looking at such characteristics as the extent to which there is electoral competition, the level of demonstrable support for law, and governmental protection of civil liberties. Obviously, the values embedded in these criteria are more likely to be found in polyarchies than in authoritarian systems.

It is a mistake, however, to conclude that polyarchic systems are all equally liberal or that authoritarian systems are all equally repressive. Potholm recognizes that significant differences exist within his classifications; hence he did not talk about a single type of system in each category but rather about a polyarchic and authoritarian spectrum.

The Polyarchic (Democratic) Spectrum

At one end of the spectrum of African polyarchies are multiparty systems, found in varying forms and degrees in the early 1990s in Botswana, the Gambia, Mauritius, Namibia, Senegal, Zambia, and Zimbabwe, to cite the most notable examples. Although these seven countries had all held free elections, only in Mauritius, Zambia, and Zimbabwe had they led to a change in government. The most notable case was in 1991 in Zambia, where President Kenneth Kaunda, the country's founder and paramount leader for twenty-seven years, was resoundingly defeated. One journalist observed, "Frederick Chiluba's victory in Zambia's first multi-party elections in nearly 20 years stands as a new highwater mark in an extraordinary process of democratization in Africa that began in earnest in Zambia and other nations several years ago."[16]

Nothing like the tidal wave of democracy that hit Eastern Europe after 1989 has occurred in sub-Saharan Africa, however. Rather, there have been democratic stirrings. In tiny Cape Verde, for example, the Marxist president, Aristedes Pereira, relinquished power to Antonio Monteiro, a free-market liberal, after a peaceful election in February 1991. Then Mathieu Kérékou, Benin's longtime military ruler, stepped down after losing an election to Nicéphore Soglo, a former World Bank governor. But elections in Côte d'Ivoire (Ivory Coast) and Gabon in the same year left autocratic presidents in power. (Critics of course charged that the elections had been rigged.)

Pressure for political change has, however, been mounting throughout the region. Governments "in transition" in the early 1990s included those of Ghana, Togo, Nigeria, Somalia, Ethiopia, Liberia, and Mali. In the last four of these, leaders were ousted by civil war or military coup in 1990 or 1991; in all seven, the shape of the future government remained indeterminate.

Some countries in the region pretend to be democratic but are clearly not. Sudan, for example, has nearly thirty political parties but has not sustained a viable system of competitive parties and elections; changes of government have been brought about by military coups, and Sudan's authoritarian rulers have never felt constrained by party leaders or democratically elected legislatures.

In truth, until very recently, only Botswana, the Gambia, and Senegal have had free and fair elections involving multiple candidates for the office of president as well as seats in the national legislature. These three states have several other features in common. They each have a unicameral legislature and a national chief executive who is also head of state and holds the title of president. Periodic elections are held by universal suffrage, and candidates seeking legislative office or the presidency conduct freewheeling campaigns. Presidential and legislative terms of office are fixed in all three countries: five years in the Gambia and Senegal, four years in Botswana. There is no limitation on reelection. In the Gambia and Senegal, the president is directly elected by a simple majority of the popular vote. The president of Botswana is indirectly elected by a simple majority of the elected members of the legislature. In each country, the vice-president is appointed by the president, at whose pleasure he or she serves.

In the first elections held after independence, the leader who was most instrumental in blazing the trail to independence was usually able to carry his party to victory. Subsequent elections have generally favored incumbent parties. Although minor parties have managed to win some legislative seats, they have not been able to muster parliamentary majorities, force the leading party into parliamentary coalitions, or capture the presidency. The results of elections in Botswana, the Gambia, and Senegal exemplify this pattern of success for the party of independence: in Botswana in 1984, the Botswana Democratic party won 29 of 34 seats; in the Gambia in 1987, the Progressive People's party won 31 of 36 seats; and in Senegal in 1988, the Socialist party won 103 of 120 seats. In subsequent elections, opposition parties made modest gains in all three countries, but the dominant parties remain firmly in the driver's seat.

Single-Party States

Single-party states are the other pole of Potholm's polyarchic spectrum, but some single-party states do not fit. If the attributes of constitutional democracy—free and fair elections involving competitive parties, rule of law, and respect for civil liberties—are lacking, the political system in question belongs on the authoritarian spectrum.

Like their multiparty counterparts, the single-party polyarchies in sub-Saharan Africa have a unicameral legislature and a chief executive, or president, who is both head of state and head of government. Periodic elections are held for members of the national assembly, and legislative seats are contested by several candidates in each voting district. In many single-party states, candidates must be party members and must receive party approval to stand for election.

Kenya, Sierra Leone, and Tanzania are all single-party polyarchies, as was Zambia before 1991. At independence, each of these countries had multiple parties but later switched to constitutional one-party systems.

In this type of system, the ruling party typically nominates only one candidate for president, and the nominee must receive a majority of the votes in the party's central committee, whose members may vote "yes" or "no." In Kenya, the president is elected indirectly by the National Assembly. Although party approval and confirmation are required for the presidential candidate, it is not always needed for candidates in legislative contests. Thus in Ethiopia's first-ever legislative election in 1987, fully 2,250 candidates contested the 835 seats, and some were nominated by mass organizations (although the great majority were handpicked by the Marxist Workers party). In Tanzania's general election in 1985, President Ali Hassan Mwinyi received a 92 percent "yes" vote—a suspiciously large share. Tanzania's ruling party also approved 238 candidates, who contested 156 legislative seats.

Zambia's United National Independence party nominated between 532 and 790 candidates to contest 125 seats in various general elections. Voter turnout averaged less than 40 percent, but voters who did go to the polls unseated nearly half the incumbents each time.[17] The combination of low turnout and substantial voting against incumbents generally suggests dissatisfaction with the system. And as noted, in the first multiparty presidential election in recent Zambian history, the voters turned President Kaunda out of office.

In Sierra Leone, legislative elections were held in 1986. The aptly named All Peoples party approved 335 candidates to contest 105 elective seats. The party typically offers at least three contestants for each seat, a common practice among one-party states in sub-Saharan Africa. Thus one-party systems are more democratic than they may at first appear to Western observers.

Why is single-party polyarchy more popular in sub-Saharan Africa than the multiparty democracy prevalent in Western Europe? First, mindful of the colonial past, Africans have sought to avoid imitating European political institutions, preferring instead to develop their own models and methods of governing. Second, the fragmented condition of many African states that resulted from the drawing of political boundaries by European colonial powers made it necessary to devise ways and means of mitigating conflict and unifying the nation. Obviously, this task is complicated by the existence of competing parties, which tend to perpetuate and institutionalize social divisions. Third, a single "umbrella party" that encompasses a variety of interests may be more appropriate for the level of development in many sub-Saharan states; a multiparty system places a premium on compromises and coalitions—a luxury that many developing countries can ill afford.

The Authoritarian Spectrum

Authoritarian regimes may be military or civilian, and they may be autocratic (ruled by one) or oligarchic (ruled by a few). In sub-Saharan Africa, the most common forms of authoritarianism are *civilian oligarchies* and *military praetorian regimes,* to use Potholm's terminology.

First, note that it is often difficult to distinguish between a single-party polyarchy and an authoritarian regime. For example, authoritarian regimes may have political parties and may hold elections. The key is not whether parties and elections are present but whether they are politically meaningful. If parties are merely symbolic and elections are nothing more than rituals, there is every likelihood that the political system that sponsors them is authoritarian.

Second, not all authoritarian regimes are brutal and repressive, although many certainly are both. Aristotle taught that monarchs may be high-minded and humane; students of history cannot help but note, however, that such enlightened despots are rare. As Lord Acton astutely observed, "Power corrupts; absolute power corrupts absolutely." The history of the twentieth century offers little to contradict this assertion.

Third, in the African context, it is important to note that some authoritarian regimes claim to be transitional, while others are well entrenched and more or less permanent. The former, often called **provisional governments**, are likely to follow a military coup.

Entrenched Authoritarian Regimes   Zaire, Somalia (until 1991), Malawi, Guinea, and Côte d'Ivoire are examples of authoritarian government in Africa. Authoritarian traits include the absence of electoral competition, repression of civil liberties, and arbitrary arrest. These regimes, except in Somalia, have remained unchanged for a quarter century or longer under the same autocratic ruler. As these leaders reach old age, it is appropriate to describe their regimes as **gerontocracies** ("rule by the aged").

Authoritarian rulers come to power in various ways: by rising through the ranks a step at a time, by a military coup d'état, or by promotion from the traditional hierarchy. Once in power, they employ age-old techniques of governing; they enforce compliance with accommodation, coercion, and co-optation of critical elites and the masses.

Accommodation may involve government programs to revive indigenous cultures and traditional values, thus neutralizing popular aspirations for liberalization and modernization. Symbols of nationalism are exploited to negate any social or political ideas that might challenge the policies of the rulers. The first president of Zaire, for example, changed the Belgian Congo's name to Zaire and all other European place names to Zairean names; he even Africanized his own name (from Joseph-Désiré Mobutu to Mobutu Sese Seko) and urged his people to do likewise. Recalling the evils of colonialism is a common device used to instill patriotism.

Elections are manipulated and modified in ways designed to mollify the people without giving them a real voice. Thus in Zaire, Somalia, and Malawi, periodic elections have been held, but they were tainted; for example, if voting is mandatory, coercion is likely to be involved. When President Mohamed Siad Barré stood for reelection in Somalia in 1986, he received a 99.9 percent "yes" vote. Similarly, President Félix Houphouët-Boigny garnered 100 percent approval in his 1988 reelection in Côte d'Ivoire, and when President Mobutu Sese Seko was reelected in 1984, he was approved by 99.6 percent of the voters. All these men, along with Hastings Kamuzu Banda of Malawi, are more like monarchs; they are essentially presidents for life.

Co-optation is entwined with carrot-and-stick methods in a strategy of divide and rule. The cabinet is frequently reshuffled, and various privileges and perquisites are given to the bureaucratic functionaries in the civil service, to the armed forces, and to the business and economic elites such that their long-term interests coincide with the status quo. The political order rests on an intricate network of patron-client relationships. In time, the authoritarian rule of a single strongman and his cronies can become self-legitimizing; in effect, the state becomes the patrimony of an autocratic or oligarchic leadership. One danger is that as the leader ages, the system can become increasingly ossified.

Another danger in personalistic authoritarian regimes arises from the absence of orderly procedures for succession. Who will replace the existing leader, and how? Such questions are especially important in a political system that concentrates power and authority in the hands of a single individual. The political climate can become extraordinarily uncertain, especially if the leader is very old, falls ill, or is the target of an assassination attempt. At such times, the possibility of a succession crisis looms large, and political stability may give way to chaos and confusion.

An illustration or two may help make the point. Sékou Touré ruled Guinea for twenty-six years (1958–1984), and his regime was harshly authoritarian. He died without making any provision for his own succession. (Often personalistic rulers are reluctant to name an heir apparent for fear of creating a rival.) His death left a power vacuum that has since been filled by the military. To cite another example, Emperor Haile Selassie of Ethiopia was dethroned after forty years of authoritarian rule; his ouster was followed by a bloody revolution. The same sort of thing happened in Somalia after Siad Barré was ousted in 1991. If history is any guide, Malawi and Côte d'Ivoire may soon face similar succession crises.

Provisional Authoritarian Regimes   Provisional regimes are self-consciously transitional and usually look ahead to a time when they will give way to constitutional government. Such regimes are usually run by the military because, typically, that is who has overthrown the old government. In sub-Saharan Africa, the military almost always proclaims its goal to be corrective—to rescue the nation from economic malaise or mismanagement, to stem subversion or national disintegration, or to stamp out graft and corruption. Even the names these provisional regimes give themselves are instructive: the Committee for National Redemption (Burundi), the Provisional National Defense Council (Ghana), the National Resistance Movement (Uganda), the Provisional Military Administrative Council (Ethiopia).

At first, military juntas almost always claim to be temporary. Some do ultimately return the government to civilian control, but most do not. Military takeovers have occurred repeatedly in Ghana, Nigeria, Sudan, and Uganda. In Ghana, for example, Flight Lieutenant Jerry Rawlings led a successful military coup in 1979. (The fact that a mere lieutenant could overthrow a government suggests that political life in some parts of sub-Saharan Africa is capricious and that political authority is precarious. A ruler with legitimacy and credibility cannot be cast aside so easily.) Rawlings returned the government to civilian rule in 1980, warning that the military would step in again if the politicians failed to govern effectively. In 1981, alleging corruption and mismanagement, Rawlings led a second coup, returning the country to military rule.

Government in Sub-Saharan Africa

Governing involves the formulation, implementation, and adjudication of rules. These functions fall correspondingly to the legislative, executive, and judicial branches. No modern polity can operate well without such a division of responsibilities. Although the societies of sub-Saharan Africa are still evolving politically, they already contain many institutional elements, including structural differentiation and functional specialization, that are associated with modern political systems.

Lawmaking and Legislatures

In the countries discussed in this chapter, the legislatures have several similarities. First, most sub-Saharan political systems, including authoritarian regimes, have a formal legislative body—a parliament, constituent assembly, or national assembly.

Election to the legislature carries great prestige for the members themselves and for their families and friends. One reason may be that African legislators typically do not have to compete with lobbyists for the government's attention. In the absence of organized interest groups, so prevalent in the West, legislators in Africa often carry a greater share of responsibility not only for lawmaking but also for focusing on special-interest issues, articulating them, and incorporating the various demands into coherent public policy. One theory argues that the prevalence of single-party polyarchies or authoritarian regimes is due in part to a distaste for interest-group politics, which many Africans view as unseemly and divisive. In African legislatures, issues tend to be debated on their merits, and relatively little attention is paid to special interests.

Legislatures in sub-Saharan Africa tend to be unicameral (Zimbabwe's is an exception). Routes to the legislature vary, but the main avenue continues to be direct appointment by the chief executive. Sometimes members can appoint additional members to represent professional organizations, tribal groups, and trade associations. Such legislators have earned recognition in their chosen fields or have demonstrated support for the ruling party. Some legislatures (Botswana, Sierra Leone, Zambia) include consultative chiefs as ex officio members.

As elaborate as legislative debates often are, the independence of the legislature is diminished by constitutional advantages given to the chief executive, who can veto legislation, dissolve the parliament, and appoint legislative members who thereafter owe a debt of loyalty. In Zaire, President Mobutu can bypass the legislative assembly altogether, making laws by personal fiat or in consultation with his ministerial council.

The Chief Executive

In the executive branch, these political systems reveal one of the ambivalences of the triple heritage discussed earlier: the head of state is adorned with traditional powers but holds a title borrowed from the West—usually president, but without presidential constraints. Presidents in sub-Saharan Africa often have powers more typical of an emperor or a king.

Generally speaking, the chief executive is both head of state and head of government, with powers and duties that are broadly and often vaguely defined. The ambiguities are deliberate, used to stretch presidential prerogatives as far as necessary. The president is always male and is expected to be fatherly, personable, and charismatic. When these expectations are met, the national leader commands popular respect and even adulation; often he will be given lofty titles bespeaking awe and deference. For example, Premier Nkrumah of Ghana was called *Osagyefu* ("Savior"), President Kenyatta of Kenya was addressed as *Mzee* ("Wise Man"), and President Nyerere of Tanzania was revered as *Mwalimu* ("Teacher"). Such titles engender both intimacy and legitimacy; at the same time, the constitution gives leaders such as these nearly absolute power.

African premiers and presidents are not constrained by checks and balances or the separation of powers. Not only do many African chief executives have the power to appoint members of the legislature (an unthinkable breach of the separation of powers in the United States), but they can also dissolve the parliament without risk of impeachment or electoral defeat.

Chief executives in sub-Saharan Africa are selected in various ways. In Botswana, Kenya, and Zimbabwe, the president is elected by the legislature. In Senegal and the Gambia, the people elect the president by secret ballot from a slate of candidates nominated by competing parties. In some one-party systems, a single candidate is nominated by the party congress, and the people simply cast a "yes" or "no" vote. Another method is military intervention, followed by the establishment of a provisional or caretaker government (which, as we have seen, tends to become permanent). The leader of the coup usually becomes the "acting" president.

The term of office is five years in most sub-Saharan countries; the president of Zimbabwe serves a six-year term, and the presidents of Gabon, Sierra Leone, and Zaire serve seven years. No country has a constitutional limitation on the number of consecutive terms that the president or legislators may serve.

In Africa's single-party states, the president heads the party, and renomination and reelection are virtually guaranteed. President Kenyatta of Kenya died in office at the age of 88. A geriatric President Senghor of Senegal resigned in 1980 for reasons of advanced age and failing health. President Julius Nyerere of Tanzania is the rare case of a one-party president who departed from office with grace and style: in 1985, he stepped down because it was time, he said, to inject new dynamism into the political system. (Nonetheless, he retained the powerful position of party chairman.) President Kenneth Kaunda of Zambia also bowed out graciously after he was defeated in a democratic election in 1991.

The Elusive Ideal of African Unity

The years since 1960 have received the most attention in the literature of comparative politics in Africa. This exciting new era of self-rule also brought enormous challenges of nation-building, including the search for unifying political philosophies and administrative systems and for models of economic development that would foster national integration and regional cooperation. The relics of colonialism have continued to work against African unity and self-reliance.

One of the most persistent problems is that the prevailing model of state administration embodies European approaches to hierarchy and authority that are alien to Africa's tradition of direct access and communication between the people and their leaders.[18] Thus Africans have had to choose whether to go back to traditional modalities, adopt colonial institutions, or try to combine the two into a unique African blend—a task that is much easier said than done.

The Early Conferences

After independence, African leaders had to walk a tightrope—trying to act independent and negotiate the best terms for self-rule, on the one hand, and having to operate within the constraints of continuing economic dependency, on the other. Many of these leaders had returned from the battle front, prison, or exile and suddenly had to master political skills, such as administration and persuasion. They attended conference after conference, seeking answers to common problems; they met in Accra, Addis Ababa, Algiers, Cairo, Casablanca, and Monrovia. They also went to non-African capitals and met with leaders of other developing nations, comparing notes and sharing ideas.

The Bandung Conference in 1955 brought together all thirty-eight of the developing countries at that time. The attendees promised to cooperate by sharing information, especially pertaining to economic and political development. A series of such conferences ensued and became institutionalized in the 1960s and 1970s in such forms as the **nonaligned movement** and the **Group of 77**.

The nonaligned movement was launched at the Bandung Conference by Third World leaders as an alternative to choosing sides in the East-West conflict. It thus helped focus attention on the **North-South conflict**—the tension resulting from the maldistribution of wealth between the industrial democracies of the Northern Hemisphere and the developing nations, most located in the Southern Hemisphere. The Group of 77, formed in 1964, is the largest caucus group in the United Nations. Its membership has grown to over 120 developing countries, and it is the primary means by which the South pressures the North to promote a **new international economic order**. The goal is to bring about greater global equity by redistributing resources (principally in the form of foreign aid and trade concessions) between North and South.

The issue of African unity topped the political agenda at the early regional gatherings. In the realm of economics, African leaders optimistically forged a consensus in favor of self-reliance. (The practical obstacles to achieving both unity and self-reliance are examined in Chapter 18.) The struggle for political independence was ending, but the struggle for economic independence was about to begin. Meeting in Accra in 1958, the first Conference of Independent African States declared that although the political domination of colonialism was over, the economic domination of neocolonialism remained.[19] Kwame Nkrumah, Ghana's premier and a participant at the meeting, wrote a book in which he asserted that neocolonialism was incompatible with economic development in the African context.[20]

Nkrumah's Vision

Pan-Africanism emerged when Ghana and Guinea gained their independence in 1957 and 1958, respectively. Nkrumah was a leading advocate of African unity, but his views were not original. They were based on the writings of African descendants like Edward Blyden, George Padmore, Marcus Garvey, and W. E. B. Du Bois, who had lived, traveled, and taught in the United States, Europe, and the West Indies.[21]

Nkrumah had become acquainted with the works of these black intellectuals as a visitor to Europe and the United States. He was captivated by the idea of promoting a collective African consciousness.[22] What Nkrumah had in mind was not only the political and economic unification of sub-Saharan Africa but also the solidarity of all Africans worldwide.[23] His was a vision of revolutionary "black power" on a global scale; he was saying, in effect, "Africans of the world, unite!" In Nkrumah's quasi-Marxist world view, Africans were the proletariat, and Europeans were the capitalist oppressors.

But Nkrumah's concept of African unity, for all its intellectual and emotional appeal, was too radical or too idealistic for many other leaders, and the unity movement soon broke into factions. The more radical Casablanca group wanted immediate political unity; the more conservative Monrovia group preferred to start with socioeconomic and cultural cooperation. Sensitive to Africa's cultural and political fragmentation, they spurned the idea of pan-African unity at a time when sub-Saharan states were facing basic nation-building tasks, including the inculcation of a sense of national identity.[24]

The Organization of African Unity

Various groups continued to hold unity conferences until a third faction emerged, taking a position midway between the radicals and the conservatives. The setting was a 1963 conference in Addis Ababa at which thirty-two independent states agreed to establish the **Organization of African Unity (OAU)**. Patterned after the United Nations, the OAU charter adheres to the basic UN principles of noninterference in the internal affairs of member states, respect for the territorial integrity of member states, human rights, and peaceful settlement of disputes.[25] Nkrumah proposed that the OAU have a standing army, but the majority of participants opposed this measure. Subsequently, most OAU member states abstained from military intervention in regional conflicts that did not affect them directly. But Libya did send troops into Chad in the 1980s in an effort to influence the outcome of a civil war there (and seize a strip of land reputed to hold deposits of uranium); Libyan forces also helped Tanzania defeat Idi Amin in the Ugandan civil war.

The ideal of African unity remains a distant hope. The OAU has played a useful role in settling conflicts among its member states, and it acts as a moral restraint on aggression. It has also helped newer members through the critical early stages of independence and has used its influence to pressure South Africa to free Namibia and to end apartheid. But it has made little headway against human rights abuses, hunger, and other forms of deprivation in many parts of the region.

Like people elsewhere, Africans have taken to nationalism much more readily than regionalism (or pan-Africanism). Julius Nyerere of Tanzania, one of the founders of the OAU, lamented the fact that the idea of Africa has faded since the days of the early conferences: "At that time we saw Africa and we talked about Africa; today we are more Tanzanian than African, and Kenyans are more Kenyan than African."[26]

Indeed, Africans are too preoccupied with national problems to put much emphasis on distant ideals like African unity. According to one interpretation, nationalism and the nation-state are legacies of colonialism; Africa's predicament, including fragmentation, is of external origin.[27] Other observers point out that Africa has had time to put its own house in order. These critics maintain that whatever the causes of Africa's current problems, only Africans can solve them.

In any event, the OAU still holds annual conferences of African political and economic leaders. Yet there have been at least seventy-five coups and military interventions since 1963, and the OAU—founded in the name of African unity—has had to devote most of its energy and resources to mediating conflicts arising from African disunity and civil wars.

Case Studies: Kenya, Nigeria, and South Africa

Kenya is a single-party polyarchy. Nigeria is in transition between a military dictatorship and a Western-type parliamentary democracy. In South Africa, the last surviving white-minority regime operated a dual system—democracy for the white minority, tyranny for the black majority—until the early 1990s, when the government began to move toward a genuine sharing of power.

Kenya

Kenya under Kenyatta   President Jomo Kenyatta enjoyed a short honeymoon period following independence in 1963, but soon the KANU coalition (described in Chapter 16) began to come unglued. Oginga Odinga and other leaders to the left became disenchanted with Kenyatta's attempt to blend capitalist and socialist policies. This ideological tension radiated down to the rank and file. Kenyatta and Odinga had a dramatic falling out; Odinga, a KANU vice-president, shrilly criticized the party's economic programs, which, he charged, pandered to the rich. Kenyatta retaliated by abolishing the position of vice-president, hoping to isolate Odinga or at least neutralize him within the party.

Odinga's response was to organize a rival political party, the Kenyan People's Union (KPU), which made Kenya a two-party state once again. In the 1966 elections, Odinga's party won 30 out of 158 seats in the legislature. Thereafter, Odinga and the KPU became increasingly strident in their opposition to Kenyatta's policies. The assassination of Tom Mboya in 1969 precipitated an outbreak of ethnic violence. Kenyatta, blaming the KPU, ordered Odinga and his disciples jailed. He then banned Odinga's KPU party. Kenyatta subsequently persuaded some KPU members to return to KANU and contest the 1974 election.

It now became clear that occasional acts of repression were merely tactical; Kenyatta's strategy was to co-opt the opposition. The 1974 election proved to be a turning point: Kenya became a one-party polyarchy as many former KPU leaders accepted "amnesty" and returned to KANU to resume their careers in public service. Even Odinga, after several stints in prison, rejoined KANU as a life member in 1980.

Given Kenya's ethnic diversity, the switch to a single-party arrangement had a major impact on internal politics. Kenyatta had surmounted the KPU challenge by skillfully using the carrot-and-stick method and by merging the two chambers of parliament into a single chamber, easier to control. To diffuse ethnic tensions, Kenyatta popularized the slogan *Harambee-uhuru* ("Unity in freedom"), chose as his vice-president Daniel arap Moi (from one of Kenya's ethnic minorities, the Kelenjins), and championed a neutral language, Swahili, as the official tongue. Swahili is the lingua franca of Africa, a logical choice for use as an official language in a multiethnic country such as Kenya.

After 1970, KANU was the only functioning political party in Kenya. Despite persistent charges of corruption and abuses of power by the regime, Kenya under Kenyatta's one-party system achieved a high degree of political stability, accompanied by steady economic growth. In 1982, a constitutional amendment officially made Kenya a single-party system.

After Kenyatta: A Slide into Authoritarianism   When Kenyatta died in 1978, at age 88, he was peacefully succeeded by Vice President Daniel arap Moi, in accordance with the constitution, which calls for a new election after a ninety-day waiting period. Exploiting Kenyans' reverence for Kenyatta, Moi capsulized his campaign in a single Swahili word, *nyayo* ("footsteps"), a clever way of promising to follow Kenyatta's course faithfully. He underscored this continuity by naming a vice-president from Kenyatta's Kikuyu ethnic group.[28]

The orderly transition from Kenyatta to Moi meant that Kenya's one-party polyarchy had survived a major test. Although Kenya encountered serious political and economic problems in the 1980s, democratic processes, limited though they are, have survived. Elections continue to offer the voters choices—not between parties but among several candidates. In the 1983 and 1988 elections, for example, as many as 900 candidates competed for 158 elective seats in the National Assembly. Incumbents are still frequently defeated, although the number ousted has been steadily declining. Some critics have charged voter intimidation.

In recent years, Kenya has experienced a political chill as Moi introduced constricting constitutional changes. Part of this turn toward authoritarianism involved official intimidation of the bar and the media, friction between the government and the National Council of Churches (a major source of opposition), and the stifling of parliamentary debate. Under heavy international pressure, Moi released political detainees in mid-1989 and offered amnesty to exiled dissidents; still, he refused to legalize opposition parties on the grounds that Kenya's propensity for interethnic violence makes multiparty democracy unworkable there.

In May 1990, Robert Ouko, Kenya's popular foreign minister, was assassinated. The fact that Ouko had publicly criticized high-level government corruption raised suspicions that Moi was somehow involved. When the subsequent investigation pointed to two of the president's closest aides as prime suspects, Moi squelched it. In the summer of 1990, the arrest of Kenneth Matiba and Charles Rubia, two former cabinet ministers who had become the most prominent advocates of multiparty elections, touched off widespread rioting. The resulting police crackdown resulted in twenty-eight deaths and more than a thousand detentions. Despite a storm of domestic and diplomatic protest, Moi remained intransigent: in February 1991, he declared Odinga's newly launched National Democratic party illegal.

The Elections of 1992   Late in 1991, Moi succumbed to diplomatic pressure and reversed his longtime stand against multiparty elections. Within a few months, no fewer than nine opposition parties were formed, the most prominent of which were the Forum for the Restoration of Democracy, headed by Oginga Odinga, and the Democratic party, led by Mwai Kibaki, a former finance minister and vice-president. At the end of 1992, a vigorously contested presidential election resulted in Moi's reelection. The opposition charged that Moi had cheated. It was clear that he used the power of his office to gain every possible advantage. But it was also clear that the opposition had been its own worst enemy. By failing to form a united front, it ensured that the anti-Moi vote would be badly divided, enabling Moi to snatch victory from the jaws of defeat.

Nigeria

Nigeria represents the military variant of African authoritarianism, but a tendency toward federalism and democracy is also clearly present. Since gaining independence from Britain in 1960, Nigeria has oscillated between civilian and military rule. Civilians were in charge for a total of ten years (1960–1966 and 1979–1983). Five military regimes have ruled the rest of the time.

The civilian regimes came to power by means of ballots; the military regimes, by means of bullets (or threats to use them). Though regimes have changed frequently and often unexpectedly, their avowed objectives have been remarkably constant: to eliminate official corruption, foster good government, improve the quality of life, and establish a pluralistic political order based on the consent of the governed. These lofty aims have so far eluded Nigeria.

Elections and Coups: A General Disorder?   The first Nigerian republic lasted only six years; it was toppled by a 1966 military coup d'état led by General Yokobu Gowon (who was in turn ousted in 1975 for failing to curb corruption and restore civilian rule). No sooner had the military government seized power than a crisis arose that imperiled the very survival of Nigeria as a nation-state: civil war. In 1967, the eastern region known as Biafra seceded. The war pitted the Ibos (the majority population in Biafra) against the politically dominant Yoruba. The Ibos believed that they were being exploited and neglected by the central government. With casualties exceeding one million—many Biafrans starved to death despite international relief efforts—the secessionists capitulated in January 1970. The central government quickly reintegrated the Ibos into national life, but mistrust among the regions persists.

The second republic came into existence in 1979, when General Olasegun Obasanjo, who took charge after the 1975 coup, kept his promise to restore civilian rule. Following national elections, General Obasanjo returned power to the victors—a new president and parliament—in accordance with a highly acclaimed democratic constitution. The election itself was vigorously contested by several national parties, including the Unity Party of Nigeria (UPN), the Peoples' Redemption party (PRP), the Greater Nigerian Peoples' party (GNP), and the National Party of Nigeria (NPN).

The NPN candidate, Shehu Shagari, narrowly won the initial presidential contest to become the first (and last) president of the second republic. Soon after Shagari had begun his second four-year term, charges of economic mismanagement and official corruption were leveled against his government, and in a now familiar pattern, he was ousted by the military on the last day of 1983, and many of his cabinet members were put on trial and barred from public life. Nigeria again reverted to military rule.

After another coup in August 1985, the Supreme Military Council and the Federal Executive Council were reconstituted as the Armed Forces Ruling Council (AFRC) and the Council of Ministers, respectively. In 1987, the ruling AFRC oligarchy announced that Nigeria would be returned to civilian government in five years and created a Constitutional Review Committee. The following year, the Constituent Assembly was set up to finish this work and give it a democratic veneer. The most controversial issue the Assembly addressed was whether or not to enshrine Islamic law, a move opposed both by the Muslim head of state, General Ibrahim Babangida, and by Nigeria's Christian population. In the end, the general and his ruling council decided to put the issue on the back burner. Other than incorporating new anticorruption measures and extending the presidential term to six years, the draft constitution of the "third republic" closely resembles the 1979 basic law.

Party Time in Nigeria: Reinventing Democracy   In Nigeria, as elsewhere, the armed forces intervene to restore public confidence in government, eradicate corruption and mismanagement, and improve living standards.[29] They also pledge to return the country to civilian rule. As a step in this direction, General Babangida created two political parties—the National Republican Convention (NRC) and the Social Democratic party (SDP)—by presidential decree in October 1989. Both are mainstream parties by design, with one "a little bit to the right" and the other "a little bit to the left."

Nigeria's coup-prone politics, recurrent civil strife, and deepening economic crisis caution against undue optimism. Domestic unrest and an attempted coup in 1990 placed the timetable for reversion to democracy in jeopardy. Even so, Babangida vowed that he would continue to "deregulate and demilitarize the process of politics." Indeed, local elections were held in December 1990; only 10 percent of the electorate actually voted, but the balloting was orderly, and the new two-party system functioned as intended. In May 1992, rioting and bloodshed in Lagos and Kaduna again called the future of democratic reforms in Nigeria into question. As in the past, the most recent violence is rooted in Nigeria's deepening poverty and reinforced by religious and ethnic divisions.

A member of the Organization of Oil Exporting Countries (OPEC), Nigeria is one of only two major oil producers in sub-Saharan Africa (Gabon is the other OPEC member; Angola and the Congo also have oil reserves). Skyrocketing prices following the 1973 OPEC oil embargo enabled Nigeria to launch a major economic development program. But this effort foundered due in part to political instability and official corruption and in part to plummeting oil prices in the early 1980s. Between 1981 and 1985, average per capita income in the OPEC nations dropped 23 percent; Nigeria, which depends on oil for 95 percent of its export revenues, was particularly vulnerable.

Given its nettlesome internal problems, Nigeria will most likely continue in a state of transition for the indefinite future, a nation in search of a viable political system, a healthy economy, and a stable society. In the meantime, Nigeria's military rulers will wear two hats, as soldier-politicians. Instead of a legislative assembly to debate policy and pass laws, the Supreme Military Council issues edicts and proclamations. The search for viable political structures continues. The government postponed the promised 1992 national election when charges of corruption and fraud on the part of civilian politicians caused a public furor. As we shall see in Chapter 18, Nigeria's best hope for a third chance at civilian democratic self-rule appeared to be slipping away in 1993.

South Africa

To the outside world, South Africa has long been synonymous with **apartheid**. In Afrikaans, *apartheid* simply means "separateness"; it refers to the legally required separation of the racial communities in the Republic of South Africa. One way to understand the apartheid system is to look at the legal structure that supports it. In all, some 350 laws were passed to implement the system. Here are a few of the most important ones:

- Land Act (1913): Prohibited Africans from acquiring land outside their native reserves
- Mines and Works Amendment Act (1926), also known as the "Color Bar" Act: Prohibited Africans from skilled work in the mines
- Group Areas Act (1950): Outlawed racially mixed residential areas; specified which races live where
- Native Building Workers' Act (1951): Extended the earlier mining color bar to skilled construction trades
- Natives Act (1952): Required all Africans over 16 to carry a passbook specifying where they may live and work
- Native Laws Amendment Act (1952): Prohibited most Africans from remaining in urban areas for more than seventy-two hours
- Separate Amenities Act (1953): Segregated virtually all public transportation, facilities, and accommodations, including beaches (led to "Whites Only" signs, which have now disappeared)
- Riotous Assemblies Act (1956): Outlawed protest gatherings
- Separate Universities Act (1959): Prohibited nonwhites from most universities except by special permission
- General Law Amendment Act (1963): Let police hold anyone considered suspicious for renewable ninety-day periods (later reduced to renewable fourteen-day periods) without trial or legal recourse
- Bantu Homelands Citizenship Act (1970): Made all Africans citizens of "tribal homelands" (*bantustans*) and deprived them of South African citizenship (the low point of apartheid)

As the list suggests, apartheid evolved through a steady accretion of laws and amendments. The cumulative effect was to create a comprehensive and deeply entrenched system of racial discrimination.

A Half-and-Half System   The popularity of apartheid and its elevation to an ideology among Afrikaners dates back to the election of 1948, when the present Nationalist party came to power. The main agenda in that early political campaign was to find a workable solution for the ethnic and racial issues that had bedeviled South Africa since the founding of the union in 1910. Having won the election, the Nationalist party sought to fulfill its campaign pledge to keep the races separated. To this end, the new government designed a set of social policies based on the permanent separation of the whites, blacks, Coloured, and Indians. The "**homelands**"—areas reserved for various black ethnic groups—were part of this policy. The overriding purpose was to exclude nonwhites from positions of power and privilege.

South Africa has a dual political system, run according to two separate sets of rules. For whites—Afrikaners and British—the system has functioned as a democracy. Free elections (for whites only) were contested by multiple parties, and voters cast secret ballots for the candidates of their choice. From 1910 to 1984, the British "Westminster model" operated: following national elections, the majority party in the all-white House of Assembly chose a prime minister (in practice, the leader of the majority party), who then formed a government.

The 1984 Constitution: A Finger in the Dike   In 1984, South Africa adopted a new constitution, which had been approved by two-thirds of the (white) electorate in a national referendum. The constitution provided for a new three-chambered parliament: the House of Assembly (whites; 178 seats), the House of Representatives (Coloured; 85 seats), and the House of Delegates (Indians; 45 seats). Thus the legislature came to include Coloured and Indian representatives but continued to exclude the black majority.

The more things changed, the more they stayed the same. The white minority remained firmly in control: the three houses met separately, and the Coloured and Indian chambers could not override the white chamber. Perhaps more significant was the adoption of a presidential model in place of the traditional parliamentary model. The president was indirectly elected by an electoral college consisting of the three chambers of the legislature. Under that system, the president could dissolve the parliament on any number of grounds. In the event of a parliamentary deadlock—a strong possibility under the new tricameral configuration—he could rule in consultation with the President's Council, a purely advisory body that he appoints. In a crisis, the president could proclaim martial law. So broad were the president's powers that some critics viewed the new system as a potential dictatorship.

Apartheid in Retreat   Thus despite the appearance of change, white minority power remained largely intact during the 1980s. But intense domestic and foreign pressures were brought to bear on the government of President Pieter W. Botha. In response, the Botha government made important, though limited, concessions. Between 1979 and 1986, blacks won the right to belong to trade unions, to own their own homes, and to move freely around the country. In 1985, the government repealed the Mixed Marriages Act and part of the Immorality Act that proscribed interracial sex. These and other concessions only fanned the flames of political protest. In July 1985, Botha declared a state of emergency in thirty-six black districts and townships where the rioting was the worst. To die-hard white supremacists, any olive branch was an invitation to anarchy; to black leaders and moderate whites, the government's peace offerings were too little too late. For his part, Botha vacillated between compromise and intransigence. Nonetheless, it was a sign of the times that an opinion poll taken in South Africa in 1986 showed that nearly three-fourths of the whites and a solid majority of the blacks believed that apartheid would be gone within ten years.[30] The last laws reserving certain jobs for whites were repealed in 1987, and in 1991, long-standing restrictions on black land purchases were lifted.

Recent progress toward genuine power sharing in South Africa is the result of a leadership change. In 1989, Frederik W. de Klerk succeeded Botha as president. Having vowed to end apartheid, de Klerk promised to allow peaceful protests. In February 1990, he legalized the African National Congress (ANC), the Pan-Africanist Congress (PAC), and the South African Communist Party (SACP) and freed Nelson Mandela, a charismatic black leader who had been a political prisoner since the 1960s. Mandela's release was a symbolic gesture designed to show de Klerk's earnest intent to bring about peaceful accommodation between whites and blacks and to set the stage for negotiations.

In March 1990, de Klerk announced that he would enter into talks with leaders of the African National Congress. But the ANC laid down conditions: an end to the four-year-old state of emergency and amnesty for all political prisoners and exiles. In June, de Klerk moved to lift the Separate Amenities Act ("petty apartheid"); later that month, de Klerk and Mandela met for the first time. We consider what this historic breakthrough has meant for the future of South Africa in the next chapter.

CONCLUSION

Authoritarian rule has been common throughout sub-Saharan Africa, but not all governments of the region are equally repressive or corrupt. Kenya was one of the best under Kenyatta, but there have been persistent reports of political persecution by Kenyatta's successor, Daniel arap Moi. In Nigeria, promises of democracy by the military rulers have not been fulfilled. South Africa has been ruled by a white minority government but is now going through a critical transition to a power-sharing system in which the black majority will be included for the first time. Throughout the region, there has been a trend toward liberalization and democratization. Black Africa's uncertain future is the focus of Chapter 18.

KEY TERMS

trusteeship	negritude
national liberation movement	Arusha Declaration
Third World	*ujamaa*
decolonization	polyarchy
African socialism	provisional government

gerontocracy
nonaligned movement
Group of 77
North-South conflict
new international economic order

pan-Africanism
Organization of African Unity (OAU)
apartheid
"homelands"

STUDY QUESTIONS

1. What factors influenced the early economic development of African countries? To what extent do these factors remain in force today?
2. Why is one-party polyarchy more common in sub-Saharan Africa than multi-party systems like those in Europe?
3. What is apartheid? How has it changed in recent years? Do you think it is on the road to extinction?

SUGGESTED READING

Baker, Pauline. "South Africa on the Move." *Current History,* May 1990.
Falola, Toyin, and Ihonvbere, Julius. *The Rise and Fall of Nigeria's Second Republic,1979–1984.* London: Zed Press, 1985.
Hull, Richard W. "United States Policy in Southern Africa." *Current History,* May 1990.
Martin, Meredith. *In the Name of Apartheid: South Africa in the Postwar Period.* New York: Harper, 1988.
Mazrui, Ali A., and Tidy, Michael. *Nationalism and New States in Africa.* London: Heinemann, 1984.
Miller, Norman. *Kenya: The Quest for Prosperity.* Boulder, Colo.: Westview Press, 1984.
Parker, Frank J. *South Africa: Lost Opportunities.* Lexington, Mass.: Lexington Books, 1984.
Potholm, Christian. *The Theory and Practice of African Politics.* Lanham, MD.: University Press, 1985.
St. Jorre, John. *A House Divided: South Africa's Uncertain Future.* Washington, D.C.: Carnegie Endowment for International Peace, 1977.
Tangri, Roger. *Politics in Sub-Saharan Africa.* London: Heinemann, 1985.
Zartman, William I., ed. *The Political Economy of Nigeria.* New York: Praeger, 1983.

NOTES

1. C. B. Wadstrom, *An Essay on Colonialization* (London: Darton & Harvey, 1794), p. 9.
2. Examples of such resistance during the early years of this century include the Ashanti rebellion in the Gold Coast (now Ghana), the Baoulé and Samory rebellion in the Ivory Coast (now Côte d'Ivoire), and the Maji-Maji rebellion in German East Africa (now part of Tanzania); see Ali A. Mazrui and Michael Tidy, *Nationalism and New States in Africa* (London: Heinemann, 1984), pp. 116–132.
3. Ibid., pp. 13–15.

4. See William Friedland and Carl G. Rosenberg, Jr., eds., *African Socialism* (Stanford, Calif.: Stanford University Press, 1964), pp. 250–258; and Tom Mboya, *Freedom and After* (Boston: Little, Brown, 1963), pp. 164–178.

5. Kwame Khrumah, *Consciencism* (London: Heinemann, 1966), p. 70.

6. Wilford Curtey and Martin Kilson, eds., *Independent Africa: A Reader* (New York: Random House, 1970), pp. 179–192.

7. Clyde R. Ingle, *From Village to State in Tanzania: The Politics of Rural Development* (Ithaca, N.Y.: Cornell University Press, 1972), p. 99.

8. Julius K. Nyerere, *Uhuru Na Moja: Freedom and Unity* (New York: Oxford University Press, 1973), p. 247.

9. Ibid., p. 232.

10. Quoted in Friedland and Rosenberg, *African Socialism,* p. 251.

11. Colin Morris, *A Humanist in Africa: Letters to Colin Morris from Kenneth Kaunda* (Nashville, Tenn.: Abingdon Press, 1966), p. 19.

12. Colin Legum, ed., *Independence and Beyond: A Collection of Speeches by Kenneth Kaunda* (London: Nelson, 1966), pp. 18–19.

13. Morris, *Humanist in Africa,* p. 63.

14. Ali A. Mazrui, *The African Condition: A Political Diagnosis* (Cambridge: Cambridge University Press, 1980), p. 92.

15. See Christian Potholm, *The Theory and Practice of African Politics* (Lanham, Md.: University Press, 1985), chaps. 5 and 6.

16. Neil Henry, "Kaunda Graciously Bows to 'Verdict,'" *Washington Post,* Nov. 3, 1991, p. A2.

17. C. Chikulo Bornwell, "The Impact of Elections in Zambia," *Africa Today,* vol. 35, no. 2 (1988), pp. 37–41.

18. Potholm, *Theory and Practice,* pp. 34–36.

19. Ali A. Mazrui, *Toward a Pax Africana: A Study of Ideology and Ambition* (Chicago: University of Chicago Press, 1967), pp. 74–75.

20. Kwame Khrumah, *Neo-Colonialism: The Last Stage of Imperialism* (New York: International Publishers, 1966), pp. 239–259.

21. See, for example, Manning Marable, *W. E. B. Du Bois: Black Radical Democrat* (Boston: Twayne, 1986), pp. 99–120; see also Mazrui and Tidy, *Nationalism and New States,* pp. xii–xvi.

22. Basil Davidson, *Africa: History of a Continent* (New York: Macmillan, 1972), pp. 294–297.

23. Mazrui and Tidy, *Nationalism and New States,* pp. 21–23.

24. Amadu Sesay, *The OAU after Twenty-five Years* (Boulder, Colo.: Westview Press, 1984), pp. 1–13 and chap. 3.

25. Roger Tangri, *Politics in Sub-Saharan Africa* (London: Heinemann, 1985), pp. 17–25.

26. *African Recovery,* May 25, 1988.

27. Mazrui and Tidy, *Nationalism and New States,* pp. 373–374.

28. Abel Ndumu, "Seven Years of *Nyayo,*" *Africa Report,* November-December 1985, pp. 51–53.

29. Toyin Falola and Julius Ihonvbere, *The Rise and Fall of Nigeria's Second Republic, 1979–1984* (London: Zed Press, 1985), pp. 248–256.

30. Adam Chimes, "Poll in South Africa Shows a Rise in Whites' Distaste for Apartheid," *New York Times,* Aug. 3, 1986, p. 1.

18

Delayed Development and Dependency

The sub-Saharan nations, with few exceptions, face daunting economic and political challenges. The most pressing need is for effective policies aimed at stabilizing population growth and boosting food production. The food-population imbalance, not simply population growth itself, is the crux of the problem.

The evidence of deprivation has at times been shockingly apparent. In recent years, pictures of emaciated and starving children in Ethiopia, Sudan, and Somalia have flashed on our television screens. The famine resulted from the combined effects of continuous warfare and a disastrous drought that struck much of the region, ultimately causing two to three million deaths and placing some thirty million at risk of starvation.[1] Angola and Mozambique in southern Africa suffered too. By the early 1990s, the most critical food shortages were occurring in Somalia, where civil war and drought conspired to cause terrible human suffering. In August 1992, the United Nations Children's Fund (UNICEF) warned that two million Somalis faced starvation within six months; that triggered an international relief effort (see box). In addition, Liberia joined the list of famine-stricken African nations.

The droughts that triggered Africa's worst famines in memory were a grim reminder of the region's fragile economic and political condition. The challenges that sub-Saharan Africa faces are further illustrated by these startling facts:[2]

- The region's forty-eight nations have 450 million people from a thousand ethnic groups speaking more than eight hundred languages.
- If present demographic trends continue, the population will double in twenty-three years.
- Since 1972, per capita food production has decreased in every year but one.

467

Horn of Sorrows: Ethiopia, Eritrea, and Somalia

The Horn of Africa has been the scene of some of the worst human tragedies in recent times. In 1975, a military coup led by Colonel Mengistu Haile Miriam ousted Ethiopian Emperor Haile Selassie from power. Mengistu established a Marxist-style police state and ruthlessly repressed all opposition. Mengistu's rise to power ushered in a period of bloody turmoil: a war with Somalia over the Ogaden (a region inside Ethiopia inhabited largely by Somalis) and major guerrilla insurgency movements in Eritrea and Tigré provinces.

In the first half of the 1980s, a severe drought caused widespread famine and threatened millions of Ethiopians with starvation. A massive international relief effort was mounted, but military victories by Eritrean rebels in 1988 forced the government to curtail the activities of relief agencies in drought-stricken areas. The corruption, brutality, and incompetence of the Mengistu regime also contributed to the economic and humanitarian crisis. Mengistu's forces were defeated by the Eritreans in May 1991, and Mengistu fled. In April 1993, Eritrea voted overwhelmingly for independence from Ethiopia. This event was the culmination of a thirty-years' war against the Ethiopian army.

The new nation of Eritrea has a population of only 3.5 million and is one of the poorest in the world. Tens of thousands of Eritreans died in the war, and some 750,000 fled its terrors, most of them landing in squalid refugee camps in Sudan.

Even without Eritrea, Ethiopia's population is around fifty million. The annual population growth rate in the 1980s was 3.1 percent. Ethiopian women have seven or eight babies, on average; the mortality rate is a staggering 193 per thousand live births. The illiteracy rate may be as high as 39 percent, and only about 15 percent of Ethiopia's teenagers attend secondary school. Ethiopia's GNP in 1991 was $6.1 billion, about half that of Luxembourg, which has a population of only 378,000. The economy grew at a snail's pace (1.5 percent) between 1980 and 1991, and the per capita growth rate was negative (-1.6

percent). Ethiopia continues to rely on agriculture for over 40 percent of its gross domestic product (GDP), while exports amounted to only 10 percent of GDP in 1991 (for neighboring Kenya, the figure was 27 percent). Investment as a share of GDP in that same year was only 10 percent (in Kenya, it was 21 percent).

Next door in Somalia, the dictator, Siad Barré, was overthrown in January 1991. Civil war and famine followed, leaving 300,000 people dead and another two million at risk of starvation (out of a total population of slightly over eight million). A near-total breakdown of law and order plunged the country into anarchy and placed women and children at the mercy of armed bandits who disrupted relief efforts by international agencies, stole food intended for starving children, and murdered relief workers. At the end of 1992, outgoing U.S. President George Bush ordered a UN-backed military intervention to safeguard relief supplies and workers. The intervention restored order and saved countless Somali lives. But there was no clear exit strategy—at least not one that would prevent a rapid slide back into chaos.

Even before the ouster of Siad Barré, Somalia was one of the poorest countries in Africa, with a per capita GNP of less than $500 and an illiteracy rate of more than 75 percent. Moreover, Somalia was underdeveloped politically as well as economically. The structure of Somali society is based on kinship ties, or clans, and the civil war was in fact a clan war. How can Somalia, facing crushing economic and social problems, build a stable, politically integrated, modern nation-state when the Somali people continue to identify so strongly with a particular clan and identify weakly or not at all with the nation? If Somalia cannot find a formula for political stability, it cannot rebuild its economy. The reverse is also true: stability depends on economic and social progress. It seems likely that only a sustained multidimensional effort by the international community can bring peace and progress to Somalia.

- Health and education standards are the worst in the world, and at least six million adults have been infected with the AIDS virus.
- Of every hundred children born in the region, twenty die before age 5, and nearly half the survivors are malnourished.

In addition to drought and famine, disease is a major killer in sub-Saharan Africa, where doctors, hospitals, clinics, and medicines are frequently unavailable even for the gravely ill. Inadequate health care has always been a major problem in developing countries, but in the 1980s, a new specter stalked Africa: acquired immunodeficiency syndrome (AIDS), a disease for which no cure is known. At present, AIDS is Africa's biggest and potentially most catastrophic health problem.

Reasons for Underdevelopment in Africa

Sub-Saharan Africa is the poorest, least developed region in the world. Many of its nations have a tiny GNP (see Tables 18.1 and 18.2)—less than even the poorest countries in Latin America—and all but one or two of the region's economies are growing at a glacial pace. What is worse, the per capita growth rate in many nations is now negative, meaning that population growth is outstripping economic development. The already low quality of life for inhabitants of these nations is actually dropping even lower.

Contending Theories

Scholars have debated the causes of Africa's economic and political problems, and a variety of theories have emerged. One view holds that the European colonial powers intentionally impeded economic and political development.[3] Another view (espoused by Julius Nyerere and others) stresses the debilitating but unintentional consequences of colonial exploitation. A variation on this theme has been offered by Adebayo Adedeji, general secretary of the United Nations Economic Commission for Africa, who charges colonialism with changing Africa's agricultural priorities from food production for local consumption to export crops such as cocoa, coffee, and tea, the prices of which depend on demand in foreign markets.[4]

More introspective African writers blame certain African traditions for creating resistance to social change and progress.[5] They also accuse political elites of abusing power and lacking the vision needed to lift Africa out of deprivation.

Western development theorists sometimes draw on social psychology and cultural anthropology to explain why some societies advance more easily than others. This perspective focuses on variations in social rules, behavioral norms, lifestyles, and expectations.[6] Other development theorists, as noted in Chapter 3, draw on political economy—more specifically, on incentives theory, which looks at the presence or absence of formal rules, legal structures, and contractual relations that undergird commercial activity, define rewards and punishments, and reinforce the work ethic.[7]

Table 18.1 Economic Profile: Selected Countries in Sub-Saharan Africa

	Gross National Product (GNP), 1991 (billions of U.S. dollars)	GNP Growth Rate, 1980–1991 (percent per year)	Per Capita GNP, 1991 (U.S. Dollars)	Per Capita Growth Rate, 1980–1991 (percent per year)
Angola	N.A.	N.A.	500–1,499	N.A.
Botswana	3.3	9.3	2,590	5.8
Burkina Faso	3.2	4.0	350	1.3
Côte d'Ivoire	8.5	0.3	690	1.0
Ethiopia*	6.1	1.5	120	− 1.6
Kenya	8.5	4.1	340	0.3
Nigeria	34.1	1.4	290	− 1.7
Senegal	5.5	2.9	720	0.0
Sierra Leone	0.9	1.1	210	− 1.3
Somalia	N.A.	N.A.	500	N.A.
South Africa	90.9	3.3	2,530†	0.9
Sudan	10.1	0.3	400†	− 2.4
Uganda	2.8	5.9	160	3.3
Zaire	8.1	1.6	220†	− 1.6
Zimbabwe	6.2	3.6	620	0.2

N.A. = not available.
* Including Eritrea.
† 1990.

Source: World Bank, *The World Bank Atlas* (Washington, D.C.: World International Bank for Reconstruction and Development/The World Bank, 1992). Published by Oxford University Press, Inc., New York.

Some African societies exhibit a kind of family-centered particularism that breeds social attitudes inimical to individual success and economic development. For example, the Oromos and Amharas of Ethiopia are very conscious of how they are perceived by others. In their culture, a person must not become too ambitious because individual achievement can bring social stigma. To ignore this norm is to be ostracized as greedy or overzealous. In principle, the morality of modesty, cooperation, and sharing is good, but in practice, the taboo on individualism both constrains competition and stifles personal aspirations.

Colonialism as the Culprit

Colonialism and certain nonindigenous socioreligious practices were equally detrimental to personal growth and national self-reliance. Colonialism undercut Africans' sense of personal efficacy; at the same time, it introduced individualism into a society that had traditionally stressed collective or community values. The colonial white man was the *Bwana*, the master benefactor, who established new values and behavioral norms. By the same token, non-African religions

Table 18.2 Indicators of Economic Dynamism: Selected Countries in
Sub-Saharan Africa

	Share of Gross Domestic Product (percent)		
	Agriculture	Exports	Investment
Angola	13	31	12
Botswana	5	59	22
Burkina Faso	32	11	24
Côte d'Ivoire	46	37	10
Ethiopia*	42	8	10
Kenya	27	27	21
Nigeria	37	38	17
Senegal	21	26	12
Sierra Leone	43	19	11
Somalia	65	10	16
South Africa	5	26	19
Sudan	29	7	9
Uganda	66	9	14
Zaire	30	25	11
Zimbabwe	13	N.A.	N.A.

N.A. = not available.

* Including Eritrea.

Source: World Bank, *The World Bank Atlas* (Washington, D.C.: World International Bank for Reconstruction and Development/The World Bank, 1992). Published by Oxford University Press, Inc., New York.

were often at odds with African belief systems and seemed self-contradictory. For example, missionaries taught the equality of all God's children, yet they themselves often behaved in a condescending manner to their converts.

Furthermore, as colonial administrators and missionaries dispensed food, medicine, and education, they created a socioeconomic environment conducive to low self-esteem and dependency. Ironically, the colonizers cast themselves in the role of givers and the Africans in the role of receivers. This ascription of roles shaped African politics: when a colonial society is judged for generations by foreign standards and its people are forced into the habit of uncritical receiving, economic development is certain to suffer once the colonizers have gone.

The benevolence of colonial administrators and the charity of missionaries were thus a mixed blessing. Religiously motivated altruism encouraged generosity, but it also stifled individual initiative and the desire for worldly possessions. Indeed, in some places, religion was a barrier to economic development. For example, the Ethiopian Orthodox church designated a great many days as religious holidays for one saint or another, and believers were encouraged to roam the streets on these days, asking for charity in the names of saints. By sanctioning such beggary, the church taught peasants who might have spent their time in productive labor instead to abandon material values and to live off the meager bread of others in return for heavenly rewards.

With respect to education, students in church-sponsored schools studied humanities rather than science, engineering, and technology, which churches spurned as too materialistic and worldly. In this way, too, the new religions discouraged attitudes and orientations associated with free enterprise in the West. The Orthodox, Roman Catholic, and Protestant churches also encouraged *tithing* (giving one-tenth of one's earnings to the church) and the belief that it is more blessed to give than to receive. Such lessons may counteract greed, but they also teach that goodness is inversely related to wealth and possessions.

Finally, the search for an alternative to the Western capitalist model of development made entrepreneurship suspect throughout much of Africa. Only a new social ethic that encourages individual initiative is likely to spur an era of progress and rapid economic growth in this region. Such a change in attitude will probably not occur at the grass-roots level unless it is fostered by African leaders—the very ones who have for decades rejected Western values while embracing dependency theory to explain Africa's ills.

Dependency Theory Revisited

Coups, revolutions, secessionist movements, civil wars, and popular disenfranchisement since independence point to the weakness of political institutions in sub-Saharan Africa and support the view that political and economic development are linked. As noted in Chapter 3, theories abound to explain this chronic instability. One approach that has gained a wide following, especially among Third World development scholars, is **dependency theory**.

The Disease and the Diagnosis

Theotonio Dos Santos has defined *dependency* as "a situation in which the economy of certain countries is conditioned by the development and expansion of another economy to which the former is subjected." He argues that interdependence gives way to dependency "when some countries (the dominant ones) can expand and can be self-sustaining, while others (the dependent ones) can do this only as a reflection of that expansion which can have either positive or negative effect on their immediate development."[8]

Dependency theory and the concept of neocolonialism gained currency in the late 1950s and early 1960s, after the United Nations Economic Commission for Latin America published a study by Raul Prebisch.[9] Originally conceived as an explanation for the consequences of Latin America's economic exploitation by the United States, the dependency perspective eventually came to be seen as especially applicable to Africa and Asia. Its relatively benign interpretation of colonialism has attracted many scholars from the United States and Europe, widening its acceptance and application to the entire Third World.

The concept of dependency transcends economic and political realms; it includes social and psychological attitudes and behaviors of dominant and dependent nations toward one another. Dependency connotes a relationship that is not equal or reciprocal.[10] Although the ties between the developed center and the underdeveloped periphery can be negative or positive, the gains for the periphery are, at best, indirect. According to Dos Santos:

> Trade relations are based on monopolistic control of the market, which leads to transfer of surplus generated in the dependent countries to the dominant countries. Financial relations . . . are based on loans and export of capital, which permit [the dominant countries] to receive interest and profits. . . . The result is to limit the development of [the dependent countries'] internal market and their technical and cultural capacity as well as the moral and physical health of their people.[11]

A Capital Offense

James Caporaso stresses the role of transnational ties between foreign and local capitalists, restricted development choices, and distortions in the domestic economy caused by the incorporation of the less developed nations into the world market system:

> Structural asymmetries are the basis for power, i.e., these asymmetries provide the resources to affect others by depriving them of the desired exchange of goods. When one actor supplies another with large amounts of important goods which cannot be easily replaced at tolerable costs, that actor is in a position to influence the dependent actor.[12]

As a consequence, domestic economic structures are distorted, and development policies are responsive to external market conditions rather than internal needs. For Africans, poverty and despair are inherent in this system, Caporaso argues, because the power to improve their plight in life is outside their own societies.

Dependent development exists where a given nation can take only limited initiatives and has limited access to such vital resources as capital and technology, which are externally controlled. According to many dependency theorists, who are heavily influenced by the turn-of-the-century writings of J. A. Hobson and V. I. Lenin, underdevelopment is perpetuated by the workings of the world capitalist systems.[13]

A. G. Frank advanced this argument:

> Underdevelopment, no less than development itself, is the product but also part of the motive power of capitalism. Capitalist development everywhere has been a fundamentally contradictory development based on exploitation and resulting simultaneously in development and underdevelopment. [Furthermore,] the growth and expansion of European mercantilism of the 16th century led to the development of a single, integrated capitalist system of worldwide scope. Associated ever since the beginning with the growth of powerful states, the expansion of mercantilism-capitalism led to the development of a metropole and, related to it through ties of commerce and force, of a periphery. Variously related to each other through colonialism, free trade, imperialism, and "neo-colonialism," the metropole exploited the periphery in such a way and extent that the metropole became what we today call developed while the periphery became what we now call underdeveloped.[14]

In sum, the economies of the underdeveloped countries have not only become "asymmetrically" integrated with those of the industrially developed nations but, in this view, have also become permanently unequal partners in the global system. Not surprisingly, dependency theorists tend to be anticapitalist and usually advocate socialism as the best cure for underdevelopment and the best hope for transforming the international economic order. They reject the existing system of foreign trade, aid, and investment as a capitalist web that ensnares developing nations and holds them in economic bondage.

Development in African Perspective

There is some truth in almost every theory of development, but none is without flaws. For example, traditional **evolutionary theory**, which seeks to explain development in terms of internal causes, largely ignores the effects of colonialism and neocolonialism. Dependency theory, by contrast, blames underdevelopment on external causes, particularly colonialism and capitalism, but ignores internal factors such as cultural and social barriers to change, political instability, and the weakness of local markets.

Evolutionary theory often prescribes a *laissez faire* policy and soft-pedals the need for concerted state action. Its bias in favor of security and stability places the highest priority on maintaining the status quo, even though social progress and economic development sometimes require radical change. Dependency theory recognizes the need to correct the structural distortions associated with neocolonialism, but it often seeks to do this through revolution. Unfortunately, revolutions may be indiscriminate, destroying both positive and negative elements of the old order and impeding rather than facilitating development. This is especially true if the revolution does not have popular support and if the new regime feels compelled to resort to repression.

For Africans, the development debate is far from academic. Development policy in the region has been entangled in an ideological rivalry between socialism and capitalism, anticolonialism and pro-Western anticommunism. One observer of this value conflict suggests that a viable strategy for developing nations may be to pursue "selective socialism" or "selective capitalism," regarding both as means to an end measured by the same yardstick: Does this approach help or hinder the achievement of society's goals?[15]

Another weakness of most development theories is their failure to give due consideration to physical environment, as opposed to history, culture, social psychology, and politics. Geography has played a major role in shaping Africa's history and politics; it is also a barrier to economic development in most of the region.

The Sahara, for example, extends across North Africa to the Atlantic Ocean. Blanketing 3.5 million square miles, it is the largest desert in the world—the contiguous United States would fit into it. Yet this arid region is inhospitable to human habitation and unsuitable for agriculture or animal husbandry. In much of sub-Saharan Africa, the blazing sun causes drought, then heavy rains erode the soil; both heat and flash floods destroy crops. To cite but one example, Sudan had barely recovered from two years of drought when in August 1988, six times as much rain fell in just two days as had fallen in all of 1987. The country was inundated, paralyzed for weeks. The floods destroyed 100,000 homes and left a million and a half people homeless.

Such catastrophes have impeded the development of many African countries. Floods, volcanic eruptions, and earthquakes occur suddenly without respect for public policy. No amount of statesmanship can influence nature's course.

Although theories of development can help diagnose Africa's economic and political ills, they cannot change the prognosis in the short run. Perhaps a better understanding of the causes of African poverty and underdevelopment will lead to wiser policies and brighter prospects. In the meantime, it must be recognized that there is no African polity, only African polities; no African problem, only African problems; no African solution, only African solutions.

Garden of Eden in Decay?

In a lecture series for the British Broadcasting Corporation, Ali Mazrui, a noted African scholar, took an unusual approach to describing Africa's condition. He used a powerful metaphor that no doubt shocked some of his audience:

> It is as if I were a doctor and Africa came to me and asked for a comprehensive medical examination on the eve of a particular anniversary. The most important century in Africa's relations with Europe is the century from the 1880s to the 1980s. It was in the 1880s that the Conference of Berlin was held to agree on the terms of the European partition of Africa. It was in the 1880s that Egypt was occupied, that the Nile Valley was scrambled for, and that the repercussions for the rest of the continent were released. It was in the 1880s that the map of Africa began to acquire more decisively the different flag colours of the occupation powers of Europe. Let us assume Africa has come to my clinic for varied medical tests on the eve of the hundredth anniversary of Europe's rape of the body and her possessions.[16]

Mazrui proceeded to diagnose Africa's condition in terms of multiple maladies, most of which, he asserted, were caused by European colonialism and economic dependency. Mazrui characterized Africa as a garden of Eden in decay—the first habitat of mankind, but the last to be truly habitable.[17]

The Global Response

In May 1986, the United Nations convened a special session devoted solely to Africa's predicament. The heads-of-state delegation of the Organization of African Unity brought a detailed relief and recovery plan totaling $128 billion, including $45.6 billion in external aid over a five-year period (primarily from the industrial nations—an increase of 130 percent). In addition, the OAU plan asked Western creditor nations to forgive debts estimated to be as high as $55 billion over the same period.[18]

Of the intended donor nations, only Canada, Denmark, and the Netherlands were willing to make specific commitments. African leaders made it clear that even without foreign aid, the recovery program would not simply disappear. Bolaji Akinyemi, Nigeria's minister of external affairs, asserted, "We are not seeking to make Africa a charity case."[19] He pointed out that more than 70 percent of the resources needed under the recovery plan would be provided by Africans themselves. Although the special session helped focus world attention on Africa's plight, the results were inconclusive, and the situation did not improve. Five years later, it was observed that "the continent is in worse shape than ever before. Reforms have faltered. Outside financial flows have actually declined. Food shortages are rampant."[20]

That the special session was called at all, however, suggested that the world could no longer ignore Africa. The drama of a continent teetering on the brink of collapse was given wide coverage in the world media. Pictures of skeletal children barely clinging to life appeared frequently in the press and on television. Emaciated mothers unable to nurse their dying babies stared with hollow eyes. People were shown traveling to relief camps with empty bowls in search of a few scoops of grain. Around them, the drought-stricken land offered no hope.

To make matters worse, Africa's economies stagger under a massive burden of foreign debt—about $270 billion in 1991. This is more than 100 percent of the region's gross national product—more than twice the ratio found in Latin America and more than four times that of East Asia. Interest payments alone amount to roughly 30 percent of the continent's export earnings.[21] Africa continues to be squeezed in an economic vise, between falling agricultural output and heavy debt service payments that sap meager hard-currency reserves.

In the mid-1980s, foreign governments and humanitarian agencies responded to this African crisis in several ways. Creditors considered various types of debt relief; celebrities turned their talents to worldwide fund-raising efforts. At the peak of the crisis, in 1985, official emergency aid reached an estimated $3.4 billion, and as many as one million lives were saved.[22] But these efforts were short-lived, and the world's attention soon turned to other regions and other problems:

> Africa has seen only a marginal increase in overseas development assistance (ODA), while international export credits and commercial bank loans have all but dried up. . . . Even as aid flows in at a lower rate, domestic resources are flowing out at a higher rate, as capital flight and high debts deplete national savings.[23]

Plenty of Blame to Go Around

One upshot of the crisis was to accentuate the failure of African nations to achieve key goals. Julius Nyerere, former president of Tanzania and longtime champion of African socialism and self-reliance, criticized fellow African leaders for reacting to the crisis of the moment but failing to engage in longer-term problem solving:

> Virtually all African governments are now almost entirely occupied with crisis management—that is, with searching for foreign capital even to maintain the very minimum administrative and economic structures, and with keeping the economy running somehow. In the process, we have ourselves begun to believe that all Africa's problems are the result of Africa's mistakes, Africa's incompetence, and its political and economic venality. We are apologetic and demoralized in the face of the rest of the world.[24]

But Nyerere failed to mention the role of African socialism itself in either causing or failing to prevent the region's economic distress. Another omission is the definition of *self-reliance*. What does it mean? Autarky? Interdependence in some sort of pan-African economic grouping? Neither alternative has been realistic at any time since decolonization. Ironically, heavy borrowing from the West—hardly consistent with self-reliance—has led to sub-Saharan Africa's most pressing economic problem, the mountain of foreign debt.

A most agonizing issue is the refugee problem. Dependency theorists argue that the militarization of African society is one of the consequences of European colonialism. One of the consequences of militarization, in turn, is refugees. Their numbers reached crisis proportions in the 1980s, when war and revolution, drought and famine produced a tidal wave of displaced and destitute souls.

Famine, Conflict, and the Refugee Problem

Africa is a war-torn region. The persistence of armed conflict, both domestic and international, has been a stubborn fact of life for many sub-Saharan nations since the early years of independence in the 1950s. Hardly a country in the region has not been involved in a civil war or a border war. Civil wars in Ethiopia and Sudan dragged on for more than a quarter century. The 1967 war in Nigeria took a heavy toll, as did the Congo crisis from 1960 to 1964. In the 1970s, Tanzania backed Ugandan rebels in overthrowing dictator Idi Amin. A territorial dispute between Ethiopia and Somalia erupted in war in 1978 and came close to engaging the superpowers. In Angola, a civil war raged from 1975 to 1988 and was internationalized when Cuban troops intervened on the side of Angola's Marxist government and South African troops buttressed Joseph Savimbi's UNITA rebels. Such conflicts have plagued the region and continue to sap its resources while undermining cooperative efforts.

In both human and economic terms, the toll of border conflicts, civil and ethnic strife, and chronic political instability is enormous. The human cost is counted not only in battle casualties but also in ordinary people fleeing war, persecution, and hunger. Of the estimated twelve million refugees worldwide in the late 1980s, nearly half of them were Africans, and more than three-fourths of those were from four nations: Ethiopia, Mozambique, Angola, and Sudan. At least an equal number of displaced Africans were living in temporary settlements in their own countries. (People who do not cross an international border are not officially considered refugees.) Black South Africans and Angolans accounted for more than 40 percent of this population. Thus there were close to seventeen million refugees and displaced persons in sub-Saharan Africa in the late 1980s.

Though impossible to quantify, the economic and human costs of conflict and famine are readily apparent. Refugees suffer severe deprivation, unfathomable indignities, and loss of self-respect. Their home governments are mired in debt and forced to seek outside help, often sacrificing independence in the process. Host governments must contend with situations not of their own making; their systems for providing education, health care, housing, sanitation, and other human services can be easily overwhelmed but cannot be rapidly expanded. Even food reserves are often insufficient, yet again leading to external dependencies.[25] It is easy to see how internal conflicts can spill over, giving rise to border tensions and international strife. Thus conflict begets conflict in a vicious cycle that only serves to perpetuate the militarization of African politics.

Some sub-Saharan countries—including Botswana, Kenya, Malawi, Tanzania, Zambia, and Zimbabwe—deserve credit for achieving political stability and for providing shelter for refugees. Domestic backlash has so far been kept in check, but no country can accommodate an unending influx of refugees without suffering severe stress. One country reached the breaking point in the early 1980s, when a faltering domestic economy induced the government of Nigeria to order the forced repatriation of thousands of laborers and refugees from neighboring Ghana.

Roots of Despair: The Economic Crisis

A year after the United Nations General Assembly emergency session on the economic crisis in sub-Saharan Africa, the UN secretary general, Javier Pérez de Cuéllar, reported that Africa's economic plight was not improving and that the industrialized nations had not fulfilled their promises to provide additional foreign aid.

Decade of Decline

During the first half of the 1980s, Africa's combined gross national product dropped steadily. Net exports were negative in every year except 1985, when exports barely exceeded imports. The trade deficit in some years amounted to 15 percent of the continent's total annual GNP. Meanwhile, the exploding population helped plunge Africa into a severe debt crisis: by 1986, its external debt equaled its GNP and was still climbing. So was the price of manufactured imports—up 20 percent in 1986–1987 alone.[26]

To meet this crisis, the African nations were to raise $82.5 billion under the plan adopted by the UN General Assembly in June 1986, and the industrial nations pledged $9 billion annually for five years. In addition, yearly debt service requirements were projected at $14.6 billion, bringing total external financing needs to about $24 billion. Despite good intentions, the net inflow of external funds amounted to $18 billion—a decrease in real terms over the 1985 level.

According to the secretary general's report, "Serious initiatives have yet to be taken by the international community . . . to respond to the increasingly tightly entwined debt, commodity, and resource-flow problem in Africa." The net flow of resources was "grossly inadequate" to compensate for Africa's drastically reduced export revenues and mounting debt service obligations. Moreover, industrialized nations had failed "to deal urgently with commodity issues." On the contrary, the report asserted that there had been almost no effort to stabilize the prices of raw materials (commodities and minerals), Africa's major exports. Indeed, falling commodity prices cost Africa $50 billion in lost export earnings between 1986 and 1990, according to UN statistics.

By contrast, the report noted that no fewer than twenty-eight African nations had adopted at least some of the recommended reforms. For example, more than four-fifths had created price incentives to boost agricultural production and rural development, two-thirds had taken steps to improve internal distribution, and even more had allocated at least 25 percent of total investment to agriculture. Furthermore, there had been movement toward privatization as public-enterprise subsidies were being curtailed in many countries and laws affecting investment and business were being liberalized.

The report also noted the downside of these economic reforms. They had adversely affected immediate social well-being (health, education, and employment) in a region with the lowest quality-of-life indicators in the world (see Table 18.3). "Africa's margins of maneuver to implement the program of action are being reduced," the secretary general inveighed. This sentiment was echoed by many African leaders, including Zambian President Kenneth Kaunda, who warned of the dangers of adopting painful economic reforms.

Zambia is a kind of microcosm of the dilemma that Africa faces. The Zambian government reduced urban food subsidies and raised farm prices in compliance with the 1986 UN blueprint. The idea was to cut deficit spending and to encourage greater agricultural output, which it did. On the one hand, food production jumped 15 percent and manufacturing rose 5 percent. On the other, food prices also rose, quite predictably, sparking urban riots that left at least fifteen people dead and forced Kaunda to rescind the offending measures.[27]

Tanzania encountered another kind of pitfall: it increased cotton production by 75 percent in 1986 but actually earned less from this export than in 1985! There were two reasons, both external: world cotton prices fell sharply in 1986, and Tanzania devalued its currency to comply with the rules of the International Monetary Fund. The Tanzanian case illustrates how dependent many African nations are on world commodity prices. Cotton is Tanzania's major export, and commodity prices on the world market often fluctuate wildly. At the same time, the IMF lends money on easy terms to finance international trade. Many countries in the developing South experience chronic hard-currency shortfalls and depend on IMF loans to facilitate imports, especially manufactures, from the industrial North. As a consequence, they are often at the mercy of external forces—one reason why neocolonialism is still a factor in sub-Saharan Africa.

Table 18.3   Development Profile: Selected Countries in Sub-Saharan Africa

	Life Expectancy at Birth, 1991 (years)	Infant Mortality Rate (per thousand live births)	Illiteracy Rate (percent)	Women's Share of Labor Force (percent)
Angola	46	215	58	38
Botswana	68	45	26	35
Burkina Faso	48	198	82	46
Côte d'Ivoire	55	135	46	34
Ethiopia*	48	193	N.A.	37
Kenya	59	102	31	40
Nigeria	52	157	49	35
Senegal	48	125	62	39
Sierra Leone	42	245	79	33
Somalia	48	208	76	39
South Africa	62	86	N.A.	36
Sudan	51	165	73	22
Uganda	46	197	52	41
Zaire	52	150	28	35
Zimbabwe	60	70	33	34

N.A. = not available.

*Including Eritrea.

Source: World Bank, The World Bank Atlas (Washington, D.C.: World International Bank for Reconstruction and Development/The World Bank, 1992). Published by Oxford University Press, Inc., New York.

The Demographics of Decline

Many observers contend that Africa's economic ills are caused primarily by overpopulation. In the West, government officials and scholars alike accept this contention almost unquestioningly, and it does seem plausible, considering that Africa's population growth rate is the highest in the world (see Table 18.4), and the region has also been hardest hit by food shortages. Thus a strong case can be made for the view that the population explosion is the root cause of deprivation and decline in Africa.

But is this argument accurate? Djibril Diallo, chief spokesman for the United Nations Office for Emergency Operations in Africa, says no:

> Of all the myths about Africa prevailing in the West, none is propagated with more vigor and regularity than the notion that overpopulation is a central cause of African poverty. The recent famine has given propagators of this myth fresh ammunition with which to press home their argument. . . .
>
> The overpopulation myth is particularly harmful because it preempts deeper probing into the complex causes of underdevelopment.[28]

Diallo argues that the popularity of this myth in the West actually complicates efforts to launch family-planning programs in Africa: "After centuries of foreign

Table 18.4 Demographic Facts: Selected Countries in Sub-Saharan Africa

	Population, 1991 (millions)	Population Growth Rate, 1980–1991 (percent per year)	Fertility Rate (births per woman)
Angola	10.3	2.6	6.6
Botswana	1.3	3.3	4.5
Burkina Faso	9.3	2.6	6.5
Côte d'Ivoire	12.3	3.8	6.6
Ethiopia*	52.9	3.1	7.5
Kenya	25.0	3.8	6.5
Nigeria	118.8	3.1	5.9
Senegal	7.6	3.8	6.5
Sierra Leone	4.3	2.4	6.5
Somalia	8.0	3.1	6.8
South Africa	36.8	2.4	4.2
Sudan	25.9	2.7	6.2
Uganda	16.9	2.5	7.3
Zaire	38.5	3.2	6.2
Zimbabwe	10.1	3.4	4.8

*Including Eritrea.

Source: World Bank, *The World Bank Atlas* (Washington, D.C.: World International Bank for Reconstruction and Development/The World Bank, 1992). Published by Oxford University Press, Inc., New York.

domination, many Africans are deeply suspicious of any campaigns designed to alter the way they live and behave." Diallo gives a clear example of how sensitive the issue of population control can be in the multiethnic context of African society:

> Just as the Kenyan government was concluding careful negotiations with the United States Agency for International Development to launch a major marketing drive for contraceptives in the rural areas, children in the central highlands areas suddenly stopped taking their free milk drinks at school. The reason became clear a few days later when a man appeared in court charged with spreading the rumor that the milk had been treated with contraceptive chemicals. The implication behind the rumor was that the authorities wished to reduce the population increase of the ethnic groups living in the region.[29]

Diallo makes several points that merit consideration. First, a double standard is often applied by experts who stress the link between food supply and population size. Japan, Switzerland, and the Netherlands are not self-sufficient in food and have relatively little available farmland, yet they are not charged with being overpopulated. By contrast, "Africa has more arable land per capita than any other developing region." Under the right conditions, Chad alone could feed the whole Sahel (the area from Chad westward to the Atlantic Ocean just south of the Sahara). Second, Africa's average population density is only 16 people per square kilometer, much lower than China's (100) and India's (225). Nonetheless,

India and China have both made impressive strides toward food self-sufficiency. According to Diallo, "In their quest for appropriate solutions to their own food predicaments, more and more Africans are making their way to India to study breakthroughs there."[30] But even Africans who criticize the critics do not argue that family planning is unnecessary in many sub-Saharan countries, only that it is not a panacea.

African Democracy: Wave of the Future?

At the beginning of the 1990s, there were signs that the trends toward democracy and respect for human rights in Latin America and Eastern Europe were also having an impact in sub-Saharan Africa. In Niger, Côte d'Ivoire, Benin, Gabon, Cameroon, Kenya, and Zaire, opponents of authoritarian government pressed for democratization.[31] In Benin, for example, President Mathieu Kérékou renounced Marxism in late 1989 and called for talks with the democratic opposition. In March 1990, he resigned and transferred power to a non-Communist prime minister. Meanwhile in Niger, government security forces responded to demands by professionals and government workers for better pay by shooting demonstrators. Following this outrage, President Ali Saibou fired his cabinet ministers and promised to introduce democracy. In Côte d'Ivoire, doctors and teachers went on strike against a government austerity program. President Houphouët-Boigny closed the schools for the year; students then clamored for multiparty elections.

But another trend was even more prominent in the early 1990s: sudden leadership changes (in Ethiopia, Somalia, Liberia, Mali, Chad, and Lesotho) threw governments into a transitional state, leaving the affected societies with no clear direction or destination. Other nations not jolted by coups (including Ghana, Togo, Angola, Kenya, Nigeria, and South Africa) also appeared to be undergoing varying degrees of liberalization, but it was not clear how far the reform process would go or where it might lead.

These developments were only straws in the wind, and it is doubtful that they portend far-reaching changes of the kind that occurred in Eastern Europe in 1989. As we have seen, authoritarian rule is deeply rooted in Africa. In one sense, a discussion of whether multiparty democracy is likely to come to the region begs the question: Is political pluralism a viable model in these multiethnic societies? Given the instability that has become a hallmark of African politics, a premature move toward democracy raises the possibility of a slide into civil strife and social chaos that could end tragically, as it did in Nigeria in the late 1960s. Otherwise put, democracy is not a cure for Africa's ills; in some cases, it might only exacerbate existing problems.

Case Studies: Nations in Transition

Kenya, Nigeria, and South Africa, like so many countries in Africa, are changing. The challenges they face are daunting but not extreme, for these are not the poorest, the most unstable, or the least developed nations on the continent. On the contrary, they are relatively representative of virtually all the problems found anywhere in Africa.

Kenya

A Rocky Regime   During the 1980s, the Moi government survived criticism of its human rights record, a coup attempt, student unrest, and a high-level scandal. The scandal involved Charles Njojo, a popular and ambitious Kikuyu politician in charge of law enforcement and internal security. Njojo was accused of colluding with foreign governments, including South Africa. Njojo was cleared of any wrongdoing by a special judicial commission, but the affair left nagging doubts about the integrity of the people around the president.

More troublesome was a coup attempt by the Kenyan air force support troops in 1982. The coup failed, but it sent shock waves through the government. Several thousand air force personnel and civilian suspects were detained and put on trial. Although twelve airmen received the death sentence, most of the others were granted amnesty.

Student demonstrations and protests against alleged mismanagement of the economy and violations of civil liberties led to the closing of Kenya's universities at times, and a small band of agitators known as **Mwakenya** became a nuisance to internal security forces. The world press put Kenya in the spotlight as critics accused Moi of trampling on human rights.

Despite these rumblings, Kenya's one-party system has proved highly resilient. KANU's membership actually increased in the 1980s (although the main reason seems to be that civil service employees were required to join the party).[32]

In 1988, the government introduced a controversial primary election system known as **queuing**. A month before the general election, voters were asked to select legislative nominees by literally lining up behind the candidate of their choice. The candidates with the longest queue proceeded to the general election.[33] Also in 1988, the number of elective seats in the Kenyan parliament was increased from 158 to 188. The new method, the added seats, and the defeat of incumbents combined to produce a large "freshmen class" in the Assembly (roughly one-third of the membership), but only at the expense of electoral controversy, allegations of voting fraud, and a spate of lawsuits.

At the end of the 1980s, many critics decried what they viewed as a tendency toward presidential dictatorship in Kenya. Several disturbing signs pointed toward this conclusion. For example, in the fall of 1988, the National Assembly, without debate, unanimously passed a constitutional amendment giving the president nearly unlimited power to fire judges. This endangered the independence of the judiciary by making judges subject to political pressures under threat of dismissal. The same amendment also extended from twenty-four hours to fourteen days the period during which police can hold suspects before bringing them to court. That this amendment was approved unanimously, with the Assembly acting as a rubber stamp, also raised questions about the future of polyarchy in Kenya.

The situation was alarming to Moi's critics because the president was becoming increasingly intolerant of opposition and was resorting to the tactics of a demagogue. The government had taken to attacking elements in society that it viewed as disloyal, including church leaders, lawyers, and students. The wealthy Asian business class—only about sixty thousand in number but in control of 70 percent of the urban retail sector and much manufacturing—also felt persecuted. In addition, the government had launched a vitriolic campaign against foreign journalists, the British Broadcasting Corporation, and Amnesty International ("an agent of imperialism"), among others.[34]

Worse still, persistent rumors of arbitrary detentions and torture made the assault on the judicial system and the legal profession seem particularly ominous. According to one close observer writing in early 1988:

> Eleven people are detained without trial under Kenya's Public Security Act, while more than 80 have been jailed in connection with a secret anti-government movement known as Mwakenya, which was uncovered in 1986. None of the 80 had legal representation in court, and both Amnesty International and the American Lawyers Committee for Human Rights have published evidence that many were tortured into pleading guilty.[35]

Plainclothes officers of the dreaded **Special Branch**, Kenya's secret police, enforced the unwritten rule against criticism of President Moi as well as laws against sabotage and sedition.

Critics also charged that Moi was using Mwakenya as a kind of hobgoblin: "The clampdown on criticism, including the fear that one may be branded a Mwakenya member for expressing disloyal thoughts, has prevented any real opposition from emerging."[36] Whether true or false in this case, the fact remains that populist tyrants in Africa and elsewhere have frequently used such tactics to stifle opposition.

It would be a mistake to conclude that President Moi lacks popular support. Despite all the controversy, the electorate gave him a renewed mandate in 1988 and again in 1992.

Economic Stability   Kenya has long had a reputation for economic vitality and political tolerance. In February 1989, the U.S. State Department concluded that Kenya "remains one of Africa's success stories" in terms of both economic growth and political stability.[37] Another observer noted that "the country feeds itself, has avoided the conflicts and bloodshed which plague its neighbors, and has enjoyed steady expansion while other countries have sunk deeper into poverty."[38] All of these accomplishments are as impressive as they are rare in the sub-Saharan region.

Although Kenya continues to face formidable tasks of economic and political development, it is better off than any of its neighbors. Conditions in Kenya are quite bearable compared to Uganda and Tanzania and even luxurious compared to Sudan, Ethiopia, and Somalia. When Moi stumps in the villages, he stresses bread-and-butter issues—roads, schools, clinics. He points out how much better things are in Kenya than in neighboring countries and promises that so long as he has the support of the ordinary citizens, living standards will continue to improve. So even if the political scene appears bleak to outsiders, the economic picture looks pretty good.

Without minimizing the dangers of interethnic violence or AIDS, Kenya's greatest challenge is to contain its population growth, which remains the highest in the world.* Economic growth, however steady, may be unable to outstrip the nation's demographic liabilities. New schools and expanded social services are needed; new jobs must be created. Unless the economy continues to grow and the government continues to deliver on its promises of a better life, pressures will inevitably build. So far, Kenya has coped remarkably well—so well that most Kenyans expect things to keep getting better. Therein lies the challenge for Moi and his successors.

Nigeria

As noted in Chapter 17, Nigeria's military government pledged to reestablish democracy by 1993. Democratic rule, however, is not a cure-all. If the social and economic ills that beset Nigerian society are not alleviated, democracy will be short-lived.

In the early 1990s, Nigeria was one of the poorest countries in the world (only twelve nations ranked below it). At the same time, its population growth rate, at 3.1 percent a year, was one of the highest in the world, outpacing both food production and new job opportunities.

Despite being a major oil exporter, Nigeria was unable to capitalize on its windfall profits in the 1970s. This combination of oil wealth and grinding poverty is rare in the world: Nigeria shares this dubious distinction with only one other nation, Indonesia. Their mushrooming populations set them apart from the oil-rich Arab states of the Persian Gulf. The contrast in per capita GNP between densely populated Nigeria ($290) and the sparsely populated United Arab Emirates ($16,870) is striking—both are members of OPEC, but that is where the similarity ends. The average per capita income of all major oil-exporting countries in 1988 was around $5,000. Gabon, the only other OPEC member-state in sub-Saharan Africa, had a per capita income in 1991 more than thirteen times that of Nigeria. Indonesia, with a population of more than 180 million, half again as large as Nigeria's, had a per capita income more than twice that of Nigeria. So Nigeria stacks up poorly against other oil-producing nations from every angle.

Poverty and degradation are the dry tinder of ethnic violence in Nigeria (as elsewhere in the region). Ethnic hatred, always seething beneath the surface of Nigerian society, once again erupted in violent clashes in 1992. The civil strife was a potential impediment to restoration of civilian rule, but the military appeared committed to its promise to hold free elections and restore civilian

---

*AIDS was reaching epidemic proportions in Kenya and neighboring Uganda as elsewhere in sub-Saharan Africa in the early 1990s. Unless this alarming trend can be reversed in coming years, AIDS could well overshadow all other economic and social problems in Kenya by the end of the decade.

rule by 1993. However, leading candidates for the presidency, according to many reports, refused to play by the rules, choosing instead to engage in unfair campaign practices. As a consequence, the Babangida government again postponed the election. In mid-1993, Nigeria was still under military rule.

The presidential election was finally held in June 1993 after it had been postponed three times. By this time, the on-again—off-again presidential election was greeted with voter apathy and turnout was correspondingly low. General Babangida quickly nullified the election when it was clear that the government did not like the results. A candidate from southern Nigeria, Chief Moshood Abiola, had won the election which Babangida and others saw as a threat to the traditional dominance of northerners' ruling hierarchy. Babangida's about-face was widely criticized in the Western press, but public opinion in Nigeria was not greatly aroused.

In the meantime, Nigeria's economic ills went untreated. Costly fuel subsidies remained in force despite the government's earlier acceptance of an IMF-structured adjustment program that called for an end to such subsidies. Inflation was climbing at an annual rate of about 50 percent and the local currency (the naira) was falling even faster. In the opinion of some close observers, Nigeria needed a changing of the guard—not so much because the military leaders had performed less well than civilians, but because new ideas and fresh faces were, in this view, necessary to rejuvenate the country.

South Africa

In early 1989, President P. W. Botha, in ailing health, stepped down as head of the ruling National party (but stayed on as president). His successor was Frederik W. de Klerk, a hard-liner on apartheid who had long opposed and obstructed proposals to lessen discrimination against blacks. In August, embittered and isolated within his own party, Botha relinquished the presidency as well, ending more than a decade in power. Botha detested de Klerk but could not block his elevation to the post.

When de Klerk took power, South Africa was in crisis. The **African National Congress (ANC)**, which had been directing the armed struggle against the Pretoria government from its headquarters in Lusaka, Zambia, intensified its campaign of violence and terrorism. As noted in Chapter 17, Botha had made some important concessions prior to 1985—he scrapped laws prohibiting interracial sex and marriage, extended rights to black trade unions, gave blacks property rights, and abolished the hated "pass laws" used to control the influx of blacks into South African cities. Botha had seriously contemplated far-reaching reforms in the apartheid system in the mid-1980s, but he succumbed to pressures from the right wing within his party and instead gave a defiant speech warning the world not to push South Africa too far.

The international reaction was swift and damaging. A spate of economic sanctions and diplomatic protests left Pretoria isolated and ostracized from the international community. Foreign banks called in loans early, multinational firms quit South Africa, and the value of the rand plummeted. These external

CONTRAST and COMPARISON

Angola: The Second Civil War

A former Portuguese colony in the east of southern Africa, Angola finally won its independence in 1975. For the next sixteen years, a civil war raged, and at least 350,000 Angolans died.

In 1991, with the Cold War ended, the United States, Russia, and Portugal brokered an Angolan peace accord. In the fall of 1992, free multiparty elections were held under close United Nations supervision. The two major candidates were Jose Eduardo dos Santos, the incumbent and head of the left-wing governing party, the Popular Movement for the Liberation of Angola (MPLA), and his archrival, Joseph Savimbi, leader of the insurgency and head of the National Union for the Total Independence of Angola (UNITA). (The United States had supported Savimbi's UNITA during the civil war, and the USSR had backed the Marxist government.) Dos Santos won convincingly over Savimbi, but other minor candidates siphoned off enough votes to force a runoff. (Dos Santos fell four-tenths of a point short of the simple majority he needed.)

The runoff was not to be. Savimbi cried election fraud (but offered no evidence) and relaunched the civil war. Although both sides had agreed to demobilize as part of the 1991 peace accord, neither side had done so. In the spring of 1993, Savimbi's forces appeared to achieve the military breakthrough that had eluded UNITA during the first civil war.

Whoever finally emerges victorious will face daunting problems of national rehabilitation and reconstruction. Angola's population is almost the same size as that of its former colonial overlord, Portugal (about 10.3 million). But Angola's GNP per capita in 1991 was about one-tenth of Portugal's (which is among the lowest in Western Europe). Life expectancy in Angola was about 45; in Portugal, it was 75. In Angola, 215 of every thousand babies born do not live beyond the age of 5; in Portugal, the figure is 15. The daily Portuguese diet contains nearly twice the calories the average Angolan consumes. In Angola, 58 percent of the population is illiterate, compared to 15 percent in Portugal. Finally, only one Angolan child in ten can expect to enroll in secondary school; in Portugal, half the children go to secondary school (again, a low figure by European standards).

Civil war is costly in human and economic terms for any society. More Americans died in the Civil War between 1861 and 1865 than in any other war in American history. But the United States was a country on the move economically in the second half of the nineteenth century. By contrast, Angola is going nowhere. So long as the fighting continues, Angola's economic development will, at best, be on hold; at worst, it will be set back by years or even decades.

pressures precipitated the deep economic recession into which the country sank in the second half of the decade.

Economic troubles were accompanied by intensified political pressures both at home and abroad. Botha was ultimately defeated by a wide array of opposition forces; his successor, de Klerk, could read the handwriting on the wall: negotiate with the black majority (and protect white interests as far as possible), or risk a convulsive end to white rule (in which case Afrikaners might lose everything). In February 1990, de Klerk not only released Nelson Mandela from prison (where he had languished since 1961) but also legalized the ANC and invited thousands of ANC exiles to return to South Africa and take part in seeking accommodation between blacks and whites.

Direct talks between Mandela, as the ANC leader, and de Klerk, beginning in the spring of 1990, brought a further dismantling of the apartheid system. During the next year, the Reservation of Separate Amenities Act establishing "petty apartheid," the Group Areas Act designating racially segregated residential zones, the Lands Acts of 1913 and 1936 setting aside 87 percent of the land for the white minority, and the Population Registration Act classifying South Africans by race were all abolished. In early 1991, the government and the ANC agreed to convene an all-party (hence multiracial) constitutional convention.

But the more conciliatory stance toward the government adopted by Mandela and the ANC was not seconded by more radical black parties and leaders, including the Pan-Africanist Congress and the South African Communist party. The politically moderate Zulu-based Inkatha Freedom party of Chief Mangosuthu Buthelezi distrusted the ANC as well. Mandela and Buthelezi met for the first time in thirty years on January 29, 1991, but they failed to defuse the fierce rivalry that had already caused four thousand deaths and divided the antiapartheid movement.

A negotiated settlement in South Africa, despite spectacular gains for the black majority, will not come easily, for several reasons. First, the extreme right within the National party is increasingly popular among ordinary Afrikaners fearful that their way of life is endangered. Hard-liners will try to block concessions to blacks at every turn. Second, it is not clear who, if anybody, can claim to speak for all of South Africa's blacks. The movement is divided and disposed to self-inflicted wounds (for example, in the spring of 1990, Mandela admitted publicly that the ANC had used torture against some of its own members accused of disloyalty). Violence involving blacks has skyrocketed. In 1992, black South Africans were reported to be "dying daily in an undeclared war apparently fueled by right-wing elements with links to the security forces."[39] Between 1984 and 1992, more than twelve thousand people, most of them black, perished in the civil turbulence.

Finally, it will be difficult to overcome the bitter legacy of years of repression: between 1961 and 1990, South Africa detained over seventy-five thousand black activists without trial; some seventy-five political prisoners (including Stephen Biko) died in prison; scores were executed, and thousands exiled; at least forty-five activists were killed by police and army "hit squads" in the late 1980s; dozens of ANC operatives were assassinated beyond South Africa's borders; and more than fifty antiapartheid organizations were banned. This brutality will continue to cast a long shadow of mistrust over efforts at power sharing between the white minority and the black majority.

South Africa's white leadership has lately acted on the principle of enlightened self-interest. Thus Botha helped bring about negotiated settlements to the protracted wars in Angola and Namibia, and de Klerk has pulled down the legal pillars of apartheid. But formal authority and a monopoly on the legitimate exercise of coercive power (as well as access to the government's huge arsenal of lethal weapons) remain in the hands of the Afrikaners.

In the early 1990s, a sullen but factionalized black majority confronted a beseiged white minority government still not entirely reconciled to the idea of sharing power. The possibility of civil war hung like a pall over South Africa. Frequent incidents of both interracial and intraracial violence, such as the 1993 assassination of a popular ANC leader by a fanatical white supremacist, continue to push tensions to a dangerously high level. Whether all parties to the conflict will show the mutual tolerance and vision necessary to bring about peaceful change in South Africa remains to be seen.

CONCLUSION

As the colonial era fades, the governments of sub-Saharan Africa will no longer be able to attribute policy failures manifested in unrelieved poverty, oppression, and stagnation solely to colonialism and neocolonialism. A trend toward democratization is evident throughout much of the region, but democracy is not likely to take root unless nurtured by economic development. Africa south of the Sahara remains the poorest region in the world, and the most unfortunate. Since independence, millions of Africans have endured natural disasters and corrupt, repressive governments—the worst of these (such as Zaire under Mobutu) are sometimes called "kleptocracies" because the leaders use political power to line their own pockets. Even Latin America, which has had its share of natural disasters, corrupt leaders, and repressive governments, looks prosperous by comparison. We turn to that region next.

KEY TERMS

dependency theory   queuing
evolutionary theory   Special Branch
Mwakenya   African National Congress (ANC)

STUDY QUESTIONS

1. In what sense is Africa a "garden of Eden in decay"?
2. To what extent are the problems faced by Kenya, Nigeria, and South Africa part of a larger pattern found throughout the region?
3. How do scholars explain Africa's social, economic, and political problems? Which theory makes the most sense to you, and why?
4. Compare Kenya and Nigeria in terms of social diversity, political stability, and economic development. Which country has the better future prospects?
5. What are the major problems facing South Africa today, and what obstacles stand in the way of solving them? Is democracy the answer?

SUGGESTED READING

Baker, Pauline. *The United States and South Africa: The Reagan Years.* New York: Ford Foundation/Foreign Policy Association, 1989.
Berger, Peter, and Godsell, Bobby. "South Africa on the Move." *Current History,* May 1990.

Berger, Peter, and Godsell, Bobby, eds. *A Future for South Africa: Visions, Strategies, and Realities.* Boulder, Colo.: Westview Press, 1988.

Mazrui, Ali A. *The African Condition: A Political Diagnosis.* Cambridge: Cambridge University Press, 1980.

McGowan, Patrick J., and Smith, Dale L. "Economic Dependency in Black Africa: An Analysis of Competing Theories." *International Organization,* Winter 1978.

Rosenblum, Mort, and Williamson, Doug. *Squandering Eden: Africa at the Edge.* San Diego, Calif.: Harcourt, 1987.

Sampson, Anthony. *Black and Gold: Tycoons, Revolutionaries, and Apartheid.* New York: Pantheon, 1987.

NOTES

1. "The President's Initiative to End Hunger in Africa," *USAID Highlights,* vol. 4, no. 3 (Summer 1987); George D. Moffett III, "Africa Teeters on Famine's Edge," *Christian Science Monitor,* June 25, 1991.

2. United States Agency for International Development.

3. See, for example, Walter Rodney, *How Europe Underdeveloped Africa* (Washington, D.C.: Howard University Press, 1974); and Samir Amin, *Imperialism and Unequal Development* (New York: Monthly Review Press, 1977).

4. *UN Chronicle,* vol. 22, no. 2 (1985), p. 7.

5. See, for example, Chinua Achebe, *Arrow of God* (London: Heinemann, 1958); Chinua Achebe, *Things Fall Apart* (London: Heinemann, 1958); T. M. Aluko, *The Gab Boys* (London: Fontana Books, 1969); Ola Rotimi, *The Gods Are Not to Blame* (London: Oxford University Press, 1971); and Ayi Kwei Armah, *The Beautiful Ones Are Not Yet Born* (Boston: Houghton Mifflin, 1968).

6. Talcott Parson, *The Social System* (New York: Free Press, 1951); see also Talcott Parson, "Evolutionary Universals in Society," in *Socialization Theory and Modern Society,* Talcott Parson, ed. (New York: Free Press, 1967).

7. See, for example, Seymour Martin Lipset, "Some Social Prerequisites of Democracy, Economic Development, and Political Legitimacy," *American Political Science Review,* vol. 53, no. 3 (March 1969).

8. Theotonio Dos Santos, "The Structure of Dependence," *American Economic Review,* vol. 60, no. 5 (May 1970), p. 231.

9. Lois Eugenio Di Marco, ed., *International Economics and Development: Essay in Honor of Raul Prebisch* (Philadelphia: Academic Press, 1972), pp. 1–34.

10. See, for example, James A. Caporaso, "Introduction," *International Organization,* vol. 32, no. 1 (Winter 1978), p. 6; James A. Caporaso, "Dependence, Dependency, and Power in the Global System: A Structural and Behavioral Analysis," *International Organization,* vol. 32, no. 1 (Winter 1978), pp. 13–43, 121–125; Patrick J. McGowan and Dale L. Smith, "Economic Dependency in Black Africa: An Analysis of Competing Theories," *International Organization,* vol. 32, no. 1 (Winter 1978), pp. 179–235; and R. Dan Walleri, "Trade Dependence and Underdevelopment: A Causal Chain Analysis," *Comparative Political Studies,* vol. 11, no. 1 (April 1978), pp. 94–121.

11. Dos Santos, "Structure of Dependence," p. 231.

12. Caporaso, "Dependence, Dependency, and Power," p. 28.

13. See Immanuel Wallerstein, *The Modern World System* (San Diego, Calif.: Academic Press, 1974), pp. 67, 301; Immanuel Wallerstein, ed., *World Inequality: Origin of*

and Perspectives on the World System (Montreal: Black Rose Books, 1975), p. 16; Celso Furtado, "Development and Stagnation in Latin America: A Structuralist Approach," *Studies in Comparative Development,* vol. 1, no. 11 (1965); and Amin, *Imperialism and Unequal Development,* pp. 12–15.

14. André Gunder Frank, *Capitalist Underdevelopment* (New York: Oxford University Press, 1976), pp. 94–95.
15. Peter Berger, *Pyramids of Sacrifice: Political Ethics and Social Change* (Garden City, N.Y.: Anchor/Doubleday, 1976), chaps. 5 and 6.
16. Ali A. Mazrui, *The African Condition: A Political Diagnosis* (Cambridge: Cambridge University Press, 1980), pp. 1–2.
17. Ibid., pp. 6–9.
18. See *UN Chronicle,* vol. 23, no. 4 (August 1986), pp. 7–20; and *Africa Report,* May-June 1986.
19. Mary Ann Weaver, "UN Plan for Africa," *Christian Science Monitor,* June 3, 1986, p. 1.
20. Amy Kaslow and George D. Moffett III, "UN Renewing Effort to Rescue Sliding African Economies," *Christian Science Monitor,* Aug. 29, 1991, p. 1.
21. Ibid.
22. *UN Chronicle,* vol. 24, no. 1 (February 1987), p. 47.
23. Kaslow and Moffett, "UN Renewing Effort," p. 1.
24. Julius K. Nyerere, *Africa Recovery,* vol. 2, no. 2 (June 1988), p. 9.
25. See, for example, Sheila Rule, "Refugees Tax Already Desperate Malawi," *New York Times,* July 18, 1988, p. 1A.
26. Ted Morello, "UN's Africa Recovery Program Fails to Make Dent in Crisis," *Christian Science Monitor,* Nov. 6, 1987, p. 14.
27. Morello, "UN's Africa Recovery Program," p. 14.
28. Djibril Diallo, "Overpopulation and Other Myths about Africa," *Christian Science Monitor,* Apr. 22, 1986, p. 15.
29. Ibid.
30. Ibid.
31. See, for example, Robert M. Press, "Africans Join Protests for Multiparty Rule," *Christian Science Monitor,* Apr. 11, 1990, p. 1.
32. Todd Shields, "Kenya: The Queuing Controversy," *Africa Report,* vol. 33, no. 3 (May-June 1988), pp. 47–49.
33. *Nairobi Weekly Review,* Feb. 12, 1988, pp. 16–18, and Apr. 1, 1988, pp. 4–26; see also Shields, "Kenya."
34. Linsey Hilsum, "The Dynamics of Discontent," *Africa Report,* vol. 33, no. 1 (January-February 1988), pp. 22–26.
35. Ibid., p. 24.
36. Ibid.
37. U.S. Department of State, Bureau of Public Affairs, *Current Policy No. 1148* (Washington, D.C.: Government Printing Office, 1989), p. 4.
38. Todd Shields, *Africa Report,* vol. 33, no. 6 (November-December 1988), p. 50.
39. John Battersby, "Violence Clouds S. African Hopes," *Christian Science Monitor,* Mar. 23, 1992, p. 2.

PART VII

Latin America

Mexico
Cuba
Dominican Republic
Virgin Islands
Belize Jamaica Haiti Puerto Rico Guadeloupe
Guatemala St. Lucia Barbados
El Salvador Nicaragua St. Vincent
Honduras Trinidad and Tobago
Costa Rica
Panama Venezuela
Colombia
Ecuador Guyana
Suriname
French Guiana
Peru Brazil
Bolivia
Paraguay
Uruguay
Chile Argentina

MEXICO

Area: 761,604 square miles
Population: 88 million
Density per square mile: 116
Languages: Spanish (official), American languages
Literacy rate: 87%
Religions: Roman Catholicism
Monetary unit: peso
GNP: (1991) $252 billion; $2,870 per capita

BRAZIL

Area: 3,286,470 square miles
Population: 153 million
Density per square mile: 47
Languages: Portuguese (official), English, German, Italian
Literacy rate: 81%
Religions: Roman Catholicism
Monetary unit: cruzeiro
GNP: (1991) $447 billion; $2,920 per capita

ARGENTINA

Area: 1,065,189 square miles
Population: 33 million
Density per square mile: 31
Languages: Spanish (official), Italian
Literacy rate: 95%
Religions: Roman Catholicism
Monetary unit: peso
GNP: (1991) $91 billion; $2,780 per capita

19

The Spanish Conquest and Its Aftermath

Latin America owes its name to the Latin-derived languages spoken there (Spanish and Portuguese). The region encompasses Mexico and Central America, the Caribbean, and South America. Its thirty-four sovereign states range in size from Brazil, which is larger than the contiguous United States, to the tiny islands of Barbados (about one-tenth the size of Rhode Island), Antigua, Barbuda, Saint Kitts, and Nevis. The actual Latin states, in which Spanish or Portuguese is the principal language, number only twenty; of these, all except Brazil, colonized by Portugal, were once under the colonial rule of Spain.

Central America comprises seven independent nations: Belize, Costa Rica, El Salvador, Guatemala, Honduras, Nicaragua, and Panama. (Mexico, though usually considered part of Central America, is historically and geographically apart from it. Central America together with Mexico is sometimes called **Middle America**.) Two years after they broke from Spain in 1823, Guatemala, Honduras, El Salvador, Costa Rica, and Nicaragua formed the United Provinces of Central America. This union lasted until 1838. Since then, repeated attempts to restore the union—some twenty-five in all—have failed.

With a land area of nearly 6.9 million square miles, **South America** is the world's fourth-largest continent. (North America's landmass is about 9.4 square miles.) South America has some of the highest mountains in the world (the Andes), the largest rain forest (the Amazon Basin), and some of the oldest advanced civilizations in the world (including the Incan). South America's multiplicity of native cultures complements its geographic diversity.

The Caribbean region consists of hundreds of islands in a chain running from northern South America to just south of Florida. The southernmost islands are Trinidad and Tobago; the northernmost are the Bahamas. Cuba is by far the biggest of these islands. Some, like Cuba and the Dominican Republic, are

Spanish-speaking; in others, the primary language is English, French, or Dutch. The Caribbean islands are culturally diverse and only tenuously connected by strands of history or commerce to the rest of Latin America. These islands are often called the **West Indies**. Geographer David Lowenthal aptly characterized the difficulty of generalizing about this subregion:

> Alike in not being Iberian [Hispanic], the West Indies are not North American either, nor indeed do they fit any ordinary regional pattern. Not so much undeveloped as overdeveloped, exotic without being traditional, they are part of the Third World yet ardent emulators of the West.[1]

Although language is a common denominator throughout most of the region, Latin America as a whole is a diverse mixture of nations and cultures, to which Spain, Portugal, England, France, Italy, the Netherlands, Africa, and the indigenous people have all contributed.

Nor do experts agree on the extent to which Latin America comprises a unity. Some, like Chilean historian Claudio Veliz, argue that the Iberian inheritance is an essential part of Latin American life. Others, like U.S. political scientist Lawrence Graham, demur. In Graham's view, "generalizations about Latin American cultural unity are no longer tenable." But he notes that nationalism is a powerful force in the region and that "one of the effects of nationalism has been to . . . lead growing numbers of individuals within the region to identify with their own nation-state before they think in terms of a more amorphous land mass called Latin America."[2]

As far as Latin America is concerned, stereotypes and generalizations impede understanding. Every state in the region has distinctive features. But the region does have a common heritage rooted in the historical influence of Spain and Portugal and thus in the cultures of the Mediterranean. This European—Iberian—connection has not resulted in carbon-copy cultures, but with few exceptions, it has profoundly influenced each individual culture.

Land, Population, and Resources

As we have seen throughout this book, physical environment influences the history of nations and regions in many ways. None of these influences is more basic than geography.

In Latin America, geographic factors have often hindered economic development and impeded state-building—the spread of the state's administrative and political institutions, popular recognition of the state's legitimate authority, and growth of a sense of citizenship as evidence in identification with the state's symbols, aims, and interests. Throughout much of the region, the progression from local to national loyalties so essential to state-building has been blocked by physical barriers—mountains, jungles, and sparsely inhabited plains. In Bolivia, for example, most natives identify themselves not as Bolivians but as members of a tribe, village, or region. The same is true in Guatemala, in Peru, and elsewhere.

Geography

The most important aspect of Latin America's geography is its location in the Southern Hemisphere, for a host of climatic, political, economic, diplomatic, and cultural reasons. Generally speaking, the climate is warmer and wetter than in North America. The vast rain forests of South America's Amazon Basin, for example, are enormously important from an environmental standpoint and have no true counterpart on other continents. Temperature, rainfall, and altitude also set South America apart environmentally. And the geographic diversity within Latin America is equally striking.

South America   The continent of South America divides quite naturally into three main parts: the northern Andean countries of Venezuela, Colombia, Ecuador, Peru, and Bolivia; the Southern Cone countries of Argentina, Uruguay, Paraguay, and Chile; and Brazil (which occupies almost the entire eastern half of the continent), plus, to its north, the small states of Guyana (formerly British), Suriname (formerly Dutch), and French Guiana (an overseas department of France).

The majestic Andes, with peaks reaching nearly 23,000 feet in Chile and Argentina, stretch all the way from Venezuela to the tip of the Southern Cone. This massive mountain range bisects South America, separating the narrow western coastal plain from the rest of the continent. It also divides the countries it passes through into separate regions, with important political, economic, social, and cultural consequences.

From the standpoint of settlement patterns, South America appears to be a "hollow" continent in that most large urban centers are coastal and interior development is minimal.

Middle America   The Andes are justly famous; less famous is the chain of volcanic mountains that extends from Mexico through Central America. These mountains have influenced history in several ways. As barriers to communication, for example, they have complicated the process of national integration. Because their terrain is difficult or impossible to cultivate, they have also impeded economic development. The mountains that form the spine of Middle America rise along major fault lines. Volcanic eruptions and earthquakes have reduced thousands of villages and nearly every major city in this region to rubble and ash at one time or another. In recent years, massive earthquakes have devastated Mexico City in the north and Managua, the capital of Nicaragua, farther south. Disastrous floods are also common, due to heavy rains from May to October, and along the coast, hurricanes are a familiar threat as well.

A kaleidoscope of microclimates and environments, Central America can be divided into four geographic subregions: northern Guatemala and Belize (an extension of Mexico's Yucatán peninsula); the Caribbean coasts of Guatemala, Honduras, and Nicaragua; the Pacific volcanic region, and the Costa Rica–Panama isthmus. The cultural and political history of Central America is anchored in the highlands and Pacific plains, the areas most hospitable to human habitation.

Population Patterns

The people of Latin America are as diverse as the land. Except in the West Indies, descendants of the Spanish or Portuguese colonial rulers form the nucleus of a social and economic elite throughout most of the region. At the bottom of the socioeconomic order is Latin America's large and culturally differentiated Indian population. For the most part, the Indians of Latin America have clung tenaciously to their traditional values and beliefs and have resisted modernization schemes drawn up by urban elites, who remain foreigners in their eyes. Attached to a particular locality and oriented toward village and family, native inhabitants still do not view themselves as Guatemalans, Nicaraguans, or Peruvians. They typically live in rural poverty, often far from the center of government, victims of benign neglect or even official abuse.

The elites are European or Europeanized, urban in outlook, university-educated, sophisticated, and stylish. They typically live in affluent neighborhoods, preferably in capital cities. They constitute the professional class—politicians, businessmen, bureaucrats, lawyers, doctors, engineers, academics, and the like. The cities are also home to absentee landlords, the scions of old money for whom land ownership is not only a source of wealth but also a status symbol and proof of pedigree, which is important to many Latin elites.

The Melting Pot   South Americans have a three-layered ethnic heritage—Iberian, Indian, and **mestizo** (mixed blood)—but intermarriage has blurred ethnic distinctions. Ethnic commingling is most dramatic in Chile, which is 95 percent European and Spanish-Indian; it is least evident in Argentina and Uruguay, which are overwhelmingly Spanish-European. Unassimilated Indians are most prevalent in the Andean countries of Bolivia, Peru, and Ecuador, a reminder of the Incan civilization that once flourished there. (For example, over half the population of Bolivia is Indian.) In Venezuela and Colombia, Spanish and Indians are outnumbered by mestizos, who constitute about 60 percent of the population. Mestizos are a major segment of society in most of Latin America. There is little or no stigma attached to mixed blood, and mestizos, though not Indians, are prominently represented among social, political, and economic elites.

In Central America, a similar pattern holds, with one notable exception: here **Ladinos** are a major element in the population. The word *Ladino* refers to anyone who has been latinized, but it means different things in different places. In Guatemala, it is synonymous with *mestizo,* a person of mixed blood;

elsewhere in Central America, it refers to an Indian who has adopted European ways.

Initially, Ladinos were caught between two cultures and rejected by both—they looked Indian and acted "white." But they excelled as entrepreneurs and became agents of social change, modernization, and national integration. Today, Ladinos are local leaders in Guatemala, Nicaragua, Honduras, and El Salvador.

Urbanization, Migration, and Poverty   Since the Spanish conquest, culture in Latin America has been inseparable from city life. A bias against the harsh, remote, and "uncivilized" world beyond the city gates permeates the thinking of the elites and the middle class, who dominate Latin society and define its values. Latin culture is highly social—networks of families and constant interaction with friends and neighbors are the norm. In fact, there are more cities with a population of over half a million in Latin America than in the United States, even though the United States is far more advanced industrially (urbanization and industrialization are often viewed as inextricably entwined).

In recent decades, Latin America has been the scene of major population shifts from the countryside to the cities. This migration cannot be explained by cultural factors or by the lure of bright city lights alone. Rather it is driven by land scarcity, population pressure, insurgency, rural poverty, and the promise of a better life. The appeal of an improved situation in the city turns out to be an illusion for most migrants.

The influx of people from impoverished rural areas has been particularly heavy in the cities of Middle America. The population of Mexico City, for example, exceeded twenty million by 1990 and continues to grow at an alarming rate. The government's capacity to provide essential services such as running water, electricity, sewage disposal and treatment, garbage removal, street maintenance, neighborhood schools, and fire and police protection is overwhelmed. Shantytowns have sprung up on the outskirts of mushrooming urban centers like Mexico City; living conditions in them are wretched by any standard. Such overcrowding and urban poverty no doubt contribute to the steady flow of illegal immigrants coming from Mexico to the United States every year—mass migration is almost always a symptom of social and economic ills. In 1992, Mexico sought a customs union with the United States and Canada. Whether a North American Free Trade Association (NAFTA) would energize the economy and improve the wretched living standards so common in Mexican society remains to be seen.

In Central America, El Salvador has experienced the most intense population pressure. There is simply too little land to go around now that the population is growing at a rate of 2.9 percent a year—second only to Nicaragua (3.0 percent) in Central America. Most of the land is devoted to export crops—primarily cotton and coffee—or to cattle raising. Thus it is little wonder that land reform has been a burning issue in El Salvador and that a rural insurgency has torn the country asunder. Nor is the problem of land scarcity in El Salvador likely to be resolved: even if agrarian reform were implemented (which is highly unlikely), there would still be too little land to go around.

Thousands of Salvadorans migrated to Honduras in the 1960s in search of land or jobs in commerce and industry. By the end of that decade, some 75 percent of all foreigners in Honduras were from El Salvador. The resulting tension was a contributing cause of the two-week war that broke out between the two countries in 1969.

Depopulation of the countryside is also occurring in South America. Peru and Bolivia provide striking illustrations. In both cases, people from the impoverished highlands, facing famine, have fled to the cities. In the case of Peru, natural disasters and a vicious guerrilla war in the southern Andes have played a role as well. At present, six million people, or nearly one-third of Peru's population, live in Lima, the capital. Most newcomers have no money, no education, no job, and therefore no choice but to become squatters, settling in squalid suburban communities that Peruvians euphemistically call *pueblos jovenes* ("new towns").

Although migration is not acute everywhere, it is pervasive throughout Latin America. Where the grass looks greener on the other side of the border, immigrants (and refugees) flock to neighboring countries. Venezuela has had an immigration problem somewhat analogous to that of the United States' problem with Mexico. Since the early 1970s, when Venezuela experienced an oil-export driven economic boom, Colombians have been crossing into Venezuela illegally in search of high-paying jobs.

Thus population movements pose serious problems for many governments in the region. If the trend reflected positive marketplace conditions—economic growth and labor shortages—this geographic mobility would be healthy. Unfortunately, in contemporary Latin America, it reflects negative conditions—poverty, hunger, insurgency, and despair.

Natural Resources

In resources, Latin America is neither rich nor poor. Mexico and Venezuela are both significant petroleum producers and exporters. Chile, Brazil, and Colombia have many kinds of minerals. Brazil and Colombia also have precious gemstone deposits. Colombia, for example, supplies 90 percent of the world's emeralds, and Brazil has diamonds. Both countries produce gold.

In addition to mining, Latin America has rivers that produce hydroelectric power, and Brazil has the world's largest rain forest. Also, the region has long been a major food producer. Although some states in Central America are sometimes derisively labeled "banana republics," they are also important producers of such export crops as cotton, sugar, and coffee. The same holds true for South America. For example, coffee accounts for 50 percent of Colombia's annual legal exports, and Brazil produces more coffee than any other nation in the world. Argentina is a leading producer of beef and feed grains.

Colombia, Bolivia, Peru, and Ecuador are the world's leading coca producers and supply most of the cocaine sold in the United States. Although coca may not be considered a commodity by many observers, it is the major export crop for several countries in the region. Coca plants are extremely hardy, grow in a variety of climates and at different altitudes, and yield by far the highest income for the peasants who cultivate them. South America's illegal drug trade is estimated in the billions of dollars.

Latin American Development and Dependency

In a 1916 essay titled "Imperialism: The Highest Stage of Capitalism," V. I. Lenin advanced a thesis about the economic causes of nineteenth-century imperialism. He characterized the processes of advanced capitalist development as follows:

1. The concentration of production and development of capital to such a high stage that monopolies come to dominate economic life.
2. The merging of bank capital with industrial capital; the resulting "finance capital" gives rise to a powerful "financial oligarchy."
3. The export of capital becomes more important than the export of commodities.
4. The internationalization of monopoly capitalism; world markets are shared for mutual profit.
5. The territorial division of the entire globe by the greatest capitalist powers is consummated.[3]

Lenin argued that imperialism could generate higher profits for monopoly corporations by exploiting cheap Third World labor and pirating natural resources. Part of these profits, in turn, could be used to buy off potentially militant unionized workers in the West (Lenin called them the "labor aristocracy").

Closely related to this line of analysis is the leftist view that Western-based multinational corporations (MNCs) have, in effect, created a new kind of colonialism, *neocolonialism*, by substituting corporate economic domination for control by imperialist powers. The MNCs allegedly manipulate Third World governments by co-opting leaders, exploiting elite fears of leftist revolution, subverting the military with arms aid, and interfering in domestic politics. An oft-cited case in point is Chile in the early 1970s. The United States government, in conjunction with U.S. corporate interests, mounted a covert operation to destabilize the government of Chile's popularly elected socialist president, Salvadore Allende. According to one critic:

> MNCs have attempted, through privileged links to the State Department, the CIA, and the Pentagon, to undermine policies and overthrow regimes that threaten their interests. . . . The MNC would of course prefer not to have to "get tough" in order to assure a favorable investment climate; but in fact it does get tough when its profit margins are at stake, and it can call in some pretty powerful friends to help it get its way.[4]

This vehement criticism of Western governments, banks, and corporations, including such U.S.-dominated world organizations as the International Monetary Fund and the World Bank, has been echoed in the writings of the so-called dependency theorists. The genesis of this school of thought, which has been extremely influential among Latin American political and intellectual elites, is instructive:

> Special hopes and much publicity had been given to the Alliance for Progress, a United States–sponsored investment and aid program of the 1960s, the goal of which was to achieve a breakthrough to sustained and independent economic development for at least several Latin American nations. The spectacular failure of the Alliance (judged by both friends and critics) led to a thorough critique of conventional Western models (Rostow, Kuznets) of economic development, which spelled out a general "do it like we did it" approach. This critique in turn led to a new theory of dependency, which accounted for the failure of Western-style development to appear in Latin America and also predicted that real development would not appear as long as the dependency syndrome lasted.[5]

Significantly, **dependency theory** was first propounded by a group of Latin American economists (Dos Santos, Sunkel, Cardoso, Casanova, and Frank). As we have seen, it has since been applied to Africa and Asia as well. Unfortunately, dependency theory tends to obscure the extremely inequitable conditions that socioeconomic elites have both created and perpetuated. Dependency theorists consider these elites to be part of a **comprador** class, created by foreign imperialists and capitalists who needed the help of local elements. Seen in this light, dependency theory is a self-serving rationalization for homegrown inadequacies and failures.

It is difficult to generalize about development in Latin America because the picture differs considerably from one state to the next and even from one part of a state to another. Many Latin American nations have made great strides politically, economically, socially, and culturally, but much remains to be done to spread the benefits of economic development to the roughly 160 million Latin Americans living in extreme poverty.[6]

Political History and Culture

Many studies dealing with the development of Latin American political institutions begin at the wrong point—the Spanish conquest or the start of the independence movement in the early nineteenth century. But the Spanish could not impose new institutions until they had displaced, destroyed, adapted, or assimilated the cultures and civilizations that were already there.

Latin America's Original Civilizations

The Incas, the Mayas, and the Aztecs developed the three most advanced native cultures in the Americas. The Incan Empire stretched two thousand miles along the high mountains and plateaus of the Andean range in South America. It was based in what is now the city of Cuzco in southern Peru, north of Lake Titicaca.

From Cuzco, the Incan monarch, or *Sapa Inca,* controlled a highly centralized empire.

When the **Incas** expanded their territories, the peoples they conquered were fully integrated into the political system and were required to learn the Incan language, **Quechua**. The empire was served by extensive transportation and communication systems of roads, supply posts, and runners and an advanced water system of aqueducts, irrigation ditches, and reservoirs.

Incan agriculture was innovative and efficient, and the administrative system was sophisticated, penetrating as far down into society as the family. The Incas had been established at least four hundred years by the time Francisco Pizarro arrived in the 1520s.

The Mayan civilization, anchored in the Yucatán peninsula of present-day Mexico, had existed for at least a thousand years before Hernán Cortés came and conquered it in 1519. The **Mayas**, like the Incas, were architects and scholars. They built large stone temples, developed an accurate calendar, and had a writing system (which the Incas did not have). The Mayas also surpassed the Incas in mathematics and astronomy. Religion was a vital part of Mayan life, and priests actually ruled for a time, turning the Mayan political system into a kind of theocracy.

In contrast to the peace-loving Mayans, the **Aztecs** were warlike, often attacking weaker neighbors. Entering Mexico in the 1200s, they too were empire builders, making alliances with neighboring tribes that they could not easily subjugate and collecting tribute wherever possible. They worshiped various deities and practiced human sacrifice. The pictorial writing system they developed was less advanced than that of the Mayas. Their administrative system was also inferior, but they excelled at architecture and sculpture, building immense religious pyramids and a capital city, Tenochtitlán, which was an engineering marvel. Situated in the center of a large lake, the fortress city, adorned by imposing temples and statuary, could be reached only by three causeways. It supported a population of sixty thousand families.

Many other less advanced Indian tribes inhabited the Americas. Millions of Native Americans lived within territorial and cultural boundaries etched into mental maps that had guided their ancestors and governed their way of life for centuries. One thing that all the indigenous peoples had in common was that they did not want to be liberated, converted, conquered, or enslaved. But there was no stopping the Iberian juggernaut borne by the winds from an alien world.

The Spanish Conquest

Christopher Columbus arrived in the New World in 1492 while on a quest for King Ferdinand and Queen Isabella of Spain to find a new route to the East Indies. The first Spanish settlements were established in the Caribbean, where the colonists had little difficulty subduing the native populations and forcing them into a slavery-based tribute system. Attempts to gain a foothold on the mainland were less successful, however; more advanced Indians attacked and killed some of the first explorers and slave catchers.

Spain had only recently become a unified state under Ferdinand and Isabella after a long war to oust the Moors (Arabs). As a consequence, a generation of Spaniards knew no life other than war. Unfortunately for Native Americans, many Spaniards became soldiers of fortune and journeyed to the New World in pursuit of adventure and riches.

Hernán Cortés first conquered Cuba, then cast about for another challenge. Against the governor's orders, he set sail for the mainland in February 1519 with eleven ships and six hundred men. After two years of bloody battles, Cortés finally conquered the Aztecs. His triumph redeemed his image as a rebel, and he was appointed Spanish proconsul in Mexico. The Spanish built Mexico City on the ruins of Tenochtitlán, the great Aztec capital.

Cortés sent armed expeditions into other parts of Mexico and Central America. In 1523–1524, a force led by Pedro de Alvarado defeated the Mayas. A second empire had fallen.

The conquest of the Incan Empire took longer, even though it was aided by internecine strife among the Incas themselves. Francisco Pizarro set out from present-day Panama in 1524 to explore South America. Having discovered the wealth of the Incas, he sought and received permission from the Spanish court to conquer and colonize the continent. Pizarro's charging horsemen and thundering artillery terrified the Incas, who had never seen horses or firearms; they panicked and fled.

Spain then progressively colonized the Andean empire of the Incas and moved into what are now Colombia and Venezuela in the north and Paraguay, Uruguay, and Argentina in the south. At the same time, the Spanish were also colonizing Central America. (They concluded in the 1540s that North America held nothing that would attract settlers.)

Spanish Colonial Rule

Colonizing Latin America proved to be more difficult than conquering it. The conquest brought chaos to areas where organization had once flourished. Now Spain had to build new institutions on the ruins of those it had destroyed. Nor was governance Queen Isabella's only concern; converting the Indians to Christianity was a high priority from the outset.

The Spanish needed laborers to build their cathedrals and cities and to work on their plantations, so they conscripted the Indians. The *encomienda* system was designed to compel the Indians to do what was supposedly in their own best interest: to work for pay while learning the Christian religion. Indian laborers were organized by villages where an *encomiendero,* who supervised work, religious instruction, and welfare, had virtually unlimited authority. He also collected all fruits of the land and labor he managed.

Had the system worked as intended, the Indians' dignity and freedom would have been respected. But flagrant abuses occurred. Many of the *encomienderos* were petty tyrants. The Indians, forced to do grueling work, became slaves. The hard labor killed many conscripts, especially in the Caribbean islands, where entire native populations were wiped out. (They were replaced with slaves from Africa, which is why blacks now make up the majority of the population throughout much of the Caribbean.)

In most of Latin America, Indians remained the primary labor source, particularly in the high elevations to which they were adapted. In these areas, the Spanish divided villages into sections and forcibly drafted about one man of every seven to work in the mines or elsewhere until another section relieved them. Laborers were supposed to be paid, and there were limits on the distance they could be taken from home. But abuses were common, and Indians were frequently overworked and poorly fed, housed, and clothed. Many died in the mines.

Despite efforts of the Spanish crown to protect Indians' rights and prevent their exploitation, the colonists always prevailed. The *encomienda* system lasted well into the eighteenth century, when it was finally outlawed. By this time, however, colonial overlords had imposed Spanish culture and Christianity on the Indians, leaving a legacy of hatred and prejudice that remains a major cause of civil strife in parts of the region (especially Peru and Guatemala).

Nor did exploitation of the Indians end with the demise of the *encomienda* system. Ironically, the natives were forced to help destroy their own empires and build a new one. Persecuted and proselytized, they found their cultures, languages, and identities threatened with extinction. That cultures are often more resilient than political systems is evident in the fact that the Spanish Empire is long gone, but some of the Indian cultures have survived. For example, 30 percent of the people in Peru still speak no Spanish; they speak Quechua, the language of the Incas.

The basic problem inherent in Spanish rule was that the crown wanted to maintain direct control over its colonial empire, but its proconsuls had to make decisions and react to conditions on the spot. (Communication between the colonies and the royal court, dependent on ship traffic, took months.) To resolve this dilemma, a system was eventually established whereby an official appointed by the crown exercised full authority within a designated territory. The **viceroys** (and their captains general) were responsible for enforcing laws, collecting taxes, running the government, spreading Christianity, and commanding the Spanish army within their jurisdiction.

Besides being inefficient in structure and practice, the colonial administration of the Spanish Empire became corrupt to the core. Some Spanish officials served with honor and distinction, but they were the exceptions. More commonly, unqualified people of poor character curried favor with the crown in order to get a colonial post in the Americas. By the end of the sixteenth century, positions were simply awarded to the highest bidder. Political favors, promotions, the legal system, tax collection—all had their price. Property ownership came with no guarantees of permanence, and even inspectors sent to check on officials were not above taking bribes. In the words of one historian, "Corruption was universal and in most cases unpunished. The public treasury was defrauded in countless ways, and justice (or more frequently injustice) was for sale in the courts."[7]

The Role of the Church   Under the Spanish colonial administration, a special relationship between church and state developed. Catholicism had been the official religion in Spain since the heyday of the Roman Empire, and the Spanish crown was determined to export the "one true faith" to the New World. To this end, Spain barred from the colonies all non-Spanish and non-Catholic immigrants.

With a near-homogeneous religious population in colonial Latin America, the Catholic church became very powerful, overseeing baptisms, weddings, registration of births and deaths, religious processions and festivals, holidays, and charities. It built and managed the schools, hospitals, asylums, missions, and cemeteries and operated its own system of civil and criminal courts. The church amassed great wealth, receiving 10 percent of the taxes as well as bequests of money and land from the estates of the rich. It also controlled much of the banking system, many mortgages on personal property, and much land in its own right. Church revenues were tax-exempt.

The power of the church reached its zenith during the **Spanish Inquisition** of the sixteenth century. The Spanish crown established tribunals in Lima in 1570 and Mexico City in 1571 to punish heretics and other religious offenders with property loss, imprisonment, exile, or even death, sometimes by burning. Other repressive measures included press censorship and book burning.

The church eventually came to be perceived as a threat to the state. In 1767, Charless III expelled the **Jesuits**—a Roman Catholic religious order founded in 1534 that had played a leading role in the colonial phase of the Spanish Inquisition—from Spain and the colonies. This battle was only the beginning of a long struggle between church and state in Latin America. The conflict pitted liberals, who wanted to reduce church power and enact religious reforms, against conservatives, who supported minor church reforms but generally aligned themselves with the clergy.

The church-versus-state dispute lasted until the 1820s—well beyond the period of Spanish rule—and became particularly acute in Mexico, Central America, Colombia, and Ecuador. The liberals, who eventually won out, instituted religious reforms that abolished many of the church's privileges. Years of struggle, however, were largely for naught:

> In most instances . . . all that the people obtained from the expensive, bloody, and prolonged conflict was a little more freedom in religion—in which they were not seriously concerned, since they were content to remain Roman Catholics—and somewhat broader opportunities for education.[8]

In the end, the church retained its religious monopoly and much of its prestige, but its power and wealth were curbed.

Control of Trade   Despite the tension between the church and the Spanish crown, religion was an instrument of Spanish imperial rule. Another was a crude form of **mercantilism**—the plundering of the region's natural resources. Spanish indifference to the material well-being of the colonies contrasted sharply with the crown's solicitude for the spiritual welfare of the Indians. Spain actually discouraged economic development in Latin America, concentrating instead on extraction and export of raw materials, particularly gold and silver. The crown never even took full advantage of potentially profitable cash crops, such as sugar, indigo, and cacao.

Besides neglecting economic growth in the colonies, Spain also imposed severe trade restrictions on them. Only two Spanish ports, Seville and Cádiz, were allowed to carry on trade with the colonies, and all imports had to pass through New Spain (Mexico) or Peru. Tough restrictions also governed trade among the colonies themselves. Lone ships sailing between Spain and the New World would often be captured by foreign powers or pirates, so after 1550, almost all trade was done in fleets of merchant ships or convoys sailing under the protection of the Spanish navy.

Class Conflict   Spanish colonial administrators also had to deal with tensions between newly developing social classes. Of particular concern was the animosity between **Creoles**, Spanish descendants born in the New World, and the *peninsulares,* immigrants from Spain. The crown persisted in giving preferential treatment to "pure" Spaniards whose ties to Spain were most direct; Creoles greatly resented this discrimination.

The mestizos ranked next in the Latin American caste system. Intermarriage between Spaniards and Indians occurred partly because few Spanish women immigrated to the New World. Mestizos were not accepted as equals by the Creoles, although some white fathers succeeded in conferring upper-class status on their children of mixed blood.

Next in rank came the **mulattoes**, of mixed Spanish and African blood, and the **zambos**, of mixed African and Indian blood. Both groups held lower status than the mestizos, but none of the mixed races suffered from open discrimination. The lowest classes were the Indians, free Africans, and African slaves, in that order. Members of these groups were discriminated against in education, employment, and other areas.

Class conflicts thus became a natural part of the Spanish Empire in Latin America. Government policy was flawed and unenlightened from start to finish. Having discovered the New World by accident, the Spanish crown did not know what to do with it. By the time Spain finally decided that its highest priority in the colonies was to keep other powers out, its conquistadors had already destroyed three native civilizations. Overlooking Latin America's long-range economic potential, Spain adopted a short-range policy of exploitation that favored extraction over cultivation. Meanwhile, the Spanish left the "Indian problem," as well as the social and cultural development of the colonies, to the Roman

Catholic Church, which itself exploited the Indians and resented every intrusion of secular authority.

The Spanish colonists could accept the sad state of affairs in Latin America out of blind loyalty. But a new class of native-born Latin Americans was emerging to challenge colonial rule. One of the most urgent tasks of the new leaders would be to fill the vacuum the Spanish would leave behind.

Independence and Self-Government in Latin America

The conquest of Spain by Napoleon and the abdication of Charles IV at Bayonne in 1808 undercut the authority of the Spanish proconsuls in the colonies. Most of the colonists, even the rising Creole and mestizo classes, had no desire to exchange Spanish tutelage for French. Latin America's turbulent independence movement grew out of the confusion and disarray that followed Spain's fall. (By contrast, Brazil, a Portuguese colony, made a peaceful transition to independence, which probably accounts for the relative stability that has characterized Brazil's political development.)

Latin Liberation

Simón Bolívar, the most famous of Latin America's early freedom fighters, led an abortive revolt against Spanish rule in the summer of 1811; two years later, he captured Caracas, the capital of Venezuela, and earned the title "the Liberator." After the British defeated Napoleon in 1815, however, Ferdinand VII ascended to the Spanish throne and sent a force of ten thousand men to crush the New World revolution. Other early insurrections met a similar fate. But the virus of revolt spread like an epidemic, and Spain could not contain it.

The conflict pitted not only Spain against the colonies but also colonist against colonist. More than a war of national liberation against Spain, the independence struggle was actually a series of civil wars. As the ranks of revolutionaries swelled, a nearly equal force of colonists loyal to Spain rose up to defend the crown's interests. Much of the fighting was thus between local royalist and revolutionary forces, a split that persisted even after independence had been won.

Order out of Chaos

Independence from Spain was achieved in the mid-1820s, but the newly independent states soon encountered many of the same problems as the Spanish had had in establishing stable systems of government. The first turbulent decades after independence were marked by power struggles in which *caudillos* (strongmen) played a prominent role in many countries. Brazil and Chile enjoyed relatively stable government, but other countries—notably Argentina, Mexico, Colombia, and Venezuela—were torn by civil war. Freed from the commercial restrictions imposed by Spain, Latin America (particularly Argentina, Brazil, and Chile) became more actively involved in international trade. However, Middle America and much of South America sank into a deep torpor. In general, the period from 1820 to 1870 brought more turmoil than prosperity to the region, and the population remained predominantly rural, illiterate, and poor.

Beginning in about 1870, Latin America entered the takeoff phase of its modern development as international capitalism expanded and opened up new markets around the globe. Latin America's exports consisted of foodstuffs and raw materials, for which demand was rising in Europe's rapidly industrializing nations (and later in the United States). Many Latin American nations, enjoying an unprecedented export boom, could now finance imported manufactured goods. Transportation and urban life were modernized. Argentina's economic development was especially rapid during this period. In other countries, too, national leaders saw export-driven growth and foreign capital as the keys to progress.

The new economic vitality stimulated social change. Cities grew, literacy spread, and a middle class came into being. At the same time, a new urban proletariat (and labor movements) also sprang up, especially in countries where a surge in exports created new domestic markets for consumer goods that could be manufactured locally. Social diversification accompanied urbanization in the early stages of industrial development, with important consequences for political life. The state became better organized. As new social groups (especially the industrial labor force) emerged to challenge traditional landowning elites, the stage was being set for future domestic tensions and power struggles.

The Impact of External Forces

A major change in hemispheric relations occurred with the rise of the United States as a great power. The emergence of the "colossus to the north" was dramatically evidenced in the Mexican-American War (1846–1848), the Spanish-American War (1898), and the seizure of Panama (1903). Numerous military interventions in the first three decades of the twentieth century confirmed the new patterns of power and influence in the Western Hemisphere.

The worldwide depression of the 1930s, followed by World War II, greatly disrupted the international economy and ushered in the third phase of modern Latin American history. The export-driven economies of the region saw their foreign markets dry up. Without export earnings, the Latin nations could not service their overseas debt and were soon cut off from foreign financial markets. Every country except Argentina and Haiti defaulted. The crisis led directly to greater state intervention in the economy, and "import-substituting industrialization" now became a prominent strategy.

World War II brought a new surge in the region's exports that in turn helped finance industrialization. By 1960, Argentina, Brazil, and Mexico had become the leading industrial nations in the Third World, with Chile and Colombia close behind. The smaller nations, however, remained dependent on agriculture and mining. All the while, the role of the state—particularly in banking, market development, and industry—continued to grow.

As industrialization advanced, the process of social differentiation also accelerated. The middle class and organized labor gained political power, although true pluralistic multiparty systems did not develop (except in Chile). Broad-based populist coalitions ruled for extended periods in some countries—for example, in Brazil under Getúlio Vargas and Argentina under Juan Perón. In Mexico, one-party rule became entrenched.

From the 1930s to the 1960s, Latin America displayed a variety of political systems, including civilian democracies and military dictatorships. Whatever the specific disposition, however, the shadow of the *caudillo* and the possibility of a coup were ever present.

Political Culture

The past impinges on the present through its power to shape the values, perceptions, and predilections of a nation or, as in Latin America, of an entire region. Many Latin leaders and academicians, as well as outside observers, blame Latin America's failure to keep pace economically with Western Europe, North America, and East Asia on basic attitudes brought from the Iberian peninsula during the period of Spanish and Portuguese colonial rule.

The Lingering Effects of Spanish Rule

Some scholars argue that a culture inhospitable to liberal democracy and innovation is to blame for Latin America's eclipse. In contrast to the settlers who colonized the United States and Canada, according to one cultural theory, the colonists of Latin America

> arrived with the notion of power and authority as invariably centralized, owing to the hierarchical organization of the Spanish crown and the conservative Spanish Catholic Church, which gave birth to the Inquisition. They saw wealth as something to be distributed rather than to be created.
>
> The English settlers of the north, on the other hand, already were used to the idea of shared power and authority and had begun to believe in the primacy of the individual, as well as the capitalistic notion of making money to make more money.[9]

The colonial experience gave Latin America a unique moral unity that was reinforced by the pervasive influence of the Roman Catholic Church and the dissemination of Spanish language and culture. The colonial administration was staffed at the highest levels by crown-appointed peninsular officials through the Council of the Indies at Seville. (After their tenure, top officials were subject to the *residencia,* an evaluation of their performance in office.)

Religious Conflict and *Caudillismo*

As mentioned earlier, when the Spanish Empire crumbled in the 1820s, a struggle developed between liberals, who were generally associated with republicanism and anticlericalism, and conservatives, who wanted to preserve the privileges of the traditional elites and saw defense of the established church as one way to do it. Liberals also came to be identified with demands for local autonomy, whereas conservatives favored a strong, centralized state. The role of Napoleon in weakening the Spanish monarchy and destroying its mystique in the colonies is significant here: Napoleon himself became a kind of model for the fledgling Latin America republics, and military prowess became the principal source of political legitimacy. Hence the military *caudillo* was institutionalized throughout the region in the first half century after independence.

Caudillismo was idiosyncratic—it depended on the personality of the leader. Simón Bolívar, liberator of Venezuela, Colombia, Ecuador, Bolivia, and Peru, epitomized this phenomenon at an early stage. Unlike Bolívar, however, most *caudillos* were pragmatic military figures who cared little about ideas, ideals, or ideologies. Constitutions were used to legitimize power seizures rather than to constrain aggressors. Venezuela, in 1811 the first to draft a constitution, has since had no fewer than twenty. Historically, law has been subordinated to order, and order has been a function of military rather than civilian leadership. A prominent military role in domestic affairs, even under civilian rule, has thus become a trademark of Latin America.

Warlords Unlimited: The Politics of *Localismo*

Localismo—a strong identity with a particular geographic area—is another salient feature of Latin American politics. Typically, *caudillos* asserted their local dominance first and only then challenged the existing ruler, if they dared. The extent of a *caudillo*'s power depended on his personal charisma, which in turn reflected his military exploits, machismo, and local reputation. If he could recruit a large enough personal army, he had a chance of toppling the current strongman (who may or may not have come to power by similar means). More likely, he would be content to rule his "fiefdom" as part of a larger and relatively loose-knit political system based on local patron-client networks.

Local political bosses were not universally loved. They were often pejoratively called *caciques* in Hispanic Latin America and *coronels* in Brazil, terms that imply a panoply of corrupt practices. *Caciquismo* is a local variant of *caudillismo*.

Militarism and localism were thus deeply embedded in the culture and even, to some degree, in the geography, which isolated small areas and made communication difficult. The Andes are seldom crossed by car or train even today. Tropical jungles also impede communication in both Central and South America. In Argentina, extensive flat grasslands (pampas) provide an excellent environment for grazing; isolation there results from the distances between haciendas or communities. Geographic isolation reinforced tendencies toward local particularism and created barriers to political integration, which helps explain why civil and, more recently, guerrilla wars have been so much a part of Latin America's history.

Hostility toward the United States, or *anti-yanquismo,* also permeates Latin American politics. This sentiment is expressed in literature as a rejection of North American materialism and in politics as a radical, sometimes revolutionary brand of left-wing extremism. The Cuban Revolution (1959), which dramatized Cuba's break with the United States, might have become a symbol throughout the region had it not been for Castro's clumsy attempts to "export revolution" by subverting other governments in Latin America. After Che Guevara, a revolutionary compadre of Fidel Castro, was killed in Bolivia in 1967, fear of communism caused a chain reaction of military coups and repressive countermeasures that wiped out all threat of revolution in most places; the anti-Americanism that helped spawn it, however, remained intact.

Damn Yankees: Bullies or Good Neighbors?

The United States is viewed with a mixture of admiration and resentment in Latin America—admiration for U.S. military prowess, power, and prestige, resentment for its "**big stick**" **diplomacy** (interventionism), which has often overshadowed U.S. efforts to be a good neighbor. The foundation of U.S. foreign policy toward Latin America was laid in the 1820s with the enunciation of the **Monroe Doctrine**, which declared the Western Hemisphere off limits to the Great Powers of Europe. In effect, the United States was replacing Spain as the dominant power in Latin America; it is no coincidence that the promulgation of the Monroe Doctrine coincided with the crumbling of the Spanish Empire in the New World. The only time the European powers violated the U.S. ban on outside interference was in Santo Domingo and in Mexico during the 1860s, when the United States was momentarily preoccupied with its own Civil War.

The United States made Mexico relinquish Texas in 1836, and after the Mexican-American War (1846–1848), it came away with Texas and the entire Southwest (California, Nevada, Utah, and most of New Mexico and Arizona). Half a century later, the United States acquired Cuba, Puerto Rico, and the Philippines in the Spanish-American War (1898). In 1903, President Theodore Roosevelt cast a covetous eye on the isthmus of Panama, wrested the desired territory from Colombia, and began construction on the Panama Canal.

Since then there has been no waning of U.S. interest or intervention in Latin American affairs. The U.S. government sent marines into Nicaragua and Honduras in 1912 (and kept a military presence in Nicaragua until the late 1920s); it sent forces to the Dominican Republic and Haiti in 1915–1916. After Pancho Villa conducted a raid against a border town in New Mexico in 1916, President Woodrow Wilson ordered a military expedition headed by General John J. Pershing into Mexico; the troops stayed nearly a year. The president

United States[4]

Atlantic Ocean

MEXICO[2]

Gulf of Mexico

Mexico City

Havana

CUBA[3]

BELIZE

JAMAICA[5]

THE BAHAMAS

HAITI[4]

DOMINICAN REPUBLIC[1]

VIRGIN ISLANDS

PUERTO RICO

GUADELOUPE

ST. LUCIA

BARBADOS

GUATEMALA[1]

EL SALVADOR[2]

HONDURAS[1]

NICARAGUA[2]

PANAMA[2]

COSTA RICA[1]

Caribbean Sea

ST. VINCENT

TRINIDAD AND TOBAGO

Caracas

VENEZUELA[2]

GUYANA[2]

Georgetown

FRENCH GUIANA

Pacific Ocean

ECUADOR[1]

Quito

Bogotá

COLOMBIA[1]

SURINAME[2]

PERU[1]

Lima

BRAZIL[2]

Recife

La Paz

BOLIVIA[2]

Brasília

PARAGUAY[1]

Asunción

Rio de Janeiro

São Paulo

CHILE[2]

Santiago

URUGUAY[3]

Buenos Aires

Montevideo

ARGENTINA[2]

Organization of American States (OAS) Member Nations:
All nations *except* Cuba and French Guiana
(United States and Canada are also OAS members)

✧ **Organization of Petroleum Exporting Countries (OPEC) Member Nations:**
Ecuador and Venezuela

☭ **Communist Government Nation:** Cuba

△ **Nations with Nuclear Weaponry**
Potential: Argentina, Brazil, and Chile

Labor Force Data: Percentage of Females in the Labor Force
[1] Less than 25%
[2] 25–29%
[3] 30–36%
[4] 37–41%
[5] 42% or more

of Mexico, though Villa's adversary, denounced the U.S. action; the venture accomplished little more than to solidify Mexican sentiment against U.S. interventionism. Anti-U.S. feeling in Mexico around this time was so intense that Mexico sided with Germany in World War I.

After World War II, the United States intervened against Guatemala's government (1953), attempted to overthrow Fidel Castro in Cuba (1961), sent marines into the Dominican Republic (1965), armed Nicaraguan rebels against Daniel Ortega's Sandinista regime (1980s), invaded Grenada (1983), and ousted Panamanian dictator Manuel Noriega (1989). In addition, the United States supported Great Britain against Argentina in the Falkland Islands War (1982).

But "big stick" diplomacy is only one side of U.S.–Latin American relations; the **"good neighbor" policy** is the other. After World War II, the United States created the **Organization of American States (OAS)** to provide a multilateral framework for hemispheric collaboration. In the early 1960s, President John Kennedy launched the **Alliance for Progress**, aimed at fostering economic cooperation and development in Latin America. More recently, the Reagan administration sponsored the **Caribbean Basin Initiative**, designed to promote prosperity, trade, and free enterprise in the Caribbean.

Today the United States is Latin America's major trading partner. Moreover, U.S. aid and investment have played a key supporting role in the region's development efforts. U.S. banks, encouraged by the government, made billions of dollars in loans available to Latin America in the 1970s, along with other Western countries; the result was a foreign debt that topped $400 billion at the end of the 1980s. The United States and the International Monetary Fund agreed to debt relief and rescheduling schemes in a number of cases, but the price that these debtor states have had to pay is high: unpopular austerity programs that put severe strains on recently established democratic institutions.

Case Studies: Mexico, Brazil, and Argentina

Now we will look closely at three Latin American countries: Mexico, Brazil, and Argentina. They are representative of the region's political patterns and trends.

Mexico

Under Spanish rule, Mexico was known as New Spain, a tribute to the flagship colony of Spain's New World empire. At independence in 1821, Mexico had the largest population in Latin America and produced two-thirds of the world's silver. Mexico City was not only the largest city in Latin America but also its cultural center. Despite these advantages, the new nation of Mexico got off to a troubled and turbulent start.

Mexico's first two constitutions were short-lived. The first election (1829) was nullified when the losing party, refusing to accept the outcome, revolted and ousted the victorious party, with help from the military. Thus precedent was set at an early stage: elections must be held for the sake of appearances, but the outcome is not sacrosanct. If the results are not satisfactory, resort to violence rather than submit; better yet, manipulate the elections to ensure the desired results.

Tug of War over Texas   The greatest figures in Mexico's political history before the Revolution of 1911 are Antonio López de Santa Anna, Benito Juárez, and Porfirio Díaz. Santa Anna, the first successful leader after independence, came to power following a revolt in 1829 and dominated politics for the next twenty-five years. He dissolved the congress and discarded the constitution. He was a tough-minded pragmatist, but his rule was destined to coincide with one of the greatest humiliations in modern Mexican history.

In 1835, the settlers of Texas revolted against Mexico City. They defeated the Mexican forces the following year and captured Santa Anna, who was forced to sign a treaty granting Texas independence from Mexico. In 1838, after several foreign powers accused Mexico of offenses against their nationals, France sent a fleet to Veracruz and demanded restitution in the form of a large cash payment. The fighting that followed is known as the Pastry War because France claimed that a baker's shop had been ransacked. Britain mediated the dispute, and Mexico paid the claim.

Worse was yet to come. In 1845, the United States annexed Texas despite a clear warning from the Mexican government that such a move would be considered an act of war. Mexico attacked but lost again. Disgraced, Santa Anna stepped down and went into exile. Mexico signed the **Treaty of Guadalupe Hidalgo** in 1848, officially making Texas, New Mexico, Arizona, Nevada, Utah, and California part of the United States. For Mexico, the loss of this vast territory was traumatic and humiliating. Nonetheless, Santa Anna returned from exile in 1853 and resumed his former role as dictator until a revolt a year later forced him to flee, thus closing one of many unhappy chapters in Mexico's history.

Mexico's Other War   The struggle between liberals and conservatives in Mexico festered. The conservatives, who identified with the church and the landed aristocracy, were in the ascendancy in the 1820s. Under Santa Anna, pragmatism had eclipsed ideology (Santa Anna and many of his contemporaries switched sides opportunistically). With the end of the Santa Anna era, the liberals, who sought to rein in the church and extend civil rights, gained the upper hand. Led by a *caudillo* named Juan Álvarez, the new liberal government embarked on major reforms aimed at reducing the power and wealth of the church. The new reforms, along with sundry individual liberties and protections, were enshrined in the constitution of 1857. But this liberal triumph did not put an end to class conflict in Mexico.

The period from 1857 to 1876 was a time of troubles for Mexico—civil war, foreign intervention, economic collapse. In 1876, Porfirio Díaz staged a *caudillo*-style military coup and embarked on the longest career of personal dictatorial rule in Mexican history (1876–1911).

The Porfiriato   The **Porfiriato**, as Díaz's rule was called, represented the triumph of pragmatism over ideology and ushered in a period of accelerated economic development. Díaz ruled as a benevolent dictator, placing prosperity ahead of liberty. Elections were rigged, and opposition was co-opted or crushed. "Plenty of administration and no politics" was a popular Porfirian slogan. Díaz stressed a state-energized market system as the key to economic revitalization. Always the pragmatist, he refused to let *anti-yanquismo* or nationalism interfere with his development strategy. He attracted foreign capital by allowing foreign investors to develop—and profit from—mining ventures, railways, and commercial agriculture.

Mexico's economic recovery under the Díaz dictatorship is the bright side; there was a dark side as well. In rural areas, the rich got richer as enterprising landlords gobbled up smallholders' lands, and protest was smothered by local *jefes politicos* (political bosses) loyal to the Porfiriato. The result was rising agrarian discontent. In the cities, too, the burgeoning middle class, educated and prosperous, resented being excluded from the political process. In the waning years of the Díaz dictatorship, the surface tranquillity was deceiving: underneath, an upheaval was in the making.

The Mexican Revolution   The upheavals that rocked Mexican society between 1911 and 1917 left the country in shambles. Francisco Madero, the leader of the revolution, wrote a widely circulated book urging the Mexican voters to reject Díaz in the 1910 election. During the presidential campaign, Díaz jailed Madero for allegedly fomenting a revolt. Díaz "won" the election, but facing the threat of civil war, he subsequently resigned.

A popular hero, Madero was elected president of Mexico in November 1911. He had little time to savor his triumph, however. The very next year, two simultaneous revolts broke out, one led by Emiliano Zapata in the south, the other led by Pancho Villa in the north. In 1913, the commander in chief, General Victoriano Huerta, overthrew Madero and assumed the presidency. Madero was killed, allegedly during an attempted escape while awaiting trial for treason.

The Mexican Revolution did not die with Madero, however. Civil war ravaged the country for several more years before the smoke cleared and Venustiano Carranza emerged as victor and president. In 1917, following seven years of turmoil, Carranza promulgated a new constitution, built on the liberal foundation of the 1857 constitution. It prescribed an impressive array of radical reforms in government, education, labor, and land tenure. For example, the new constitution prohibited presidential self-succession; embraced the principle of universal compulsory education as a responsibility of the state (rather than of the church); created a labor code that guaranteed workers' rights to organize, strike, and engage in collective bargaining; expropriated all property of religious orders; and restored communal lands to the Indians. The constitution also reduced the role of the church in political life. By secularizing Mexican society, it sought to undercut the moral authority of the power elite, whose legitimacy depended on the church, and at the same time to remove a major impediment to modernization.

Sonoran Rule and More Civil War   Scintillating in theory, the 1917 constitution was never fully observed in practice. In 1920, Álvaro Obregón, a *caudillo* from the state of Sonora who had earlier defeated Pancho Villa, came to power following the overthrow and assassination of President Carranza. His successor, Plutarco Elías Calles, dominated Mexican politics for a decade. The "Sonoran dynasty" pared down the army and drastically reduced the military budget. It sought the support of urban workers and land-poor *campesinos* as a counterweight to the military, which revolted on three separate occasions (1923, 1927, 1929) without success.

Sonoran policies combined conservative and liberal elements. Moderate land reform and anticlericalism coexisted with a preference for a strong centralized state, a capitalist economy, and a placid, productive society. In many respects, Sonoran rule resembled Porfirian rule. For example, foreign investment was encouraged, although it was more closely regulated than during the Díaz dictatorship. The 1920s brought economic progress, tarnished at times by violent social and religious strife.

A civil war over the issue of church rights raged for three years (1926–1929). In 1928, Obregón was elected to a second term as president but was assassinated by a Catholic fanatic before his inauguration. This act prompted former President Calles to found the **National Revolutionary party (PNR)**, precursor of the **Institutional Revolutionary party (PRI)**, which has dominated Mexican politics since its inception in 1946. By further institutionalizing civilian rule, the PNR in effect demilitarized the political system.

The Cárdenas Era   The PNR helped Calles maintain his dominance until 1934, when Lázaro Cárdenas, a Calles protégé, was elected president but proved to be too independent and too radical for his mentor. The resulting power struggle was won decisively by Cárdenas (Calles was sent into exile), and a period of genuine agrarian reform began.

Cárdenas also courted organized labor. In 1936, the Confederation of Mexican Workers (CTM) was founded and became an integral part of a newly constituted official party. Cárdenas pleased labor by arbitrating generous wage settlements, nationalizing the railways, and expropriating foreign oil companies (1938). Cárdenas was thus instrumental in building a broad farm-labor coalition and paving the way for Mexico's economic resurgence after 1940.

Since World War II, Mexico has undergone substantial economic development. With the PRI monopolizing power and setting priorities, the Mexican government was able to launch a modernization drive with single-minded determination. The results were extraordinary: industry surged ahead of agriculture, and manufacturing displaced mining as Mexico's economic engine. Between 1940 and 1965, the economy grew fivefold overall, agricultural output quadrupled, and population doubled. Mostly fortuitous events kept the bubble from bursting until the 1980s.

Brazil

Portugal's colonial claim to Brazil dates back to the middle of the fifteenth century, but the first settlement was not established there until 1530. Phillip II of Spain extended his royal authority to Portugal in 1580, and after a war between the Spanish and the Dutch, the latter dominated Portugal for a time. This period coincided with the heyday of the Dutch East India Company, which effectively controlled Brazil after overcoming some resistance by Portuguese settlers. The Dutch opened up trade with Brazil, but the colonists continued to revolt, eventually with Portugal's aid. The ensuing struggle ended in 1654, and the Dutch abandoned claims to Brazil in 1661.

Portugal's interest in Brazil was desultory. Gold was discovered in 1695, and diamonds were found in 1729. Settlements had been confined to the coast, but the gold rush sent a flood of fortune seekers into the interior, and towns sprang up there. In contrast to the Spanish colonies, the church in Brazil was poor and thus less politically influential. Britain helped Portugal hold Brazil in the 1700s in return for trade privileges.

When Napoleon invaded Portugal in 1807, the royal family took refuge in Brazil. This happenstance helped reverse Brazil's status as a benighted colonial backwater. Under direct rule of the Portuguese monarch, Rio de Janeiro became the capital of Portugal, and a colonial culture blossomed, complete with schools, libraries, newspapers, and banks. The king returned to Portugal in 1821, but his son, Prince Pedro, stayed behind.

Pedro, Emperor of Brazil   Back in Portugal, the ruling council tried to enact restrictions that would be harmful to Brazil. When Pedro was ordered to return to Portugal, he refused, and with a rallying cry of "Independence or death!" he declared himself emperor of Brazil on October 12, 1822. Brazil thus achieved independence without bloodshed or upheaval—in sharp contrast to the turbulence of Spanish America. Pedro ruled until 1831, when, having lost a short war with Argentina and alienated Brazilians in various ways, he abdicated in favor of his 5-year-old son.

The triumvirate-style regency that succeeded Pedro was replaced by a single regent in 1835. Five years later, the parliament ousted the regent and pronounced the youngster, age 14, old enough to rule. The coronation of Pedro II, who reigned for the next half century, ushered in a period of stability and economic development.

The First Republic   The monarchy ultimately became arthritic and inflexible in the face of social change, which, ironically, it had done much to foster. A military coup was mounted in November 1889, and the empire was replaced by a republic. General Deodoro da Fonseca headed a coalition government in which Ruy Barbosa was the outstanding figure. Barbosa drew up a constitution patterned after the federal government of the United States. The first five years, however, were characterized by power struggles among oligarchies controlling the various states. For the winner, the prize would be control of the national government. After 1894, three civilian presidents, all from São Paulo, brought a period of peace and prosperity to Brazil—the Golden Age of the first republic.

In 1922, a group of radical young army officers rebelled; in 1924, another army revolt occurred, but loyal troops suppressed it and established martial law. The first republic collapsed in 1930, a casualty of both the Great Depression, which devastated Brazil's export-dependent economy, and an increasingly chaotic political system. The military's power seizure this time was intended in part to avert civil war. Fractious rivalries among the politicians themselves is what finally doomed the republic.

The Vargas Presidency and the Estado Novo

The 1930 revolution put Getúlio Vargas in the presidential palace, where he remained until 1945. He was elected president in 1933, in Brazil's first secret ballot. In 1937, he suspended the constitution rather than relinquish the presidency. From that point on, he ruled as a relatively benevolent dictator, banning political parties, censoring the press, and creating a corporatist state, the *Estado Novo* ("New State"), in which the interests of business, labor, landowners, and bureaucrats were fused.

Brazil sided with the United States and the Allies in World War II and even sent troops to fight on the Italian front. After the war, Vargas agreed to free elections, but the military was not taking any chances: believing that Vargas would not give up power without a fight, the generals plotted a successful coup d'état and established a democratic republic that lasted until 1964.

Brazil's Short-Lived Democracy

The most important figure during this period was President Juscelino Kubitschek, who took office in 1955 vowing to give Brazil "fifty years' progress in five." During his tenure, industrial production rose by 80 percent, and economic growth averaged 7 percent a year. Brazil became self-sufficient in auto production and operated an international airline. Kubitschek's most flamboyant project was building a new capital city, Brasília, in the interior of the country on a previously barren site. But Kubitschek's profligate spending (financed, in part, by heavy international borrowing) led to debt-servicing problems and spiraling inflation. The resulting disillusionment brought a surprise winner in the 1960 election—an independent candidate named Jânio Quadros.

Quadros had a reputation for integrity and competence; for reasons that remain unclear, however, he resigned after less than a year in office. The vice-president, João Goulart, was seen by some critics as incompetent and politically inept; others view him more kindly as an embattled figure who paid a high price for trying to pull his country back from undue U.S. influence. As the economy declined and inflation soared, Goulart pursued a vaguely leftist course that antagonized not only the military but also the upper and middle classes. In the spring of 1964, the military staged a coup that had widespread civilian support. More than two decades were to pass before civilian rule was restored.

From Repression to "Decompression"   It gradually became apparent that what appeared to be just another military coup was in fact a revolution. The military junta proceeded to centralize power, drive the traditional parties into the political wilderness, and ruthlessly rid Brazil of subversive and leftist elements. Newspaper editors were harassed, all dissent was suppressed, and opponents were arrested. Torture and death squads were the junta's gruesome trademarks.

Old-guard politicians were muzzled, but the military called on civilian technocrats to engineer Brazil's economic recovery. Chief among these was the finance minister, Antonin Delfim Neto, who worked a short-lived economic miracle in the early 1970s by obtaining new loans, retiring old debts, and attracting foreign investment. Thus reinvigorated, the economy grew at an annual rate of 10 percent, inflation dropped to respectable levels (15 to 25 percent), and Brazil finally began exporting manufactures.

But the oil crisis spoiled Brazil's economic recovery. The economy slowed, and inflation rose sharply. After 1974, the military regime, now headed by Ernesto Geisel, a pragmatist, moved to ease the repressive measures still in effect. His successor, João Baptista Figueiredo, continued on this course, allowing an independent trade union movement to develop and lifting the ban on political parties. This process culminated in the election of a civilian president in 1985.

Argentina

Although Argentina's rolling plains and pampas region were ideally suited for agriculture and cattle grazing, the Spanish paid it little attention. Europe was not interested in agricultural products, and the country did not have mineral wealth to match that of Mexico and Peru.

In some ways, this benign neglect turned out to be advantageous. The process of social diversification was delayed in Argentina because economic development lagged behind that in other parts of Latin America. As a result, the class conflicts that typically accompany rapid social change were absent. Also, the Catholic church never became entrenched in Argentina the way it did elsewhere in the region. This accident of history helped Argentina avoid the religious strife that rent the social fabric of some other nations.

Argentina's stability, abundant land, and temperate climate made it attractive to European immigrants, who began arriving around 1810. A great influx of Spanish and Italian immigrants lasted through 1930, boosting the population and transforming the nation's character. Wild and lawless *gauchos* (cowboys) had once roamed the plains, but the new cattle-raising settlers created a more structured and more sedentary society. The gauchos' way of life also changed as they were integrated into the work routine of the large ranches. With ranching and meat processing to underpin it, Argentina's economy began to prosper.

A Nation in Search of a State   When Argentina declared its independence from Spain in 1816, it was a collection of "united provinces" and regions encompassing not only present-day Argentina but also Bolivia, Paraguay, and Uruguay. The hope of keeping the entire Viceroyalty of the River Plate together was soon abandoned, and attention turned to uniting the provinces of Argentina. The various parts of the new nation were controlled by *caudillos.*

The first issue to be settled was whether Argentina's structure should be federal (decentralized) or unitary (centralized). Buenos Aires favored a unitary system because it would give the capital power over the provinces. The *caudillo* rulers in the provinces favored a federal system because they wanted to retain independence from Buenos Aires. The issue sparked a civil war that finally ended in 1835 when Juan Manuel de Rosas, a provincial leader, defeated the forces of Buenos Aires and became its governor. With Buenos Aires under his control, Rosas dominated the entire country, creating an extensive domestic spy system and terrorizing his opponents. Rosas appears to have been a demagogue of the first order who ruled Argentina as a ruthless dictator.

In 1852, Justo José de Urquiza defeated Rosas in the battle of Monte Caseros and became chief executive of the Argentine federation. Buenos Aires refused to join. National unification was not achieved until a decade later, following another civil war between Buenos Aires and the federation. Urquiza withdrew from politics after the indecisive battle of Pavon (1861), whereupon Bartolomé Mitre, the governor of Buenos Aires, gained the ascendancy and persuaded the *caudillos* in the provinces to make Buenos Aires the national capital for five years.

Argentina Emerges   During the 1860s, Argentina entered a lengthy period of stability and steady economic growth. With agricultural exports leading the way, profitable farming and ranching continued to take precedence over industrial development. The large landowners were the predominant economic interest, and they enjoyed far greater political influence than any other class. New political parties emerged in the 1890s, but not until 1912 did electoral reform law create a genuine multiparty system. As a result of the new law, the nation's first popularly elected president took office in 1916. World War I brought the economic boom to an end, but the economy bounced back in the 1920s. By this time, Argentina had become the most prosperous nation in Latin America.

The Great Depression threw Argentina's export-oriented economy into a tailspin and provoked a military coup that ended fourteen years of representative democracy. A coalition of several parties, known as the *Concordancia,* held power until 1943, when the army staged another coup. The outbreak of World War II badly disrupted world trade once again and thus dealt another blow to Argentina's beleaguered economy.

For the remainder of the war, Argentina was ruled by the military. It was during this interregnum that Colonel Juan Domingo Perón, minister of war and head of the Secretariat of Labor and Social Welfare, began his ascent.

A Coup-Prone Past   Argentina, like Brazil, has a history of military intervention in the political process as well as some limited experience with democracy and civilian rule. As mentioned, an army coup in 1930 ended fourteen years of democracy. Civilian rule was restored in 1936; this time it lasted about a decade before the military again stepped in.

Juan Perón was elected president in 1946. He extended the franchise to women in 1947 and founded the **Peronist party** the following year. On the negative side, Perón's critics contend that he bankrupted Argentina and set the stage for its future economic troubles. His second wife, Eva ("Evita") Duarte de Perón, was widely admired and extremely popular, especially among Argentina's industrial workers. Perón was reelected in November 1951. (Eva Perón died the following year at the age of 33. The personality cult that soon developed around her memory became a rallying point for the Peronist party and the nation's poor.) As president, Perón stressed nationalism and social progress through an alliance between the state and organized labor. His attempt to secularize Argentina and to legalize divorce led to confrontations with the Roman Catholic Church. In 1955, he was ousted by a military coup and went into exile in Spain.

In 1973, having returned to Argentina after eighteen years in the political wilderness, Juan Perón was once again elected president of Argentina—this time with more than 60 percent of the popular vote. During Perón's enforced absence, Argentina had been plagued by political instability and a pervasive sense of drift. Many Argentines viewed Perón as a national savior; for these believers, his return was a second coming in more ways than one. But he died in 1974, leaving the task of saving the nation to his politically ambitious third wife, Vice President Isabel ("Isabelita") Martínez Perón—whose official image was calculated to capitalize on the Evita cult.

The miracle was not to be. Economic problems forced Isabel Perón to adopt unpopular austerity measures. The resulting discontent, coupled with spiraling inflation, prompted the military to intervene yet again. Following this 1976 armed forces coup, a three-man junta was set up, and Lieutenant General Jorge Videla was sworn in as president.

Argentina's "Dirty War"   During the 1970s, a left-wing guerrilla group, the Monteñeros, carried out violent acts against the government. One particularly heinous deed was the kidnapping and killing of General Pedro Aramburu, a former president. The military regime that took power in 1976 reintroduced the death penalty for abduction, subversion, and terrorism as part of a major offensive against the guerrillas. The anti-insurgency campaign worked; unfortunately, this success came at the expense of human rights. For two years, the regime waged a "**dirty war**" against subversion: people were arbitrarily arrested, imprisoned, tortured, and murdered by the security forces, who were given carte blanche to do whatever was necessary to crush the insurgency. Thousands of people the junta suspected of disloyalty simply disappeared. The odious methods epitomized by Argentina's *desaparecidos* ("disappeared ones")—estimates go as high as thirty thousand—provoked outrage in the United States and elsewhere.

(Argentina was a prime target of U.S. President Jimmy Carter's human rights crusade.)

The "dirty war" succeeded in destroying the insurgency, but it caused an international furor. In 1978, after the guerrillas had been quashed, the government eased the repression. Pressures for political liberalization mounted, and in 1981, the military government made overtures to political parties as a prelude to eventually restoring democracy. A coalition of five parties, the so-called *Multipartidaria,* urged the military junta to hold general elections. But tensions between the government and the people were exacerbated by a rapidly degenerating economic situation.

CONCLUSION

Just as sub-Saharan Africa continues to struggle with the unhappy legacy of colonialism, the countries of Latin America still bear the imprint of the brutal Spanish conquest and of repressive Spanish rule. The United States has long since replaced Spain as the dominant power in the region; the U.S. habit of military intervention in Latin America, inspired by the Monroe Doctrine and reinforced by the perceived Soviet threat after World War II, has left a residue of bitter anti-American feelings in many Latin American societies.

Unlike other former colonial areas of the world, the Americas came to be dominated by descendants of the European colonizers rather than by indigenous political elites. Historically, the most important local rulers, the *caudillos,* came to power by force and fraud more often than by free elections. The native peoples became oppressed minorities in their own homelands both in the United States and in Latin America. After World War II, the military juntas that have traditionally ruled throughout most of Latin America often enjoyed the support of the United States, despite egregious violations of human rights in some cases. This U.S. policy was an outgrowth of the Cold War: basically, any anticommunist government in Latin America, especially if it was threatened by a left-wing insurgency, could count on American military and economic aid.

Argentina did not suffer the disruptive and destabilizing effects of church-state conflict that divided Mexico in its early history. Nor did it suffer the humiliating foreign interventions, military defeats, and losses of territory that marred Mexico's debut as an independent republic. Unlike Brazil, it did not have the advantage of a unifying monarchy during most of its first half century of independence. Instead, it had to struggle long and hard with the problem of political integration. Mexico faced similar nation-building problems—how to stitch separate regions into a tightly knit union. In all three countries, the military played a major role in domestic politics. A major difference, however, is that Mexico managed to demilitarize the political process in the twentieth century; the same cannot be said of Brazil and Argentina.

Latin America does have a weak tradition of democracy, but throughout most of its history, nearly every country in the region has been ruled by military juntas or personal dictatorships. The military plays a much larger role in Latin American politics than it does in the United States or in Europe. In the 1980s, one South American government after another switched from dictatorship to democracy. Why and how are taken up in Chapter 20.

KEY TERMS

Latin America	zambos
Central America	*caudillos*
Middle America	*caudillismo*
South America	*localismo*
West Indies	*cacique*
mestizos	*coronels*
Ladinos	*caciquismo*
dependency theory	*anti-yanquismo*
comprador	"big stick" diplomacy
Incas	Monroe Doctrine
Quechua	"good neighbor" policy
Mayas	Organization of American States (OAS)
Aztecs	Alliance for Progress
encomienda system	Caribbean Basin Initiative
encomiendero	Treaty of Guadalupe Hidalgo
viceroy	Porfiriato
Spanish Inquisition	National Revolutionary party (PNR)
Jesuits	Institutional Revolutionary party (PRI)
mercantilism	*Estado Novo*
Creoles	Peronist party
peninsulares	"dirty war"
mulattoes	*desaparecidos*

STUDY QUESTIONS

1. How do Latin American political traditions and institutions differ from those of the United States?
2. Compare and contrast political development in Mexico, Brazil, and Argentina. What role did the military play in the history of these countries? How did the world wars and the Great Depression affect political development in these countries?
3. Does Latin America have abundant natural resources? Fertile farmland? Climatic conditions conducive to agriculture? Should Latin America be poor? (Use the case studies as focal points in developing a thoughtful response.)
4. What do you think it means to be Mexican, Brazilian, or Argentine? Do

Mexicans see the world much differently than Argentines or Brazilians? What similarities and differences would you expect among citizens of these countries?

SUGGESTED READING

Burns, E. Bradford. *A History of Brazil.* 2nd ed. New York: Columbia University Press, 1980.

Burns, E. Bradford. *Latin America.* 5th ed. Englewood Cliffs, N.J.: Prentice Hall, 1990.

Hopkins, Jack W., ed. *Latin America: Perspectives on a Region.* New York: Holmes & Meier, 1987.

Lowenthal, Abraham F., and Fitch, Samuel J., eds. *Armies and Politics in Latin America.* 2nd ed. New York: Holmes & Meier, 1986.

Meyer, Michael C., and Sherman, William L. *The Course of Mexican History.* 4th ed. New York: Oxford University Press, 1991.

Scobie, James R. *Argentina: A City and a Nation.* 2nd ed. New York: Oxford University Press, 1971.

NOTES

1. Paul B. Goodwin, Jr., *Latin America,* 3rd ed. (Guilford, Conn.: Dushkin, 1988), pp. 81–82.
2. Ibid., p. 3.
3. See V. I. Lenin, *Imperialism: The Highest Stage of Capitalism* (New York: International Publications, 1969), p. 16.
4. John D. Nagle, *Comparative Politics: Political System Performance in Three Worlds* (Chicago: Nelson-Hall, 1985), p. 229.
5. Ibid.
6. Lucrecia Lozano, quoted in David Clark Scott, "Ibero-Americans to Move toward Integration," *Christian Science Monitor,* July 17, 1991, p. 4.
7. Dana Gardner Munro, *The Latin American Republics: A History* (Englewood Cliffs, N.J.: Prentice Hall, 1950), p. 81.
8. J. Fred Rippy, *Latin America: A Modern History* (Ann Arbor: University of Michigan Press, 1958), p. 185.
9. Eugene Robinson, "The Battle for the Soul of Latin America," *Washington Post,* Nov. 3, 1991, p. 1.

20

Caudillos, Coups, and Constitutions

Latin America differs from North America in many ways, but no difference has been more striking than the regions' political traditions. But in the 1980s that began to change as one Latin American country after another switched from military rule to civilian government based on popular election. Democratization is suddenly a major theme in Latin America, where the tradition has been authoritarian. To dramatize the significance of this turnaround, we will begin by sketching a hypothetical Latin American government before the democratic revolution of the 1980s.

The Latin Authoritarian Model

Throughout Latin America, authoritarian regimes, often dominated by or dependent on the military, have restricted civil liberties and have paid lip service to free elections. In most cases, dictators or military juntas were closely linked to a deeply entrenched economic elite, and the most common method for replacing a government was the military coup d'état.

Patterns of Military Rule

There are several identifiable patterns of military involvement in Latin American politics. In some countries, such as Brazil and Uruguay, the army has ruled in coalition with civilian leaders. In other countries, including Peru and Ecuador, military and civilian rulers have tended to alternate in power. In still others, among them Argentina and Bolivia, the military is entrenched in the political system, but military rule, when it occurs, is unstable. Personalistic rule by a general turned president is yet another familiar pattern; recent examples include Panama under Noriega, Chile under Pinochet, and Paraguay under Stroessner. Finally, in countries such as Venezuela, Colombia, Mexico, and Cuba, the military plays a key role but has not actually ruled for many decades. Costa Rica is a genuine exception to the militarism found throughout the region: it has no standing army.

Until the 1960s, most military dictatorships fit the personalistic *caudillo* model to the extent that their legitimacy depended heavily on the prestige and personal authority of a single individual. During the 1960s and 1970s, the military in many Latin American countries entered into a limited partnership with civilian politicians, holding elections or plebiscites without giving up real power. In the 1980s, the military stepped back (except in Panama, Chile, and Paraguay) and let the politicians grapple with growing domestic problems.

Dictators or juntas sometimes held elections, but these were seldom either free or fair. More often, the government banned opposition parties (and jailed their leaders); muzzled the press; harassed, threatened, and intimidated voters; stuffed ballot boxes; manipulated voter registration rolls; bought votes; and, if all else failed, falsified election returns.

Human Rights and Wrongs

Corruption has been rampant in Latin American politics. Election fraud is just one example; bribery and extortion have also been pervasive. Worse still, politically motivated violence has afflicted many Latin American societies. Horrendous government repression has occurred in Guatemala, Nicaragua, Argentina, Chile, and Brazil. The most notorious case was Argentina's "dirty war" (1976–1982) in which as many as thirty thousand people vanished. In Argentina, as elsewhere, repression came in response to a leftist threat. Earlier in the 1970s, a military junta seized power in Uruguay after the civilian president turned to the army for help in fighting urban guerrillas. In both countries, repressive state policies had probably played a role in bringing the insurgencies into being; the insurgencies in turn prompted the governments to step up the repression. Thus in Latin America, power struggles between ruling oligarchies and disaffected leftist groups have led to violence on both sides.

Insurgencies are a fact of political life in many Latin American countries. At the start of the 1990s, guerrilla groups were engaging in armed struggle against the government in Nicaragua, Guatemala, El Salvador, Colombia, Chile, Peru, and Ecuador. The persistence and magnitude of the guerrilla problem has varied from country to country: in Venezuela, Uruguay, and Argentina, the guerrillas have been defeated, for now. In Colombia, where several insurgent groups are active, kidnapping and other terrorist acts occur regularly. In Peru, a vicious Maoist guerrilla movement, *Sendero Luminoso* ("Shining Path"), has been terrorizing the countryside and the capital since 1980; some 25,000 people have been massacred by both guerrilla and government forces.[1] By contrast, Mexico has not had an insurgency since the Revolution of 1911, but that raged for seven years and cost over a million lives.

Latin American Democracy: The Domino Effect

Until recently, to speak of Latin American democracy was almost a contradiction in terms. Excluding the Caribbean, only three nations in the region—Costa Rica, Colombia, and Venezuela—had a democratic tradition. Costa Rica is a small, neutral country with no army whose president, Oscar Arias Sánchez, was awarded the Nobel Peace Prize in 1987 for his Central American peace plan. Colombia is a troubled nation with a violent history that has nonetheless managed to function as a constitutional democracy with a two-party system and an elected president since the end of a twelve-year civil war (1946–1958). Venezuela is an oil-rich nation with a democratic political system and a federal structure that closely resemble those of the United States.

Other Latin American nations began converting to civilian democratic rule in the late 1970s, and dictatorships toppled like dominoes. In South America, the new democracies included Brazil, Argentina, Uruguay, Peru, and Bolivia. In Central America, four nations—El Salvador, Honduras, Nicaragua, and Guatemala—have instituted fragile democratic processes, but the military is still waiting in the wings in case the civilian leaders falter. Mexico remains a mixed regime, half democratic and half authoritarian; although elections occur every six years, the dominant Institutional Revolutionary party (PRI) has not lost an election in more than six decades.

The most recent elections in Latin America have been free and unfettered. Candidates have had access to newspapers, radio, and television and have campaigned without interference. Political rallies are no longer considered subversive, and elections have been intensely competitive.

Case Studies: Mexico, Brazil, and Argentina

We will now examine the contemporary political systems of Mexico, Brazil, and Argentina—three countries that fairly well represent the political traditions and institutions of Latin America; since two of them, Brazil and Argentina, have recently switched from military dictatorships to civilian democratic rule, we will also examine that trend. Together, these three countries have a larger population than that of the United States, and their combined landmass exceeds that of the United States by nearly 1.7 million square miles. Because population growth in these countries is higher than in the United States, the demographic gap will widen.

Mexico

As already noted, Mexico's political system originated in the Revolution of 1911, and the 1917 constitution was forged in a protracted and violent struggle. Recall that the Mexican Revolution was a class struggle—not between "proletariat" and "capitalists" but between the wealthy, landed aristocracy and impoverished peasants who were much like serfs in a semifeudal order. The convulsive nature of the revolt was intensified by the excesses that spawned it—extreme inequality, extreme poverty, extreme injustice, and extreme indifference to mass suffering. This was the legacy of General Porfirio Díaz (1876–1911), Mexico's last and most infamous military dictator.

The long and bitter fight against a tyrant who ruled with an iron fist for thirty-five years (a lifetime for the Mexican underclass in that dark age) produced a generation of revolutionary leaders who were determined to create a just social order. The constitution of 1917 was the instrument designed to achieve that lofty aim.

The Constitution of 1917   In theory, Mexico is a federal republic comprising thirty-one states and one federal district (around Mexico City, the capital). The constitution of 1917 assigned legislative power to the bicameral National Congress, elected by universal adult suffrage (all nationals 18 and older who have "an honorable means of livelihood"). The Senate (upper house) has sixty-four members (two from each state and the Federal District), who serve a six-year term. The Chamber of Deputies (lower house) has five hundred members directly elected to a three-year term. Three hundred seats are filled from single-member districts, and nearly all are traditionally won by the majority Institutional Revolutionary party (PRI). In 1986, the number of seats reserved for minority parties was doubled to two hundred. These seats are allocated under a scheme of proportional representation.

Executive power is given to the president, directly elected to a single, nonrenewable six-year term. He appoints both the Council of Ministers (cabinet), whose members head the various government departments, and senior military and civilian officers. The constitution of 1917 also created an independent judiciary. The federal Supreme Court has twenty-six members including a chief justice. Supreme Court justices, who must be native-born, are appointed by the president with Senate approval. The thirty-one state governors are popularly elected to a six-year term; like the president, they can never serve again. Under Article 76 of the constitution, the president can ask the Senate to remove the governor of any state in which law and order has broken down.

In sum, the constitution of 1917 set up a federal democratic republic in which powers are clearly separated among the three branches of government. The constitution also enshrined the aims of the Mexican Revolution by mandating radical land reform, drafting a labor code, and sharply curtailing the power of the Catholic church. Its provisions dealing with religion, education, and the exploitation of mineral wealth reflect the long struggle against dictatorship, the church, large landowners, and "economic imperialism."

The Mexican constitution is a thoroughly democratic document. Drafted just months before the October Revolution in Russia, it outdid even the Bolsheviks in putting workers on a pedestal. For example, Article 123 deals with labor rights. Its provisions include an eight-hour workday, a minimum wage, twelve weeks' pregnancy leave, two extra rest periods each day for nursing mothers, equal pay for equal work regardless of sex or nationality, profit sharing for workers, double pay for overtime, and appropriate compensation for job-related injuries or diseases. This list of workers' rights sounds impressive today; in 1917, it was groundbreaking.

Leaders of a party in power often pretend that things are better than they actually are. Nowhere is the contrast between appearance and reality sharper in Mexican life than in the difference between the formal workings of government (the constitution) and the informal workings (the system).

The Mexican System   "Effective suffrage, no reelection"—this was democracy in a nutshell for Francisco Madero, president of Mexico from 1911 to 1913. Half of this formula—no reelection—has been put into practice. The idea behind the one-term rule was to prevent dictatorships like that of Porfirio Díaz. The rule also prohibits members of the Congress, the state legislatures, and municipal councils from serving two consecutive terms, again to prevent an entrenched elite from regaining a monopoly on power and wealth. But almost every rule can be circumvented. In Mexico, this rule is observed in a formal sense; informally, however, the system is a game of musical chairs in which majority-party (PRI) politicians rotate from one position to another.

Though different in practice from the original intent of its authors, this system has produced nearly eight decades of political stability in Mexico. For the entire period, the government has been controlled by one party, the PRI, which has in turn fashioned a powerful coalition of government, party, labor, industrial, and agrarian leaders.

The president is the key figure in the system. To become president, a politician must have previous experience as a cabinet member; be male, youthful, and physically vigorous; and be able to mediate between the left and right wings of the PRI. The party's inner circle, headed by the incumbent president, chooses the nominee, who is always elected. In effect, the outgoing president handpicks his successor. There is no vice-president; if necessary, the congress chooses an interim chief executive. Since 1946, every president of Mexico has been a civilian.

Although the constitution gives the congress extensive power to make laws, in reality the president dominates the legislative branch. He can introduce legislation directly into both houses and can set the legislative agenda. He can also veto legislation but has never had to do so because no law that was opposed by a sitting president has ever been enacted!

The president can also make laws by decree in most areas of public policy. For example, Mexico's income tax was created by decree; only years later did the congress get around to enacting it formally. Presidential decrees have created cabinet ministries, government departments, public corporations, and major public-works projects. The budget, family planning, and nuclear energy are all areas in which policy—later to be rubber-stamped by the congress—has been effected by presidential fiat.

The most important cabinet officer is the *secretario de gobernación* (minister of internal affairs), who supervises intragovernmental relations, liaison with the congress, elections, voter and party registration, immigration and emigration, motion picture production, radio and television airtime, the federal police, and federal prisons. Other key cabinet positions include planning and budget, finance, commerce and industry, public enterprises, foreign affairs, and labor. President José López Portillo (1976–1982), for example, had been the finance minister; President Miguel de la Madrid Hurtado (1982–1988) was previously planning and budget minister.

Because the congress is dominated by the PRI, it debates the form rather than the substance of legislation. Floor debates are often vigorous but have little effect. Criticism of government policies is frequently voiced by opposition party leaders, but even this is softened by the media, which pander to the all-powerful PRI-dominated state. Seniority is not an issue in Mexico's congress for two reasons: committees do not wield real power in a legislature that is dominated by the executive branch, and members cannot serve consecutive terms.

The judiciary is independent, but judges owe their jobs to a highly politicized patron-client system. Since 1929, every Supreme Court justice has belonged to the PRI. Although corruption is endemic throughout the government, justice is frequently served anyway. The major restraint on presidential power is the **writ of *amparo*** (protection), by which federal judges can protect citizens from violations of their constitutional rights by stopping a government agency from taking action until the Supreme Court has ruled on appeal. The court may halt government action, compel officials to carry out constitutional obligations, or force judges to specify or clarify the charges against a defendant in a criminal case. Some 5,500 writs of *amparo* were issued against the president or cabinet ministers between 1917 and 1980; the Supreme Court ruled against the government in about a third of these cases.

The PRI's control extends to the thirty-one states as well. Governors are popularly elected, but the PRI inner circle, dominated by the incumbent president, decides whose name will appear on the ballot. Nomination is tantamount to election; since 1929, every state governor has been a member of the PRI. In all but six states, governors' terms do not coincide with the presidential elections, which means that each new president inherits twenty-five governors who were chosen by his predecessor. As mentioned earlier, the president can ask the Senate to remove a governor. Since 1964, presidents have exercised this prerogative on the average of only once per term; before 1964, it was used far more frequently.

The Party Machine   Mexico is a prime example of a **one-party-dominant system**. Although regular elections are held, the PRI always wins control of the government. The federal government sets the rules for the creation and operation of political parties. These rules are fairly liberal, but parties must obtain 1.5 percent of the national vote to retain their legal status. The fact that as many as nine parties have been represented in the congress at any given time suggests that the right of free association is respected and that minority parties do not have to overcome insurmountable legal or bureaucratic obstacles.

The PRI monopolizes the non-Marxist center-left on the political spectrum. Since 1933, the party has developed six-year plans for the economy; each such plan then becomes the basis for the government's official program. As its name suggests, the party claims to be the permanent custodian of an ongoing and institutionalized revolution. It embraces welfare-state policies (even though the state lacks the resources to support them), state ownership of major industries, and individual or communal ownership of land. Two of the party's most fundamental principles are "no reelection" and the right of all workers (including public employees) to strike.

In foreign policy, the PRI stresses Mexico's independence. Distancing itself from the U.S. imperialism was until recently a major motif; indeed, the PRI was long sympathetic to left-wing, anti-imperialist regimes in Cuba, Nicaragua, and Peru. The fact that Mexico lost about half its total area to the United States in the Mexican-American War accounts for some of the tension between these two "distant neighbors," as journalist Alan Riding once called them.[2]

Minority parties run the gamut from conservative to collectivist. On the right is the Partido Democrata Mexicano (PDM), which advocates reprivatization of the economy, reduction of welfare programs, an end to the PRI patronage system, and a "union of church and state." Another right-of-center party is the Partido Acción Nacional (PAN), which in the 1980s became a serious challenger to PRI control in parts of Mexico, especially in Chihuahua, Duranga, Hermosillo, and Ciudad Juárez.

On the far left, there has been an array of Marxist parties, including the pro-Soviet Communist Party of Mexico (PCM), also known as the Unified Socialist Party of Mexico (PSUM); a Trotskyite party called the Revolutionary Party of the Workers (PRT); and several other socialist and workers' parties. The PRI could not have wished for a better divide-and-conquer scenario.

Mexico's 1988 Presidential Elections   A challenge was mounted on the left in the 1988 presidential election when a new populist party, the Democratic National Front (FDN), led by Cuauhtemoc Cárdenas (son of Lázaro Cárdenas, one of the most popular presidents in modern Mexican history), forged an alliance with the Mexican Socialist Party (PMS). The PMS was created the previous fall when six leftist parties formed a coalition led by Herberto Castillo. Castillo stepped aside to clear the way for Cárdenas to run against the PRI candidate, Carlos Salinas de Gortari. Cárdenas, a disaffected former PRI leader, had forged his party in 1987 out of more than fifteen center-left groups.

The alliance between the FDN and the PMS was thus an untested merger made up of two equally untested coalitions. Although PRI candidate Salinas was declared the winner, there were allegations of massive ballot-box fraud. The

Cuba: Marxist Holdout

Cuba became a virtual U.S. protectorate after the Spanish-American War in 1898. In 1952, Fulgencio Batista seized power and established a repressive dictatorship. Seven years later, Fidel Castro led a successful guerrilla insurgency movement against Batista.

Castro denounced American imperialism and nationalized or expropriated all industrial assets and banks in Cuba, including over $1 billion in U.S.-owned properties. These actions prompted the Eisenhower administration to organize a force of Cuban exiles as the cornerstone of a covert attempt to overthrow Castro. The resulting Bay of Pigs invasion, ordered by President Kennedy in 1961, was a debacle of the first order. Not only did Castro survive it, but he emerged with enhanced prestige in the eyes of most Cubans.

The United States, which had always been Cuba's main market for sugar (its most important export), suspended trade and refused to recognize Castro's regime. Facing diplomatic and economic isolation, Castro declared himself a Marxist and turned to the Soviet Union for help. Moscow was at first reluctant to accept Cuba into the "socialist commonwealth." Perhaps as a quid pro quo for Moscow's economic subventions, Castro agreed to allow the Soviet Union to place medium-range nuclear missiles in Cuba. This decision led to the Cuban Missile Crisis in 1962, in which the Soviet leader, Nikita Khrushchev, came into an eyeball-to-eyeball confrontation with President Kennedy. Khrushchev blinked first.

Thereafter, the United States used its economic and military might to make Cuba the pariah of the Western Hemisphere. Cuba under Castro survived but did not thrive. Dependent entirely on the Soviet Union for lavish subsidies, Castro allowed Cuba to be used as an instrument of Soviet foreign policy, especially in Africa. Cuban "proxy" forces were inserted into various regional conflicts, mostly notably in Ethiopia and Angola.

At home, Castro's government was highly centralized and authoritarian. Cuba became a closed society. Castro was an absolute dictator, but apparently not an unpopular one, despite perennial allegations of human rights violations. Castro blamed Cuba's ills on the Americans.

By any standards, Cuba is economically underdeveloped. The World Bank estimates that Cuba's per capita GNP in 1991 was less than $1,500 and possibly as low as $500. One indication of Cuba's poverty is the fact that the government will not disclose any economic statistics—most likely to avoid embarrassing itself. By contrast, Cuba's social policies have apparently been quite successful. Annual population growth in the 1980s averaged 0.9 percent (in Honduras, for example, it was 3.3 percent). Life expectancy was equal to that in the United States (76 years); infant mortality was the lowest in Latin America (fourteen per thousand live births, compared to eleven in the United States); school enrollment was nearly 90 percent in 1989; and illiteracy was a mere 6 percent (it was 45 percent in Guatemala).

The dissolution of the Soviet Union deprived Cuba of its patron and protector. Whether Cuba can afford to pursue its current course is unclear. One thing is very clear, however: the costs and risks associated with past policies have escalated, while the benefits are now more in question than ever before.

---

very fact that the left managed to unite even temporarily was unprecedented and represented a significant new development in Mexican party politics.

The attempt to unite the left followed in the wake of labor unrest in Mexico. Until recently, government and organized labor worked hand in glove, but economic difficulties have led to serious friction between the PRI and the Confederation of Mexican Workers (CTM). Independent labor unions made rapid gains and for the first time posed a potential challenge to the traditional PRI domination of the political system.

In 1990, the government sponsored an election reform bill designed in part to perpetuate PRI control of the Mexican political system. Among other changes in election procedures, the new law barred electoral alliances and provided that any party receiving 35 percent of the vote would be guaranteed a majority (50 percent plus one seat) in the Chamber of Deputies. With the PRI's popularity fading but the opposition splintered, this law stacks the deck in favor of the PRI so long as it can garner slightly more than one-third of the votes.

Nonetheless, the reforms did contain measures aimed at curbing ballot-box fraud, compiling a new voter roll, and creating an independent electoral commission. These steps, among other factors, boosted Salinas's personal popularity, and in federal legislative and state gubernatorial elections in August 1991, the PRI's candidates won over 60 percent of the votes and all six of the governorships at stake.

A Revitalized Mexican Economy?   A deepening economic crisis formed the backdrop to public disenchantment with the PRI in the late 1980s. A monstrous external debt, mounting budget deficits, skyrocketing inflation, massive unemployment, a sharp decline in consumer purchasing power, a plummeting peso—these were the conditions that greeted the incoming president in 1988. Salinas lost no time in instituting new policies and programs that restored the PRI's popularity and revitalized Mexico's sluggish economy. One key element in the Salinas government's economic development strategy was the proposed North American Free Trade Agreement (NAFTA) with the United States and Canada. Mexico's economic problems and prospects in the wake of this historic treaty are explored in Chapter 21.

Brazil

Just as Mexico's constitution is far more democratic than its political system, Brazil's movement toward democracy, known as the *aberatura,* did not fix everything that was wrong with Brazilian politics. Even so, the holding of free elections in January 1985 signaled the end of two decades of military rule and the beginning of a new era in Brazilian political life.

Brazil's motto, *Ordem e Progresso* ("Order and Progress"), has been emblazoned on its flag since the founding of the republic in 1889, and those two aims have been paramount ever since. Liberty is not mentioned; nor is equality—these democratic virtues are subsumed under "progress," which ranks after "order." The motto sums up over a century of Brazilian history.

Radicals in Uniform: Military Modernizers   In Brazil, the concept of progress has always been closely linked with the stabilizing presence of a protective and centralized authoritarian state. In the 1920s, disenchanted middle-class groups joined junior military officers (*tenentes*) in opposing an oligarchy representing the interests of entrenched coffee plantation owners. They believed that the

Brazil's Constitution and Government

The constitution of 1969, amended by presidential decree in 1977 and 1978, made Brazil a federal republic comprising twenty-three states, three territories, and a federal district (Brasília). The president is the linchpin in the system. He is the supreme commander of the armed forces, issues decrees and regulations, sets the budget, proposes legislation, and appoints cabinet ministers. A legislative majority in the hands of the opposition does not block presidential action. Any measure introduced by the president automatically becomes law after forty days, even without congressional approval. The president can intervene in any of the twenty-three states without consulting the congress, and he can declare a state of siege and rule by decree.

Under the 1969 constitution, the president served a six-year term and was chosen by an electoral college made up of the members of the congress and delegates from state legislatures. In May 1985, the congress approved a constitutional amendment that provided for direct election of the president by universal suffrage. The 1988 constitution incorporated those changes and set the president's term at five years.

Brazil's congress is bicameral and, except for one-third of the senators, is directly elected. Members of the Chamber of Deputies (lower house) are elected to four-year terms, and Senate members are elected to eight-year terms. The number of deputies is based on population. The congress has the formal power to approve legislation, as well as budgets, taxes, and treaties. But most legislative power is vested in the president.

military alone could awaken the nation, unlock its pent-up energies, and spearhead modernization. They wanted to oust conservative politicians who blocked the path of progress. The *tenentes'* program included labor reforms such as recognition of trade unions, a minimum wage and a maximum workweek, and regulation of child labor. It also called for land reform, state ownership of natural resources, and expansion of the public school system. The *tenentes* faded into history, but many of their ideas were adopted by Getúlio Vargas, who staged a revolution in 1930, established a fascist-style corporatist state, and ruled as a benevolent dictator until 1945, when the generals forced him to resign.

The 1964 Coup: Revolution from Above   For the next eighteen years, Brazil was governed by a parade of civilian presidents. The parade ended abruptly in 1964 when the military—disgruntled by the leftist leanings of President João Goulart and by his failure to curb rampant inflation and official corruption—staged a bloodless coup. The military did not view this intervention as anything ordinary; it was the start of a revolution from above. As if to pick up where the *tenentes* and Vargas had left off, the military launched a major modernization drive. They would have order with progress, but it would come at the expense of freedom and dignity. Strict press censorship was imposed, and flagrant abuses of human rights became commonplace.

During the decade following the revolution of 1964, Brazil experienced an economic miracle, with growth rates averaging 10 percent a year. But the benefits went primarily to the upper and middle classes; they did not trickle down to the vast majority of Brazilians, who continued to live in poverty. Furthermore,

Brazil's development strategy was fundamentally flawed: it stressed industrialization, mechanization, and capital-intensive investment and neglected agriculture, appropriate technologies, and public-works projects that would benefit the whole nation.

During the 1970s, the miracle turned into a nightmare for Brazil's military rulers. A worldwide recession triggered by the OPEC oil embargo hit Brazil especially hard. Energy import prices shot skyward, while the price of agricultural products (about 40 percent of Brazil's exports) fell sharply. Meanwhile, the deteriorating rural economy led to a mass migration into overcrowded cities, where basic services could not keep pace. Brazil's military rulers were rediscovering the advantages of civilian government.

The Great Aberatura   The reforms of the late 1970s set the stage for a democratic reform movement, the *aberatura*. Hundreds of political exiles were allowed to return, and political parties were permitted, as long as they were not ideological and did not target a single class: the Communist party was outlawed, and a workers' party was expressly forbidden as well. (The ban on parties of the Left was lifted in 1985.)

The prohibition against a British-style labor party reflected the regime's preoccupation with order and its awareness that the crippled economy, coupled with the mass discontent it engendered, could be profoundly destablizing. This situation was alarming, in part because government and labor in Brazil had long enjoyed a relationship of mutual trust and dependency. Organized labor expected the state to protect its interests; demands for democracy were secondary. If the government, be it authoritarian or democratic, could deliver on promises of benefits to the workers, labor would support it. The government's failure in the 1970s and early 1980s to protect the workers in conditions of economic crisis severely strained this long-standing compact. Facing hyperinflation, surging food prices, and massive unemployment, labor defected in 1983, joining the rising chorus of voices demanding direct elections and civilian rule. After 1985, President José Sarney sought to placate organized labor, which remains a potent force in Brazilian politics.

Labor militancy was not the only challenge for Brazil's embattled rulers prior to 1985. New political parties proliferated.* In Brazil, party organizations are notoriously weak and often personalistic, and coalitions tend to be fragile and shifting. From 1965 to 1979, there were only two legal parties in Brazil: the progovernment ARENA party and the opposition Brazilian Democratic Movement (MDB). The former was reconstituted as the Social Democratic party (PDS) in the early 1980s; by that time, the old MDB had become the new PMDB (its founders simply added the word *party* to the name). As the 1985 elections approached, political maneuvering intensified. A dissident faction of the right-wing PDS split away to form the Liberal Front party (PFL), which subsequently entered into a coalition with the center-left PMDB. The coalition, known as the

---

* As noted earlier, the previous strictures against parties of the Left were formally abolished in 1985.

Democratic Alliance, challenged the PDS in the electoral college and won. José Sarney was the PFL's candidate; when the coalition was formed, Sarney was given the number two spot on the ticket. Tancredo Neves, the PMDB candidate, headed the winning ticket but did not live to serve. Thus as the leader of a small splinter party, Sarney become Brazil's first civilian president in over twenty years.

In addition, the Democratic Labor party (PDT), the Brazilian Labor party (PTB), and the Party of Workers (PT) merit brief attention. All three are center-left, non-Marxist, pro-labor parties. The PDT favors welfare-state policies and considers itself a social democratic party. The PTB and the PT both stress the need for further democratization of the political process.

There are also a dozen or so smaller parties that are legally registered but have negligible impact. The two most important are the Communist party (PCB) and the Socialist party (PSB). In part because the left is so badly fragmented in Brazil (as elsewhere in Latin America), the probability of a serious challenge from this side of the political spectrum is low.

One measure of Brazil's gradual march toward democracy is the number of political parties that now contest elections. Before 1979, there were just two official parties. In the 1982 elections, there were five parties; in 1986, there were more than a dozen, and eleven of these won at least one seat in the congress. This proliferation of parties is a crude gauge of the liberal democratic reforms enacted in Brazil during the 1980s.

Liberalization was advanced in the spring of 1985 when the congress legislated several significant changes in the electoral system. First, as mentioned earlier, it abolished the electoral college and provided for direct election of the president. Second, it required direct election of mayors in all municipalities and state capitals. Third, it eliminated literacy as a voting requirement, thereby

Brazil's Disappearing Rain Forest

The tropical rain forests of South America and sub-Saharan Africa generate not only oxygen but also exports worth a total of $8 billion a year. Brazil's rain forest, the world's largest, is being destroyed at an alarming rate. Vast tracts of jungle forest are being burned, adding to already dangerously high carbon dioxide levels, thinning the ozone layer over the Antarctic, and contributing to the "greenhouse effect," or global warming.

Much of the devastation of the rain forest is the result of government policies that are aimed at encouraging Brazil's land-hungry peasants (70 percent of the rural population is landless) to resettle in Amazonia, a "land without men for men without land," as a way to sidestep the politically delicate issue of land reform (0.7 percent of the farms occupy 43 percent of the cultivated land area). Brazil's disappearing rain forest provides a clear illustration of the tensions that exist between environment and development in the Third World and suggests that in a conflict between the two, the environment is likely to lose unless something is done to change the public's perceptions and policymakers' priorities.

expanding the electorate by twenty million voters. Fourth, it abolished the party loyalty rule, which obligated members of the congress to vote the party line and penalized party defectors. Fifth, it eased the establishment of new political parties and legalized Communist parties.

The Bumpy Road Back to Democracy   It took several years to effect an orderly transition from military to civilian rule. As the economy continued its early-1980s tailspin, inflation soared past 200 percent a year, and workers' incomes plunged by 30 percent. Mass protests involving as many as 1.5 million marchers erupted in the spring of 1984.

In 1985, José Sarney assumed the presidency with an impressive array of new constitutional tools. But Sarney was unable to turn the economy around. Bloated government budgets contributed to galloping inflation; in 1988, consumer prices rose 692 percent.

In November 1989, Fernando Collor was directly elected to the presidency. The transfer of power from one civilian chief executive to another was a remarkable event, given Brazil's recent history. Collor promptly initiated spending cuts and market-oriented reforms, including a liberalized trade policy that pleased the United States and the International Monetary Fund. The new president also put tough anti-inflation measures into effect, raising taxes on high incomes, freezing large savings accounts, and introducing Brazil's fourth new currency in as many years. These steps failed to stabilize the economy, however, and Collor's political fortunes went from bad to worse in 1992 as a corruption scandal led to calls for his impeachment and gave new impetus to a movement to institute a parliamentary system of government.[3]

Argentina

When Raúl Alfonsín was sworn in as president of Argentina in December 1983, it marked the end of an era of extraordinarily repressive and brutal military dictatorship. The Argentina that Alfonsín inherited was a nation in chaos. The economy was hurtling downhill like a runaway locomotive, the political system had come unhinged following an ignominious defeat in the Falkland Islands War, and the society was sullen and seething from the atrocities perpetrated by Argentina's former military rulers.

The Falkland Islands War   To divert attention from domestic problems, the government, headed by Lepoldo Galtieri, manufactured an external crisis. Argentina had long claimed sovereignty over nearby British islands that the Argentines called the Malvinas and the British called the Falklands. When negotiations failed, Argentina invaded the islands, and a short but ferocious naval war with Great Britain ensued. The British administered a humiliating defeat to Argentina in general and to the ruling military junta in particular.

Huge demonstrations against the government were followed by strikes and social chaos. The military rulers tried to stem the protest with renewed repression, but the embattled regime was now bankrupt, morally and politically. In early 1983, the government announced that general and presidential elections would be held at the end of October.

Popular Rule Again: A "Radical" Restoration   The Peronist party, which had never lost an election it contested, was the favorite to win again in 1983, but Alfonsín, the leader of the Radical party, pulled an upset by garnering 50.5 percent of the vote; his Peronist opponent could muster only 39.1 percent. (A decade earlier, Perón himself had won over 60 percent of the popular vote to the Radicals' 24 percent.) Despite this setback, the Peronists were far from dead: they won control of the Senate and many provincial legislatures and governments. The Radicals managed a slim majority in the Chamber of Deputies and captured over half of the provincial governorships.

President Alfonsín had to confront two critical issues: the economy, which was in a nosedive, and the "dirty war," whose perpetrators had mostly gone unpunished. Both issues were explosive. Inflation was soaring to new heights (well over 400 percent in 1983), gross domestic product was falling, and capital flight—a barometer of domestic investors' confidence in the future—was estimated at $2 billion.

The question of how to punish the former military rulers and their henchmen for the atrocities committed against Argentine citizens during the "dirty war" was in some ways more explosive than the economic situation. Alfonsín faced a dilemma: given the propensity of the armed forces to revolt, any move against the military risked a coup, but given public anger, any attempt to sweep the "dirty war" under the rug would provoke a groundswell of indignation. If he lost control of the situation, Alfonsín either would have to ask the security forces to intervene (shades of the dark past) or would have to wait for the army to stage another coup. Either way, he would lose—and so would the cause of democracy in Argentina.

President Alfonsín managed to finesse the situation by steering a middle course. The former military rulers were tried, and some were convicted; their sentences ranged from four-and-a-half years to life in prison. Although many Argentines thought the government had been too lenient, the military brooded, and rumors of coup plotting circulated. Nor did the matter end with the trial of the highest authorities. Several hundred lower-ranking officers were also implicated in "dirty war" atrocities, and Alfonsín promised that they too would be brought to justice. In the end, however, Alfonsín was not able to keep his promise.

Argentina's Constitution and Government   The return to civilian rule in 1983 restored the principles of Argentina's original constitution, drafted in 1853. The "Declarations, Rights and Guarantees" gave the Roman Catholic religion "State protection" but guaranteed "freedom of religious belief" to all. It also granted freedom of association and expression; made everyone equal before the law; protected citizens against arbitrary arrest, ex post facto laws, and unwarranted search and seizure; enshrined property rights ("no one may suffer expropriation"); and expressly prohibited confiscation of property as a judicial remedy or penalty.

Argentina's political-administrative system comprises a federal district, twenty-three provinces, and one national territory, Tierra del Fuego. Executive power is vested in the president, who is chief of state, head of government, and commander in chief of the armed forces. The president "issues the instructions and rulings necessary for the execution of the laws, and himself takes part in drawing up and promulgating those laws." He also appoints judges of the Supreme Court and other tribunals, ambassadors, top-echelon civil servants, the senior officers of the armed forces, and his cabinet ministers. All but the cabinet ministers require Senate approval.

The president and vice-president run on a single ticket and are elected to a six-year term. Members of the electoral college are chosen from each province, the Federal District, and the national territory, each having twice as many electors as it has representatives to the national congress. Candidates must be Argentine-born Catholics at least 30 years old.

The constitution gives the president broad executive powers, including the right to introduce and veto legislation, conduct foreign affairs, and suspend citizens' constitutional guarantees by declaring a state of emergency. The president is not eligible to succeed himself.

The parallels with the Constitution of the United States are many. Even the method of choosing presidents is similar: the U.S. electoral college is a reminder that, in a strictly formal sense, American presidents are still elected indirectly, although this practice is now little more than an empty ritual in the United States. One difference, however, is that although Argentina's constitution dates back to the mid-nineteenth century, it has been inoperative during most of its existence.

One key to popular self-government is a freely elected legislature. In Argentina, lawmaking power is vested in a bicameral congress, comprising the lower Chamber of Deputies (254 directly elected members, chosen for four years and eligible for reelection) and the upper Senate (forty-six members, chosen by provincial legislatures for nine-year terms, with one-third of the seats being renewed every three years).

Argentina's congress has powers similar to those of the U.S. Congress, including the power to regulate foreign trade, fix import and export duties, levy taxes, contract loans, regulate debt and currency, and determine the budget. The congress also approves or rejects treaties, authorizes the president to declare war or make peace, and sets the strength of the armed forces. Legislation relating to taxes and the military draft must start in the Chamber of Deputies. Impeachment procedures are like those in the United States: the lower house decides whether there are grounds for a trial, which is then conducted in the upper house, where a verdict is rendered.

Most bills may be introduced in either house; all must be approved by both houses to become law. Traditionally, legislative initiative was primarily a presidential prerogative; now, however, the congress is more assertive than in the past, a development that President Alfonsín encouraged. As in the U.S. Congress, proposed legislation is referred to standing committees for preliminary action before it goes to the full chamber for final vote. Unlike its U.S. counterpart, the Argentine congress does not use conference committees to resolve differences. Instead, bills must be sent back and forth between the two chambers until agreement is reached. Finally, a presidential veto can be overridden by a two-thirds vote of both houses.

The fact that the constitution makes the congress an equal partner with the president is highly significant in this regard. Logically, a strong legislature goes hand in hand with a strong party system. In a true democratic republic, political parties often operate most effectively and purposefully through the legislative branch. The reverse is also true: the legislative branch operates best when political parties function so as to articulate and aggregate interests within the larger society. When the system provides incentives for political parties to compete vigorously, they tend to flourish; and when political parties flourish, a president cannot afford to ignore them. Such a system requires that the chief executive be a skilled mediator and conciliator.

In a country beset by internal problems, there are pros and cons to this type of system. Since in Argentina, the president is indirectly elected (unlike American presidents who are, for all practical purposes, elected by a popular vote), he does not have the same sort of popular mandate as the president of, say, Mexico or France. This fact, combined with the relatively powerful role given to Argentina's legislative branch, might weaken the moral authority and credibility of the chief executive in a time of trouble.

Passing the Torch: A Peronist without Peronism   Argentina's democratic institutions have so far survived the economic instability that has plagued the country in recent years. President Alfonsín was defeated by the Peronist party's candidate, Carlos Saul Menem, in May 1989; not only was the transfer of power peaceful, but it also took place early. Alfonsín—a lame-duck president—stepped aside in July, five months before his term expired, when rapidly escalating commodity prices led to food riots that forced the government to declare a state of siege. Menem alone had the mandate to deal forcefully with this crisis.

But the pragmatic and charismatic new president's popularity was short-lived: his public-approval rating dropped from 74 percent in September 1989 to 31 percent by the end of the year because he was unable to stop the Argentine economy's tailspin, despite austerity measures and other seemingly appropriate economic policies. His popularity rebounded in mid-1990 to a peak of 63 percent, only to fall to a new low of 16 percent in May 1991. This public opinion roller coaster reflected two major issues that cast a shadow over the Menem presidency: the economy (which ultimately showed signs of recovery by 1992) and scandals involving members of Menem's own family. Surprisingly, no rumors of coup plotting by the military surfaced, and opposition to the government remained polite. Despite erratic helmsmanship, Argentina seems to be on a relatively steady course.

CONCLUSION

During the 1980s, much of Latin America underwent a remarkable political metamorphosis from military to civilian rule—in many cases, engineered by the military. The new democratically elected leaders, however, faced daunting tasks. In most countries, the military had badly mismanaged the economy; in a few, a huge foreign debt had accumulated. Economic crisis has contributed to social unrest, exacerbated by the severe maldistribution of wealth and the resulting class tensions that have always characterized these societies. Although the transition to democracy was accomplished without bloodshed or social upheaval, the consolidation of constitutional government continues to be impeded by economic ills, social inequities, and political corruption in many countries. Democracy in Brazil and Argentina, two key countries in South America, is still shaky. By contrast, in Mexico, the election of Salinas de Gortari as president in 1988 ushered in a period of political stability and economic growth there. Given Latin America's many domestic problems, the new democracies must alleviate widespread poverty, gain the confidence of the middle class, and placate the military. Can they do it? We turn to this question in Chapter 21.

KEY TERMS

writ of *amparo*   *aberatura*
one-party-dominant system

STUDY QUESTIONS

1. How is Mexico ruled? Is the Mexican political system democratic or authoritarian? Is it repressive or tolerant of dissent? Is it a multiparty or one-party system? Are the leaders civilian or military?
2. How is Brazil ruled? What is the role of the military? How, when, and why did political change come to Brazil? Is the chief executive directly or indirectly elected? Is he or she a president or prime minister? Civilian or military? Constitutionally strong or weak?
3. How is Argentina ruled? What is the role of the military? How and why has this role changed? What is Peronism, and is it a threat to Argentine democracy at present?
4. Compare and contrast politics and government in Mexico, Brazil, and Argentina. What are the most important features that they have in common? What are the most striking differences?
5. If you were hired as a political consultant to diagnose the causes of Argentina's governmental instability, would you recommend any constitutional changes as part of the cure? Do the same exercise for Brazil and Mexico. (In the case of Mexico, has the government been unstable in recent times?)

SUGGESTED READING

Black, Jan K. *Sentinels of Empire: The United States and Latin American Militarism.* Westport, Conn.: Greenwood Press, 1986.

Loveman, Brian, and Davies, Thomas M., Jr., eds. *The Politics of Antipolitics: The Military in Latin America.* Lincoln: University of Nebraska Press, 1989.

Postash, Robert A. *The Army and Politics in Argentina, 1928–1945.* Stanford, Calif.: Stanford University Press, 1980.

Riding, Alan. *Distant Neighbors: A Portrait of the Mexicans.* New York: Random House, 1989.

Wynia, Gary W. *The Politics of Latin American Development.* 2nd ed. New York: Cambridge University Press, 1984.

NOTES

1. Sally Bowen, "Peru's President Steps Up Battle with Terrorists," *Christian Science Monitor,* May 19, 1992, p. 5.
2. Alan Riding, *Distant Neighbors: A Portrait of the Mexicans* (New York: Random House, 1989).
3. Julia Michaels, "Brazilian President Reels from Charges," *Christian Science Monitor,* May 28, 1992, p. 3.

21

The Politics of Miracles

In the 1980s, two major trends defined the contours of Latin American politics. On the one hand, the violent forces of revolution and repression that had ravaged the region for nearly two decades were finally subdued as moderate civilian governments replaced military regimes in Guatemala, El Salvador, Honduras, Ecuador, Bolivia, Peru, Brazil, Uruguay, and Argentina. Add to this list the countries where civilians have long ruled—Mexico, Costa Rica, Venezuela, and Colombia—and a pattern becomes clear: the role of the military in Latin America has receded, and popular self-government has made unprecedented gains. In South America, the present situation marks a dramatic turnabout from just a decade or two earlier, when military rule and brutal repression were so widespread that only two countries had civilian governments, competitive elections, opposition parties, and a free press.

On the other hand, the economic dynamism of the 1960s and 1970s gave way to an epidemic of debt and decline that weakened the social fabric and threatened the stability of the region's fledgling democracies. These problems were exacerbated in some instances by average annual population growth rates in excess of 2 percent (see Table 21.1).

In the early 1990s, a third trend emerged as Latin American countries moved toward greater regional economic integration. These moves were motivated by the success of the European Community and by the need of recently reinstituted democratic governments to chart a new economic course. The first Ibero-American summit, which brought together leaders from nineteen Latin American countries plus Spain and Portugal, was convened in Guadalajara, Mexico, in July 1991 and is now an annual event. Three months earlier, Argentina, Brazil, Paraguay, and Uruguay had agreed to create a common market known as Mercosur by 1995, and Colombia, Mexico, and Venezuela agreed to create a free-trade zone by 1994. Earlier in 1991, Mexico and Central American nations had vowed to remove trade barriers by 1996. At the same time, Colombia,

Table 21.1 Demographic Facts: Selected Countries in Latin America

	Population in 1991 (millions)	Annual Growth Rate, 1980–1991 (percent)	Fertility Rate (births per woman)
Argentina	32.6	1.3	2.8
Bolivia	7.4	2.5	4.8
Brazil	153.2	2.2	3.1
Chile	13.4	1.7	2.5
Colombia	32.9	2.0	2.6
Costa Rica	2.9	2.4	3.0
Guatemala	9.5	2.9	5.4
Mexico	87.8	2.0	3.2
Nicaragua	4.0	3.0	5.3
Panama	2.5	2.1	2.8
Peru	22.1	2.3	3.7
Venezuela	20.2	2.7	3.5

Source: Data from the World Bank, *The World Bank Atlas* (Washington, D.C.: World International Bank for Reconstruction and Development/The World Bank, 1992). Published by Oxford University Press, Inc., New York.

Venezuela, Ecuador, Peru, and Bolivia resurrected the Andean Pact, a moribund 1960s integration plan. Finally, regionalism in the Western Hemisphere gained new impetus in the early 1990s when Mexico joined the United States and Canada in moving toward the creation of a North American Free Trade Agreement (NAFTA).

Transition to Civilian Rule

The onset of economic difficulties in the 1970s deepened into a full-blown crisis in the early 1980s and sent the military scurrying for cover. In Argentina, the generals, looking for a diversion, conjured up the Falkland Islands War, which they lost. Elsewhere, they bowed out more gracefully. Nearly everywhere, the key question was not whether the military would relinquish power but precisely when and how.

By the mid-1980s, the transition from dictatorship to democracy, from military to civilian rule, was well under way. The last country in South America to make this switch was Chile, where General Pinochet was defeated in a plebiscite and so allowed free elections in November 1989. As noted in Chapter 20, Brazil's generals had allowed a civilian chief to take charge in 1985. But could the newly chartered governments consolidate power when doing so meant having to overcome a daunting array of domestic and especially economic problems (see Tables 21.2 and 21.3)?

Table 21.2 Development Profile: Selected Countries in Latin America

	Life Expectancy at Birth, 1991 (years)	Infant Mortality Rate (per thousand live births)	Illiteracy Rate (percent)	Female Share of the Labor Force (percent)
Argentina	71	34	5	28
Bolivia	60	115	23	26
Brazil	67	66	19	28
Chile	72	20	7	29
Colombia	69	43	13	22
Costa Rica	75	20	7	22
Guatemala	64	81.	45	17
Mexico	70	45	13	27
Nicaragua	65	70	N.A.	26
Panama	73	24	12	27
Peru	63	82	15	24
Venezuela	70	40	12	28

N.A. = not available.

Source: Data from the World Bank, *The World Bank Atlas* (Washington, D.C.: World International Bank for Reconstruction and Development/The World Bank, 1992). Published by Oxford University Press, Inc., New York.

Table 21.3 Indicators of Economic Dynamism: Selected Countries in Latin America

	Share of Gross Domestic Product (percent)		
	Agriculture	Exports	Investment
Argentina	15	11	13
Bolivia	24	18	14
Brazil	10	7	22
Chile	9	36	19
Colombia	16	18	16
Costa Rica	18	39	23
Guatemala	25	18	13
Mexico	9	14	25
Nicaragua	35	19	10
Panama	10	29	15
Peru	7	8	16
Venezuela	6	31	21

Source: Data from the World Bank, *The World Bank Atlas* (Washington, D.C.: World International Bank for Reconstruction and Development/The World Bank, 1992). Published by Oxford University Press, Inc., New York.

Peru was an important test case. There, a charismatic young politician, Alan Garcia Pérez, was elected president in 1985. His victory was impressive for several reasons. First, he was only 36 years old, one of the youngest chief executives in the world. Second, he was the head of the Popular American Revolutionary Alliance (APRA), a left-leaning party with a history of opposition to the military; never before had an APRA candidate been allowed to assume the presidency. Third, his election marked the first time in many decades that power had been transferred by free election and without fraud or foul play from one civilian president to another. Fourth, Peru faced excruciating economic difficulties, including runaway inflation, massive unemployment, and a burdensome foreign debt (Garcia vowed to limit debt payments to no more than 10 percent of Peru's export earnings). Fifth, the nation was in the midst of a bloody and protracted guerrilla war.

After a year of shock treatment, Peru's economy showed early signs of revival. Measures taken included a freeze on prices, exchange rates, dollar deposits, and wage hikes. The result was a surge in consumer spending and factories working at full tilt for the first time in years. Most of the economic vital signs suddenly perked up: industrial output, construction starts, and imports all rose sharply. Gross domestic product climbed, and inflation tumbled (from 183 percent in 1985 to 63 percent a year later). These positive indicators created false hopes that were soon dashed: by the end of Garcia's term, the socioeconomic ills that had plunged the nation into poverty—hyperinflation, budget deficits, stagnant output, strikes, and trade deficits—were once again ravaging Peru. President Garcia's popularity had faded, and the future of Peru's fledgling democracy was in doubt.

In 1990, despite the economic stagnation and the ongoing **Shining Path** insurgency, elections were held, and the military, for the third time in a decade, allowed power to be transferred from one freely elected civilian leader to the next. Alberto Fujimori, the son of Japanese immigrants, defeated popular novelist Mario Vargas Llosa in a runoff election in June. Fujimori promised to promote exports and discourage food imports. But he could not reverse Peru's economic decline, nor could he stop the Shining Path's relentless offensive. On April 5, 1992, he suspended the constitution and dissolved the congress. "Chaos and corruption" in the congress and the judiciary, the president declared, meant that the state "could not combat the combined power of terrorism and drug traffickers." He vowed to "defeat terrorism before 1995."[1]

The illegal drug industry poses serious political and social problems for the Andean countries. Cracking down on coca cultivation is tantamount to threatening the livelihood of many peasants in the remote and impoverished highland regions where most of the crop is grown. In Peru, government workers sent out to eradicate coca crops have been attacked and even murdered. Coca growers have rioted on occasion. At the same time, there is considerable domestic and international pressure on these governments to combat the drug kingpins who build their own little empires complete with armed contingents, processing labs, airfields, and transportation systems. Faced with the prospect of extradition for trial in the United States, the drug cartel in Colombia has waged a campaign of crime and terror aimed at intimidating politicians, judges, and other government officials. Drug lords have also infiltrated the courts, the bureaucracy, the police, and even the armed forces, using bribery and extortion to neutralize the government.

In Uruguay, Bolivia, and Ecuador, civilians were in charge, but the military stood ready to intervene at any time. Elections in Ecuador in 1988 transferred power peacefully from a right-wing president to a left-wing one. In Bolivia, a dreadful economic situation and chronic instability dimmed prospects for continued civilian rule. In Uruguay, President Sanguinetti grappled with economic problems while trying to restore both civilian rule and civilized politics, but he was forced to pay a heavy price—ignoring past human rights abuses. In Argentina, President Alfonsín had managed to place former military rulers on trial; remarkably, several were sentenced to long prison terms.

Until the late 1980s, Chile and Paraguay were authoritarian holdouts. Isolated internationally and facing wide opposition at home, the Chilean regime held a plebiscite on a new constitution in 1989 that would automatically renew General Augusto Pinochet's term in office for another decade. (Pinochet had seized power in a military coup in 1973.) Voters rejected the new constitution, which then paved the way for national elections in November 1989. In Paraguay, a military coup led by General Andres Rodriguez ousted aging dictator Alfredo Stroessner, who had ruled since 1954. Rodriguez then won the presidency in multicandidate elections and vowed that his successor would be a freely elected civilian.

South America's two longtime democratic showcases, Colombia and Venezuela, were not immune to destabilizing forces. Colombia reeled from the combined impact of natural disasters (including a major volcanic eruption in 1985), multiple guerrilla insurgencies, and illegal drug trafficking (Colombia is the world's primary source of cocaine). When President Betancur's domestic peace initiative collapsed in 1985, guerrillas stormed the Supreme Court building in Bogotá, seized scores of hostages, and executed some of them (including eleven justices) before being killed themselves by security forces.

Venezuela, once awash in oil profits, had to adopt austerity measures after oil prices plunged in the early 1980s. A declining standard of living threatened to crack the broad consensus that had undergirded Venezuelan democracy since the late 1950s. Venezuela's economic problems prompted President Carlos Andres Pérez to institute austerity measures that provoked a coup attempt in February 1992. But both the president and Venezuelan democracy survived: unlike Fujimori in Peru, Pérez did not suspend the constitution or shut down the legislature.

In Middle America, Mexico and Costa Rica were joined by Guatemala, El Salvador, and Honduras under civilian rule. But only Costa Rica was unambiguously democratic. Turmoil continued in El Salvador, with violence on both the left and the right. As many as 62,000 people were dying each year. Only recently has the violence subsided.

Central America forms the land bridge between North America and South America. Excluding Mexico, the area had a population of 29.5 million in 1991—roughly half the population of the United Kingdom or Italy. Between 1980 and 1991, annual population growth rates varied from a high of 3 percent in Honduras and Nicaragua to a still lofty low of 2.1 percent in Panama and El Salvador. For the region as a whole, the natural rate of increase averaged 2.7 percent per year in the 1980s (in Western Europe, the rate is below 0.5 percent).

Central America is impoverished, but it is not as blighted as sub-Saharan Africa. Life expectancy ranges from 64 in Guatemala and El Salvador to 75 in Costa Rica. In 1991, infant mortality rates (per thousand live births) ranged from lows of 20 and 24 in Costa Rica and Panama, respectively, to highs of 75 and 81 in Honduras and Guatemala. (By comparison, the figure is 212 in Niger and 245 in Sierra Leone; the rates in Western Europe are generally 10 or below.) In most developed countries, the daily diet averages about 3,500 calories; in Central America, the figure is slightly less than 2,500 calories—better than most countries in sub-Saharan Africa but still quite low. Only 21 percent of the youth attend secondary school in Guatemala, and 26 percent in El Salvador; in Panama (59 percent), Nicaragua (43 percent), and Costa Rica (41 percent), educational opportunities are somewhat better. Illiteracy is highest in Guatemala (45 percent), lowest in Costa Rica (7 percent) and Panama (12 percent).

Women make up 23 percent of the labor force in Central America (compared to 40 percent in most industrially developed countries). The percentage of women in the labor force is more than twice as high in the four Scandinavian countries—this is an interesting measure of how progressive a particular society really is.

The combined GNP for the region in 1991 was $31.2 billion—considerably smaller than that of the former Czechoslovakia, which had about half the population of Central America. Real GNP growth rates for the 1980s averaged only 1.7 percent; for the four largest countries (Guatemala, Honduras, El Salvador, and Nicaragua), they averaged less than 1 percent. Worse still, yearly real per capita growth rates were negative in every Central American state except Belize, ranging from -0.2 in Costa Rica to -4.6 in Nicaragua. The economies of Nicaragua, Honduras, Costa Rica, and Belize still depend heavily on agriculture, and most countries in the region are dependent on agricultural exports. Excluding Belize and Costa Rica, investment as a percentage of GDP in 1991 was slightly under 15 percent; the comparative figure for the Asian NICs is instructive: 39 percent for South Korea, 37 percent for Singapore, 29 percent for Hong Kong.

Only Costa Rica has a well-rooted democratic tradition. El Salvador and Nicaragua were consumed by civil war in the 1980s, and both countries are still struggling with that bitter legacy. Honduras and Guatemala are nominal democracies in which the military continues to play a prominent political role and reports of human rights violations are common. The insurgency in El Salvador is still smoldering, and in Nicaragua, the government of Violeta Chamorro, who defeated former Sandinista strongman Daniel Ortega in free elections in 1990, braced itself against a rising tide of opposition in the face of deteriorating economic and social conditions. In Panama, civilian government was restored after a U.S. expeditionary force seized military dictator Manuel Noriega, who had been indicted by two U.S. federal grand juries on drug-trafficking charges.

This litany of political troubles in Central America does not tell the whole story. The festering problem of the region's oppressed native populations (especially in Guatemala) has yet to be addressed. Also, coups are so much a part of the political culture of these countries that it would be remarkable if the military were to stay on the sidelines should social unrest or economic breakdown threaten the established order. There is a vicious cycle at work here: social inequality and economic mismanagement are only likely to be overcome through liberal reforms, but the elected governments most likely to institute such reforms are too easily destabilized when they fail to produce quick results—a virtual impossibility in light of the challenges and obstacles implicit in Central America's bleak development profile.

In Guatemala and Honduras, where democracy had sprouted in the mid-1980s, the military continued to play an important behind-the-scenes role in the government, which, in both cases, was headed by an elected civilian. But Honduras remained the poorest state in Latin America after Haiti, and Guatemala continued to be plagued by violence and disappearances. Democratic Costa Rica was flanked by the area's two remaining authoritarian regimes, Nicaragua and Panama.

The year 1990 brought dramatic changes in both those countries. In national elections in Nicaragua, Violeta Barríos de Chamorro defeated Daniel Ortega, whose Marxist-military junta had ruled for a decade. In Panama, the personal dictatorship of General Manuel Noriega ended when the Bush administration ordered a military intervention, captured Noriega, and brought him to the United States to stand trial for drug trafficking. Though El Salvador remained a battle-ground, the Central American peace process entered the 1990s with growing impetus.

Finally, Mexico's pseudodemocratic system, which had exhibited remarkable resilience over the years, began to come unglued in the late 1980s. Tremendous difficulties—a severe economic crunch compounded by low oil prices and a huge external debt; mounting social problems epitomized by the polluted, crime-ridden, congested, and overcrowded capital; and rising discontent across the entire social spectrum—threatened the PRI's six-decade-long domination of the political system. In the 1988 elections, the PRI's candidate, Carlos Salinas de Gortari, won by the smallest margin in the party's history. Two opposition candidates, one from the left and the other from the right, made strong showings.

Throughout the region, political stability is a dependent variable: peace, order, and progress hinge above all on economic performance, and progress is being hindered in several key countries by enormous foreign debt.

Foreign Debt and Domestic Distress

A 1987 article summed up the situation in many of Latin America's new democracies:

> Democracy has returned at an inconvenient time: elected governments have had to plunge their countries into unpopular austerity so that they can service the foreign debts piled up by the generals and put their internal economies in order. Standards of living, already miserably low, have gone down almost everywhere. There have been demonstrations and strikes against austerity in Argentina, Brazil, Uruguay, Bolivia, Panama, Guatemala, and El Salvador. Yet extremists of left and right are failing to take advantage of what ought to be a splendid opportunity. Elections are regularly won by middle-of-the-roaders (though left-wing parties seem to be on the rise).[2]

The region's total debt had reached $416 billion by the end of the 1980s. Paying off this debt strained the economies of Mexico, Venezuela, Brazil, Argentina, and Peru—the major Latin American debtor nations—and, according to some observers, placed debt and democracy on a collision course. Many Latin American countries still depend heavily on a single export: copper (Peru), oil (Venezuela and Mexico), bananas (Honduras), coffee (Colombia), sugar (Cuba). For Colombia, Peru, Bolivia, and Mexico, another commodity—illegal drugs—has become a major source of export earnings. In addition, severe income maldistribution—extremes of wealth and poverty—continues to threaten stability in Latin American societies.

The economic picture was not entirely bleak in the mid-1980s. Latin America's combined GDP grew by 3.4 percent in 1986. Interest rates on the region's onerous external debt fell from 8.6 percent to about 6 percent. In South America, countries with the best growth rates were Brazil and Peru (roughly 8 percent), followed by Argentina, Chile, Uruguay, and Colombia (5 to 6 percent). Inflation fell from a runaway regional average of 275 percent to 70 percent—still far too high but a giant step in the right direction. Monetary reform in Brazil, Argentina, and Peru brought dramatic short-term reductions in inflation.

In some parts of the region, even foreign-debt pressures were alleviated. Mexico negotiated a sizable new loan package, Uruguay signed a multiyear restructuring agreement and obtained new capital from abroad, and Venezuela succeeded in restructuring its public-sector debt. Other countries—including Brazil, Argentina, and Peru—were also maneuvering for international debt relief.

The financial dilemma for most of Latin America, however, was not to be resolved soon. To avoid losing IMF borrowing privileges and to obtain new loans from the World Bank, foreign governments, and overseas commercial banks, the debtor nations were under great pressure to adopt IMF austerity programs. These generally involved budget cuts, constricted money supplies, tax increases, wage restraints—any belt-tightening measures that might restore solvency and stability. But there is a serious downside to this formula:

> Since the debt crisis, the poor in Latin America have gotten poorer and the middle class has moved down a peg or two; austerity policies have been unpopular. Letting off steam, voters kicked unpopular austerity-minded governments out of office in Colombia (1982), Venezuela (1983), Ecuador (1984), Peru (1986), and the Dominican Republic (1986).[3]

Decade of Decline

Despite hopeful signs, Latin America during the 1980s suffered the worst recession in half a century. Production per capita declined by 7 or 8 percent over the decade, and real income per capita dropped by approximately 10 percent (see Table 21.4).

When an economy spins out of control, unemployment and inflation rise. People lack purchasing power and cannot translate basic needs into effective demand. Business and industry are hurt by shrinking domestic markets. Individ-

Table 21.4   Economic Profile: Selected Countries in Latin America

	Gross National Product (GNP), 1991 (billions of U.S. dollars)	GNP Growth Rate, 1980–1991 (percent per year)	Per Capita GNP, 1991 (U.S. dollars)	Per Capita Growth Rate, 1980–1991 (percent per year)
Argentina	91.2	−0.2	2,780	−1.5
Bolivia	4.8	0.5	650	−2.0
Brazil	447.3	2.5	2,920	0.4
Chile	28.9	3.4	2,160	1.7
Colombia	41.9	3.2	1,280	1.2
Costa Rica	6.2	3.4	1,930	1.0
Guatemala	8.8	1.0	930	−1.8
Mexico	252.4	1.5	2,870	−0.5
Nicaragua	1.9	−1.4	340	−4.6
Panama	5.3	0.3	2,180	−1.8
Peru	38.3	−0.4	1,020	−2.6
Venezuela	52.8	1.1	2,610	−1.5

Source: Data from the World Bank, *The World Bank Atlas* (Washington, D.C.: World International Bank for Reconstruction and Development/The World Bank, 1992). Published by Oxford University Press, Inc., New York.

ual hardships are compounded by austerity-induced budget cuts for health, education, social security, defense, and public works and curbs on state subsidies for food, fuel, housing, and transportation.

In the industrial democracies, any double-digit jobless rate is perceived as a policy failure. In Latin America, however, it is not uncommon to find 40 percent of the labor force unemployed or underemployed. The combination of unemployment, soaring inflation, and a shrinking social safety net is particularly deadly in developing countries where poverty is endemic and maldistribution of wealth is built into the social structure.

Losing Interest

Exacerbating Latin America's domestic economic problems is the debt burden being borne by Mexico, Brazil, Argentina, Venezuela, Chile, Colombia, Peru, and Ecuador. The region's debt-to-export ratio, a measure of repayment capacity, deteriorated rapidly in the early 1980s. As a result, over one-third of Latin America's export earnings were devoted to interest payments.

Beginning in 1981, the outflow of funds for interest payments and repatriated profits of foreign firms exceeded the inflow from new loans and investments—in other words, Latin America had a net loss of capital every year. Between 1981 and 1987, the region transferred some $150 billion to the industrial democracies, about 5 percent of its GDP. Interest payments cut deeply into savings, and capital flight further reduced domestic investment and consumption. For the region as a whole, investment shrank by about 25 percent during the 1980s.

The debt crunch thus set up a vicious cycle. Devoting savings to debt service rather than to investment stunted economic growth. Slow growth, in turn, meant that debtor nations had to choose between external and internal priorities (loan repayment versus wage concessions, tax cuts, subsidies, and so on). This predicament generated politically charged controversy. In 1985, Peru's President Garcia bitterly denounced the IMF and the United States and announced that Peru would limit its loan repayments to one-tenth of its annual export earnings. The IMF withdrew Peru's borrowing privileges, and the United States declared outstanding loans to Peru "value-impaired," blocking future credit from U.S. commercial banks. Garcia's unilateral solution to Peru's debt problem was less drastic than it might have been: there had been fears that Peru might actually default. President Garcia seemed to be launching a debtors' revolt, with the enthusiastic endorsement of his compatriots.

The political impact of the debt issue pervaded Latin America. Economic ills led to the downfall or decimation of incumbent governments in Mexico, Brazil, Argentina, Peru, Ecuador, Venezuela, and Bolivia. The message from the voters was clear: provide economic relief, or do not expect any more self-sacrifice. By the end of 1987, eight Latin American countries were substantially in arrears on their external debt payments, and governments were under mounting pressure to take drastic action. A single default could touch off a chain reaction.

Boom Ahead?

Almost miraculously, the situation in Latin America began to undergo a metamorphosis. The United States spearheaded debt relief under the **Brady Plan**, and world interest rates dropped, consequently easing the debt-servicing burden. Inflation slowed dramatically throughout the region, and economies revived. Mexico's net external debt equaled 60 percent of its GDP in 1988; by 1992, that had shrunk to 20 percent of GDP.[4]

What accounted for the turnaround? First, inefficient state-run corporations were privatized throughout the region. Chile and Costa Rica led the way, followed by Argentina and Mexico. By selling off airlines and telephone companies to private investors, Argentina reduced its debt load by $7 billion in one year and planned to raise another $20 billion from privatization the next. Similarly, Mexico netted $16 billion over a three-year period.

Second, trade blocs were springing up all over Latin America in the early 1990s. Trade patterns shifted to reflect a greater intraregional emphasis. In 1991, Brazil's exports within South America rose 54 percent to $4.9 billion (15 percent of its total exports), while its exports to the United States fell 19 percent to $6.3 billion (20 percent of the total). Brazil and Argentina formed the core of **Mercosur**, the Southern Common Market, in 1986; Paraguay and Uruguay joined in 1991. The four nations plan to eliminate internal trade barriers by 1995 and levy a 15 percent tariff on imports from outside. With a combined population of 190 million and a combined gross domestic product of $420 billion, Mercosur has great potential.

The **Andean Pact**, linking Ecuador, Colombia, Peru, Bolivia, Chile, and Venezuela, is the region's other large trade bloc. Several member countries have been plagued by drug trafficking and terrorism, which continue to impede progress toward integration. Nonetheless, in 1988, they set the goal of establishing a unified economy like that of the European Community by 1996. Two other trade blocs, the Central American Common Market and the Caribbean Community (Caricom), have taken more cautious steps in the same direction. In addition, Mexico, Colombia, and Venezuela set up the Group of Three, and Chile created its own intraregional market through a series of bilateral agreements.

Mexico also plans to join the Central American Common Market, slated to start in 1996, and entered into an open trade agreement with Chile in 1991, but both of these initiatives pale by comparison with the **North American Free Trade Agreement (NAFTA)**, which was signed in August 1992 by Mexico, the United States, and Canada. Although the NAFTA treaty was signed by all three countries in 1992, the treaty was not approved by the U.S. Senate until November 1993. This pact will eliminate customs duties on tens of thousands of items "from car windshields to tomatoes" and "will make it possible for a Mexican trucker earning $7 a day to climb into an 18-wheeler in Monterrey and drive a load of auto parts all the way to Detroit."[5] NAFTA was hotly debated in the 1992 presidential election campaign when then-candidate Bill Clinton promised to renegotiate parts of the treaty. Ross Perot, another 1992 presidential candidate, vigorously opposed NAFTA and continued to campaign and lobby against it even after the election.

NAFTA created a single market of 360 million consumers—bigger than the European Community. Opposed by organized labor in the United States, NAFTA brought benefits to Mexico even before the agreement was signed—in 1991, foreign investment nearly doubled over the previous year, reaching $9.2 billion. The inflow of foreign investment accelerated even more as the agreement came closer to completion: in the eighteen months leading up to the signing, $20 billion poured into Mexico.

It is too early to tell how far the economic revival will go or how long it will last, but the combination of political and economic change occurring in Latin America has provided grounds for greater optimism than at any other time in this century.

Case Studies: Mexico, Brazil, and Argentina

Mexico

Prior to 1988, Mexican elections had been cut and dried: the PRI candidates always won. But this time, things were different. Two opposition candidates ran strong campaigns against the PRI's standard-bearer, Carlos Salinas de Gortari. One was Cuauhtemoc Cárdenas, the son of former populist president Lázaro Cárdenas. For days after the election, the Federal Election Commission was silent. The PRI claimed victory but did not indicate by what margin. Salinas's predecessor, PRI candidate Miguel de la Madrid Hurtado, had received "only" 71 percent of the vote in 1982—a record low for the party. This time it appeared that Salinas had failed to attract even half of the votes cast. Salinas was declared president (amid charges of election fraud), but the PRI's monopoly of power was being challenged like never before. What caused this sudden change in voting behavior? In a word, the economy.

The Lost Decade   After decades of steady growth, Mexico was engulfed in a deepening economic crisis in the 1980s. Between 1950 and 1981, the Mexican economy grew at the brisk pace of 6.6 percent a year; per capita GNP growth rates averaged an equally impressive 3.4 percent. In the 1970s, the pace quickened to about 8 percent a year, due to high oil prices and easily obtainable foreign loans.

At the start of the 1980s, however, the picture clouded over as oil prices fell sharply. By this time, Mexico was well on its way to accumulating a $100 billion foreign debt; at the end of 1982, the interest payments alone were devouring as much as 45 percent of the nation's total annual export earnings. Between 1982 and 1988, the economy stalled at zero growth (per capita GNP actually declined by 2 percent a year), inflation averaged around 100 percent, and unemployment was estimated as high as 45 percent of the labor force. The value of the peso plunged from 48 to the dollar in 1982 to 500 to the dollar in 1986. (It would ultimately reach nearly 3,000 to the dollar before monetary reforms were put in place.)

The crisis forced Mexico's government to take drastic action. Currency controls had been put into effect in 1982. Under growing pressure from the International Monetary Fund and foreign creditors, President de la Madrid adopted unpopular austerity measures including reductions in state subsidies for food and fuel. Other spending cuts were also made in an effort to curb the escalating budget deficits.

Mexico was also hit by a natural disaster in September 1985 when a massive earthquake rocked Mexico City and five states. The greatest loss of life and property occurred in the capital, where official estimates put the death toll at seven thousand. Other sources estimated as many as twenty thousand deaths. Moreover, some 300,000 people were left homeless, and property damage was estimated at $4 billion. The government was scathingly criticized for doing too little too late. There were also allegations that international relief funds had been misappropriated by corrupt Mexican officials.

From Bust to Boom   When Salinas was elected in 1988, there was little reason to cheer and even less reason to believe that the new president could slow the slide into economic oblivion. Within a few short years, however, he managed to work a small miracle, revitalizing an economy that had been heading toward collapse for a decade.

Salinas warmly embraced economic liberalism and gave new impetus to the free-trade policies initiated by his predecessor, Miguel de la Madrid. Under de la Madrid, Mexico had moved away from traditional protectionism, opening up large parts of its economy to foreign competition. Accordingly, it joined the General Agreement on Trade and Tariffs (GATT) in 1987 and thereafter dropped its import tariffs on average from 45 percent to 9 percent. It was President Salinas, however, who first proposed a free-trade agreement with the United States and Canada and then spearheaded the negotiations that led to the signing of such an agreement in 1992.

But the good news for Mexico was not confined to trade relations. Real wages in manufacturing, which had fallen by more than 30 percent in the 1982–1988 period, climbed steadily. Inflation dropped from nearly 160 percent in 1987 to 12 percent in 1992, thanks to a tough austerity program Salinas put in place. Governmental belt-tightening turned a huge budget deficit (16 percent of GDP in 1987) into a 1 percent surplus in 1991. In addition, Salinas pushed through an ambitious privatization program, selling off billions of dollars' worth of state-owned industrial assets, using most of the proceeds to reduce the national debt.

The key to Salinas's export-driven economic development strategy is the free-trade agreement with the United States and Canada. When it joined the GATT in 1987, Mexico's trade with the United States stood at $21 billion; by 1991, that figure had risen to $62 billion. Trade with the United States accounted for about 70 percent of Mexico's total trade in the early 1990s.

Thus prospects for Mexico, more than any other Latin American country, are tied to actions and decisions in Washington. As mentioned, the NAFTA issue was hotly debated during the 1992 U.S. presidential campaign. Of the three major candidates, only George Bush unequivocally endorsed the agreement; his opponents, Bill Clinton and Ross Perot, both raised objections to parts of it.

As president, Clinton repeatedly reiterated his support in principle for NAFTA and wholeheartedly campaigned for it when the treaty went to the House of Representatives for approval in November 1993. Clinton's narrow success with that vote secured quick approval of the treaty by the Senate. Mexico's economic recovery is hanging in the balance.

Mexico's Unfinished Business   Mexico is still a developing country in many respects. Politically, the tasks of nation-building—integrating the various parts of the country into a unified state and society—have not yet been completed. The challenge of integration is complicated by three types of inequality in Mexican society: economic, ethnic, and regional. The first form is related to class and caste, the second involves the oppressed condition of the Indian population, and the third is the result of geographically unbalanced economic development.

The mestizo population greatly outnumbers both Indian and Spanish elements in Mexico. Nonetheless, distinct Indian tribes or ethnic groups still number more than two hundred and speak some fifty languages and dialects. Indians are often the victims of discrimination, and many Spanish-speaking Mexicans see them as hindering social progress.

Another obstacle to integration is Mexico's regionalism. Many Mexicans identify with a specific region more strongly than with the nation itself. One observer has argued that there are actually five Mexican nations:[6]

1. Metromex—Mexico City and its environs
2. New Spain—the old colonial heartland
3. Mexamerica—the progressive northern region along the Mexican-American border
4. South Mexico—the poor, underdeveloped, predominantly Indian nation between Mexico City and Guatemala
5. Club Mex—the wealthy resort areas of both coasts

Mexico City alone accounted for one-half of Mexico's industry and 38 percent of its GDP in 1987. But "Metromex" also illustrates the sharp class divisions within Mexican society. In addition to the wealthy elite, some two to three million government employees, entrepreneurs, and unionized workers enjoyed job security and a rising standard of living before the slump in the 1980s eroded the income security of this sizable middle class. The teeming underclass, however, remained terribly deprived: half of Mexico City's poor lived without running water, 40 percent had no health care, and a quarter had too little to eat.

One of Mexico City's worst health problems, smog, was not confined in its effects on the poor. Air pollution in the capital assaulted everyone. Nor were environmental issues confined to Mexico City or even to domestic politics. Mexico's failure to enforce environmental policies was a major issue for some opponents of NAFTA in the United States.

In sum, Mexico has a wide array of domestic problems but has also made significant progress toward alleviating many of them in recent years. The population explosion is being contained—average annual growth rates dropped from the 3 to 4 percent range in the 1970s to about 2 percent in the 1980s. The economy is reviving, and President Salinas enjoys growing popular support. Under Salinas's leadership, Mexico has instituted market reforms as part of an export-driven development strategy. At the same time, it has exposed its own industries to foreign competition. These measures were a tonic for a society that had fallen into a deep malaise in the 1980s.

Brazil

Unlike Mexico, Brazil has endured frequent changes in its political and constitutional system over the past half century. The most dramatic change occurred in 1985, when the military junta relinquished power to a civilian president. The promised new constitution was completed in 1988, after the Constituent Assembly considered more than ten thousand proposals. Two critical issues were resolved. First, the Constituent Assembly decided to maintain a presidential system rather than switching to a parliamentary system, and second, it extended the president's term from four years to five.

The Politics of Confusion   The proceedings of the Constituent Assembly reflected the nation's confused and chaotic political situation. In November 1986, Brazilians elected 559 delegates (*constituintes*) to the Assembly to draft the new constitution. The Brazilian Democratic Movement party (PMDB) controlled 307 delegates on paper; in reality, nearly three-fourths of the PMDB's original *constituintes* came from the extinct ARENA party. As a result of opportunistic party switching and reshuffling that took place after the ban on new political parties was lifted in the early 1980s, party affiliations were neither a reliable guide to political convictions nor even a sure sign of party loyalties. The Assembly resembled a three-ring circus.

The confusion in drafting the new constitution was mirrored in the government, where the majority PMDB was a hodgepodge of right-wing, moderate, liberal, and left-wing politicians. The PMDB was hampered by intense factionalism, and there was some speculation that it might even break up into rival parties. One Brazilian party had already self-destructed recently: the Social Democratic party (PDS), the descendant of the right-wing ARENA party once headed by President Sarney himself, disintegrated in 1985 when its members defected. Sarney had virtually no power base of his own. Instead, he had to court PMDB chieftains in the congress and try to ingratiate himself with the electorate by pretending to be a born-again populist. The result was disarray and drift.

The Debt Moratorium   By 1991, Brazil's external debt had ballooned to $115 billion—the largest in Latin America. President Sarney's economic cabinet had been a revolving door: three finance ministers, two economic planning ministers, and four central bank presidents in the first eighteen months. In late February 1987, Brazil suspended interest payments on its huge commercial bank debt (then $67 billion), which amounted to roughly 60 percent of its total foreign debt. It was, in effect, a moratorium, although Sarney refused to use the word—one step away from a default. What motivated him to take such drastic action?

Brazil's debt pressures during the late 1980s must be seen against a backdrop of hyperinflation, austerity, budget deficits, and high unemployment. Even in less extreme circumstances, the debt burden might have been unbearable. From 1983 to 1986, Brazil made interest payments totaling some $40 billion while imposing austerity measures prescribed by the IMF. (During that period, Brazil's debt payments alone accounted for almost 20 percent of Citicorp's profits.) Meanwhile, the country was enduring a recession and receiving little new money from overseas commercial banks. Brazil's trade surplus was $8 billion in 1986; the same year, it had to pay $10 billion to service its external debt.

Sarney's initial efforts to deal with the nation's economic problems had an Alice-in-Wonderland quality about them. The **Cruzado Plan** created a new unit of currency, the *cruzado;* it froze wages and prices and abolished indexation (pay hikes pegged to inflation). At first, the plan seemed to work, but not for long:

> One month after it was introduced in February 1986, inflation fell to zero. An artificial boom followed as wages temporarily outpaced inflation. Profits soared. The São Paulo stock market doubled in a single month. The unknown Sarney became popular. But by the summer of 1986 acute shortages had appeared. . . . Relative prices became absurd. Typewriters, assuming you could find them, were cheaper than shoes. Meanwhile the Central Bank kept money loose, feeding inflation. By fall inflation was raging. By June 1987 it exceeded 1,900 percent and interest rates were nearly 30 percent a month. The stock market fell 90 percent in real terms. The country's trade surplus nearly disappeared, despite falling prices and interest rates.[7]

In April 1987, Sarney again changed his economic team and unveiled a new stabilization plan, which called for a ninety-day freeze on wages and prices, forbade automatic wage adjustments, and accelerated currency devaluation to spur exports. These measures achieved at least partial success as Brazil's trade balance improved and inflation came down somewhat.

Slight improvements, however, could hardly mitigate the effects of previous policies. Hyperinflation and unemployment had hit labor and the poor in a way that spurred economic crimes such as robbery and shoplifting. Bizarre events suggested the dimensions of social discontent:

> In late May, near São Paulo, hungry people attacked garbage workers and battled them for the garbage. In early June, Rio bus ticket prices were raised by 50 percent, provoking huge downtown riots. . . . The situation has become even worse in . . . Brazil's poorest areas. Each week about 200 buses arrive in São Paulo from northern regions filled with refugees. They survive in makeshift huts, huddled against the city's damp nights.[8]

Changing his mind again, Sarney announced in February 1988 that Brazil would pay $350 million to banks around the world and would cover part of the $850 to $900 million in back interest that was due in January. He also agreed to negotiate an austerity program with the IMF—a clear signal of his intention to shift from confrontation to conciliation.

Even defusing the crisis atmosphere generated by the 1987 debt moratorium raised doubts about whether President Sarney had a plan or was improvising. Would he make the necessary deep cuts in the bloated national budget? Once before, his economic advisers had urged him to reduce government spending by trimming 300,000 federal jobs; Sarney had refused, expanding the public payrolls instead. Lacking a solid power base, dependent on opportunistic PMDB politicians, and incapable of forging a national consensus, Sarney had not been willing or able to administer the medicine Brazil's sickly economy needed. In the twilight of the 1980s, Brazil had neither order nor progress; the generals and the voters demanded both, and they turned to Fernando Collor de Mello, who took office in March 1990.

Brazil's Embattled Democracy   After a year in office, Collor had failed to make progress in stabilizing Brazil's economy, and public discontent with his anti-inflation program was rising. In 1991, he announced a new "national reconstruction plan." The plan called for a wide array of tax and administrative reforms, incentives for business, greater privatization, debt renegotiation, and many other bold features—it contained something for everyone. Collor's plan and the swearing in of newly elected governors in twenty-four states raised the hopes of some political analysts. But events dashed the prospects for a new order in Brazil. In August 1991, newspaper reports linked the Bank of Credit and Commerce International (BCCI) to prominent Brazilian citizens.* The BCCI scandal did not touch President Collor, but it proved to be the tip of an iceberg of corruption in Brazilian politics. In 1992, another scandal involving millions of dollars in illegal payments and benefits from business interests to Collor and his inner circle outraged the public. The funds were received by a cabal made up of Collor's family and friends in exchange for lucrative government contracts. Congress impeached Collor, but not before these new revelations of official misconduct at the highest levels had undermined public trust in Brazil's teetering democratic institutions.

Argentina

Argentina was in decay when democracy arrived in December 1983. The signs were easy to see: a $45 billion foreign debt, an inflation rate of 600 percent a year, and real incomes that had fallen below 1970 levels. More than a decade of economic progress had been lost. President Raúl Alfonsín's early assurances that the economy would recover and the standard of living would improve turned out to be dead wrong. Over the next eighteen months, the economy's decline quickened: by June 1985, inflation had skyrocketed to an annual rate of 1,900 percent, and gross domestic product had dropped by 5 percent during the first half of the year.

The Austral Plan   Facing the worst economic crisis in Argentina's history, Alfonsín unveiled an austerity program, the **Austral Plan**, in mid-1985. The program's drastic belt-tightening measures, including a ninety-day wage and

---

* BCCI has been widely reported to have engaged in illegal financial operations involving international drug trafficking, arms trading, and perhaps other illicit activities.

price freeze and extensive budget cuts, were immediately denounced by Argentina's largest trade union and by the Peronist party. The general public was more receptive, however, and the inflation rate did fall dramatically in the first few months after the plan went into effect. Although inflation inched up later, it stayed well below preplan levels. In the 1985 congressional elections, Alfonsín's Radical Civic Union (UCR) outpolled the Peronists, 43 percent to 34 percent.

Economic news in 1986 was upbeat. Inflation for the year was down to 82 percent, and the economy grew by 5.5 percent (after shrinking by 4.8 percent the previous year). In April 1987, the government announced with much fanfare that it had renegotiated the country's foreign debt on highly favorable terms. Praise for Alfonsín's economic policies poured in from all directions—most notably from Barber Conable, the World Bank president, who called the Austral Plan "an excellent program."

Just when it appeared that Argentina's diseased economy was finally recovering, Alfonsín found himself in a confrontation with the military. The circumstances surrounding Argentina's transition to civilian rule made the danger of a military coup greater there than elsewhere in Latin America. The military had relinquished power following Argentina's defeat at the hands of Great Britain in the Falkland Islands War—in other words, the junta had been brought down by the British, not by the Argentines. As Alfonsín himself put it, "It wasn't exactly the storming of the Bastille."[9]

The Law of Due Obedience   When Alfonsín took office, a dark cloud hung over Argentina: the military had committed atrocities against thousands of Argentine citizens and had gone unpunished—without atoning, repenting, or even admitting any wrongdoing. This was a delicate issue because the officers would likely stage another coup rather than permit politicians to heap public scorn on the armed forces. But the public clamored for justice.

As noted in Chapter 20, Alfonsín tried to escape from this trap by placing only a few officers (former junta members) on trial. To prevent the net from being cast too widely, he pushed a law through the congress that set a sixty-day deadline for indictments. Much to the government's chagrin, the courts moved swiftly to indict hundreds of officers.

In April 1987, the crisis came to a head when 150 officers and troops seized an army training facility on the outskirts of Buenos Aires. This provoked a tremendous outpouring of popular support in favor of Alfonsín and constitutional government. The tension mounted as the army's Second Corps advanced, on Alfonsín's orders, and then stopped: no military unit was willing to use force against the mutinous troops. It was a stalemate.

No one knows for certain what deal Alfonsín made with the military, but a settlement was reached. One upshot was the **Law of Due Obedience**, which granted most officers immunity from prosecution on the grounds that they were simply obeying orders when they committed crimes in the conduct of Argentina's "dirty war" against subversives.

The crisis was resolved, but not to the public's satisfaction. The military had been pardoned for appalling human rights abuses without the slightest apology. Alfonsín had won the battle with the rebel officers, but he was losing the war against military tyranny.

Argentina's Economic Relapse   Alfonsín's problems with the military were compounded by another economic downturn. By mid-1987, inflation was again surging, and other economic indicators were equally alarming: the budget deficit was much bigger than expected, the trade surplus was smaller, the market value of the currency was eroding, and foreign currency reserves were seriously depleted.

In the fall elections, the Peronists turned the tables on the UCR, outstripping the president's party in the congressional races and also winning sixteen of the twenty-two provinces, including the largest one, Buenos Aires, with one-third of Argentina's population. This setback for the UCR had two consequences: first, it meant that any hope of a constitutional change that would allow Alfonsín to seek a second term was gone; second, it meant that the two largest parties would have to cooperate if the Alfonsín government were to avoid paralysis. The approach of the 1989 campaign, however, seemed to preclude all but the most grudging cooperation in the meantime.

Peronist candidate Carlos Menem won the May 1989 national elections, and Alfonsín transferred power to him in June, six months earlier than required. Menem received a strong popular mandate, sweeping all electoral districts but one and garnering 49 percent of the popular vote (against 37 percent for the UCR's candidate). Even so, his presidency faced formidable obstacles: inflation was up to 2,000 percent annually, and the country's foreign debt was nearly $60 billion. Having paid no interest on this in more than a year, Menem had to win the confidence of Western banks and governments, as well as the IMF. At a minimum, this meant an austerity program complete with spending cuts and tax reform. In addition, Menem surprisingly moved to privatize state-owned companies and deregulate the economy.

Argentina's new free-market reforms were clearly aimed at pleasing the United States and the IMF, whose financial goodwill and support were necessary for Menem to have any chance of restarting the economy. Menem lost little time in serving notice that he would abandon the Peronist tradition of keeping the United States at arm's length. In September, he became the first Peronist president to visit Washington while in office. He also moved toward normalization of relations with Great Britain and vigorously backed U.S. antidrug efforts in South America (he even refused to recognize Noriega's government in Panama). The reason behind Argentina's new foreign policy was clear: the debt had to be reduced before the economy could be restructured, and that objective could not be achieved without the cooperation of the United States.

As in Mexico and Brazil, democracy in Argentina faced several major tests. Putting the nation's economic house in order was one. Reining in inflation was another. In February 1991, economic minister Domingo Cavallo launched his Autumn Plan to balance the state budget, a prime cause of Argentina's inflation problem. The plan rapidly improved tax collection, cut federal outlays, and restricted the money supply. By mid-1991, the rate of inflation had dropped to about 3 percent a month.

Restructuring the external debt in the light of the 1987–1988 relapse was still another problem. The twin difficulties of inflation and debt no longer seemed insurmountable, but they did not go away. In the absence of rapid economic recovery, there was always the possibility of a military coup. As Piero Gleijeses observed:

> For Argentines, their country's straits are all the more painful because they are haunted by a past that the passage of time and a succession of failures have made all the more alluring. There was a time—the first three decades of this century—when Argentina had a strong economy and the sixth highest per capita income in the world; a time when Argentina seemed poised to become the leader of Spanish America.[10]

Rumors of corruption in high places persist. Like Brazil, Argentina faces a crisis of public confidence in its leaders and democratic institutions.

CONCLUSION

Many Latin American countries have made great strides in recent years toward enfranchising previously excluded segments of their societies, liberalizing their political systems, and opening up their economies to foreign competition. For traditionally class-ridden societies based on the gross maldistribution of wealth, liberalization is risky and potentially explosive. Throughout this comparative study, we have shown how politics and economics are inextricably intertwined. Unless Latin America can put its economy in order, democracy cannot last. Conversely, unless the underprivileged majority in these countries is given a real voice in politics, social progress will be stultified. Economic gains for the few will create ever-greater resentment and misery for the many. Since the time of Aristotle, wise observers have understood that injustice (often in the form of glaring economic and social inequality) is the root cause of revolution. In some countries, winds of change are stirring. Stopgap measures will not suffice: Latin America needs a quiet revolution if it is to escape chronic instability and achieve sustainable economic growth in the decades ahead.

KEY TERMS

Shining Path
Brady Plan
Mercosur
Andean Pact
North American Free Trade
   Association (NAFTA)

Cruzado Plan
Austral Plan
Law of Due Obedience

STUDY QUESTIONS

1. Is there a Latin American "underdevelopment syndrome"? What patterns are discernible throughout the region? What is the cause of this seemingly pervasive economic malaise? What is the cure?
2. How are the current economic predicaments of Brazil and Mexico similar? How are they different?
3. Would it be wiser to invest in Brazil or Argentina? Why?
4. In what sense can it be said that there is not one Mexico but five?
5. Of Mexico, Brazil, and Argentina, which is most likely to be plunged into turmoil in the coming years? Which is least likely to face a revolution? If a regime change does occur in one or more of these states, how do you think it will happen, and with what results?

SUGGESTED READING

Casagrande, Louis B. "The Five Nations of Mexico." *Focus,* Spring 1987.

Gleijeses, Piero. "The Decay of Democracy in Argentina." *Current History,* January 1988.

Pang, Eul-Soo. "The Darker Side of Brazil's Democracy." *Current History,* January 1988.

Stallings, Barbara, and Kaufman, Robert, eds. *Debt and Democracy in Latin America.* Boulder, Colo.: Westview Press, 1989.

Wiarda, Howard J. *Latin America at the Crossroads: Debt, Development, and the Future.* Washington, D.C.: American Enterprise Institute, 1987.

NOTES

1. Sally Bowen, "Peru's President Steps Up Battle with Terrorists," *Christian Science Monitor,* May 19, 1992, p. 5.
2. "Will Latin America Last?" *The World Today,* April 1987; reprinted in Paul Goodwin, Jr., ed., *Latin America,* 3rd ed. (Guilford, Conn.: Dushkin, 1988), p. 120.
3. Ibid.
4. David Clark Scott, "South in Transformation: Nations Sell State Firms and Tackle Inflation, Debt," *Christian Science Monitor,* Mar. 18, 1992, p. 10.
5. Keith Bradsher, "Free Trade Accord for North America Is Expected Today," *New York Times,* Aug. 12, 1992, p. 1.
6. Louis B. Casagrande, "The Five Nations of Mexico," *Focus,* Spring 1987, pp. 2–9.
7. James S. Henry, "Brazil Says: Nuts," *New Republic,* Oct. 12, 1987, p. 25.
8. Ibid., pp. 28–29.
9. See Piero Gleijeses, "The Decay of Democracy in Argentina," *Current History,* January 1988, p. 6.
10. Ibid., p. 5.

Index